STUDY GUIDE

Avi J. Cohen   Harvey B. King

York University   *University of Regina*

MICROECONOMICS

CANADA IN THE GLOBAL ENVIRONMENT

SIXTH EDITION

MICHAEL PARKIN   ROBIN BADE

PEARSON
Addison Wesley
Toronto

ISBN 0-321-41845-X

Editor-in-Chief, Business & Economics: Gary Bennett
Senior Developmental Editor: Madhu Ranadive
Production Editor: Jen Handel
Production Coordinator: Andrea Falkenberg

3 4 5 11 10 09 08 07

Printed and bound in Canada.

PEARSON
Addison Wesley

Contents

Acknowledgments

This sixth edition of the *Study Guide* has benefited from help and advice from Beverly Cameron, University of Manitoba; Glen Stirling, University Western Ontario; Andrew Wong, Grant MacEwan College; and from students who pointed out mistakes and ambiguities they found in using the *Study Guide*. Thanks to Joshua Borg, Ka Sin Chui, Elian Demangos, Ying Liu, Hyunseok Park, Anthony Patmanidis, Wai Pho, Amir Shuster, Joanna Warren, and Yunyun Wu for helping us in this area. Thanks also to Robin Bade and Michael Parkin for their dedication to the continuous improvement of the textbook, the *Study Guide*, and the teaching of economics.

Harvey King dedicates this edition to Morgan, for showing me how much fun life can be, to Harrison for explaining the intricacies of the undead, and to Tracy for putting up with all of us. Avi Cohen dedicates this edition to Robert Cohen, my father, whose extraordinary qualities as a teacher make him my role model.

Harvey King
Avi Cohen
March 2006

Introduction

Before You Begin …

Our experience has taught us that what first-year economics students want most from a *Study Guide* is help in mastering course material in order to do well on examinations. We have developed this *Study Guide* to respond specifically to that demand. Using this *Study Guide* alone, however, is not enough to guarantee that you will do well in your course. In order to help you overcome the problems and difficulties that most first-year students encounter, we have some general advice on how to study, as well as some specific advice on how to best use this *Study Guide*.

Some Friendly Advice

The study of economics requires a different style of thinking from what you may encounter in other courses. Economists make extensive use of assumptions to break down complex problems into simple, analytically manageable parts. This analytical style, while not ultimately more demanding than the styles of thinking in other disciplines, feels unfamiliar to most students and requires practice. As a result, it is not as easy to do well in economics simply on the basis of your raw intelligence and high-school knowledge as it is in many other first-year courses. Many students who come to our offices are frustrated and puzzled by the fact that they are getting As and Bs in their other courses but only a C or worse in economics. They have not recognized that the study of economics is different and requires practice. In order to avoid a frustrating visit to your instructor after your first test, we suggest you do the following.

Don't rely solely on your high-school economics. If you took high-school economics, you will have seen the material on demand and supply which your instructor will lecture on in the first few weeks. Don't be lulled into feeling that the course will be easy. Your high-school knowledge of economic concepts will be very useful, but it will not be enough to guarantee high marks on exams. Your college or university instructors will demand much more detailed knowledge of concepts and ask you to apply them in new circumstances.

Keep up with the course material on a weekly basis. Read the appropriate chapter in the textbook before your instructor lectures on it. In this initial reading, don't worry about details or arguments you can't quite follow—just try to get a general understanding of the basic concepts and issues. You may be amazed at how your instructor's ability to teach improves when you come to class prepared. As soon as your instructor has finished covering a chapter, complete the corresponding *Study Guide* chapter. Avoid cramming the day before or even just the week before an exam. Because economics requires practice, cramming is an almost certain recipe for failure.

Keep a good set of lecture notes. Good lecture notes are vital for focusing your studying. Your instructor will only lecture on a subset of topics from the textbook. The topics your instructor covers in a lecture should usually be given priority when studying. Also give priority to studying the figures and graphs covered in the lecture.

Instructors do differ in their emphasis on lecture notes or the textbook, so early on in the course ask which is more important in reviewing for exams—lecture notes or the textbook. If your instructor answers that both are important, then ask the following, typically economic question: at the margin, which will be more beneficial—spending an extra hour rereading your lecture notes or an extra hour rereading the textbook? This question assumes that you have read each textbook chapter twice (once before lecture for a general understanding, and then later for a thorough understanding); that you have prepared a good set of lecture notes; and that you have worked through all of the problems in the appropriate *Study Guide* chapters. By applying this style of analysis to the problem of efficiently allocating your study time, you are already beginning to think like an economist!

Use your instructor and/or teaching assistants for help. When you have questions or problems with course material, come to the office to ask questions. Remember, you are paying for your education and instructors are there to help you learn. We are often amazed at how few students come to see us during office hours. Don't be shy. The personal contact that comes from one-on-one tutoring is professionally gratifying for us as well as (hopefully) beneficial to you.

Form a study group. A very useful way to motivate your studying and to learn economics is to discuss the course material and problems with other students. Explaining the answer to a question out loud is a very effective way of discovering how well you understand the question. When you answer a question only in your head, you often skip steps in the chain of reasoning without realizing it. When you are forced to explain your reasoning aloud, gaps and mistakes quickly appear, and you (with your fellow group members) can quickly correct your reasoning. The true/false and explain questions in the *Study Guide* and the critical thinking questions at the end of each textbook chapter are good study-group material. You might also get together after having worked the *Study Guide* problems, but before looking at the answers, and help each other solve unsolved problems.

Work old exams. One of the most effective ways of studying is to work through exams your instructor has given in previous years. Old exams give you a feel for the style of question your instructor may ask, and give you the opportunity to get used to time pressure if you force yourself to do the exam in the allotted time. Studying from old exams is not cheating, as long as you have obtained a copy of the exam legally. Some institutions post old exams online, others keep them in the library, the department or at the student union. Upper-year students who have previously taken the course are usually a good source as well. Remember, though, that old exams are a useful study aid only if you use them to understand the reasoning behind each question. If you simply memorize answers in the hopes that your instructor will repeat the identical question, you are likely to fail. From year to year, instructors routinely change the questions or change the numerical values for similar questions.

Use the MyEconLab Web site. In addition to this *Study Guide*, we believe the MyEconLab site (www.pearsoned.ca/myeconlab) is worth using for the valuable help it will provide in mastering course material and doing well on examinations. However, don't just take our word for it—ask students who have used it for their opinions. MyEconLab is an online homework and tutorial system that includes practice tests, personalized study plans, practice exercises, tutorial instruction, a powerful graphing tool, Economics in the News updates, and a virtual Office Hours feature that enables you to get help by email from Michael Parkin and Robin Bade.

Using the *Study Guide*

You should only attempt to complete a chapter in this *Guide* after you have read the corresponding textbook chapter and listened to your instructor lecture on the material. Each *Study Guide* chapter contains the following sections.

Key Concepts This first section is a one-to-two-page summary, in point form, of all key definitions, concepts, and material from the textbook chapter. The summary is organized using the same major section headings from the textbook chapter. Key terms from the textbook appear in bold. This section is designed to focus you quickly and precisely on the core material that you must master. It is an excellent study aid for the night before an exam. Think of it as crib notes that will serve as a final check of the key concepts you have studied.

Helpful Hints When you encounter difficulty in mastering concepts or techniques, you will not be alone. Many students find certain concepts difficult and often make the same kinds of mistakes. We have seen these common mistakes often enough to have learned how to help students avoid them. The hints point out these mistakes and offer tips to avoid them. The hints focus on the most important concepts, equations, and techniques for problem solving. They also review crucial graphs that appear on every instructor's exams. We hope that this section will be very useful, since instructors always ask exam questions designed to test these possible mistakes in your understanding.

This section sometimes includes extra material that your instructor may add to the course, but is not in textbook chapters. An example is the discussion in Chapter 2 of mathematics of the slope of the production possibilities frontier. Such extra material is marked with the symbol ⓔ ("e" for "extra") and may be skipped if your instructor does not cover it.

The same symbol is used throughout the *Study Guide* to identify questions and answers based on extra material.

Self-Test This should be one of the most useful sections of this *Study Guide*. The questions are designed to give you practice and to test skills and techniques you must master to do well on exams. You are encouraged to write directly in the *Guide*. There are plenty of the multiple-choice questions (25 for each chapter) you are most likely to encounter on course tests and exams. There are also other types of questions, described below, each with a specific pedagogical purpose. Questions (and answers) based on extra material covered in the Helpful Hints are marked with the "extra" symbol ⓔ so that you can easily skip them if your instructor does not assign that material.

Before we describe the three parts of the Self-Test section, here are some tips that apply to all parts:

Use a pencil. This will allow you to erase your mistakes and have neat, completed pages from which to study. Draw graphs wherever applicable. Some questions will ask explicitly for graphs; many others will not, but will require a chain of reasoning that involves shifts of curves on a graph. *Always draw the graph.* Don't try to work through the reasoning in your head—you are much more likely to make mistakes that way. Whenever you draw a graph, even in the margins of this *Guide*, label the axes. You may think that you can keep the labels in your head, but you will be confronting many different graphs with many different variables on the axes. Avoid confusion: label. As an added incentive, remember that on exams where graphs are required, instructors will deduct marks for unlabelled axes.

Do the Self-Test questions as if they were real exam questions, which means do them without looking at the answers. This is the single most important tip we can give you. Struggling for the answers to questions that you find difficult is one of the most effective ways to learn. The athletic adage "No pain, no gain" applies equally to studying. You will learn the most from right answers you had to struggle for and from your wrong answers and mistakes. Only after you have attempted all the questions should you look at the answers. When you finally do check the answers, be sure to understand where you went wrong and why the right answer is right.

If you want to impose time pressure on yourself to simulate the conditions of a real exam, allow two minutes for each true/false and multiple-choice question. The short answer problems vary considerably in their time requirements, so it is difficult to give time estimates for them. However, we believe that such time pressure is probably not a good idea for Study Guide questions. A state of relaxed concentration is best. If you want practice with time pressure, use old exams, or use the Part Wrap Up Midterm Examinations (see description on page x).

There are many questions in each chapter, and it will take you somewhere between two and five hours to answer all of them. If you get tired (or bored), don't burn yourself out by trying to work through all of the questions in one sitting. Consider breaking up your Self-Test over two (or more) study sessions.

One other tip about the Self-Test. *Before* you jump in and do the questions, be sure to read through the Key Concepts and Helpful Hints. This will save you frustration at getting wrong answers to questions. When you do get wrong answers, you will often find an explanation of the right answers in Key Concepts or Helpful Hints.

The three parts of the Self-Test section are:

True/False and Explain These questions test basic knowledge of chapter concepts and your ability to apply the concepts. Some challenge your understanding, to see if you can identify mistakes in statements using basic concepts. These questions will quickly identify gaps in your knowledge and are useful to answer out loud in a study group. There are 15 of these questions, organized using the same major section headings from the textbook. The Test Bank that your instructor will likely use to make up tests and exams also contains true/false questions like those in the Self-Test.

When answering, identify each statement as *true* or *false*. Explain your answer in one sentence. The space underneath each question should be sufficient in every case for writing your answer.

Multiple-Choice These more difficult questions test your analytical abilities by asking you to apply concepts to new situations, manipulate information, and solve numerical and graphical problems.

This is the most frequently used type of test and exam question, and the Self-Test contains 25 of them organized using the same major section headings from the textbook. Your instructor's Test Bank contains all of the *Study Guide* multiple-choice questions, numerous questions that closely parallel the *Study Guide* questions, plus many similar questions.

Before you answer, read each question and all five choices carefully. Many of the choices will be plausible and will differ only slightly. You must choose the one *best* answer. A useful strategy is to first eliminate any obviously wrong choices and then focus on the remaining alternatives. Be aware that sometimes the correct answer will be "none of the above." Don't get frustrated or think that you are dim if you can't immediately see the correct answer. These questions are designed to make you work to find the correct choice.

Short Answer Problems The best way to learn to do economics is to do problems. Problems are also a popular type of test and exam question—practise them as much as possible! Each Self-Test concludes with ten short answer, numerical, or graphical problems, often based on economic policy issues. In many chapters, this is the most challenging part of the Self-Test. It is also likely to be the most helpful for deepening your understanding of the chapter material. We have, however, designed the questions to teach as much as to test. We have purposely arranged the parts of each multipart question to lead you through the problem-solving analysis in a gradual and sequential fashion, from easier to more difficult parts.

Problems that require critical thinking are marked with the symbol ct, to alert you to the need for extra time and effort. This symbol gives you the same indication you would have on a test or exam from the number of marks or minutes allocated to a problem.

Answers The Self-Test is followed by a section that gives answers to all the questions. But do not look at any answer until you have attempted the question.

When you finally do look, use the answer to understand where you went wrong, and think about why the answer is right. Every true/false and multiple-choice answer includes a brief, point-form explanation to suggest where you might have gone wrong and the economic reasoning behind the answer. At the end of each answer are page references to the textbook, so you can read a more complete explanation.

Answers to critical thinking questions are marked with ct to indicate why you might have struggled with that question! (We purposely did not mark which true/false and multiple-choice questions were critical thinking, to stay as close as possible to a real test or exam format. In an exam, all multiple-choice questions, for example, are worth the same number of marks, and you would have no idea which questions are the more difficult ones requiring critical thinking.)

The detailed answers to the short answer problems should be especially useful in clarifying and illustrating typical chains of reasoning involved in economic analysis. Answers to critical thinking problems are marked with (ct). If the answers alone do not clear up your confusion, go back to the appropriate sections of the textbook and to Key Concepts and Helpful Hints in this *Study Guide*. If that still does not suffice, go to your instructor's or teaching assistants' office, or to your study-group members, for help and clarification.

Part Wrap Up Problem and Midterm Examination

Every few chapters, at the end of each of the nine Parts of the textbook, you will find a special multipart problem (and answer). These problems draw on material from all chapters in the Part, and emphasize policy and real-world questions (e.g., the impact of cigarette smuggling on tax revenues). They will help you integrate concepts from different chapters that may seem unrelated, but actually are. We often design exam questions similar to these problems.

Each Wrap Up also contains a Midterm Examination, consisting of four or more multiple-choice questions from each chapter in the textbook part. The midterm is set up like a real examination or test, with a scrambled order and a time limit for working the questions. Like the other multiple-choice questions, there are answers with point-form explanations as well as page references to the textbook so you can go find more complete explanations.

If you effectively combine the use of the textbook, the *Study Guide*, MyEconLab, and all other course resources, you will be well prepared for exams. Equally importantly, you will also have developed analytical skills and powers of reasoning that will benefit you throughout life and in whatever career you choose.

Do You Have Any Friendly Advice for Us?

We have attempted to make this *Study Guide* as clear and as useful as possible, and to avoid errors. No doubt, we have not succeeded entirely, and you are the only judges who count in evaluating our attempt. If you discover errors, or if you have other suggestions for improving the *Guide*, please write to us. In future editions, we will try to acknowledge the names of all students whose suggestions help us improve this supplement. Send your correspondence or email to either of us:

Professor Avi J. Cohen
Department of Economics
Vari Hall, York University
Toronto, Ontario M3J 1P3
avicohen@yorku.ca

Professor Harvey B. King
Department of Economics
University of Regina
Regina, Saskatchewan S4S 0A2
Harvey.King@uregina.ca

Should the Study of Economics Be Part of Your Future?

By Harvey King (University of Regina) and
Robert Whaples (Wake Forest University)

Should You Take More Economics Courses?

Soon you will learn about supply and demand, utility and profit maximization, employment and unemployment. First, however, let's take a moment to look to the future.

- Should you take more classes or maybe even major in economics?
- What about graduate school in economics?

Economists generally assume that people try to make rational choices to maximize their own well-being. The purpose of this chapter is help you make that rational maximizing choice by providing low-cost information. Let us assess the benefits and see whether they outweigh the costs of studying economics.

Benefits from Studying Economics

Knowledge, Enlightenment, and Liberation

As John Maynard Keynes, a famous British economist, said, "The ideas of economists … both when they are right and when they are wrong, are more powerful than is commonly understood. Indeed the world is ruled by little else. Practical men, who believe themselves to be quite exempt from any intellectual influences, are usually the slaves of some defunct economist." Studying economics is a liberating and enlightening experience. You don't want to be the slave of a defunct economist, do you? Liberate yourself. It's better to bring your ideas out in the open, to confront and understand them, rather than to leave them buried.

Knowledge, Understanding, and Satisfaction

Many of the most important problems in the world are economic. Studying economics gives you a practical set of tools to understand and solve them. Every day, on television and in the newspapers, we hear and read about big issues such as economic growth, inflation, unemployment, health care reform, welfare reform, the environment, and the transition away from Communism. Your introduction to economics will let you watch the news or pick up a newspaper and better understand these issues. As an added bonus, economics helps you understand smaller, more immediate concerns, such as: How much Spam should I buy? Is skipping class today a good idea? Should I put my retirement funds in government bonds or in the stock market? After all, as George Bernard Shaw put it, "Economy is the art of making the most of life." Mick Jagger, who dropped out of the London School of Economics, complains that he "can't get no satisfaction." Maybe he should have studied more economics. The economic way of thinking will help you maximize your satisfaction.

Career Opportunities

All careers are not equal. While the wages in many occupations have not risen much lately, the wages of "symbolic analysts" who "solve, identify, and broker problems by manipulating symbols" are soaring.[1] These people "simplify reality into abstract images that can be rearranged, juggled, experimented with, communicated to other specialists, and then, eventually, transformed back into reality." Their wages have been rising as the globalization of the economy increases the demand for their insights and as technological developments (especially computers) have enhanced their productivity. Economists are the quintessential symbolic analysts as we manipulate ideas about abstractions such as supply and demand, cost and benefits, and equilibrium. You can think of your training in economics as an exercise regimen, a workout for your brain.

You will use many of the concepts you will learn in introductory economics during your career, but it is the practice in abstract thinking that will really pay off. In fact, most economics majors do not go on to become economists. They enter fields that use their analytical abilities, including business, management, insurance, finance, real estate, marketing, law, education, policy analysis, consulting, government, planning, and even medicine, journalism, and the arts.

A recent survey of 100 former economics majors at one university included all of these careers. If you want to verify that economics majors graduate to successful and rewarding careers, just ask your professors or watch what happens to economics majors from your school as they graduate.

Statistics from the 2001 Canadian census (the most recent available at the time of writing) show that economics majors earn a healthy salary. Table 1 shows the average yearly earnings for females who worked full-year, full-time by age and type of education, while Table 2 shows the same data for males. (Want to understand why women get paid less than men? Take some more economics!)

We can also see that economics degrees do well by examining data on entry-level wages (***Source:*** *Job Futures, Part 2: Career Outlooks for Graduates*, Human Resources and Development Canada, accessed at www.jobfutures.ca). The average starting salary for a B.A. in economics is $31,600. Although this is lower than degrees in engineering ($39,200) or computing science, it is higher than the starting salary for a B.A. in humanities

TABLE 1 AVERAGE YEARLY EARNINGS, FULL-YEAR, FULL-TIME WORKERS (FEMALE), 2000

	Age				
Highest Degree and Major Field of Study	**20–24**	**25–34**	**35–44**	**45–54**	**55–64**
High school graduation certificate	18,449	27,144	31,529	33,176	31,663
Trade certificate or diploma	19,297	25,836	29,896	31,236	30,004
College certificate or diploma	22,169	30,506	36,890	38,212	36,358
Bachelor's degree					
Educational, recreational and counselling services	23,403	35,819	45,312	49,630	44,942
Humanities and related fields	23,747	37,132	47,962	51,401	46,477
Social sciences and related fields	24,913	39,070	53,562	53,770	51,050
Economics	**27,605**	**44,266**	**57,493**	**52,086**	**57,313**
Geography	24,211	38,054	48,861	47,835	41,194
Political science	26,345	40,916	54,701	53,173	55,676
Psychology	23,724	36,282	47,095	49,385	48,534
Sociology	23,525	36,533	46,783	51,178	44,526
Commerce, management, and business administration	28,383	44,097	56,189	54,434	46,102

Source: Statistics Canada "Highest Degree, Certificate or Diploma (12), Major Field of Study (122), 2000 Employment Income (3), Work Activity in 2000 (2), Age Groups (13B) and Sex (3) for Total Population 15 Years and Over, for Canada, Provinces and Territories, 2001 Census—20% Sample Data," 2001 Census, with calculations by H. King, Catalogue no. 97F0018XCB2001043 <www12.statcan.ca/english/census01/products/standard/themes/AboutProduct.cfm?Temporal=2001&APATH=3&ALEVEL=9&THEME=52&VID=0&FL=0&RL=0&GK=NA&GC=99&IPS=97F0018XCB2001043&CATNO=97F0018XCB2001043&FREE=0&S=1>, accessed June 26, 2006.

TABLE 2 AVERAGE YEARLY EARNINGS, FULL-YEAR, FULL-TIME WORKERS (MALE), 2000

	Age				
Highest Degree and Major Field of Study	**20–24**	**25–34**	**35–44**	**45–54**	**55–64**
High school graduation certificate	14,400	30,971	40,375	44,334	40,497
Trade certificate or diploma	20,178	34,172	41,683	44,460	39,857
College certificate or diploma	16,259	35,770	47,829	51,016	46,234
Bachelor's degree					
Educational, recreational and counselling services	22,830	40,155	52,256	56,662	50,625
Humanities and related fields	25,827	42,191	55,915	64,407	69,687
Social sciences and related fields	26,659	51,863	75,689	85,429	107,034
Economics	**28,656**	**58,012**	**81,049**	**79,961**	**152,870**
Geography	23,946	45,027	62,531	66,531	55,349
Political science	26,801	51,639	68,645	73,960	78,127
Psychology	25,506	45,056	56,913	66,708	84,615
Sociology	28,557	46,833	55,340	64,905	62,609
Commerce, management, and business administration	31,595	54,926	81,890	87,062	98,484

Source: Same as for Table 1.

(English degrees earned $27,600, French degrees $29,500), or for a B.A. in the other social sciences (psychology degrees earned $28,000, sociology degrees $27,800), or for a B.Sc. in many of the sciences (physics degrees earned $31,600, biology degrees $27,400). In addition, employment rates for economics B.A.s were higher than average, and salaries grew over the first five years at a higher-than-average rate.

You might like to consider graduate school in economics—the entry-level wage for an M.A. in economics is roughly $42,100.

The Costs of Studying Economics

Since the "direct" costs of studying economics (tuition, books, supplies) aren't generally any higher or lower than the direct costs of other courses, indirect costs will be the most important of the costs to studying economics.

Forgone Knowledge

If you study economics, you can't study something else. This forgone knowledge could be very valuable.

Time and Energy

Economics is a fairly demanding major. Although economics courses do not generally take as much time as courses in English and history (in which you have to read a lot of long books) or anatomy and physiology (in which you have to spend hours in the lab and hours memorizing things), they do take a decent amount of time. In addition, some people find the material "tougher" than most subjects because memorizing is not the key. In economics (like physics), analyzing and solving are the keys.

Grades

As Table 3 shows, grades in introductory economics courses are generally lower than grades in some other majors, including other social sciences and the humanities. On the other hand, grades in economics are similar to grades in some sciences and math.

TABLE 3 AVERAGE GRADES AND GRADE DISTRIBUTION IN INTRODUCTORY COURSES AT SEVEN ONTARIO UNIVERSITIES

Department	Mean Grade*	% (A + B)	% (D + F)
Music	3.02	72.1	9.7
English	2.76	64.0	9.4
French	2.69	61.1	12.4
Philosophy	2.54	57.6	15.3
Biology	2.52	54.5	19.7
Sociology	2.51	52.8	14.2
Political Science	2.49	55.6	14.1
Psychology	2.40	48.4	20.6
Physics	2.38	46.1	28.4
Mathematics	2.19	44.4	33.9
Chemistry	2.18	42.9	30.9
Economics	2.18	41.6	30.7

*A = 4, B = 3, C = 2, D = 1, F = 0.

Source: Paul Anglin and Ronald Meng, "Evidence on Grades and Grade Inflation at Ontario's Universities," *University of Windsor Working Paper*, November 1999. Used with permission.

Caveat Emptor (Buyer Beware): Interpreting Your Grades Is Not Straightforward

High grades provide direct satisfaction to most students, but they also act as a signal about the student's ability to learn the subject material. Unfortunately, because the grade distribution is not uniform across departments, you may be confused and misled by your grades. You may think that you are exceptionally good at a subject because of a high grade, when in fact nearly everyone gets a high grade in that subject. The important point here is that you should be informed about your own school's grade distribution. Just because you got a B in economics and an A in history does not necessarily mean that your comparative advantage is in learning history rather than economics. Everyone—or virtually everyone—may receive an A in history. Earning a B or a C in economics might mean that it is the best major for you, because high grades are much harder to earn in economics. It is fun to have a high GPA in college, but maximizing GPA should not be your goal. Maximizing your overall well-being is probably your goal, and this might be obtained by trading off a tenth or so of your GPA for a more rewarding major—perhaps economics.

Potential Side Effects from Studying Economics

Studying economics has some potential side effects. We're not sure whether they are costs or benefits and will let you decide.

Changing Ideas About What Is Fair

One study compared students at the beginning and end of the semester in an introductory economics course.[2] It found that by the end of the semester, significantly more of the students thought that the functioning of the market is "fair." This was especially true for female students. The results were consistent across a range of professors who fell across the ideological spectrum.

For example, the proportion of students who regarded it as unfair to increase the price of flowers on a holiday fell almost in half. The proportion that favoured government control over flower prices, rather than market determination, fell by over 60 percent. The study argues that these responses do not reflect changes in deep values, but instead represent the discovery of previous inconsistencies and their modification in the light of new information learned during the semester.

Changing Behaviour

Many people believe that the study of economics changes students' values and behaviour. Some think that it changes them for the worse. Others disagree. In particular, it is argued that economics students become more self-interested and less likely to cooperate, perhaps because they spend so much time studying economic models, which often assume that people are self-interested. For example, one study reports experimental evidence that economics students are more likely than nonmajors to behave self-interestedly in prisoners' dilemma games and ultimatum bargaining games.[3]

This need not mean that studying economics will change you, however. Another study compares beginning freshmen and senior economics students and concludes that economics students "are already different when they begin their study of economics."[4] In other words, students signing up for economics courses are already different; studying economics doesn't change them. However, there are reasons to question both of these conclusions, because it is not clear whether these laboratory experiments using economic games reflect reality. One experiment asked students whether they would return money that had been lost. It found that economics students were more likely than others to say that they would keep the cash.

However, what people say and what they do are sometimes at odds. In a follow-up experiment, this theory was tested by dropping stamped, addressed envelopes containing $10 in cash in different campus classrooms. To return the cash, the students had only to seal the envelopes and mail them. The results were that 56 percent of the envelopes dropped in economics classes were returned, while only 31 percent of the envelopes dropped in history, psychology, and business classes were sent in.[5] Perhaps economics students are less selfish than others!

Obviously, no firm conclusions have been reached about whether or how studying economics changes students' behaviour.

Cost Versus Benefits

Suppose that you've weighed the costs and benefits of studying economics and you've decided that the benefits are greater than or equal to the costs. Obviously, then, you should continue to take economics courses. If you can't decide whether the benefits outweigh the costs, then you should probably collect more information—especially if it is good but inexpensive. In either case, read the rest of this section.

The Economics Major

The study of economics is like a tree. The introductory microeconomics and macroeconomics courses you begin with are the tree's roots. Most colleges and universities require that you master this material before you go on to any other courses. The way of thinking, the language, and the tools that you acquire in the introductory course are usually reinforced in intermediate microeconomics and macroeconomics courses before they are applied in more specialized courses that you take. The intermediate courses are the tree's trunk. Among the specialized courses that make up the branches of economics are econometrics (statistical economics), financial economics, labour economics, resource economics, international trade, industrial organization, public finance, public choice, economic history, the history of economic thought, mathematical economics, current economic issues, and urban economics. The branches of the tree vary from department to department, but these are common. It will pay to check your school calendar and discuss these courses with professors and other students.

Graduate School in Economics

Preparing for Graduate School in Economics

You can prepare for graduate school in economics by taking several math classes. This would probably include one year of calculus plus a couple of courses in probability and statistics and linear/matrix algebra. Ask your advisor about the particular courses to take at your university. In addition, the mathematical economics and econometrics courses in the economics department are essential. (*Hint:* Even if you aren't going to graduate school, these mathematical courses can be valuable to you, just as more economics courses can be valuable for nonmajors.)

If your school offers graduate level economics courses, you might want to sit in on a few to get accustomed to the flavour of graduate school.

Most graduate programs require strong grades in economics, a good score on the Graduate Record Examination (GRE) for U.S. schools, and solid letters of recommendations. It is a good idea to get to know a few professors very well and to go above and beyond what is expected so that they can write glowing letters about you.

Financing Graduate School

Unlike some other graduate and professional degree programs, you probably won't need to pile up a massive amount of debt while pursuing an M.A. or Ph.D. in economics. Most graduate programs hire their economics graduate students as teaching or research assistants. Teaching assistants begin by grading papers and running review sessions and can advance to teaching classes on their own. Research assistants generally do data collection, statistical work, and library research for professors and often jointly write papers with them. Most assistantships will pay for tuition and provide you with enough money to live on.

Where Should You Apply?

The best graduate school for you depends on a lot of things, especially your ability level, geographical location, areas of research interests, and, of course, financing. You should talk with your professors about ability level and areas of research. In addition, for U.S. schools there are informative articles that give overall departmental rankings and rankings by subfield. See especially John Tschirhart, "Ranking Economics Department in Areas of Expertise," *Journal of Economic Education*, Spring 1989, and Richard Dusansky and Clayton J. Vernon, "Rankings of U.S. Economics Departments," *Journal of Economic Perspectives*, vol. 12, no. 1 (Winter 1998), pp. 157–70.

What You Will Do in Graduate School

Most students who go on to graduate school do only an M.A. These degrees typically take one year for the non-thesis route and about two years for the thesis route. Course work will include 2–4 courses in economic theory, plus 4–6 courses in specific subfields.

Most Ph.D. programs in economics begin with a year of theory courses in macroeconomics and microeconomics. After a year you will probably take a series of tests to show that you have mastered this core theory. If you pass these tests, in the second and third year of courses you will take more specialized subjects and perhaps take lengthy examinations in a couple of subfields. After this you will be required to write a dissertation—original research that will contribute new knowledge to one of the fields of economics. These stages are intertwined with work as a teaching and/or research assistant, and the dissertation stage can be quite drawn out. In the social sciences the median time it takes for a student to complete the Ph.D. degree is about 7.5 years.[6] Be aware that a high percentage (roughly 50%) of students do not complete their doctoral degree.

What Is Graduate School Like?

Graduate school in economics comes as a surprise to many students. The material and approach are distinctly different from what you will learn as an undergraduate. The textbooks and journal articles you will read in graduate school are often very theoretical and abstract. A good source of information is sitting in on courses or reading the reflections of recent students. See especially *The Making of an Economist* by Arjo Klamer and David Colander (Boulder, CO: Westview Press, 1990).

The Committee on Graduate Education in Economics (COGEE) undertook an important review of graduate education in economics and reported its findings in the September 1991 issue of the *Journal of Economic Literature*. COGEE asked faculty members, graduate students, and recent Ph.D.s to rank the most important skills needed to be successful in the study of graduate economics. At the top of the list were analytical skills and mathematics, followed by critical judgment, the ability to apply theory, and computational skills. At the bottom of the list were creativity and the ability to communicate. If you are interested in economic issues but do not have the characteristics required by graduate economics departments, there are other economics-related fields to consider, such as graduate school in public policy. Many economics majors go to business schools to obtain an MBA and are often better prepared than students who have undergraduate degrees in business.

Economics Reading

If you decide to make studying economics part of your future, or if you're hungry for more economics, you should immediately begin reading the economic news and books by economists. Life is short. Why waste it watching TV?

The easiest way to get your daily recommended dose of economics is to keep up with current economic events. Here are a few sources to pick up at the newsstand, bookstore, or library over your summer or winter break.

The Globe and Mail *or* The National Post

Many undergraduates subscribe to *The Globe and Mail* or *The National Post* at low student rates. Join them! Not only are these well-written business newspapers, but they also have articles on domestic and international news, politics, the arts, travel, and sports, as well as lively editorial pages. Reading one of these papers is one of the best ways to tie the economics you are studying to the real world and to prepare for your career.

Magazines and Journals

The Economist, a weekly magazine published in England, is available at a student discount rate. Pick up a copy at your school library and you will be hooked by its informative, sharp writing. *Business Week* is also well worth the read.

Also recommended are *Challenge* magazine and *The Public Interest*, two quarterlies that discuss economic policy, as well as *Policy Options*, a bimonthly publication of the Institute for Research on Public Policy. Finally, there is the *Journal of Economic Perspectives*, which is published by the American Economic Association and written to be accessible to undergraduate economics students.

Books by Economists

Below is a list of suggested readings, compiled from asking other professors, and from our own readings.

Steven Levitt and Stephen Dubner, *Freakonomics: A Rogue Economist Explores the Hidden Side of Everything*.

Milton Friedman, *Capitalism and Freedom*.

Robert Heilbroner, *The Worldly Philosophers: The Lives, Times, and Ideas of the Great Economic Thinkers*.

Steve Landsburg, *The Armchair Economist: Economics and Everyday Life*.

Jared Diamond, *Guns, Germs, and Steel: The Fates of Human Societies*.

Diane Coyle, *Sex, Drugs and Economics: An Unconventional Introduction to Economics*.

Patrick Luciani, *Economics Myths: Making Sense of Canadian Policy Issues*.

Hernando deSoto, *The Mystery of Capital: Why Capitalism Triumphed in the West and Failed Everywhere Else*.

David Friedman, *Hidden Order: The Economics of Everyday Life*.

Adam Smith's *The Wealth of Nations* is a must-read for every student of economics. It was written in 1776, yet it is the most influential work of economics ever and its insights are still valuable.

Endnotes

1. This term is used by Robert Reich in *The Work of Nations*. The quote is from p. 178.

2. Robert Whaples, "Changes in Attitudes About the Fairness of Free Markets Among College Economics Students," *Journal of Economic Education*, vol. 26, no. 4 (Fall 1995).

3. Robert H. Frank, Thomas Gilovich, and Dennis T. Regan, "Does Studying Economics Inhibit Cooperation?' *Journal of Economic Perspectives*, vol. 7, no. 2 (Spring 1993), pp. 159–171.

4. John R. Carter and Michael D. Irons, "Are Economists Different, and If So, Why?" *Journal of Economic Perspectives*, vol. 5, no. 2 (Spring 1991), pp. 171–177.

5. "Economics Students Aren't Selfish, They're Just Not Entirely Honest," *Wall Street Journal*, January 18, 1995, B1.

6. See Ronald Ehrenberg, "The Flow of New Doctorates," *Journal of Economic Literature*, vol. 30, June 1992, pp. 830–875. If breaks in school attendance are included, this climbs to 10.5 years. Of course, some students attend only part time, and most have some kind of employment while completing their degrees.

Chapter 1
What Is Economics?

KEY CONCEPTS

Definition of Economics

All economic questions arise from **scarcity**.

- Because wants exceed the resources available to satisfy them, we cannot have everything we want and must make choices.
  - Choices depend on **incentives**—rewards that encourage actions and penalties that discourage action.
- **Economics** is the social science that studies the choices people make to cope with scarcity.
  - **Microeconomics** studies choices of individuals and businesses.
  - **Macroeconomics** studies national and global economies.

Two Big Economic Questions

Two questions summarize the scope of economics:

- How do choices determine *what*, *how*, and *for whom* **goods and services** are produced, and in what quantities?
- When do choices made in the pursuit of self-interest also promote the social interest?

The **factors of production** used to produce goods and services are

- **land** (shorthand for all natural resources) which earns **rent**.
- **labour** (includes **human capital**—knowledge and skills from education, training, experience) which earns **wages**.
- **capital** (machinery) which earns **interest**.
- entrepreneurship which earns profit.

Choices made in **self-interest** are best for the person making them. Choices that are in the **social interest** are best for society as a whole.

- Markets often provide incentives so that the pursuit of our self-interest also promotes the social interest; but self-interest and social interest sometimes conflict.
- Economic principles allow us to understand when self-interest promotes the social interest, when they conflict, and policies to reduce those conflicts.

The Economic Way of Thinking

A choice is a **tradeoff**—we give up one thing to get something else—and the **opportunity cost** of any action is the highest-valued alternative forgone. Opportunity cost is the single most important concept for making choices.

Economic tradeoffs:

- "guns" versus "butter" tradeoffs (between any pair of goods).
- "what," "how," and "for whom" tradeoffs.
- the **big tradeoff**—between equality and efficiency. Government redistribution using taxes and transfers weaken incentives, so a more equally shared pie results in a smaller pie.

We make choices in small steps, or at the **margin**, and choices are influenced by incentives.

- Economic choices are made by comparing the *additional* benefit—**marginal benefit**—and *additional* cost—**marginal cost**—of a small increase in an activity. If marginal benefit exceeds marginal cost, we choose to increase the activity.
- By choosing only activities that bring greater benefits than costs, we use our scarce resources in the way that makes us as well off as possible.
- Given a change in incentives—rewards and penalties for particular actions—we can predict how choices will change by looking for changes in marginal benefit and marginal cost.

Economists assume that it is human nature for all people—consumers, producers, politicians, public servants—to pursue their self-interest. Incentives are key for reconciling self-interest and the social interest. Economists identify incentive systems and institutions (like a legal system protecting personal security and private property) that result in self-interested choices leading to the social interest.

Economics: A Social Science

Economics, as a social science, distinguishes between

- *positive* statements—statements about what *is*, that can be tested by checking them against the facts.
- *normative* statements—statements about what *ought* to be, that depend on values and cannot be tested.

Economic science attempts to understand the economic world and is concerned with positive statements. Economists try to discover positive statements that are consistent with observed facts by

- observation and measurement.
- building **economic models**—abstract, simplified representations of the real world with two components:
  - *assumptions* about what is essential versus inessential detail.
  - *predictions* that can be tested by comparison with observed facts.
- testing economic models to develop **economic theories**—generalizations for understanding economic choices and economic performance.

Useful economic models and theories isolate important economic forces and disentangle cause and effect. This requires

- ***ceteris paribus*** assumptions to hold other things equal to isolate the effects of one force at a time.
- avoiding errors of reasoning, including the
  - fallacy of composition—the false statement that what is true of the parts is true of the whole, or what is true of the whole is true of the parts.
  - *post hoc* fallacy—the false claim that event *a* caused event *b* just because event *a* occurred first.

Economists agree on a wide range of questions about how the economy works.

HELPFUL HINTS

1 The definition of economics (explaining the choices we make using limited resources to try to satisfy unlimited wants) leads us directly to two important economic concepts—choice and opportunity cost. If wants exceed resources, we cannot have everything we want and therefore must make *choices* among alternatives. In making a choice, we forgo other alternatives, and the *opportunity cost* of any choice is the highest-valued alternative forgone.

2 Marginal analysis is a fundamental tool economists use to predict people's choices. The key to understanding marginal analysis is to focus on *additional*, rather than total, benefits and costs. For example, to predict whether or not Taejong will eat a fourth Big Mac, the economist compares Taejong's *additional* benefit or satisfaction from the fourth Big Mac with its *additional* cost. The total benefits and costs of all four Big Macs are not relevant. Only if the marginal benefit exceeds the marginal cost will Taejong eat a fourth Big Mac.

3 In attempting to understand how and why something works (e.g., an airplane, a falling object, an economy), we can try to use description or theory. A description is a list of facts about something. But it does not tell us which facts are essential for understanding how an airplane works (the shape of the wings) and which facts are less important (the colour of the paint).

Scientists use theory to abstract from the complex descriptive facts of the real world and focus only on those elements essential for understanding. Those essential elements are fashioned into models—highly simplified representations of the real world.

In physics and some other natural sciences, if we want to understand the essential force (gravity) that causes objects to fall, we use theory to construct a simple model, then test it by performing a controlled experiment. We create a vacuum to eliminate less important forces like air resistance.

Economic models are also attempts to focus on the essential forces (competition, self-interest) operating in the economy, while abstracting from less important forces (whims, advertising, altruism). Unlike physicists, economists cannot easily perform controlled experiments to test their models. As a result, it is difficult to conclusively prove or disprove a theory and its models.

4 Models are like maps, which are useful precisely because they abstract from real-world detail. A map that reproduced all of the details of the real world (street lamps, fireplugs, electric wires) would be useless. A useful map offers a simplified view, which is carefully selected according to the purpose of the map. Remember that economic models are not claims that the real world is as simple as the model. Models claim to capture the simplified effect of some real force operating in the economy. Before drawing conclusions about the real economy from a model, we must be careful to consider whether, when we reinsert all of the real-world complexities the model abstracted from, the conclusions will be the same as in the model.

5 The most important purpose of studying economics is not to learn what to think about economics but rather *how* to think about economics. The "what"—the facts and descriptions of the economy—can always be found in books. The value of an economics education is the ability to think critically about economic problems and *to understand how* an economy works. This understanding of the essential forces governing how an economy works comes through the mastery of economic theory and model-building.

SELF-TEST

True/False and Explain

Definition of Economics

1 Economics explains how we use unlimited resources to satisfy limited wants.

2 Economics studies the choices people make to cope with scarcity and the institutions that influence and reconcile choices.

Two Big Economic Questions

3 In economics, the definition of "land" includes nonrenewable resources but excludes renewable resources.

4 In economics, the definition of "capital" includes financial assets like stocks and bonds.

5 Entrepreneurs bear the risks arising from the business decisions they make.

6 "How do choices determine *what*, *how* and *for whom* goods and services are produced?" is one of the big economic questions.

7 "When do choices made in the pursuit of the social interest also promote self-interest?" is one of the big economic questions.

8 Choices made in the pursuit of self-interest always promote the social interest.

The Economic Way of Thinking

9 When the opportunity cost of an activity increases, the incentive to choose that activity increases.

10 Tradeoffs and opportunity costs are the key concepts for understanding the economic way of thinking.

11 Economists assume that it is human nature for all people to act selfishly.

Economics: A Social Science

12 A positive statement is about what is, while a normative statement is about what will be.

13 Economics is not a science since it deals with the study of willful human beings and not inanimate objects in nature.

14 *Ceteris paribus* means "after this, therefore because of this."

15 Observers are correct in noting that economists disagree on most questions.

Multiple-Choice

Definition of Economics

1 The fact that human wants cannot be fully satisfied with available resources is called the problem of
- a opportunity cost.
- b scarcity.
- c normative economics.
- d what to produce.
- e who will consume.

2 The problem of scarcity exists
- a only in economies with government.
- b only in economies without government.
- c in all economies.
- d only when people have not optimized.
- e now, but will be eliminated with economic growth.

3 Scarcity differs from poverty because
- a resources exceed wants for the rich.
- b wants exceed resources even for the rich.
- c the rich do not have to make choices.
- d the poor do not have any choices.
- e the poor do not have any wants.

4 The branch of economics that studies the choices of individual households and firms is called
- a macroeconomics.
- b microeconomics.
- c positive economics.
- d normative economics.
- e home economics.

5 Microeconomics studies all of the following *except* the
- a decisions of individual firms.
- b effects of government safety regulations on the price of cars.
- c global economy as a whole.
- d prices of individual goods and services.
- e effects of taxes on the price of beer.

Two Big Economic Questions

6 The two big economic questions
- a arise from scarcity.
- b summarize the scope of economics.
- c describe choices we make.
- d examine incentives that influence choices.
- e are all of the above.

7 The first big economic question about goods and services includes all of the following *except*
- a *what* to produce.
- b *why* produce.
- c *how* to produce.
- d *what* quantities to produce.
- e *who* gets what is produced.

8 The trends over the past 60 years in what we produce show that __________ has expanded and __________ has shrunk.
- a manufacturing; services
- b manufacturing; agriculture
- c agriculture; services
- d agriculture; manufacturing
- e services; agriculture

9 All of the following are resources *except*
- a natural resources.
- b tools.
- c entrepreneurship.
- d government.
- e land.

10 The knowledge and skill obtained from education and training is
- **a** labour.
- **b** human capital.
- **c** physical capital.
- **d** entrepreneurship.
- **e** technological know-how.

11 Which statement about incomes earned by factors of production is *false*?
- **a** Land earns rent.
- **b** Natural resources earn rent.
- **c** Labour earns wages.
- **d** Capital earns profit.
- **e** Entrepreneurship earns profit.

12 When a drug company pursuing maximum profits charges $5,000 per dose for a new HIV drug, that is certainly a(n)
- **a** self-interested choice.
- **b** altruistic choice.
- **c** globalization choice.
- **d** factor of production choice.
- **e** choice in the social interest.

The Economic Way of Thinking

13 When the government chooses to use resources to build a dam, those resources are no longer available to build a highway. This illustrates the concept of
- **a** a market.
- **b** macroeconomics.
- **c** opportunity cost.
- **d** a "how" tradeoff.
- **e** the big tradeoff.

14 The big tradeoff is between
- **a** taxes and transfers.
- **b** equality and efficiency.
- **c** current consumption and a higher future standard of living.
- **d** guns and butter.
- **e** personal security and private property.

15 Renata has the chance to either attend an economics lecture or play tennis. If she chooses to attend the lecture, the value of playing tennis is
- **a** greater than the value of the lecture.
- **b** not comparable to the value of the lecture.
- **c** equal to the value of the lecture.
- **d** the opportunity cost of attending the lecture.
- **e** zero.

16 Which of the following sayings best describes opportunity cost?
- **a** "Make hay while the sun shines."
- **b** "Money is the root of all evil."
- **c** "Boldly go where no one has gone before."
- **d** "There's no such thing as a free lunch."
- **e** "Baseball has been very good to me."

17 Marginal benefit is the
- **a** total benefit of an activity.
- **b** additional benefit of a decrease in an activity.
- **c** additional benefit of an increase in an activity.
- **d** opportunity cost of a decrease in an activity.
- **e** opportunity cost of an increase in an activity.

18 Monika will choose to eat a seventh pizza slice if
- **a** the marginal benefit of the seventh slice is greater than its marginal cost.
- **b** the marginal benefit of the seventh slice is less than its marginal cost
- **c** the total benefit of all seven slices is greater than their total cost.
- **d** the total benefit of all seven slices is less than their total cost.
- **e** she is training to be a Sumo wrestler.

19 Economists assume that
- **a** self-interested actions are all selfish actions.
- **b** consumers and producers pursue their self-interest while politicians and public servants pursue the social interest.
- **c** incentives are key in reconciling self-interest and the social interest.
- **d** all people pursue the social interest.
- **e** human nature changes as incentives change.

Economics: A Social Science

20 A positive statement is
- **a** about what ought to be.
- **b** about what is.
- **c** always true.
- **d** capable of evaluation as true or false by observation and measurement.
- **e** **b** and **d**.

21 Which of the following is a positive statement?
- **a** Low rents will restrict the supply of housing.
- **b** High interest rates are bad for the economy.
- **c** Housing costs too much.
- **d** Owners of apartment buildings ought to be free to charge whatever rent they want.
- **e** Government should control the rents that apartment owners charge.

22 A normative statement is a statement regarding
- **a** what is usually the case.
- **b** the assumptions of an economic model.
- **c** what ought to be.
- **d** the predictions of an economic model.
- **e** what is.

23 Which of the following statements is/are normative?
- **a** Scientists should not make normative statements.
- **b** Warts are caused by handling toads.
- **c** As compact disc prices fall, people will buy more of them.
- **d** If income increases, sales of luxury goods will fall.
- **e** None of the above.

24 An economic model is tested by
- **a** examining the realism of its assumptions.
- **b** comparing its predictions with the facts.
- **c** comparing its descriptions with the facts.
- **d** the Testing Committee of the Canadian Economic Association.
- **e** all of the above.

25 The Latin term *ceteris paribus* means
- **a** "Innocent until proven guilty."
- **b** "Fallacies are composed."
- **c** "Compositions are fallacious."
- **d** "The whole is not the sum of the parts."
- **e** "If all other relevant things remain the same."

Short Answer Problems

1 What is meant by scarcity, and why does the existence of scarcity mean that we must make choices?

2 "If all people would only economize, the problem of scarcity would be solved." Agree or disagree, and explain why.

3 Ashley, Doug, and Mei-Lin are planning to travel from Halifax to Sydney. The trip takes one hour by airplane and five hours by train. The air fare is $100 and train fare is $60. They all have to take time off from work while travelling. Ashley earns $5 per hour in her job, Doug $10 per hour, and Mei-Lin $12 per hour.

Calculate the opportunity cost of air and train travel for each person. Assuming they are all economizers, how should each of them travel to Sydney?

4 Suppose the government builds and staffs a hospital in order to provide "free" medical care.
- **a** What is the opportunity cost of the free medical care?
- **b** Is it free from the perspective of society as a whole?

ⓒⓣ 5 Branko loves riding the bumper cars at the amusement park, but he loves the experience a little less with each successive ride. In estimating the benefit he receives from the rides, Branko would be willing to pay $10 for his first ride, $7 for his second ride, and $4 for his third ride. Rides actually cost $5 apiece for as many rides as Branko wants to take. This information is summarized in Table 1.1.

TABLE **1.1**

Ride	1st	2nd	3rd
Marginal benefit	10	7	4
Marginal cost	5	5	5

- **a** If Branko chooses by comparing total benefit and total cost, how many rides will he take?
- **b** If Branko chooses by comparing marginal benefit and marginal cost, how many rides will he take?
- **c** Is Branko better off by choosing according to total or marginal benefit and cost? Explain why.

ⓒⓣ 6 Assume Branko's benefits are the same as in Short Answer Problem **5**. Starting fresh, if the price of a bumper car ride rises to $8, how many rides will Branko now take? Explain why.

7 Indicate whether each of the following statements is positive or normative. If it is normative (positive), rewrite it so that it becomes positive (normative).
- **a** The government ought to reduce the size of the deficit in order to lower interest rates.
- **b** Government imposition of a tax on tobacco products will reduce their consumption.

8 Consider the following paradox. If one farmer has a bumper crop, her income increases. On the basis of the experience of the individual farmer, you predict that, in general, bumper crops cause

rising farm incomes. But when all farmers have bumper crops, the excess supply causes prices to fall drastically and farm income actually decreases. What error in reasoning ruined your prediction? Explain.

9 Suppose we examine a model of plant growth that predicts that, given the amount of water and sunlight, the application of fertilizer stimulates plant growth.

a How might you test the model?

b How is the test different from what an economist could do to test an economic model?

ⓒⓣ 10 Suppose your friend, who is a history major, claims that economic theories are useless because the models on which they are based are so unrealistic. He claims that since the models leave out so many descriptive details about the real world, they can't possibly be useful for understanding how the economy works. How would you defend your decision to study economic theory?

ANSWERS

True/False and Explain

1 F Limited resources and unlimited wants. (2)

2 T This is the full definition of economics—the institutional aspect is often omitted for brevity. (2)

3 F "Land" includes all natural resources, whether nonrenewable (oil) or renewable (forests). (3)

4 F "Capital" only consists of physical equipment like tools and buildings used in production. (4)

5 T Entrepreneurs earn profits in return for bearing the risks of organizing labour, land, and capital. (4)

6 T See text discussion. (3–4)

7 F When do choices made in the pursuit of self-interest also promote the social interest? (5)

8 F Markets often provide incentives so that pursuit of self-interest also promotes social interest, but self-interest and social interest sometimes conflict. (5–8).

9 F Incentive decreases because activity is now more expensive. (11)

10 T Scarcity requires choice, choice involves tradeoffs, and tradeoffs involve opportunity cost. (9–11)

11 F Economists assume people act in their self-interest, but self-interested actions are not necessarily selfish actions, if what makes you happy is to help others. (11)

12 F Normative statements are about what *ought* to be. (12)

13 F Science not defined by subject, but by method of observation, measurement, and testing of theoretical models. (12–13)

14 F *Ceteris paribus* means "other things being equal." Other quote is *post hoc ergo propter hoc*. (13–14)

15 F There is agreement on a wide range of (mostly positive) questions. (14)

Multiple-Choice

1 b Definition. (2)

2 c With infinite wants and finite resources, scarcity will never be eliminated. (2)

3 b Poverty is a low level of resources. But wants exceed resources for everyone, necessitating choice. (2)

4 b Definition. (2)

5 c Macroeconomic topic. (2)

6 e Economics explains choices created by scarcity and incentives that help reconcile self-interest and social interest. (2–5)

7 b *Why* is not part of first big question. (3–8)

8 e Services have expanded; agriculture and manufacturing have shrunk. See Text Figure 1.1. (3)

9 d Government is a social institution. (3–4)

10 b Definition. (3)

11 d Capital earns interest. (4)

ⓒⓣ **12 a** Certainly in company's self-interest; may or may not be altruistic or in social interest depending on cost of producing drug. (5–8)

13 c Highway is forgone alternative. (9–11)

14 **b** Greater equality (using taxes and transfers) reduces efficiency by weakening incentives. **c**, **d**, are other tradeoffs, **e** nonsense. (9–11)

15 **d** Choosing lecture means its value > tennis. Tennis = (highest-valued) forgone alternative to lecture. (9–11)

16 **d** Every choice involves a cost. (10)

17 **c** Definition; **e** is marginal cost, **b** and **d** are nonsense. (11)

18 **a** Choices are made at the margin, when marginal benefit exceeds marginal cost. (11)

19 **c** Assume human nature given and all people pursue self-interest. When self-interested choices not in social interest, there are wrong incentives. (11)

20 **e** Definition. (12)

21 **a** While **a** may be evaluated as true or false, other statements are matters of opinion. (12)

22 **c** Key word for normative statements is *ought*. (12)

23 **a** Key word is *should*. Even statement **b** is positive. (12)

24 **b** Assumptions not realistic descriptions; are simplified representations of world. (12–13)

25 **e** Definition. **a**, **b**, and **c** are nonsense. **d** is fallacy of composition. (13)

Short Answer Problems

1 Scarcity is the universal condition that human wants always exceed the resources available to satisfy them. The fact that goods and services are scarce means that individuals cannot have all of everything they want. It is therefore necessary to choose among alternatives.

2 Disagree. If everyone economized, then we would be making the best possible use of our resources and would be achieving the greatest benefits or satisfaction possible, given the limited quantity of resources. But this does not mean that we would be satisfying all of our limitless needs. The problem of scarcity can never be "solved" as long as people have infinite needs and finite resources for satisfying those needs.

3 The main point is that the total opportunity cost of travel includes the best alternative value of travel time as well as the train or air fare. The total costs of train and air travel for Ashley, Doug, and Mei-Lin are calculated in Table 1.2.

TABLE **1.2**

Traveller	Train	Plane
Ashley		
(a) Fare	$ 60	$100
(b) Opportunity cost of travel time at $5/hr	$ 25	$ 5
Total cost	**$ 85**	**$105**
Doug		
(a) Fare	$ 60	$100
(b) Opportunity cost of travel time at $10/hr	$ 50	$ 10
Total cost	**$110**	**$110**
Mei-Lin		
(a) Fare	$ 60	$100
(b) Opportunity cost of travel time at $12/hr	$ 60	$ 12
Total cost	**$120**	**$112**

On the basis of the cost calculation in Table 1.2, Ashley should take the train, Mei-Lin should take the plane, and Doug could take either.

4 **a** Even though medical care may be offered without charge ("free"), there are still opportunity costs. The opportunity cost of providing such health care is the highest-valued alternative use of the resources used in the construction of the hospital, and the highest-valued alternative use of the resources (including human resources) used in the operation of the hospital.

b These resources are no longer available for other activities and therefore represent a cost to society.

ⓒⓣ 5 **a** If Branko rides as long as total benefit is greater than total cost, he will take 3 rides.

Total benefit (cost) can be calculated by adding up the marginal benefit (cost) of all rides taken. Before taking any rides, his total benefit is zero and his total cost is zero. The first ride's marginal benefit is $10, which when added to 0 yields a total benefit of $10. The first ride's marginal cost is $5, which when added to zero yields a total cost of $5. Total cost is greater than total benefit, so Branko takes the first ride. For the first and second rides together, total benefit is $17, which is greater than total cost of $10. For all 3 rides together, total benefit is $21, which is greater than total cost of $15.

b If Branko compares the marginal benefit of each ride with its marginal cost, he will only take 2 rides. He will take the first ride because its marginal benefit ($10) is greater than its marginal cost ($5). After the first ride, he will still choose to take the second ride because its marginal benefit ($7) is greater than its marginal cost ($5). But he will quit after the second ride. The third ride would add a benefit of $4, but it costs $5, so Branko would be worse off by taking the third ride.

c The marginal rule for choosing will make Branko better off. It would be a mistake to pay $5 for the third ride when it is only worth $4 to Branko. He would be better off taking that final $5 and spending it on something (the roller coaster?) that gives him a benefit worth at least $5.

You will learn much more about applying marginal analysis to choices like Branko's in Chapters 2 and 5.

6 If the price of a bumper car rises to $8, Branko now takes only 1 ride. He will take the first ride because its marginal benefit ($10) is greater than its marginal cost ($8). After the first ride, he will quit. The marginal benefit of the second ride ($7) is now less than its marginal cost ($8).

7 a The given statement is normative. The following is positive: If the government reduces the size of the deficit, interest rates will fall.

b The given statement is positive. The following is normative: The government ought to impose a tax on tobacco products.

8 The paradox is an example of the fallacy of composition—the (false) statement that what is true of the parts is true of the whole. We cannot always generalize from the parts to the whole, and the prediction that bumper crops cause rising incomes for all farmers is a false generalization from the parts to the whole.

9 a The prediction of the model can be tested by conducting the following controlled experiment and carefully observing the outcome. Select a number of plots of ground of the same size that have similar characteristics and are subject to the same amount of water and sunlight. Plant equal quantities of seeds in all the plots. In some of the plots apply no fertilizer and in some of the plots apply (perhaps varying amounts of) fertilizer. When the plants have grown, measure the growth of the plants and compare the growth of the fertilized plots and the unfertilized plots. If plant growth is greater in fertilized plots, we provisionally accept the model and the theory on which it is based. If plant growth is not greater in fertilized plots, we discard the theory (model), or modify its assumptions. Perhaps the effective use of fertilizer requires more water.

Then construct a new model that predicts that, given more water (and the same amount of sunlight), fertilized plants will grow larger than equivalently watered unfertilized plants. Test that model and continue modifying assumptions until predictions are consistent with the facts.

b Economists cannot easily perform such controlled experiments and instead must change one assumption at a time in alternative models and compare the results. Then differences in outcomes can only be tested against variations in data that occur naturally in the economy. This is a more difficult and less precise model-building and testing procedure than exists for the controlled fertilizer experiment.

10 A brief answer to your friend's challenge appears in Helpful Hint **3**. Models are like maps, which are useful precisely because they abstract from real-world detail. A useful map offers a simplified view, which is carefully selected according to the purpose of the map. No mapmaker would claim that the world is as simple as her map, and economists do not claim that the real economy is as simple as their models. What economists claim is that their models isolate the simplified effect of some real forces (like optimizing behaviour) operating in the economy, and yield predictions that can be tested against real-world data.

Another way to answer your friend would be to challenge him to identify what a more realistic model or theory would look like. You would do well to quote Milton Friedman (a Nobel Prize winner in economics) on this topic: "A theory or its 'assumptions' cannot possibly be thoroughly 'realistic' in the immediate descriptive sense. … A completely 'realistic' theory of the wheat market would have to include not only the conditions directly underlying the supply and demand for wheat but also the kind of coins or credit instruments used to make exchanges; the personal characteristics of wheat-traders such as the color of each trader's hair and eyes, … the number of members of his family, their characteristics, … the kind of soil on which the wheat was grown, … the weather prevailing during the growing season; … and so on indefinitely. Any attempt to move very far in achieving this kind of 'realism' is certain to render a theory utterly useless." From Milton Friedman, "The Methodology of Positive Economics," in *Essays in Positive Economics* (Chicago: University of Chicago Press, 1953), p. 32.

Chapter 1 Appendix: Graphs in Economics

KEY CONCEPTS

Graphing Data

Graphs represent quantity as a distance. On a two-dimensional graph,

- ♦ horizontal line is *x-axis*.
- ♦ vertical line is *y-axis*.
- ♦ intersection (0) is the *origin*.

Main types of economic graphs:

- ♦ **Time-series graph**—shows relationship between time (measured on *x*-axis) and other variable(s) (measured on *y*-axis). Reveals variable's level, direction of change, speed of change, and **trend** (general tendency to rise or fall).
- ♦ **Cross-section graph**—shows level of a variable across different groups at a point in time.
- ♦ **Scatter diagram**—shows relationship between two variables, one measured on *x*-axis, the other measured on *y*-axis. Correlation between variables does not necessarily imply causation.

Misleading graphs often break the axes or stretch/compress measurement scales to exaggerate or understate variation. Always look closely at the values and labels on axes before interpreting a graph.

Graphs Used in Economic Models

Graphs showing relationships between variables fall into four categories:

- ♦ **Positive (direct) relationship**—variables move together in same direction: upward-sloping.
- ♦ **Negative (inverse) relationship**—variables move in opposite directions: downward-sloping.
- ♦ Relationships with a maximum/minimum:
  - Relationship slopes upward, reaches a maximum (zero slope), and then slopes downward.
  - Relationship slopes downward, reaches a minimum (zero slope), and then slopes upward.
- ♦ Unrelated (independent) variables—one variable changes while the other remains constant; graph is vertical or horizontal straight line.

The Slope of a Relationship

Slope of a relationship is change in value of variable on *y*-axis divided by change in value of variable on *x*-axis.

- ♦ Δ means "change in."
- ♦ Formula for slope is $\Delta y/\Delta x$ = rise/run.
- ♦ Straight line (**linear relationship**) has constant slope.
  - A positive, upward-sloping relationship has a positive slope.
  - A negative, downward-sloping relationship has a negative slope.
- ♦ Curved line has varying slope, which can be calculated
  - *at a point*—by drawing straight line tangent to the curve at that point and calculating slope of the line.
  - *across an arc*—by drawing straight line across two points on the curve and calculating slope of the line.

Graphing Relationships Among More Than Two Variables

Relationships among more than two variables can be graphed by holding constant the values of all variables except two. This is done by making a *ceteris paribus* assumption—"other things remain the same."

HELPFUL HINTS

1 Throughout the text, relationships among economic variables will almost invariably be represented and analyzed graphically. An early, complete understanding of graphs will greatly facilitate your mastery of the economic analysis of later chapters. Avoid the common mistake of assuming that a superficial understanding of graphs will be sufficient.

2 If you have limited experience with graphical analysis, this appendix is crucial to your ability to understand later economic analysis. You will likely find significant rewards in occasionally returning to this appendix for review. If you are experienced in constructing and using graphs, this appendix may be "old hat." Even so, you should skim it and work through the Self-Test in this *Study Guide*.

3 Slope is a *linear* concept since it is a property of a straight line. For this reason, the slope is constant along a straight line but is different at different points on a curved (nonlinear) line. For the slope of a curved line, we actually calculate the slope of a straight line. The text presents two alternatives for calculating the slope of a curved line: (1) slope at a point and (2) slope across an arc. The first of these calculates the slope of the *straight line* that just touches (is tangent to) the curve at a point. The second calculates the slope of the *straight line* formed by the arc between two points on the curved line.

4 A straight line on a graph can also be described by a simple equation (see Text Mathematical Note, pages 28–29). The general form for the equation of a straight line is

$$y = a + bx$$

If you are given such an equation, you can graph the line by finding the y-intercept (where the line intersects the vertical y-axis), finding the x-intercept (where the line intersects the horizontal x-axis), and then connecting those two points with a straight line:

To find the y-intercept, set $x = 0$.

$$y = a + b(0)$$

$$y = a$$

To find the x-intercept, set $y = 0$.

$$0 = a + bx$$

$$x = -a/b$$

Connecting these two points $((x = 0, y = a)$ and $(x = -a/b, y = 0))$ or $(0, a)$ and $(-a/b, 0)$ allows you to graph the straight line. For any straight line with the equation of the form $y = a + bx$, the slope of the line is b. Figure A1.1 illustrates a line where b is a *negative* number, so there is a *negative* relationship between the variables x and y.

FIGURE A1.1

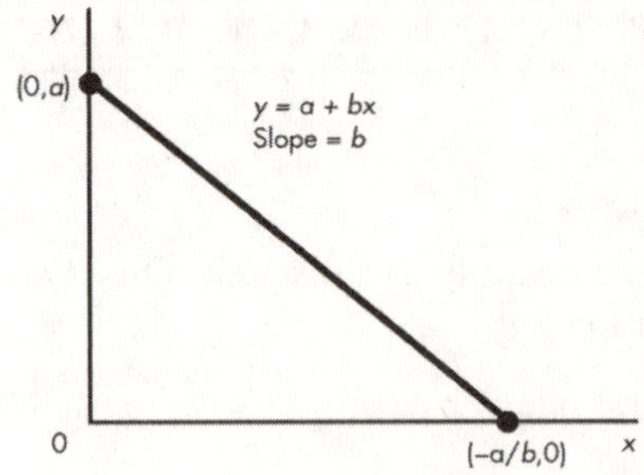

To see how to apply this general equation, consider this example:

$$y = 6 - 2x$$

To find the y-intercept, set $x = 0$.

$$y = 6 - 2(0)$$

$$y = 6$$

To find the x-intercept, set $y = 0$.

$$0 = 6 - 2x$$

$$x = 3$$

Connecting these two points, (0, 6) and (3, 0), yields the line in Figure A1.2.

FIGURE A1.2

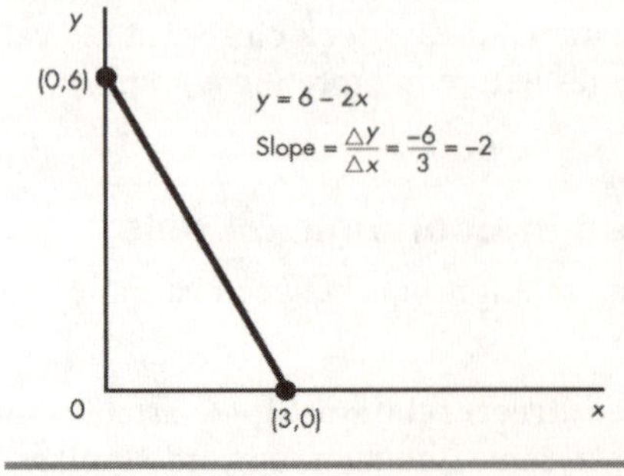

The slope of this line is –2. Since the slope is negative, there is a negative relationship between the variables x and y.

SELF-TEST

True/False and Explain

Graphing Data

1 A time-series graph shows the level of a variable across different groups at a point in time.

2 A graph with a break in the axes must be misleading.

3 If a scatter diagram shows a clear relationship between variables *x* and *y*, then *x* must cause *y*.

Graphs Used in Economic Models

4 If the graph of the relationship between two variables slopes upward (to the right), the graph has a positive slope.

5 The graph of the relationship between two variables that are in fact unrelated is always vertical.

6 In Figure A1.3, the relationship between *y* and *x* is first negative, reaches a minimum, and then becomes positive as *x* increases.

FIGURE **A1.3**

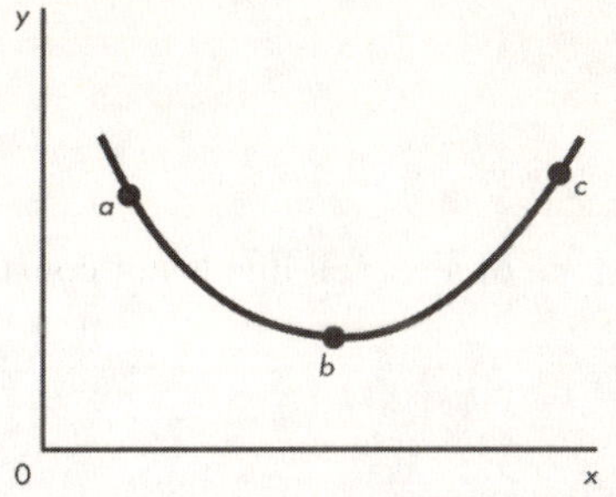

7 In Figure A1.3, the value of *x* is a minimum at point *b*.

The Slope of a Relationship

8 In Figure A1.3, the slope of the curve is increasing as we move from point *b* to point *c*.

9 In Figure A1.3, the slope of the curve is approaching zero as we move from point *a* to point *b*.

10 The slope of a straight line is calculated by dividing the change in the value of the variable measured on the horizontal axis by the change in the value of the variable measured on the vertical axis.

11 For a straight line, if a small change in *y* is associated with a large change in *x*, the slope is large.

12 For a straight line, if a large change in y is associated with a small change in x, the line is steep.

13 The slope of a curved line is not constant.

Graphing Relationships Among More Than Two Variables

14 *Ceteris paribus* means "other things change."

15 Relationships between three variables can be displayed on a two-dimensional graph.

Multiple-Choice

Graphing Data

1 Figure A1.4 is a time-series graph. The horizontal axis measures __________ and the vertical axis measures __________.
- **a** time; the variable of interest
- **b** time; slope
- **c** the variable of interest in one year; the variable of interest in another year
- **d** the variable of interest; time
- **e** slope; time

FIGURE **A1.4**

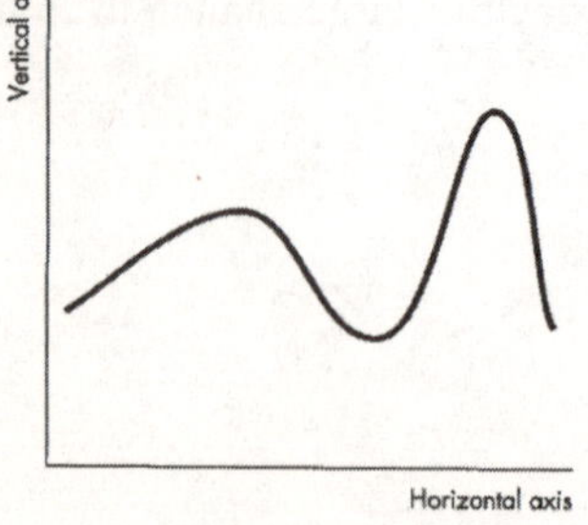

2 The tendency for a variable to rise or fall over time is called its
- **a** slope.
- **b** trend.
- **c** y-coordinate.
- **d** level.
- **e** correlation.

3 Which type of graph can mislead?
- **a** Time-series graphs only
- **b** Cross-section graphs only
- **c** Scatter diagrams only
- **d** Graphs with correlations between variables only
- **e** Any of the above

Graphs Used in Economic Models

4 From the data in Table A1.1, it appears that
- **a** x and y have a negative relationship.
- **b** x and y have a positive relationship.
- **c** there is no relationship between x and y.
- **d** there is first a negative and then a positive relationship between x and y.
- **e** there is first a positive and then a negative relationship between x and y.

TABLE **A1.1**

Year	x	y
2004	6.2	143
2005	5.7	156
2006	5.3	162

5 If variables x and y move up and down together, they are said to be
- **a** positively related.
- **b** negatively related.
- **c** conversely related.
- **d** unrelated.
- **e** trendy.

6 The relationship between two variables that move in opposite directions is shown graphically by a line that is
- **a** positively sloped.
- **b** relatively steep.
- **c** relatively flat.
- **d** negatively sloped.
- **e** curved.

The Slope of a Relationship

7 In Figure A1.5 the relationship between *x* and *y* as *x* increases is
- **a** positive with slope decreasing.
- **b** negative with slope decreasing.
- **c** negative with slope increasing.
- **d** positive with slope increasing.
- **e** positive with slope first increasing then decreasing.

FIGURE **A1.5**

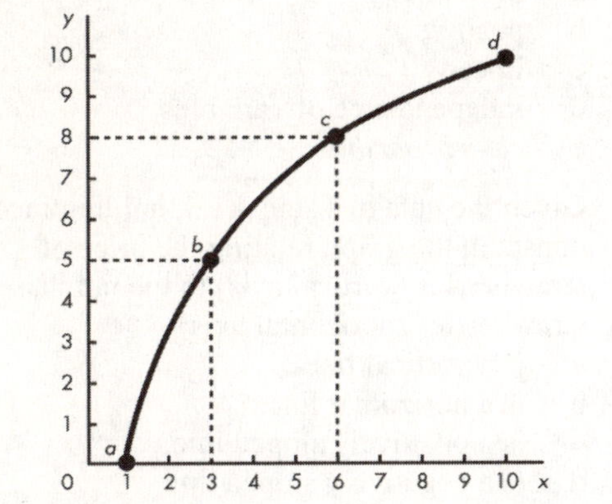

8 What is the slope across the arc between *b* and *c* in Figure A1.5?
- **a** 1/2
- **b** 2/3
- **c** 1
- **d** 2
- **e** 3

9 In Figure A1.5, consider the slopes of arc *ab* and arc *bc*. The slope at point *b* is difficult to determine exactly, but it must be
- **a** greater than 5/2.
- **b** about 5/2.
- **c** between 5/2 and 1.
- **d** about 1.
- **e** less than 1.

10 In Table A1.2, suppose that *w* is the independent variable measured along the horizontal axis. The slope of the line relating *w* and *u* is
- **a** positive with a decreasing slope.
- **b** negative with a decreasing slope.
- **c** positive with an increasing slope.
- **d** negative with a constant slope.
- **e** positive with a constant slope.

TABLE **A1.2**

w	2	4	6	8	10
u	15	12	9	6	3

11 Refer to Table A1.2. Suppose that *w* is the independent variable measured along the horizontal axis. The slope of the line relating *w* and *u* is
- **a** +3.
- **b** –3.
- **c** –2/3.
- **d** +3/2.
- **e** –3/2.

12 In Figure A1.6, if household income increases by $1,000, household expenditure will
- **a** increase by $1,333.
- **b** decrease by $1,333.
- **c** remain unchanged.
- **d** increase by $1,000.
- **e** increase by $750.

FIGURE **A1.6**

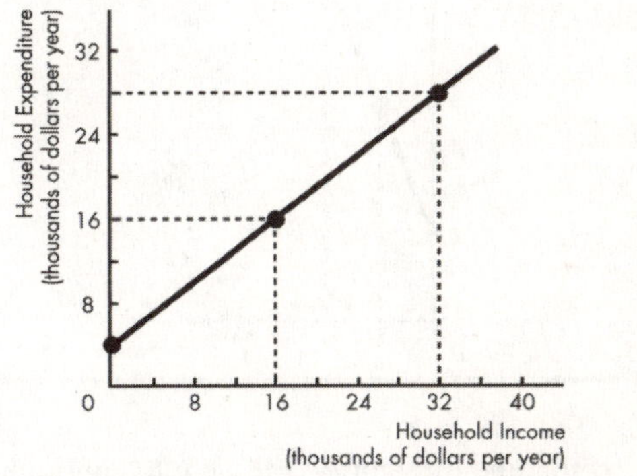

13 In Figure A1.6, if household income is zero, household expenditure is
- **a** 0.
- **b** –$4,000.
- **c** $4,000.
- **d** $8,000.
- **e** impossible to determine from the graph.

14 In Figure A1.6, if household expenditure is \$28,000, household income is
- **a** \$36,000.
- **b** \$32,000.
- **c** \$28,000.
- **d** \$25,000.
- **e** none of the above.

15 At all points along a straight line, slope is
- **a** positive.
- **b** negative.
- **c** constant.
- **d** zero.
- **e** none of the above.

16 What is the slope of the line in Figure A1.7?
- **a** 2
- **b** 1/2
- **c** 3
- **d** 1/3
- **e** –3

FIGURE **A1.7**

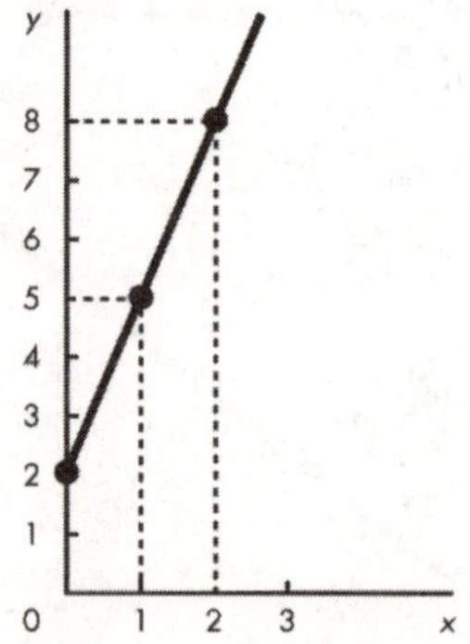

17 If the line in Figure A1.7 were to continue down to the x-axis, what would the value of x be when y is zero?
- **a** 0
- **b** 2
- **c** 2/3
- **d** –2/3
- **e** –3/2

18 If the equation of a straight line is $y = 6 + 3x$, the slope is
- **a** –3 and the y-intercept is 6.
- **b** –3 and the y-intercept is –2.
- **c** 3 and the y-intercept is 6.
- **d** 3 and the y-intercept is –2.
- **e** 3 and the y-intercept is –6.

19 If the equation of a straight line is $y = 8 - 2x$, then the slope is
- **a** –2 and the x-intercept is –4.
- **b** –2 and the x-intercept is 4.
- **c** –2 and the x-intercept is 8.
- **d** 2 and the x-intercept is –4.
- **e** 2 and the x-intercept is 4.

Graphing Relationships Among More Than Two Variables

20 To graph a relationship among more than two variables, what kind of assumption is necessary?
- **a** normative
- **b** positive
- **c** linear
- **d** independence of variables
- **e** *ceteris paribus*

21 Given the data in Table A1.3, holding income constant, the graph relating the price of strawberries (vertical axis) to the purchases of strawberries (horizontal axis)
- **a** is a vertical line.
- **b** is a horizontal line.
- **c** is a positively sloped line.
- **d** is a negatively sloped line.
- **e** reaches a minimum.

TABLE **A1.3**

Weekly Family Income (\$)	Price per Box of Strawberries (\$)	Number of Boxes Purchased per Week
300	\$1.00	5
300	\$1.25	3
300	\$1.50	2
400	\$1.00	7
400	\$1.25	5
400	\$1.50	4

22 Given the data in Table A1.3, suppose family income decreases from \$400 to \$300 per week. Then the graph relating the price of strawberries (vertical axis) to the purchases of strawberries (horizontal axis) will
- **a** become negatively sloped.
- **b** become positively sloped.
- **c** shift rightward.
- **d** shift leftward.
- **e** no longer exist.

23 Given the data in Table A1.3, holding price constant, the graph relating family income (vertical axis) to the purchases of strawberries (horizontal axis) is a

- **a** vertical line.
- **b** horizontal line.
- **c** positively sloped line.
- **d** negatively sloped line.
- **e** positively or negatively sloped line, depending on the price that is held constant.

24 In Figure A1.8, *x* is

- **a** positively related to *y* and negatively related to *z*.
- **b** positively related to both *y* and *z*.
- **c** negatively related to *y* and positively related to *z*.
- **d** negatively related to both *y* and *z*.
- **e** greater than *z*.

FIGURE **A1.8**

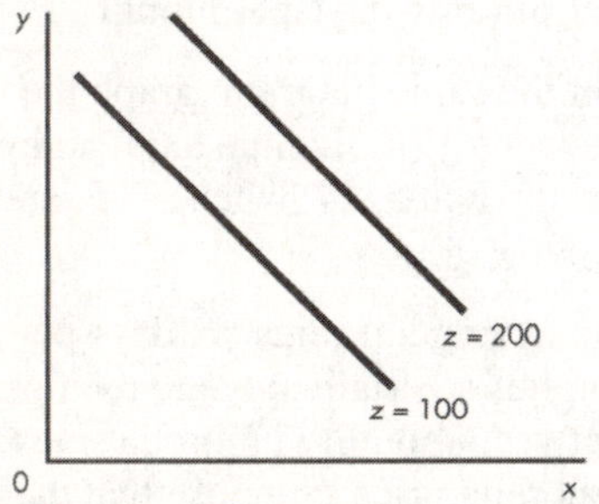

25 In Figure A1.8, a decrease in the value of *z* will cause, *ceteris paribus*,

- **a** a decrease in the value of *x*.
- **b** an increase in the value of *x*.
- **c** an increase in the value of *y*.
- **d** no change in the value of *y*.
- **e** no change in the value of *x*.

Short Answer Problems

1 Consider the data in Table A1.4.

- **a** Draw a time-series graph for the interest rate.
- **b** Draw a time-series graph for the inflation rate.
- **c** Draw a scatter diagram for the inflation rate (horizontal axis) and the interest rate (vertical axis).
- **d** Would you describe the general relationship between the inflation rate and the interest rate as positive, negative, or unrelated?

TABLE **A1.4**

Year	Inflation Rate (%)	Interest Rate (%)
1970	5.4	6.4
1971	3.2	4.3
1972	3.4	4.1
1973	8.3	7.0
1974	11.8	7.9
1975	6.7	5.8
1976	4.9	5.0
1977	6.5	5.3
1978	8.6	7.2
1979	12.3	10.0

2 Draw a graph of variables *x* and *y* that illustrates each of the following relationships:

- **a** *x* and *y* move up and down together.
- **b** *x* and *y* move in opposite directions.
- **c** as *x* increases *y* reaches a maximum.
- **d** as *x* increases *y* reaches a minimum.
- **e** *x* and *y* move in opposite directions, but as *x* increases *y* decreases by larger and larger increments for each unit increase in *x*.
- **f** *y* is unrelated to the value of *x*.
- **g** *x* is unrelated to the value of *y*.

3 What does it mean to say that the slope of a line is –2/3?

4 Compute the slopes of the lines in Figure A1.9(a) and (b).

FIGURE **A1.9**

(a)

(b)

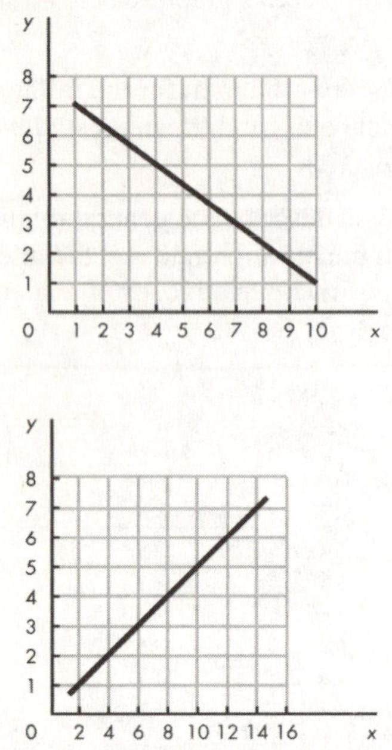

5 Draw each of the following:

a a straight line with slope –10 and passing through the point (2, 80).

b a straight line with slope 2 and passing through the point (6, 10).

6 The equation for a straight line is $y = 4 - 2x$.

a Calculate the y-intercept; the x-intercept; the slope.

b Draw the graph of the line.

7 Explain two ways to measure the slope of a curved line.

8 Use the graph in Figure A1.10 to compute the slope

a across the arc between points *a* and *b*.

b at point *b*.

c at point *c*, and explain your answer.

FIGURE **A1.10**

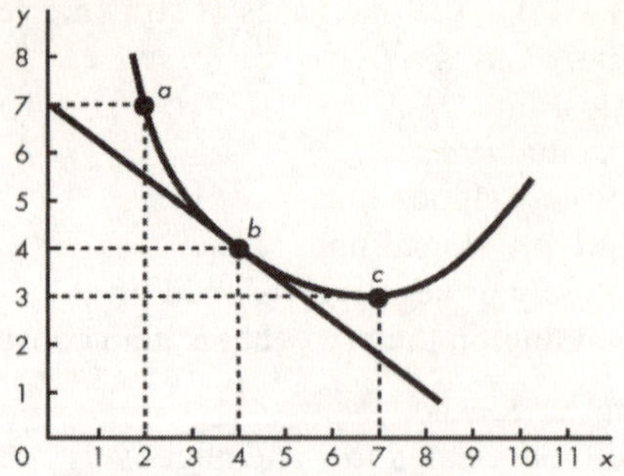

9 How do we graph a relationship among more than two variables using a two-dimensional graph?

10 In Table A1.5, x represents the number of umbrellas sold per month, y represents the price of an umbrella, and z represents the average number of rainy days per month.

a On the same diagram, graph the relationship between x (horizontal axis) and y (vertical axis) when $z = 4$, when $z = 5$, and when $z = 6$.

b On average, it rains six days per month. This implies a certain average relationship between monthly umbrella sales and umbrella price. Suppose that the "greenhouse effect" reduces the average monthly rainfall to four days per month. What happens to the graph of the relationship between umbrella sales and umbrella prices?

c On a diagram, graph the relationship between x (horizontal axis) and z (vertical axis) when $y = \$10$ and when $y = \$12$. Is the relationship between x and z positive or negative?

d On a diagram, graph the relationship between y (horizontal axis) and z (vertical axis) when $x = 120$ and when $x = 140$. Is the relationship between y and z positive or negative?

TABLE **A1.5**

Umbrellas Sold per Month (x)	Price per Umbrella (y)	Average Number of Rainy Days per Month (z)
120	$10	4
140	$10	5
160	$10	6
100	$12	4
120	$12	5
140	$12	6
80	$14	4
100	$14	5
120	$14	6

ANSWERS

True/False and Explain

1 F Definition of a cross-section graph. Time-series graph shows relationship between time (on x-axis) and other variable(s) (on y-axis). (18)

2 F Breaks in the axes may be misleading, or may bring information into clearer view. (20)

3 F x and y are correlated, but correlation does not guarantee causation. (20)

4 T Upward-sloping curves/lines have positive slopes. (20–21)

5 F Graph of unrelated variables may be vertical or horizontal. (23)

6 T Arc *ab* would have negative slope, arc *bc* positive slope. (22–26)

7 F Value of y is minimum at point *b*. (22–23)

8 T Curve becomes steeper, meaning Δy increasing faster than Δx, so slope increasing. (24–26)

9 T At *b*, tangent has slope = 0, since $\Delta y = 0$ along horizontal line through *b*. (24–26)

10 F Slope = (Δ variable on vertical (y) axis)/(Δ variable on horizontal (x) axis). (24–25)

11 F Large slope means large Δy associated with small Δx. (24–25)

12 T Steep line has large slope, meaning large Δy associated with small Δx. (24–25)

13 T Slope of straight line is constant. (24–25)

14 F "Other things remain the same." Only variables being studied are allowed to change. (26)

15 T See Text Figure A1.12. A *ceteris paribus* assumption holds one variable constant, allowing other two variables to be plotted in two dimensions. (26–27)

Multiple-Choice

1 a Time is measured on the x-axis and the variable in which we are interested on the y-axis. (18)

2 b Definition. (18)

3 e Any type of graph can mislead with breaks in the axes or stretched/compressed measurement scales. (20)

4 a Higher values x (6.2) associated with lower values y (143). (20–22)

5 a Definition. (20–22)

6 d Graph may be steep, flat, or curved, but must have negative slope. (21–22)

7 a Slope of arc *ab* = +2.5. Slope of arc *bc* = +1. (24–26)

8 c $\Delta y = 3(8 - 5)$; $\Delta x = 3(6 - 3)$. (25–26)

9 c 5/2 is slope of *ab*, while 1 is slope of *bc*. (25–26)

10 d As w increases, u decreases. $\Delta u/\Delta w$ is constant. (24–26)

11 e Between any two points, $\Delta u = 3$, $\Delta w = -2$. (24–26)

12 e Slope ($\Delta y/\Delta x$) = 3/4. If Δx (Δ household income) = \$1,000, then Δy (Δ household expenditure) = \$750 = ¾ of \$1,000. (24–26)

13 c Where the line intersects the household expenditure (y) axis. (24–26)

14 b From \$28,000 on vertical (expenditure) axis, move across to line, then down to \$32,000 on horizontal (income) axis. (24–26)

15 c Along straight line, slope may or may not be **a**, **b**, or **d**. (24–25)

16 c Between any two points, $\Delta y = 3$ and $\Delta x = 1$. (24–25)

17 d Equation of line is $y = 2 + 3x$. Solve for x-intercept (set $y = 0$). (24–26, 28–29)

18 c Use formula $y = a + bx$. Slope = b, y-intercept = a. (24–26, 28–29)

19 b Use formula $y = a + bx$. Slope = b, x-intercept = $-a/b$. (24–26, 28–29)

20 e Must hold constant other variables to isolate relationship between two variables. (26–27)

21 d Look either at data in top 3 rows (income = 300) or data in bottom 3 rows (income = 400). Higher price associated with lower purchases. (26–27)

22 d At each price, fewer boxes will be purchased. (26–27)

23 c For $P = 1$, two points on line are (5 boxes, \$300) and (7 boxes, \$400). Same relationship for other prices. (26–27)

24 c Increased y causes decreased x holding z constant. Increased z causes increased x holding y constant. (26–27)

25 a Decreased z causes decreased x holding y constant. Decreased z causes decreased y holding x constant. (26–27)

Short Answer Problems

1 a A time-series graph for the interest rate is given in Figure A1.11(a).

b A time-series graph for the inflation rate is given in Figure A1.11(b).

c The scatter diagram for the inflation rate and the interest rate is given in Figure A1.11(c).

d From the graph in Figure A1.11(c), we see that the relationship between the inflation rate and the interest rate is generally positive (upward-sloping).

FIGURE **A1.11**

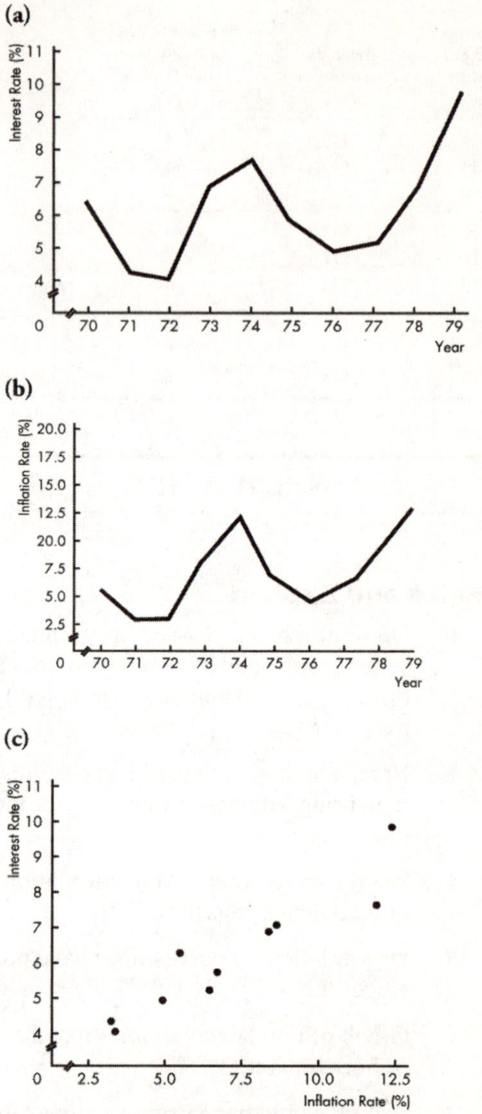

2 Figures A1.12(a) through (g) illustrate the desired graphs.

FIGURE **A1.12**

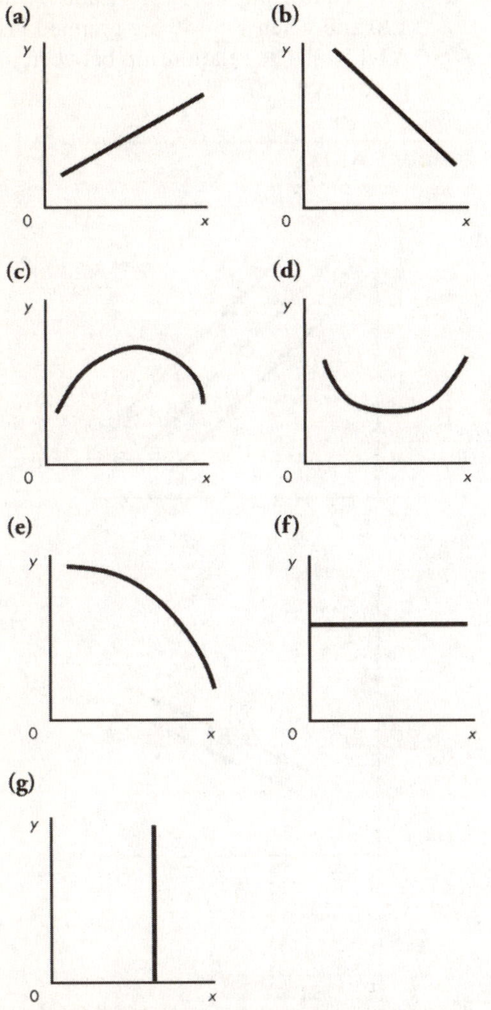

3 The negative sign in the slope of –2/3 means that there is a negative relationship between the two variables. The value of 2/3 means that when the variable measured on the vertical axis decreases by 2 units (the rise or Δy), the variable measured on the horizontal axis increases by 3 units (the run or Δx).

4 To find the slope, pick any two points on a line and compute $\Delta y/\Delta x$. The slope of the line in Figure A1.9(a) is –2/3, and the slope of the line in Figure A1.9(b) is 1/2.

5 a The requested straight line is graphed in Figure A1.13(a). First plot the point (2, 80). Then pick a second point whose *y*-coordinate decreases by 10 for every 1 unit increase in the *x*-coordinate, for example, (5, 50). The slope between the two points is –30/3 = –10.

b The requested straight line is graphed in Figure A1.13(b). First plot the point (6, 10). Then pick a second point whose *y*-coordinate decreases by 2 for every 1 unit decrease in the *x*-coordinate, for example, (5, 8). The slope between the two points is –2/–1 = 2.

FIGURE **A1.13**

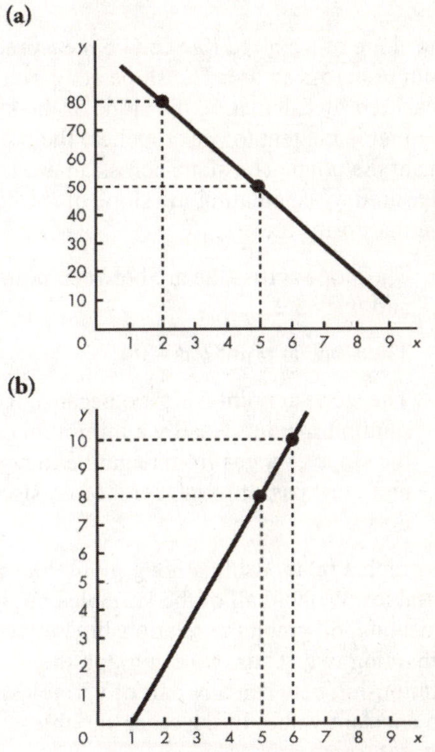

6 a To find the *y*-intercept, set $x = 0$.

$$y = 4 - 2(0)$$

$$y = 4$$

To find the *x*-intercept, set $y = 0$.

$$0 = 4 - 2x$$

$$x = 2$$

The slope of the line is –2, the value of the "*b*" coefficient on *x*.

b The graph of the line is shown in Figure A1.14.

FIGURE **A1.14**

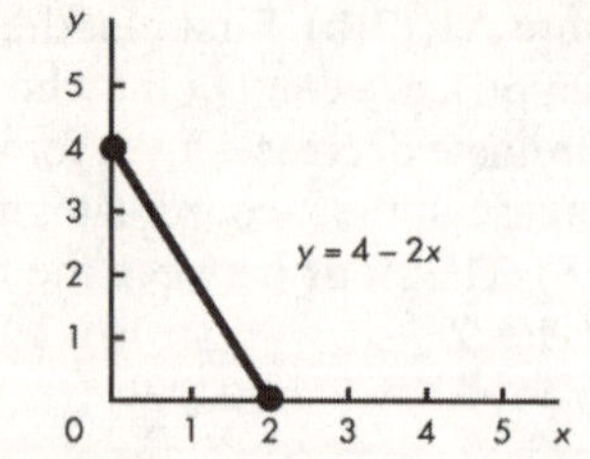

7 The slope of a curved line can be measured at a point or across an arc. The slope at a point is measured by calculating the slope of the straight line that is tangent to (just touches) the curved line at the point. The slope across an arc is measured by calculating the slope of the straight line that forms the arc.

8 **a** The slope across the arc between points *a* and *b* is –3/2.

b The slope at point *b* is –3/4.

c The slope at point *c* is zero because it is a minimum point. Nearby a minimum point the slope changes from negative to positive and must pass through zero, or no slope, to do so.

9 To graph a relationship among more than two variables, we hold all of the variables but two constant, and graph the relationship between the remaining two. Thus, we can graph the relationship between any pair of variables, given the constant values of the other variables.

10 **a** The relationships between *x* and *y* for *z* = 4, 5, and 6 are graphed in Figure A1.15(a).

b If the average monthly rainfall drops from 6 days to 4 days, the curve representing the relationship between umbrella sales and umbrella prices will shift from the curve labelled *z* = 6 to *z* = 4.

c The relationships between *x* and *z* when *y* is \$10 and when *y* is \$12 are graphed in Figure A1.15(b). The relationship between *x* and *z* is positive.

d The relationships between *y* and *z* when *x* = 120 and when *x* = 140 are graphed in Figure A1.15(c). The relationship between *y* and *z* is positive.

FIGURE **A1.15**

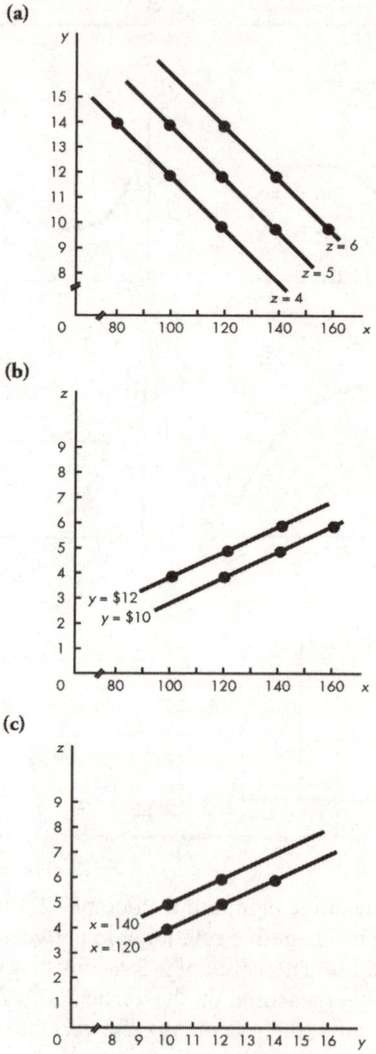

Chapter 2 The Economic Problem

KEY CONCEPTS

Production Possibilities and Opportunity Cost

The production possibility frontier (*PPF*)

- ♦ is the boundary between unattainable and attainable production possibilities.
- ♦ shows maximum combinations of outputs (goods and services) that can be produced with given resources and technology.

PPF characteristics:

- ♦ points on *PPF* represent **production efficiency**—more of one good cannot be produced without producing less of another good.
- ♦ points inside *PPF* are inefficient—attainable, but not maximum combinations of outputs; they represent unused or misallocated resources.
- ♦ points on *PPF* are preferred to points inside *PPF*.
- ♦ points outside *PPF* are unattainable.
- ♦ choosing among efficient points on *PPF* involves an *opportunity cost* and a *tradeoff*.

*PPF*s are generally bowed outward (concave), reflecting increasing opportunity costs as more of a good is produced.

- ♦ *PPF* is bowed outward because resources are not equally productive in all activities (nonhomogeneous). Resources most suitable for a given activity are the first to be used.
- ♦ Bowed-out-shaped *PPF* represents increasing opportunity cost—opportunity cost of good increases as its quantity produced increases.
- ♦ In moving between two points on *PPF* more good *X* can be obtained only by producing less good *Y*. Opportunity cost on *PPF* of additional *X* is amount of *Y* forgone.
- ♦ No opportunity cost in moving from point inside *PPF* to point on *PPF*.

Using Resources Efficiently

To choose among points on *PPF*, compare

- ♦ **marginal cost**—opportunity cost of producing one more unit of a good.
  - • marginal cost curve slopes upwards because of *increasing opportunity cost*.
- ♦ **marginal benefit**—benefit (measured in willingness to forgo other goods) from consuming one more unit of a good. Depends on a person's **preferences**—likes and dislikes.
  - • **marginal benefit curve** slopes downwards because of *decreasing marginal benefit*.

We choose a point on *PPF* of **allocative efficiency**

- ♦ where we produce the goods and services valued most highly
- ♦ where marginal benefit = marginal cost.

Economic Growth

Economic growth is the expansion of production possibilities—an outward shift of *PPF*.

- ♦ *PPF* shifts from changes in resources or technology.
- ♦ **Capital accumulation** and **technological change** shift *PPF* outward—economic growth.
- ♦ Opportunity cost of increased goods and services in future (economic growth through capital accumulation and technological progress) is decreased consumption today.

Gains from Trade

Production increases if people *specialize* in the activity in which they have a comparative advantage.

- Person has **comparative advantage** in producing a good if she can produce at lower opportunity cost than anyone else.
- When each person specializes in producing a good at which she has comparative advantage and exchanges for other goods, there are gains from trade.
- Specialization and exchange allow consumption (not production) at points outside *PPF*.
- Person has **absolute advantage** in producing a good if, using the same quantity of resources, she can produce more than anyone else.
    - Absolute advantage is irrelevant for specialization and gains from trade.
    - Even a person with an absolute advantage in producing all goods gains by specializing in activity in which she has a comparative advantage and trading.
- **Dynamic comparative advantage** results from specializing in an activity, **learning-by-doing**, and over time becoming the producer with the lowest opportunity cost.

Economic Coordination

Gains from trade and specialization require coordination. Decentralized coordination through markets depends on the social institutions of

- **firms**—hire and organize factors of production to produce and sell goods and services. Firms coordinate much economic activity, but the efficient size of a firm is limited.
- **property rights**—governing ownership, use, and disposal of resources, goods, and services.
- **markets**—coordinating buying and selling decisions through price adjustments.
- **money**—any generally acceptable means of payment; makes trading more efficient.

HELPFUL HINTS

1 This chapter reviews the absolutely critical concept of opportunity cost—the best alternative forgone—that was introduced in Chapter 1. Opportunity cost is a *ratio*. A very helpful formula for opportunity cost, which works well in solving problems, especially problems that involve moving up or down a production possibility frontier (*PPF*), is:

$$\text{Opportunity Cost} = \frac{\text{Give Up}}{\text{Get}}$$

Opportunity cost equals the quantity of goods you must give up divided by the quantity of goods you will get. This formula applies to all *PPF*s, whether they are bowed out as in Text Figure 2.1 or linear as in Text Figure 2.7. To illustrate, look again at the bowed-out *PPF*.

FIGURE 2.1 Production Possibilities Frontier

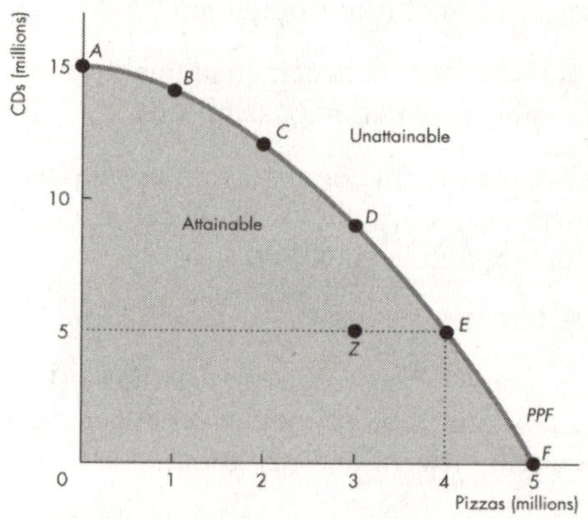

First, consider an example of moving down the *PPF*. In moving from *C* to *D*, what is the opportunity cost of an additional pizza? This economy must give up 3 CDs (12 – 9) to get 1 pizza (3 – 2). Substituting into the formula, the opportunity cost is:

$$\frac{3 \text{ CDs}}{1 \text{ pizza}} = 3 \text{ CDs per pizza}$$

Next, consider an example of moving up the *PPF*. In moving from *D* to *C*, what is the opportunity cost of an additional CD? We must give up 1 pizza (3 – 2) to get 3 CDs (12 – 9). Substituting into the formula, the opportunity cost is:

$$\frac{1 \text{ pizza}}{3 \text{ CDs}} = \frac{1}{3} \text{ pizza per CD}$$

Opportunity cost is always measured in the units of the forgone good.

ⓔ 2 Opportunity cost can also be related to the slope of the *PPF*. As we move down between any two points on the *PPF*, the opportunity cost of an additional unit of the good on the horizontal axis is:

$$|\text{slope of } PPF|$$

The slope of the *PPF* is negative, but economists like to describe opportunity cost in terms of a positive quantity of forgone goods. Therefore, we must use the absolute value of the slope to calculate the desired positive number.

As we move up between any two points on the *PPF*, the opportunity cost of an additional unit of the good on the vertical axis is:

$$\left|\frac{1}{\text{slope of } PPF}\right|$$

This is the *inverse* relation we saw between possibilities *C* and *D*. The opportunity cost of an additional pizza (on the horizontal axis) between *C* and *D* is 3 CDs. The opportunity cost of an additional CD (on the vertical axis) between *D* and *C* is 1/3 pizza.

3 All points on a *PPF* achieve productive efficiency in that they fully employ all resources. But how do we pick a point on the *PPF* and decide *what* combination of goods we want? The *PPF* provides information about resources and *costs*. But choosing what goods we want also requires information about *benefits*.

This choice, like all economic choices, is made at the margin. To decide what goods we want, compare the marginal cost (*MC*) and marginal benefit (*MB*) of different combinations. Marginal cost is the opportunity cost of producing one more unit. The marginal cost of producing more of any good increases as we move along the *PPF*. Marginal benefit is the benefit received from consuming one more unit. Marginal benefit decreases as we consume more of any good.

If the marginal cost of a good exceeds the marginal benefit, we decrease production of the good. If the marginal benefit exceeds the marginal cost, we increase production. When marginal cost equals marginal benefit for every good, we have chosen the goods that we value most highly. The decision rule of $MB = MC$ yields an *efficient* allocation of resources.

Text Figure 2.4 is crucial for explaining all economic decisions. Make sure you spend time on it even though it may be hard to fully understand. You will understand Text Figure 2.4 better after we spend time in future chapters elaborating the concepts of marginal cost and marginal benefit.

4 The CDs and pizza production possibility frontier assumes that resources are *not* equally productive in all activities. Resources with such differences are also called nonhomogeneous resources. As a result of this assumption, opportunity cost increases as we increase the production of either good. In moving from possibility *C* to *D*, the opportunity cost per unit of pizza is 3 CDs. But in increasing pizza production from *D* to *E*, the opportunity cost per unit of pizza increases to 4 CDs. In producing the first 1 (million) pizzas, we use the resources best suited to pizza production. As we increase pizza production, however, we must use resources that are less well suited to pizza production—hence increasing opportunity cost. A parallel argument accounts for the increasing opportunity cost of increasing CD production.

It is also possible to construct an even simpler model of a *PPF* that assumes resources are equally productive in all activities, or homogeneous resources. As a result of this assumption, opportunity cost is constant as we increase production of either good. Constant opportunity cost means that the *PPF* will be a straight line (rather than bowed out). As you will see in some of the following exercises, such a simple model is useful for illustrating the principle of comparative advantage, without having to deal with the complications of increasing opportunity cost.

ⓔ 5 The text defines absolute advantage as a situation where one person is more productive than another in the producing one or more goods. We can also define *absolute advantage in the production of one good.* In comparing the productivity of two persons, this narrower concept of absolute advantage can be defined in terms of either greater output of the good per unit of resource inputs or fewer resource inputs per unit of output. It is useful to understand these definitions of absolute advantage only to demonstrate that absolute advantage has no role in explaining specialization and trade. The gains from trade depend only on differing comparative advantages. People have a comparative advantage in producing a good if they can produce it at lower opportunity cost than others.

6 This chapter gives us our first chance to develop and use economic models. It is useful to think about the nature of these models in the context of the general discussion of models in Chapter 1. For example, one model in this chapter is a representation of the production possibilities in the two-person and two-good world of Liz and Joe. The model abstracts greatly from the complexity of the real world in which there are billions of people and numerous different kinds of goods and services. The model allows us to explain a number of phenomena that we observe in the world such as specialization and exchange.

The production possibilities model also has some implications or predictions. For example, countries that devote a larger proportion of their resources to capital accumulation will have more rapidly expanding production possibilities. The model can be subjected to "test" by comparing these predictions to the facts we observe in the real world.

SELF-TEST

True/False and Explain

Production Possibilities and Opportunity Cost

Refer to the production possibility frontier (*PPF*) in Figure 2.2 for Questions **1** to **4**.

FIGURE **2.2**

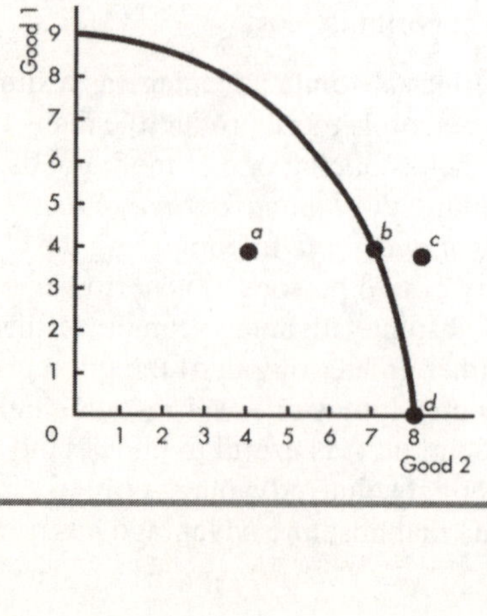

1 Point *a* is not attainable.

2 The opportunity cost of increasing the production of good 2 from 7 to 8 units is 4 units of good 1.

3 Point *c* is not attainable.

ⓔ 4 In moving from point *b* to point *d*, the opportunity cost of increasing the production of good 2 equals the absolute value of the slope of the *PPF* between *b* and *d*.

Using Resources Efficiently

5 The marginal cost of the 4th pizza is the cost of producing all 4 pizzas.

6 The marginal benefit of good *X* is the amount of good *Y* a person is willing to forgo to obtain one more unit of *X*.

7 The principle of decreasing marginal benefit states that the more we have of a good, the *less* we are willing to pay for an additional unit of it.

8 All points on a *PPF* represent both production efficiency and allocative efficiency.

Economic Growth

9 Economic growth, by shifting out the *PPF*, eliminates the problem of scarcity.

10 In a model where capital resources can grow, points on the *PPF* that have more consumption goods yield faster growth.

Gains from Trade

11 With specialization and trade, a country can produce at a point outside its *PPF*.

12 Canada has no incentive to trade with a cheap-labour country like Mexico.

13 Nadim definitely has a comparative advantage in producing skateboards if he can produce more than Elle.

Economic Coordination

14 The incentives for specialization and exchange do not depend on property rights but only on differing opportunity costs.

15 Price adjustments coordinate decisions in goods markets but not in factor markets.

Multiple-Choice

Production Possibilities and Opportunity Cost

1 If Harold can increase production of good *X* without decreasing the production of any other good, he
- **a** is producing on his *PPF*.
- **b** is producing outside his *PPF*.
- **c** is producing inside his *PPF*.
- **d** must have a linear *PPF*.
- **e** must prefer good *X* to any other good.

2 The bowed-out (concave) shape of a *PPF*
- **a** is due to the equal usefulness of resources in all activities.
- **b** is due to capital accumulation.
- **c** is due to technological change.
- **d** reflects the existence of increasing opportunity cost.
- **e** reflects the existence of decreasing opportunity cost.

3 The economy is at point *b* on the *PPF* in Figure 2.3. The opportunity cost of producing one more unit of *X* is
- **a** 1 unit of *Y*.
- **b** 20 units of *Y*.
- **c** 1 unit of *X*.
- **d** 8 units of *X*.
- **e** 20 units of *X*.

FIGURE **2.3**

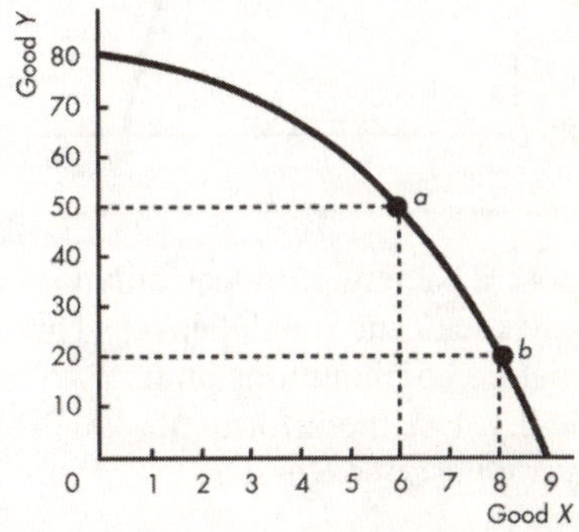

4 Refer to the *PPF* in Figure 2.3. Which of the following statements is *false*?
- **a** Resources are not equally productive in all activities.
- **b** Points inside the frontier represent unemployed resources.
- **c** Starting at point *a*, an increase in the production of good *Y* will shift the frontier out.
- **d** The opportunity cost of producing good *Y* increases as production of *Y* increases.
- **e** Shifts in preferences for good *X* or good *Y* will not shift the frontier.

5 Refer to Figure 2.4, which shows the *PPF* for an economy without discrimination operating at maximum efficiency. If discrimination against women workers is currently occurring in this economy, the elimination of discrimination would result in a(n)
- **a** movement from *a* to *b*.
- **b** movement from *b* to *c*.
- **c** movement from *a* to *c*.
- **d** outward shift of the *PPF*.
- **e** inward shift of the *PPF*.

FIGURE **2.4**

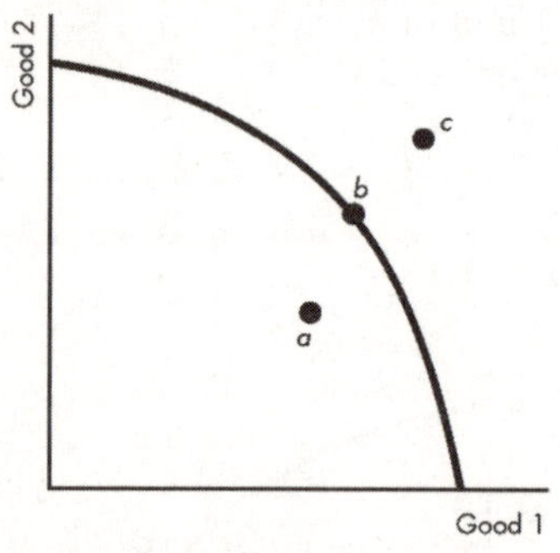

Suppose a society produces only two goods—hockey sticks and maple leaves. Three alternative combinations on its *PPF* are given in Table 2.1. Use the information in Table 2.1 to answer Questions **6** and **7**.

TABLE **2.1** PRODUCTION POSSIBILITIES

Possibility	Units of Hockey Sticks	Units of Maple Leaves
a	3	0
b	2	3
c	0	9

6 In moving from combination *c* to combination *b*, the opportunity cost of producing one additional hockey stick is
- **a** 2 maple leaves.
- **b** 1/2 maple leaves.
- **c** 6 maple leaves.
- **d** 1/6 maple leaves.
- **e** 3 maple leaves.

7 According to this *PPF*
- **a** resources are equally productive in all activities.
- **b** a combination of 3 hockey sticks and 9 maple leaves is attainable.
- **c** a combination of 3 hockey sticks and 9 maple leaves would not employ all resources.
- **d** the opportunity cost of producing hockey sticks increases as more hockey sticks are produced.
- **e** the opportunity cost of producing hockey sticks decreases as more hockey sticks are produced.

Using Resources Efficiently

8 The marginal benefit curve for a good
- **a** shows the benefit a firm receives from producing one more unit.
- **b** shows the amount a consumer is willing to pay for one more unit.
- **c** is upward-sloping.
- **d** is bowed out.
- **e** is none of the above.

9 With increasing production of food, its marginal benefit
- **a** increases and marginal cost increases.
- **b** increases and marginal cost decreases.
- **c** decreases and marginal cost increases.
- **d** decreases and marginal cost decreases.
- **e** decreases and marginal cost is constant.

10 Suppose the *PPF* for skirts and pants is a straight line. As the production of skirts increases, the marginal benefit of skirts
- **a** increases and marginal cost is constant.
- **b** is constant and marginal cost increases.
- **c** decreases and marginal cost decreases.
- **d** decreases and marginal cost increases.
- **e** decreases and marginal cost is constant.

11 With allocative efficiency, for each good produced, marginal
- a benefit equals marginal cost.
- b benefit is at its maximum.
- c benefit exceeds marginal cost by as much as possible.
- d cost exceeds marginal benefit by as much as possible.
- e cost is at its minimum.

Economic Growth

12 The *PPF* for wine and wool will shift if there is a change in
- a the price of resources.
- b the unemployment rate.
- c the quantity of resources.
- d preferences for wine and wool.
- e all of the above.

13 A movement *along* a given *PPF* will result from
- a technological change.
- b change in the stock of capital.
- c change in the labour force.
- d all of the above.
- e none of the above.

14 The opportunity cost of pushing the *PPF* outward is
- a capital accumulation.
- b technological change.
- c reduced current consumption.
- d the gain in future consumption.
- e all of the above.

15 In general, the higher the proportion of resources devoted to technological research in an economy, the
- a greater will be current consumption.
- b faster the *PPF* will shift outward.
- c faster the *PPF* will shift inward.
- d closer it will come to having a comparative advantage in the production of all goods.
- e more bowed out the shape of the *PPF* will be.

16 Refer to the *PPF* in Figure 2.5. A politician who argues that "if our children are to be better off, we must invest now for the future" is recommending a current point like
- a *a.*
- b *b.*
- c *c.*
- d *d.*
- e *e.*

FIGURE **2.5**

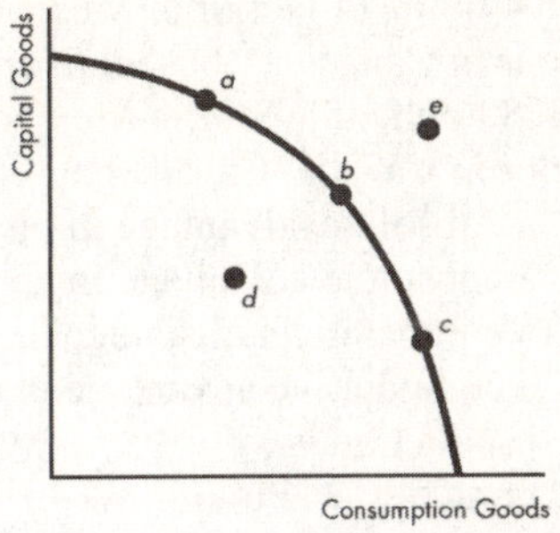

17 Refer to the *PPF* in Figure 2.5. The statement that "unemployment is a terrible waste of human resources" refers to a point like
- a *a.*
- b *b.*
- c *c.*
- d *d.*
- e *e.*

Gains from Trade

In an eight-hour day, Andy can produce either 24 loaves of bread or 8 kilograms of butter. In an eight-hour day, Rolfe can produce either 8 loaves of bread or 8 kilograms of butter. Use this information to answer Questions **18** and **19**.

18 Which of the following statements is *true*?
- a Andy has an absolute advantage in butter production.
- b Rolfe has an absolute advantage in butter production.
- c Andy has an absolute advantage in bread production.
- d Andy has a comparative advantage in butter production.
- e Rolfe has a comparative advantage in bread production.

19 Andy and Rolfe
- a can gain from exchange if Andy specializes in butter production and Rolfe specializes in bread production.
- b can gain from exchange if Andy specializes in bread production and Rolfe specializes in butter production.
- c cannot gain from exchange.
- d can exchange, but only Rolfe will gain.
- e can exchange, but only Andy will gain.

20 Mexico and Canada produce both oil and apples using labour only. A barrel of oil is produced with 4 hours of labour in Mexico and 8 hours of labour in Canada. A bushel of apples is produced with 8 hours of labour in Mexico and 12 hours of labour in Canada. Canada has
- **a** an absolute advantage in oil production.
- **b** an absolute advantage in apple production.
- **c** a comparative advantage in oil production.
- **d** a comparative advantage in apple production.
- **e** none of the above.

21 In Portugal, the opportunity cost of a bale of wool is 3 bottles of wine. In England, the opportunity cost of 1 bottle of wine is 3 bales of wool. Given this information,
- **a** England has an absolute advantage in wine production.
- **b** England has an absolute advantage in wool production.
- **c** Portugal has a comparative advantage in wine production.
- **d** Portugal has a comparative advantage in wool production.
- **e** no trade will occur.

22 To gain from comparative advantage, countries must not only trade, they must also
- **a** save.
- **b** invest.
- **c** engage in research and development.
- **d** engage in capital accumulation.
- **e** specialize.

23 Learning-by-doing is the basis of
- **a** absolute comparative advantage.
- **b** dynamic comparative advantage.
- **c** intellectual property rights.
- **d** financial property rights.
- **e** none of the above.

Economic Coordination

24 Trade is organized using the social institutions of
- **a** firms.
- **b** property rights.
- **c** money.
- **d** markets.
- **e** all of the above.

25 Markets

1 enable buyers and sellers to get information.

2 are defined by economists as geographical locations where trade occurs.

3 coordinate buying and selling decisions through price adjustments.

- **a** 1 only
- **b** 3 only
- **c** 1 and 3 only
- **d** 2 and 3 only
- **e** 1, 2, and 3

Short Answer Problems

1 Why is a *PPF* negatively sloped? Why is it bowed out?

2 Suppose that an economy has the *PPF* shown in Table 2.2.

TABLE **2.2** PRODUCTION POSSIBILITIES

Possibility	Maximum Units of Butter per Week	Maximum Units of Guns per Week
a	200	0
b	180	60
c	160	100
d	100	160
e	40	200
f	0	220

- **a** On graph paper, plot these possibilities, label the points, and draw the *PPF*. (Put guns on the *x*-axis.)
- **b** If the economy moves from possibility *c* to possibility *d*, the opportunity cost *per unit of guns* will be how many units of butter?
- **c** If the economy moves from possibility *d* to possibility *e*, the opportunity cost *per unit of guns* will be how many units of butter?
- **d** In general terms, what happens to the opportunity cost of guns as the output of guns increases?
- **e** In general terms, what happens to the opportunity cost of butter as the output of butter increases? What do the results in parts **d** and **e** imply about resources?

f If (instead of the possibilities given) the *PPF* were a straight line joining points *a* and *f*, what would that imply about opportunity costs and resources?

g Given the original *PPF* you have plotted, is a combination of 140 units of butter and 130 units of guns per week attainable? Would you regard this combination as an efficient one? Explain.

h Given the original *PPF*, is a combination of 70 units of butter and 170 units of guns per week attainable? Does this combination achieve productive efficiency? Explain.

3 If the following events occurred (each is a separate event, unaccompanied by any other event), what would happen to the *PPF* in Short Answer Problem **2**?

a A new, easily exploited, energy source is discovered.

b A large number of skilled workers immigrate into the country.

c The output of butter increases.

d A new invention increases output per person in the butter industry but not in the guns industry.

e A new law is passed compelling workers, who could previously work as long as they wanted, to retire at age 60.

4 The Borg produce only two goods—cubes and transwarp coils—and want to decide where on their *PPF* to operate. Table 2.3 shows the marginal benefit and marginal cost of cubes, measured in the number of transwarp coils per cube.

TABLE **2.3**

Borg Cubes	Marginal Benefit	Marginal Cost
1	12	3
2	10	4
3	8	5
4	6	6
5	4	7
6	2	8

a If the Borg are efficient (and they are!), what quantity of cubes will they produce?

b If the Borg were to produce one more cube than your answer in **a**, why would that choice be inefficient?

5 Suppose the country of Quark has historically devoted 10 percent of its resources to the production of new capital goods. Use *PPF* diagrams like Text Figures 2.5 and 2.6 on pages 40–41 to compare the consequences (costs and benefits) of each of the following:

a Quark continues to devote 10 percent of its resources to the production of capital goods.

b Quark begins now to permanently devote 20 percent of its resources to the production of capital goods.

6 Lawyers earn $200 per hour while secretaries earn $15 per hour. Use the concepts of absolute and comparative advantage to explain why a lawyer who is a better typist than her secretary will still specialize in doing only legal work and will trade with the secretary for typing services.

7 France and Germany each produce both wine and beer, using a single, homogeneous input—labour. Their production possibilities are:

- France has 100 units of labour and can produce a maximum of 200 bottles of wine or 400 bottles of beer.
- Germany has 50 units of labour and can produce a maximum of 250 bottles of wine or 200 bottles of beer.

a Complete Table 2.4.

TABLE **2.4**

	Bottles Produced by 1 Unit of Labour		Opportunity Cost of 1 Additional Bottle	
	Wine	Beer	Wine	Beer
France				
Germany				

Use the information in part **a** to answer the following questions.

b Which country has an absolute advantage in wine production?

c Which country has an absolute advantage in beer production?

d Which country has a comparative advantage in wine production?

e Which country has a comparative advantage in beer production?

f If trade is allowed, describe what specialization, if any, will occur.

8 Tova and Ron are the only two remaining inhabitants of the planet Melmac. They spend their 30-hour days producing widgets and woggles, the only two goods needed for happiness on Melmac. It takes Tova 1 hour to produce a widget and 2 hours to produce a woggle, while Ron takes 3 hours to produce a widget and 3 hours to produce a woggle.

a For a 30-hour day, draw an individual *PPF* for Tova, then for Ron.

b What does the shape of the *PPF*s tell us about opportunity costs? about resources?

c Assume initially that Tova and Ron are each self-sufficient. Define self-sufficiency. Explain what the individual consumption possibilities are for Tova, then for Ron.

d Who has an absolute advantage in the production of widgets? of woggles?

e Who has a comparative advantage in the production of widgets? of woggles?

f Suppose Tova and Ron each specialize in producing only the good in which she/he has a comparative advantage (one spends 30 hours producing widgets, the other spends 30 hours producing woggles). What will be the total production of widgets and woggles?

g Suppose Tova and Ron exchange 7 widgets for 5 woggles. On your *PPF* diagrams, plot the new point of Tova's consumption, then of Ron's consumption. Explain how these points illustrate the gains from trade.

9 The Netsilik and Oonark families live on the Arctic coast, west of Hudson Bay. They often go fishing and hunting for caribou together. During an average working day, the Netsiliks can, at most, either catch 6 kilograms of fish or kill 6 caribou. The Oonarks can either catch 4 kilograms of fish or kill 4 caribou.

a Assuming linear *PPF*s, draw each family's *PPF* on the same diagram. Put fish on the horizontal axis and caribou on the vertical axis.

b Complete Table 2.5.

TABLE **2.5**

	Opportunity Cost of 1 Additional	
	Fish (kg)	**Caribou**
Netsiliks		
Oonarks		

c Which family has a comparative advantage in catching fish? in hunting caribou?

d Can specialization and trade increase the total output of fish and caribou produced by the two families? Explain.

10 Explain the interdependence that exists between households and firms in Text Figure 2.8 on page 47.

ANSWERS

True/False and Explain

1 F Attainable but not an efficient point. (34–35)

2 T Moving from *b* to *d*, production good 1 decreases by 4 units. (35–36)

3 T Outside *PPF*. (34–35)

4 T See Helpful Hint **2**. (35–36)

5 F Marginal cost is *additional* cost of producing the 4th pizza alone. (37)

6 T Marginal benefit is also the amount a person is willing to pay for one more unit, but payment in money ultimately represents an opportunity cost in goods forgone. (38)

7 T The more we have of a good, the smaller is the marginal benefit and hence the willingness to pay for it. (38)

8 F All points represent productive efficiency (efficient use of resources). But allocative efficiency only occurs at the single point (combination of goods) that we prefer above all others (where *MB* = *MC*). (39)

9 F Cost of growth is forgone current consumption. (40)

10 F Points with more capital goods yield faster growth. (40–41)

11 F Can *consume* at point outside *PPF*. (43–44)

12 F Mutually beneficial trade depends on comparative advantage, not absolute advantage. (42–45)

13 F Nadim has absolute advantage in skateboard production, but without information about opportunity costs, we don't know if he has comparative advantage. (45)

14 F Property rights are prerequisite for specialization and exchange. (46)

15 F Price adjustments coordinate buying and selling decisions in all markets. (46–47)

Multiple-Choice

1 c For 0 opportunity cost, must be unemployed resources. (34–35)

2 d **a** would be true if *un*equal resources; **b** and **c** shift *PPF*. (36)

3 b To increase quantity *X* to 9, must decrease quantity *Y* from 20 to 0. (35–36)

ⓒⓣ **4 c** Increased production *Y* moves up *along* *PPF*. (34–36)

5 a Discrimination causes underemployment of resources. Women not allowed to produce up to full abilities. (34–36)

6 e Give up 6 maple leaves to get 2 hockey sticks: 6/2 = 3 maple leaves per hockey stick. (35–36)

ⓒⓣ **7 a** Constant opportunity cost means resources equally productive for producing all goods—see Helpful Hint **4**. (34–36)

8 b Benefits apply to consumers; curve is downward-sloping. (38)

9 c Principles of diminishing marginal benefit and increasing marginal cost. (37–39)

ⓒⓣ **10 e** Diminishing marginal benefit, but linear *PPF* means constant opportunity and marginal costs. (37–39)

11 a Whenever $MB \neq MC$, efficiency improves by reallocating resources to produce more goods with high marginal benefits, causing a decrease in their marginal benefit and increase in marginal cost. (39)

12 c Only changes in resources or technology shift *PPF*. (40)

ⓒⓣ **13 e** **a**, **b**, and **c** all shift *PPF*. (40–41)

14 c **a** and **b** cause outward shift *PPF*, not opportunity cost; **d** effect of outward shift *PPF*. (40–41)

15 b Technological change shifts *PPF* outward at cost of current consumption. (40–41)

16 a Producing more capital goods now, shifts *PPF* outward in future. (40–41)

17 d Points inside *PPF* represent unemployed resources, whether labour, capital, or land. (34–35, 40–41)

ⓔ **18 c** Andy produces 3 loaves bread per hour; Rolfe produces 1 loaf per hour—see Helpful Hint **5**. (42–45)

19 b Andy has comparative advantage (lower opportunity cost) bread, Rolfe has comparative advantage butter production. (42–45)

ⓒⓣ **20 d** Opportunity cost oil in bushels of apples—Canada 2/3, Mexico 1/2. Opportunity cost apples in barrels of oil—Canada 3/2, Mexico 2. (42–45)

21 c Opportunity cost wine in bales of wool—Portugal 1/3, England 3. Opportunity cost wool in bottles of wine—Portugal 3, England 1/3. (42–45)

22 e Gains from trade require specialization based on comparative advantage. **a**–**d** may increase productivity and absolute advantage, not necessarily comparative advantage. (42–45)

23 b Definition. (45)

24 e All 4 institutions required for gains from trade and specialization through decentralized coordination. (46)

25 c 2 is the ordinary meaning of markets, not the economist's definition. (45–46)

Short Answer Problems

1 The negative slope of the *PPF* reflects opportunity cost: in order to have more of one good, some of the other must be forgone. It is bowed out because the existence of resources not equally productive in all activities creates increasing opportunity cost as we increase the production of either good.

2 a The graph of the *PPF* is given in Figure 2.6.

FIGURE **2.6**

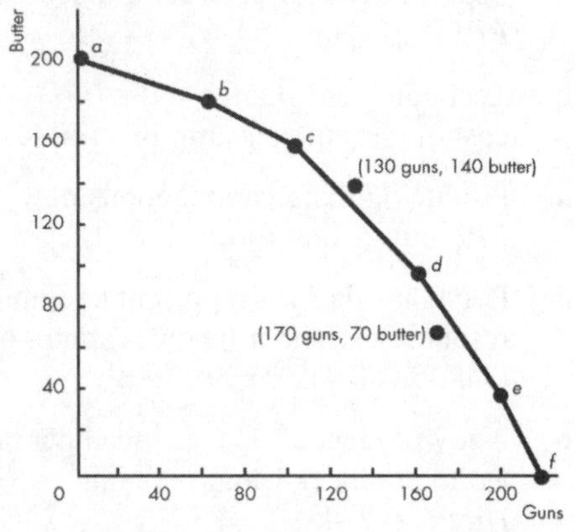

b In moving from *c* to *d*, in order to gain 60 units of guns, we must give up 160 – 100 = 60 units of butter. The opportunity cost per unit of guns is

$$\frac{60 \text{ units butter}}{60 \text{ units guns}} = 1 \text{ unit butter per unit of guns}$$

c In moving from *d* to *e*, in order to gain 40 units of guns, we must give up 100 – 40 = 60 units of butter. The opportunity cost per unit of guns is

$$\frac{60 \text{ units butter}}{40 \text{ units guns}} = 1.5 \text{ unit butter per unit of guns}$$

d The opportunity cost of producing more guns increases as the output of guns increases.

e Likewise, the opportunity cost of producing more butter increases as the output of butter increases. Increasing opportunity costs imply that resources are not equally productive in gun and butter production; that is, they are nonhomogeneous.

f Opportunity costs would always be constant, regardless of the output of guns or butter. The opportunity cost per unit of guns would be

200/220 = 10/11 units of butter

The opportunity cost per unit of butter would be

220/200 = 1.1 units of guns

Constant opportunity costs imply that resources are equally productive in gun and butter production; that is, they are homogeneous.

g This combination is outside the *PPF* and therefore is not attainable. Since the economy cannot produce this combination, the question of efficiency is irrelevant.

h This combination is inside the *PPF* and is attainable. It is inefficient because the economy could produce more of either or both goods without producing less of anything else. Therefore some resources are not fully utilized.

3 a Assuming that both goods require energy for their production, the entire *PPF* shifts out to the northeast as in Figure 2.7(a).

b Assuming that both goods use skilled labour in their production, the entire *PPF* shifts out to the northeast.

c The *PPF* does not shift. An increase in the output of butter implies a movement along the *PPF* to the left, not a shift of the *PPF* itself.

d The new invention implies that for every level of output of guns, the economy can now produce more butter. The *PPF* swings to the right, but remains anchored at point *f* as in Figure 2.7(b).

e The entire *PPF* shifts in toward the origin.

FIGURE **2.7**

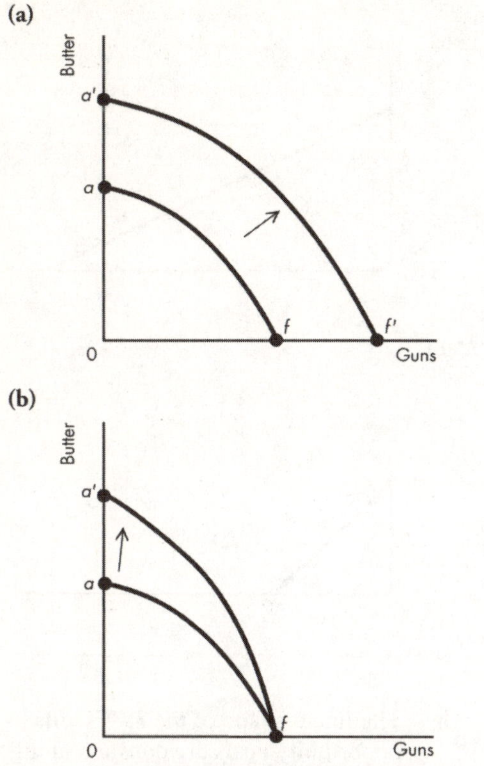

4 a At the efficient quantity of output, marginal benefit = marginal cost. The Borg will produce 4 cubes ($MB = MC = 4$ transwarp coils/cube).

b At 5 cubes, marginal benefit = 4 and marginal cost = 7. Since $MC > MB$, the Borg could get better use from their resources by shifting production out of cubes and into transwarp coils.

5 a The situation for Quark is depicted by Figure 2.8. Suppose Quark starts on PPF_1. If it continues to devote only 10 percent of its resources to the production of new capital goods, it is choosing to produce at a point like *a*. This will shift the *PPF* out in the next period, but only to the curve labelled 2 (where, presumably, Quark will choose to produce at point *b*).

FIGURE **2.8**

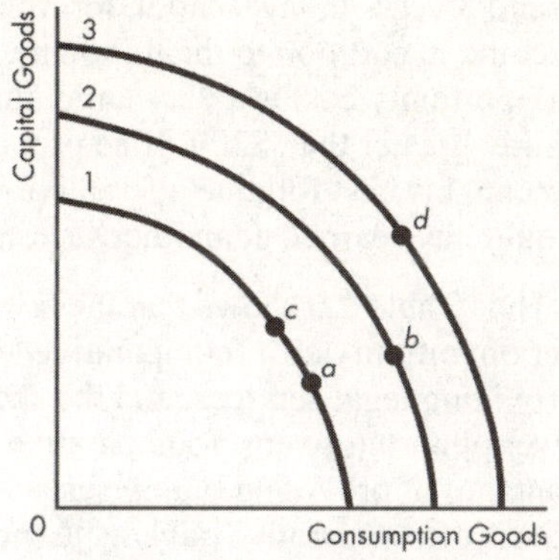

b Starting from the same initial *PPF*, if Quark now decides to increase the resources devoted to the production of new capital to 20 percent, it will be choosing to produce at a point like *c*. In this case, next period's *PPF* will shift further—to curve 3, and a point like *d*, for example.

Thus in comparing points *a* and *c*, we find the following costs and benefits: point *a* has the benefit of greater present consumption but at a cost of lower future consumption; point *c* has the cost of lower present consumption, but with the benefit of greater future consumption.

6 The lawyer has an absolute advantage in producing both legal and typing services relative to the secretary. Nevertheless, she has a comparative advantage in legal services, and the secretary has a comparative advantage in typing. To demonstrate these comparative advantages, we can construct Table 2.6 of opportunity costs.

TABLE **2.6**

	Opportunity Cost of 1 Additional Hour ($)	
	Legal Services	**Typing**
Lawyer	200	200
Secretary	>200	15

Consider first the lawyer's opportunity costs. The lawyer's best forgone alternative to providing 1 hour of legal services is the $200 she could earn by providing another hour of legal services. If she provides 1 hour of typing, she is also forgoing $200 (1 hour) of legal services.

What would the secretary have to forgo to provide 1 hour of legal services? He would have to spend 3 years in law school, forgoing 3 years of income in addition to the tuition he must pay. His opportunity cost is a very large number, certainly greater than $200. If he provides 1 hour of typing, his best forgone alternative is the $15 he could have earned at another secretarial job.

Thus Table 2.6 shows that the lawyer has a lower opportunity cost (comparative advantage) of providing legal services, and the secretary has a lower opportunity cost (comparative advantage) of providing typing services. It is on the basis of comparative advantage (not absolute advantage) that trade will take place from which both parties gain.

7 a The completed table is shown here as Table 2.4 Solution.

TABLE **2.4** SOLUTION

	Bottles Produced by 1 Unit of Labour		Opportunity Cost of 1 Additional Bottle	
	Wine	**Beer**	**Wine**	**Beer**
France	2	4	2.0 beer	0.50 wine
Germany	5	4	0.8 beer	1.25 wine

b Germany, which can produce more wine (5 bottles) per unit of input, has an absolute advantage in wine production.

c Neither country has an absolute advantage in beer production, since beer output (4 bottles) per unit of input is the same for both countries.

d Germany, with the lower opportunity cost (0.8 beer), has a comparative advantage in wine production.

e France, with the lower opportunity cost (0.5 wine), has a comparative advantage in beer production.

f The incentive for trade depends only on differences in comparative advantage. Germany will specialize in wine production and France will specialize in beer production.

8 a The individual *PPF*s for Tova and Ron are given by Figure 2.9(a) and (b) respectively.

FIGURE **2.9**

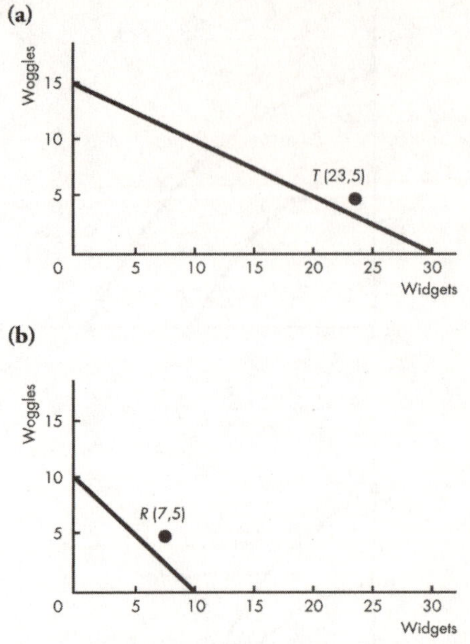

b The linear shape of the *PPF*s tells us that opportunity costs are constant along each frontier and that resources are homogeneous.

These linear *PPF*s with constant opportunity costs abstract from the complexity of the real world. The world generally has increasing opportunity costs, but that fact is not essential for understanding the gains from trade, which is the objective of this problem. Making the model more complex by including increasing opportunity costs would not change our results, but it would make it more difficult to see them.

c Individuals are self-sufficient if they consume only what they produce. This means there is no trade. Without trade, Tova's (maximum) consumption possibilities are exactly the same as her production possibilities—points along her *PPF*. Ron's (maximum) consumption possibilities are likewise the points along his *PPF*.

d Tova has an absolute advantage in the production of both widgets and woggles. Her absolute advantage can be defined either in terms of greater output per unit of inputs or fewer inputs per unit of output. A comparison of the *PPF*s in Figure 2.9 shows that, for given inputs of 30 hours, Tova produces a greater output of widgets than Ron (30 versus 10) and a greater output of woggles than Ron (15 versus 10). The statement of the problem tells us equivalently that, per unit of output, Tova uses fewer inputs than Ron for both widgets (1 hour versus 3 hours) and woggles (2 hours versus 3 hours). Since Tova has greater productivity than Ron in the production of all goods (widgets and woggles), we say that overall she has an absolute advantage.

e Tova has a comparative advantage in the production of widgets, since she can produce them at lower opportunity cost than Ron (1/2 woggle versus 1 woggle). On the other hand, Ron has a comparative advantage in the production of woggles, since he can produce them at a lower opportunity cost than Tova (1 widget versus 2 widgets).

f Tova will produce widgets and Ron will produce woggles, yielding a total production between them of 30 widgets and 10 woggles.

g After the exchange, Tova will have 23 widgets and 5 woggles (point *T*). Ron will have 7 widgets and 5 woggles (point *R*). These new post-trade consumption possibility points lie outside Tova's and Ron's respective pre-trade consumption (and production) possibilities. Hence trade has yielded gains that allow the traders to improve their consumption possibilities beyond those available with self-sufficiency.

9 a The *PPF*s of the Netsiliks and Oonarks are shown in Figure 2.10.

FIGURE **2.10**

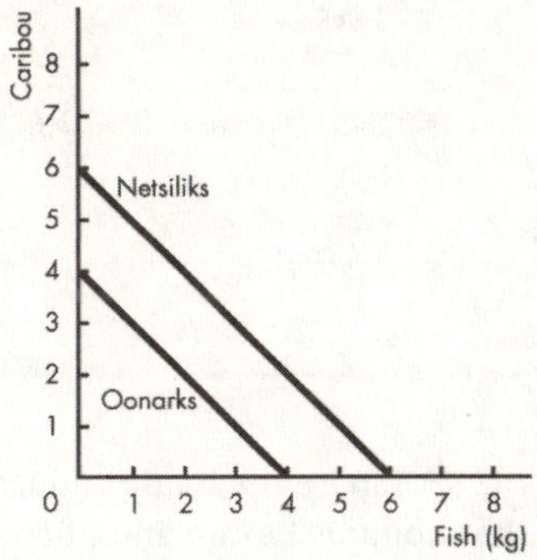

b The completed table is shown here as Table 2.5 Solution.

TABLE **2.5** SOLUTION

	Opportunity Cost of 1 Additional	
	Fish (kg)	**Caribou**
Netsiliks	1 caribou	1 kg fish
Oonarks	1 caribou	1 kg fish

c Neither family has a comparative advantage in catching fish, since the opportunity cost of fish is the same (1 caribou) for each family. Similarly, neither family has a comparative advantage in hunting caribou, since the opportunity cost of a caribou is the same (1 kilogram of fish) for each family.

d Gains from specialization and trade are due to the existence of comparative advantage. In this case, no family has a comparative advantage in either fishing or hunting, so there are no gains from specialization and trade.

To illustrate the absence of gains, suppose that initially each family devoted half of its time to each activity. Then suppose that the Netsiliks specialized completely in catching fish and the Oonarks specialized completely in hunting caribou. Production before and after specialization is shown in Table 2.7.

TABLE **2.7**

	Before Specialization		After Specialization	
	Fish (kg)	**Caribou**	**Fish (kg)**	**Caribou**
Netsiliks	3	3	6	0
Oonarks	2	2	0	4
Total Production	5	5	6	4

Compare the total production of both commodities before and after specialization.

Specialization has increased the total production of fish by 1 kilogram, but it has also led to a decrease in the total production of caribou by 1. There are no clear gains in consumption from specialization and trade.

10 Firms depend on households for the supply of factors of production. In exchange, households depend on firms for income. Households use that income to buy goods and services from firms, while firms depend on the money they get from household purchases to purchase more factors of production in the next period and renew the circular flow.

CHAPTERS 1–2

Part 1 Wrap Up

Understanding the Scope of Economics

PROBLEM

The economy is a mechanism that allocates scarce resources among competing uses. But how do those allocation decisions get made? In the Canadian economy, markets are the primary institutions that coordinate individual decisions through price adjustments.

Suppose, for simplicity, the Canadian economy produced only two outputs—child-care services and televisions. The production possibility frontier (*PPF*) for the economy appears in Figure P1.1 below. The economy is operating at point *a*, producing Q^0_{cc} units of child-care services and Q^0_{tv} televisions.

FIGURE **P1.1**

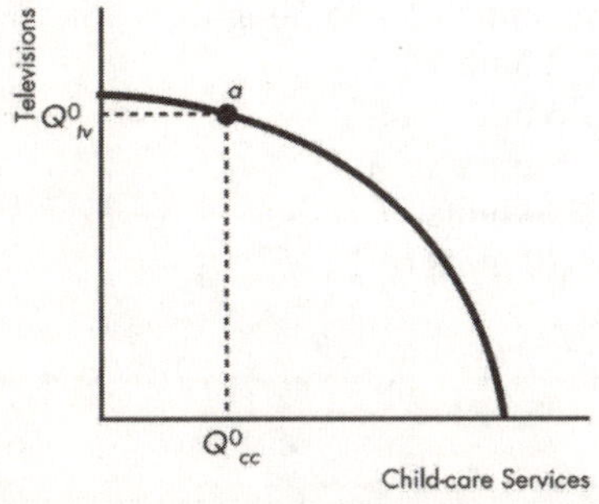

a What does the bowed-out (concave) shape of the *PPF* imply about resources? opportunity costs?

b As more women enter the labour force, there is increased demand for child-care services. As a result, the price and quantity of child-care services both increase. At the same time, the demand for televisions falls (perhaps to save money to pay for the additional child-care services). As a result, the price and quantity of televisions both decrease.

On the *PPF* in Figure P1.1, label as point *b* a new combination of child-care services and televisions reflecting the changes in demand.

c Explain how the economy came to produce these new quantities in response to the changing demands of households.

d What determines the distance of the *PPF* from the origin? What determines the precise point on the *PPF* at which the economy operates? What is the true cost of moving from point *a* to point *b* on the *PPF?*

MIDTERM EXAMINATION

You should allocate 30 minutes for this examination (15 questions, 2 minutes per question). For each question, choose the one *best* answer.

1 A *PPF* shows that
- **a** there is a limit to the production of any one good.
- **b** to produce more of one good, we must produce less of another good.
- **c** there are limits to total production with given resources and technology.
- **d** all of the above are true.
- **e** none of the above is true.

2 The graph showing the level of a variable across different groups at a point in time is a
- **a** linear graph.
- **b** time-series graph.
- **c** cross-section graph.
- **d** misleading graph.
- **e** scatter diagram.

Suppose a society produces only two goods—guns and butter. Three alternative combinations on its *PPF* are given in Table P1.1. Use the information in Table P1.1 to answer Questions **3** and **4**.

TABLE **P1.1** PRODUCTION POSSIBILITIES

Possibility	Units of Butter	Units of Guns
a	8	0
b	6	1
c	0	3

3 In moving from combination *b* to combination *c*, the opportunity cost of producing *one* additional unit of guns is
- **a** 2 units of butter.
- **b** 1/2 unit of butter.
- **c** 6 units of butter.
- **d** 1/6 unit of butter.
- **e** 3 units of butter.

4 According to this *PPF*
- **a** a combination of 6 butter and 1 gun would not employ all resources.
- **b** a combination of 0 butter and 4 guns is attainable.
- **c** resources are equally productive in all activities.
- **d** the opportunity cost of producing guns increases as more guns are produced.
- **e** the opportunity cost of producing guns decreases as more guns are produced.

5 Which of the following is a normative statement?
- **a** Pollution is an example of an external cost.
- **b** Pollution makes people worse off.
- **c** Firms that pollute should be forced to shut down.
- **d** Pollution imposes opportunity costs on others.
- **e** None of the above.

6 The graph of the relationship between two variables that are negatively related
- **a** is horizontal.
- **b** slopes upward to the right.
- **c** is vertical.
- **d** slopes downward to the right.
- **e** is linear.

7 In Figure P1.2, the slope of the line is
- **a** 1.50.
- **b** 1.25.
- **c** 1.00.
- **d** 0.75.
- **e** 0.50.

FIGURE **P1.2**

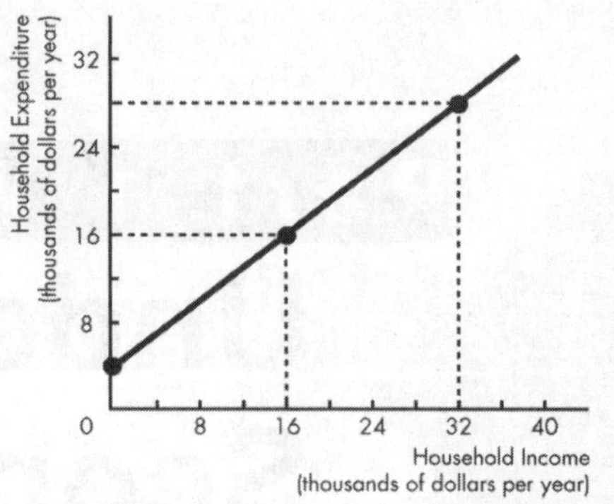

8 Other things being equal, which of the following statements is correct?

1 If unemployment increases, the opportunity cost of attending university decreases.

2 If men generally earn more than women in the labour market, the opportunity cost of attending university is higher for men than for women.

- **a** 1 only
- **b** 2 only
- **c** 1 and 2
- **d** Neither 1 nor 2
- **e** Impossible to judge without additional information

9 The economy is at point *b* on the *PPF* in Figure 1.3. The opportunity cost of increasing the production of *Y* to 50 units is
- **a** 2 units of *X*.
- **b** 6 units of *X*.
- **c** 8 units of *X*.
- **d** 20 units of *Y*.
- **e** 30 units of *Y*.

FIGURE **P1.3**

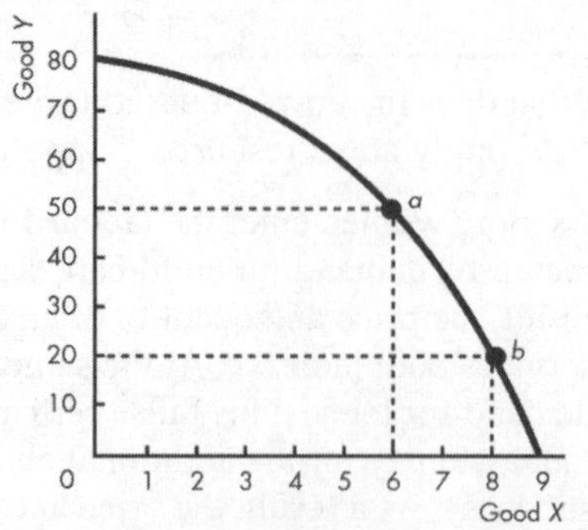

10 Because productive resources are scarce, we must give up some of one good in order to acquire more of another. This is the essence of the concept of
- **a** specialization.
- **b** monetary exchange.
- **c** comparative advantage.
- **d** absolute advantage.
- **e** opportunity cost.

11 The scarcity of resources implies that the *PPF* is
- **a** bowed inward (convex).
- **b** bowed outward (concave).
- **c** positively sloped.
- **d** negatively sloped.
- **e** linear.

12 If additional units of any good can be produced at a constant opportunity cost, the *PPF* is
- **a** bowed inward (convex).
- **b** bowed outward (concave).
- **c** positively sloped.
- **d** perfectly horizontal.
- **e** linear.

13 Marginal cost is the
- **a** total cost of an activity.
- **b** additional benefit of a decrease in an activity.
- **c** additional benefit of an increase in an activity.
- **d** opportunity cost of a decrease in an activity.
- **e** opportunity cost of an increase in an activity.

14 If variables *x* and *y* move in opposite directions, they are said to be
- **a** positively related.
- **b** negatively related.
- **c** intimately related.
- **d** unrelated.
- **e** siblings.

15 *Ceteris paribus* is a Latin term meaning
- **a** "After this, therefore because of this."
- **b** "What is true of the parts is true of the whole."
- **c** "What is true of the parts is *not* true of the whole."
- **d** "Other things being equal."
- **e** "Your place or mine."

ANSWERS

Problem

a The bowed-out shape of the *PPF* implies that resources are not equally productive in all activities; they are nonhomogeneous. With nonhomogeneous resources, there are increasing opportunity costs as production increases of either child-care services or televisions.

b See Figure P1.1 Solution.

FIGURE **P1.1** SOLUTION

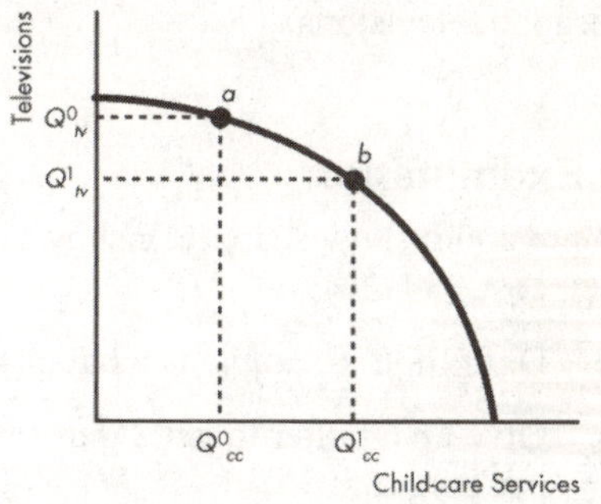

c The increased demand for child-care services puts upward pressure on the price of child-care services, making it more profitable to produce them. The higher price serves as a signal to firms to shift additional resources to producing child-care services.

Those additional resources come from the television market. The decreased demand for televisions puts downward pressure on the price of televisions, making it less profitable to produce them. The lower price serves as a signal to firms to shift resources to more profitable uses (in child care).

Thus the market economy responds to the changing demands of households by reallocating resources into child-care services from television production. Prices are the signals that coordinate the demand decisions of households with the resource allocation decisions of firms. The market—operating through a combination of price signals, self-interest, and competition—acts like an "invisible hand" to guide resources to the uses that households desire.

d The distance of the *PPF* from the origin is determined by the quantities of resources and the technology in the economy. The *PPF* shows maximum combinations of outputs (goods and services) that can be produced with given resources and technology.

The precise point on the *PPF* at which the economy operates (e.g., the combination at point *a* of child-care services and televisions) is determined by the demands of households.

The true cost of moving from point *a* to point *b* is the televisions that must be forgone as scarce resources are shifted to produce more child-care services. In other words, the true cost of additional child care is an opportunity cost—forgone televisions.

Midterm Examination

1 d **a** and **b** show scarcity, **c** shows opportunity cost. (34–36)

2 c Definition. Example is a bar chart. (18–20)

3 e Give up 6 butter to get 2 guns: 6/2 = 3 butter per gun. (34–36)

4 d Opportunity cost gun between *a* and *b* = 2 butter; between *b* and *c* = 3 butter. *a* on *PPF*, *b* outside *PPF*. (34–36)

5 c **a** is a true statement (definition); **d** and **b** are positive statements that can be tested. (12–13)

6 d As x increases, y decreases. (20–22)

7 d For example, using points (0, 4) and (16, 16): $\Delta y = 12\ (16 - 4)$, $\Delta x = 16\ (16 - 0)$. (24–26)

8 c Unemployment decreases expected average income from working. Higher opportunity cost for men may not be fair, but is a fact. (11)

9 a To move from *b* to *a*, quantity *X* decreases from 8 to 6. (35–36)

10 e Definition. (35–36)

11 d Scarcity implies opportunity cost, which involves a negative relationship—to get more of *X* you must give up *Y*. (34–36)

12 e Constant opportunity cost yields constant slope *PPF*. (36)

13 e Definition; **c** is marginal benefit, **b** and **d** are nonsense. (11, 37)

14 b Definition. (21–22)

15 d Definition; **a** is *post hoc ergo propter hoc*. (13–14)

Chapter 3
Demand and Supply

KEY CONCEPTS

Markets and Prices

Competitive market—many buyers and sellers so no one can influence prices.

Relative price of a good is

- its *opportunity cost*—the other goods that must be forgone to buy it.
- ratio of its **money price** to the money price of another good.
- determined by demand and supply.

Demand

The **quantity demanded** of a good is the amount consumers plan to buy during a given time period at a particular price. The **law of demand** states: "Other things remaining the same, the higher the price of a good, the smaller is the quantity demanded." Higher price reduces quantity demanded for two reasons:

- *substitution effect*—with an increase in the relative price of a good, people buy less of it and more of substitutes for the good.
- *income effect*—with an increase in the relative price of a good and unchanged incomes, people have less money to spend on all goods, including the good whose price increased.

The **demand curve** represents the inverse relationship between quantity demanded and price, *ceteris paribus*. The demand curve also is a willingness-and-ability-to-pay curve, which measures marginal benefit.

- A change in price causes movement along the demand curve. This is called a **change in the quantity demanded**. The higher the price of a good, the lower the quantity demanded.
- A shift of the demand curve is called a **change in demand**. The demand curve shifts from changes in
  - prices of related goods.
  - expected future prices.
  - income.
  - expected future income.
  - population.
  - preferences.
- Increase in demand—demand curve shifts rightward.
- Decrease in demand—demand curve shifts leftward.
- For an increase in
  - price of a **substitute**—demand shifts rightward.
  - price of a **complement**—demand shifts leftward.
  - expected future prices—demand shifts rightward.
  - income (**normal good**)—demand shifts rightward.
  - income (**inferior good**)—demand shifts leftward.
  - expected future income (**normal good**)—demand shifts rightward.
  - expected future income (**inferior good**)—demand shifts leftward
  - population—demand shifts rightward.
  - preferences—demand shifts rightward.

Supply

The **quantity supplied** of a good is the amount producers plan to sell during a given time period at a particular price. The **law of supply** states: "Other things remaining the same, the higher the price of a good, the greater is the quantity supplied." Higher price increases quantity supplied because marginal cost increases with increasing quantities. Price must rise for producers to be willing to increase production and incur higher marginal cost.

The **supply curve** represents the positive relationship between quantity supplied and price, *ceteris paribus*. The supply curve is also a minimum-supply-price curve, showing the lowest price at which a producer is willing to sell another unit.

- ♦ A change in price causes movement along the supply curve. This is called a **change in the quantity supplied**. The higher the price of a good, the greater the quantity supplied.
- ♦ A shift of the supply curve is called a **change in supply**. The supply curve shifts from changes in
  - prices of productive resources.
  - prices of related goods produced.
  - expected future prices.
  - number of suppliers.
  - technology.
- ♦ Increase in supply—supply curve shifts rightward.
- ♦ Decrease in supply—supply curve shifts leftward.
- ♦ For an increase in
  - prices of productive resources—supply shifts leftward.
  - price of a *substitute in production*—supply shifts leftward.
  - price of a *complement in production*—supply shifts rightward.
  - expected future prices—supply shifts leftward.
  - number of suppliers—supply shifts rightward.
  - technology—supply shifts rightward.

Market Equilibrium

The **equilibrium price** is where the demand and supply curves intersect, where quantity demanded equals quantity supplied.

- ♦ Above the equilibrium price, there is a surplus (quantity supplied > quantity demanded), and price will fall.
- ♦ Below the equilibrium price, there is a shortage (quantity demanded > quantity supplied), and price will rise.
- ♦ Only in equilibrium is there no tendency for the price to change. The **equilibrium quantity** is the quantity bought and sold at the equilibrium price.

Predicting Changes in Price and Quantity

For a single change *either* in demand *or* in supply, *ceteris paribus*, when

- ♦ demand increases, P rises and Q increases.
- ♦ demand decreases, P falls and Q decreases.
- ♦ supply increases, P falls and Q increases.
- ♦ supply decreases, P rises and Q decreases.

When there is a simultaneous change *both* in demand *and* supply, we can determine the effect on either price or quantity. But without information about the relative size of the shifts of the demand and supply curves, the effect on the other variable is ambiguous. *Ceteris paribus*, when

- ♦ both demand and supply increase, P may rise/fall/remain constant and Q increases.
- ♦ both demand and supply decrease, P may rise/fall/remain constant and Q decreases.
- ♦ demand increases and supply decreases, P rises and Q may rise/fall/remain constant.
- ♦ demand decreases and supply increases, P falls and Q may rise/fall/remain constant.

HELPFUL HINTS

1 When you are first learning about demand and supply, think of specific examples to help you understand how to use the concepts. For example, in analyzing complementary goods, think about hamburgers and french fries; in analyzing substitute goods, think of hamburgers and hot dogs. This will reduce the "abstractness" of the economic theory and make concepts easier to remember.

2 The statement that "price is determined by demand and supply" is a shorthand way of saying that price is determined by all of the factors affecting demand (prices of related goods, expected future prices, income, expected

future income, population, preferences) and all of the factors affecting supply (prices of productive resources, prices of related goods produced, expected future prices, number of suppliers, technology). The benefit of using demand and supply curves is that they allow us to systematically sort out the influences on price of each of these separate factors. Changes in the factors affecting demand shift the demand curve and move us up or down the given supply curve. Changes in the factors affecting supply shift the supply curve and move us up or down the given demand curve.

Any demand and supply problem requires you to sort out these influences carefully. In so doing, *always draw a graph*, even if it is just a small graph in the margin of a true/false or multiple-choice problem. Graphs are a very efficient way to "see" what happens. As you become comfortable with graphs, you will find them to be effective and powerful tools for systematically organizing your thinking.

Do not make the common mistake of thinking that a problem is so easy that you can do it in your head, without drawing a graph. This mistake will cost you dearly on examinations. Also, when you do draw a graph, be sure to label the axes. As the course progresses, you will encounter many graphs with different variables on the axes. It is easy to become confused if you do not develop the habit of labelling the axes.

3 Another very common mistake among students is failing to *distinguish* correctly between *a shift in a curve* and *a movement along a curve*. This distinction applies both to demand and to supply curves. Many questions in the Self-Test are designed to test your understanding of this distinction, and you can be sure that your instructor will test you heavily on this. The distinction between "shifts in" versus "movements along" a curve is crucial for systematic thinking about the factors influencing demand and supply, and for understanding the determination of equilibrium price and quantity.

Consider the example of the demand curve. The quantity of a good demanded depends on its own price, the prices of related goods, expected future prices, income, expected future income, population, and preferences. The term "demand" refers to the relationship between the price of a good and the quantity demanded, holding constant all of the other factors on which the quantity demanded depends. This demand relationship is represented graphically by the demand curve. Thus, the effect of a change in price on quantity demanded is already reflected in the slope of the demand curve; the effect of a change in the price of the good itself is given by a movement along the demand curve. This is referred to as a **change in quantity demanded**.

On the other hand, if one of the other factors affecting the quantity demanded changes, the demand curve itself will shift; the quantity demanded *at each price* will change. This shift of the demand curve is referred to as a **change in demand**. The critical thing to remember is that a change in the price of a good will not shift the demand curve; it will only cause a movement along the demand curve. Similarly, it is just as important to distinguish between shifts in the supply curve and movements along the supply curve.

To confirm your understanding, consider the effect (draw a graph!) of an increase in household income on the market for compact discs (CDs). First note that an increase in income affects the demand for CDs and not supply. Next we want to determine whether the increase in income causes a shift in the demand curve or a movement along the demand curve. Will the increase in income increase the quantity of CDs demanded even if the price of CDs does not change? Since the answer to this question is yes, we know that the demand curve will shift rightward. Note further that the increase in the demand for CDs will cause the equilibrium price to rise. This price increase will be indicated by a movement along the supply curve (an increase in the quantity supplied) and will not shift the supply curve itself.

Remember: It is shifts in demand and supply curves that cause the market price to change, not changes in the price that cause demand and supply curves to shift.

4 When analyzing the shifts of demand and supply curves in related markets (for substitute goods like beer and wine), it often seems as though the feedback effects from one market to the other can go on endlessly. To avoid confusion, stick to the rule that each curve (demand and supply) for a given market can shift a maximum of *once*. (See Short Answer Problems **4** and **6** for further explanation and examples.)

5 The relationships between price and quantity demanded and supplied can be represented in three equivalent forms: demand and supply schedules, curves, and equations. Text Chapter 3 illustrates schedules and curves, but demand and supply equations are also powerful tools of economic analysis. The Mathematical Note to Chapter 3 provides the general form of these equations. The purpose of this Helpful Hint and the next is to further explain the equations and how they can be used to determine the equilibrium values of price and quantity.

Figure 3.1 presents a simple demand and supply example in three equivalent forms: (a) schedules, (b) curves, and (c) equations. The demand and supply schedules in (a) are in the same format as Text Figure 3.7. The price-quantity combinations from the schedules are plotted on the graph in (b), yielding linear demand and supply curves. What is new about this example is the representation of those curves by the equations in (c).

If you recall (Chapter 1 Appendix) the formula for the equation of a straight line ($y = a + bx$), you can see that the demand equation is the equation of a straight line. Instead of y, P is the dependent variable on the vertical axis, and, instead of x, Q_D is the independent variable on the horizontal axis. The intercept on the vertical axis a is +5, and the slope b is –1. The supply equation is also linear and graphed in the same way, but with Q_S as the independent variable. The supply curve intercept on the vertical axis is +1, and the slope is +1. The negative slope of the demand curve reflects the law of demand, and the positive slope of the supply curve reflects the law of supply.

You can demonstrate the equivalence of the demand schedule, curve, and equation by substituting various values of Q_D from the schedule into the demand equation, and calculating the associated prices. These combinations of quantity demanded and price are the coordinates (Q_D, P) of the points on the demand curve. You can similarly demonstrate the equivalence of the supply schedule, curve, and equation.

FIGURE **3.1**

(a) Demand and Supply Schedules

Price ($)	Q_D	Q_S	Shortage (–)/ Surplus (+)
1	4	0	–4
2	3	1	–2
3	2	2	0
4	1	3	+2
5	0	4	+4

(b) Demand and Supply Curves

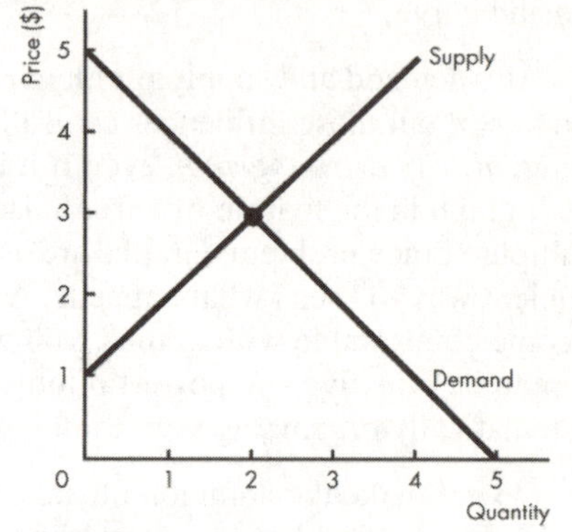

(c) Demand and Supply Equations

Demand: $P = 5 - 1Q_D$
Supply: $P = 1 + 1Q_S$

The demand and supply equations are very useful for calculating the equilibrium values of price and quantity. As the schedules and curves both show, two things are true in equilibrium: (1) the price is the same for consumers (the highest price they are willing to pay for the last unit) and producers (the lowest price they are willing to accept for the last unit) and (2) the quantity demanded equals the quantity supplied, so that there are no surpluses or shortages. In terms of the demand and supply equations, this means that, *in equilibrium*,

(1) The price in both equations is the same. We will denote the equilibrium price as P^*.

(2) $Q_D = Q_S$ = the equilibrium quantity bought and sold. We will denote the equilibrium quantity as Q^*.

In equilibrium, the equations become

Demand: $P^* = 5 - 1Q^*$

Supply: $P^* = 1 + 1Q^*$

These equilibrium equations constitute a simple set of simultaneous equations. Since there are two equations (demand and supply) and two unknowns (P^* and Q^*), we can solve for the unknowns.

Begin the solution by setting demand equal to supply:

$$5 - 1Q^* = 1 + 1Q^*$$

Collecting like terms, we find

$$4 = 2Q^*$$

$$2 = Q^*$$

Once we have Q^* (equilibrium quantity), we can solve for the equilibrium price using either the demand or the supply equations. Look first at demand:

$$P^* = 5 - 1Q^*$$

$$P^* = 5 - 1(2)$$

$$P^* = 5 - 2$$

$$P^* = 3$$

Alternatively, substituting Q^* into the supply equation yields the same result:

$$P^* = 1 + 1Q^*$$

$$P^* = 1 + 1(2)$$

$$P^* = 1 + 2$$

$$P^* = 3$$

Once you have solved for Q^*, the fact that substituting it into either the demand or the supply equation yields the correct P^* provides a valuable check on your calculations. If you make a mistake in your calculations, when you substitute Q^* into the demand and supply equations, you will get two different prices. If that happens, you know to recheck your calculations. If you get the same price when you substitute Q^* into the demand and supply equations, you know your calculations are correct.

6 Economists have developed the convention of graphing quantity as the independent variable (on the horizontal x-axis) and price as the dependent variable (on the vertical y-axis), and the foregoing equations reflect this. Despite this convention, economists actually consider real-world prices to be the independent variables and quantities the dependent variables. In that case, the equations would take the form

Demand: $Q_D = 5 - 1P$
Supply: $Q_S = -1 + 1P$

You can solve these equations for yourself to see that they yield exactly the same values for P^* and Q^*. (*Hint:* First solve for P^* and then for Q^*.) Whichever form of the equations your instructor may use, the technique for solving the equations will be similar and the results identical.

SELF-TEST

True/False and Explain

Markets and Prices

1 In a competitive market, every single buyer and seller influences price.

2 The relative price of a good is the other goods that must be forgone to buy it.

3 A good's relative price can fall even when its money price rises.

Demand

4 The law of demand tells us that as the price of a good rises, demand decreases.

5 The demand curve is a willingness-and-ability-to-pay curve that measures marginal cost.

6 Hamburgers and fries are complements. If Burger Bar reduces the price of fries, the demand for hamburgers increases.

7 A decrease in income always shifts the demand curve leftward.

Supply

8 A supply curve shows the maximum price at which the last unit will be supplied.

9 If *A* and *B* are substitutes, an increase in the price of *A* always shifts the supply curve of *B* leftward.

10 When a cow is slaughtered for beef, its hide becomes available to make leather. Thus beef and leather are substitutes in production.

11 If the price of beef rises, there will be an increase in both the supply of leather and the quantity of beef supplied.

Market Equilibrium

12 When the actual price is above the equilibrium price, a shortage occurs.

Predicting Changes in Price and Quantity

13 If the expected future price of a good increases, there will always be an increase in equilibrium price and a decrease in equilibrium quantity.

14 Suppose new firms enter the steel market. *Ceteris paribus*, the equilibrium price of steel will always fall and the quantity will rise.

15 Suppose the demand for personal computers increases while the cost of producing them decreases. The equilibrium quantity of personal computers will rise and the price will always fall.

Multiple-Choice

Markets and Prices

1 A relative price is
- **a** the ratio of one price to another.
- **b** an opportunity cost.
- **c** a quantity of a "basket" of goods and services forgone.
- **d** determined by demand and supply.
- **e** all of the above.

Demand

2 If an increase in the price of good *A* causes the demand curve for good *B* to shift leftward,
- **a** *A* and *B* are substitutes in consumption.
- **b** *A* and *B* are complements in consumption.
- **c** *A* and *B* are complements in production.
- **d** *B* is an inferior good.
- **e** *B* is a normal good.

3 Which of the following could *not* cause an increase in demand for a commodity?
- **a** an increase in income
- **b** a decrease in income
- **c** a decrease in the price of a substitute
- **d** a decrease in the price of a complement
- **e** an increase in preferences for the commodity

4 Some sales managers are talking shop. Which of the following quotations refers to a movement along the demand curve?
- **a** "Since our competitors raised their prices our sales have doubled."
- **b** "It has been an unusually mild winter; our sales of wool scarves are down from last year."
- **c** "We decided to cut our prices, and the increase in our sales has been remarkable."
- **d** "The Green movement has sparked an increase in our sales of biodegradable products."
- **e** none of the above.

5 If Hamburger Helper is an inferior good, then, *ceteris paribus*, a decrease in income will cause
- **a** a leftward shift of the demand curve for Hamburger Helper.
- **b** a rightward shift of the demand curve for Hamburger Helper.
- **c** a movement up along the demand curve for Hamburger Helper.
- **d** a movement down along the demand curve for Hamburger Helper.
- **e** none of the above.

6 A decrease in quantity demanded is represented by a
- **a** rightward shift of the supply curve.
- **b** rightward shift of the demand curve.
- **c** leftward shift of the demand curve.
- **d** movement upward and to the left along the demand curve.
- **e** movement downward and to the right along the demand curve.

7 Which of the following "other things" are *not* held constant along a demand curve?
- **a** income
- **b** prices of related goods
- **c** the price of the good itself
- **d** preferences
- **e** all of the above

Supply

8 The fact that a decline in the price of a good causes producers to reduce the quantity of the good supplied illustrates
- **a** the law of supply.
- **b** the law of demand.
- **c** a change in supply.
- **d** the nature of an inferior good.
- **e** technological improvement.

9 A shift of the supply curve for rutabagas will be caused by
- **a** a change in preferences for rutabagas.
- **b** a change in the price of a related good that is a substitute in consumption for rutabagas.
- **c** a change in income.
- **d** a change in the price of rutabagas.
- **e** none of the above.

10 If a resource can be used to produce either good *A* or good *B*, then *A* and *B* are
- **a** substitutes in production.
- **b** complements in production.
- **c** substitutes in consumption.
- **d** complements in consumption.
- **e** normal goods.

11 Which of the following will shift the supply curve for good *X* leftward?
- **a** a decrease in the wages of workers employed to produce *X*
- **b** an increase in the cost of machinery used to produce *X*
- **c** a technological improvement in the production of *X*
- **d** a situation where quantity demanded exceeds quantity supplied
- **e** all of the above

12 Some producers are chatting over a beer. Which of the following quotations refers to a movement along the supply curve?
- **a** "Wage increases have forced us to raise our prices."
- **b** "Our new, sophisticated equipment will enable us to undercut our competitors."
- **c** "Raw material prices have skyrocketed; we will have to pass this on to our customers."
- **d** "We anticipate a big increase in demand. Our product price should rise, so we are planning for an increase in output."
- **e** "New competitors in the industry are causing prices to fall."

13 If an increase in the price of good *A* causes the supply curve for good *B* to shift rightward,
- **a** *A* and *B* are substitutes in consumption.
- **b** *A* and *B* are complements in consumption.
- **c** *A* and *B* are substitutes in production.
- **d** *A* and *B* are complements in production.
- **e** *A* is a factor of production for making *B*.

Market Equilibrium

14 If the market for Twinkies is in equilibrium,
- **a** Twinkies must be a normal good.
- **b** producers would like to sell more at the current price.
- **c** consumers would like to buy more at the current price.
- **d** there will be a surplus.
- **e** equilibrium quantity equals quantity demanded.

15 The price of a good will tend to fall if
- **a** there is a surplus at the current price.
- **b** the current price is above equilibrium.
- **c** the quantity supplied exceeds the quantity demanded at the current price.
- **d** all of the above are true.
- **e** none of the above is true.

16 A surplus can be eliminated by
- **a** increasing supply.
- **b** government raising the price.
- **c** decreasing the quantity demanded.
- **d** allowing the price to fall.
- **e** allowing the quantity bought and sold to fall.

17 A shortage is the amount by which quantity
- **a** demanded exceeds quantity supplied.
- **b** supplied exceeds quantity demanded.
- **c** demanded increases when the price rises.
- **d** demanded exceeds the equilibrium quantity.
- **e** supplied exceeds the equilibrium quantity.

Predicting Changes in Price and Quantity

18 Which of the following will definitely cause an increase in the equilibrium price?
- **a** an increase in both demand and supply
- **b** a decrease in both demand and supply
- **c** an increase in demand combined with a decrease in supply
- **d** a decrease in demand combined with an increase in supply
- **e** none of the above

19 Coffee is a normal good. A decrease in income will
- **a** increase the price of coffee and increase the quantity demanded of coffee.
- **b** increase the price of coffee and increase the quantity supplied of coffee.
- **c** decrease the price of coffee and decrease the quantity demanded of coffee.
- **d** decrease the price of coffee and decrease the quantity supplied of coffee.
- **e** cause none of the above.

20 An increase in the price of Pepsi (a substitute for coffee) will
- **a** increase the price of coffee and increase the quantity demanded of coffee.
- **b** increase the price of coffee and increase the quantity supplied of coffee.
- **c** decrease the price of coffee and decrease the quantity demanded of coffee.
- **d** decrease the price of coffee and decrease the quantity supplied of coffee.
- **e** cause none of the above.

21 A technological improvement lowers the cost of producing coffee. At the same time, preferences for coffee decrease. The *equilibrium quantity* of coffee will
- **a** rise.
- **b** fall.
- **c** remain the same.
- **d** rise or fall depending on whether the price of coffee falls or rises.
- **e** rise or fall depending on the relative shifts of demand and supply curves.

22 Since 1980, there has been a dramatic increase in the number of working mothers. On the basis of this information alone, we can predict that the market for child-care services has experienced a(n)
- **a** increase in demand.
- **b** decrease in demand.
- **c** increase in quantity demanded.
- **d** decrease in quantity supplied.
- **e** increase in supply.

23 If *A* and *B* are complementary goods (in consumption) and the cost of a resource used in the production of *A* decreases, the price of
- **a** both *A* and *B* will rise.
- **b** both *A* and *B* will fall.
- **c** *A* will fall and the price of *B* will rise.
- **d** *A* will rise and the price of *B* will fall.
- **e** *A* will fall and the price of *B* will remain unchanged.

24 The demand curve for knobs is $P = 75 - 6Q_D$ and the supply curve for knobs is $P = 35 + 2Q_S$. What is the equilibrium price of a knob?
- **a** \$5
- **b** \$10
- **c** \$40
- **d** \$45
- **e** None of the above

25 The demand curve for tribbles is $P = 300 - 6Q_D$. The supply curve for tribbles is $P = 20 + 8Q_S$. If the price of a tribble was set at \$120, the tribble market would experience
- **a** equilibrium.
- **b** excess demand causing a rise in price.
- **c** excess demand causing a fall in price.
- **d** excess supply causing a rise in price.
- **e** excess supply causing a fall in price.

Short Answer Problems

1 Explain the difference between wants and demands.

2 The price of personal computers has continued to fall even in the face of increasing demand. Explain.

ⓒⓣ 3 A tax on crude oil would raise the cost of the primary resource used in the production of gasoline. A proponent of such a tax has claimed that it will not raise the price of gasoline using the following argument. While the price of gasoline may rise initially, that price increase will cause the demand for gasoline to decrease, which will push the price back down. What is wrong with this argument?

4 Brussels sprouts and carrots are substitutes in consumption and, since they can both be grown on the same type of land, substitutes in production too. Suppose there is an increase in the demand for brussels sprouts. Trace the effects on price and quantity traded in both the brussels sprout and the carrot market. (Keep in mind Helpful Hint **4**.)

5 The information given in Table 3.1 is about the behaviour of buyers and sellers of fish at the market on a particular Saturday.

TABLE **3.1** DEMAND AND SUPPLY SCHEDULES FOR FISH

Price (per fish)	Quantity Demanded	Quantity Supplied
$0.50	280	40
$1.00	260	135
$1.50	225	225
$2.00	170	265
$2.50	105	290
$3.00	60	310
$3.50	35	320

a On graph paper, draw the demand curve and the supply curve. Be sure to label the axes. What is the equilibrium price?

b We will make the usual *ceteris paribus* assumptions about the demand curve so that it does not shift. List six factors that we are assuming do not change.

c We will also hold the supply curve constant by assuming that five factors do not change. List them.

d Explain briefly what would happen if the price was initially set at $3.

e Explain briefly what would happen if the price was initially set at $1.

f Explain briefly what would happen if the price was initially set at $1.50.

6 The market for wine in Canada is initially in equilibrium with supply and demand curves of the usual shape. Beer is a close substitute for wine; cheese and wine are complements. Use demand and supply diagrams to analyze the effect of each of the following (separate) events on the equilibrium price and quantity in the Canadian wine market. Assume that all of the *ceteris paribus* assumptions continue to hold except for the event listed. For both equilibrium price and quantity you should indicate in each case whether the variable rises, falls, remains the same, or moves ambiguously (may rise or fall).

a The income of consumers falls (wine is a normal good).

b Early frost destroys a large part of the world grape crop.

c A new churning invention reduces the cost of producing cheese.

d A new fermentation technique is invented that reduces the cost of producing wine.

e A new government study is published that links wine drinking and increased heart disease.

f Costs of producing both beer and wine increase dramatically.

ⓒⓣ 7 A newspaper reported, "Despite a bumper crop of cherries this year, the price drop for cherries won't be as much as expected because of short supplies of plums and peaches."

a Use a demand and supply graph for the cherry market to explain the effect of the bumper crop alone.

b On the same graph, explain the impact on the cherry market of the short supplies of plums and peaches.

8 Table 3.2 lists the demand and supply schedules for cases of grape jam.

TABLE **3.2** DEMAND AND SUPPLY SCHEDULES FOR GRAPE JAM PER WEEK

Price (per case)	Quantity Demanded (cases)	Quantity Supplied (cases)
$70	20	140
$60	60	120
$50	100	100
$40	140	80
$30	180	60

a On the graph in Figure 3.2, draw the demand and supply curves for grape jam. Be sure to properly label the axes. Label the demand and supply curves D_0 and S_0 respectively.

FIGURE **3.2**

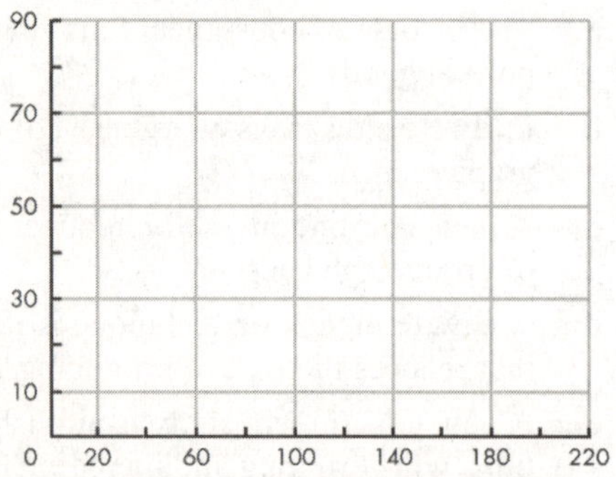

b What are the equilibrium price and quantity in the grape jam market? On your diagram, label the equilibrium point *a*.

c Is there a surplus or shortage at a price of $40? How much?

d The demand and supply schedules can also be represented by the following demand and supply equations:

Demand: $P = 75 - 0.25Q_D$

Supply: $P = 0.5Q_S$

Use these equations to solve for the equilibrium quantity (Q*); equilibrium price (P*). (*Hint:* Your answers should be the same as those in **8b**.)

e Suppose the population grows sufficiently that the demand for grape jam increases by 60 cases per week at every price.

i Construct a table (price, quantity demanded) of the new demand schedule.

ii Draw the new demand curve on your original graph and label it D_1.

iii Label the new equilibrium point *b*. What are the new equilibrium price and quantity?

iv What is the new demand equation? (*Hints:* What is the new slope? What is the new price-axis intercept?)

9 The demand equation for dweedles is

$$P = 8 - 1Q_D$$

The supply equation for dweedles is

$$P = 2 + 1Q_S$$

where P is the price of a dweedle in dollars, Q_D is the quantity of dweedles demanded, and Q_S is the quantity of dweedles supplied. The dweedle market is initially in equilibrium and income is $300.

a What is the equilibrium quantity (Q*) of dweedles?

b What is the equilibrium price (P*) of a dweedle?

c As a result of an increase in income to $500, the demand curve for dweedles shifts (the supply curve remains the same). The new demand equation is

$$P = 4 - 1Q_D$$

Use this information to calculate the new equilibrium quantity of dweedles; calculate the new equilibrium price of a dweedle.

d On the graph in Figure 3.3, draw and label: (1) the supply curve, (2) the initial demand curve, (3) the new demand curve.

e Are dweedles a normal or inferior good? How do you know?

FIGURE **3.3**

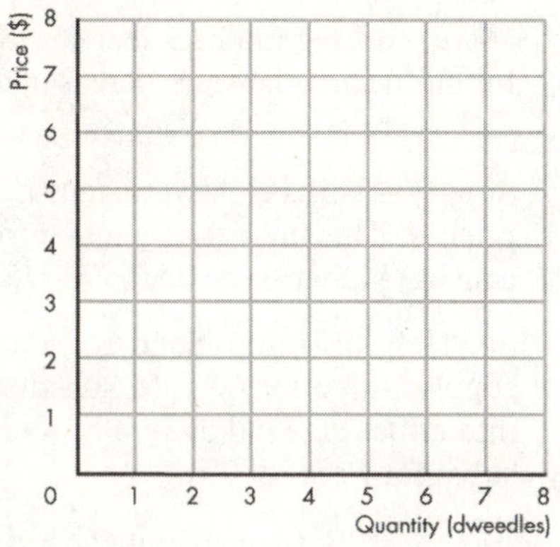

10 The demand equation for flubits is

$$P = 80 - 2Q_D$$

The supply equation for flubits is

$$P = 50 + 1Q_S$$

where P is the price of a flubit in dollars, Q_D is the quantity of flubits demanded, and Q_S is the quantity of flubits supplied. Assume that there are no changes in *ceteris paribus* assumptions.

a If the price of flubits was set at $56, calculate the exact surplus or shortage of flubits.

b Explain the adjustment process that will bring the situation above to equilibrium.

c What is the equilibrium quantity (Q^*) of flubits?

d What is the equilibrium price (P^*) of a flubit?

e Now assume that as a result of technological advance, the supply curve for flubits shifts (the demand curve remains the same). The new supply equation is

$$P = 20 + 1Q_S$$

Use this information to calculate the new equilibrium quantity of flubits; calculate the new equilibrium price of a flubit.

ANSWERS

True/False and Explain

1 F No single buyer or seller influences price. (60)

2 T Relative price is an opportunity cost. (60)

(ct) **3 T** If money prices of other goods rise even more, a good's relative price falls. If price of gum rises from $1 to $2, but price of coffee rises from $1 to $4, opportunity cost of pack of gum falls from 1 to 0.5 coffee forgone. (60)

4 F As price rises, *quantity demanded* decreases. (61)

5 F Measures marginal benefit. (62)

6 T Combined meal of hamburger and fries now cheaper. (63)

(ct) **7 F** Leftward shift for normal good, rightward shift for inferior good. (64)

8 F Supply curve shows minimum price at which last unit supplied. (67)

(ct) **9 F** True if *A* and *B* substitutes in production, but false if substitutes in consumption. (68–69)

(ct) **10 F** Beef and leather complements in production because produced together of necessity. (67–68)

11 T For complements in production, higher price for one good causes increased quantity supplied and increase in supply other good. (67–68)

12 F At $P >$ equilibrium P, there is surplus (quantity supplied > quantity demanded). (70–71)

(ct) **13 F** Higher expected future prices cause rightward shift demand and leftward shift supply. Price rises, but Δ quantity depends on relative magnitude shifts. (63–64, 68, 75)

14 T Increased number of firms causes rightward shift supply leading to fall in price and increased quantity. (73)

15 F Quantity will increase but Δ price depends on relative magnitude shifts in demand and supply. (75)

Multiple-Choice

1 e Definitions. (60)

2 b For example, higher-price fries causes decreased demand for hamburgers. (63)

3 c Both income answers could be correct if commodity were normal (**a**) or inferior (**b**). (63–64)

4 c Other answers describe shifts of demand curve. (63–65)

5 b Changes in income shift demand curve rather than causing movement along demand curve. (64)

6 d Decreased quantity demanded is movement up along demand curve. Could also be caused by leftward shift supply. (64–65)

7 c "Other things" shift demand curve. Only price can change along fixed demand curve. (65)

8 a Question describes movement down along supply curve. (66–67)

9 e Answers **a**, **b**, and **c** shift demand, while **d** causes movement along supply curve. (67–69)

10 a Definition of substitute in production. (67–68)

11 b Higher price productive resource shifts supply leftward. (67–68)

12 d Other answers describe shifts of supply curve. (68–69)

13 d Definition of complements in production. Price changes related goods in consumption shift demand. (67–68)

14 e At equilibrium price, plans producers and consumers match; quantity demanded = quantity supplied. (70–71)

15 d All answers describe price above equilibrium price. (70–71)

16 d Other answers make surplus (excess quantity supplied) larger. (70–71)

17 a Shortage is horizontal distance between demand and supply curves at price below equilibrium price. (70–71)

18 c Answers **a** and **b** have indeterminate effect on price, while **d** causes lower price. (74–75)

19 d Demand shifts leftward. (72–73)

20 b Demand shifts rightward. (72–73)

21 e Supply shifts rightward, demand shifts leftward, price definitely falls. (75)

22 a More working mothers increases preferences for child care, causing increased demand for child-care services. (72–75)

23 c Supply *A* shifts rightward causing lower-price *A*. This increases demand for *B*, causing higher price of *B*. (72–75)

24 d See Helpful Hint **5**. Set demand equal to supply, solve for $Q^* = 5$. Substitute $Q^* = 5$ into either demand or supply equation to solve for P^*. (78–79)

25 b At $P = \$120$, $Q_D = 30$, and $Q_S = 12.5$. Excess demand so price will rise. (71, 78–79)

Short Answer Problems

1 Wants are our unlimited desires for goods and services without regard to our ability or willingness to make the sacrifices necessary to obtain them. The existence of scarcity means that many of those wants will not be satisfied. On the other hand, if we demand something, then we want it, can afford it, and have made a definite plan to buy it. Demands reflect decisions about which wants to satisfy.

2 Due to the tremendous pace of technological advance, not only has the demand for personal computers been increasing, but the supply has been increasing as well. Indeed, supply has been increasing much more rapidly than demand, which has resulted in falling prices. Thus *much* (but not all) of the increase in sales of personal computers reflects a movement down along a demand curve rather than a shift in demand.

3 This argument confuses a movement along an unchanging demand curve with a shift in the demand curve. The proper analysis is as follows. The increase in the price of oil (the primary resource in the production of gasoline) will shift the supply curve of gasoline leftward. This will cause the equilibrium price of gasoline to increase and thus the quantity demanded of gasoline will decrease. Demand itself will not decrease—that is, the demand curve will not shift. The decrease in supply causes a movement along an unchanged demand curve.

4 The answer to this question requires us to trace through the effects on the two graphs in Figure 3.4: (a) for the brussels sprout market and (b) for the carrot market. The sequence of effects occurs in order of the numbers on the graphs.

Look first at the market for brussels sprouts. The increase in demand shifts the demand curve rightward from D_0 to D_1 (1), and the price of brussels sprouts rises. This price rise has two effects (2) on the carrot market. Since brussels sprouts and carrots are substitutes in consumption, the demand curve for carrots shifts rightward from D_0 to D_1. And, since brussels sprouts and carrots are substitutes in production, the supply curve of carrots shifts leftward from S_0 to S_1. Both of these shifts in the carrot market raise the price of carrots, causing feedback effects on the brussels sprout market. But remember the rule (Helpful Hint **4**) that each curve (demand and supply) for a given market can shift a maximum of *once*. Since the demand curve for brussels sprouts has already shifted, we can only shift the supply curve from S_0 to S_1 (3) because of the substitutes in production relationship. Each curve in each market has now shifted once and the analysis must stop. We can predict that the net effects are increases in the equilibrium prices of both brussels sprouts and carrots, and indeterminate changes in the equilibrium quantities in both markets.

FIGURE **3.4**

(a) Brussel Sprout Market

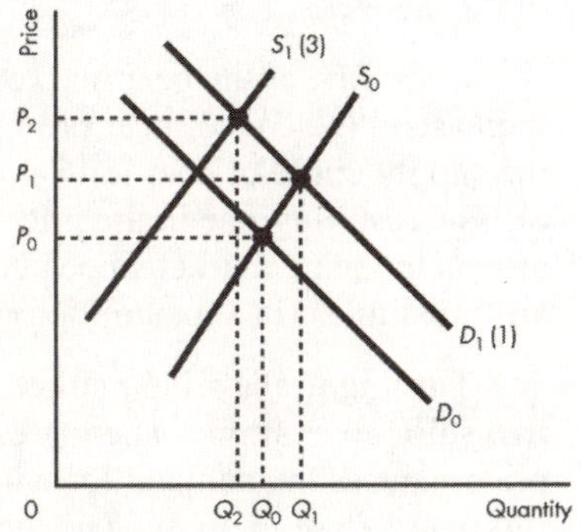

(b) Carrot Market

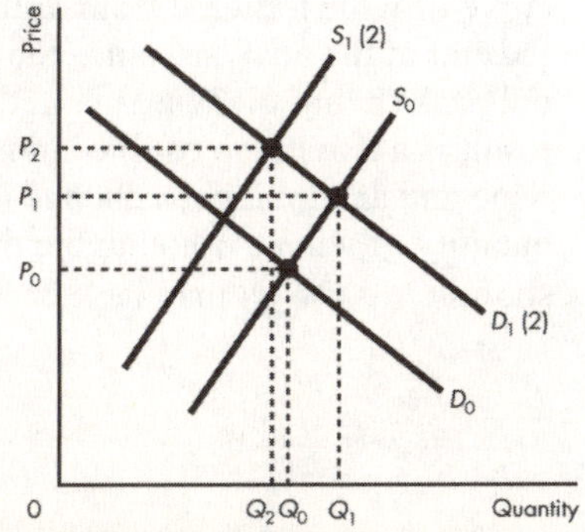

5 **a** The demand and supply curves are shown in Figure 3.5. The equilibrium price is $1.50 per fish.

FIGURE **3.5**

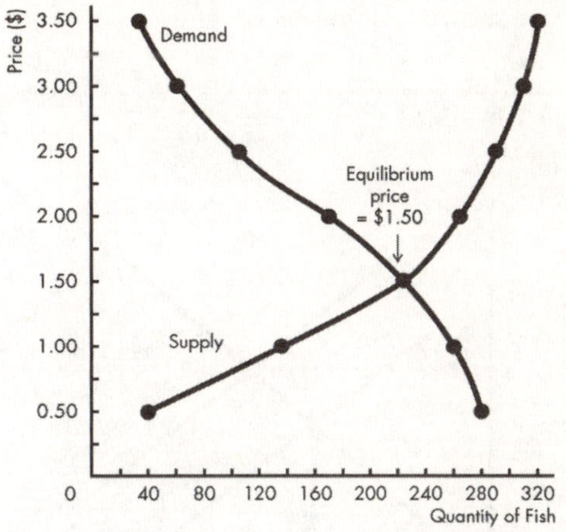

b Prices of related goods; expected future prices; income; expected future income; population; preferences.

c Prices of productive resources; prices of related goods produced; expected future prices; number of suppliers; technology.

d At a price of $3, quantity supplied (310) exceeds quantity demanded (60). Fish sellers find themselves with surplus fish. Rather than be stuck with unsold fish (which yields no revenue), some sellers cut their price in an attempt to increase the quantity of fish demanded. Competition forces other sellers to follow suit, and the price falls until it reaches the equilibrium price of $1.50, while quantity demanded increases until it reaches the equilibrium quantity of 225 units.

e At a price of $1, the quantity demanded (260) exceeds the quantity supplied (135)—there is a shortage. Unrequited fish buyers bid up the price in an attempt to get the "scarce" fish. As prices continue to be bid up as long as there is excess demand, quantity supplied increases in response to higher prices. Price and quantity supplied both rise until they reach the equilibrium price ($1.50) and quantity (225 units).

f At a price of \$1.50, the quantity supplied exactly equals the quantity demanded (225). There is no excess demand (shortage) or excess supply (surplus), and therefore no tendency for the price or quantity to change.

6 The demand and supply diagrams for parts **a** to **e** are shown in Figure 3.6.

FIGURE **3.6**

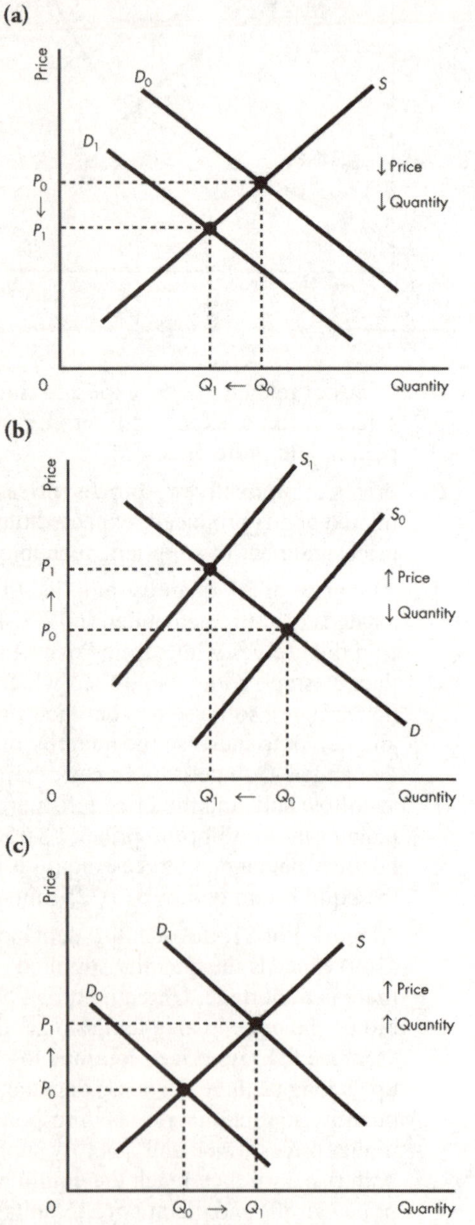

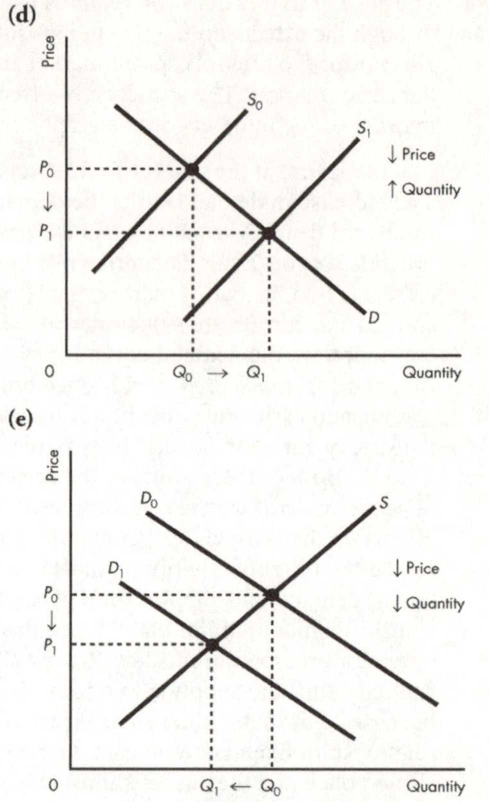

f Questions like this require the examination of two separate but related markets—the beer and wine markets. Since this kind of question often causes confusion for students, Figure 3.7 gives a more detailed explanation of the answer.

Look first at the beer market. The increase in the cost of beer production shifts the supply curve of beer leftward from S_0 to S_1. The resulting rise in the price of beer affects the wine market since beer and wine are substitutes (in consumption).

Turning to the wine market, there are two shifts to examine. The increase in beer prices causes the demand for wine to shift rightward from D_0 to D_1. The increase in the cost of wine production shifts the supply curve of wine leftward from S_0 to S_1. This is the end of the analysis, since the question only asks about the wine market. The final result is a rise in the equilibrium price of wine and an ambiguous change in the quantity of wine. Although the diagram shows $Q_1 = Q_0$, Q_1 may be $\geq$ or $\leq Q_0$.

FIGURE **3.7**

(a) Beer Market

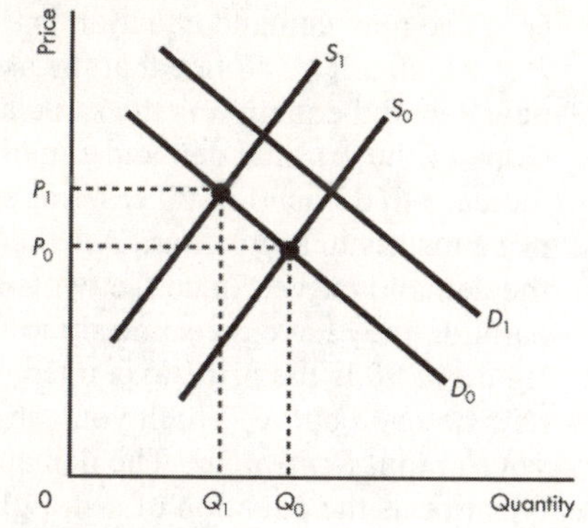

(b) Wine Market

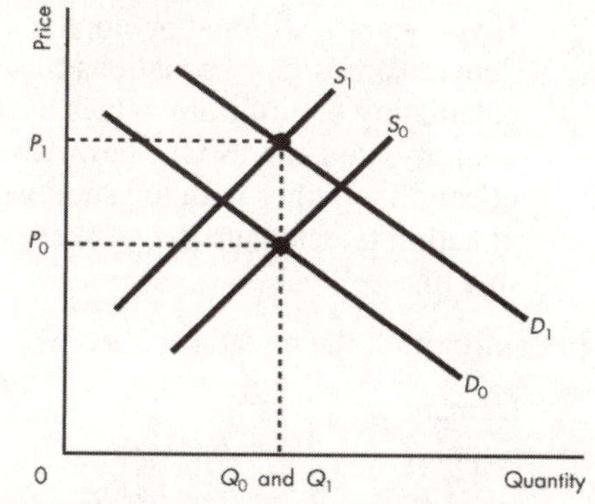

Many students rightfully ask, "But doesn't the rise in wine prices then shift the demand curve for beer rightward, causing a rise in beer prices and an additional increase in the demand for wine?" This question, which is correct in principle, is about the dynamics of adjustment, and these graphs are only capable of analyzing once-over shifts of demand or supply. We could shift the demand for beer rightward, but the resulting rise in beer prices would lead us to shift the demand for wine a *second time*. In practice, stick to the rule that each curve (demand and supply) for a given market can shift a maximum of *once*.

ⓒⓣ **7** **a** The demand and supply curves for the cherry market are shown in Figure 3.8.

FIGURE **3.8**

Cherry Market

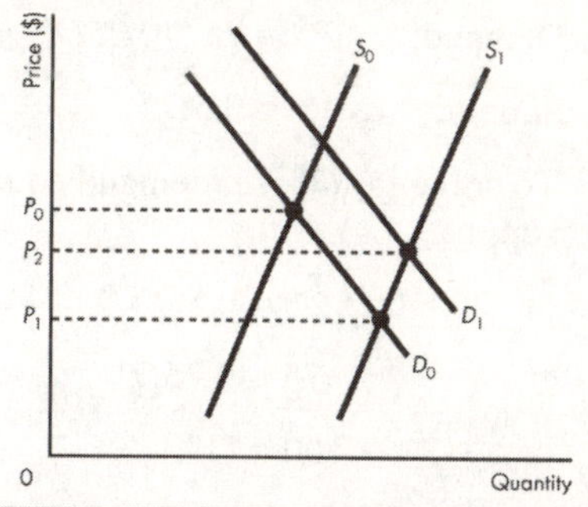

Suppose D_0 and S_0 represent the demand and supply curves for cherries last year. This year's bumper crop increases supply to S_1. Other things being equal, the price of cherries would fall from P_0 to P_1.

b But other things are not equal. Short supplies of plums and peaches (their supply curves have shifted leftward) drive up their prices. The increase in the prices of plums and peaches, which are substitutes in consumption for cherries, increases the demand for cherries to D_1. The net result is that the price of cherries only falls to P_2 instead of all the way to P_1.

8 **a** The demand and supply curves for grape jam are shown in Figure 3.2 Solution.

FIGURE **3.2** SOLUTION

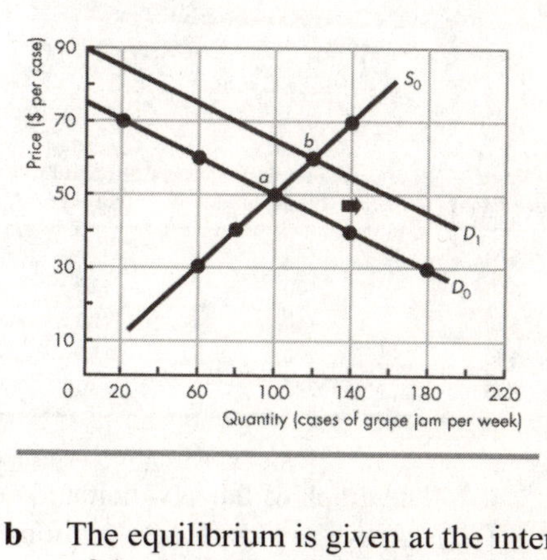

b The equilibrium is given at the intersection of the demand and supply curves (labelled point *a*). The equilibrium price is $50 per case and the equilibrium quantity is 100 cases per week.

c At a price of $40 there is a shortage of 60 cases per week.

d In equilibrium, the equations become:

Demand: $P^* = 75 - 0.25Q^*$

Supply: $P^* = 0.5Q^*$

To solve for Q^*, set demand equal to supply:

$$75 - 0.25Q^* = 0.5Q^*$$

$$75 = 0.75Q^*$$

$$100 = Q^*.$$

To solve for P^*, we can substitute Q^* into either the demand or supply equations. Look at demand first:

$$P^* = 75 - 0.25Q^*$$

$$P^* = 75 - 0.25(100)$$

$$P^* = 75 - 25$$

$$P^* = 50$$

Alternatively, substituting Q^* into the supply equation yields the same result:

$$P^* = 0.5Q^*$$

$$P^* = 0.5(100)$$

$$P^* = 50$$

e **i** Table 3.3 also contains the (unchanged) quantity supplied, for reference purposes.

TABLE **3.3** NEW DEMAND AND UNCHANGED SUPPLY SCHEDULES FOR GRAPE JAM PER WEEK

Price (per case)	Quantity Demanded (cases)	Quantity Supplied (cases)
$70	80	140
$60	120	120
$50	160	100
$40	200	80
$30	240	60

ii The graph of the new demand curve, D_1, is shown in Figure 3.2 Solution.

iii The new equilibrium price is $60 per case and the quantity is 120 cases of grape jam per week.

iv The new demand equation is $P = 90 - 0.25Q_D$. Notice that the slope of the new demand equation is the same as the slope of the original demand equation. An increase in demand of 60 cases at every price results in a rightward *parallel* shift of the demand curve. Since the two curves are parallel, they have the same slope. The figure of 90 is the price-axis intercept of the new demand curve, which you can see on your graph. *Remember:* The demand equation is the equation of a straight line ($y = a + bx$)—in this case, $a = 90$.

If you want additional practice in the use of demand and supply equations for calculating equilibrium values of price and quantity, you can use the new demand curve equation together with the supply curve equation to calculate the answers you found in **e iii**.

9 In equilibrium, the equations become

Demand: $P^* = 8 - 1Q^*$
Supply: $P^* = 2 + 1Q^*$

a To solve for Q^*, set demand equal to supply:

$$8 - 1Q^* = 2 + 1Q^*$$

$$6 = 2Q^*$$

$$3 = Q^*$$

b To solve for P^*, we can substitute Q^* into either the demand or supply equations. Look first at demand:

$$P^* = 8 - 1Q^*$$

$$P^* = 8 - 1(3)$$

$$P^* = 8 - 3$$

$$P^* = 5$$

Alternatively, substituting Q^* into the supply equation yields the same result:

$$P^* = 2 + 1Q^*$$

$$P^* = 2 + 1(3)$$

$$P^* = 2 + 3$$

$$P^* = 5$$

c In equilibrium, the equations are

Demand: $P^* = 4 - 1Q^*$
Supply: $P^* = 2 + 1Q^*$

To solve for Q^*, set demand equal to supply:

$$4 - 1Q^* = 2 + 1Q^*$$

$$2 = 2Q^*$$

$$1 = Q^*$$

To solve for P^*, we can substitute Q^* into either the demand or supply equations. Look first at demand:

$$P^* = 4 - 1Q^*$$

$$P^* = 4 - 1(1)$$

$$P^* = 4 - 1$$

$$P^* = 3$$

Alternatively, substituting Q^* into the supply equation yields the same result:

$$P^* = 2 + 1Q^*$$

$$P^* = 2 + 1(1)$$

$$P^* = 2 + 1$$

$$P^* = 3$$

d The supply curve, initial demand curve, and new demand curve for dweedles are shown in Figure 3.3 Solution.

FIGURE **3.3** SOLUTION

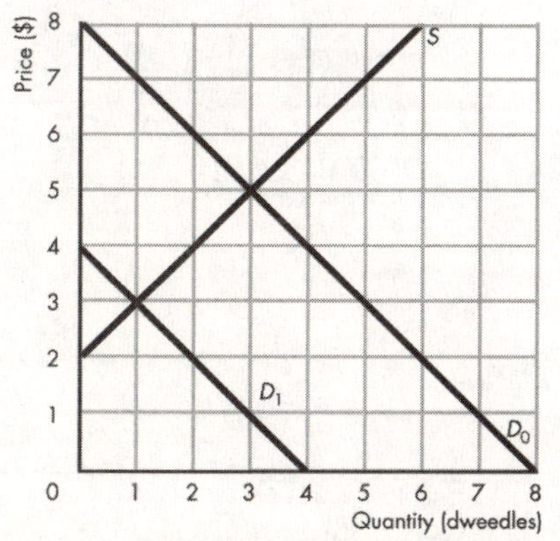

e Dweedles are an inferior good. An increase in income (from \$300 to \$500) caused a decrease in demand—the demand curve for dweedles shifted leftward.

10 a Substitute the price of \$56 into the demand and supply equations to calculate the quantities demanded and supplied at that price. This is the mathematical equivalent of what you do on a graph when you identify a price on the vertical axis, move your eye across to the demand (or supply) curve, and then move your eye down to read the quantity on the horizontal axis.

Substituting into the demand equation, we find

$$P = 80 - 2QD$$

$$56 = 80 - 2QD$$

$$2QD = 24$$

$$QD = 12.$$

Substituting into the supply equation,

$$P = 50 + 1QS$$

$$56 = 50 + 1QS$$

$$6 = QS$$

Quantity demanded exceeds quantity supplied by 6 (12 – 6), so there is a shortage of 6 flubits.

b A shortage means the price was set below the equilibrium price. Competition between consumers for the limited number of flubits will bid up the price and increase the quantity supplied until we reach the equilibrium price and quantity.

c In equilibrium, the equations are

Demand: $P^* = 80 - 2Q^*$

Supply: $P^* = 50 + 1Q^*$

To solve for Q^*, set demand equal to supply:

$$80 - 2Q^* = 50 + 1Q^*$$

$$30 = 3Q^*$$

$$10 = Q^*$$

d To solve for P^*, substitute Q^* into the demand equation:

$$P^* = 80 - 2Q^*$$

$$P^* = 80 - 2(10)$$

$$P^* = 80 - 20$$

$$P^* = 60$$

You can check this answer yourself by substituting Q^* into the supply equation.

e The new equilibrium equations are

Demand: $P^* = 80 - 2Q^*$

Supply: $P^* = 20 + 1Q^*$

To solve for Q^*, set demand equal to supply:

$$80 - 2Q^* = 20 + 1Q^*$$

$$60 = 3Q^*$$

$$20 = Q^*$$

To solve for P^*, substitute Q^* into the supply equations:

$$P^* = 20 + 1Q^*$$

$$P^* = 20 + 1(20)$$

$$P^* = 20 + 20$$

$$P^* = 40$$

You can check this answer yourself by substituting Q^* into the demand equation.

Chapter 4 Elasticity

KEY CONCEPTS

Price Elasticity of Demand

Price elasticity of demand (η) measures responsiveness of quantity demanded to change in price.

- η is units-free measure of responsiveness.

$$\eta = \left| \frac{\%\ \Delta \text{ quantity demanded}}{\%\ \Delta \text{ price}} \right| = \left| \frac{\Delta Q / Q_{ave}}{\Delta P / P_{ave}} \right|$$

- Elasticity is *not* equal to slope. Moving down along a linear demand curve, slope ($\Delta P/\Delta Q$) is constant but elasticity decreases as P_{ave} falls and Q_{ave} increases.

When	Demand Is
$\eta = \infty$	**perfectly elastic** (horizontal)
$1 < \eta < \infty$	**elastic**
$\eta = 1$	**unit elastic**
$0 < \eta < 1$	**inelastic**
$\eta = 0$	**perfectly inelastic** (vertical)

Elasticity and **total revenue** ($P \times Q$)—the **total revenue test**:

When Demand Is	Price Cut Causes
elastic ($\eta > 1$)	increased total revenue
unit elastic ($\eta = 1$)	no change total revenue
inelastic ($\eta < 1$)	decreased total revenue

Elasticity of demand depends on

- *closeness of substitutes*—closer substitutes for a good yield higher elasticity.
  - Goods defined more narrowly have higher elasticity.
  - Necessities generally have poor substitutes and inelastic demands.
  - Luxuries generally have many substitutes and elastic demands.
- *proportion of income spent on good*—greater proportion of income spent on a good yields higher elasticity.
- *time elapsed since price change*—longer time elapsed yields higher elasticity.
  - Short-run demand describes responsiveness to a change in price *before* sufficient time for all substitutions to be made.
  - Long-run demand describes responsiveness to a change in price *after* sufficient time for all substitutions to be made.
  - Short-run demand is usually less elastic than long-run demand.

More Elasticities of Demand

Cross elasticity of demand (η_x) measures the *responsiveness* of quantity demanded of good *A* to a change in price of good *B*.

- $$\eta_x = \frac{\%\ \Delta \text{ quantity demanded good } A}{\%\ \Delta \text{ price good } B}$$
- $\eta_x > 0$ Goods are substitutes.
- $\eta_x = 0$ Goods are independent.
- $\eta_x < 0$ Goods are complements.

Income elasticity of demand (η_y) measures *responsiveness* of demand to change in income.

- $$\eta_y = \frac{\%\ \Delta \text{ quantity demanded}}{\%\ \Delta \text{ income}}$$

When	Demand Is
$\eta_y > 1$	income elastic (normal good)
$0 < \eta_y < 1$	income inelastic (normal good)
$\eta_y < 0$	negative income elasticity (inferior good)

Elasticity of Supply

Elasticity of supply (η_s) measures *responsiveness* of quantity supplied to change in price.

- $\eta_s = \frac{\%\ \Delta \text{ quantity supplied}}{\%\ \Delta \text{ price}}$

When	Supply Is
$\eta_s = \infty$	perfectly elastic (horizontal)
$1 < \eta_s < \infty$	elastic
$\eta_s = 1$	unit elastic
$0 < \eta_s < 1$	inelastic
$\eta_s = 0$	perfectly inelastic (vertical)

Elasticity of supply depends on

- *resources substitution possibilities*—the more common the productive resources used, the higher η_s.
- *time frame for supply decision*—the longer the time elapsed, from momentary to short-run to long-run supply, the higher η_s.
  - Momentary supply describes responsiveness of quantity supplied immediately following a price change.
  - Short-run supply describes responsiveness of quantity supplied to a price change when *some* technologically possible adjustments to production have been made.
  - Long-run supply describes responsiveness of quantity supplied to a price change when *all* technologically possible adjustments to production have been made.

HELPFUL HINTS

1 There are many elasticity formulas in this chapter, but they are all based on the same simple, intuitive principle—*responsiveness*. All of the demand and supply elasticity formulas measure the *responsiveness* (sensitivity) *of quantity* (demanded or supplied) to changes in something else. Thus percentage change in quantity is always in the numerator of the relevant formula. As you come to understand how quantity responds to changes in price, income, and prices of related goods, you will be able to work out each elasticity formula, even if you have temporarily forgotten it.

2 The complete formula (see Text Figure 4.2, page 85) for calculating the price elasticity of demand between two points on the demand curve is

$$\eta = \frac{\%\ \Delta \text{ quantity demanded}}{\%\ \Delta \text{ price}}$$

$$= \left| \left(\frac{\Delta Q}{Q_{ave}}\right) \Big/ \left(\frac{\Delta P}{P_{ave}}\right) \right|$$

The law of demand assures us that price and quantity demanded always move in opposite directions along any demand curve. Thus without the absolute value sign, the formula for the price elasticity of demand would yield a negative number. Because our main interest is in the *magnitude* of the response in quantity demanded to a change in price, for simplicity's sake we take the absolute value to guarantee a positive number. Whenever you see the often-used shorthand term "*elasticity* of demand," remember that it means the absolute value of the *price* elasticity of demand.

3 Elasticity is *not* the same as slope (although they are related). Along a straight-line demand curve the slope is constant, but the elasticity varies from infinity to zero as we move down the demand curve. To see why, look at the formula below, which is just a rearrangement of the elasticity formula in Helpful Hint **2**.

$$\eta = \left| \left(\frac{\Delta Q}{\Delta P}\right) \times \left(\frac{P_{ave}}{Q_{ave}}\right) \right|$$

The term in the first parentheses is simply the inverse of the slope. Since the slope is constant everywhere along a straight-line demand curve, so is the inverse of the slope. Consider, however, what happens to the term in the second parentheses as we move down the demand curve. At the "top" of the demand curve, P_{ave} is very large and Q_{ave} is very small, so the term in the second parentheses is large. As we move down the demand curve, P_{ave} becomes smaller and Q_{ave} becomes larger, so the term in the second parentheses falls in value. The net result is that the absolute value of the price elasticity of demand falls as we move down the demand curve.

4 One of the most practical and important uses of the concept of price elasticity of demand is that it allows us to predict the effect on total revenue of a change in price. A fall in price will increase total revenue if demand is elastic, leave total revenue unchanged if demand is unit elastic, and decrease total revenue if demand is inelastic. Because price and quantity demanded always

move in opposite directions along a demand curve, a fall in price will cause an increase in quantity demanded. Since total revenue equals price times quantity, the fall in price will tend to decrease total revenue, while the increase in quantity demanded will increase total revenue. The net effect depends on which of these individual effects is larger.

The concept of price elasticity of demand conveniently summarizes the net effect. For example, if demand is elastic, the percentage change in quantity demanded is greater than the percentage change in price. Hence, with a fall in price, the quantity effect dominates and total revenue will increase. If, however, demand is inelastic, the percentage change in quantity demanded is less than the percentage change in price. Hence, with a fall in price, the price effect dominates and total revenue will decrease.

5 Two other important elasticity concepts are the income elasticity of demand and the cross elasticity of demand.

Income elasticity of demand:

$$\eta_y = \frac{\%\ \Delta \text{ quantity demanded}}{\%\ \Delta \text{ income}}$$

$$= \left(\frac{\Delta Q}{Q_{ave}}\right) / \left(\frac{\Delta Y}{Y_{ave}}\right)$$

Cross elasticity of demand:

$$\eta_x = \frac{\%\ \Delta \text{ quantity demanded good } A}{\%\ \Delta \text{ price good } B}$$

$$= \left(\frac{\Delta Q^A}{Q^A_{ave}}\right) / \left(\frac{\Delta P^B}{P^B_{ave}}\right)$$

Notice that these two elasticity formulas do *not* have absolute value signs and can take on either positive or negative values. While these formulas measure responsiveness, both the magnitude *and the direction* of the response are important. In the case of income elasticity of demand, the response of quantity demanded to an increase in income will be positive for a normal good and negative for an inferior good. In the case of cross elasticity of demand, the response of the quantity demanded of good *A* to an increase in the price of good *B* will be positive if the goods are substitutes and negative if the goods are complements.

In calculating an income elasticity or a cross elasticity, be alert to the fact that the *price of the good in the numerator* of the formula *is assumed constant*. Income elasticity measures the quantity response to a change in income, *ceteris paribus*. Cross elasticity measures the quantity response of good *A* to a change in the price of good *B*, *ceteris paribus*. This means that we cannot simply read numerical values for calculating these elasticities from the equilibrium positions of a set of demand and supply curves. For example, when income increases, demand shifts rightward (for a normal good), and the new equilibrium quantity will also have a higher equilibrium price. To calculate income elasticity correctly, we compare the income and quantity demanded of the initial equilibrium with the new income and quantity demanded. To obtain the correct new quantity demanded, we must use the new demand curve, but must calculate the quantity demanded that would have prevailed at the *initial*, unchanged price. (See Short Answer Problems **9** and **10** for examples.)

SELF-TEST

True/False and Explain

Price Elasticity of Demand

1 The price elasticity of demand measures how responsive prices are to changes in demand.

2 Price elasticity of demand is constant along a linear demand curve.

3 If a decrease in supply causes total revenue to increase, demand must be inelastic.

4 If a 9 percent increase in price leads to a 5 percent decrease in quantity demanded, total revenue has decreased.

5 If you like Pepsi Cola and Coca-Cola about the same, your demand for Pepsi is likely to be elastic.

6 The more narrowly we define a good, the more elastic its demand.

7 If your expenditures on toothpaste are a small proportion of your total income, your demand for toothpaste is likely to be inelastic.

8 The demand for gasoline is likely to become more inelastic with the passage of time after a price increase.

More Elasticities of Demand

9 An inferior good has a negative cross elasticity of demand.

10 If a 10 percent increase in the price of widgets causes a 6 percent increase in the quantity of woozles demanded, then widgets and woozles must be complements.

11 We would expect a negative cross elasticity of demand between hamburgers and hamburger buns.

Elasticity of Supply

12 Elasticity of supply equals the change in quantity supplied divided by the change in price.

13 A horizontal supply curve is perfectly elastic.

14 Goods produced with rare resources have a low elasticity of supply.

15 Supply is generally more inelastic in the long run than in the short run.

Multiple-Choice

Price Elasticity of Demand

1 There are two points on the demand curve for volleyballs, as shown in Table 4.1.

TABLE **4.1**

Price per Volleyball	Quantity Demanded
$19	55
$21	45

What is the elasticity of demand between these two points?

a 2.5
b 2.0
c 0.5
d 0.4
e None of the above

2 If the price elasticity of demand is 2, a 1 percent decrease in price will

a double the quantity demanded.
b reduce the quantity demanded by half.
c increase the quantity demanded by 2%.
d reduce the quantity demanded by 2%.
e increase the quantity demanded by 0.5%.

3 If price elasticity of demand is zero, then as the price falls

a total revenue does not change.
b quantity demanded does not change.
c quantity demanded falls to zero.
d total revenue increases from zero.
e none of the above occurs.

4 A perfectly vertical demand curve has a price elasticity of
- **a** zero.
- **b** greater than zero but less than one.
- **c** one.
- **d** greater than one.
- **e** infinity.

5 A union leader who claims that "higher wages increase living standards without causing unemployment" believes that the demand for labour is
- **a** income elastic.
- **b** income inelastic.
- **c** perfectly elastic.
- **d** perfectly inelastic.
- **e** unit elastic.

6 Business people talk about price elasticity of demand without using the actual term. Which of the following statements reflect elastic demand for a product?
- **a** "A price cut won't help me. It won't increase sales, and I'll just get less money for each unit that I was selling before."
- **b** "I don't think a price cut will make any difference to my bottom line. What I may gain from selling more I would lose on the lower price."
- **c** "My customers are real bargain hunters. Since I set my prices just a few cents below my competitors', customers have flocked to the store and sales are booming."
- **d** "With the recent economic recovery, people have more income to spend and sales are booming, even at the same prices as before."
- **e** None of the above.

7 A technological breakthrough lowers the cost of photocopiers. If the demand for photocopiers is price inelastic, we predict that photocopier sales will
- **a** fall and total revenue will rise.
- **b** fall and total revenue will fall.
- **c** rise and total revenue will rise.
- **d** rise and total revenue will fall.
- **e** rise but changes in total revenue will depend on elasticity of supply.

8 A decrease in tuition fees will decrease the university's total revenue if the price elasticity of demand for university education is
- **a** negative.
- **b** greater than zero but less than one.
- **c** equal to one.
- **d** greater than one.
- **e** less than the price elasticity of supply.

9 If the demand for orange juice is price elastic, a severe frost that destroys large quantities of oranges will likely
- **a** reduce the equilibrium price of juice, but increase total consumer spending on it.
- **b** reduce the equilibrium quantity of juice as well as total consumer spending on it.
- **c** reduce both the equilibrium quantity and the price of juice.
- **d** increase the equilibrium price of juice as well as total consumer spending on it.
- **e** increase the equilibrium price of juice, but leave total consumer spending on it constant.

10 If a 4 percent rise in the price of peanut butter causes total revenue to fall by 8 percent, demand for peanut butter
- **a** is elastic.
- **b** is inelastic.
- **c** is unit elastic.
- **d** has an elasticity of 1/2.
- **e** has an elasticity of 2.

11 Tina and Brian work for the same recording company. Tina claims that they would be better off by increasing the price of their CDs while Brian claims that they would be better off by decreasing the price. We can conclude that
- **a** Tina thinks the demand for CDs has price elasticity of zero, and Brian thinks price elasticity equals one.
- **b** Tina thinks the demand for CDs has price elasticity equal to one, and Brian thinks price elasticity equals zero.
- **c** Tina thinks the demand for CDs is price elastic, and Brian thinks it is price inelastic.
- **d** Tina thinks the demand for CDs is price inelastic and Brian thinks it is price elastic.
- **e** Tina and Brian should stick to singing and forget about economics.

12 Given the relationship shown in Figure 4.1 between total revenue from the sale of a good and the quantity of the good sold,
- **a** this is an inferior good.
- **b** this is a normal good.
- **c** the elasticity of demand is zero.
- **d** the elasticity of demand is infinity.
- **e** the elasticity of demand is one.

FIGURE 4.1

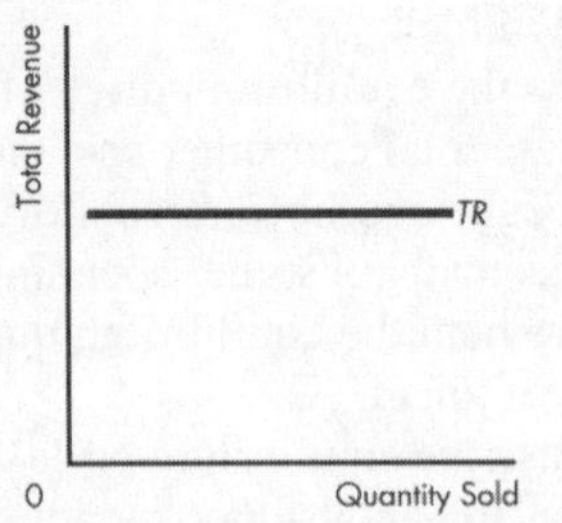

13 If the Jets decrease ticket prices and find that total revenue does not change, the price elasticity of demand for tickets is
a zero.
b greater than zero, but less than one.
c equal to one.
d greater than one.
e inferior.

14 The fact that butter has margarine as a close substitute in consumption
a makes the supply of butter more elastic.
b makes the supply of butter less elastic.
c makes the demand for butter more elastic.
d makes the demand for butter less elastic.
e does not affect butter's elasticity of supply or demand.

15 A given percentage increase in the price of a good is likely to cause a larger percentage decline in quantity demanded
a the shorter the passage of time.
b the larger the proportion of income spent on it.
c the harder it is to obtain good substitutes.
d all of the above.
e none of the above.

More Elasticities of Demand

16 A negative value for
a price elasticity of supply implies an upward-sloping supply curve.
b cross elasticity of demand implies complementary goods.
c price elasticity of demand implies an inferior good.
d income elasticity of demand implies a normal good.
e income elasticity of demand implies an error in your calculation.

17 The cross elasticity of the demand for white tennis balls with respect to the price of yellow tennis balls is probably
a negative and high.
b negative and low.
c positive and high.
d positive and low.
e zero.

18 If a 10 percent increase in income causes a 5 percent increase in quantity demanded (at a constant price), what is the income elasticity of demand?
a 0.5
b –0.5
c 2.0
d –2.0
e none of the above

19 Luxury goods tend to have income elasticities of demand that are
a greater than one.
b greater than zero but less than one.
c positive.
d negative.
e first positive and then negative as income increases.

20 If a 4 percent decrease in income (at a constant price) causes a 2 percent decrease in the consumption of dweedles,
a the income elasticity of demand for dweedles is negative.
b dweedles are a necessity and a normal good.
c dweedles are a luxury and a normal good.
d dweedles are an inferior good.
e **a** and **d** are true.

Elasticity of Supply

21 When price goes from $1.50 to $2.50, quantity supplied increases from 9,000 to 11,000 units. What is the price elasticity of supply?
a 0.4
b 0.8
c 2.5
d 4.0
e none of the above

22 Preferences for brussels sprouts increase. The price of brussels sprouts will not change if the price elasticity of
a demand is 0.
b demand is 1.
c supply is 0.
d supply is 1.
e supply is infinity.

23 A sudden end-of-summer heat wave increases the demand for air conditioners and catches suppliers with no reserve inventories. The momentary supply curve for air conditioners is
- a perfectly elastic.
- b perfectly inelastic.
- c elastic.
- d upward-sloping.
- e horizontal.

24 The long-run supply curve is likely to be
- a more elastic than momentary supply, but less elastic than short-run supply.
- b less elastic than momentary supply, but more elastic than short-run supply.
- c less elastic than both momentary and short-run supply curves.
- d more elastic than both momentary and short-run supply curves.
- e vertical.

25 Long-run elasticity of supply of a good is greater than short-run elasticity of supply because
- a more substitutes in consumption for the good can be found.
- b more complements in consumption for the good can be found.
- c more technological ways of adjusting supply can be exploited.
- d income rises with more elapsed time.
- e the long-run supply curve is steeper.

Short Answer Problems

1 Why is elasticity superior to slope as a measure of the responsiveness of quantity demanded to changes in price?

2 In each of the following, compare the price elasticity of demand for each pair of goods and explain why the demand for one of the goods is more elastic than demand for the other.

- a IBM personal computers before the development of other "clone" personal computers versus IBM personal computers after the production of such clones
- b Television sets versus matches
- c Electricity just after an increase in its price versus electricity two years after the price increase
- d Acetaminophen versus Tylenol-brand acetaminophen

3 Why does supply tend to be more elastic in the long run?

4 In Figure 4.2, which demand curve (D_A or D_B) is more elastic in the price range P_1 to P_2? Explain why. (*Hint:* Use the formula for price elasticity of demand.)

FIGURE **4.2**

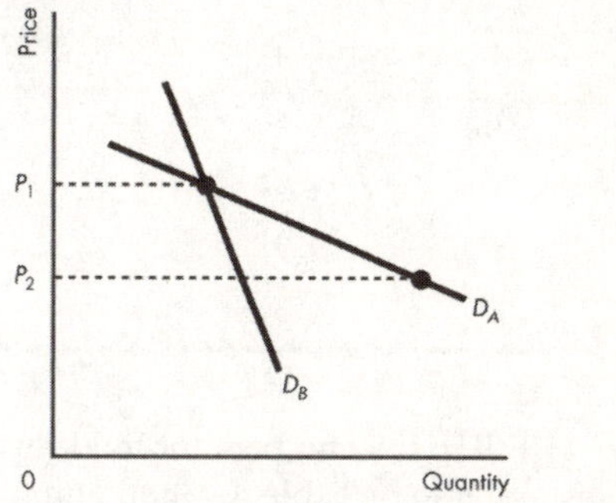

5 Consider the demand curve in Figure 4.3(a). A portion of the demand curve is also described by the demand schedule in Table 4.2.

FIGURE **4.3**

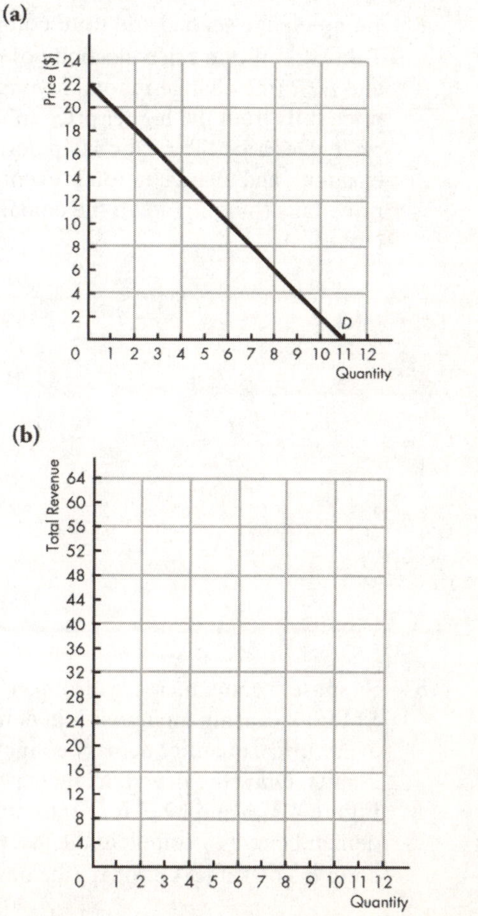

TABLE **4.2**

Price ($)	Quantity Demanded	Total Revenue
22	0	
20	1	
18	2	
16	3	
14	4	
12	5	
10	6	
8	7	
6	8	

Fill in the numbers for total revenue in the last column of Table 4.2, and graph your results on Figure 4.3(b). Describe the shape of the total revenue curve as quantity increases (price decreases).

6 Using the same information for the demand curve in Short Answer Problem **5**:

a Complete the second and third columns of Table 4.3: η (the price elasticity of demand) and ΔTR (the change in total revenue) as the price falls from the higher price to the lower price. Describe the relationship between elasticity and change in total revenue as price falls (moving down the demand curve).

TABLE **4.3**

ΔP ($)	η	ΔTR ($)	η′	$\Delta TR'$ ($)
16 — 14				
14 — 12				
12 — 10				
10 — 8				
8 — 6				

b Suppose income increases from $10,000 to $14,000, causing an increase in demand: at every price, quantity demanded increases by 2 units. Draw the new demand curve on Figure 4.3(a) and label it *D*'. Use this new demand curve to complete the last two columns of Table 4.3 for η' (the new price elasticity of demand) and $\Delta TR'$ (the new change in total revenue).

c Using the price range between $16 and $14, explain why *D*' is more inelastic than *D*.

d Calculate the income elasticity of demand, assuming the price remains constant at $12. Is this a normal or inferior good? Explain why you could have answered the question even without calculating the income elasticity of demand.

ⓒⓣ 7 The demand equation for woozles is $P = 60 - 2Q_D$. The supply equation for woozles is $P = 32 + 5Q_S$, where *P* is the price of a woozle in dollars, Q_D is the quantity of woozles demanded, and Q_S is the quantity of woozles supplied.

a Calculate the price elasticity of demand for woozles between $Q_D = 4$ and $Q_D = 6$.

b Initially, the woozle market is in equilibrium with $P^* = 52$ and $Q^* = 4$. Then, the supply curve shifts (the demand curve remains constant) yielding a new equilibrium price of $P^* = 48$.

Using all of the relevant information above, show *two separate methods* for determining whether total revenue increases, decreases, or remains constant in moving from the initial equilibrium to the new equilibrium.

8 Suppose Jean loses his present job and his monthly income falls from $10,000 to $6,000, while his monthly purchases of grits increase from 200 to 400.

a Calculate his income elasticity of demand for grits.

b Are grits a normal or inferior good? Explain why.

9 The demand equation for tribbles is $P = 50 - 1Q_D$. The supply equation for tribbles is $P = 20 + 0.5Q_S$, where *P* is the price of a tribble in dollars, Q_D is the quantity of tribbles demanded, and Q_S is the quantity of tribbles supplied. The tribble market is initially in equilibrium, and income is $180.

a What is the equilibrium quantity (Q^*) of tribbles?

b What is the equilibrium price (P^*) of a tribble?

c As a result of a decrease in income to $120, the demand curve for tribbles shifts (the supply curve remains the same). The new demand equation is:

$$P = 110 - 1Q_D$$

Use this information to calculate the new equilibrium quantity of tribbles; calculate the new equilibrium price of a tribble.

d Calculate the income elasticity of demand for tribbles. Are tribbles a normal or inferior good? (*Hint*: In your calculation be sure to: (1) use the information about the *initial* equilibrium conditions [price, quantity, and income] and (2) keep in mind that price is assumed *constant* in calculating income elasticity. Only income and quantity change.)

10 Table 4.4 gives the demand schedules for good A when the price of good B (P_B) is $8 and $12. Complete the last column of the table by computing the cross elasticity of demand between goods A and B for each of the three prices of A. Are A and B complements or substitutes?

TABLE **4.4** DEMAND SCHEDULES FOR GOOD A

	P_B = $8	P_B = $12	
P_A	Q_A	Q'_A	η_x
$8	2,000	4,000	
$7	4,000	6,000	
$6	6,000	8,000	

ANSWERS

True/False and Explain

1 F Responsiveness quantity demanded to ΔP. (84)

2 F Slope constant; η falls as move down demand curve. (87)

3 T Decreased S causes increased P and increased total revenue, so demand inelastic. (88)

4 F (% increase P) > (% decrease Q), so total revenue ($P \times Q$) increases. (88)

5 T Colas are substitutes for you. (89)

6 T With narrower definition, more substitutes. (89)

7 T Lower proportion income spent on good, more inelastic demand. (90)

8 F Elasticity increases with elapsed time. (90)

9 F Inferior good has negative income elasticity; cross elasticity sign depends on whether substitute or complement. (91–92)

10 F η_x positive so goods are substitutes. (91–92)

11 T η_x negative for complements. (91–92)

12 F η_s equals *percentage* change in quantity supplied divided by *percentage* change in price. (94)

13 T η_s = infinity. (95)

14 T $\eta_s < 1$. (95)

15 F Supply more elastic in long run. (96)

Multiple-Choice

1 b $|(-10/50)/(2/20)| = 2$. (85–86)

2 c $\eta = |(\%\ \Delta Q_D)/(\%\ \Delta P)| = |(1/5)/(1/10)| = 2$. Q_D and P always inversely related on demand curve. (85–86)

3 b Demand curve vertical so lower P does not Δ quantity demanded. (86–87)

4 a Definition. (86–87)

5 d Labour demand curve would be vertical. (86–87)

6 c Small fall P causes large increase quantity demanded. **a** inelastic, **b** unit elastic, **d** on income elasticity. (86–87)

7 d Rightward shift supply causes increased quantity sold and lower P; with inelastic demand causes decreased total revenue. (88)

8 b Lower P causes decreased total revenue when $\eta < 1$. η never negative. (88)

9 b Decreased S causes decreased Q_D and higher P. Since $\eta > 1$, higher P causes decreased expenditure. (88)

10 a If higher P causes decreased total revenue, η must be > 1. Must know (% ΔQ_D) to precisely calculate η. (88)

11 d Better off means increased total revenue. By definition of relation between higher P, η, and total revenue. (88)

12 e Note total revenue (TR) on y-axis. Since TR constant as increased Q (and presumably lower P), $\eta = 1$. **a**, **b** depend on η_y. (88)

13 c Total revenue test. (88)

14 c Closer substitutes yield higher elasticity demand. (89)

15 b η increases with increased proportion income spent on good. η increases when longer time passage and easier to obtain substitutes. (89–90)

16 b η_s and η never negative. η_y negative for inferior good. (91–92)

17 c Close substitutes so η_x positive and very elastic (high). (91)

18 a η_y = (% ΔQ_D)/(% Δ income) = 5/10 = 0.5. (92)

19 a See answer to **20** below. **c** correct, but **a** best answer. (92–93)

20 b $\eta_y > 0$ so normal good. Necessities tend to have $\eta_y < 1$, while luxuries tend to have $\eta_y > 1$. (92–93)

21 a η_s = (% ΔQ_S)/(% ΔP) = (2,000/10,000)/(1/2) = 0.4. (94–95)

22 e Increased D causes no ΔP if supply curve horizontal (η_s = infinity). (94–95)

23 b Definition. (86)

24 d Definition. Momentary supply curve most vertical. (96)

25 c Definition. **a**, **b**, **d** affect demand, not supply. Long-run supply curve flatter than short-run. (95–96)

Short Answer Problems

1 The slope of a demand curve tells us how much quantity demanded changes when price changes. However, the numerical value of the slope depends on the units we use to measure price and quantity and will change if the unit of measure is changed even though demand is unchanged. For example, if we change the unit of measure for quantity from tonnes to kilograms, the new slope of the (same) demand curve will be 1,000 times the old slope. On the other hand, elasticity gives a unit-free measure of the responsiveness of quantity demanded to price changes.

2 a The demand for IBM personal computers will be more elastic after the production of clone personal computers, since there would then be more readily available substitutes.

b The demand for television sets will be more elastic, since they will generally take a larger proportion of consumer income.

c The demand for electricity after the passage of two years will be more elastic, since consumers will have more time to find substitutes for electricity, for example a gas stove.

d The demand for Tylenol is more elastic. There are far more substitutes for Tylenol (other brands of acetaminophen) than for acetaminophen in general.

3 Supply is more elastic in the long run, because the passage of time allows producers to find better (more efficient) ways of producing that are not available in the short run. The responsiveness of production to an increase in price will increase as firms have time to discover and implement new technologies or to increase the scale of operation.

4 D_A is more elastic than D_B. To see why, look at the formula for price elasticity of demand:

$$\eta = \left| \frac{\%\ \Delta\ \text{quantity demanded}}{\%\ \Delta\ \text{price}} \right|$$

The percentage change in price is the same for the two demand curves. But the percentage change in quantity is greater for D_A. At P_1, the initial quantity demanded is the same for both demand curves (Q_1). With the fall in price to P_2, the increase in quantity demanded is greater for D_A (to Q_{2A}) than for D_B (to Q_{2B}). Therefore D_A is more elastic than D_B.

FIGURE **4.2** SOLUTION

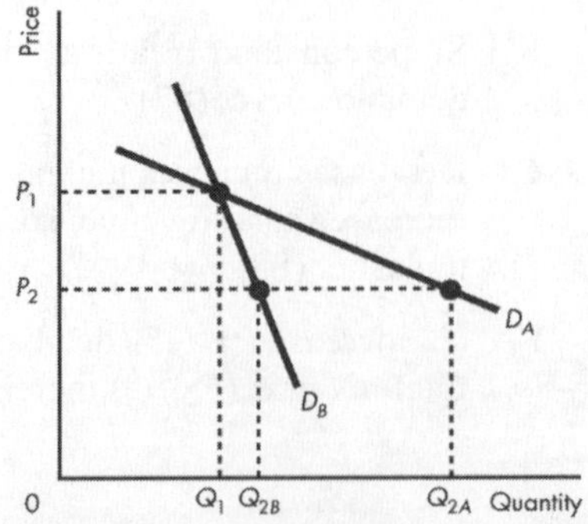

5 The numbers for total revenue are shown in Table 4.2 Solution. The total revenue curve is shown in Figure 4.3(b) Solution. The total revenue curve first increases (at a diminishing rate—its slope is decreasing as we move up the curve), then reaches a maximum between $Q = 5$ and $Q = 6$, then decreases. We will encounter this pattern of changing total revenue again in studying monopoly in Chapter 12.

TABLE **4.2** SOLUTION

Price ($)	Quantity Demanded	Total Revenue
22	0	0
20	1	20
18	2	36
16	3	48
14	4	56
12	5	60
10	6	60
8	7	56
6	8	48

FIGURE **4.3(b)** SOLUTION

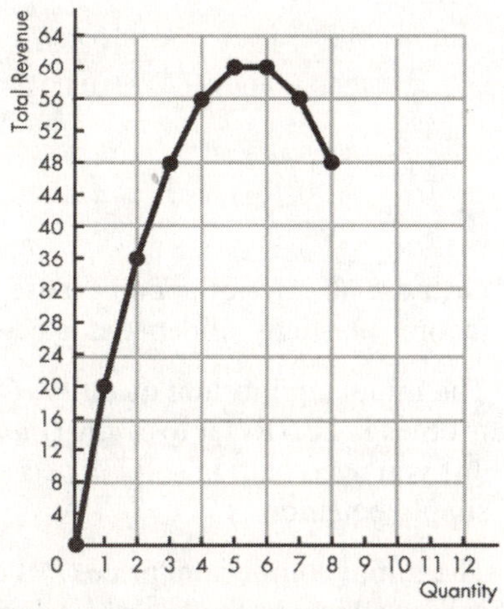

6 a The completed columns of Table 4.3 are shown here. The second and third columns of the table show that as price falls, total revenue increases when demand is elastic; total revenue remains constant when demand is unit elastic; total revenue falls when demand is inelastic.

TABLE **4.3** SOLUTION

ΔP($)	η	ΔTR($)	η′	ΔTR′ ($)
16 — 14	2.14	+8	1.36	+4
14 — 12	1.44	+4	1.00	0
12 — 10	1.00	0	0.73	–4
10 — 8	0.69	–4	0.53	–8
8 — 6	0.47	–8	0.37	–12

b The new demand curve is labelled *D*' in Figure 4.3(a) Solution. The last two columns of the table have been completed on the basis of the new demand curve.

FIGURE **4.3(a)** SOLUTION

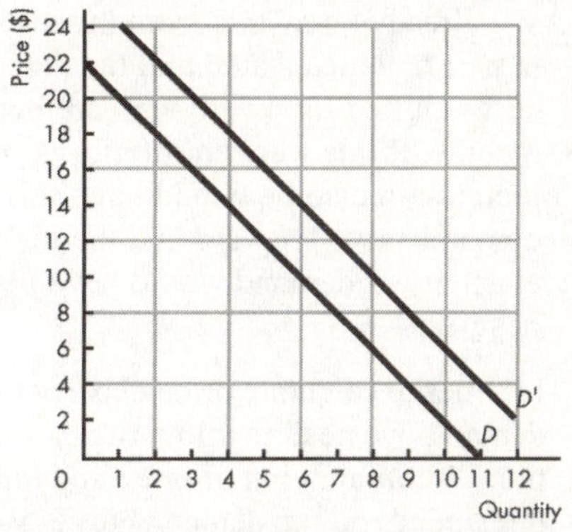

c Since they are parallel, *D*' and *D* have exactly the same slope. Thus we know that for a given change in price, the change in quantity demanded will be the same for the two curves. However, elasticity is determined by *percentage* changes, and the percentage change in quantity demanded is different for the two curves, although the percentage change in price will be the same. For a given percentage change in price, the percentage change in quantity demanded will always be less for *D*'. For example, as the price falls from $16 to $14 (a 13 percent change), the quantity demanded increases from 5 to 6 units along *D*', but from 3 to 4 along *D*. The percentage change in quantity demanded is only 18 percent along *D*' and 29 percent along *D*. Since the percentage change in price is the same for both curves, *D*' is more inelastic than *D*.

d Income increases from $10,000 to $14,000. At a constant price of $12, the increase in income, which shifts out the demand curve to D', increases the quantity consumers will demand from 5 units to 7 units. Substituting these numbers into the formula for the income elasticity of demand yields

$$\eta_y = \left(\frac{\Delta Q}{Q_{ave}}\right) \Big/ \left(\frac{\Delta Y}{Y_{ave}}\right)$$

$$= \left(\frac{2}{6}\right) \Big/ \left(\frac{4{,}000}{12{,}000}\right) = +1$$

The income elasticity of demand is a positive number, since both ΔQ and ΔY are positive. Therefore this is a normal good. We already knew that from the information in part **b**, which stated that the demand curve shifted rightward with an increase in income. If this were an inferior good, the increase in income would have shifted the demand curve leftward and the income elasticity of demand would have been negative.

ⓒⓣ **7 a** In order to calculate price elasticity of demand, we need to know two points (each point a combination of price and quantity demanded) on the demand curve. We only are given the quantity demanded coordinate of each point. By substituting $Q_D = 4$ and $Q_D = 6$ into the demand equation, we can solve for the two price coordinates:

At $Q_D = 4$; $P = 60 - 2(4) = 52$

At $Q_D = 6$; $P = 60 - 2(6) = 48$

These price and quantity demanded coordinates can now be substituted into the formula for the price elasticity of demand:

$$\eta = \left|\left(\frac{\Delta Q}{Q_{ave}}\right) \Big/ \left(\frac{\Delta P}{P_{ave}}\right)\right|$$

$$= \left|\left(\frac{-2}{5}\right) \Big/ \left(\frac{4}{50}\right)\right| = 5$$

b One method is simply to compare total revenue ($P \times Q$) at each equilibrium:

- Initial equilibrium:

Total revenue = $(P \times Q) = (52 \times 4) = 208$.

- New equilibrium:

If $P^* = 48$, Q^* can be calculated by substituting P^* into the demand equation:

$$48 = 60 - 2Q^*$$

$$2Q^* = 12$$

$$Q^* = 6$$

So total revenue = $(P \times Q) = (48 \times 6) = 288$. In moving from the initial to the new equilibrium, total revenue has increased.

A second method is to use the information from part **a** on the price elasticity of demand. We know that between $Q_D = 4$ and $Q_D = 6$ on the demand curve, demand is elastic. These two points correspond to the initial equilibrium and, after the shift of the supply curve, the new equilibrium. Since demand here is elastic, we know that the fall in price from $P = 52$ to $P = 48$ will increase total revenue.

8 a Using the formula for income elasticity of demand:

$$\eta_y = \left(\frac{\Delta Q}{Q_{ave}}\right) \Big/ \left(\frac{\Delta Y}{Y_{ave}}\right)$$

$$= \left(\frac{200 - 400}{½(200 + 400)}\right) \Big/ \left(\frac{10{,}000 - 6{,}000}{½(10{,}000 + 6{,}000)}\right)$$

$$= \left(\frac{-200}{300}\right) \Big/ \left(\frac{4{,}000}{8{,}000}\right) = -\frac{4}{3}$$

b Grits are an inferior good because the income elasticity of demand is negative.

9 a The initial equilibrium quantity (Q^*) of tribbles is 20. (Refer to *Study Guide* Chapter 3 if you need help in solving demand and supply equations.)

b The initial equilibrium price (P^*) of a tribble is $30. (Refer to *Study Guide* Chapter 3 if you need help in solving demand and supply equations.)

c The new equilibrium quantity of tribbles is 60. The new equilibrium price of a tribble is $50.

d At the initial income of $180 and price of $30, the quantity of tribbles demanded is 20. In order to find the new quantity demanded at income of $120, we have to use the new demand equation. But since *price* is assumed constant in calculating income elasticity, we have to substitute $P = 30$ into the new demand equation to get the appropriate new quantity. It would be *incorrect* to use the new equilibrium quantity, because that quantity corresponds to a *different price* ($50).

$$P = 110 - 1Q_D$$

$$30 = 110 - 1Q_D$$

$$Q_D = 80$$

We now have appropriate information about the initial quantity demanded (20) and income ($180), and about the new quantity demanded (80) and income ($120). Substituting this information into the formula for income elasticity of demand yields

$$\eta_y = \left(\frac{\Delta Q}{Q_{ave}}\right) \Big/ \left(\frac{\Delta Y}{Y_{ave}}\right)$$

$$= \left(\frac{-60}{50}\right) \Big/ \left(\frac{60}{150}\right) = -3$$

Since the income elasticity of demand for tribbles is negative, tribbles are an inferior good.

10 The cross elasticities of demand between *A* and *B* are listed in Table 4.4 Solution. Since the cross elasticities are positive, we know that *A* and *B* are substitutes.

TABLE **4.4** SOLUTION
DEMAND SCHEDULES FOR GOOD A

	P_B = $8	P_B = $12	
P_A	Q_A	Q'_A	η_x
$8	2,000	4,000	1.67
$7	4,000	6,000	1.00
$6	6,000	8,000	0.71

Chapter 5
Efficiency and Equity

KEY CONCEPTS

Resource Allocation Methods

Alternative methods for allocating scarce resources are: market price (resources go to those most willing and able to pay); **command system** (by order of authority); majority rule; contest; first-come, first-served; lottery; personal characteristics; force.

Demand and Marginal Benefit

Value is what consumers are willing to pay; price is what consumers actually pay.

- ♦ Demand curve is a marginal benefit curve.
  - Marginal benefit = value = maximum willing to pay for additional unit.

Individual demand and market demand:

- ♦ individual demand—relationship between quantity demanded and price for single individual.
- ♦ market demand—sum of individual demands; relationship between total quantity demanded and price.
- ♦ market demand curve—horizontal sum of individual demand curves.
  - Market demand curve is economy's marginal social benefit (*MSB*) curve.
- ♦ **Consumer surplus** is the value of a good minus its price, summed over the quantity bought. It is the triangular area under the demand curve, but above market price (see Text Figure 5.2, page 107).

Supply and Marginal Cost

Opportunity cost is what producers pay; price is what producers receive.

- ♦ Supply curve is a marginal cost curve.
  - Marginal cost = minimum producers must receive to produce additional unit.

Individual supply and market supply:

- ♦ individual supply—relationship between quantity supplied and price for single producer.
- ♦ market supply—sum of individual supplies; relationship between total quantity supplied and price.
- ♦ market supply curve—horizontal sum of individual supply curves.
  - Market supply curve is economy's marginal social cost (*MSC*) curve.
- ♦ **Producer surplus** is the price of a good minus its opportunity cost of production, summed over the quantity sold. It is the triangular area below market price, but above the supply curve (see Text Figure 5.4, page 109).

Is the Competitive Market Efficient?

In competitive equilibrium

- ♦ marginal social benefit = marginal social cost.
- ♦ resource allocation is efficient.
- ♦ *total surplus* (= consumer surplus + producer surplus) is maximized.

Inefficiency (from underproduction or overproduction) is measured by **deadweight loss**—decrease in total surplus below efficient levels.

Obstacles to efficient resource allocation:

- ♦ price and quantity regulations, taxes, subsidies (Chapter 6).

- *externalities*—cost or benefit affecting others besides the buyers and sellers of a good (Chapter 15).
  - Competitive markets overproduce goods and services that have external costs.
  - Competitive markets underproduce goods and services that have external benefits.
- *public goods*—consumed simultaneously by all, even if they don't pay for it (Chapter 16).
  - Competitive markets produce less than the efficient quantity of public goods because of the free-rider problem.
- *monopolies*—firms that restrict output and raise price, creating deadweight loss (Chapter 12).
- high **transactions costs**—opportunity costs of making trades in a market—lead to underproduction.

Is the Competitive Market Fair?

Ideas about fairness divide into two approaches:

- Fair results—there should be equality of incomes.
  - **Utilitarianism**—result should be "greatest happiness for the greatest number." Requires income transfers from rich to poor.
  - Income transfers create the "**big tradeoff**" between efficiency and fairness. Transfers use scarce resources and weaken incentives, so a more equally shared pie results in a smaller pie.
  - Modified utilitarianism—after incorporating costs of income transfers, result should make the poorest person as well off as possible.
- Fair rules—people in similar situations should be treated similarly.
  - **Symmetry principle.**
  - Equality of opportunity.
  - Requires property rights and voluntary exchange.

HELPFUL HINTS

1 This chapter provides important tools for analyzing economic policies. Policy analysis involves judgements of efficiency and fairness (or equity). The concepts of consumer and producer surplus allow us to evaluate efficiency—efficient outcomes maximize total surplus—the sum of consumer and producer surplus. Efficiency is a positive concept. The outcomes of different policies can be measured and compared objectively (at least in principle) to see which is more efficient.

Fairness is another important aspect of any economic policy. Fairness is a normative concept, depending on value judgements about which reasonable people can differ. But policymakers must make decisions, and it is helpful to be explicit about what ideas of fairness are used to judge policy. The two main normative ideas developed in this chapter are fair results and fair rules.

2 There are two ways to interpret or "read" a demand curve—as a demand curve and as a marginal benefit curve. Both readings are correct, but each provides slightly different information. You can see the two readings in Text Figures 5.1 and 5.2 on pages 106–107.

The first reading (Figure 5.1) starts with price. For a given price, the demand curve tells us the quantity demanded. Pick a price on the vertical axis. To find quantity demanded, we go "over" to the demand curve and "down" to the quantity axis. This is the standard demand curve of Chapter 3.

The second reading (Figure 5.2) starts with quantity. For a given quantity, the demand curve tells us the maximum price people are willing to pay. Pick a quantity on the horizontal axis. To find the maximum price people are willing to pay, we go "up" to the demand curve and "over" to the price axis. This is a reading of the demand curve as a marginal benefit curve. For a given quantity, the marginal benefit curve tells us the value (equals the maximum price people are willing to pay) of that unit of the good.

We read a demand curve "over and down." But we read a marginal benefit curve "up and over." Each reading is helpful, depending on the problem you are trying to solve or the issue you are trying to analyze. If you get stuck with a demand or marginal benefit curve problem, you may not be using the most suitable reading. Try reading the curve both ways and see which one is most helpful.

3 As with the demand curve, there are two ways to interpret or "read" a supply curve—as a supply curve and as a marginal cost curve. Both readings are correct, but each provides slightly different information. You can see the two readings in Text Figures 5.3 and 5.4 on pages 108–109.

The first reading (a) starts with price. For a given price, the supply curve tells us the quantity supplied. Pick a price on the vertical axis. To find quantity supplied, we go "over" to the supply curve and "down" to the quantity axis. This is the standard supply curve of Chapter 3.

The second reading (b) starts with quantity. For a given quantity, the supply curve tells us the minimum price producers are willing to accept. Pick a quantity on the horizontal axis. To find the minimum price producers are willing to accept, we go "up" to the supply curve and "over" to the price axis. This is a reading of the supply curve as a marginal cost curve. For a given quantity, the marginal cost curve tells us the opportunity cost of producing that unit of the good.

Thus we read a supply curve "over and down," while we read a marginal cost curve "up and over." Each reading is helpful, depending on the problem you are trying to solve or the issue you are trying to analyze. If you get stuck with a supply or marginal cost curve problem, you may not be using the most suitable reading. Try reading the curve both ways and see which one is most helpful.

4 The market demand curve is a marginal social benefit curve and the market supply curve is a marginal social cost curve *as long as there are no external benefits or costs*. Once you think of demand and supply curves as marginal social benefit and cost curves, the concepts of consumer surplus and producer surplus follow directly. Consumer surplus is the difference between the maximum amount people are willing to pay and the price actually paid. At any price, consumer surplus for the market is the area below the demand (marginal social benefit) curve but above the horizontal line at market price. Producer surplus is the difference between the minimum amount producers are willing to accept and the price actually received. At any price, producer surplus for the market is the area above the supply (marginal social cost) curve but below the horizontal line at market price.

5 An efficient allocation of resources occurs at the quantity of output that maximizes total surplus (= consumer surplus + producer surplus). Total surplus is maximized at the quantity where marginal social benefit (*MSB*) equals marginal social cost (*MSC*). To see why the *MSB* = *MSC* condition signals maximum efficiency, consider outputs less than and greater than the efficient quantity of output.

If output is less than the efficient quantity (to the left), *MSB* is greater than *MSC*. Resources are creating more value (*MSB*) than they cost (*MSC*). By shifting more resources into production of this good and out of production of other goods where *MSB* is only equal to or less than *MSC*, total surplus will increase.

Similarly, if output is greater than the efficient quantity (to the right), *MSC* is greater than *MSB*. Resources cost more (*MSC*) than the value (*MSB*) that they are creating. By shifting more resources out of production of this good and into production of other goods where *MSB* is at least equal to or greater than *MSC*, total surplus will increase.

Only at the output where *MSB* = *MSC* is total surplus at a maximum, and no reallocation of resources can increase the sum of consumer surplus and producer surplus.

6 Fairness is a normative issue. But note that the tradeoff between economic efficiency and fairness (the "big tradeoff") is a positive issue. Income transfers to achieve fairness norms have real impacts on economic output due to administrative costs and incentive effects. The loss of output and reduced efficiency can be measured. Even though fairness has a cost, policymakers may still come to the conclusion that improved fairness or equity is worth the loss in efficiency. That is the normative issue.

True/False and Explain

Resource Allocation Methods

1 A command system can work well to allocate resources when it is easy to monitor activities.

Demand and Marginal Benefit

2 The value of a good is its consumer benefit.

3 The market demand curve is the horizontal sum of all individual demand curves.

4 The market demand curve is formed by adding the willingness to pay for each individual at each price.

5 Consumer surplus is the value of a good minus the price paid for it.

6 Consumer surplus equals the area above the demand curve, but below market price.

Supply and Marginal Cost

7 The market supply curve is the vertical sum of the individual firm supply curves.

8 The opportunity cost of producing a given quantity of a good is the area under the supply curve.

9 Producer surplus is the opportunity cost of producing a good minus its price.

Is the Competitive Market Efficient?

10 Adam Smith's "invisible hand" suggests that competitive markets send resources to their highest-valued use.

11 Markets always use resources efficiently.

12 Deadweight loss is a loss to consumers and a gain to producers.

Are Markets Fair?

13 Utilitarianism is an example of a fair results idea.

14 If we think of the total income of a society as a pie, a more equally shared pie results in a larger pie.

15 In economic life, the symmetry principle translates into equality of outcomes.

Multiple-Choice

Resource Allocation Methods

1 An efficient method to allocate resources when the efforts of the participants are hard to monitor and reward directly is a
- **a** command system.
- **b** lottery.
- **c** contest.
- **d** first-come, first-served rule.
- **e** market price.

Demand and Marginal Benefit

2 The maximum price a consumer is willing to pay for a good is known as the
- **a** consumer surplus.
- **b** value of a good.
- **c** relative price of a good.
- **d** money price of a good.
- **e** marginal cost of a good.

3 Market demand is the
- a sum of the prices that each individual is willing to pay for each quantity demanded.
- b sum of the quantities demanded by each individual at each price.
- c sum of the consumer surplus of each individual.
- d difference between the maximum amount each individual is willing to pay for a good and the market price.
- e difference between the market price and the maximum amount each individual is willing to pay for a good.

4 Consumer surplus is the
- a difference between the maximum price consumers are willing to pay and the minimum price producers are willing to accept.
- b difference between the value of a good and the price paid for the good.
- c total value to consumers of a good.
- d area under the demand curve.
- e total amount paid for the good.

5 Consider the demand curve in Figure 5.1. What is the value of the first unit of the good?

FIGURE **5.1**

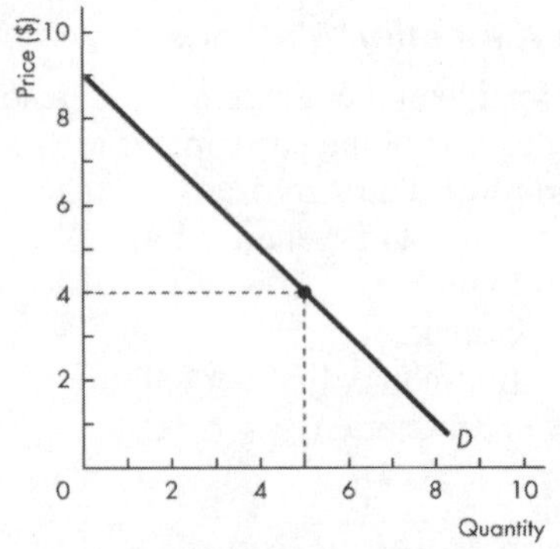

- a $10
- b $9
- c $8
- d $5
- e $4

6 Consider the demand curve in Figure 5.1. If the price of the good is $4, what is the total consumer surplus?
- a $32.50
- b $25.00
- c $20.00
- d $12.50
- e None of the above

Supply and Marginal Cost

7 The marginal cost of a service is
- a the opportunity cost of the first unit produced.
- b the maximum price producers must receive to induce them to supply an additional unit of the service.
- c the value of all alternatives forgone.
- d increasing with increased output.
- e decreasing with increased output.

8 A supply curve is
- a a marginal cost curve.
- b a minimum supply-price curve.
- c an opportunity cost of production curve.
- d all of the above.
- e none of the above.

9 Producer surplus is the
- a difference between the maximum price consumers are willing to pay and the minimum price producers are willing to accept.
- b difference between producers' revenues and opportunity costs of production.
- c opportunity cost of production.
- d area under the supply curve.
- e total amount paid for the good.

10 Consider the demand and supply curves in Figure 5.2. Which area in the diagram indicates the opportunity cost of production?
- a *abc*
- b *aec*
- c *ebc*
- d *0bcd*
- e *0ecd*

FIGURE **5.2**

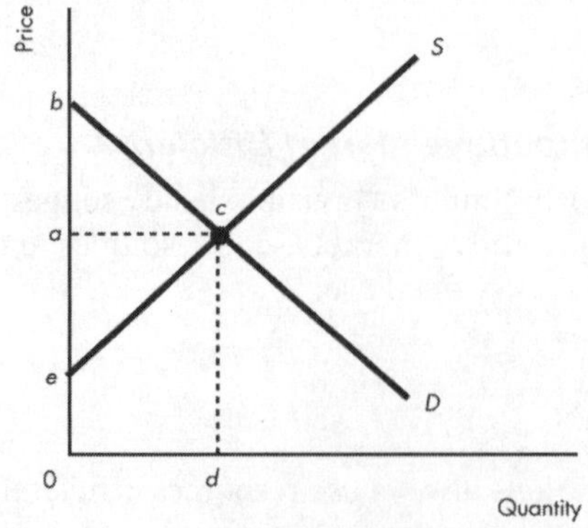

11 Consider the demand and supply curves in Figure 5.2. Which area in the diagram indicates producer surplus?
- a *abc*
- b *aec*
- c *ebc*
- d 0*bcd*
- e 0*ecd*

Is the Competitive Market Efficient?

12 At current output, the marginal benefit of Furbys is greater than marginal cost. To achieve an efficient allocation,

1 Furby output must increase.
2 Furby output must decrease.
3 the marginal benefit of Furbys will rise.
4 the marginal cost of Furbys will fall.

- a 1 and 3
- b 1 and 4
- c 2 and 3
- d 2 and 4
- e 1 only

13 If production is not at an efficient level, which of the following *must* be true?
- a Marginal benefit exceeds marginal cost.
- b Marginal cost exceeds marginal benefit.
- c Production will increase.
- d Production will decrease.
- e None of the above.

14 In competitive equilibrium, which of the following statements is *false*?
- a Marginal social benefit equals marginal social cost.
- b Willingness to pay equals opportunity cost.
- c The sum of consumer surplus and producer surplus is maximized.
- d Deadweight loss is maximized.
- e Resources are used efficiently to produce goods and services that people value most highly.

15 If resources are allocated efficiently,
- a consumer surplus exceeds producer surplus.
- b producer surplus exceeds consumer surplus.
- c the sum of consumer surplus and producer surplus is maximized.
- d marginal social benefit is maximized.
- e marginal social cost is minimized.

16 Markets may not achieve an efficient allocation of resources when there are
- a public goods.
- b external benefits.
- c monopolies.
- d subsidies.
- e all of the above.

17 The overproduction of a good means that
- a deadweight loss has been eliminated.
- b the sum of consumer surplus and producer surplus is greater than the sum for an efficient allocation.
- c marginal social cost exceeds marginal social benefit.
- d marginal social benefit exceeds marginal social cost.
- e this is a public good.

18 Deadweight loss is
- a borne entirely by consumers.
- b gained by producers.
- c the social loss from inefficiency.
- d not a problem with overproduction.
- e all of the above.

19 Consider the demand and supply curves in Figure 5.3. Which area in the diagram indicates the deadweight loss from underproduction?
- a *eacf*
- b *acd*
- c *abd*
- d *bcd*
- e *kaci*

FIGURE **5.3**

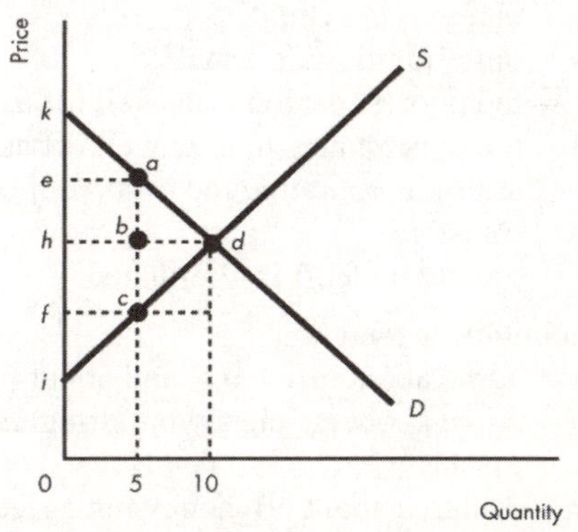

20 Consider the demand and supply curves in Figure 5.3. Which area in the diagram indicates the loss in consumer surplus from underproduction?
- a *eacf*
- b *acd*
- c *abd*
- d *bcd*
- e *kaci*

Are Markets Fair?

21 Which of the following applies to the *results* principle of fairness?
- a Symmetry principle
- b Equality of opportunity
- c The big tradeoff
- d Protection of private property
- e Purely voluntary exchange

22 A principle of fairness that emphasizes equality of opportunity is
- a fair results.
- b fair rules.
- c fair incomes.
- d utilitarianism.
- e modified utilitarianism.

23 According to the "big tradeoff,"
- a income transfers reduce efficiency.
- b efficiency requires income transfers.
- c a more equally shared pie results in a larger pie.
- d property rights and voluntary exchange insure equality of opportunity.
- e income transfers should make the poorest person as well off as possible.

24 According to John Rawls' modified utilitarianism, income should be redistributed until
- a incomes are equal.
- b opportunities are equal.
- c the poorest person is as well off as possible.
- d the poorest person is as well off as possible, after incorporating the costs of income transfers.
- e the big tradeoff is eliminated.

25 Economists tend to
- a agree about efficiency and about fairness.
- b agree about efficiency but disagree about fairness.
- c disagree about efficiency but agree about fairness.
- d be more agreeable than philosophers about fairness.
- e be more disagreeable than philosophers about fairness.

Short Answer Problems

1 Table 5.1 gives the demand schedules for broccoli for three individuals: Tom, Jana, and Ted.

TABLE **5.1** INDIVIDUAL DEMAND FOR BROCCOLI

Price ($ per kilogram)	Quantity Demanded (kilograms per week)		
	Tom	Jana	Ted
0.50	10	4	10
0.75	9	2	7
1.00	8	0	4
1.25	7	0	1

- a Calculate the market demand schedule.
- b On a single diagram, draw the individual demand curves for Tom, Jana, and Ted, as well as the market demand curve.

2 Figure 5.4 shows the market for champagne. Note that the demand curve is also a marginal social benefit curve, and the supply curve is also a marginal social cost curve. Use this information to answer Questions 2–5.

FIGURE **5.4** THE CHAMPAGNE MARKET

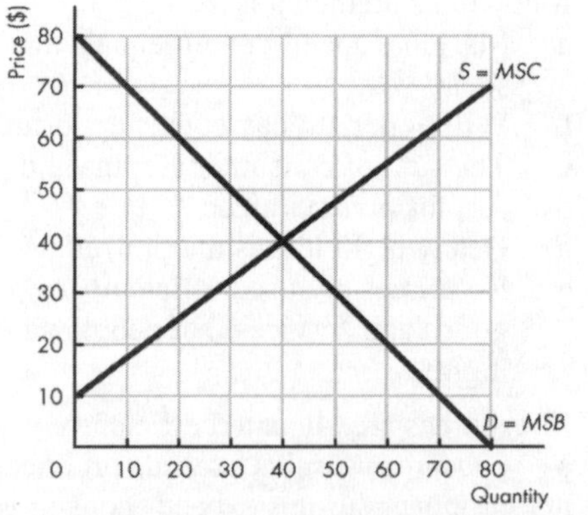

- a If the price of a bottle of champagne is $60, what is the quantity demanded? the quantity supplied?
- b At the price of $60, is there a shortage or a surplus of champagne? Explain the forces that will move the market toward equilibrium.

c If the quantity sold of champagne is 20 bottles, what is the marginal social benefit of the 20th bottle to consumers? the marginal social cost to producers?

d At the quantity of 20 bottles, what is the relationship between the value of the 20th bottle of champagne and the value of the resources forgone to make it? Explain the forces that will move the market toward an efficient allocation of resources.

3 Suppose the champagne market in Figure 5.4 is in equilibrium.

a Calculate the consumer surplus.

b Calculate the producer surplus.

c What is the sum of consumer surplus and producer surplus?

d What is the condition for economic efficiency?

4 Suppose now that that there is underproduction in the champagne market in Figure 5.4 and output is restricted to 20 bottles.

a List three kinds of obstacles to efficiency that might cause underproduction.

b Calculate the deadweight loss.

c What is the sum of consumer surplus and producer surplus?

d How does the sum compare to the sum in Problem **3c**? Is the output of 20 bottles efficient?

5 Suppose instead that there is overproduction in the champagne market and output increases to 60 bottles.

a List one kind of obstacle to efficiency that might cause overproduction.

b Calculate the deadweight loss.

c What is the sum of consumer surplus and producer surplus?

d How does the sum compare to the sum in Problem **3c**? Is the output of 60 bottles efficient?

6 a Define deadweight loss.

b Who gains from deadweight loss? Who loses?

c Explain how a policymaker would use the concept of deadweight loss to decide between two alternative economic policies.

d What other issue would the policymaker have to consider in her decision?

ⓒⓣ 7 There appears to be a contradiction between the Chapter 1 claim that the basic economic problem is scarcity and the Chapter 5 claim that there can be a problem of "overproduction." When the basic problem is that there is too little to meet our wants, how can there be too much of a good?

8 Ideas about fairness divide into two groups—fair results and fair rules.

a What is the basic principle of fair-results ideas? What is the basic principle of fair-rules ideas?

b What is utilitarianism? Explain why it is a fair-results or fair-rules idea.

9 Why is there a "big tradeoff" between fairness and efficiency?

ⓒⓣ 10 Suppose two political parties are vying for your vote in an upcoming election. The "Rights" advocate a more privatized health care system, where the market sets the price for medical services and individuals pay more of their own bills. The "Lefts" advocate more government subsidies in health care, that would extend free coverage to preventative dental care and prescription drugs.

a As an intelligent and economically informed citizen, use the concepts of efficiency and fairness (equity) to evaluate the likely pros and cons of each party's policy.

b Which policy would you likely support? What does this say about your personal valuation of efficiency versus equity?

ANSWERS

True/False and Explain

1 **T** Works badly when many, difficult-to-monitor activities. (104)

2 **F** Value = *MB*. (106)

3 **T** Definition. (106)

4 **F** Adding the quantities demanded by each individual at each price. (106)

5 T Definition. (107)

6 F Area under the demand curve, but above market price. (107)

7 F Horizontal sum of individual firm supply curves. (108)

8 T That area sums opportunity cost of production for each unit of good produced. (108–109)

9 F Price of a good minus its opportunity cost of production. (109)

10 T Competitive markets are "led by an invisible hand" to promote efficient resource use which benefits all. (111)

11 F Not when there are obstacles to efficiency like price and quantity regulations, externalities, monopoly, high transactions costs. (112–113)

12 F Social loss borne by entire society. (112)

13 T For utilitarianism, only equality of results is fair, bringing "the greatest happiness for the greatest number." (114)

14 F A more equally shared pie results in a smaller pie because of the "big tradeoff" between efficiency and fairness. (115)

15 F The symmetry principle—treat others as you would like to be treated—translates into equality of *opportunity*. (116)

Multiple-Choice

1 c Only a few end up with a big prize, but many work harder trying to win. (104–105).

2 b Value = marginal benefit. (106)

3 b See text discussion. (106)

4 b Definition. Area under demand curve but above market price. (106–107)

5 c From $Q = 1$, go up to demand curve to read over to maximum price willing to pay. (106)

6 d Area of triangle ($1/2ba$) below demand and above $P = 4$. (107)

7 d Principle of increasing marginal cost; MC = value of *best* alternative forgone. (108–109)

8 d All definitions of supply curve. (108–109)

9 b Definition. Area below market price but above supply curve. (109)

10 e Area below supply curve. (108–109)

11 b Area below market price but above supply curve. (109)

12 e With increasing Q, MSB must fall and MSC rise. (110)

13 e If production below efficient level, **a** and **c** true; if production above efficient level, **b** and **d** true. (110)

14 d No deadweight loss. All other answers are definitions of competitive equilibrium. (110)

15 c Definition where marginal benefit equals marginal cost. No other necessary relation between consumer and producer surplus. (110)

16 e All change quantity produced above (**d**) or below (**a**, **b**, **c**) efficient quantity. (112–113)

17 c Production beyond efficient level creates deadweight loss, reducing total surplus. (111–112)

18 c Borne by consumers and producers when underproduction or overproduction. (111–112)

19 b Decrease in consumer and producer surplus compared to efficient quantity (10) of production. (111–112)

20 c Area subtracted from consumer surplus at efficient quantity (10) of production (*hkd*). (111–112)

21 c Other answers apply to *rules* principle of fairness. (114–116)

22 b Other answers apply to *results* principle of fairness. (114–116)

23 a Tradeoff between equity (which requires income transfers) and efficiency. (115)

24 d Rawls' idea incorporates the effects of the big tradeoff in trying to redistribute income more equally, but not totally equally. (115)

25 b Efficiency is a positive issue; fairness is a normative issue. (114)

Short Answer Problems

1 a The market demand schedule is obtained by adding the quantities demanded by Tom, Jana, and Ted at each price (see Table 5.2).

TABLE **5.2** MARKET DEMAND SCHEDULE FOR BROCCOLI

Price ($ per kilogram)	Quantity Demanded (kilograms per week)
0.50	24
0.75	18
1.00	12
1.25	8

b Figure 5.5 illustrates the individual demand curves for Tom, Jana, and Ted as well as the market demand curve.

FIGURE **5.5**

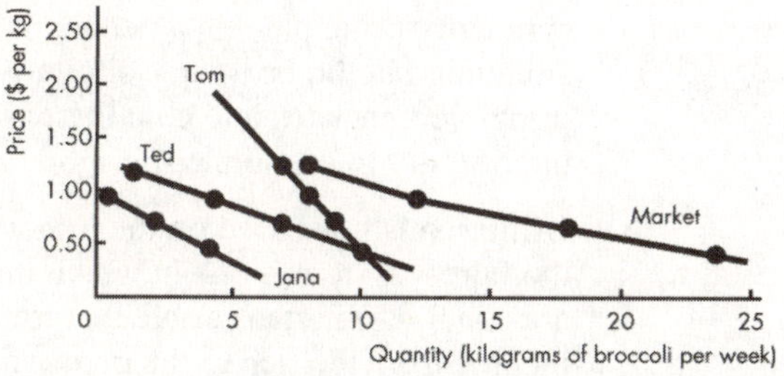

2 a Quantity demanded is 20 bottles; quantity supplied is approximately 67 bottles. We find these quantities by starting with the price of $60 and reading "over" to each curve and "down" to the quantity.

b There is a surplus because quantity supplied exceeds quantity demanded. Producers have excess supplies, so they will cut prices rather than be stuck with unsold goods. Quantity demanded will increase as price falls, until we end up at the equilibrium price of $40/bottle and the equilibrium quantity of 40 bottles.

c Marginal social benefit is $60; marginal social cost is $25. We find these values by starting with the quantity of 20 bottles and reading "up" to each curve and "over" to the marginal social benefit and cost (measured in prices).

d The 20th bottle of champagne is valued by consumers at $60, but uses only $25 worth of resources to make. With marginal social benefit exceeding marginal social cost, consumers would happily pay more than $25 for an additional bottle of champagne and will bid up the price. Producers will increase the quantity supplied until the market reaches the equilibrium price of $40/bottle and the equilibrium quantity of 40 bottles. Producers increase champagne output by transferring resources from other uses. Resources, which were being used elsewhere to create value just equal to their cost, are now being used more efficiently in that they create more value in champagne production than their cost.

3 a Consumer surplus is the triangular area under the demand curve but above the horizontal line at the market price of $40. The formula for the area of a triangle is 1/2(base)(altitude), so consumer surplus = 1/2(40)(40) = 800.

b Producer surplus is the triangular area above the supply curve but below the horizontal line at the market price of $40. Producer surplus = 1/2(40)(30) = 600.

c The sum of consumer and producer surplus is 800 + 600 = 1,400.

d Economic efficiency occurs when the sum of consumer surplus and producer surplus is maximized. Is this specific outcome efficient? We can't be sure if 1,400 is a maximum until we compare other situations in the champagne market.

4 a Price and quantity regulations, taxes, external benefits, public goods, monopoly and high transactions costs all might cause output to be restricted.

b Deadweight loss is the decrease in consumer surplus and producer surplus that results from an inefficient level of production. It is equal to the triangular area between the demand and supply curves from quantity = 20 to quantity = 40. Deadweight loss = 1/2(35)(20) = 350.

c The new sum of consumer and producer surplus is the original amount of 1,400 minus the deadweight loss: 1,400 – 350 = 1,050.

d The sum of consumer and producer surplus (1,050) is less than the equilibrium sum in Problem **3c** at an output of 40 bottles. Since an efficient output maximizes the sum of consumer and producer surplus, the output of 20 bottles is not efficient.

5 a Subsidies to producers or external costs can cause overproduction.

b Deadweight loss is equal to the triangular area between the demand and supply curves from quantity = 40 to quantity = 60. Deadweight loss = 1/2(35)(20) = 350. (It is just a coincidence that this deadweight loss from overproduction happens to be equal to the deadweight loss from underproduction. In general these losses are not necessarily equal.)

c The new sum of consumer and producer surplus is the original amount of 1,400 minus the deadweight loss: 1,400 – 350 = 1,050.

d The sum of consumer and producer surplus (1,050) is less than the equilibrium sum in Problem **3c** at an output of 40 bottles. Since an efficient output maximizes the sum of consumer and producer surplus, the output of 60 bottles is not efficient.

6 a Deadweight loss is the decrease in consumer surplus and producer surplus that results from an inefficient level of production.

b No one gains from deadweight loss. It is a social loss borne by the entire society—consumers and producers.

c A policymaker would choose the most efficient policy—the one with the smallest deadweight loss.

d Fairness or equity would be the other consideration in deciding between alternative policies.

ct **7** Because wants *in general* exceed the resources available to satisfy them, we cannot have everything we want and must make choices. This basic problem leads to economizing behaviour—choosing the best or optimal use of available resources. But *specific* wants can be satisfied. Each of us has relatively limited wants, for example, for salt, for heat in our houses during the winter, or for nail clippers. If these or other goods are produced beyond the point where the marginal benefit equals the marginal cost, there is a problem of overproduction.

Overproduction is a problem because the resources could be *better used* to produce different goods that could meet still-unsatisfied wants. The money invested in excessive salt production could be diverted to health research to find a cure for cancer, or to schools to allow more demands for education to be satisfied. Because wants *in general* are unlimited, producing too much of a good to satisfy a *specific* want actually prevents us from making optimal use of available resources. So the ideas of scarcity and overproduction are not contradictory. In fact, overproduction of a *specific* good is a problem precisely because there is a problem of scarcity in satisfying wants *in general*.

8 a Fair-results ideas are based on the principle that results are most important, and that the fairest economic result is equal incomes for all. Fair-rules ideas are based on the symmetry principle—that people in similar situations should be treated similarly. This principle translates into equality of opportunity in economic life.

b Utilitarianism is based on the principle that the fairest system is one in which incomes are equal. Utilitarians argue that transferring income from the rich to the poor will result in "the greatest happiness for the greatest number," since the marginal benefit of an additional dollar to the poor person is greater than the benefit to the rich person. Only at equal incomes for all is total social benefit at a maximum. Since utilitarianism focuses on equal incomes or results, it is a fair-results idea.

9 If greater fairness means increasing the equality of income, it can only be achieved by income redistribution. The income of some must be taxed in order to pay for the transfer payments and administrative costs of a redistribution policy. However, there are incentive effects that reduce the total amount of income available to be distributed.

If productive activities such as work are taxed, there will be a tendency to reduce time spent in those activities. Furthermore, any redistribution program requires the use of resources to administer it and thus leave fewer resources for other productive activities. Thus we arrive at this insight: A more equally shared pie results in a smaller pie.

ⓒⓣ **10** **a** The "Rights" market-oriented health care policy likely is more efficient. It requires less government administration, and would probably allow lower taxes because less is being spent by government and more by private individuals. With lower taxes, incentives to work might increase, and the size of the economic pie might be larger.

With lower government subsidies, the price of health care to individuals will rise. Health care may become unaffordable to some members of society, so the "Rights" policy may be less fair from a "fair results" perspective. From a "fair rules" perspective, the "Rights" policy is fair as long as everyone faces the same opportunities.

The "Lefts" subsidized health care policy likely is less efficient, because it would require subsidies to health care providers and require more government administration and higher taxes to pay for the policy. With higher taxes, incentives to work might decrease, and the size of the economic pie might be smaller. On the other hand, with a healthier population, productivity might increase because fewer work days would be lost to illness. So the net effect on efficiency is unclear.

More health care services will become available to a greater number of people, so the "Lefts" policy may be fairer from a fair-results perspective. From a fair-rules perspective, the "Lefts" policy may be less fair if, to pay for the policy, individuals with higher incomes are taxed more than those with lower incomes.

b There is obviously no single correct answer to this question. The important thing is to think explicitly about your personal valuation of efficiency versus equity, and which idea of fairness appeals most to you.

Chapter 6 Markets in Action

KEY CONCEPTS

Housing Markets and Rent Ceilings

In an unregulated housing market

- shortages cause rising rents, economizing on space, and increased quantity supplied (short run).
- in the long run, building activity shifts supply rightward, rents fall, and the housing stock increases.

In a regulated housing market

- a **rent ceiling** (a **price ceiling** applied to rents) makes it illegal to raise rents.
- housing stocks are lower than in an unregulated market both in short and long run; no incentive to economize on space or build new housing.
- shortages cause excess demand and
  - **search activity** (time spent looking for someone with whom to do business).
  - **black markets** (illegal markets where prices exceed ceilings).

Unregulated markets allocate housing resources efficiently, while rent ceilings create inefficiencies (deadweight loss) without necessarily improving equity.

The Labour Market and the Minimum Wage

A **minimum wage** (a **price floor** applied to wages) makes it illegal to hire labour below a specified wage.

- Minimum wages create excess supply of labour (unemployment) and lower the quantity of labour demanded and hired.
- Unemployed workers willing to work at a lower wage spend more time searching for work.
- Employment effects of a **living wage**—wage rate enabling a person working 40 hours/week to rent housing for 30 percent or less of income earned—similar to minimum wage.

Taxes

Tax on sellers shifts up supply curve by vertical distance equal to amount of tax. Tax on buyers shifts demand curve down by vertical distance equal to amount of tax. Results are the same.

Tax incidence—division of the burden of a tax between buyers and sellers—depends on elasticities of supply and demand.

Supply elasticity and tax division:

- Perfectly inelastic supply—sellers pay all.
- More inelastic supply—sellers pay more.
- More elastic supply—buyers pay more.
- Perfectly elastic supply—buyers pay all.

Demand elasticity and tax division:

- Perfectly inelastic demand—buyers pay all.
- More inelastic demand—buyers pay more.
- More elastic demand—sellers pay more.
- Perfectly elastic demand—sellers pay all.

Taxes decrease quantity produced and consumed, creating deadweight loss.

Subsidies and Quotas

Demand for most farm products is inelastic, creating large variations in farm revenue.

- Poor harvest (decreased S) causes rising P, increased total revenue.
- Bumper harvest (increased S) causes falling P, decreased total revenue.

Farm stabilization agencies (**farm marketing boards**) limit price fluctuations by setting

- price floors, which increase market price and surpluses.
- **production quotas** (quantity restrictions on production), which increase market price and decrease Q grown.
- **subsidies** (payments by governments to producers), which increase supply and decrease market price (but farmers receive market price plus subsidy).

Farm marketing boards are inefficient and redistribute income from consumers to farmers. The equity of the redistribution is a normative question.

Markets for Illegal Goods

Penalizing dealers for selling illegal goods increases cost of selling goods and decreases supply. Penalizing buyers for consuming illegal goods decreases willingness to pay and decreases demand.

- When (sellers' penalties > buyers' penalties), Q decreases, P rises.
- When (sellers' penalties < buyers' penalties), Q decreases, P falls.
- Taxing (decriminalized) goods can achieve the same consumption levels as prohibition.

HELPFUL HINTS

1 In the real world, governments often regulate markets using price constraints, so it is important to study the effects of such regulation. Another benefit of studying government regulation is to understand how markets work when, by contrast, the government does *not* affect the normal operation of markets.

Whenever something disturbs an equilibrium in an unregulated (free) market, the desires of buyers and sellers are brought back into balance by price movements. If prices are controlled by government regulation, however, the price mechanism can no longer serve this purpose. Thus *balance* must be restored in some other way. In the case of price ceilings, black markets are likely to arise. If black markets cannot develop because of strict enforcement of price ceilings, demanders will be forced to bear the costs of increased search activity, waiting in line, or something else.

2 This chapter discusses government price constraints in three specific markets: rental housing, labour, and farm products. The basic principles, however, can be generalized to other markets.

In any market with a legal price ceiling set below the market-clearing price, we will observe excess quantity demanded, because price cannot increase to eliminate it. As a consequence, the marginal benefit of the last unit of the good available will exceed the controlled price. Demanders are willing to engage in costly activities up to the marginal benefit of that last unit (search activity, waiting lines, and black market activity) in order to obtain the good.

Furthermore, if price is allowed to increase in response to a decrease in supply or an increase in demand, there are incentive effects for suppliers to produce more and demanders to purchase less (movements along the supply and demand curves). Indeed, it is the response to these incentives that restores equilibrium in markets with freely adjusting prices. If the price cannot adjust, these price-induced incentive effects do not have a chance to operate. In the case of rent ceilings, the inability of rents (price) to rise means that: (1) there is no inducement to use the current stock of housing more intensively in the short run and (2) there is no incentive to construct new housing in the long run. Similarly, the effects on any market in which a minimum price (price floor) is set above the market-clearing (equilibrium) price will be similar to those discussed in the text for the labour market under minimum wage or price floors in agricultural markets.

3 The division of the burden of a tax is called tax incidence. Who pays a sales tax imposed on producers depends on the elasticities of demand and supply. The general principles of tax incidence are

- more inelastic demand—consumers pay more.
- more elastic demand—producers pay more.
- more inelastic supply—producers pay more.
- more elastic supply—consumers pay more.

SELF-TEST

True/False and Explain

Housing Markets and Rent Ceilings

1 In an unregulated housing market, higher rents increase the short-run quantity of housing supplied.

2 When rents in an unregulated housing market rise due to a decrease in supply, people who are unable to pay the higher rents will not get housing.

3 If a rent ceiling exceeds people's willingness to pay, search activity and black markets will increase.

The Labour Market and Minimum Wage

4 In an unregulated labour market, a decrease in the demand for labour causes the wage rate to rise.

5 An increase in the minimum wage will reduce the number of workers employed.

6 Most economists believe that raising the minimum wage has no effect on unemployment.

7 Minimum wage laws increase the amount of time people spend searching for work.

Taxes

8 The more elastic demand is for a product, the larger the fraction of a sales tax paid by consumers.

9 A sales tax always creates deadweight loss.

10 The deadweight loss from a sales tax equals the tax revenue collected by government.

Subsidies and Quotas

11 Suppose the supply curve for corn fluctuates widely but the demand curve is stable. The price of corn will fluctuate more if demand is elastic rather than inelastic.

12 A production quota creates inefficiency through overproduction.

13 A subsidy paid to producers shifts the demand curve for a good rightward.

Markets for Illegal Goods

14 The statement "If we legalize and tax drugs, tax revenues could be used to finance more drug education programs" is normative.

15 If penalties are imposed on both sellers and buyers in a market for prohibited goods, the price may rise, fall, or remain constant, while the quantity bought always decreases.

Multiple-Choice

Housing Markets and Rent Ceilings

1 The short-run supply curve for rental housing is positively sloped because
- a the supply of housing is fixed in the short run.
- b the current stock of buildings will be used more intensively as rents rise.
- c the cost of constructing new buildings increases as the number of buildings increases.
- d the cost of constructing new buildings is about the same regardless of the number of buildings in existence.
- e new buildings will be constructed as rents rise.

2 Rent ceilings imposed by governments
- a keep rental prices below the unregulated market price.
- b keep rental prices above the unregulated market price.
- c keep rental prices equal to the unregulated market price.
- d increase the stock of rental housing.
- e increase the intensity of use of the current stock of rental housing.

3 A price ceiling set below the equilibrium price will result in
- a excess supply.
- b excess demand.
- c the equilibrium price.
- d an increase in supply.
- e a decrease in demand.

4 Which of the following is *not* a likely outcome of rent ceilings?
- a a black market for rent-controlled housing
- b long waiting lists of potential renters of rent-controlled housing
- c a short-run shortage of housing
- d black market prices below the rent ceiling prices
- e increased search activity for rent-controlled housing

The Labour Market and the Minimum Wage

5 If the minimum wage is set at $2 per hour in Figure 6.1, what is the level of unemployment in millions of hours?
- a 50
- b 40
- c 20
- d 10
- e 0

FIGURE **6.1**

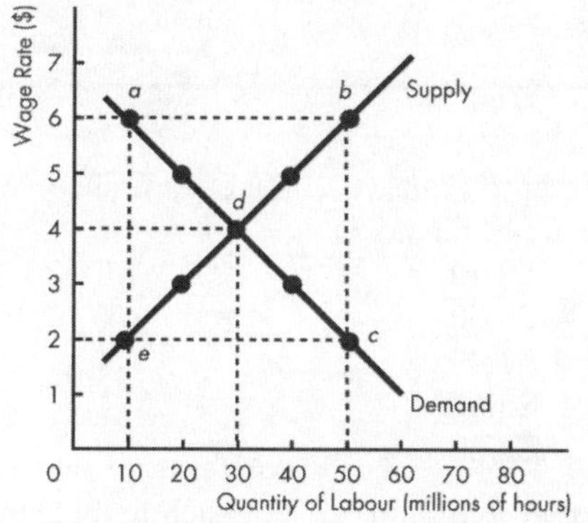

6 In Figure 6.1, if the minimum wage is set at $6 per hour, what is the level of unemployment in millions of hours?
- a 50
- b 40
- c 20
- d 10
- e 0

7 In Figure 6.1, if the minimum wage is set at $6 per hour, what is the area of deadweight loss?
- a *abd*
- b *bcd*
- c *cde*
- d *ade*
- e 0

Taxes

8 Figure 6.2 shows the market for frisbees before and after a sales tax is imposed. The sales tax on each frisbee is
- a $0.40.
- b $0.60.
- c $1.00.
- d $5.60.
- e $6.60.

FIGURE 6.2

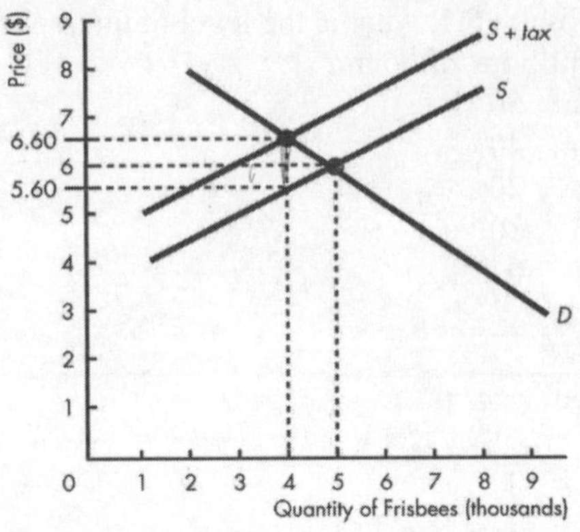

9 Refer to Figure 6.2. For each frisbee, the sellers' share of the tax is
- a $0.40.
- b $0.60.
- c $1.00.
- d $5.60.
- e $6.60.

10 Refer to Figure 6.2. For each frisbee, the buyers' share of the tax is
- a $0.40.
- b $0.60.
- c $1.00.
- d $5.60.
- e $6.60.

11 Refer to Figure 6.2. Government revenue from the tax is
- a $4,000.
- b $5,000.
- c $22,400.
- d $26,400.
- e $30,000.

12 From Figure 6.2 we can deduce that between 4,000 and 5,000 units, the demand for frisbees is
- a inelastic.
- b unit elastic.
- c elastic.
- d more elastic than the supply (*S*) of frisbees.
- e soaring.

13 Refer to Figure 6.2. Deadweight loss from the tax is
- a $500.
- b $1,000.
- c $3,600.
- d $4,000.
- e $5,000.

14 A tax on buyers
- a shifts the demand curve up by a vertical distance equal to the tax.
- b shifts the supply curve up by a vertical distance equal to the tax.
- c has the same effect on price and quantity as a tax on sellers.
- d has a different effect on price and quantity as a tax on sellers.
- e increases the price received by sellers.

15 If the price of a good is not affected by a sales tax,
- a supply is perfectly elastic.
- b demand is perfectly elastic.
- c elasticity of supply is greater than elasticity of demand.
- d elasticity of demand is greater than elasticity of supply.
- e none of the above.

Stabilizing Farm Revenue

16 A momentary supply curve is
- a elastic, since price is fixed.
- b relatively more elastic than a short-run supply curve.
- c relatively inelastic, since yields are known but sales are not.
- d inelastic, since output is fixed.
- e as ephemeral as gossamer wings.

17 Which of the following combinations would generally yield the greatest price fluctuation?
- a large supply shifts and inelastic demand
- b large supply shifts and elastic demand
- c large supply shifts and perfectly elastic demand
- d small supply shifts and inelastic demand
- e small supply shifts and elastic demand

18 Figure 6.3 illustrates the short-run demand and supply curves in the wheat bran market. If the Wheat Marketing Board sets a quota of 50 million bushels, the market-clearing price of a bushel of wheat bran is
- a $1.
- b $3.
- c $5.
- d two scoops of raisins.
- e none of the above.

FIGURE 6.3

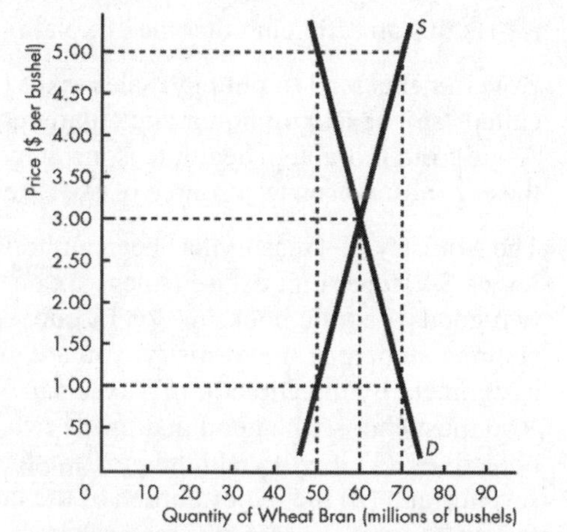

19 Refer to Figure 6.3. With the quota of 50 million bushels, farmers have an incentive to
- **a** decrease output because the market-clearing price is below cost of production.
- **b** decrease output because there is a surplus at the market-clearing price.
- **c** increase output because the market-clearing price is above cost of production.
- **d** increase output because there is a shortage at the market-clearing price.
- **e** stick to the quota.

20 Refer to Figure 6.3. Suppose the marketing board develops a new kind of subsidy called a direct payment plan. Farmers are told, "We will guarantee you $5 per bushel, but everything you produce at this price must be sold on the market for whatever buyers will pay; then we will give you (at taxpayers' expense) the difference between the market price and $5 per bushel." How many bushels of wheat bran will be sold?
- **a** 20 million
- **b** 50 million
- **c** 60 million
- **d** 70 million
- **e** none of the above

21 Refer to Figure 6.3. The amount of taxpayers' money that the marketing board pays to farmers in Question **20** is
- **a** zero.
- **b** $70 million.
- **c** $250 million.
- **d** $280 million.
- **e** $350 million.

22 European Union (EU) countries have been accumulating butter and cheese mountains and wine lakes. These surpluses are consistent with
- **a** floor prices for agricultural products that are below market prices.
- **b** floor prices for agricultural products that are above market prices.
- **c** ceiling prices for agricultural products that are below market prices.
- **d** ceiling prices for agricultural products that are above market prices.
- **e** quotas for agricultural products.

23 An agricultural subsidy
- **a** shifts the supply curve rightward.
- **b** benefits consumers by lowering product prices.
- **c** benefits farmers by raising the price they receive.
- **d** imposes major costs on taxpayers.
- **e** does all of the above.

Markets for Illegal Goods

24 If enforcement is aimed at sellers of a prohibited good,
- **a** price and quantity bought will decrease.
- **b** price and quantity bought will increase.
- **c** price will increase and quantity bought will decrease.
- **d** price will decrease and quantity bought will increase.
- **e** price change will be uncertain and quantity bought will decrease.

25 Which of the following statements about prohibited goods is *true*?
- **a** Taxes are more effective in changing preferences than prohibition.
- **b** Prohibition is more effective in generating revenue than an equivalent tax.
- **c** Taxes and penalties cannot be set so as to yield equivalent outcomes.
- **d** Taxes generate revenues, while prohibition generates more enforcement expenses.
- **e** None of the above is true.

Short Answer Problems

1 Suppose that the market for rental housing is initially in long-run equilibrium. Use graphs to answer the following:

- **a** Explain how an unregulated market for rental housing would adjust, if there is a sudden significant increase in demand. What will happen to rent and the quantity of units rented in the short run and in the long run? Be sure to discuss the effect on incentives (in both the short and the long run) as the market-determined price (rent) changes.

b Now explain how the market would adjust to the increase in demand, if rent ceilings are established at the level of the initial equilibrium rent. What has happened to supplier incentives in this case?

2 The demand for and supply of gasoline are given in Table 6.1.

a What are the equilibrium price and quantity of gasoline?

TABLE **6.1**

Price ($ per litre)	Quantity Demanded (millions of litres per day)	Quantity Supplied (millions of litres per day)
1.40	8	24
1.30	10	22
1.20	12	20
1.10	14	18
1.00	16	16
0.90	18	14

b Suppose that the quantity of gasoline supplied suddenly declines by 8 million litres per day at every price. Construct a new table of price, quantity demanded, and quantity supplied, and draw a graph of the demand curve and the initial and new supply curves. Assuming that the market for gasoline is unregulated, use either your table or your graph to find the new equilibrium price and quantity of gasoline.

c How has the change in price affected the behaviour of demanders? the behaviour of suppliers?

3 Suppose that the government imposes a price ceiling of $1 per litre of gasoline at the same time as the decrease in supply reported in Short Answer Problem **2b**.

a What is the quantity of gasoline demanded? quantity supplied?

b What is the quantity of gasoline actually sold?

c What is the excess quantity of gasoline demanded?

d For the last litre of gasoline sold, what is the marginal benefit? marginal cost?

e Is this an efficient outcome? Explain.

4 Governments tend to put high sales taxes (often called "sin" taxes) on liquor and cigarettes. Aside from moral and health reasons, why are these goods chosen as a source of tax revenue?

5 The Ministry of Treasury has been authorized to levy a $0.15 per unit excise (sales) tax on one of two goods—comic books or dog biscuits. As a summer student at the Ministry, you are given an assignment by the Director of Taxes, Dr. More. You must choose the good that meets two objectives: (1) it will yield the greatest tax revenue and (2) the major burden of the tax will fall on consumers. Ministry researchers have estimated the supply and demand curves (without the tax) for each market. The comic book market is shown in Figure 6.4 and the dog biscuit market in Figure 6.5. The following questions will help you complete your assignment.

FIGURE **6.4** COMIC BOOK MARKET

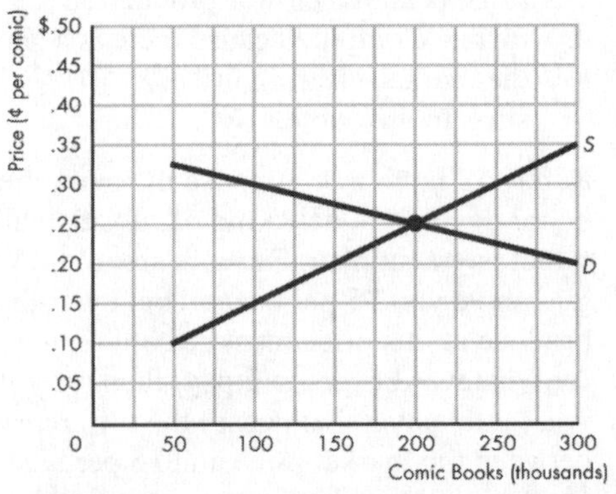

a For the comic book market, shift the appropriate curve to reflect the tax and draw it on Figure 6.4. Label the curve either "*S + tax*" or "*D + tax*." Identify the new equilibrium price and quantity. Compare the total expenditure in the original and new equilibriums.

b Calculate the total tax revenue collected, and indicate it as an area on Figure 6.4.

c How much of the tax is paid by consumers? by producers?

FIGURE **6.5** DOG BISCUIT MARKET

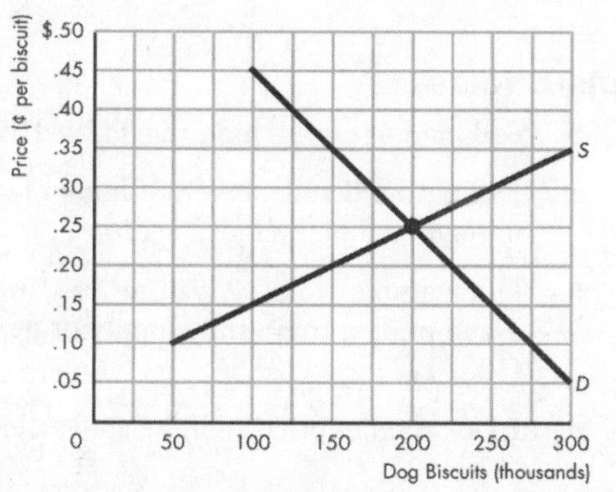

d Now perform the same analysis on the dog biscuit market. Shift the appropriate curve to reflect the tax and draw it on Figure 6.5. Label the curve either "*S* + *tax*" or "*D* + *tax*." Identify the new equilibrium price and quantity. Compare the total expenditure in the original and new equilibriums.

e Calculate the total tax revenue collected, and indicate it as an area on Figure 6.5.

f How much of the tax is paid by consumers? by producers?

g What is your recommendation to Dr. More? Explain.

ⓒⓣ **6** Dr. More was pleased with your excise tax recommendation in Short Answer Problem **5**, but you can't stop wondering about his comment, "Hmm, I thought you would do it the other way." If you haven't already figured out to what he was referring, the following questions will help.

a For the comic book market, calculate the elasticity of demand between the original and new equilibrium points. Is demand elastic or inelastic?

b Perform the same calculation for the dog biscuit market. Is demand elastic or inelastic?

c What do you know about demand elasticities that would have allowed you to complete your assignment "the other way" and predict which market would yield maximum tax revenue, and which market would place most of the tax burden on consumers?

7 After spending so much time on Dr. More's tax assignment in Short Answer Problems **5** and **6**, you realize you have one last chance to impress the boss. While your previous tax assignment had two important policy objectives—maximum tax revenue and appropriate tax burden—no one asked you about the relative efficiency loss of a tax on comic books versus dog biscuits. If the policy objective is to minimize deadweight loss, which good do you recommend be taxed?

8 Figure 6.6 shows the demand curve in the market for grinola seeds. Grinola is difficult to grow—simply a frown from a farmer in the field causes the seeds to develop split ends, which makes them worthless. As a result, grinola harvests fluctuate widely.

FIGURE **6.6** DEMAND FOR GRINOLA

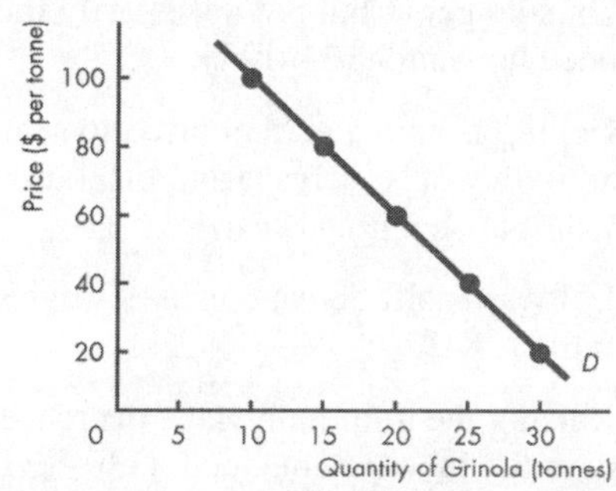

a If there are no subsidies or quotas in the grinola market, what will be the market price and total revenue when momentary supply is 30 tonnes?

b After a sad year (*The Simpsons* finally goes off the air), momentary supply drops to 20 tonnes. What will be the new market price and total revenue?

c On the basis of the total revenue information above, what can you conclude about the elasticity of demand for grinola between the quantities of 30 and 20 tonnes? Calculate the elasticity of demand between the quantities of 30 and 20 tonnes to check your conclusion.

9 Because the demand for most agricultural products is inelastic, poor harvests increase total farm revenue. Explain the fallacy that is involved in jumping to the conclusion that poor harvests make all farmers better off.

10 Suppose the Nudist Party wins the next federal election because all the clothed citizens forgot to vote. The Nudists pass a law making clothes illegal. Unfortunately for the Nudists, the police don't take the law seriously (where would officers pin their badges?) and put almost no effort into enforcement. Use a diagram to explain why the black market price of now illegal clothes will be close to the unregulated market equilibrium price.

ANSWERS

True/False and Explain

1 T Higher rents create incentives to use current buildings more intensively. (124)

2 T At equilibrium rent, all who can afford housing get it, but not necessarily those who need housing. (124–127)

3 F Ceiling is above market price so search activity won't increase and black markets won't arise. (125–126)

4 F Leftward shift demand causes wage rate to fall. (128–129)

5 T Raising the minimum wage decreases quantity labour demanded. (130–131)

6 F Exceptions are economists Card and Krueger. (131)

7 T Compared to unregulated market, increased job search by labour in excess supply at minimum wage. (130–131)

8 F More elastic demand means more substitutes available and consumers better able to escape tax by not buying. (134)

9 F Usually true; false if demand or supply perfectly inelastic. (136)

10 F See Text Figure 6.11. Tax revenue and deadweight loss come from lost surplus, but not equal. (136)

11 F Fluctuate more if demand inelastic. (137–138)

12 F Creates inefficiency through underproduction. (139)

13 F Shifts supply rightward. (138)

14 F Positive statement; can be verified by observation. (140–141)

15 T Effect on *P* depends on relative magnitude of penalties. (140–141)

Multiple-Choice

1 b **c**, **d**, and **e** refer to long run. (124–125)

2 a Definition. **d** and **e** result of higher rent in unregulated market. (125–126)

3 b Draw graph. No Δ *ceteris paribus* assumptions, so no shift supply or demand. (125–127)

4 d Black market prices will be above ceiling. (126–127)

5 e Floor below equilibrium *P* doesn't prevent market from reaching equilibrium. (129–130)

6 b Quantity supplied (50) > quantity demanded (10). (129–130)

7 d Half of loss is consumer surplus, half is producer surplus. (129–130)

8 c Equals the vertical distance between the two supply curves. (131–132)

9 a Original *P* = \$6, new *P* = \$6.60. Sellers pay \$1 tax and get \$0.60 more from buyers, so sellers pay \$0.40. (131–133)

10 b See previous answer. (131–133)

11 a \$1 per frisbee × 4,000 units sold. (131–134)

12 c Rise in *P* (\$6 to \$6.60) decreases total revenue (\$30,000 to \$26,400). **d** wrong: $\eta = 2.3$ and $\eta_s = 3.2$. (131–134)

13 a Area of triangle (1/2*ba*) with base = \$1 (\$6.60 – \$5.60) and altitude = 1,000 (5,000 – 4,000). (136)

14 c See Text Figure 6.8. Shifts demand curve down by vertical distance tax and decreases price received by sellers. (133)

15 b **a** would raise *P* by full amount tax. **c** and **d** affect *P* but amounts uncertain. (134–135)

16 d Definition. (137)

17 a Draw graphs to see. (137–138)

18 c Where momentary supply curve at 50 million bushels intersects demand. (139)

19 c Farmers receiving \$5 but willing to supply this quantity at (their cost of) \$1. (139)

20 d Quantity supplied at *P* = \$5. (138)

ⓔ 21 d 70 million bushels sell for $1 per bushel. Taxpayers make up difference of $4 per bushel × 70 million. (138)

22 b Floor above market P creates excess supply. (138–139)

23 e Definition. (138)

24 c Supply shifts leftward as penalties are added to other costs. (140–141)

25 d Reverse taxes and prohibition to make **a** and **b** true. (140–141)

Short Answer Problems

1 a Figure 6.7 corresponds to an unregulated market for rental housing. The initial demand, short-run supply, and long-run supply curves are D_0, SS_0, and LS respectively. The market is initially in long-run equilibrium at point *a* corresponding to rent R_0 and quantity of rental units Q_0. Demand then increases to D_1, creating excess quantity demanded of $Q_2 - Q_0$ at the initial rent. In the short run, in an unregulated market, rent will rise to R_1 to clear the markets and the equilibrium quantity of housing rented is Q_1 (point *b*). Note that as the rent rises, the quantity of rental housing supplied increases (a movement from point *a* to point *b* along supply curve SS_0) as the existing stock of housing is used more intensively. Also the quantity of housing demanded decreases (a movement from point *c* to point *b* along demand curve D_1). Together, these movements eliminate the excess quantity demanded. The higher rent also provides an incentive to construct new housing in the long run. This is illustrated by the shift in the supply curve from SS_0 to SS_1. Finally, a new long-run equilibrium is achieved at point *c*, with rent restored to its original level and the number of units rented equal to Q_2.

FIGURE **6.7**

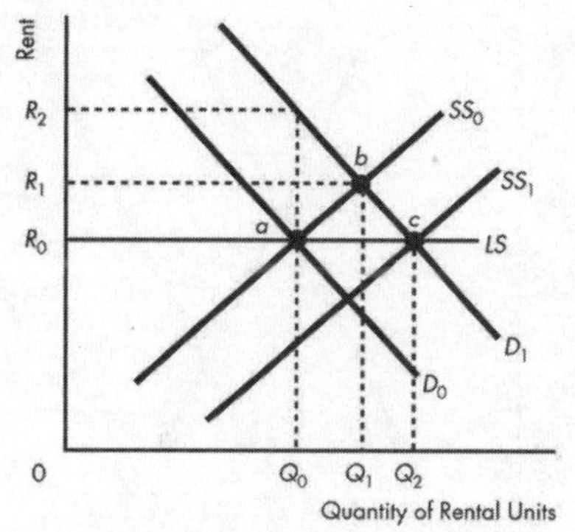

b We can also use Figure 6.7 to discuss the behaviour of a market with a rent ceiling set at R_0. Start in the same long-run equilibrium at point *a*. Once again we observe an increase in demand from D_0 to D_1. In this case, however, the rent cannot rise to restore equilibrium. There will be no incentive to use the existing stock of housing more intensively in the short run or to construct new housing in the long run. The quantity of rental housing supplied will remain at Q_0. Since the last unit of rental housing is valued at R_2, but rent is fixed at R_0, demanders of rental housing will be willing to bear additional costs up to $R_2 - R_0$ (in the form of additional search activity or illegal payments) in order to obtain rental housing.

2 a The equilibrium price of gasoline is $1 per litre, since at that price the quantity of gasoline demanded is equal to the quantity supplied (16 million litres per day). The equilibrium quantity of gasoline is 16 million litres per day.

b The new table and graph are shown in Table 6.2 and Figure 6.8.

TABLE **6.2**

Price	Quantity Demanded (millions of litres per day)	Quantity Supplied (millions of litres per day)
1.40	8	16
1.30	10	14
1.20	12	12
1.10	14	10
1.00	16	8
0.90	18	6

FIGURE **6.8**

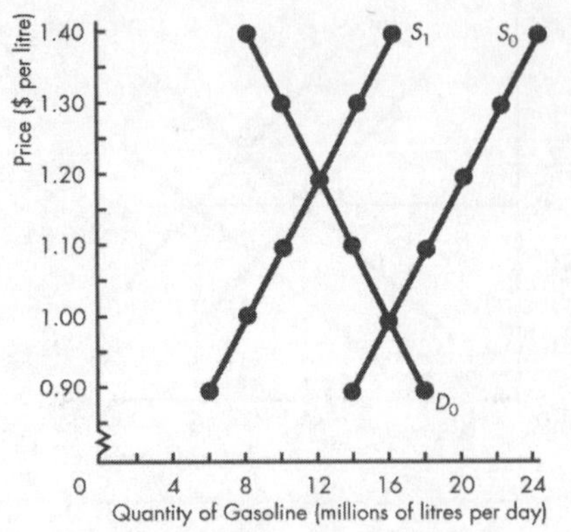

The new equilibrium price is $1.20 per litre, since at that price the quantity of gasoline demanded equals the new quantity supplied (12 million litres per day). The new equilibrium quantity is 12 million litres of gasoline per day.

c The increase in price has caused the quantity of gasoline demanded to decrease by 4 million litres per day (from 16 to 12 million). Given the new supply curve S_1, the increase in price from $1 to $1.20 per litre increases the quantity of gasoline supplied by 4 million litres per day (from 8 to 12 million).

3 a At the ceiling price of $1, quantity demanded is 16 million litres per day, quantity supplied is 8 million litres per day.

b The quantity of gasoline actually sold is 8 million litres per day. When, at a given price, quantity demanded and quantity supplied differ, whichever quantity is *less* determines the quantity actually sold.

c The excess quantity of gasoline demanded is 8 million litres per day.

d The marginal benefit of the 8-millionth litre per day of gasoline sold is $1.40. You can obtain this answer from your graph by imagining a vertical line from the quantity 8 million litres up to where it intersects the demand curve at $1.40. The demand curve is also a marginal benefit curve, showing the highest price consumers are willing to pay for each additional litre.

The marginal cost of the 8-millionth litre per day of gasoline sold is $1. The imaginary vertical line from the quantity 8 million litres intersects the supply curve S_1 at $1. The supply curve is also a marginal cost curve, showing the minimum producers must receive to produce an additional litre.

e Since marginal benefit ($1.40) > marginal cost ($1), the outcome is *not* efficient. The sum of consumer and producer surplus could be increased by allowing the price to rise, which would shift more resources into production of this good and out of production of other goods where marginal benefit is only equal to or less than marginal cost.

4 Because alcohol and nicotine are addictive, the demands for liquor and cigarettes are relatively inelastic. When liquor and cigarette prices are increased by "sin" taxes, the percentage fall in quantity demanded is less than the percentage increase in price. Thus total revenue increases as does tax revenue. To raise a fixed amount of revenue, it takes a much smaller per-unit tax on goods with inelastic demand than on goods with elastic demand. Inelastic demand also means, *ceteris paribus*, that a greater portion of the tax is borne by consumers rather than producers.

5 a See Figure 6.4 Solution. In the comic book market, the supply curve shifts up vertically by an amount equal to the tax ($0.15). The original equilibrium price is $0.25 and quantity is 200,000. The new equilibrium price is $0.30 and quantity is 100,000. Total expenditure has decreased, from $50,000 ($0.25 × 200,000) to $30,000 ($0.30 × 100,000).

FIGURE **6.4** SOLUTION
COMIC BOOK MARKET

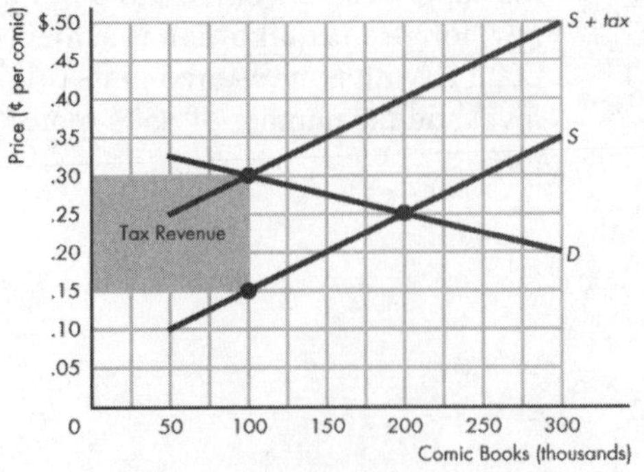

b Total tax revenue is \$0.15 per comic book × 100,000 units sold = \$15,000 and is indicated by the shaded area on Figure 6.4 Solution.

c As a result of the tax, the price to consumers has gone up by \$0.05 (from \$0.25 to \$0.30). Consumers' share of the tax burden is \$5,000 (\$0.05 × 100,000). Producers pay the \$0.15 tax to government, but only get back \$0.05 of it from consumers. Therefore producers' share of the tax burden is \$10,000 (\$0.10 × 100,000).

d See Figure 6.5 Solution. In the dog biscuit market, the supply curve shifts up vertically by an amount equal to the tax (\$0.15). The original equilibrium price is \$0.25 and quantity is 200,000. The new equilibrium price is \$0.35 and quantity is 150,000. Total expenditure has increased, from \$50,000 (\$0.25 × 200,000) to \$52,500 (\$0.35 × 150,000).

FIGURE **6.5** SOLUTION
DOG BISCUIT MARKET

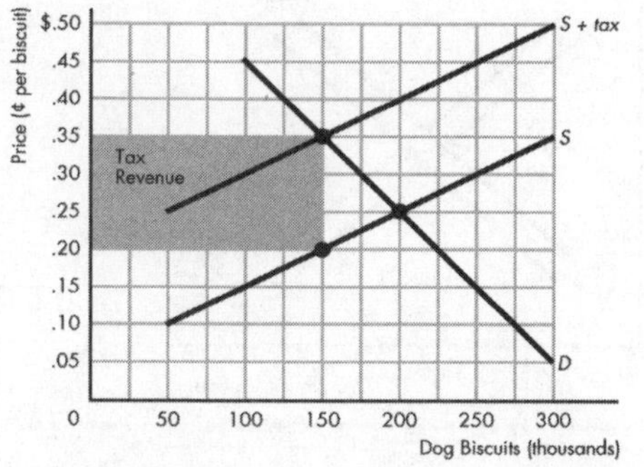

e Total tax revenue is \$0.15 per dog biscuit × 150,000 units sold = \$22,500 and is indicated by the shaded area on Figure 6.5 Solution.

f As a result of the tax, the price to consumers has gone up by \$0.10 (from \$0.25 to \$0.35). Consumers' share of the tax burden is \$15,000 (\$0.10 × 150,000). Producers pay the \$0.15 tax to government, and get back \$0.10 of it from consumers. Therefore producers' share of the tax burden is \$7,500 (\$0.05 × 150,000).

g You confidently recommend to Dr. More that the Ministry tax dog biscuits. An excise tax on dog biscuits meets both objectives: (1) it will raise more tax revenue than a tax on comic books (\$22,500 versus \$15,000) and (2) it will put more of the tax burden on consumers. In the dog biscuit market, consumers will pay \$15,000, which is 67 percent of the tax burden. In the comic book market, consumers will pay only \$5,000, which is 33 percent of the tax burden.

6 You are kicking yourself because you forgot that there is a relationship between elasticity of demand and both (1) a change in total revenue for a (tax-induced) increase in price, and (2) whether consumers or producers bear more of the burden of a tax.

a For the comic book market, the elasticity of demand calculation is

$$\eta = \left|\left(\frac{\Delta Q}{Q_{ave}}\right) \Big/ \left(\frac{\Delta P}{P_{ave}}\right)\right|$$

$$= \left|\left(\frac{100 - 200}{150}\right) \Big/ \left(\frac{.30 - .25}{.275}\right)\right|$$

$$= \left|\left(\frac{-.667}{.182}\right)\right| = 3.67$$

Demand is elastic.

b For the dog biscuit market, the elasticity of demand calculation is

$$\eta = \left|\left(\frac{\Delta Q}{Q_{ave}}\right) \Big/ \left(\frac{\Delta P}{P_{ave}}\right)\right|$$

$$= \left|\left(\frac{150 - 200}{175}\right) \Big/ \left(\frac{.35 - .25}{.30}\right)\right|$$

$$= \left|\left(\frac{-.286}{.333}\right)\right| = 0.86$$

Demand is inelastic.

c You forgot that an increase in price increases total expenditure when demand is inelastic, and decreases total expenditure when demand is elastic. Thus you could have used elasticity data to predict that expenditure would increase in the dog biscuit market. An increase in expenditure is not the same as an increase in tax revenue, but if more money is being spent, there is more to be spent on taxes. You also forgot that the more inelastic demand is, the more of a tax consumers pay.

If you had thought of the elasticity approach without prompting, good for you! Dr. More will be calling on you again for advice. If you didn't think of it, time to return to Drs. Parkin and Bade for a refresher.

7 Deadweight loss can be calculated from Figure 6.4 Solution and Figure 6.5 Solution. The loss is area of the triangle bordered by the three black dots. For comic books, the triangle has a base of \$0.15 and altitude of 100,000, so the area = 1/2*ba* = 1/2(\$0.15)(100,000) = \$7,500.

For dog biscuits, the triangle has a base of \$0.15 and altitude of 50,000, so the area = 1/2*ba* = 1/2(\$0.15)(100,000) = \$3,750.

Once again, your recommendation is to tax dog biscuits. Dr. More is impressed—you are offered full-time employment!

8 a When momentary supply is 30 tonnes, *P* = \$20/tonne. Total revenue is \$600 (\$20/tonne × 30 tonnes).

b When momentary supply is 20 tonnes, *P* = \$60/tonne. Total revenue is \$1,200 (\$60/tonne × 20 tonnes).

c Because an increase in price from \$20/tone to \$60/tonne increases total revenue from \$600 to \$1,200, demand must be inelastic.

The elasticity of demand calculation between the points in parts **a** and **b** is

$$\eta = \left|\left(\frac{\Delta Q}{Q_{ave}}\right) / \left(\frac{\Delta P}{P_{ave}}\right)\right|$$

$$= \left|\left(\frac{30-20}{25}\right) / \left(\frac{20-60}{40}\right)\right|$$

$$= \left|\left(\frac{0.4}{-1}\right)\right| = 0.4$$

9 The fallacy of composition falsely assumes that what is true of the whole is also true of the parts. Although total farm revenue increases when there is a poor harvest, revenue decreases for those individual farmers whose entire crop is wiped out. So a poor harvest is not necessarily good news for all farmers.

10 The clothing market is illustrated in Figure 6.9. The demand curve is *D* and the supply curve is *S*. The equilibrium price is P_c and the quantity is Q_c. Since police enforcement is lax, the cost of breaking the law (*CBL*) is very small for both buyers and sellers. Thus the curves that incorporate *CBL* are very close to the original demand and supply curves. The intersection of *D* – *CBL* and *S* + *CBL* yields a new equilibrium price identical to the original price (the price may be slightly higher or lower depending on the relative magnitude of the shifts of demand and supply) and a new equilibrium quantity (Q_P) only slightly less than the original quantity.

FIGURE **6.9**

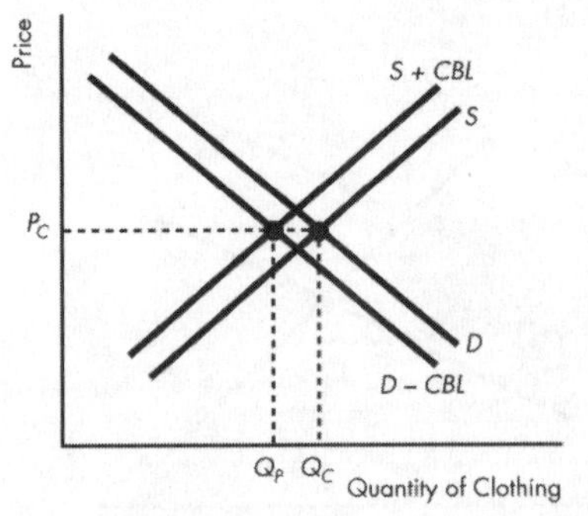

CHAPTERS 3–6

Part 2 Wrap Up

Understanding How Markets Work

PROBLEM

The finance minister has asked your boss at the finance department, Dr. Ina Lastic, to estimate the effects of levying a $24-per-carton tax on cigarettes. Dr. Lastic predicts that the tax will raise significant tax revenues (at least $30 million) because cigarette demand is inelastic.

Unfortunately, Dr. Lastic is unaware of a recent study you read in *The Globe and Mail* about past tax increases that found "Ottawa has not received the entire tax windfall it expected from increased cigarette levies because of growing tobacco smuggling."

She has asked you to perform the following detailed analysis for her predictions. The demand and supply curves (without taxes) for cigarettes are given in Figure P2.1. The before-tax price is $28 per carton, and the before-tax quantity is 2.25 million cartons per year.

a Draw the new "S + tax" curve on Figure P2.1.

b According to Dr. Lastic's predictions, what is the after-tax equilibrium price? equilibrium quantity?

c Calculate her predicted tax revenues.

d Check to see if Dr. Lastic's claim that the demand for cigarettes is inelastic is correct by calculating η between the before-tax equilibrium and the after-tax equilibrium. Was she right?

FIGURE **P2.1** CANADIAN CIGARETTE MARKET

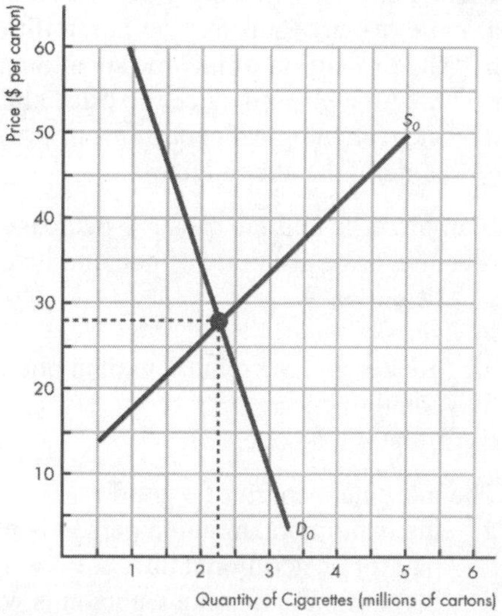

ct **e** Dr. Lastic gets high marks for economics so far. Nonetheless, you respectfully point out that her revenue prediction is wrong because she hasn't taken into account the effects of smuggling. Showing an uncharacteristic willingness to stretch herself, she replies, "I'm listening. What's *your* prediction of tax revenue?"

Here's your chance to impress the boss. You know that the supply curve of cigarettes in the United States is the same as the before-tax supply curve in Canada. You have estimated the cost of breaking the law (*CBL*) to suppliers at $16 per carton and risk to consumers of buying smuggled cigarettes is so small that their *CBL* is effectively zero. Use this information to answer the following questions.

i Draw and label any appropriate new curve(s) on Figure P2.1.

ii What is *your* prediction of the after-tax price of a carton of cigarettes? the quantity of cigarettes sold legally? the quantity of smuggled cigarettes sold illegally? (*Hint:* The price of legal and illegal cigarettes will be equal because they are perfect substitutes.)

iii What is your prediction of tax revenue?

MIDTERM EXAMINATION

You should allocate 32 minutes for this examination (16 questions, 2 minutes per question). For each question, choose the one *best* answer.

1 The magnitude of *both* the elasticity of demand and the elasticity of supply depends on
a the resource substitution possibilities.
b the proportion of income spent on a good.
c the time elapsed since the price change.
d the technological conditions of production.
e none of the above factors.

2 If an increase in price causes a decrease in total revenue, price elasticity of demand is
a negative.
b zero.
c greater than zero but less than one.
d equal to one.
e greater than one.

3 The marginal benefit of a good is
a the maximum amount a person is willing to pay for an additional unit.
b the minimum amount a person is willing to pay for an additional unit.
c equal to marginal cost.
c greater than marginal cost.
e less than marginal cost.

4 The proportion of a sales tax paid by consumers will be greater the more
1 elastic is demand.
2 inelastic is demand.
3 elastic is supply.
4 inelastic is supply.
a 2 only
b 1 and 3
c 1 and 4
d 2 and 3
e 2 and 4

5 The "big tradeoff" is between
a efficiency and fairness.
b fair results and fair rules.
c equality of income and equality of opportunity.
d the symmetry principle and utilitarianism.
e consumer surplus and producer surplus.

6 If both demand and supply increase, equilibrium price
a will rise and quantity will increase.
b will fall and quantity will increase.
c could rise or fall and quantity will increase.
d will rise and quantity could either increase or decrease.
e will fall and quantity could either increase or decrease.

7 If turnips are an inferior good, then, *ceteris paribus*, a rise in the price of turnips will cause
a a decrease in the demand for turnips.
b an increase in the demand for turnips.
c a decrease in the supply of turnips.
d an increase in the supply of turnips.
e none of the above.

8 In Figure P2.2, if the minimum wage is set at $6 per hour, what is the level of unemployment in millions of hours?
a 50
b 40
c 20
d 10
e 0

FIGURE **P2.2**

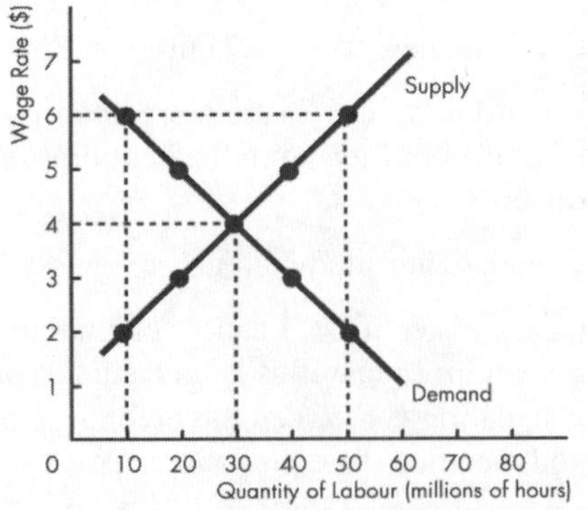

9 A demand curve is
a a consumer surplus curve.
b a marginal benefit curve.
c a minimum-willingness-to-pay curve.
d all of the above.
e none of the above.

10 If a 10 percent increase in income causes a 10 percent decrease in the consumption of widgets (at a constant price),
- **a** the price elasticity of demand for widgets equals 1.
- **b** the income elasticity of demand for widgets is negative.
- **c** the income elasticity of demand for widgets equals 1.
- **d** widgets are a normal good.
- **e** none of the above is true.

11 A price floor set below the equilibrium price results in
- **a** excess supply.
- **b** excess demand.
- **c** the equilibrium price.
- **d** an increase in supply.
- **e** a decrease in demand.

12 When there is underproduction of a good,
- **a** the sum of consumer surplus and producer surplus is greater than the sum for an efficient allocation.
- **b** the sum of consumer surplus and producer surplus is less than the sum for an efficient allocation.
- **c** deadweight loss is less than for an efficient allocation.
- **d** consumer surplus only is lost.
- **e** producer surplus only is lost.

13 A decrease in the price of *X* from \$6 to \$4 causes an increase in the quantity of *Y* demanded (at the current price of *Y*) from 900 to 1,100 units. What is the cross elasticity of demand between *X* and *Y*?
- **a** 0.5
- **b** –0.5
- **c** 2
- **d** –2
- **e** **a** or **b**, depending on whether *X* and *Y* are substitutes or complements

14 A decrease in quantity supplied is represented by a
- **a** movement down the supply curve.
- **b** movement up the supply curve.
- **c** leftward shift of the supply curve.
- **d** rightward shift of the supply curve.
- **e** rightward shift of the demand curve.

15 At current output, the marginal benefit of shoehorns is less than marginal cost. To achieve an efficient allocation,
1. shoehorn output must increase.
2. shoehorn output must decrease.
3. the marginal benefit of shoehorns will rise.
4. the marginal cost of shoehorns will rise.

- **a** 1 and 3
- **b** 1 and 4
- **c** 2 and 3
- **d** 2 and 4
- **e** 1 only

16 Farmland can be used to produce either cattle or corn. If the demand for cattle increases,
- **a** demand for corn will increase.
- **b** supply of corn will increase.
- **c** demand for corn will decrease.
- **d** supply of corn will decrease.
- **e** **b** and **c**.

ANSWERS

Problem

a See Figure P2.1 Solution. Ignore the curve *S* + *CBL* for now.

FIGURE **P2.1** SOLUTION
CANADIAN CIGARETTE MARKET

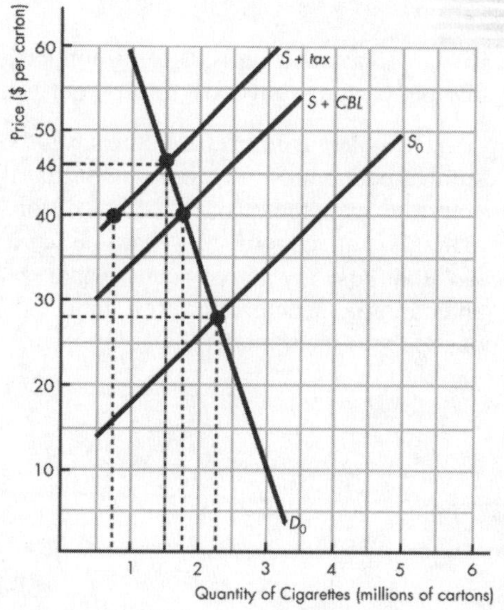

b The after-tax equilibrium price is \$46 per carton. The after-tax equilibrium quantity is 1.5 million cartons per year.

c Tax revenue is 1.5 million cartons × \$24 per carton = \$36 million per year.

d

$$\eta = \left| \frac{\frac{\Delta Q}{Q_{ave}}}{\frac{\Delta P}{P_{ave}}} \right|$$

$$\eta = \left| \frac{\frac{-.75}{1.875}}{\frac{18}{37}} \right| = \frac{.4}{.486} = .82$$

The demand curve is inelastic ($\eta < 1$) between the two equilibrium points. Dr. Lastic's predictions about tax revenue (without smuggling) and elasticity were correct.

e i See Figure P2.1 Solution. Since the *CBL* to consumers is zero, the demand curve does not shift. The smugglers' supply curve is *S* + *CBL*.

ii Since consumers can buy cigarettes from smugglers at a price of \$40 per carton, no one is willing to buy at the higher legal price of \$46. The legal price is bid down to \$40. At that price, legal suppliers will supply 0.75 million cartons (read off of the *S* + *tax* curve), and total market demand is 1.75 million cartons. Smugglers supply the difference, 1 million cartons.

iii Tax revenue is 0.75 million cartons × \$24 per carton = only \$18 million per year.

Dr. Lastic is impressed. She says, "When I studied economics, we were taught that illegal activities were the business of law enforcement officials, not economists. What you have shown is that almost any activity can be analyzed from an economic perspective. Well done. Let's draft our reply to the minister."

Midterm Examination

ⓒⓣ **1 c** **a, d** affect η_s only. **b** affects η only. (89–90, 95–96)

2 e Total revenue test. (88–89).

3 a Definition. Relation to *MC* depends if allocation is efficient or not. (106–107)

4 d Definition. (134–135)

5 a Definition. (115)

6 c Rightward shifts demand and supply must increase equilibrium quantity, but effect on price indeterminate. (74)

ⓒⓣ **7 e** Rise in *P* causes movement along demand curve. (61–65)

8 b Quantity supplied (50) > quantity demanded (10). (128–130)

9 b Also a *maximum* willingness to pay curve. (106–107)

10 b $\eta_y = (\%\ \Delta Q_D)/(\%\ \Delta \text{ income}) = -10/10 = -1$; widgets inferior good. (92)

ⓒⓣ **11 c** Draw graph. Floor doesn't prevent *P* rising from excess demand. (129–130)

12 b Deadweight loss reduces both consumer and producer surplus relative to an efficient allocation. (111–112)

13 b $\eta_x = (\%\ \Delta Q^Y_D)/(\%\ \Delta P^X) = (200/1{,}000)/(-2/5) = -0.5$. (91–92)

14 a Illustration of law of supply. (66–69)

15 c With decreasing *Q*, *MB* must rise and *MC* fall. (110)

16 d Cattle and corn substitutes in production. Increased demand for cattle raises price of cattle, causing decreased supply of corn. (67–68)

Chapter 7
Utility and Demand

KEY CONCEPTS

The Household's Budget

Household consumption choices are determined by budget and preferences.

Budget line

- Income and prices (P) of goods and services are given.
- Budget line marks boundary between affordable (points on line or inside) and unaffordable (outside line) choices.
- **Relative price** is the slope of the budget line, and **real income** is income expressed as a quantity of goods household can afford.

Preferences and Utility

Preferences (likes and dislikes) are based on **utility**—benefit or satisfaction from consumption.

- **Total utility** (*TU*) is total benefit or satisfaction from consumption of goods and services. Increased consumption increases total utility.
- **Marginal utility** (*MU*) is Δ total utility from one-unit increase in quantity good consumed. *MU* positive, but due to **diminishing marginal utility**, decreases as consumption good increases.

Maximizing Utility

Consumers strive for utility maximization—maximum attainable benefit.

- Given income and the prices of goods and services, **consumer equilibrium** occurs when consumer allocates income in way that maximizes total utility.
- Total utility is maximized when all income is spent and **marginal utility per dollar** spent is equal for all goods. For substitute goods movies (*M*) and pop (*P*), this occurs when

$$\frac{MU_M}{P_M} = \frac{MU_P}{P_P}$$

The power of marginal analysis for predicting economic choices stems from a simple rule—if the marginal gain from an action exceeds the marginal loss, take the action.

- The rule applied to the utility maximization example is—if the marginal utility per dollar spent on movies exceeds the marginal utility per dollar spent on pop, buy more movies and less pop.
- The marginal gain from more movies exceeds the marginal loss from less pop.

Predictions of Marginal Utility Theory

Ceteris paribus, if P_M falls, Q_M consumed increases (movement down along demand curve for movies); also causes leftward shift demand curve for pop.

Ceteris paribus, if P_P rises, Q_P consumed decreases (movement up along demand curve for pop); also causes rightward shift demand curve for movies.

Movies and pop normal goods. *Ceteris paribus*, increased income causes increased consumption movies and pop (rightward shifts both demand curves).

Marginal utility theory allows us to derive and predict the above results which, in Chapter 3, were just *assumptions* about consumer demand.

Efficiency, Price, and Value

Value is related to total utility or consumer surplus. Price is related to marginal utility. Distinction between total utility and marginal utility resolves diamond-water paradox.

- Diamonds, though less useful (low *TU* and small consumer surplus) than water, have higher price (high *MU*).
- Water more useful (high *TU* and large consumer surplus), but has lower price (low *MU*).

HELPFUL HINTS

1 Utility is a very useful abstract concept that allows us to think more clearly about consumer choice. Do not be concerned that arbitrary units are used to measure utility. The only important basis for marginal utility theory is that you can judge whether the additional satisfaction per dollar spent on good *X* is greater or less than the additional satisfaction per dollar spent on *Y*. If it is greater, then you decide to consume an additional unit of *X*. How much greater is irrelevant for the decision.

2 The marginal utility per dollar spent on good *X* can be written as MU_X/P_X, where MU_X is the marginal utility of the last unit of *X* consumed and P_X is the price of a unit of good *X*. The consumer equilibrium (utility-maximizing) condition for goods *X* and *Y* can be written

$$\frac{MU_X}{P_X} = \frac{MU_Y}{P_Y}$$

This implies that, in consumer equilibrium, the ratio of marginal utilities will equal the ratio of prices of the two goods:

$$\frac{MU_X}{MU_Y} = \frac{P_X}{P_Y}$$

This result is often useful.

3 If an individual is not in consumer equilibrium, then the preceding equation is not satisfied. For example, consider spending all of your income on a consumption plan where

$$\frac{MU_X}{P_X} > \frac{MU_Y}{P_Y}$$

or, equivalently,

$$\frac{MU_X}{MU_Y} > \frac{P_X}{P_Y}$$

Since P_X and P_Y are given, this means that MU_X is "too large" and MU_Y is "too small." Total utility can be increased by increasing consumption of *X* (and thereby decreasing MU_X due to the principle of diminishing marginal utility) and decreasing consumption of *Y* (and thereby increasing MU_Y due to diminishing marginal utility).

4 Text Table 7.7 on page 163 is a good review device.

SELF-TEST

True/False and Explain

The Household's Budget

1 All points inside a consumer's budget line are unaffordable.

2 In comparing two goods, their relative price is the price of one good minus the price of the other.

3 An increase in income causes an outward parallel shift of the budget line.

Preferences and Utility

4 The principle of diminishing marginal utility means that as consumption of a good increases, total utility increases but at a decreasing rate.

Maximizing Utility

5 A household is maximizing utility if the marginal utility per dollar spent is equal for all goods and all its income is spent.

6 If the marginal utilities from consuming two goods are not equal, the consumer cannot be in equilibrium.

7 If the marginal utility per dollar spent on good *X* exceeds the marginal utility per dollar spent on good *Y*, total utility will increase by increasing consumption of *X* and decreasing consumption of *Y*.

Predictions of Marginal Utility Theory

8 When the price of good *X* rises, the marginal utility from the consumption of *X* decreases.

9 When income decreases, the marginal utility derived from a good will always increase.

10 When the price of one good rises, demand decreases for goods that are substitutes.

11 When income increases, the quantity demanded of all goods increases.

Efficiency, Price, and Value

12 In consumer equilibrium, price equals marginal benefit for the last unit consumed.

13 A demand curve describes the quantity demanded at each price when marginal utility is maximized.

14 Consumer surplus for relatively cheap goods like water will be relatively low.

15 If a shift in supply decreases the price of a good, consumer surplus increases.

Multiple-Choice

The Household's Budget

1 A household's consumption choices are determined by
- **a** prices of goods and services.
- **b** income.
- **c** preferences.
- **d** all of the above.
- **e** **a** and **b** only.

2 If income decreases, the budget line will
- **a** shift outward.
- **b** shift inward.
- **c** become steeper.
- **d** become flatter.
- **e** become sadder.

3 If the price of the good on the horizontal axis rises, the budget line will
- **a** shift outward.
- **b** shift inward.
- **c** become steeper.
- **d** become flatter.
- **e** become madder.

Preferences and Utility

4 Total utility equals
- **a** the sum of the marginal utilities of each unit consumed.
- **b** the area below the demand curve but above the market price.
- **c** the slope of the marginal utility curve.
- **d** the marginal utility of the last unit divided by price.
- **e** the marginal utility of the last unit consumed multiplied by the total number of units consumed.

5 Total utility is always
a greater than marginal utility.
b less than marginal utility.
c decreasing when marginal utility is decreasing.
d decreasing when marginal utility is increasing.
e increasing when marginal utility is positive.

6 According to the principle of diminishing marginal utility, as consumption of a good increases, total utility
a decreases and then eventually increases.
b decreases at an increasing rate.
c decreases at a decreasing rate.
d increases at an increasing rate.
e increases at a decreasing rate.

Maximizing Utility

7 If a consumer is in equilibrium,
a total utility is maximized given the consumer's income and the prices of goods.
b marginal utility is maximized given the consumer's income and the prices of goods.
c marginal utility per dollar spent is maximized given the consumer's income and the prices of goods.
d the marginal utility of each good will be equal.
e none of the above is true.

8 Suppose that Ally spends her entire income of $10 on law books and miniskirts. Law books cost $2 and miniskirts cost $4 (see Table 7.1). The marginal utility of each good is independent of the amount consumed of the other good.

TABLE **7.1** ALLY'S MARGINAL UTILITY

	Marginal Utility	
Quantity	**Law Books**	**Miniskirts**
1	12	16
2	10	12
3	8	8
4	6	4

If Ally is maximizing her utility, how many miniskirts does she buy?
a 0
b 1
c 2
d 3
e 4

9 If potato chips were free, individuals would consume
a an infinite quantity of chips.
b the quantity of chips at which total utility from chips falls to zero.
c the quantity of chips at which marginal utility from chips falls to zero.
d zero chips, since this equates marginal utility and price.
e none of the above.

10 In consumer equilibrium, a consumer equates the
a total utility from each good.
b marginal utility from each good.
c total utility per dollar spent on each good.
d marginal utility per dollar spent on each good.
e total income spent on each good with total utility from each good.

11 Samir consumes apples and bananas and is in consumer equilibrium. The marginal utility of the last apple is 10 and the marginal utility of the last banana is 5. If the price of an apple is $0.50, what is the price of a banana?
a $0.05
b $0.10
c $0.25
d $0.50
e $1.00

12 If Ms. Petersen is maximizing her utility in the consumption of goods *A* and *B*, which of the following statements must be *true*?

a $MU_A = MU_B$
b $\frac{MU_A}{P_A} = \frac{MU_B}{P_B}$
c $\frac{MU_A}{P_B} = \frac{MU_B}{P_A}$
d $TU_A = TU_B$
e $\frac{TU_A}{P_A} = \frac{TU_B}{P_B}$

13 Squid costs $2 per kilogram and octopus costs $1 per kilogram. Jacques buys only octopus and gets 10 units of utility from the last kilogram he buys. Assuming that Jacques has maximized his utility, his marginal utility, in units, from the first kilogram of squid must be
a more than 10.
b less than 10.
c more than 20.
d less than 20.
e zero.

14 If Soula is maximizing her utility and two goods have the same marginal utility, she will
- **a** buy only one.
- **b** buy equal quantities of both.
- **c** be willing to pay the same price for each.
- **d** get the same total utility from each.
- **e** do none of the above.

15 Suppose that Madonna spends her entire income of $6 on purple nail polish and leather outfits. Nail polish costs $1 per unit and outfits cost $2 per unit (see Table 7.2). The marginal utility of each good is independent of the amount consumed of the other good.

TABLE **7.2** MADONNA'S MARGINAL UTILITY

	Marginal Utility	
Quantity	**Nail Polish**	**Outfits**
1	8	16
2	6	12
3	4	10
4	3	6

If Madonna is maximizing her utility, what is her *total* utility?
- **a** 19
- **b** 28
- **c** 38
- **d** 42
- **e** None of the above

16 Sergio is maximizing his utility in his consumption of beer and bubblegum. If the price of beer is greater than the price of bubblegum, then we know with *certainty* that
- **a** Sergio buys more beer than bubblegum.
- **b** Sergio buys more bubblegum than beer.
- **c** the marginal utility of the last purchased beer is greater than the marginal utility of the last purchased bubblegum.
- **d** the marginal utility of the last purchased bubblegum is greater than the marginal utility of the last purchased beer.
- **e** the marginal utilities of the last purchased beer and bubblegum are equal.

Predictions of Marginal Utility Theory

17 Bikes and roller blades are substitutes. Marginal utility theory predicts that when the price of bikes increases, the quantity demanded of bikes
- **a** decreases and the demand curve for roller blades shifts rightward.
- **b** decreases and the demand curve for roller blades shifts leftward.
- **c** decreases and the demand curve for roller blades will not shift.
- **d** increases and the demand curve for roller blades shifts rightward.
- **e** increases and the demand curve for roller blades shifts leftward.

18 Which of the following is *not* a prediction of marginal utility theory?
- **a** Other things remaining the same, the higher the price of a good, the lower the quantity demanded.
- **b** Other things remaining the same, the higher the price of a good, the higher the consumption of substitutes for that good.
- **c** Other things remaining the same, the lower the price of a good, the lower the consumption of substitutes for that good.
- **d** the law of demand
- **e** diminishing marginal utility

19 Chuck and Barry have identical preferences but Chuck has a much higher income. If each is maximizing his utility,
- **a** they will have equal total utilities.
- **b** Chuck will have lower total utility than Barry.
- **c** Chuck will have lower marginal utility than Barry for each normal good consumed.
- **d** Chuck will have higher marginal utility than Barry for each normal good consumed.
- **e** they will have equal marginal utilities for each normal good consumed.

20 The relative prices of beer to back bacon are 2:1. If Bob's current consumption is at a level where $MU_{BEER}/MU_{BACKBACON}$ is 1:2, to achieve maximum utility Bob must
- **a** consume more beer and less back bacon.
- **b** not change his current consumption of beer and back bacon.
- **c** consume less beer and more back bacon.
- **d** increase the price of beer.
- **e** consume twice as much beer and one-half as much back bacon.

21 Broomhilda is initially maximizing her utility in her consumption of goods *X* and *Y*. The price of good *X* doubles, *ceteris paribus*. For Broomhilda to once again maximize her utility, her *quantity* of *X* consumed must
- a rise until the marginal utility of *X* has doubled.
- b fall to one-half its previous level.
- c fall until the marginal utility of *X* has doubled.
- d fall until the marginal utility of *X* falls to one-half its previous level.
- e yield infinite bliss.

22 Beverly is currently in consumer equilibrium. An increase in her income will
- a increase her total utility.
- b decrease her total utility.
- c increase her marginal utility of all goods.
- d decrease her marginal utility of all goods.
- e increase her consumption of all goods.

Efficiency, Price, and Value

23 The value of a good relates to
- a total utility while price relates to consumer surplus.
- b consumer surplus while price relates to total utility.
- c marginal utility while price relates to consumer surplus.
- d marginal utility while price relates to total utility.
- e total utility while price relates to marginal utility.

24 Bill and Ted consume 15 chocolate bars each at the current price. If Bill's demand curve is more elastic than Ted's demand curve,
- a Bill's willingness to pay for the 15th chocolate bar is greater than Ted's.
- b Ted's willingness to pay for the 15th chocolate bar is greater than Bill's.
- c Bill's consumer surplus is greater than Ted's.
- d Ted's consumer surplus is greater than Bill's.
- e Bill's consumer surplus equals Ted's.

25 The high price of diamonds relative to the price of water reflects the fact that, at typical levels of consumption,
- a the total utility of water is relatively low.
- b the total utility of diamonds is relatively high.
- c the marginal utility of water is relatively high.
- d the marginal utility of diamonds is relatively low.
- e none of the above is true.

Short Answer Problems

1 Explain why the consumer equilibrium condition and the principle of diminishing marginal utility imply the law of demand.

2 Consider the following information for a consumer who is trying to allocate her income between goods *X* and *Y* so as to maximize utility. The price of *X* is $2 and the price of *Y* is $1 per unit. When all income is spent, the marginal utility of the last unit of *X* is 20 and the marginal utility of the last unit of *Y* is 16.
- a Why is the consumer not in equilibrium?
- b To increase utility, which good should this consumer consume more of and which less of?

3 A consumer is initially maximizing his utility in the consumption of goods *A* and *B* so that

$$\frac{MU_A}{P_A} = \frac{MU_B}{P_B}$$

The price of *A* then rises as a result of the shift in supply shown in Figure 7.1.

FIGURE **7.1**

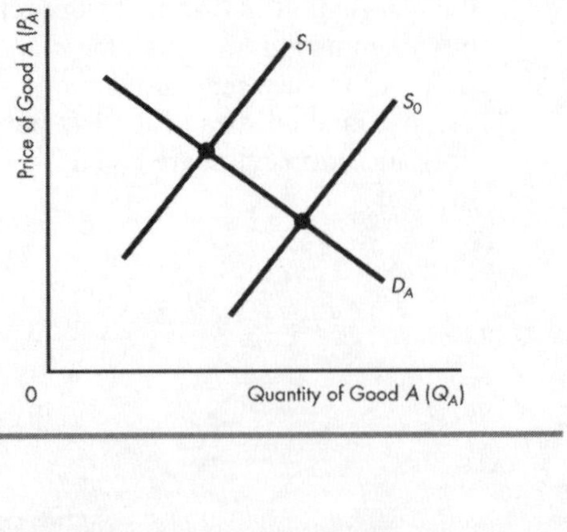

Use the above condition for utility maximization to explain how the consumer will move to a new utility-maximizing equilibrium. Show the connection between your explanation and the change on the diagram.

4 Tables 7.3 and 7.4 give Amy's utility from the consumption of popcorn and candy bars during a week.

TABLE **7.3** AMY'S UTILITY FROM POPCORN

Bags of Popcorn	Total Utility	Marginal Utility
1	20	
2	36	
3	50	
4		12
5	72	
6	80	

TABLE **7.4** AMY'S UTILITY FROM CANDY BARS

Number of Candy Bars	Total Utility	Marginal Utility
1	14	
2	26	
3		10
4	44	
5	51	
6	57	

a Complete the tables.

b Suppose the price of a bag of popcorn is $1 and the price of a candy bar is $0.50. Given the information in Tables 7.3 and 7.4, complete Table 7.5 where *MU/P* means marginal utility divided by price, which is equivalent to marginal utility per dollar spent.

TABLE **7.5** AMY'S *MU/P*

Bags of Popcorn	*MU/P*	Number of Candy Bars	*MU/P*
1		1	
2		2	
3		3	
4		4	
5		5	
6		6	

5 Amy's weekly allowance is $4. Using your answers to Short Answer Problem **4** above, answer the following if Amy spends her entire allowance on popcorn and candy.

a How much popcorn and how many candy bars will Amy consume each week if she maximizes her utility?

b Show that the utility maximum condition is satisfied.

c What is total utility?

d If, instead, Amy consumed 3 bags of popcorn and 2 candy bars, explain why she would not be maximizing her utility using figures both for total utility and for the terms *MU/P*.

6 Suppose that Amy's preferences remain as they were in Short Answer Problem **4**, but the price of a candy bar doubles to $1.

a Construct a new table (similar to Table 7.5) of *MU/P* for popcorn and candy bars.

b Amy's allowance continues to be $4. After the price change, how much popcorn and how many candy bars will she consume each week?

c Are popcorn and candy bars substitutes or complements for Amy? Why?

d On the basis of the information you have obtained, draw Amy's demand curve for candy bars.

e Suppose that both bags of popcorn and candy bars continue to sell for $1 each, but now Amy's allowance increases to $6 per week.

i How many candy bars and bags of popcorn will Amy choose to consume per week under the new situation?

ii Are popcorn and candy bars normal goods? Why or why not?

7 Suppose that Andre Agassi spends his entire income of $8 on razors and toy tennis rackets (see Table 7.6). The price of a razor is $2 and the price of a tennis racket is $4. The marginal utility of each good is independent of the amount consumed of the other good.

TABLE 7.6 ANDRE'S MARGINAL UTILITY

	Marginal Utility	
Quantity	Razors	Rackets
1	20	36
2	18	32
3	16	20
4	8	16

a If Andre is maximizing his utility, how many units of each good should he purchase?

b If Andre's income rises to $24, how many units of each good should he purchase?

c Using the information above, calculate Andre's income elasticity of demand for razors.

8 Suppose that Igor maximizes his utility by spending his entire income on bats and lizards (see Table 7.7). The marginal utility of each good is independent of the amount consumed of the other good.

TABLE 7.7 IGOR'S MARGINAL UTILITY

	Marginal Utility	
Quantity	Bats	Lizards
1	20	45
2	18	40
3	16	25
4	8	20

Igor's income is $16. The price of a bat is $2, and he buys 3 bats. If the marginal utility of the last lizard he buys is 40, calculate the price of a lizard using two separate methods.

9 How does utility theory resolve the diamond-water paradox?

ⓒⓣ 10 An apparent paradox that bothers many people is that although child-care workers are usually paid low salaries, it is often said that "they have the most important job in the world." Use economic reasoning to resolve this paradox.

ANSWERS

True/False and Explain

1 F Points on and inside budget line are affordable; points outside are unaffordable. (154)

2 F Relative price is price of one good divided by price of the other good. (154–155)

3 T With more income, household can buy more of both goods. (155)

4 T Because *MU* positive but diminishing. (156–157)

5 T Rules for maximizing total utility. (158–159)

6 F Ratios of MU/P are crucial. If prices unequal, marginal utilities unequal in consumer equilibrium. (158–160)

ⓒⓣ **7 T** Increased consumption *X* causes decreased MU_X. Decreased consumption *Y* causes increased MU_Y. Moves ratios MU/P toward equality and total utility maximization. (158–160)

8 F Rising *P* causes decreased *Q* and increased *MU*. (160–162)

ⓒⓣ **9 F** True for normal good; may be false for inferior good. (163)

10 F Demand increases for substitutes because now relatively cheaper. (160–162)

ⓒⓣ **11 F** Quantity demanded increases for normal goods, but decreases for inferior goods. (163)

12 T Consumer on demand curve = willingness-to-pay curve. (164–165)

13 F When *total* utility maximized. (164–165)

14 F Since many units consumed, many earlier units have willingness to pay > price. (164–165)

15 T With fall in price and increased quantity consumed, more units with willingness-to-pay > price. (164–165)

Multiple-Choice

1 **d** Consumption possibilities (constraints) and preferences. (154)

2 **b** Decreased income causes inward shift with no change in slope. (155)

3 **c** From fixed intercept on vertical axis, budget line rotates inward, becoming steeper. (155)

4 **a** **b** is consumer surplus. For **c**, *MU* = slope *TU* curve. **d** and **e** nonsense. (156–157)

5 **e** *TU* increasing when *MU* positive, whether *MU* decreasing or increasing. *TU* may be $\lesseqgtr$ *MU*. (156–157)

ⓔ 6 **e** Because marginal utility is positive but diminishing with increased consumption. (156–157)

7 **a** Consumers maximize *TU*. **c** and **d** wrong because *MU*/*P* equal for *TU* maximization. (158–159)

8 **b** Buys 1 miniskirt (*MU*/*P* = 16/4) and 3 books (*MU*/*P* = 8/2). (158–160)

ⓔ 9 **c** Maximizes *TU*. With fewer chips, *MU* still positive, so *TU* could increase. With more, *MU* turns negative so *TU* would decrease. (158–160)

10 **d** Definition. *MU*/*P* key to utility maximization. (158–160)

11 **c** Solve 10/0.5 = 5/P_{BANANA} for P_{BANANA}. (158–160)

12 **b** Definition. (158–160)

ⓔ 13 **d** For octopus, MU_O/P_O = 10. For squid, MU_S/2 would need to be < 10, so MU_S must be < 20. (158–160)

ⓔ 14 **c** From maximum condition of equal *MU*/*P*. No necessary relation between *MU* and quantity or *TU*. (158–160)

15 **d** Buys 2 polish and 2 outfits. *TU* = 8 + 6 + 16 + 12. (158–160)

16 **c** From maximum condition of equal *MU*/*P*. No necessary relation between *MU* and quantity. (158–160)

17 **a** See text discussion. (160–163)

18 **e** Diminishing *MU* is *assumption* of theory. (160–163)

19 **c** Chuck consumes greater quantities of each good, so *MU* lower. (160–163)

20 **c** To equalize *MU*/*P* must increase MU_{BEER} and decrease $MU_{BACKBACON}$. **d** wrong because no control over prices. (160–163)

21 **c** From maximum condition of equal *MU*/*P*. No necessary relation between *MU* and quantity consumed. (160–163)

ⓔ 22 **a** For inferior goods, consumption may decrease and *MU* increase. (163)

23 **e** Value relates to total utility and consumer surplus; price relates to marginal utility. (164–165)

24 **d** Ted's steeper demand curve means greater willingness to pay for previous units. Willingness to pay for last unit equal. (164–165)

25 **e** For diamonds: *TU* relatively low, *MU* relatively high. For water: *TU* relatively high, *MU* relatively low. (164–165)

Short Answer Problems

1 Suppose we observe an individual in consumer equilibrium consuming X_0 units of good *X* and Y_0 units of good *Y*, with the prices of *X* and *Y* given by P_X and P_Y respectively. This means that at consumption levels X_0 and Y_0, the marginal utility per dollar spent on *X* equals the marginal utility per dollar spent on *Y*. Now let the price of *X* increase to P^1_X. The marginal utility per dollar spent on *X* declines and thus is now less than the marginal utility per dollar spent on *Y*. To restore equilibrium, our consumer must increase the marginal utility of *X* and decrease the marginal utility of *Y*. From the principle of diminishing marginal utility we know that the only way to do this is to decrease the consumption of *X* and increase the consumption of *Y*. This demonstrates the law of demand, since an increase in the price of *X* has been shown to require a decrease in the consumption of *X* to restore consumer equilibrium.

2 **a** This consumer is not in equilibrium because the marginal utility per dollar spent is not the same for goods *X* and *Y*. The marginal utility per dollar spent on *X* is MU_X/P_X = 20/2 = 10, which is less than the marginal utility per dollar spent on *Y*: MU_Y/P_Y = 16.

b To equate the marginal utilities per dollar spent (and thus increase utility), this consumer should increase consumption of *Y* and decrease consumption of *X*. The principle of diminishing marginal utility implies that this will decrease the marginal utility of *Y* and increase the marginal utility of *X*.

3 When the price of *A* rises, *ceteris paribus*,

$$\frac{MU_A}{P_A} < \frac{MU_B}{P_B}$$

The consumer is no longer in equilibrium. In order to restore the equality in the equilibrium condition, the consumer must change his consumption to make MU_A rise and MU_B fall. (The consumer cannot change the prices of *A* and *B*.) Since marginal utility diminishes with increases in quantity consumed, the consumer must decrease consumption of *A* and increase consumption of *B*. Decreased consumption of *A* moves the consumer up to the left on the demand curve, from the initial intersection of *D* and S_0 to the new intersection of *D* and S_1. In the new consumer equilibrium, equality will be restored in the equilibrium condition.

4 **a** The tables are completed in Table 7.3 Solution and Table 7.4 Solution.

TABLE **7.3** SOLUTION
AMY'S UTILITY FROM POPCORN

Bags of Popcorn	Total Utility	Marginal Utility
1	20	20
2	36	16
3	50	14
4	62	12
5	72	10
6	80	8

TABLE **7.4** SOLUTION
AMY'S UTILITY FROM CANDY BARS

Number of Candy Bars	Total Utility	Marginal Utility
1	14	14
2	26	12
3	36	10
4	44	8
5	51	7
6	57	6

b The table is completed in Table 7.5 Solution.

TABLE **7.5** SOLUTION
AMY'S *MU/P*

Bags of Popcorn	*MU/P*	Number of Candy Bars	*MU/P*
1	20	1	28
2	16	2	24
3	14	3	20
4	12	4	16
5	10	5	14
6	8	6	12

5 **a** 2 bags of popcorn and 4 candy bars.

b The utility maximum condition is satisfied, since Amy spends all of her income ($4), and the marginal utility per dollar spent is the same for popcorn and candy bars (16).

c Total utility is the utility from the consumption of 2 bags of popcorn (36) plus the utility from the consumption of 4 candy bars (44) = 80.

d If Amy consumed 3 bags of popcorn and 2 candy bars, total utility would be 76, which is less than 80, the total utility from the consumption of 2 bags of popcorn and 4 candy bars. For the combination of 3 bags of popcorn and 2 candy bars, *MU/P* for popcorn is 14 while *MU/P* for candy bars is 24. Since *MU/P* is not the same for both goods, this combination does not meet the condition for utility maximization.

6 **a** See Table 7.8.

TABLE **7.8** AMY'S *MU/P*

Bags of Popcorn	*MU/P*	Number of Candy Bars	*MU/P*
1	20	1	14
2	16	2	12
3	14	3	10
4	12	4	8
5	10	5	7
6	8	6	6

b 3 bags of popcorn and 1 candy bar. Amy spends all of her income ($4) and the marginal utility per dollar spent is the same for popcorn and candy bars (14).

c Popcorn and candy bars are substitutes for Amy, since an increase in the price of a candy bar causes an increase in the demand for popcorn.

d Amy's demand curve for candy bars is given in Figure 7.2. Two points on the demand curve have been identified: when the price of a candy bar is \$1, one candy bar will be demanded, and when the price is \$0.50, 4 candy bars will be demanded. The demand curve is a line through these two points.

FIGURE **7.2**

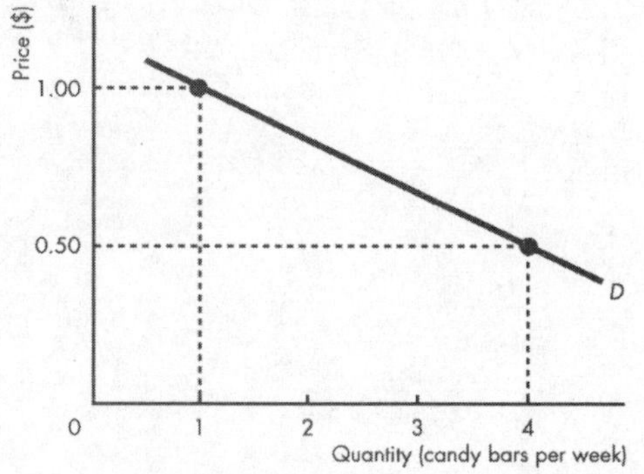

e **i** Now, Amy will choose to consume 4 bags of popcorn and 2 candy bars (instead of 3 bags of popcorn and 1 candy bar). Amy spends all of her income (\$6) and the marginal utility per dollar spent is the same for popcorn and candy bars (12).

ii Popcorn and candy bars are both normal goods for Amy, since the increase in income (allowance) leads to increases in the demand for both goods.

7 **a** The utility-maximizing combination of goods is shown in Table 7.9.

TABLE **7.9** ANDRE'S *MU/P*

Quantity	*MU/P* Razors	Rackets
1	10	9
2	9	8
3	8	5
4	4	4

Andre should purchase 2 razors and 1 racket. Andre spends all of his income (\$8), and the marginal utility per dollar spent is the same for razors and rackets (9).

b Andre should purchase 4 razors and 4 rackets. He spends all of his income (\$24), and the marginal utility per dollar spent is the same for razors and rackets (4).

c The income elasticity of demand for razors is

$$\eta_y = \frac{\dfrac{\Delta Q}{Q_{ave}}}{\dfrac{\Delta Y}{Y_{ave}}} = \frac{\dfrac{4-2}{\frac{1}{2}(4+2)}}{\dfrac{24-8}{\frac{1}{2}(24+8)}} = \frac{\frac{2}{3}}{\frac{16}{16}} = \frac{2}{3}$$

8 There are two methods for calculating the price of a lizard. One method is based on the fact that Igor spends all of his income on bats and lizards. This means that

$$Y = P_B Q_B + P_L Q_L$$

where Y = income, P_B = the price of a bat, Q_B = the quantity of bats purchased, P_L = the price of a lizard, and Q_L = the quantity of lizards purchased. We know $Y = 16$, $P_B = 2$, $Q_B = 3$, and if the marginal utility of the last lizard is 40, then $Q_L = 2$. Substituting these values, we can solve for P_L.

$$16 = 2(3) + P_L(2)$$
$$10 = P_L(2)$$
$$5 = P_L$$

The second method uses the condition for utility maximization:

$$\frac{MU_B}{P_B} = \frac{MU_L}{P_L}$$

We know that $MU_L = 40$, $P_B = 2$, and if Igor buys 3 bats $MU_B = 16$. Substituting these values, we can solve for P_L.

$$\frac{16}{2} = \frac{40}{P_L}$$
$$80 = 16P_L$$
$$5 = P_L$$

9 The distinction between total utility and marginal utility resolves the diamond-water paradox. The total utility from consuming water is large, but because we consume so much water the marginal utility from the last litre of water is small. The total utility from consuming diamonds is small, but because we consume so few diamonds the marginal utility from the last diamond is large. Since price is related to marginal utility, not total utility, the price of water is low and the price of diamonds is high.

CT 10 While most parents put a high value on child-care services, many child-care workers are willing to provide those services. While the total utility provided by the services of child-care workers is high, the marginal utility of those (abundantly supplied and therefore low-wage) services is low.

Chapter 8 Possibilities, Preferences, and Choices

KEY CONCEPTS

Consumption Possibilities

Budget line shows limits to household consumption, given income, and prices of goods and services. Consider example of movies (horizontal axis) and pop (vertical axis).

- Budget equation is

$$Q_P = \frac{Y}{P_P} - \frac{P_M}{P_P} Q_M$$

- Magnitude of slope of budget equation (P_M/P_P) equals **relative price** of movies in terms of pop.
- Intercepts measure household's **real income** in movies (*x*-intercept) and pop (*y*-intercept).
- Higher P_M yields steeper budget line, fixed pop-intercept.
- Higher P_P yields flatter budget line, fixed movie-intercept.
- Higher Y yields rightward parallel shift budget line.

Preferences and Indifference Curves

Indifference curve maps household preferences, joining combinations goods giving equal satisfaction.

- Indifference curves generally slope downward and bow toward the origin (convex).
- Indifference curves farther from the origin represent higher levels of satisfaction.
- Indifference curves never intersect.
- **Marginal rate of substitution** (*MRS*) is magnitude of slope of indifference curve—rate at which household gives up good *y* (pop) for additional unit good *x* (movies) and remains indifferent (remains on same indifference curve).
- **Diminishing marginal rate of substitution** is tendency for *MRS* to diminish as move down along an indifference curve. Accounts for bowed-toward-the-origin shape of indifference curves.
  - More substitutability between goods yields straighter indifference curves.
  - Less substitutability between goods yields more tightly curved indifference curves.

Predicting Consumer Behaviour

Given income and prices of goods, household allocates income to maximize satisfaction. Household chooses best-affordable point, which is on budget line and on highest possible indifference curve. At the best-affordable point,

- household spends all its income and achieves maximum possible satisfaction.
- budget line and indifference curve are tangent and have same slope—*MRS* equals the relative price.

Price effect is Δ consumption resulting from Δ price of a good. Price effect = substitution effect + income effect.

- **Substitution effect**—Δ consumption resulting from Δ price accompanied by (hypothetical) Δ income leaving household indifferent between initial and new situations. For normal and inferior goods, substitution effect of falling price is increased consumption.
- **Income effect**—Δ consumption resulting from (hypothetically) restoring original income but keeping prices constant at new level. For normal

goods, income effect of (hypothetically) increased income is increased consumption. For inferior goods, (hypothetically) increased income yields decreased consumption.

- The downward-sloping demand curve is a consequence of the consumer choosing his best-affordable combination of goods. The demand curve can be derived from the price effect—by tracing the best-affordable quantity of a good as its price changes.

For normal goods, substitution and income effects work in same direction, so falling price yields increased consumption.

For inferior goods, substitution and income effects work in opposite directions, but net effect of falling price usually yields (smaller) increased consumption.

Work-Leisure Choices

The labour supply curve is a consequence of the consumer choosing a utility-maximizing allocation of time between labour and leisure.

- An *income-time budget line* and indifference curves describe constraints and preferences for the choice between labour (income) and leisure.
- A rising wage changes the slope of the budget line yielding
  - substitution effects—more time spent labouring.
  - income effects—more income for consuming more of all normal goods, including leisure.
- The labour supply curve is
  - upward-sloping when substitution effect > income effect.
  - backward-bending when income effect > substitution effect.

HELPFUL HINTS

1 The consumer's basic problem is to do the best given her constraints. These constraints, which limit possible choices, depend on income and the prices of goods and are represented graphically by the budget line. Doing the best means finding the most preferred outcome consistent with those constraints. In this chapter, preferences are represented graphically by indifference curves.

Graphically, the consumer problem is to find the highest indifference curve attainable given the budget line. To make graphical analysis easier, we examine choices between only two goods, but the same principles apply in the real world to many choices, including the choice between labour and leisure.

2 The budget equation for pop and movies on text page 173 is

$$Q_P = \frac{Y}{P_P} - \frac{P_M}{P_P} Q_M$$

This is the type of straight-line equation ($y = a + bx$) that we discussed in Chapter 1 appendix. The differences are that Q_P is the dependent variable (instead of y) and Q_M is the independent variable (instead of x). We can use the budget equation to graph the budget line by finding the Q_P-intercept (where the line intersects the vertical Q_P axis), finding the Q_M-intercept (where the line intersects the horizontal Q_M axis), and then connecting those two points with a straight line.

To find the Q_P-intercept, set $Q_M = 0$.

$$Q_P = \frac{Y}{P_P} - \frac{P_M}{P_P}(0)$$

$$Q_P = \frac{Y}{P_P}$$

To find the Q_M-intercept, set $Q_P = 0$.

$$0 = \frac{Y}{P_P} - \frac{P_M}{P_P} Q_M$$

$$\frac{P_M}{P_P} Q_M = \frac{Y}{P_P}$$

$$Q_M = \frac{Y}{P_M}$$

The Q_P-intercept, $Q_P = Y/P_P$, is the consumer's real income in terms of pop. It tells us how much pop could be purchased if all income was spent on pop. The Q_M-intercept, $Q_M = Y/P_M$, is the consumer's real income in terms of movies. It tells us how many movies could be purchased if all income was spent on movies. These intercepts provide an easy method for drawing a budget line. Each of the two endpoints (the intercepts) is just income divided by the price of the good on that axis. Connecting those endpoints with a straight line yields the budget line.

The slope of the budget line provides additional information for the consumer's choice. The magnitude (absolute value) of the slope equals the relative price (or opportunity cost) of movies in terms of pop. In other words, the magnitude of the slope equals the number of units of pop it takes to buy one movie. More generally, the magnitude of the slope of the budget line (P_X/P_Y) equals the relative price (or opportunity cost) of the good on the horizontal *x*-axis in terms of the good on the vertical *y*-axis; or the number of units of vertical-axis goods it takes to buy one unit of the horizontal-axis good.

3 The marginal rate of substitution (*MRS*) is the rate at which a consumer gives up good *Y* for an additional unit of good *X* and still remains indifferent (on the same indifference curve). The *MRS* equals the magnitude of the slope of the indifference curve, $\Delta Q_Y/\Delta Q_X$.

Because indifference curves are bowed toward the origin (convex), the magnitude of the slope and hence the *MRS* diminish as we move down an indifference curve. The diminishing *MRS* means that the consumer is willing to give up less of good *Y* for each additional unit of good *X*. As the consumer moves down an indifference curve, she is coming to value good *Y* more and value good *X* less. This is easily explained by the principle of diminishing marginal utility, which underlies the following equation.

$$\text{Marginal rate of substitution} = \frac{MU_X}{MU_Y}$$

At the top of the indifference curve, the consumer is consuming little *X* and much *Y*, so the marginal utility of *X* (MU_X) is high and the marginal utility of *Y* (MU_Y) is low. Moving down the curve, as the quantity of *X* consumed increases, MU_X decreases; and as the quantity of *Y* consumed decreases, MU_Y increases. Thus the principle of diminishing marginal utility provides an intuitive understanding of why the *MRS* diminishes as we move down an indifference curve.

4 At the consumer's best-affordable point, the budget line is just tangent to the highest-affordable indifference curve, so the magnitude of the slope of the budget line equals the magnitude of the slope of the indifference curve. Combining the information from Helpful Hint **2** (the magnitude of the slope of the budget line equals P_X/P_Y) and Helpful Hint **3** (the magnitude of the slope of the indifference curve equals MU_X/MU_Y) yields

$$\frac{P_X}{P_Y} = \frac{MU_X}{MU_Y}$$

Rearranging terms yields

$$\frac{MU_X}{P_X} = \frac{MU_Y}{P_Y}$$

This is the equation for utility maximization from Chapter 7. You can now see why the budget equation/indifference curve analysis of consumer choice developed in Chapter 8 complements the marginal utility analysis of Chapter 7. See the Appendix to Chapter 8 for more details.

5 Understanding the distinction between the income and substitution effects of a change in the price of a good is often challenging for students. Consider a decrease in the price of good *A*. This has two effects that will influence the consumption of *A*. First, the decrease in the price of *A* will reduce the relative price of *A*, and, second, it will increase real income. The substitution effect is the answer to the question: How much would the consumption of *A* change as a result of the relative price decline if we also (hypothetically) reduce income by enough to leave the consumer indifferent between the new and original situations? The income effect is the answer to the question: How much more would the consumption of *A* change if we (hypothetically) restore the consumer's real income but leave relative prices at the new level?

SELF-TEST

True/False and Explain

Consumption Possibilities

1 The graph of a budget line will be bowed toward the origin.

2 At any point on a budget line, all income is spent.

3 *Ceteris paribus*, an increase in the price of goods means that real income falls.

4 An increase in income causes a leftward parallel shift of the budget line.

Preferences and Indifference Curves

5 We assume that more of any good is preferred to less of the good.

6 Higher indifference curves represent higher levels of income.

7 The principle of the diminishing marginal rate of substitution explains why indifference curves are bowed toward the origin.

8 Perfect substitutes will have L-shaped indifference curves.

Predicting Consumer Behaviour

9 At the best-affordable consumption point of movies and pop, the marginal rate of substitution equals the ratio of the price of movies to the price of pop.

10 When the relative price of a good decreases, the income effect always leads to increased consumption of the good.

11 The law of demand can be derived from an indifference curve model by tracing the impact on quantity demanded of an increase in price.

12 When the price of an inferior good falls, the substitution effect increases consumption and the income effect decreases consumption.

Work-Leisure Choice

13 An income-time budget line describes preferences for income versus leisure.

14 When the labour supply curve is upward-sloping, the substitution and income effects work in the same direction.

15 When the labour supply curve is backward-bending, the income effect dominates the substitution effect.

Multiple-Choice

Consumption Possibilities

1 Which of the following statements best describes a consumer's budget line?

a the amount of each good a consumer can purchase
b the limits to a consumer's set of affordable consumption choices
c the desired level of consumption for the consumer
d the consumption choices made by a consumer
e the set of all affordable consumption choices

2 Real income is measured in
- a monetary units.
- b price units.
- c units of satisfaction.
- d units of indifference.
- e units of goods.

3 Consider the budget line and indifference curve in Figure 8.1. If the price of good *X* is \$2, what is the price of good *Y*?
- a \$0.37
- b \$0.67
- c \$1.50
- d \$2.67
- e impossible to calculate without additional information

FIGURE **8.1**

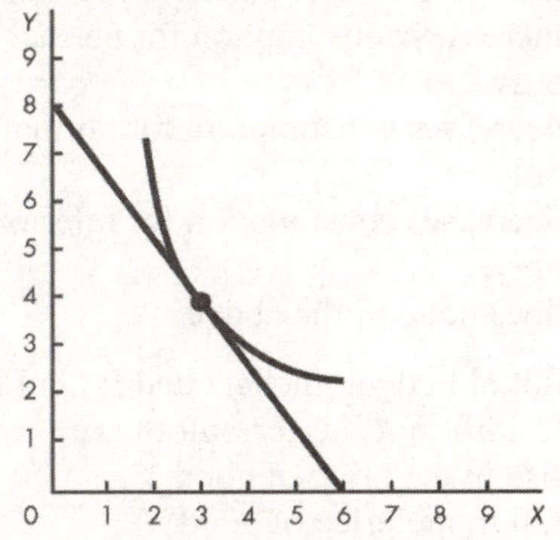

4 The budget line depends on
- a income only.
- b prices only.
- c income and prices.
- d preferences only.
- e preferences and prices.

5 Bill consumes apples and bananas. Suppose Bill's income doubles and the prices of apples and bananas also double. Bill's budget line will
- a shift left but not change slope.
- b remain unchanged.
- c shift right but not change slope.
- d shift right and become steeper.
- e shift right and become flatter.

6 The initial budget equation for pop and movies is $Q_P = 20 - 4Q_M$, and the price of pop (P_P) is \$5. If the price of pop falls to \$4, which of the following is the new budget equation?
- a $Q_P = 25 - 2Q_M$
- b $Q_P = 25 - 4Q_M$
- c $Q_P = 25 - 5Q_M$
- d $Q_P = 20 - 5Q_M$
- e None of the above

7 Zarina's income allows her to afford 3 tomatoes and no toothbrushes, or 2 toothbrushes and no tomatoes. The relative price of toothbrushes (price toothbrush/price tomato) is
- a 2/3.
- b 3/2.
- c 6/1.
- d 1/6.
- e impossible to calculate without additional information.

8 If the price of the good measured on the vertical axis increases, the budget line will
- a become steeper.
- b become flatter.
- c shift leftward but parallel to the original budget line.
- d shift rightward but parallel to the original budget line.
- e shift leftward and become steeper.

9 If income increases, the budget line will
- a become steeper.
- b become flatter.
- c shift leftward but parallel to the original budget line.
- d shift rightward but parallel to the original budget line.
- e shift parallel but leftward or rightward depending on whether a good is normal or inferior.

Preferences and Indifference Curves

10 The shape of an indifference curve depends on
- a the prices of goods.
- b household income.
- c the substitutability between goods for the household.
- d the level of satisfaction for the household.
- e all of the above.

11 In general, as a consumer moves down an indifference curve, increasing consumption of good *X* (measured on the horizontal axis),
- a more of *Y* must be given up for each additional unit of *X*.
- b a constant amount of *Y* must be given up for each additional unit of *X*.
- c less of *Y* must be given up for each additional unit of *X*.
- d the relative price of *Y* increases.
- e the relative price of *Y* decreases.

12 Which of the following statements is *false*?
- a Indifference curves are negatively sloped.
- b A preference map consists of a series of nonintersecting indifference curves.
- c Indifference curves are bowed out from the origin.
- d The marginal rate of substitution is the magnitude of the slope of an indifference curve.
- e The marginal rate of substitution increases with movement up an indifference curve.

13 In moving down along an indifference curve, the marginal rate of substitution (*MRS*) for complements will
- a increase faster than the *MRS* for substitutes.
- b increase more slowly than the *MRS* for substitutes.
- c be relatively constant.
- d decrease faster than the *MRS* for substitutes.
- e decrease more slowly than the *MRS* for substitutes.

14 If two goods are perfect substitutes, their
- a indifference curves are positively sloped straight lines.
- b indifference curves are negatively sloped straight lines.
- c indifference curves are L-shaped.
- d marginal rate of substitution is zero.
- e marginal rate of substitution is infinity.

Predicting Consumer Behaviour

15 Which of the following statement(s) about Figure 8.2 is/are *true*?
- a Point *s* is preferred to point *q*, but *s* is not affordable.
- b Points *q* and *r* yield the same utility, but *q* is more affordable.
- c Point *t* is preferred to point *q*, but *t* is not affordable.
- d Points *q* and *s* cost the same, but *q* is preferred to *s*.
- e All of the above statements are true.

FIGURE **8.2**

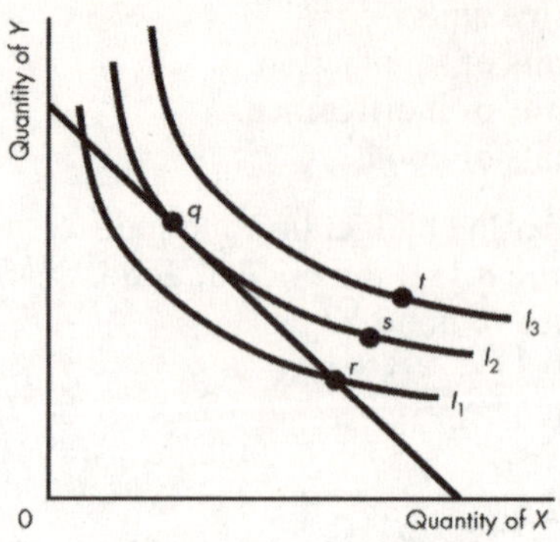

16 For a rise in price, the substitution effect
- a always increases consumption.
- b increases consumption for normal goods only.
- c decreases consumption for normal goods only.
- d decreases consumption for inferior goods only.
- e does none of the above.

17 The initial budget line labelled *RS* in Figure 8.3 would shift to *RT* as a result of a(n)
- a rise in the price of good *X*.
- b fall in the price of good *X*.
- c decrease in preferences for good *X*.
- d rise in the price of good *Y*.
- e increase in real income.

FIGURE **8.3**

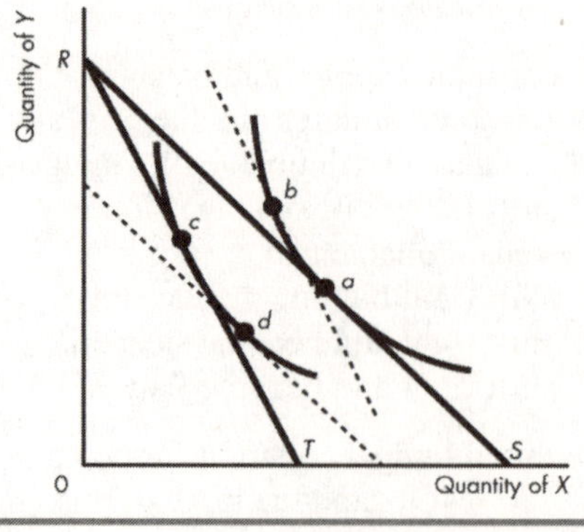

18 When the initial budget line labelled *RS* in Figure 8.3 shifts to *RT*, the substitution effect is illustrated by the move from point
- **a** *a* to *b*.
- **b** *a* to *c*.
- **c** *a* to *d*.
- **d** *b* to *d*.
- **e** *d* to *c*.

19 When the initial budget line labelled *RS* in Figure 8.3 shifts to *RT*, the income effect is illustrated by the move from point
- **a** *a* to *b*.
- **b** *a* to *c*.
- **c** *a* to *d*.
- **d** *b* to *c*.
- **e** *b* to *d*.

20 If the price of good *X* (measured on the horizontal axis) falls, the substitution effect is represented by a movement to a
- **a** higher indifference curve.
- **b** lower indifference curve.
- **c** steeper part of the same indifference curve.
- **d** flatter part of the same indifference curve.
- **e** flatter part of a higher indifference curve.

21 When Clark Gable took off his shirt in *It Happened One Night*, he was not wearing an undershirt. As a result, men's undershirt sales plummeted. *Ceteris paribus*, we can conclude that men's undershirt
- **a** preferences changed when prices changed.
- **b** preferences changed when income changed.
- **c** choices changed when preferences changed.
- **d** choices changed when prices changed.
- **e** choices changed when income changed.

22 When the price of an inferior good falls, the
1. income and substitution effects both move quantity demanded in the same direction.
2. income and substitution effects move quantity demanded in opposite directions.
3. income effect is usually larger than the substitution effect.
4. substitution effect is usually larger than the income effect.

- **a** 1 and 2
- **b** 1 and 4
- **c** 2 and 3
- **d** 2 and 4
- **e** None of the above

Work-Leisure Choices

23 The opportunity cost of an hour of leisure is
- **a** $0.
- **b** the value of time spent watching television.
- **c** the hourly wage rate.
- **d** the income effect.
- **e** the substitution effect.

24 Over the past century, the quantity of labour supplied has fallen as wages have increased because the
- **a** income and substitution effects both increased leisure.
- **b** income and substitution effects both decreased leisure.
- **c** income effect decreasing leisure dominated the substitution effect increasing leisure.
- **d** income effect increasing leisure dominated the substitution effect decreasing leisure.
- **e** substitution effect increasing leisure dominated the income effect decreasing leisure.

25 When the substitution effect dominates the income effect, the labour supply curve is
- **a** positively sloped.
- **b** horizontal.
- **c** negatively sloped.
- **d** vertical.
- **e** shifting rightward.

Short Answer Problems

1 Why is an indifference curve negatively sloped?

2 Explain why it is logically impossible for indifference curves to intersect each other, by comparing points *a*, *b*, and *c* in Figure 8.4.

FIGURE **8.4**

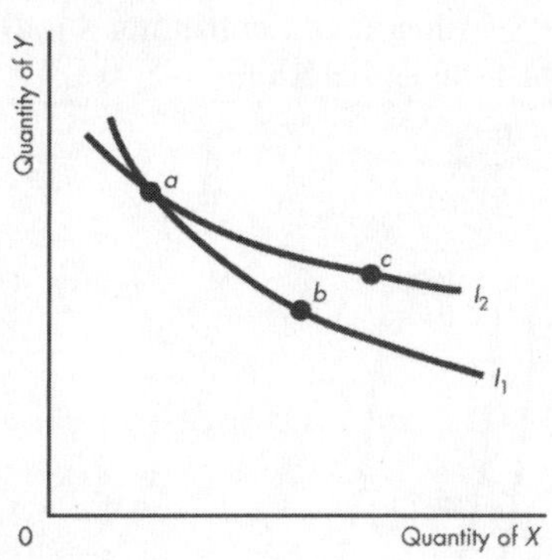

3 Helpful Hint **3** establishes that the

$$\text{Marginal rate of substitution} = \frac{\text{Marginal utility of movies}}{\text{Marginal utility of pop}}$$

As we move down an indifference curve, use the principle of diminishing marginal utility to explain why the marginal rate of substitution diminishes.

ⓒ 4 For normal goods,

- an increase in income causes an *increase in demand* (demand curve shifts to the right).
- the income effect (due to a decrease in price) causes an *increase in quantity demanded.*

Explain why these two statements are or are not contradictory. Be sure to define clearly any important concepts.

5 Jan and Dan both like bread and peanut butter and have the same income. Since they face the same prices, they have identical budget lines. Currently, Jan and Dan consume exactly the same quantities of bread and peanut butter; they have the same best-affordable consumption point. Jan, however, views bread and peanut butter as close (though not perfect) substitutes, while Dan considers bread and peanut butter to be quite (but not perfectly) complementary.

a On the same diagram, draw a budget line and representative indifference curves for Jan and Dan. (Measure the quantity of bread on the horizontal axis.)

b Now, suppose the price of bread declines. Graphically represent the substitution effects for Jan and Dan. For whom is the substitution effect greater?

ⓒ 6 Figure 8.5 illustrates a consumer's indifference map for food and clothing.

FIGURE **8.5**

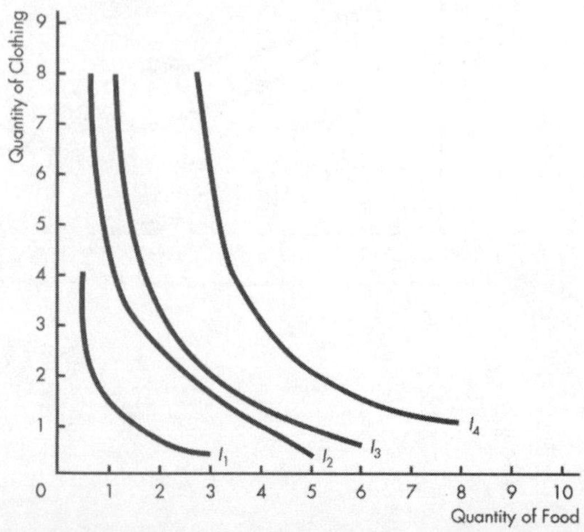

a **i** Initially, the price of a unit of clothing is $P_C = \$1$ and the price of a unit of food is $P_F = \$1.50$. If income is $Y = \$9$, draw the consumer's budget line on Figure 8.5 and label the best-affordable point as point *a*. What is the quantity of food consumed?

ii What is the equation of the budget line in terms of P_C, P_F, and Y? What is the equation of the budget line in numerical terms? Express the magnitude (absolute value) of the slope of the budget line as a ratio of P_C and P_F.

iii At point *a*, what is the value of the marginal rate of substitution (or equivalently, MU_F/MU_C)?

iv Use your answers in parts **ii** and **iii** to derive the formula for utility maximization. Explain.

b If P_F increases to \$3 per unit while income and P_C remain unchanged, draw the new budget line and label the new best-affordable point as point *b*. What is the new quantity of food consumed?

c If P_F increases again to \$4.50 per unit while income and P_C remain unchanged, draw the corresponding budget line and label the best-affordable point as point *c*. What is the quantity of food consumed?

d On a separate graph, plot and draw the demand curve for food that corresponds to points *a*, *b*, and *c*. Be sure to clearly label the axes.

e Suppose prices remain at their initial values ($P_C = \$1$, $P_F = \$1.50$) but income falls to \$3. Draw the new budget line and label the best-affordable point as point *z*. What is the quantity of food consumed? Is food a normal or inferior good? Explain. On your demand curve graph from part **d**, plot point *z* and roughly sketch a demand curve corresponding to the new income level.

7 Sharon, a fitness fanatic, plays squash and takes aerobics classes at her health club. Squash courts rent for \$2 per hour and aerobics classes are \$1 per hour. Sharon has decided to spend \$12 per week for fitness activities. Figure 8.6 illustrates several indifference curves for squash and aerobics on Sharon's preference map.

FIGURE **8.6**

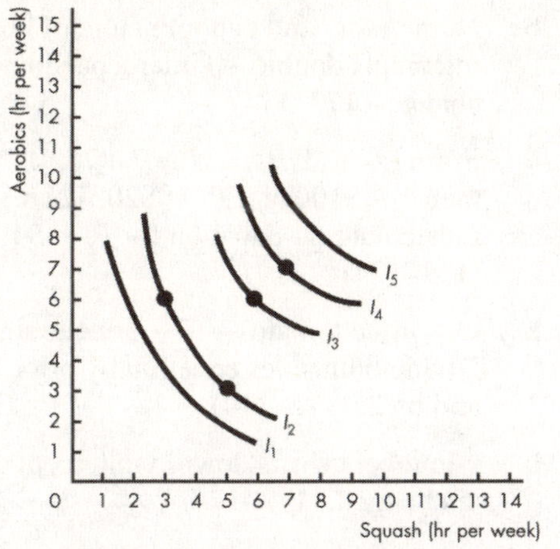

a How many hours of squash and aerobics will Sharon consume at her best-affordable point?

b Suppose that squash rentals fall to $1 per hour.

i How many hours of squash and aerobics will Sharon now consume? What is the increase in her hours of squash?

ii Of the total increase in hours of squash, how many hours are due to the substitution effect of the price fall?

iii Of the total increase in hours of squash, how many hours are due to the income effect of the price fall?

c On a separate graph, plot two points on Sharon's demand curve for squash and draw her straight-line demand curve.

d The price of squash continues to be $1 but Sharon's fitness budget increases to $14. How many hours of squash and aerobics will Sharon now consume?

Ⓔ **8** Ms. Muffet consumes both curds and whey. The initial price of curds is $1 per unit, and the price of whey is $1.50 per unit. Ms. Muffet's initial income is $12.

a What is the relative price of curds?

b Derive Ms. Muffet's budget equation and draw her budget line on a graph. (Measure curds on the horizontal axis.)

c On your graph, draw an indifference curve so that the best-affordable point corresponds to 6 units of curds and 4 units of whey.

d What is the marginal rate of substitution of curds for whey at this point?

e Show that any other point on the budget line is inferior.

9 Given the initial situation described in Short Answer Problem **8**, suppose Ms. Muffet's income now increases.

a Illustrate graphically how the consumption of curds and whey are affected if both goods are normal. (Numerical answers are not necessary. Just show whether consumption increases or decreases.)

b Draw a new graph showing the effect of an increase in Ms. Muffet's income if whey is an inferior good.

10 Return to the initial circumstances described in Short Answer Problem **8**. Now, suppose the price of curds doubles to $2 a unit, while the price of whey remains at $1.50 per unit and income remains at $12.

a Draw the new budget line.

b Why is the initial best-affordable point (label it point *r*) no longer the best-affordable point?

c Using your graph, show the new best-affordable point and label it *t*. What has happened to the consumption of curds?

d Decompose the effect on the consumption of *X* into the substitution effect and the income effect. On your graph, indicate the substitution effect as movement from point *r* to point *s* (which you must locate) and indicate the income effect as movement from point *s* to point *t*.

ANSWERS

True/False and Explain

1 **F** Budget lines straight. Indifference curves bowed toward origin. (172–173)

2 **T** Expenditure = income along budget line. (172–173)

3 **T** Real income = income/price goods. (173)

4 **F** Rightward parallel shift. (174)

5 **T** See text discussion. (175–176)

6 **F** Represent higher levels satisfaction. (175–176)

7 **T** See text discussion. (176–177)

8 **F** True for perfect complements. (177–178)

ⓔ 9 **T** Budget line tangent to indifference curve. (178–179)

ⓔ 10 **F** True for normal, false for inferior goods. (181–182)

11 **T** See text discussion. (179–180)

12 **T** Income effect decreases consumption—higher real income means household can afford to buy higher-quality (normal) goods instead. (181–182)

13 **F** Describes *constraints* on income (labour) versus leisure choice. (182–183)

14 **F** Higher wages cause substitution effect of more labour and income effect of more leisure, but substitution effect dominates. (182–183)

15 **T** At higher wage, use increased real income to consume more leisure, dominating the substitution effect of more labour supplied. (182–183)

Multiple-Choice

1 **b** **a** should be combinations of goods; **c** about indifference curves; **d** about best-affordable point; **e** includes area inside budget line. (172–173)

2 **e** Quantity goods household can buy. (173)

3 **c** Income = \$12 (\$2 × 6 units *X*), so price *Y* = \$12/8 units *Y*. (172–174)

4 **c** See text discussion. Indifference curves depend on preferences. (172–173)

5 **b** Numerators and denominators of both intercepts double, so intercepts do not change. (173–174)

ⓔ 6 **c** From $Q_P = (Y/P_P) - (P_M/P_P)Q_M$. If $P_P = \$5$, then $Y = \$100$ and $P_M = \$20$. Then recalculate Q_P equation for $P_P = \$4$. (173–174)

ⓔ 7 **b** (3 × price tomato) = (2 × price toothbrush). Divide both sides equation by price tomato and by 2. (172–174)

8 **b** *y*-intercept shifts down, *x*-intercept unchanged. (173–174)

9 **d** Increased income does not change slope but increases *x*- and *y*-intercepts. (173–174)

10 **c** Budget line depends on **a** and **b**. At any level satisfaction, indifference curve could be any shape. (175–178)

11 **c** Due to diminishing *MRS*. **d** and **e** wrong since relative price relates to budget line, not indifference curve. (175–178)

12 **c** Indifference curves bow in toward the origin. (175–178)

ⓔ 13 **d** *MRS* always diminishing moving down indifference curve. Complements have more tightly curved indifference curves. (177–178)

14 **b** With constant slope = 1. (177–178)

15 **c** *t* on higher indifference curve, but outside budget line. *s* and *q* yield same utility so **a**, **d** wrong. *q* preferred to *r* so **b** wrong. (178–179)

16 **e** For rising price, substitution effect always decreases consumption for both normal and inferior goods. (181–182)

17 **a** With same income, less *X* can be purchased. **c** relates to indifference curves. Increase in real income is move from point *b* to *c*. (179–180)

18 **a** Budget line with new prices tangent to original indifference curve. (181–182)

19 **d** Hypothetically restore original income (reverse the increase in real income) but keep prices constant at new level. (181–182)

ⓔ 20 **d** New budget line flatter and drawn tangent to same indifference curve. (181–182)

21 c Gable's influence caused decreased preference for undershirts. Combined with unchanged prices and incomes, caused decreased consumption. (178–182)

ⓔ **22 d** See text discussion. (181–182)

23 c Forgone hourly wage from working. (182–183)

24 d Higher wages increase opportunity cost of leisure and cause substitution of time away from leisure; higher wages increase income causing (greater) income effect toward leisure. (182–183)

25 a See Text Figure 8.10. Negatively sloped (backward-bending) when income effect dominates. (182–183)

Short Answer Problems

1 An indifference curve tells us how much the consumption of one good must increase as the consumption of another good decreases in order to leave the consumer indifferent (no better or worse off). It is negatively sloped because the goods are both desirable. As we decrease the consumption of one good, in order to not be made worse off, consumption of the other good must increase. This implies a negative slope.

2 The explanation takes the form of a proof by contradiction. Since points *a* and *b* are on the same indifference curve (I_1), the consumer is indifferent between them. Since points *a* and *c* are on the same indifference curve (I_2), the consumer is also indifferent between them. If the consumer is indifferent between *a* and *b* and between *a* and *c*, this implies an indifference between *b* and *c*. But indifference between points *b* and *c* is logically impossible, because we assume that more of any good is preferred to less of that good. Since point *c* has more of both good *X* and good *Y* than point *b*, the consumer cannot be indifferent between *b* and *c*. Indifference between *b* and *c* contradicts the assumption that more is preferred to less. Hence indifference curves cannot intersect.

3 As we move down an indifference curve for pop and movies, such as in Text Figure 8.4 on page 176, we increase the quantity of movies consumed and decrease the quantity of pop consumed. As movie consumption increases, each additional movie yields lower marginal utility because of the principle of diminishing marginal utility. Thus the value of the numerator on the right-hand side of the equation below decreases.

$$\text{Marginal rate of substitution} = \frac{\text{Marginal utility of movies}}{\text{Marginal utility of pop}}$$

As pop consumption decreases, each previous pop consumed yields higher marginal utility. Thus, the value of the denominator on the right-hand side of the equation increases. The combined effect of a decrease in the numerator and an increase in the denominator is that the ratio MU_{MOVIES}/MU_{POP} falls as we move down an indifference curve, corresponding to a diminishing marginal rate of substitution on the left-hand side of the equation.

ⓔ 4 These statements appear to be contradictory because an increase in income leads, in the first statement, to a shift of the demand curve but, in the second statement, to a movement along the demand curve. The reason the statements are *not* contradictory has to do with a crucial distinction between *nominal* income and *real* income.

The first statement (an *increase* in income causes an increase in *demand* [demand curve shifts rightward]) describes how an increase in *nominal* income shifts the demand curve. *Nominal* income is measured in dollars.

The second statement (the income effect [due to a decrease in price] causes an increase in *quantity demanded*) describes how an increase in *real* income causes a movement along the stationary demand curve.

Real income is measured in purchasing power, or the quantities of goods that nominal income can buy. When the price of a good decreases, your *real* income goes up because you can now purchase more of that good with the same, unchanged, *nominal* income. Because *nominal* income is unchanged in the second statement, the demand curve does not shift. But because *real* income has increased, the decrease in price leads to an increase in *quantity demanded*.

5 **a** Initially, Jan and Dan are at point *c* on the budget line labelled *AB* in Figure 8.7. Jan's indifference curve is illustrated by I_J. Note that her indifference curve is close to a straight line, reflecting the fact that bread and peanut butter are close substitutes. On the other hand, since Dan considers bread and peanut butter to be complementary, his indifference curve, I_D, is more tightly curved.

FIGURE **8.7**

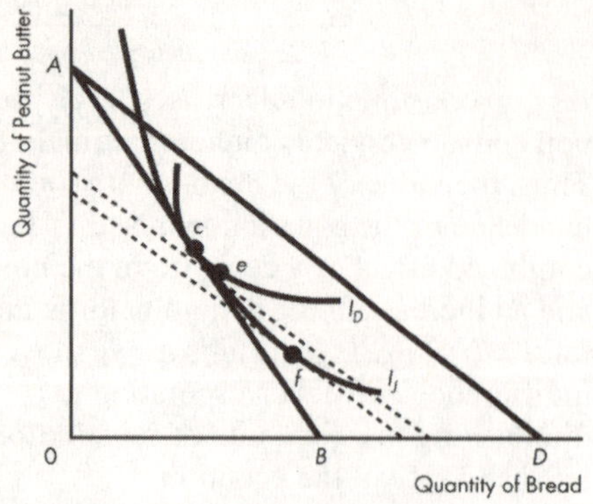

b If the price of bread declines, the budget line will become flatter, such as the line labelled *AD* in Figure 8.7. In order to measure the substitution effect, find the point on the original indifference curve that has the same slope as the new budget line. Since Dan's indifference curve is more sharply curved, it becomes flatter quite rapidly as we move away from point *c*. Thus the substitution effect is quite small, from *c* to point *e*. Since Jan's indifference curve is almost a straight line, the substitution effect must be much larger, from *c* to point *f*.

ⓒ **6** The consumer's budget line is shown in Figure 8.5 Solution.

FIGURE **8.5** SOLUTION

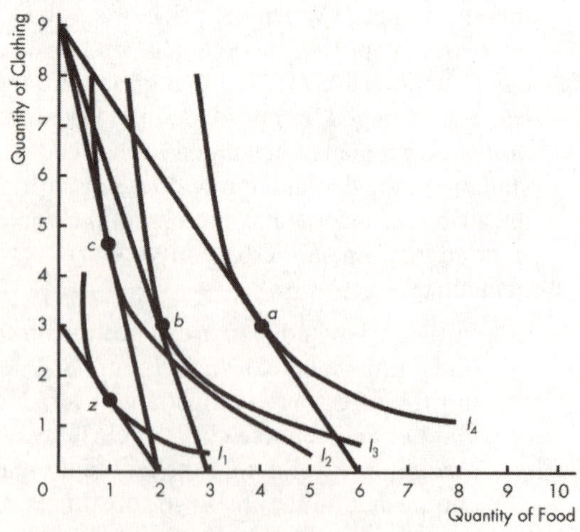

a **i** 4 units of food.

ii The consumer's budget is given by

$$P_C Q_C + P_F Q_F = Y$$

To obtain the budget equation, follow the calculation procedure on text page 173. Divide by P_C to obtain

$$Q_C + \frac{P_F}{P_C} Q_F = \frac{Y}{P_C}$$

Subtract $(P_F/P_C)Q_F$ from both sides to obtain

$$Q_C = \frac{Y}{P_C} - \frac{P_F}{P_C} Q_F$$

To obtain the budget equation in numerical terms, substitute in the values P_C = \$1, P_F = \$1.50, and Y = \$9.

$$Q_C = \frac{9}{1} - \frac{1.50}{1} Q_F$$

The magnitude (absolute value) of the slope of the budget line is 3/2, which is the ratio of P_F/P_C. Note that this price ratio cannot be read directly off the graph, since the axes measure quantities, not prices.

iii The marginal rate of substitution at point *a* is defined as the magnitude of the slope of the indifference curve at point *a*. Since the slope of the indifference curve at point *a* is equal to the slope of the tangent at *a*, and since the budget line is tangent at *a*, the magnitude of the slope of the indifference curve is 3/2. This magnitude is equivalent to MU_F/MU_C.

iv The magnitude of the slope of the budget line is P_F/P_C and the magnitude of the slope of the indifference curve at *a* is MU_F/MU_C. Since the two magnitudes are equal, $P_F/P_C = MU_F/MU_C$ or $MU_F/P_F = MU_C/P_C$.

b See Figure 8.5 Solution: 2 units of food.

c See Figure 8.5 Solution: 1 unit of food.

d The demand curve for food is shown in Figure 8.8.

FIGURE **8.8**

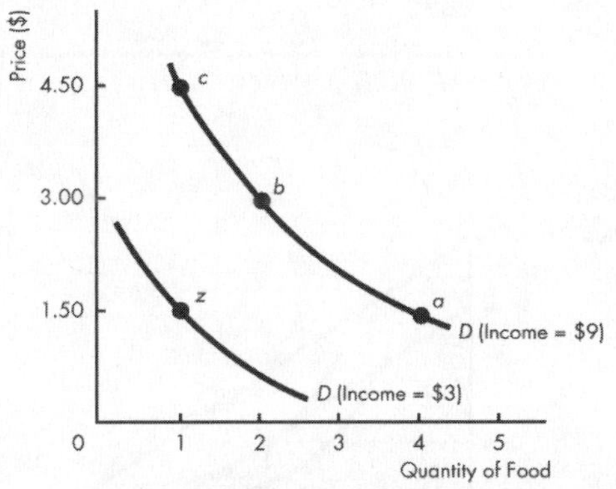

e See Figure 8.5 Solution. 1 unit of food. Food is a normal good because a *decrease* in income (with prices constant) causes a decrease in food consumption (from 4 units to 1 unit). See Figure 8.8 for the new demand curve (income = $3).

7 a In order to find Sharon's best-affordable point, draw the budget line in Figure 8.6 Solution. The initial budget line is labelled *AB* and Sharon's best-affordable point is point *c* on indifference curve I_2. Thus Sharon consumes 3 hours of squash and 6 hours of aerobics per week.

FIGURE **8.6** SOLUTION

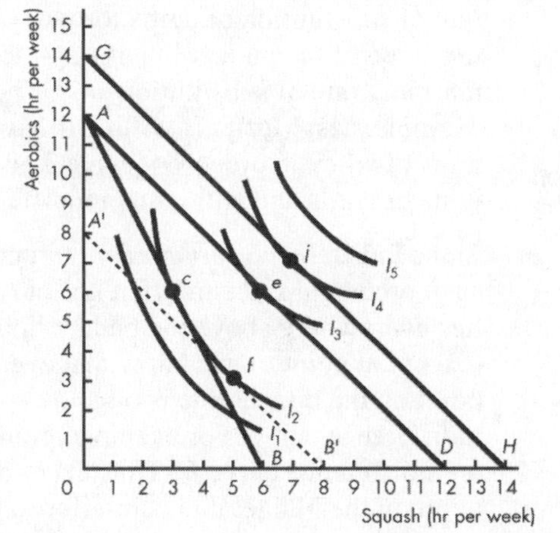

b If the price of squash falls to $1, the budget line becomes *AD*.

i Now Sharon's best-affordable point is point *e* on indifference curve I_3. This corresponds to consumption of 6 hours of squash and 6 hours of aerobics per week. Her squash consumption has increased by 3 hours.

ii To measure the substitution effect, shift the new budget line leftward in parallel fashion until it is tangent to the indifference curve I_2, where Sharon was before the fall in the price of squash. In effect, budget line *A'B'* removes the increase in real income due to the price fall in order to isolate the substitution effect of the price fall on Sharon's consumption of squash. Point *f* is what Sharon would have consumed at the new prices if her income fell just enough to return her to her original indifference curve. The substitution effect of the fall in the price of squash is the movement from initial point *c* to point *f*, which is an increase in squash hours consumed of 2 (from 3 to 5 hours).

iii To measure the income effect, shift the budget line *A'B'* rightward in parallel fashion until it is tangent to the indifference curve I_3, where Sharon was before we hypothetically reduced her real income. In effect, this shift isolates the income effect by restoring the increase in real income due to the price fall while keeping prices constant at their new values. The income effect of the fall in the price of squash is the movement from point *f* to point *e*, which is an increase in squash hours consumed of 1 (from 5 to 6 hours).

The results are summarized in Table 8.1.

TABLE **8.1** PRICE EFFECT FROM FIGURE 8.6 SOLUTION

Effect	Move from Point	Δ Hours Squash
Substitution effect	*c* to *f*	2
+ Income effect	*f* to e	1
= Price effect	c to e	3

c In parts **a** and **b**, income spent on fitness was constant at $12 and the price of aerobics was constant at $1 per hour. When the price of squash was $2 per hour, Sharon wanted to consume 3 hours of squash and when the price of squash was $1, Sharon wanted to consume 6 hours of squash. This gives us two points on Sharon's demand curve for squash, which are labelled *a* and *b* in Figure 8.9. Drawing a line passing through these points allows us to obtain her straight-line demand curve, labelled *D*.

FIGURE **8.9**

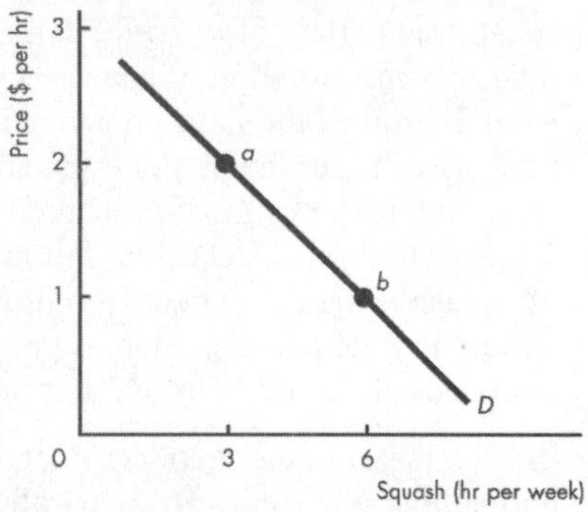

d When Sharon's fitness budget increases to $14, the budget line shifts right to the line labelled *GH* in Figure 8.6 Solution. Sharon's best-affordable point is now at *j*, which corresponds to 7 hours of squash and 7 hours of aerobics consumed per week.

ⓒ **8 a** The relative price of curds is the price of curds divided by the price of whey:

$1/$1.50 = 2/3

b Let P_C = the price of curds, P_W = the price of whey, Q_C = quantity of curds, Q_W = quantity of whey, and Y = income. The budget equation, in general form, is

$$Q_W = \frac{Y}{P_W} - \frac{P_C}{P_W} Q_C$$

Since $P_C = \$1$, $P_W = \$1.50$, and $Y = \$12$, Ms. Muffet's budget equation is specifically given by

$$Q_W = 8 - 2/3Q_C$$

The graph of this budget equation, the budget line, is given by the line labelled *AB* in Figure 8.10.

FIGURE **8.10** CURDS & WHEY NORMAL GOODS

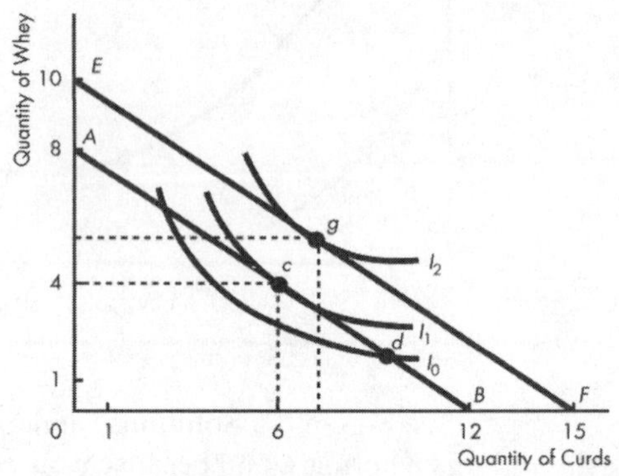

c If the best-affordable point corresponds to 6 units of curds and 4 units of whey, then the relevant indifference curve must be tangent to (just touch) the budget line *AB* at *c*, which is indifference curve I_1.

d The marginal rate of substitution is given by the magnitude of the slope of the indifference curve at point *c*. We do not know the slope of the indifference curve directly, but we can easily compute the slope of the budget line. Since, at point *c*, the indifference curve and the budget line have the same slope, we can obtain the marginal rate of substitution of curds for whey. Since the slope of the budget line is –2/3, the marginal rate of substitution is 2/3. For example, Ms. Muffet is willing to give up 2 units of whey in order to receive 3 additional units of curds and still remain indifferent.

e Since indifference curves cannot intersect each other and since indifference curve I_1 lies everywhere above the budget line (except at point *c*), we know that every other point on the budget line is on a lower indifference curve. For example, point *d* lies on indifference curve I_0. Thus every other point on the budget line is inferior to point *c*.

9 a An increase in income will cause a parallel rightward shift of the budget line, for example to *EF* in Figure 8.10. If both curds and whey are normal goods, Ms. Muffet will move to a point like *g* at which the consumption of both goods has increased.

b If whey is an inferior good, its consumption will fall as income rises. This is illustrated in Figure 8.11. Once again the budget line shifts from *AB* to *EF*, but Ms. Muffet's preferences are such that her new consumption point is a point like *g'* where the consumption of whey has actually declined.

FIGURE **8.11** WHEY AS INFERIOR GOOD

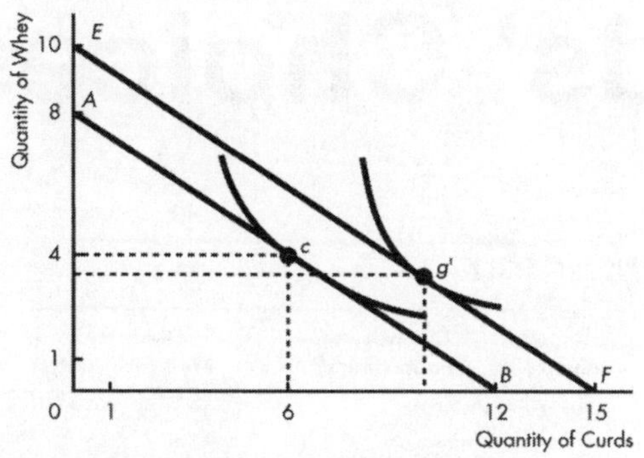

10 a Ms. Muffet's initial budget line is *AB* and the initial best-affordable point is *r* in Figure 8.12. Note that point *r* in Figure 8.12 is the same as point *c* in Figure 8.10. The new budget line following an increase in the price of curds to $2 (income remains at $12) is *AH*.

FIGURE **8.12**

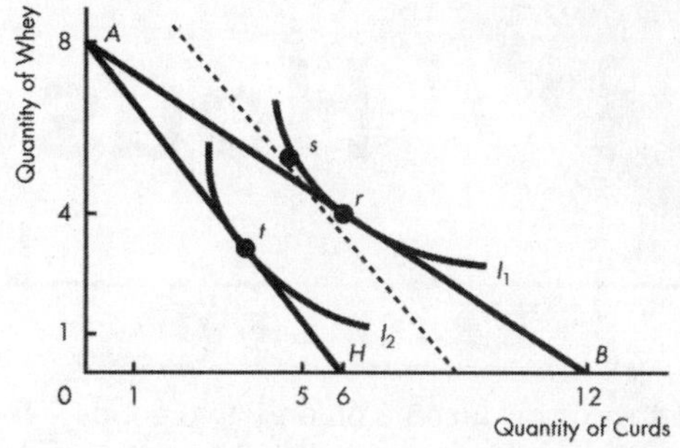

b After the price increase, point *r* is no longer the best-affordable point, since it is no longer even affordable.

c The new best-affordable point (labelled *t* in Figure 8.12) indicates a decrease in the consumption of curds.

d The substitution effect of the increase in the price of curds is indicated by the movement from *r* to *s* in Figure 8.12. This gives the effect of the change in relative prices while keeping Ms. Muffet on the same indifference curve. The income effect is indicated by movement from *s* to *t*.

CHAPTERS 7–8

Part 3 Wrap Up

Understanding Households' Choices

PROBLEM

Michael spends his income on only two goods—food and medicine. The indifference map and budget line in Figure P3.1 show different combinations of food and medicine that Michael prefers given different incomes. The combinations can also be described as the points *a* to *f* in Table P3.1. Use this information to answer the following questions.

FIGURE **P3.1**

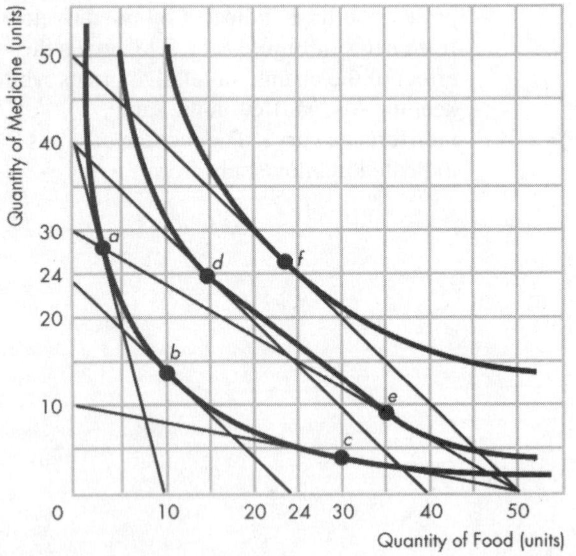

TABLE **P3.1**

Point	Quantity of Food (units)	Quantity of Medicine (units)
a	3	28
b	10	14
c	30	4
d	15	25
e	35	9
f	23	27

a Assume Michael's income is \$300 and the price of food is \$6 per unit. Using the information in Table P3.1, derive the coordinates (combinations of price and quantity) of three points on Michael's demand curve for medicine. Record the points in Table P3.2.

TABLE **P3.2** MICHAEL'S DEMAND CURVE FOR MEDICINE

Price (\$)	Quantity (units)

b Now assume Michael's income is \$600, the price of food is \$12 per unit, and the price of medicine is \$20 per unit. At Michael's best affordable point (consumer equilibrium), what is the ratio of $MU_{FOOD}/MU_{MEDICINE}$?

c Starting from Michael's best affordable point in part **b**, suppose the price of medicine then falls to $12 per unit and we want to separate the substitution and income effects of the price change.

i The substitution effect moves Michael from point __________ to point __________ (fill in the blanks).

ii The income effect moves Michael from point __________ to point __________ (fill in the blanks).

d Define the substitution effect and explain how your answer to part **c i** illustrates the substitution effect *alone*.

e Define the income effect and explain how your answer to part **c ii** illustrates the income effect *alone*.

f Is medicine a normal or inferior good for Michael? Explain your answer.

MIDTERM EXAMINATION

You should allocate 20 minutes for this examination (10 questions, 2 minutes per question). For each question, choose the one *best* answer.

1 Marginal utility equals
- **a** total utility divided by price.
- **b** total utility divided by the total number of units consumed.
- **c** the slope of the total utility curve.
- **d** the inverse of total utility.
- **e** the area below the demand curve but above market price.

2 A consumer maximizes his utility by purchasing 2 units of good *X* at $5/unit and 3 units of good *Y* at $7/unit. What is the ratio of the marginal utility of *X* to the marginal utility of *Y*?
- **a** 5/7
- **b** 7/5
- **c** 2/3
- **d** 3/2
- **e** 10/21

3 A change in the price of the good measured on the horizontal (*x*) axis changes which aspect(s) of the budget equation?
- **a** slope and *y*-intercept
- **b** slope and *x*-intercept
- **c** *x*- and *y*-intercepts but not slope
- **d** slope only
- **e** none of the above

4 Which of the following statements about the budget line is *false*? The budget line
- **a** divides affordable from unaffordable consumption points.
- **b** is based on fixed prices.
- **c** is based on fixed income.
- **d** is based on fixed quantities.
- **e** constrains consumer choices.

5 Suppose good *X* is measured on the horizontal axis and good *Y* on the vertical axis. The marginal rate of substitution is best defined as the
- **a** relative price of good *X* in terms of good *Y*.
- **b** relative price of good *Y* in terms of good *X*.
- **c** rate at which a person will give up good *Y* to get more of good *X* and remain indifferent.
- **d** rate at which a person will give up good *X* to get more of good *Y* and remain indifferent.
- **e** slope of the budget line.

6 When the price of a good changes, the change in consumption that leaves the consumer indifferent is called the
- **a** utility effect.
- **b** substitution effect.
- **c** income effect.
- **d** price effect.
- **e** inferior effect.

7 Shelley is maximizing her utility in her consumption of mink coats and Porsches. If the marginal utility of her last purchased mink coat is twice the marginal utility of her last purchased Porsche, we know with certainty that
- **a** Shelley buys twice as many mink coats as Porsches.
- **b** Shelley buys twice as many Porsches as mink coats.
- **c** Shelley buys more Porsches than mink coats, but we do not know how many more.
- **d** the price of a mink coat is twice the price of a Porsche.
- **e** the price of a Porsche is twice the price of a mink coat.

8 The difference between the value of a good and its price is known as
- **a** excess demand.
- **b** excess supply.
- **c** consumer surplus.
- **d** consumer excess.
- **e** marginal utility.

9 A change in income changes which aspect(s) of the budget equation?
- **a** slope and y-intercept only
- **b** slope and x-intercept only
- **c** x- and y-intercepts but not slope
- **d** slope only
- **e** none of the above

10 When the price of a normal good rises, the income effect
- **a** increases consumption of the good and the substitution effect decreases consumption.
- **b** decreases consumption of the good and the substitution effect increases consumption.
- **c** and the substitution effect both increase consumption of the good.
- **d** and the substitution effect both decrease consumption of the good.
- **e** is always larger than the substitution effect.

ANSWERS

Problem

a If Michael spends his entire income of \$300 on food (at \$6 per unit), he can buy 50 units of food. This gives us the quantity-of-food intercept of his budget line. There are three alternative budget lines with that intercept. If Michael can also buy 50 units of medicine with \$300, the price of a unit a medicine must be \$6. That budget line is tangent to the highest indifference curve at point *f*, where Michael would consume 27 units of medicine. So one point on Michael's demand curve for medicine is (price = \$6, quantity = 27 units). The other two points in Table P3.2 Solution (points *e* and *c* in Figure P3.1) can be derived in the same way.

TABLE **P3.2** SOLUTION
MICHAEL'S DEMAND CURVE FOR MEDICINE

Price (\$)	Quantity (units)
6	27
10	9
30	4

b At the best affordable point (see Chapter 7's Helpful Hint **2**, page 104)

$$MU_{FOOD}/MU_{MEDICINE} = P_{FOOD}/P_{MEDICINE}$$

Since $P_{FOOD}/P_{MEDICINE} = 12/20$,

$$MU_{FOOD}/MU_{MEDICINE} = 12/20 = 3/5$$

c **i** The substitution effect moves Michael from point *e* to point *d*.

ii The income effect moves Michael from point *d* to point *f*.

d The substitution effect is the effect of a change in price on the quantity bought when the consumer (hypothetically) remains indifferent between the original and new situation.

In moving from point *e* to point *d*, the new price of medicine is reflected in the budget line tangent to the indifference curve at point *d*. This budget line eliminates the increase in real income that resulted from the decrease in the price of medicine. Michael is indifferent between the original (point *e*) and the new situation (point *d*) since both are on the same indifference curve.

e The income effect is the change in consumption resulting from (hypothetically) restoring the consumer's original income but keeping prices constant at new level.

In moving from point *d* to point *f*, the prices of medicine (and food) stay constant at their new level, but Michael's real income is (hypothetically) restored to what it would have been as a result of the fall in the price of medicine.

f Medicine is a normal good for Michael because the income effect is positive—consumption of medicine increases from 25 to 27 units between points *d* and *f*.

Midterm Examination

1 c $MU = \Delta$ total utility/Δ quantity. (156–157)

2 a Quantities irrelevant. Ratio of *MU*s must be equal to ratio prices. (158–159)

3 b See Chapter 8 Helpful Hint **2** and analyze ΔP_M (movies on horizontal axis). (172–174)

4 d Quantities vary along budget line. (154)

5 c Definition. **a** and **b** relate to slope budget line. MRS = **e** only at best affordable point. (176)

6 b Definition. (181)

7 d From maximum condition of equal *MU*/*P*. No necessary relation between *MU* and quantity. (158–159)

8 c See Text Figure 7.7. (164–165)

9 c See Chapter 8 Helpful Hint **2**. Δ income (Y) does not change slope (P_M/P_P) but does Δ intercepts (Y/P_M) and (Y/P_P). (172–174)

10 d Both work in same direction. Rising *P* causes decreased quantity consumed. (180–182)

Chapter 9 Organizing Production

KEY CONCEPTS

The Firm and Its Economic Problem

A **firm** is an institution that hires and organizes factors of production to produce and sell goods and services. Firm's goal is profit maximization.

- Accounting costs = explicit costs + conventional depreciation
- Accounting profit = revenues – (explicit costs + conventional depreciation)

Opportunity costs of production consist of explicit costs (paid in money) and implicit costs (opportunities forgone but not paid in money). A firm's major implicit costs are

- **implicit rental rate**—opportunity cost of using its own capital. Equals **economic depreciation** (change in market value of capital) + forgone interest.
- cost of owner's resources—(wage income forgone) + normal profit. **Normal profit** is the expected return to *entrepreneurial ability* and is part of a firm's opportunity costs of production. Normal profit is the average profit in industry.

Economists' costs and profits:

- *Opportunity costs* = explicit costs + implicit costs
- **Economic profit** = revenues – (explicit costs + implicit costs)
- Because normal profit is part of implicit costs, economic profit (when positive) is over and above normal profit.
- Opportunity cost and economic profit are the key to correctly predicting firm behaviour.

Limits to profit maximization are:

- **technology** constraints—available resources and technology.
- information constraints—limited information and uncertainty about firm's workforce, potential customers, and competitors.
- market constraints—limited demand for firm's output; marketing efforts of competitors.

Technology and Economic Efficiency

Technological efficiency—using least inputs to produce given output.

Economic efficiency—least cost of producing given output.

Information and Organization

Firms organize production by using

- **command systems** based on a managerial hierarchy.
- **incentive systems** to overcome problems of limited information and uncertainty.

With limited information, the **principal–agent problem** arises when *agents* (those employed by others) do not act in the best interests of the *principals* (employers of the agents).

- Strategies for coping with the principal–agent problem and inducing agents to act in the best interests of the principals include ownership, incentive pay, and long-term contracts.
- To cope with limited information and uncertainty, firms have devised different forms of business organization:
  - *sole proprietorship*—single owner with unlimited liability

- *partnership*—two or more owners with unlimited liability.
- *corporation*—owned by limited-liability stockholders.

Markets and the Competitive Environment

Types of market structure:

- **Perfect competition**—many firms; identical products; easy entry of new firms.
- **Monopolistic competition**—many firms; slightly differentiated products (**product differentiation**); easy entry.
- **Oligopoly**—few firms; identical or differentiated products; some barriers to entry.
- **Monopoly**—single firm; product with no close substitutes; high barriers to new entry.

Market structure of most industries lies between extremes of perfect competition and monopoly.

- To evaluate competitiveness of a market, economists use two measures of industrial concentration:
  - **four-firm concentration ratio**—percentage of industry sales made by largest four firms.
  - **Herfindahl–Hirschman Index** (HHI)—sum of squared market shares of 50 largest firms in industry.
- High concentration ratios usually indicate low degree competition.
- Problems with concentration ratios:
  - national, but many industries regional/global.
  - no indication of entry barriers and turnover.
  - firms operate in other industries.

Markets and Firms

Firms coordinate economic activity when they perform task more efficiently than markets. Firms often have advantages of

- lower **transactions costs**—costs arising from finding someone with whom to do business.
- **economies of scale**—lower unit cost of producing good as output rate increase.
- **economies of scope**—lower unit cost from producing range of goods and services.
- economies of team production—individuals in production process specializing in mutually supportive tasks.

HELPFUL HINTS

1 In this chapter, we again meet our old friend opportunity cost. Here we look at the costs firms face and examine the differences between *opportunity cost* measures used by economists and *accounting cost* measures. Opportunity cost, which is the relevant cost concept for economic decisions, includes *explicit* and *implicit costs*. Important examples of implicit costs include economic depreciation, the owner's forgone interest and forgone wages, and normal profits. Accounting cost includes only explicit, out-of-pocket costs, and conventional depreciation. These differences in cost measures between accountants and economists also lead to the following differences in profit measures.

Economists

Opportunity costs = Explicit costs + Implicit costs

Economic profit = Revenues – (Explicit costs + Implicit costs)

Accountants

Accounting costs = Explicit costs + Conventional depreciation

Accounting profit = Revenues – (Explicit costs + Conventional depreciation)

Implicit costs, which economists include but accountants exclude, are the key difference between economists' and accountants' measures of cost and profit. Accounting profit does *not* subtract normal profits or other implicit costs, so accounting profit is generally greater than economic profit.

Because normal profit is part of implicit costs, economic profit is profit over and above normal profit. If we think of normal profit as average profit, economic profit is *above-average* profit. Economic profit is a signal to firms that they are earning a greater return on investment than could be earned on average elsewhere in the economy.

Economic profit can also be negative if revenues are less than opportunity costs. As we will see in Chapter 11, such an *economic loss* is a signal to firms that they are earning a lower return on investment than could be earned on average elsewhere.

2 The difference between *technological efficiency* and *economic efficiency* is critical since economic decisions are made only on the basis of economic efficiency. Technological efficiency is an engineering concept and occurs when the firm produces a given output using the least inputs. There is no consideration of input costs. Economic efficiency occurs when the firm produces a given output at least cost. All technologically efficient production methods are not economically efficient. But all economically efficient methods are also technologically efficient. Competition favours firms that choose economically efficient production methods, and penalizes firms that do not.

3 This chapter introduces four types of market structure—perfect competition, monopolistic competition, oligopoly, and monopoly. These market structures will not mean that much to you now, but you are about to learn more about them in Chapters 11–13. Pay attention to Table 9.6 (page 210), which summarizes the characteristics of the different market structures and gives you a sense how the structures differ. As you study each market structure in the following chapters, refer back to Table 9.6 to put it in perspective.

SELF-TEST

True/False and Explain

The Firm and Its Economic Problem

1 The goal of the firm is to maximize market share.

2 Normal profit is the expected return for supplying entrepreneurial ability.

3 Implicit costs include economic profit.

4 A firm's opportunity cost of using its own machine is lower than if it had rented the machine.

Technological and Economic Efficiency

5 Economically efficient production methods use relatively less of higher-cost resources and relatively more of lower-cost resources.

6 An economically efficient production process can become economically inefficient if the relative prices of inputs change.

7 All economically efficient production methods are also technologically efficient.

Information and Organization

8 Giving corporate managers stock in their companies is a strategy for coping with a principal–agent problem.

9 In a principal–agent relationship between the stockholders and managers of Scotiabank, the stockholders are agents and the managers principals.

10 Owners of a corporation have limited liability.

Markets and the Competitive Environment

11 Product differentiation gives a monopolistically competitive firm some monopoly power.

12 A high concentration ratio always indicates a low degree of competition.

13 Concentration ratios measure barriers to entry in a market.

Markets and Firms

14 Outsourcing is an example of firm coordination of economic activity.

15 Markets will coordinate economic activity in situations where there are economies of scale.

Multiple-Choice

The Firm and Its Economic Problem

1 Abdul operates his own business and pays himself a salary of $20,000 per year. He refused a job that pays $30,000 per year. What is the opportunity cost of Abdul's time in the business?

a $10,000
b $20,000
c $30,000
d $50,000
e Zero

2 Economic profit is revenues minus

a explicit costs.
b implicit costs.
c opportunity costs.
d accounting costs.
e (explicit costs + conventional depreciation).

3 The rate of interest is 10 percent per year. You invest $50,000 of your own money in a business and earn *accounting* profit of $20,000 after one year. *Ceteris paribus*, what is your *economic* profit?

a $20,000
b $15,000
c $5,000
d $2,000
e –$15,000

4 In general,

1 opportunity cost is greater than accounting cost.
2 opportunity cost is less than accounting cost.
3 economic profit is greater than accounting profit.
4 economic profit is less than accounting profit.

a 1 only
b 1 and 3
c 1 and 4
d 2 and 3
e 2 and 4

5 A profit-maximizing firm is constrained by

a demand for its product.
b limited resources.
c available technology.
d limited information.
e all of the above.

Technology and Economic Efficiency

6 In Table 9.1, which method(s) of making a photon torpedo is/are technologically efficient?

a 1 only
b 2 only
c 3 only
d all of the above
e 1 and 3 only

TABLE **9.1** THREE METHODS OF MAKING ONE PHOTON TORPEDO

	Quantities of Inputs	
Method	**Labour**	**Capital**
1	5	10
2	10	7
3	15	5

7 Refer to Table 9.1. If the price of labour is $10 per unit and the price of capital is $20 per unit, which method(s) is/are economically efficient?

a 1 only
b 2 only
c 3 only
d all of the above
e 1 and 3 only

8 Which of the following statements is *true*?
- **a** All technologically efficient methods are also economically efficient.
- **b** All economically efficient methods are also technologically efficient.
- **c** Technological efficiency changes with changes in relative input prices.
- **d** Technologically efficient firms will be more likely to survive than economically efficient firms.
- **e** None of the above.

9 The business people are still talking over coffee. Which of their statements below describes *economic* efficiency?
- **a** "The new production process we've installed uses less capital and labour than the old one."
- **b** "The new assembly line has higher capital costs, but the fall in workers' hours has lowered overall costs."
- **c** "The costs per unit fell dramatically as we increased the length of our production runs."
- **d** "Despite the higher costs of negotiating the contracts, hiring the cleaning firm is much cheaper than using our own staff."
- **e** "The computer servicing people we hired work well as an integrated problem-solving group."

10 To produce a unit of output, Alphaworks uses 10 hours of labour and 5 kilos of material, Betaworks uses 5 hours of labour and 10 kilos of material, and Gammaworks uses 10 hours of labour and 10 kilos of material. If labour costs $10/hour and material costs $5/kilo, which firm(s) is/are economically efficient?
- **a** Alphaworks only
- **b** Betaworks only
- **c** Gammaworks only
- **d** Alphaworks and Betaworks
- **e** Alphaworks and Gammaworks

Information and Organization

11 Firms organize production using
- **a** command systems only.
- **b** incentive systems only.
- **c** command and incentive systems.
- **d** market systems only.
- **e** principal–agent systems only.

12 The possibility that an employee may not work hard is an example of the
- **a** limited liability problem.
- **b** principal–agent problem.
- **c** transactions cost problem.
- **d** technological efficiency problem.
- **e** partnership problem.

13 Firm strategies for coping with the principal–agent problem are
- **a** ownership, incentive pay, and long-term contracts.
- **b** proprietorship, partnership, and the corporation.
- **c** economies of scale, scope, and team production.
- **d** technology, information, and the market.
- **e** none of the above.

14 A firm that has two or more owners with joint unlimited liability is
- **a** a proprietorship.
- **b** a partnership.
- **c** a conglomerate.
- **d** a corporation.
- **e** none of the above.

15 What is a *disadvantage* of a corporation relative to a proprietorship or partnership?
- **a** owners' unlimited liability
- **b** profits are taxed twice as corporate profits and stockholders' dividends
- **c** high cost of capital
- **d** perpetual life
- **e** none of the above

16 The majority of business revenues are accounted for by
- **a** proprietorships.
- **b** partnerships.
- **c** corporations.
- **d** cooperatives.
- **e** not-for-profit organizations.

Markets and the Competitive Environment

17 The most extreme *absence* of competition is
- **a** perfect competition.
- **b** monopolistic competition.
- **c** product differentiation.
- **d** oligopoly.
- **e** monopoly.

18 A market structure where a small number of firms compete is
a perfect competition.
b monopolistic competition.
c product differentiation.
d oligopoly.
e monopoly.

19 Product differentiation is an important feature of the market structure of
a perfect competition.
b monopolistic competition.
c oligopoly.
d monopoly.
e all of the above.

20 The four-firm concentration ratio measures the share of the largest four firms in total industry
a profits.
b sales.
c cost.
d capital.
e none of the above.

21 Which of the following statements is *false*? Concentration ratios
a are national measures, but firms in some industries operate in regional markets.
b are national measures, but firms in some industries operate in global markets.
c tell us nothing about barriers to entry in the industry.
d tell us nothing about how sales vary among firms in the industry.
e have difficulty classifying multi-product firms by industry.

Markets and Firms

22 Which of the following statements is *false*?
a Firms and markets are institutions for coordinating economic activity.
b Firms organize productive resources in order to produce goods and services.
c Firms sell goods and services.
d Technologically efficient firms can eliminate scarcity.
e Firms use command systems to organize production.

23 Firms coordinate economic activity more efficiently than markets when firms have
a lower transactions costs.
b economics of scale.
c economies of scope.
d economies of team production.
e all of the above.

24 Economies of scale exist when
a transactions costs are high.
b transactions costs are low.
c hiring additional inputs does not increase the price of inputs.
d the cost of producing a unit of output falls as the output rate increases.
e the firm is too large and too diversified.

25 A firm with lower unit cost from producing a wider range of goods and services has economies of
a transactions costs.
b scale.
c scope.
d team production.
e market coordination.

Short Answer Problems

1 A year ago, Frank, the bricklayer, decided to start a business manufacturing doll furniture. Frank has two sisters; Angela is an accountant and Edith is an economist. (Both sisters are good with numbers, but Edith doesn't have enough personality to be an accountant.) Each of the sisters computes Frank's cost and profit for the first year using the following information.

1 Frank took no income from the firm. He has a standing offer to return to work as a bricklayer for $30,000 per year.

2 Frank rents his machinery for $9,000 a year.

3 Frank owns the garage in which he produces, but could rent it out at $3,000 per year.

4 To start the business, Frank used $10,000 of his own money and borrowed $30,000 at the market rate of interest of 10 percent per year.

5 Frank hires one employee at an annual salary of $20,000.

6 The cost of materials during the first year is $40,000.

7 Frank's entrepreneurial abilities are worth $14,000.

8 Frank's revenue for his first year is $100,000.

a Set up a table indicating how Angela and Edith would compute Frank's cost. Ignore any depreciation. What is Frank's cost as computed by Angela? by Edith?

b What is Frank's profit (or loss) as computed by Angela? by Edith?

2 According to your roommate, it is always more economically efficient to produce wheat using some machinery than using only labour. Suppose that there are two technologically efficient methods of producing one tonne of wheat.

- Method 1 requires 20 machine hours plus 20 hours of labour.
- Method 2 requires 100 hours of labour.

Country *A* has a highly developed industrial economy, while country *B* is less developed. In country *A* the price of an hour of labour (the wage rate) is $8, while the wage rate in country *B* is $4. The price of a machine hour is $20 in both countries. Which method is economically efficient in country *A*? in country *B*? Explain.

ⓒⓣ 3 Consider countries *A* and *B* described in Short Answer Problem **2**.

a What wage rate in country *B* would make the two methods equally efficient in country *B*?

b What price of a machine hour would make the two methods equally efficient in country *A*?

ⓒⓣ 4 Explain why an economically efficient production method must be technologically efficient.

5 The standard tip in a restaurant is 15 percent. Restaurants could raise their prices 15 percent, set a no-tipping policy, and pay servers the extra 15 percent. Use principal–agent analysis to explain why most restaurants prefer tipping.

6 The annual sales for firms in the Canadian thingamabob industry are reported in Table 9.2.

TABLE **9.2** THINGAMABOB INDUSTRY SALES

Firm	Sales ($)
Things 'R' Us	500
ThingMart	400
The Thing Club	350
Thingmania	250
All other firms	13,500

a Calculate the four-firm concentration ratio for the thingamabob industry.

b How competitive is the industry according to the ratio?

7 The U.S. yadayada industry consists of only five firms, whose markets shares are reported in Table 9.3.

TABLE **9.3** YADAYADA INDUSTRY MARKET SHARE

Firm	Market Share (%)
Jerry's Yadayadas	30
Elaine's Yadayadas	40
George's Yadayadas	20
Kramer's Yadayadas	5
Neuman's Yadayadas	5

a Calculate the Herfindahl–Hirschman Index for the yadayada industry.

b How competitive is the industry according to the index?

8 Considering the geographical scope of markets, how might a concentration ratio *understate* the degree of competitiveness in an industry? How might it *overstate* the degree of competitiveness?

9 a List and describe briefly the four types of market structure.

b For each of the four types of market structure, what, in general terms, is the value of the four-firm concentration ratio?

10 Markets and firms are alternative ways of coordinating economic activity that arise because of scarcity. Why do both firms and markets exist?

ANSWERS

True/False and Explain

1 F Maximize profit. (198)

2 T Definition. (199)

3 F Implicit costs include normal profit. (198–199)

4 F Opportunity cost equal for ownership or rental. Explicit cost lower for ownership. (198–199)

5 T That achieves lowest per-unit cost. (201–202)

6 T Technological efficiency does not change with price changes, but economic efficiency can. (201–202)

7 **T** But reverse is false—technological efficiency does not guarantee economic efficiency. (201–202)

8 **T** Makes managers' (agents) incentives same as shareholders' (principal). (203–204)

9 **F** Stockholders' (principals) profits depend on job done by managers (agents). (203–204)

10 **T** Liability only for value of investment. Sole proprietorship has unlimited liability. (204–205)

11 **T** Firm is sole producer of differentiated version of good. (207)

12 **F** Often true, but depends on geographical scope market, barriers to entry, and multi-product firms. (208–211)

13 **F** Small town with 4 restaurants has high concentration ratio but low entry barriers. (208–211)

14 **F** Example of market coordination. (212–213)

15 **F** Firms more efficient if economies of scale. (212–213)

Multiple-Choice

1 **c** Forgone income. (198–199)

2 **c** Definition. (198–199)

ⓔ 3 **b** Economic profit = accounting profit – implicit costs = $20,000 – (0.10 × $50,000). (198–199)

4 **c** See formulas in Helpful Hint **1**. (198–199)

5 **e** Technology, information, and market constraints. (200)

6 **d** No method has more of one input and same amount of other input, compared with alternative method. (201–202)

7 **b** 2 costs $240 while 1 and 3 cost $250. (201–202)

8 **b** **c** true for economic efficiency. Reverse of **d** true. (201–202)

9 **b** Lowest cost. **c** describes economies of scale. **d** and **e** describe market coordination of production. (201–202)

10 **b** Costs are Alphaworks = $125, Betaworks = $100, Gammaworks = $150. (201–202)

11 **c** Principal–agent solutions are part of incentive system. (203–204)

12 **b** See text discussion. (203–204)

13 **a** All create incentives for agent to work in interests of principal. **b** lists types of business organization, **c** lists advantages of firms over markets, **d** lists constraints on firms. (204)

14 **b** Definition. (204–205)

15 **b** See Text Table 9.4; **d** advantage, **a** and **c** disadvantages proprietorship and partnership. (205)

16 **c** See Text Figure 9.1. (206)

17 **e** Monopoly is least competition, perfect competition is the most. (207–208)

18 **d** Definition. (207–208)

19 **b** Many firms producing slightly differentiated products. (207–208)

20 **b** Definition. (208)

21 **d** Concentration ratios measure sales by size of firm. (209–210)

22 **d** Scarcity can never be eliminated. (212–213)

23 **e** See text discussion. (212–213)

24 **d** See text discussion. (212–213)

25 **c** Definition. (213)

Short Answer Problems

1 **a** Table 9.4 gives the cost as computed by Angela and Edith. The item numbers correspond to the item numbers in the problem.

TABLE **9.4**

Item Number	Angela's Accounting Computation (accounting cost)	Edith's Economic Computation (opportunity cost)
1.	$0	$30,000
2.	9,000	9,000
3.	0	3,000
4.	3,000	4,000
5.	20,000	20,000
6.	40,000	40,000
7.	0	$14,000
Total Cost	$72,000	$120,000

b Revenue is \$100,000. Angela's accounting computation of profit uses this formula:

Accounting profit = Revenues – Explicit costs

= \$100,000 – \$72,000

= \$28,000

Edith's economic computation of profit uses this formula:

Economic profit = Revenues – Opportunity costs

= \$100,000 – \$120,000

= –\$20,000 (an economic loss)

2 Both production methods are technologically efficient. The economically efficient production method has the lower cost of producing a tonne of wheat. In country *A*, the price of an hour of labour is \$8 and the price of a machine hour is \$20. The cost of producing a tonne of wheat is \$560 using method 1 and \$800 using method 2. Therefore method 1 is economically efficient for country *A*.

The price of an hour of labour is \$4 in country *B*, and thus it will face different costs of producing a tonne of wheat. Under method 1, the cost will be \$480 but under method 2, which uses only labour, the cost will be \$400. So method 2 is economically efficient for country *B*.

The reason for this difference is that economic efficiency means producing at lowest cost. If the relative prices of inputs are different in two countries, there will be differences in the relative costs of production using alternative methods. Therefore your roommate is wrong.

ⓔ **3** **a** If the wage rate in country *B* were to increase to \$5 an hour, then production of a tonne of wheat would be \$500 under either method. How did we obtain this answer? Express the cost under method 1 (C_1) and the cost under method 2 (C_2) as follows:

$$C_1 = 20P_m + 20P_h$$

$$C_2 = 100P_h$$

where P_m is the price of a machine hour and P_h is the price of an hour of labour (the wage rate). We are given that $P_m = \$20$ and asked to find the value of P_h that makes the two methods equally efficient; the value of P_h that makes $C_1 = C_2$. Thus we solve the following equation for P_h:

$$20P_m + 20P_h = 100P_h$$

$$20(\$20) + 20P_h = 100P_h$$

$$\$400 = 80P_h$$

$$\$5 = P_h$$

b If the price of a machine hour is \$32, production of a tonne of wheat would be \$800 under either method in country *A*. This question asks: Given the wage rate of \$8 (P_h) in country *A*, what value of P_m makes $C_1 = C_2$? Thus we solve the following equation for P_m:

$$20P_m + 20P_h = 100P_h$$

$$20P_m + 20(\$8) = 100(\$8)$$

$$20P_m = \$640$$

$$P_m = \$32$$

ⓔ **4** If a production method is economically efficient, then it is the least-cost method of producing a given level of output. Why does this imply that the method must also be technologically efficient—using the least inputs?

Try to imagine an economically efficient production method that is technologically *inefficient*. The method would *not* use the least inputs. No matter what the price of those inputs, there would always be a method that uses less inputs and therefore costs less. So a technologically inefficient method could *not* be economically efficient. Economic efficiency implies technological efficiency.

5 Restaurants face a classic principal–agent problem because servers may provide poor service to customers and drive away future business. Instead of having managers try to closely monitor each server, it is more efficient to delegate monitoring to customers. Customers tip on the basis of quality of service, creating an incentive for the server—the agent—to provide good service. This is exactly what the restaurant owner—the principal—wants.

6 a The four-firm concentration ratio is the percentage of the value of sales accounted for by the four largest firms in an industry. For thingamabobs, sales of the four largest firms are 500 + 400 + 350 + 250 = 1,500. Total industry sales are 1,500 + 13,500 = 15,000. So the ratio is 1,500/15,000 = 10 percent.

b Since a ratio of less than 40 percent indicates a competitive market, the thingamabob industry is very competitive.

7 a The Herfindahl–Hirschman Index, for an industry of fewer than 50 firms, is the square of the percentage market share of each firm. For the yadayada industry, the index is

$$30^2 + 40^2 + 20^2 + 5^2 + 5^2 = 2,950$$

b Since an index of greater than 1,800 indicates a concentrated market, the yadayada industry is very concentrated.

8 Concentration ratios are calculated from a national geographical perspective. If the actual scope of the market is not national, the concentration ratio will likely misstate the degree of competitiveness in an industry. If the actual market is global, the concentration ratio will understate the degree of competitiveness. A firm may have a concentration ratio of 100 as the only producer in the nation, but may face a great deal of international competition. When the scope of the market is regional, the concentration ratio will overstate the degree of competitiveness. The concentration ratio includes firms elsewhere in the nation that are not real competitors in the region.

9 a Perfect competition—many firms; identical products; easy entry of new firms.

Monopolistic competition—many firms; slightly differentiated products; easy entry.

Oligopoly—few firms; identical or differentiated products; some barriers to entry.

Monopoly—single firm; product with no close substitutes; high barriers to new entry.

b Perfect competition—close to 0 percent.
Monopolistic competition—low.
Oligopoly—high.
Monopoly—100 percent.

10 As we saw in the example on text pages 212–213, car repair can be coordinated by the market or by a firm. The institution (market or firm) that actually coordinates will be the one that is more efficient. Where there are significant transactions costs, economies of scale, or economies of team production, firms are likely to be more efficient, and firms will dominate the coordination of economic activity. But the efficiency of firms is limited, and there are many circumstances where market coordination of economic activity dominates because it is more efficient.

Chapter 10
Output and Costs

KEY CONCEPTS

Decision Time Frames

Firm has two decision time frames.

- ♦ **Short run**—quantities of some resources fixed. Quantities of other resources are variable.
  - Fixed resources are called the firm's fixed *plant*—usually technology, buildings, capital, and management.
  - Variable resources—usually labour.
  - Short-run decisions are easily reversed.
- ♦ **Long run**—quantities of all resources variable.
  - **Sunk cost**—*past* cost of buying a new plant. Firm's decisions depend only on short-run cost of changing labour input and long-run cost of changing plant. Sunk costs are irrelevant.
  - Long-run decisions are *not* easily reversed.

Short-Run Technology Constraint

Short-run production described by

- ♦ **total product** curve (*TP*)—maximum attainable output with fixed quantity capital as quantity labour varies.
- ♦ **marginal product** curve (*MP*)—ΔTP resulting from one-unit increase variable input.
- ♦ **average product** curve (*AP*)—*TP* per unit variable input.

As increase variable input, *MP* increases (increasing marginal returns), reaches maximum, and then decreases (**diminishing marginal returns**). When $MP > AP$, *AP* increasing. When $MP < AP$, *AP* decreasing. When $MP = AP$, maximum *AP*.

- ♦ **Law of diminishing returns**—with given quantity fixed inputs, as firm uses more variable input, its *MP* eventually diminishes.

Short-Run Cost

Short-run cost curves determined by technology and prices of productive resources.

- ♦ **Total cost** (*TC*) = *TFC* + *TVC*
  - **Total fixed cost** (*TFC*)—cost of fixed inputs (including normal profit)
  - **Total variable cost** (*TVC*)—cost of variable inputs
- ♦ **Marginal cost** (*MC*)—ΔTC resulting from one-unit increase in output
- ♦ **Average total cost** (*ATC*) = *AFC* + *AVC*
  - **Average fixed cost** (*AFC*)—total fixed cost per unit output
  - **Average variable cost** (*AVC*)—total variable cost per unit output
  - *AFC* curve decreases constantly as output increases.
  - *AVC*, *ATC*, and *MC* curves are U-shaped.
  - As output increases, *MC* decreases, reaches minimum, and then increases.
  - When $MC < ATC$, *ATC* decreases.

    When $MC > ATC$, *ATC* increases.

    When $MC = ATC$, minimum *ATC*.

    Same relation *MC* and *AVC*.

Long-Run Cost

Long-run cost—cost of production when all inputs (capital and labour) adjusted to economically efficient quantities.

- ♦ *Production function*—relationship between maximum attainable output and quantities of all inputs—describes long-run costs.

Long-run average cost curve (*LRAC*)—a planning curve that tells the firm the plant size and quantity of labour to use at each output to minimize cost. Consists of the segments of different short-run *ATC* curves along which average total cost is lowest.

- ♦ In the long run, when all inputs increase by same percentage, increases in output can show three different returns to scale.
  - **Economies of scale** (increasing returns to scale)—percentage increase firm's output > percentage increase inputs. *LRAC* slopes downward.
  - **Constant returns to scale**—percentage increase firm's output = percentage increase inputs. *LRAC* horizontal.
  - **Diseconomies of scale** (decreasing returns to scale)—percentage increase firm's output < percentage increase inputs. *LRAC* slopes upward.
- ♦ **Minimum efficient scale**—smallest quantity of output yielding minimum *LRAC*.

HELPFUL HINTS

1 Be sure to understand how economists use the terms *short run* and *long run*. These terms do *not* refer to calendar time. Think of them as planning horizons. The short run is a planning horizon short enough that while some resources are variable, at least one resource cannot be varied but is fixed. The long run refers to a planning horizon that is long enough that all resources can be varied.

2 This chapter introduces many new concepts and graphs and may at first appear overwhelming. Don't get lost among the trees and lose sight of the forest. There is a simple and fundamental relationship between product curves and cost curves.

The chapter explains the short-run product curves and concepts of total product, marginal product, and average product. This is followed by the short-run cost function and concepts of total cost, marginal cost, average variable cost, and average total cost.

But all of these seemingly separate concepts are related to the *law of diminishing returns*. The law states that as a firm uses more of a variable input, with a given quantity of fixed inputs, the marginal product of the variable input eventually diminishes. This law explains why the marginal product and average product curves eventually fall, and why the total product curve becomes flatter. When productivity falls, costs increase, and the law explains the eventual upward slope of the marginal cost curve. When marginal product falls, marginal cost increases.

The marginal cost curve, in turn, explains the U-shape of the average variable cost and average total cost curves. When the marginal cost curve is below the average variable (or total) cost curve, the average variable (or total) cost curve is falling. When marginal cost is above the average variable (or total) cost curve, the average variable (or total) cost curve is rising. The marginal cost curve intersects the average variable (or total) cost curve at the minimum point on the average variable (or total) cost curve.

Use the law of diminishing returns as the key to understanding the relationships between the many short-run concepts and graphs in the chapter. But all concepts and graphs are not equally important. Pay most attention to the unit-cost concepts and graphs—especially marginal cost, average variable cost, and average total cost—because these will be used the most in later chapters to analyze the behaviour of firms.

3 Be sure to thoroughly understand Figure 10.1 (Text Figure 10.5 on page 225). It is the most important graph in the chapter and one of the most important graphs in all of microeconomics.

FIGURE **10.1**

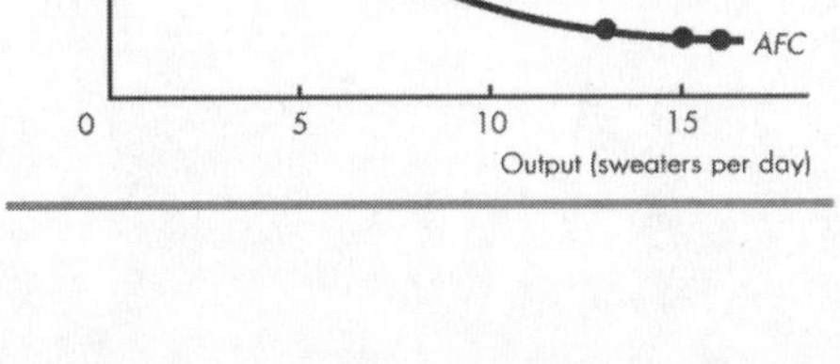

The curves for average total cost (*ATC*), average fixed cost (*AFC*), and average variable cost (*AVC*) are derived by taking the values for *TC*, *TFC*, and *TVC* and dividing by quantity of output. Since these are average values for a fixed quantity of output, they are plotted directly above the corresponding units of output.

On the other hand, marginal cost (*MC*) is the *change* in total cost (or equivalently, in total variable cost) resulting from a one-unit increase in output. It is plotted *midway* between the corresponding units of output. The *ATC*, *AVC*, and *MC* curves are crucially important. The *ATC* and *AVC* curves are both U-shaped. The *MC* curve is also U-shaped and intersects the *ATC* and *AVC* curves at their minimum points. The *MC* curve is below the *ATC* and *AVC* curves when *ATC* and *AVC* are falling, and above the *ATC* and *AVC* curves when they are rising. The less important *AFC* curve falls continuously as output increases.

4 You will probably draw a graph like the one in Figure 10.1 at least a hundred times in this course. Here are some hints on drawing the graph quickly and easily:

- Be sure to label the axes: quantity of output (*Q*) on the horizontal axis and average cost on the vertical axis.
- Draw an upward-sloping marginal cost curve, as shown here in Figure 10.2. The marginal cost curve can have a small downward-sloping section at first, but this is not important. Next, draw a shallow U-shaped curve that falls until it intersects the marginal cost curve, and then rises. Then pick a point further up the marginal cost curve. Draw another shallow U-shaped curve whose minimum point passes through your second point. Finally, label the curves.

Any time a test question (including those in the Self-Test) asks about these curves, *draw a graph* before you answer.

FIGURE **10.2**

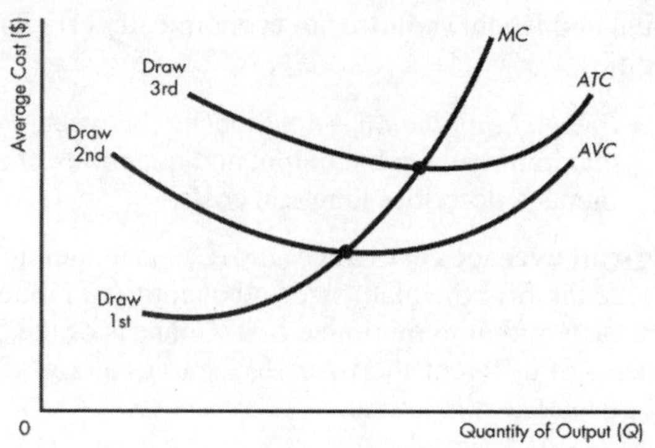

5 The later sections of the chapter explain long-run costs using a production function where both labour and capital inputs are variable. While diminishing returns is the key for understanding short-run costs, the concept of *returns to scale* is the key for understanding long-run costs. Returns to scale are the increase in output relative to the increase in inputs when all inputs are increased by the same percentage. Returns to scale can be increasing, constant, or decreasing, and correspond to the downward-sloping, horizontal, and upward-sloping sections of the long-run average cost curve.

SELF-TEST

True/False and Explain

Decision Time Frames

1 All resources are fixed in the short run.

2 The firm's short-run decisions are easily reversed.

3 The firm's long-run decisions depend on sunk costs.

Short-Run Technology Constraint

4 Given a fixed quantity of capital, if 2 additional labourers produce 15 additional units of output, the marginal product of labour is 15 units of output.

5 The law of diminishing returns implies that eventually the marginal product curve will be negatively sloped as the variable input increases.

6 Marginal product is measured by the slope of the total product curve.

7 The law of diminishing returns implies that we will not observe a range of increasing marginal returns.

8 If the marginal product of labour is greater than the average product of labour, average product is increasing.

Short-Run Cost

9 Average variable cost reaches its minimum at the same level of output at which average product is a maximum.

10 If average variable cost is decreasing, then marginal cost must be decreasing.

11 The average total cost curve always intersects the minimum point of the marginal cost curve.

Long-Run Cost

12 No part of any short-run average total cost curve can lie below the long-run average cost curve.

13 Economies of scale means that the long-run average cost curve is positively sloped.

14 If a firm can double its output by building a second plant identical to its first plant, there are constant returns to scale.

15 Minimum efficient scale occurs at the minimum point on the average total cost curve.

Multiple-Choice

Decision Time Frames

1 In economics, the short run is a time period in which
- **a** one year or less elapses.
- **b** all resources are variable.
- **c** all resources are fixed.
- **d** some resources are variable but some resources are fixed.
- **e** all resources are variable but the technology is fixed.

2 Long-run decisions
- **a** are not easily reversed.
- **b** do not depend on sunk costs.
- **c** involve changes in a firm's plant.
- **d** can vary all resources of a firm.
- **e** are all of the above.

Short-Run Technology Constraint

3 The average product of labour is
- **a** the slope of the total product curve.
- **b** the slope of the marginal product curve.
- **c** the increase in total product divided by the increase in labour employed.
- **d** the total product divided by the quantity of labour employed.
- **e** none of the above.

4 When the marginal product of labour is less than the average product of labour,
  a the average product of labour is increasing.
  b the marginal product of labour is increasing.
  c the total product curve is negatively sloped.
  d the firm is experiencing diminishing returns.
  e none of the above is true.

5 Refer to Figure 10.3 illustrating Swanky's short-run total product curve. Which of the following statements is *true*?
  a Points above the curve are attainable and inefficient.
  b Points below the curve are attainable and inefficient.
  c Points below the curve are unattainable and inefficient.
  d Points on the curve are unattainable and efficient.
  e Points on the curve all have equal marginal products.

FIGURE **10.3**

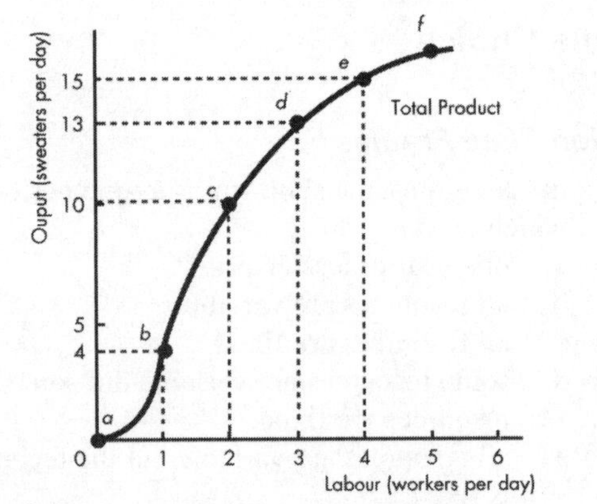

6 Refer to Figure 10.3 illustrating Swanky's short-run total product curve. Marginal product reaches a maximum when you add which labourer?
  a 1st labourer
  b 2nd labourer
  c 3rd labourer
  d 4th labourer
  e 5th labourer

7 Which of the following statements by a restaurant owner refers to the law of diminishing returns?
  a "The higher the quality of the ingredients we use, the higher the cost of producing each meal."
  b "If we double the size of our premises and double everything else—kitchen staff, serving staff, equipment—we can increase the number of meals we serve, but not to double current levels."
  c "We can increase the number of meals we serve by just adding more kitchen staff, but each additional worker adds fewer meals than the previous worker because traffic in the kitchen will get worse."
  d "We can serve the same number of meals with fewer kitchen staff, but we would have to buy more labour-saving kitchen equipment."
  e "We can serve the same number of meals with less kitchen equipment, but we would have to hire more kitchen staff."

Short-Run Cost

8 The vertical distance between the *TC* and *TVC* curves is
  a decreasing as output increases.
  b increasing as output increases.
  c equal to *AFC*.
  d equal to *TFC*.
  e equal to *MC*.

9 Total cost is $20 at 4 units of output and $36 at 6 units of output. Between 4 and 6 units of output, marginal cost
  a is less than average total cost.
  b is equal to average total cost.
  c is equal to average variable cost.
  d is greater than average total cost.
  e cannot be compared with any average cost without additional information.

10 Marginal cost is the amount that
  a total cost increases when one more labourer is hired.
  b fixed cost increases when one more labourer is hired.
  c variable cost increases when one more labourer is hired.
  d total cost increases when one more unit of output is produced.
  e fixed cost increases when one more unit of output is produced.

11 A firm's fixed costs are $100. If total costs are $200 for one unit of output and $310 for two units, what is the marginal cost of the second unit?
- **a** $100
- **b** $110
- **c** $200
- **d** $210
- **e** $310

12 If *ATC* is falling *MC* must be
- **a** rising.
- **b** falling.
- **c** equal to *ATC*.
- **d** above *ATC*.
- **e** below *ATC*.

13 Which of the following does *not* cause decreasing *ATC*?
- **a** decreasing marginal cost
- **b** decreasing average variable cost
- **c** decreasing average fixed cost
- **d** increasing marginal product
- **e** increasing returns to scale

14 The average variable cost curve will shift up if
- **a** there is an increase in fixed costs.
- **b** there is a technological advance.
- **c** the price of a variable input decreases.
- **d** the price of a variable input increases.
- **e** the price of output increases.

15 The marginal cost (*MC*) curve intersects the
- **a** *ATC*, *AVC*, and *AFC* curves at their minimum points.
- **b** *ATC* and *AFC* curves at their minimum points.
- **c** *AVC* and *AFC* curves at their minimum points.
- **d** *ATC* and *AVC* curves at their minimum points.
- **e** *TC* and *TVC* curves at their minimum points.

16 According to the law of diminishing returns,
1. marginal productivity eventually rises.
2. marginal productivity eventually falls.
3. marginal cost eventually rises.
4. marginal cost eventually falls.

- **a** 1 and 3
- **b** 1 and 4
- **c** 2 and 3
- **d** 2 and 4
- **e** 4 only

17 Average variable cost is at a minimum at the same output where
- **a** average product is at a maximum.
- **b** average product is at a minimum.
- **c** marginal product is at a maximum.
- **d** marginal product is at a minimum.
- **e** marginal cost is at a minimum.

18 A rise in the price of a fixed input will cause a firm's
- **a** average variable cost curve to shift up.
- **b** average total cost curve to shift up.
- **c** average total cost curve to shift down.
- **d** marginal cost curve to shift up.
- **e** marginal cost curve to shift down.

19 A technological advance will shift
1. *TP*, *AP*, and *MP* curves up.
2. *TP*, *AP*, and *MP* curves down.
3. *TC*, *ATC*, and *MC* curves up.
4. *TC*, *ATC*, and *MC* curves down.

- **a** 1 and 3
- **b** 1 and 4
- **c** 2 and 3
- **d** 2 and 4
- **e** none of the above

Long-Run Cost

20 In the long run,
- **a** only the plant size is fixed.
- **b** all inputs are variable.
- **c** all inputs are fixed.
- **d** a firm must experience diseconomies of scale.
- **e** none of the above is true.

21 The long-run average cost curve
- **a** is a planning curve.
- **b** identifies the cost-minimizing plant size and quantity of labour for each output level.
- **c** is the relation between lowest attainable *ATC* and output when both plant size and labour are variable.
- **d** consists of the segments of different short-run *ATC* curves along which average total cost is lowest.
- **e** is all of the above.

22 Constant returns to scale means that as all inputs are increased,
- **a** total output remains constant.
- **b** average total cost remains constant.
- **c** average total cost increases at the same rate as inputs.
- **d** long-run average cost remains constant.
- **e** long-run average cost rises at the same rate as inputs.

23 If all inputs are increased by 10 percent and output increases by less than 10 percent, it must be the case that
- a average total cost is decreasing.
- b average total cost is increasing.
- c the *LRAC* curve is negatively sloped.
- d there are economies of scale.
- e there are diseconomies of scale.

24 Minimum efficient scale is the smallest quantity of output at which
- a the *LRAC* curve reaches it lowest level.
- b the *ATC* curve reaches its lowest level.
- c the *AFC* curve reaches its lowest level.
- d economies of scale begin.
- e diminishing returns begin.

25 A firm will always want to increase its scale of plant if
- a it persistently produces on the upward-sloping part of its short-run average total cost curve.
- b it persistently produces on the downward-sloping part of its short-run average total cost curve.
- c it is producing below minimum efficient scale.
- d marginal cost is below average total cost.
- e marginal cost is below average variable cost.

Short Answer Problems

1 Why must the marginal cost curve intersect the average total cost curve at the minimum point of the average total cost curve?

2 Explain the connection, if any, between the U-shape of the average total cost curve and (a) fixed costs and (b) the law of eventually diminishing returns.

ⓔ 3 Use the concepts of marginal and average to answer the following question. Suppose the worst student at Hubertville High School transfers to Histrionic High School. Is it possible that the average grade-point of the students at each school rises? Explain.

4 What is the difference, if any, between diminishing returns and diseconomies of scale?

5 For a given scale of plant, Table 10.1 gives the total monthly output of golf carts attainable using varying quantities of labour.

TABLE **10.1** MONTHLY GOLF CART PRODUCTION

Labourers (per month)	Output (units per month)	Marginal Product	Average Product
0	0		
1	1		
2	3		
3	6		
4	12		
5	17		
6	20		
7	22		
8	23		

- a Complete the table for the marginal product and average product of labour. (Note that marginal product should be entered *midway* between rows to emphasize that it is the result of *changing* inputs—moving from one row to the next. Average product corresponds to a fixed quantity of labour and should be entered on the appropriate row.)
- b Label the axes and draw a graph of the total product curve (*TP*).
- c On a separate piece of paper, label the axes and draw a graph of both marginal product (*MP*) and average product (*AP*). (Marginal product should be plotted *midway* between the corresponding units of labour, as in Text Figure 10.2(b) on page 223, while average product should be plotted directly above the corresponding units of labour, as in Text Figure 10.3 on page 224.)

6 Now let's examine the short-run costs of golf cart production. The first two columns of Table 10.1 are reproduced in the first two columns of Table 10.2. The cost of 1 labourer (the only variable input) is $2,000 per month. Total fixed cost is $2,000 per month.

TABLE **10.2** SHORT-RUN COSTS (MONTHLY)

L	*Q*	*TFC* ($)	*TVC* ($)	*TC* ($)	*MC* ($)	*AFC* ($)	*AVC* ($)	*ATC* ($)
0	0	2,000						
1	1							
2	3							
3	6							
4	12							
5	17							
6	20							
7	22							
8	23							

a Given this information, complete Table 10.2 by computing total fixed cost (*TFC*), total variable cost (*TVC*), total cost (*TC*), marginal cost (*MC*), average fixed cost (*AFC*), average variable cost (*AVC*), and average total cost (*ATC*). Your completed table should look like the table in Text Figure 10.5 on page 227, with marginal cost entered *midway* between the rows.

b Label the axes and draw the *TC*, *TVC*, and *TFC* curves on a single graph.

c Label the axes and draw the *MC*, *ATC*, *AVC*, and *AFC* curves on a single graph. Be sure to plot *MC midway* between the corresponding units of output.

7 Now suppose that the price of a labourer increases to $2,500 per month. Construct a table for the new *MC* and *ATC* curves (output, *MC*, *ATC*) for golf cart production. Label the axes and draw a graph of the new *MC* and *ATC* curves. What is the effect of the increase in the price of the variable input on these curves?

8 Return to the original price of labour of $2,000 per month. Now suppose that we double the quantity of fixed inputs so that total fixed costs also double to $4,000 per month. This increases the monthly output of golf carts for each quantity of labour as indicated in Table 10.3.

TABLE **10.3** NEW MONTHLY PRODUCTION OF GOLF CARTS

Labourers (per month)	Output (units per month)
0	0
1	1
2	4
3	10
4	19
5	26
6	31
7	34
8	36

a Construct a table for the new *MC* and *ATC* curves (output, *MC*, *ATC*). Label the axes and draw a graph of the new *MC* and *ATC* curves.

b What is the effect on these curves (compared with the original *MC* and *ATC* curves in Short Answer Problem **6c**) of an increase in "plant size"? Are there economies of scale?

c Draw the long-run average cost (*LRAC*) curve if these are the only two plant sizes available.

9 At a firm's minimum efficient scale of plant, long-run average cost is at its lowest level. Therefore, firms should always build plants at minimum efficient scale. Agree or disagree with this statement and explain your answer.

10 Figure 10.4 gives a sequence of short-run *ATC* curves numbered 1 through 7 corresponding to seven different plant sizes.

FIGURE **10.4**

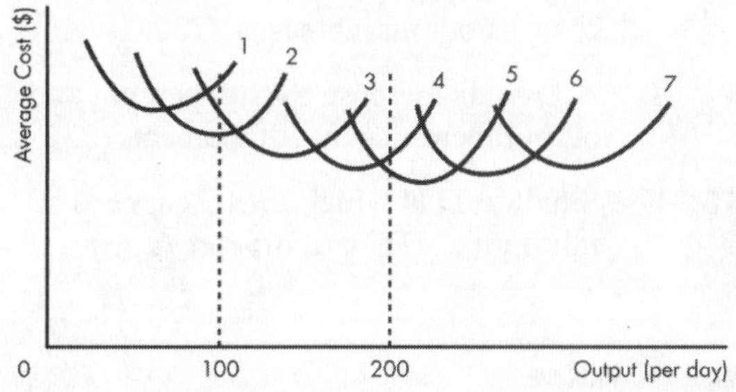

a Draw the long-run average cost curve on Figure 10.4.

b If the desired level of output is 100 units per day, what is the best plant size? (Give the number of the associated short-run *ATC* curve.) What if the desired level of output is 200 units per day?

ANSWERS

True/False and Explain

1 F Some resources fixed, some variable. (220)

2 T Firm can change output by changing quantity of labour hired. Long-run decisions not easily reversed. (220)

3 F Sunk costs are past costs and are irrelevant to all firm decisions about present or future. (220)

4 F $\Delta TP/\Delta L = 15/2 = 7.5$. (221–223)

5 T *MP* must eventually diminish with increasing *L*. (222–223)

6 T $\Delta TP/\Delta L$. (222–223)

7 F *Eventually* diminishing returns. *MP* can initially increase. (222–223)

8 T See Text Figure 10.3 and grade-point discussion for intuition. (224)

9 T $AVC = TVC/Q = WL/Q = W/(Q/L) = W/AP$. (228)

10 F *MC* must be below *AVC*, but *MC* may be increasing or decreasing. (226–228)

11 F *MC* intersect minimum *ATC*. (226–227)

12 T *LRAC* consists of lowest-cost segments of all average total cost curves. (231–232)

13 F Negatively sloped; falling long-run average costs as output increases. (232)

14 T All inputs increase by 100 percent and output increases by 100 percent. (232–233)

15 F Smallest *Q* at which *LRAC* curve is at minimum. *ATC* is short-run. (233)

Multiple-Choice

1 d Definition. (220)

2 e From definition of long run. (220)

3 d Definition. (221–223)

4 d When $MP < AP$, *MP* is decreasing (diminishing returns), *AP* is decreasing, and *TP* is positively sloped. (221–223)

5 b Attainable but not maximum *TP*. (221–222)

6 b MP = slope TP curve = 6 for 2nd labourer. (221–223)

7 c *MP* decreases as restaurant uses more variable resource (labour). (223)

8 d $TC = TFC + TVC$. Distance constant. (225–226)

9 d $MC = 16/2 = 8$. *ATC* is \$5 at 4 units and \$6 at 6 units. (225–227)

10 d Definition; **b** and **e** wrong because fixed costs don't change; **a** and **c** wrong because *MC* can also decrease and may be affected by costs other than labour. (226)

11 b Fixed costs irrelevant. $\Delta TC/\Delta Q = (\$310 - \$200)/(2 - 1)$. (225–226)

12 e *MC* could be increasing or decreasing below *ATC* when *ATC* is decreasing. (226–227)

13 e Increasing returns to scale is long-run concept; *ATC* is short-run concept. (226–228)

14 d **a** and **e** don't affect *AVC*; **b** and **c** shift *AVC* down. (228–229)

15 d *AFC* always decreases, *TC* and *TVC* always increase. (226–228)

16 c Decreasing *MP* causes increasing *MC*. (226–228)

17 a *AVC* decreases as long as *AP* is increasing. See Text Figure 10.6. (228)

18 b Won't affect *AVC* or *MC*. (228–227)

19 b Productivity increases, costs decrease. (228–229)

20 b Definition. All returns to scale possible in long run. (220, 230)

21 e All definitions of *LRAC*. (231–232)

22 d *LRAC* horizontal. (233)

23 e Definition. Since all resources variable, **a** and **b** irrelevant. (232–233)

24 a Definition of a long-run concept; **b**, **c**, **e** are short-run concepts; **d** would be correct if where economies of scale *end*. (233)

25 a Plant already too big in **b**; for **c**, sales may not justify a plant that big; **d** and **e** relate to short run. (230–233)

Short Answer Problems

1 The average total cost curve is U-shaped, first falling and then rising as output increases. When average total cost is falling, marginal cost must be less than average total cost, and when average total cost is rising, marginal cost must be greater than average total cost. Therefore the marginal cost curve must intersect the average total cost curve at its minimum point. In order for average total cost to fall, it must have been *pulled down* by a smaller increase in cost from the last unit of output. Therefore marginal cost is lower than average total cost. Similarly, when average total cost is rising, it must be that it has been *pulled up* by a higher marginal cost. When average total cost is at its minimum, it is neither falling nor rising, so marginal cost cannot be lower or higher than average total cost. Therefore, marginal cost must be equal to average total cost.

2 The U-shape of the average total cost (*ATC*) curve arises from the opposing forces of (a) spreading fixed costs over a larger output and (b) the law of eventually diminishing returns.

As output increases, fixed costs are spread over a larger output so average fixed cost (*AFC*) falls. Initially, as output increases, the marginal productivity of the variable resource rises, causing average variable cost (*AVC*) to fall. Falling *AVC*, together with falling *AFC*, causes average total cost (*ATC*) to fall, contributing to the downward-sloping portion of *ATC*. Eventually, as output increases, diminishing returns set in, marginal productivity falls, and *AVC* rises. Eventually, *AVC* rises more quickly than *AFC* falls, contributing to the upward-sloping portion of *ATC*.

3 Yes, it is possible that the average grade-point of the students at each school rises. Think of the transferring student as the *marginal* student. If his grade-point average, although the lowest at Hubertville High, is higher than the *average* grade-point at Histrionic High, then the results are: the *average* grade-point at Hubertville High rises with the elimination of the lowest grade-point; and the average grade-point at Histrionic High rises because the transferring (*marginal*) student's grade-point pulls up the *average* grade-point.

4 The law of diminishing returns states that as a firm uses more of a variable input, with a given quantity of fixed inputs, the marginal product of the variable input eventually diminishes. Diseconomies of scale occur when a firm increases all of its inputs by an equal percentage, and this results in a lower percentage increase in output. Diminishing (marginal) returns is a short-run concept since there must be a fixed input. Diseconomies of scale is a long-run concept since all inputs must be variable.

5 a The completed Table 10.1 is shown here as Table 10.1 Solution.

TABLE **10.1** SOLUTION
MONTHLY GOLF CART PRODUCTION

Labourers (per month)	Output (units per month)	Marginal Product	Average Product
0	0		0
		1	
1	1		1.00
		2	
2	3		1.50
		3	
3	6		2.00
		6	
4	12		3.00
		5	
5	17		3.40
		3	
6	20		3.33
		2	
7	22		3.14
		1	
8	23		2.88

b Figure 10.5 gives the graph of the total product curve.

FIGURE **10.5**

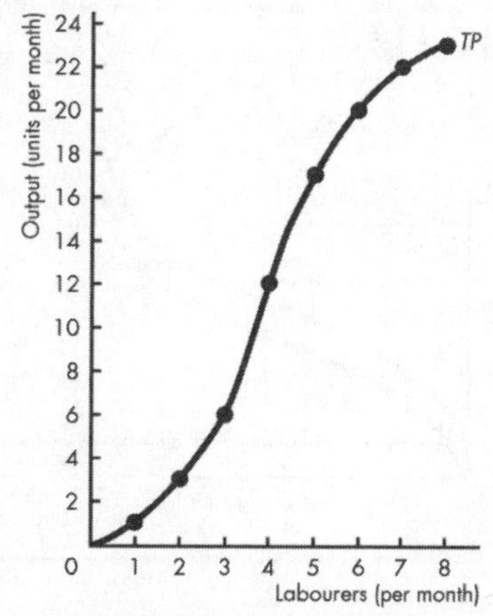

c Figure 10.6 gives the graphs of marginal product and average product.

FIGURE **10.6**

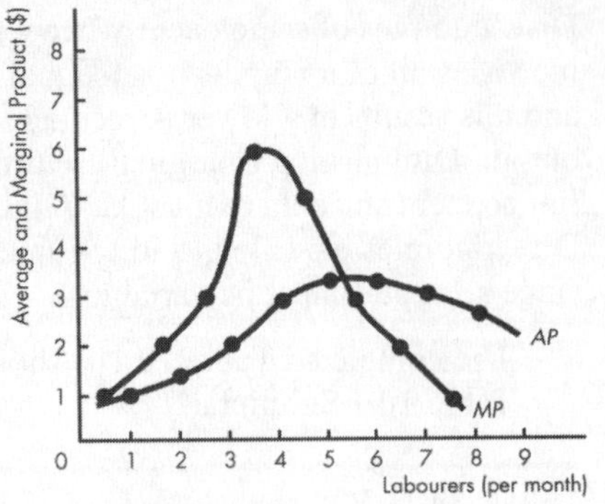

6 a Completed Table 10.2 is given here as Table 10.2 Solution.

TABLE **10.2** SOLUTION
SHORT-RUN COSTS (MONTHLY)

L	Q	TFC ($)	TVC ($)	TC ($)	MC ($)	AFC ($)	AVC ($)	ATC ($)
0	0	2,000	0	2,000		—	—	—
					2,000			
1	1	2,000	2,000	4,000		2,000	2,000	4,000
					1,000			
2	3	2,000	4,000	6,000		667	1,333	2,000
					667			
3	6	2,000	6,000	8,000		333	1,000	1,333
					333			
4	12	2,000	8,000	10,000		167	667	833
					400			
5	17	2,000	10,000	12,000		118	588	706
					667			
6	20	2,000	12,000	14,000		100	600	700
					1,000			
7	22	2,000	14,000	16,000		91	636	727
					2,000			
8	23	2,000	16,000	18,000		87	696	783

b The *TC, TVC,* and *TFC* curves are graphed in Figure 10.7.

FIGURE **10.7**

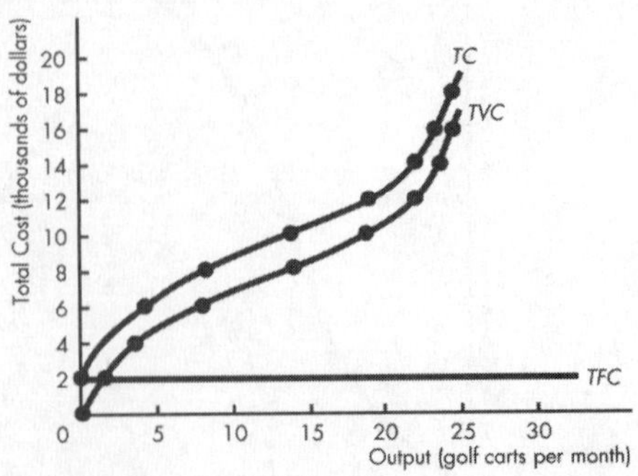

c The *MC*, *ATC*, *AVC*, and *AFC* curves are graphed in Figure 10.8.

FIGURE **10.8**

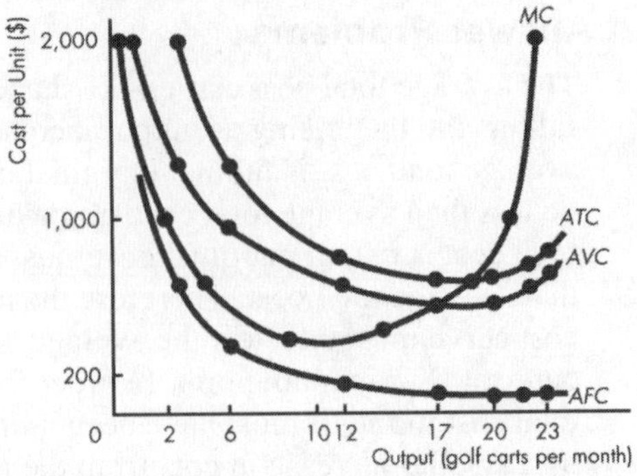

7 The new *MC* and *ATC* curves (and the associated table) for golf cart production are given in Figure 10.9. The original curves, MC_0 and ATC_0, are indicated for reference. The new curves are labelled MC_1 and ATC_1. Both curves have shifted up as a result of an increase in the price of labour.

FIGURE **10.9**

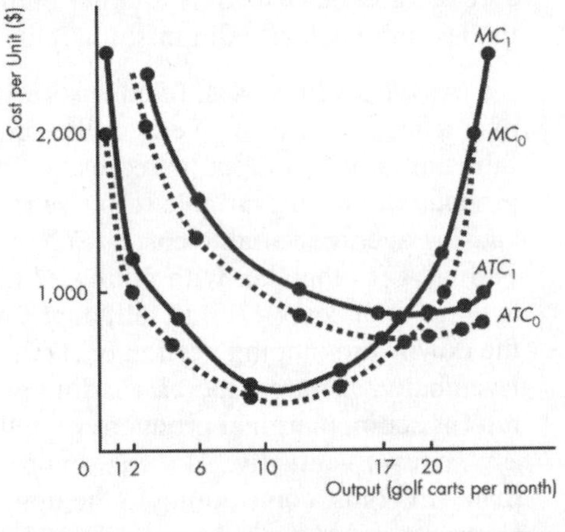

Output	MC ($)	ATC ($)
0		0
	2,500	
1		4,500
	1,250	
3		2,333
	833	
6		1,583
	417	
12		1,000
	500	
17		853
	833	
20		850
	1,250	
22		886
	2,500	
23		957

8 a The new MC and ATC curves (and the associated table) are given in Figure 10.10. The new curves are labelled MC_2 and ATC_2. The original curves, MC_0 and ATC_0, are indicated for reference.

FIGURE **10.10**

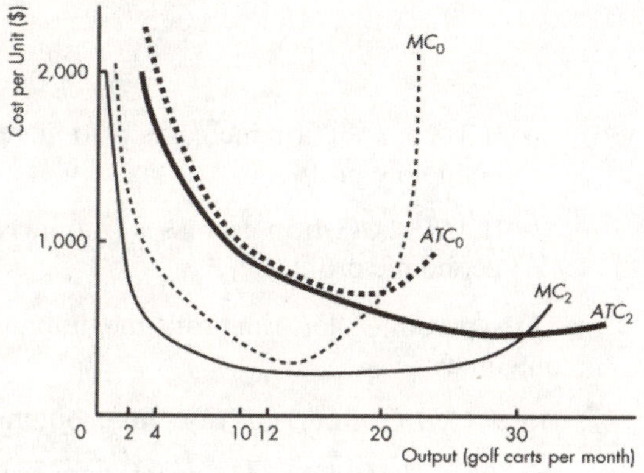

Output	MC ($)	ATC ($)
0		0
	2,000	
1		6,000
	667	
4		2,000
	333	
10		1,000
	222	
19		632
	286	
26		538
	400	
31		516
	667	
34		529

b The curves have shifted (generally) down and to the right as a result of increasing the plant size. There are economies of scale (increasing returns to scale) up to the level of output at which MC_2 intersects ATC_2 (approximately 32 units).

c The long-run average cost curve is indicated in Figure 10.10 by the heavy line tracing out the lowest short-run average total cost of producing each level of output. In this example, that happens to correspond entirely to ATC_2.

9 Disagree. To produce at minimum efficient scale, a firm must have a certain quantity of output. If demand for the firm's product does not justify that quantity of output, the firm with a minimum efficient scale plant may actually have higher short-run average total costs. Consider Text Figure 10.7. The minimum efficient scale plant has ATC_2. But if the firm is producing less than 9 units of output, average total cost would actually be lower with plant having ATC_1.

10 a The long-run average cost curve is indicated in Figure 10.4 Solution by the heavy scalloped-shaped curve tracing out the lowest short-run average cost of producing each level of output.

b For output of 100 units, the best plant size is associated with short-run average total cost curve 2. For output of 200 units, the best plant size is associated with short-run average total cost curve 5.

FIGURE **10.4** SOLUTION

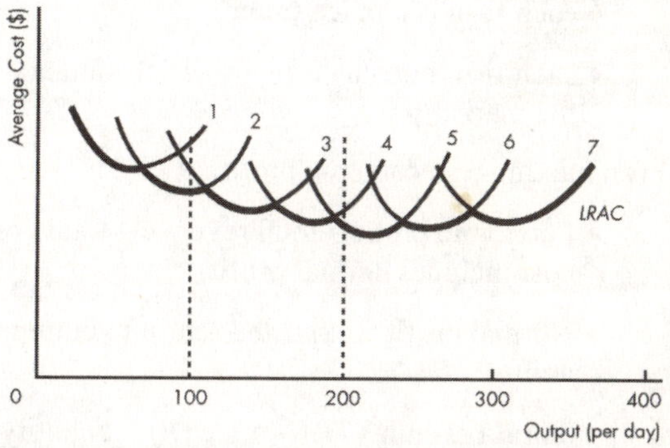

Chapter 11 Perfect Competition

KEY CONCEPTS

Competition

Perfect competition is a model of market structure where the force of *competition* is extreme and firms have no *market power*. Assumptions include many firms; identical products; many buyers; free entry; no advantages for existing firms over new firms; complete information.

Perfect competition can arise when

- ♦ industry demand is *large* relative to the minimum efficient scale of a firm (smallest quantity of output yielding minimum *LRAC*).
- ♦ products of each firm are identical.

In perfect competition,

- ♦ each firm is a **price taker**.
- ♦ each firm faces a perfectly elastic demand curve at the market price.

Firm maximizes economic profit.

- ♦ Economic profit = total revenue – total cost (total cost includes normal profit)
- ♦ Normal profit = expected return to entrepreneurial ability
- ♦ **Total revenue** (*TR*)—price (*P*) × quantity (*Q*)
  - Average revenue (*AR*)—TR/Q
  - Marginal revenue (*MR*)—$\Delta TR/\Delta Q$
  - In perfect competition, $AR = MR = P$

The Firm's Decisions in Perfect Competition

In the short run, firm decides what quantity to produce or to shut down.

- ♦ Economic profit maximized at quantity where $MR = MC$:
  - If $MR > MC$, firm increases *Q* to increase economic profit.
  - If $MR < MC$, firm decreases *Q* to increase economic profit.
- ♦ Three possible short-run profit-maximizing outcomes:
  - $P (= AR = MR) > ATC$ yields economic profit.
  - $P (= AR = MR) = ATC$ yields zero economic profit (*break-even point* at minimum *ATC*; firm just earning normal profit).
  - $P (= AR = MR) < ATC$ yields economic loss (firm earning less than normal profit).
- ♦ For firm incurring economic loss:
  - if $P > AVC$, firm will continue to produce.
  - if $P < AVC$, firm will temporarily shut down.
  - **shutdown point** at minimum *AVC*.

Perfectly competitive firm's supply curve is its *MC* curve above minimum *AVC*.

Short-run industry supply curve is horizontal sum of individual firm supply curves.

Output, Price, and Profit in Perfect Competition

Equilibrium market price and quantity determined by industry demand and supply curves.

In the short run,

- ♦ perfectly competitive firms can make an economic profit, normal profit (zero economic profit), or incur an economic loss.
- ♦ the number of firms and their plant size are fixed.

In the long run, the number of firms in the industry and the plant size of each firm can adjust. Economic profit/loss are signals for firms to enter/exit the industry and cause reallocation of resources.

- Economic profit attracts new entry, causing a rightward shift of industry supply, causing falling *P* and the elimination of economic profit.
- Economic loss induces existing firms to exit, causing a leftward shift of industry supply, causing rising *P* and the elimination of economic loss.

In long-run competitive equilibrium,

- *MR* = *P* = *MC*; firms maximize short-run profit.
- *P* = minimum *ATC*; economic profit is zero; no incentive for firms to enter or exit industry.
- *P* = minimum *LRAC*; optimum plant size; no incentive for firm to change plant size.

Changing Tastes and Advancing Technology

For a permanent shift in demand,

- decreased demand causes falling *P*, economic loss and exit, decreased industry supply, causing rising *P*. In the long run, enough firms exit so remaining firms earn normal profit.
- increased demand causes rising *P*, economic profit and entry, increased industry supply, causing falling *P*. In the long run, enough firms enter so economic profit is eliminated and firms earn normal profit.

The change in long-run equilibrium price from a permanent shift in demand depends on

- **external economies**—factors beyond control of firm that lower costs as industry output increases.
- **external diseconomies**—factors beyond control of firm that raise costs as industry output increases.

The shape of the **long-run industry supply curve** depends on existence of external economies or diseconomies. The long-run industry supply curve shows how industry quantity supplied varies as market price varies after all possible adjustments, including changes in plant size and number of firms. Shape may be

- horizontal for constant-cost industry.
- upward-sloping for increasing cost industry with external diseconomies.
- downward-sloping for decreasing cost industry with external economies.

New technology lowers costs, increases industry supply, causing falling *P*. New technology firms make economic profit and enter. Old technology firms incur economic loss and exit or switch to new technology. In the long run, all firms use new technology and earn zero economic profit (normal profit only).

Competition and Efficiency

Resource use is efficient when the most highly valued goods are produced; when no one can become better off without someone else becoming worse off; when marginal benefit equals marginal costs. Requires

- consumers are on their demand = marginal social benefit curves, and are getting the most value from their resources.
- firms are on their supply = marginal social cost curves, and are technologically efficient and economically efficient (lowest possible *LRAC*).
- equilibrium where price = marginal social benefit = marginal social cost; maximum gains from trade (consumer surplus + producer surplus).

Perfect competition achieves efficient use of resources at the market equilibrium price and quantity if there are no external benefits and external costs (Ch. 5).

HELPFUL HINTS

1 Although perfectly competitive markets are rare in the real world, there are three important reasons to develop a thorough understanding of their behaviour.

First, many markets closely approximate perfectly competitive markets. The analysis in this chapter gives direct and useful insights into the behaviour of these markets.

Second, the theory of perfect competition allows us to isolate the effects of competitive forces that are at work in *all* markets, even in those that do not match the assumptions of perfect competition.

Third, the perfectly competitive model serves as a useful benchmark for evaluating the relative efficiency of different market structures in subsequent chapters.

2 In the short run, a perfectly competitive firm cannot change the size of its plant—it has fixed inputs. The firm is also a price taker; it always sells at the market price, which it cannot influence. The only variable that the firm controls is its level of output. The short-run condition for profit maximization is to choose the level of output at which marginal revenue

equals marginal cost. This is a general condition which, as we will see in subsequent chapters, applies to other market structures such as monopoly and monopolistic competition. Since for the perfectly competitive firm, marginal revenue is equal to price, this profit-maximizing condition takes a particular form; choose the level of output at which price is equal to marginal cost ($P = MC$).

3 Many students have trouble understanding why a firm continues to operate at the break-even point, where economic profit is zero. The key to understanding lies in the definition of which costs are included in the average total cost curve. Recall from Chapter 9 that the economist defines a firm's total costs as *opportunity costs*, which include both explicit costs and *implicit costs*.

Implicit costs include forgone interest, forgone rent, and forgone cost of the owner's resources. Owners supply their time, which could have been used to earn income elsewhere. Owners also supply entrepreneurial ability. Normal profit is the expected return to entrepreneurial ability and is part of a firm's implicit costs.

At the break-even point where total revenue equals total cost (or, equivalently, average revenue equals average total cost), the owners of the firm are still earning a return on their investment, time, and entrepreneurial ability, which is equal to the best return that they could earn elsewhere. That is the definition of opportunity cost—the best alternative forgone. As the phrase "normal profit" implies, this profit could normally be earned as a return to entrepreneurial ability, on average, in any other industry. At the break-even point, the firm is earning normal profit even though its economic profit (sometimes called "extra-normal," or "above-average," profit) is zero. In earning normal profit, the firm is earning just as much profit as it could anywhere else, and is therefore totally content to continue producing in this industry.

4 When the price of output falls below the break-even point, but is above the shutdown point, the firm will continue to produce even though it is incurring economic losses. In this price range, the firm is no longer earning normal profit and theoretically could earn more by switching to another industry. Nonetheless, the firm will continue to operate in the short run because switching has costs. In order to switch industries, the firm must shut down, which entails still paying its total fixed costs.

As long as price is above the shutdown point (minimum average variable cost), a firm will decide to produce since it will be covering total variable cost and part of total fixed cost. Its loss will be less if it continues to produce at the output where $P = MC$ than if it shuts down.

If price falls below the shutdown point, a firm that produces output will not only lose its total fixed costs, it will lose *additional* money on every unit of output produced, since average revenue is less than average variable cost. Thus when price is less than average variable cost, the firm will choose to minimize its loss by shutting down.

5 In the long run, fixed costs disappear, and the firm can switch between industries and change plant size without cost. Economic profit serves as the signal for the movement or reallocation of firm resources until long-run equilibrium is achieved. Firms will move out of industries with negative economic profit (economic loss) and into industries with positive economic profit. Only when economic profit is zero will there be no tendency for firms to exit or enter industries.

The fact that there are no restrictions on entry into the industry is what assures that economic profit will be zero and that firms will be producing at the minimum of their long-run average cost curves in long-run equilibrium.

6 In long-run equilibrium, three conditions are satisfied for each firm in an industry:

i $MR = P = MC$. This implies that profits are maximized for each firm.

ii $P = ATC$. This implies that economic profit is zero and each firm is just earning normal profit.

iii $P =$ minimum $LRAC$. This implies that production takes place at the point of minimum long-run average cost.

SELF-TEST

True/False and Explain

Competition

1 A firm in a perfectly competitive industry cannot influence price.

2 The industry demand curve in a perfectly competitive industry is horizontal.

3 The objective of firms in a competitive industry is to maximize revenue.

The Firm's Decision in Perfect Competition

4 Firms will incur an economic loss in the long run but not the short run.

5 At prices below minimum average total cost, a firm will always shut down.

6 The supply curve of a perfectly competitive firm gives the quantities of output supplied at alternative prices as long as the firm earns economic profit.

Output, Price, and Profit in Perfect Competition

7 In long-run equilibrium, each firm in a perfectly competitive industry will choose the plant size associated with minimum long-run average cost.

8 Suppose a perfectly competitive industry is in long-run equilibrium when there is a substantial increase in total fixed costs. All firms will now incur economic losses and some firms will go out of business.

9 Suppose a perfectly competitive industry is in long-run equilibrium when there is an increase in demand. As new firms start entering the industry, the output of each existing firm will increase.

Changing Tastes and Advancing Technology

10 Suppose a perfectly competitive industry is in long-run equilibrium when there is a permanent increase in demand. In the short run, firms will earn an economic profit.

11 Suppose a perfectly competitive industry is in long-run equilibrium when there is a permanent decrease in demand. In the long run, firms will incur an economic loss.

12 In a perfectly competitive industry with external economies, the long-run industry supply curve is positively sloped.

Competition and Efficiency

13 Resource use is efficient as long as marginal benefit is greater than marginal cost.

14 Resource use is efficient as long as consumer surplus equals producer surplus.

15 A perfectly competitive industry will achieve efficiency if there are no external costs or external benefits.

Multiple-Choice

Competition

1 Which of the following is *not* a characteristic of a perfectly competitive industry?
- **a** downward-sloping industry demand curve
- **b** perfectly elastic demand curve for each individual firm
- **c** each firm decides its quantity of output
- **d** slightly differentiated products
- **e** many firms each supplying a small fraction of industry supply

2 For perfect competition to arise it is necessary that industry demand be
- **a** inelastic.
- **b** elastic.
- **c** perfectly elastic.
- **d** large relative to the minimum efficient scale of a firm.
- **e** small relative to the minimum efficient scale of a firm.

3 If a firm faces a perfectly elastic demand for its product,
- **a** it is not a price taker.
- **b** it will want to lower its price to increase sales.
- **c** it will want to raise its price to increase total revenue.
- **d** its marginal revenue curve is equal to the price of the product.
- **e** it will always earn zero economic profit.

The Firm's Decisions in Perfect Competition

4 In a perfectly competitive industry, the market price is \$10. An individual firm is producing the output at which $MC = ATC = \$15$. AVC at that output is \$10. What should the firm do to maximize its short-run profits?
- **a** shut down
- **b** expand output
- **c** contract output
- **d** leave output unchanged
- **e** insufficient information to answer

5 In which of the following situations will a perfectly competitive firm earn economic profit?
- **a** $MR > AVC$
- **b** $MR > ATC$
- **c** $ATC > MC$
- **d** $ATC > AR$
- **e** $AR > AVC$

6 In the price range below minimum average variable cost, a perfectly competitive firm's supply curve is
- **a** horizontal at the market price.
- **b** vertical at zero output.
- **c** the same as its marginal cost curve.
- **d** the same as its average variable cost curve.
- **e** none of the above.

7 A firm in a perfectly competitive industry is maximizing its short-run profits by producing 500 units of output. At 500 units of output, which of the following *must be false*?
- **a** $MC < AVC$
- **b** $MC < ATC$
- **c** $MC > ATC$
- **d** $AR < ATC$
- **e** $AR > AVC$

8 If a profit-maximizing firm in perfect competition is earning economic profit, it must be producing a level of output where
- **a** price is greater than marginal cost.
- **b** price is greater than marginal revenue.
- **c** marginal cost is greater than marginal revenue.
- **d** marginal cost is greater than average total cost.
- **e** average total cost is greater than marginal cost.

9 If a perfectly competitive firm in the short run is able to pay its variable costs and part, but not all, of its fixed costs, then it is operating in the range on its marginal cost curve that is anywhere
- **a** above the break-even point.
- **b** below the break-even point.
- **c** above the shutdown point.
- **d** below the shutdown point.
- **e** between the shutdown and break-even points.

10 The short-run industry supply curve is
- **a** the horizontal sum of the individual firms' supply curves.
- **b** the vertical sum of the individual firms' supply curves.
- **c** vertical at the total level of output being produced by all firms.
- **d** horizontal at the current market price.
- **e** none of the above.

11 The supply curve for an individual firm in a perfectly competitive industry is $P = 1 + 2Q_S$. If the industry consists of 100 identical firms, then what is industry supply when $P = 7$?
- **a** 300
- **b** 400
- **c** 600
- **d** 800
- **e** None of the above

Output, Price, and Profit in Perfect Competition

12 Refer to Fact 11.1. If the price of fiddleheads last month was $15 per bag, Franklin
- **a** should have shut down because total revenue did not cover total variable cost.
- **b** incurred an economic loss of $135.
- **c** earned zero economic profit.
- **d** earned economic profit of $50.
- **e** earned economic profit of $100.

FACT 11.1

Franklin is a fiddlehead farmer. He sold 10 bags of fiddleheads last month, with total fixed cost of $100 and total variable cost of $50.

---

13 Refer to Fact 11.1. If fiddlehead prices fell to $10 per bag while production and cost figures remained the same, Franklin would
- **a** shut down immediately.
- **b** break even because total revenues just cover total fixed costs.
- **c** be indifferent between producing and shutting down because his loss of $50 just covers total variable costs.
- **d** continue producing despite his loss of $50.
- **e** continue producing despite his loss of $100.

14 Refer to Fact 11.1. Suppose the price of fiddleheads is expected to stay at $10 per bag, and Franklin's production and cost figures are expected to stay the same. His total fixed cost consists entirely of rent on land, and his five-year lease on the land runs out at the end of the month. Should Franklin renew the lease?
- **a** Yes, because total revenue will still cover total fixed cost.
- **b** Yes, because total revenue will still cover total variable cost and a portion of total fixed cost.
- **c** No, because total revenue must cover all costs for resources to remain in fiddlehead farming in the long run.
- **d** No, because in the long run, zero economic profit is a signal to move resources out of fiddlehead farming.
- **e** Insufficient information to answer.

15 The maximum loss for a firm in long-run equilibrium is
- **a** zero.
- **b** its total cost.
- **c** its total variable cost.
- **d** its average total cost.
- **e** none of the above.

16 For a perfectly competitive firm in long-run equilibrium, which of the following is *not* equal to price?
- **a** short-run average total cost
- **b** short-run average variable cost
- **c** short-run marginal cost
- **d** long-run average cost
- **e** average revenue

17 When economic profit is zero
- **a** the product will not be produced in the short run.
- **b** the product will not be produced in the long run.
- **c** firms will leave the industry.
- **d** revenues are not covering implicit costs.
- **e** none of the above will occur.

Changing Tastes and Advancing Technology

18 A perfectly competitive industry is in short-run equilibrium with price below average total cost. Which of the following is *not* a prediction of the long-run consequences of such a situation?
- **a** price will increase.
- **b** the output of the industry will increase.
- **c** firms will leave the industry.
- **d** the output of each remaining firm will increase.
- **e** economic profit will be zero.

19 Figure 11.1 illustrates the cost curves for a perfectly competitive firm. The current market price is \$11 and the firm has the plant size shown by $SRAC_1$. The firm's short-run equilibrium output is

- **a** 7 units.
- **b** 9 units.
- **c** 10 units.
- **d** 17 units.
- **e** 18 units.

FIGURE **11.1**

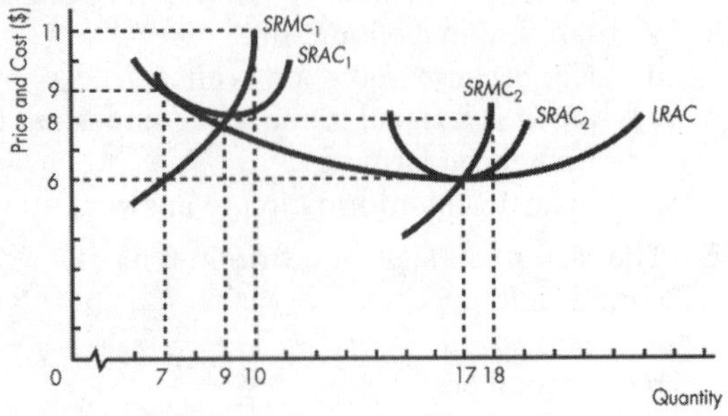

20 Refer to Figure. 11.1. The current market price is \$11 and the firm has the plant size shown by $SRAC_1$. In the long run, the firm will

- **a** exit from the industry.
- **b** keep its current plant size, and other firms will enter the industry.
- **c** keep its current plant size, and other firms will exit from the industry.
- **d** increase its plant size, and other firms will enter the industry.
- **e** increase its plant size, and other firms will exit from the industry.

21 Refer to Figure. 11.1. The long-run equilibrium price and quantity combination is

- **a** \$6 and 7 units.
- **b** \$6 and 17 units.
- **c** \$8 and 9 units.
- **d** \$8 and 18 units.
- **e** \$9 and 7 units.

22 If an industry experiences external economies as the industry expands in the long run, the long-run industry supply curve will

- **a** be perfectly inelastic.
- **b** be perfectly elastic.
- **c** have a positive slope.
- **d** have a negative slope.
- **e** have allocative inefficiency.

23 Which of the following is *not* true of a new long-run equilibrium resulting from a new technology in a perfectly competitive industry?

- **a** price will be lower
- **b** industry output will be greater
- **c** firm profits will be greater
- **d** all firms in the industry will be using the new technology
- **e** average total cost will be lower

Competition and Efficiency

24 A long-run equilibrium in a perfectly competitive industry would *not* be efficient if

- **a** firms are price takers.
- **b** new technologies are developed.
- **c** there are external economies or external diseconomies.
- **d** there are external costs or external benefits.
- **e** there is free entry to the industry.

25 Resources are used efficiently when

- **a** consumers are on their marginal social benefit curves.
- **b** firms are economically efficient.
- **c** price = marginal social benefit = marginal social cost.
- **d** there are no external benefits or external costs.
- **e** there are all of the above.

Short Answer Problems

1 Why will a firm in a perfectly competitive industry choose *not* to charge a price either above or below the market price?

2 Why will economic profit tend to zero in long-run equilibrium in a perfectly competitive industry?

3 Table 11.1 gives the total cost structure for one of many identical firms in a perfectly competitive industry.

a Complete the table by computing total variable cost, average total cost, average variable cost, and marginal cost at each level of output. (*Remember:* As in the problems in Chapter 10, marginal cost should be entered *midway* between rows.)

TABLE **11.1**

Quantity (units per day)	Total Cost ($)	Total Variable Cost ($)	Average Total Cost ($)	Average Variable Cost ($)	Marginal Cost ($)
0	12				
					...
1	24				
					...
2	32				
					...
3	42				
					...
4	54				
					...
5	68				
					...
6	84				

b Complete Table 11.2 by computing the profit (per day) for the firm at each level of output if the price of output is $9; $11; $15.

TABLE **11.2**

Quantity (units per day)	Profit P = $9	Profit P = $11	Profit P = $15
0			
1			
2			
3			
4			
5			
6			

c Consider the profit-maximizing output decision of the firm at alternative prices. How much will the firm produce if the price of output is $9? $11? $15? Explain each of your answers.

4 A firm will maximize profit if it produces every unit of output for which marginal revenue exceeds marginal cost. This is called the *marginal analysis* of profit maximization. Using marginal analysis, determine the profit-maximizing level of output for the firm in Short Answer Problem **3** when the price of output is $15. How does your answer here compare with your answer in **3c**?

5 This problem concerns a hypothetical pottery manufacturing firm that produces ceramic mugs for sale in a purely competitive market. With a plant of given size, the firm can turn out the quantities of ceramic mugs shown in Table 11.3, by varying the amount it uses of a single variable input, labour.

TABLE **11.3**

Number of Mugs	Labour-Hours (per day)
20	6.50
40	11.00
60	14.50
80	17.50
100	20.50
120	23.75
140	27.50
160	32.00
180	37.50
200	44.50
220	53.50
240	65.00
260	79.50
280	97.50

Suppose the firm can hire all the labour it would ever want at the going wage of $8 per labour-hour. The firm's total fixed costs are $64 per day.

a Draw a table showing output, total variable cost (*TVC*), total cost (*TC*), average variable cost (*AVC*), average total cost (*ATC*), and marginal cost (*MC*). (*Remember:* Marginal cost should be entered *midway* between rows of output.)

b On a graph with *Mugs (per day)* on the horizontal axis, draw the three "per-unit" cost curves, *AVC*, *ATC*, and *MC*. (Note that the marginal cost values from your table should be plotted on the graph *midway* between the corresponding units of output.)

c Consider (separately) the following alternative market prices that the firm might face:

$P = \$3.20$, $P = \$2$, $P = \$1.65$, $P = \$1.40$.

Assuming that the firm wants to maximize its profit, for *each* of the above prices, answer the following questions: Approximately how many mugs per day would the firm produce? How do you know? Is the firm making a profit at that price? And if so, approximately how much?

6 Suppose that the ceramic pottery mug industry consists of 60 firms, each identical to the single firm discussed in Short Answer Problem **5**. Table 11.4 represents some points on the industry demand schedule for ceramic pottery mugs.

TABLE **11.4**

Price ($)	Quantity Demanded
1.00	15,900
1.60	14,400
2.20	12,900
2.80	11,400
3.40	9,900
4.00	8,400
4.60	6,900
5.20	5,400
5.80	3,900
6.40	2,400
7.00	900

a On a new graph, draw the industry short-run supply curve. Draw the industry demand curve on the same graph.

b What is the short-run equilibrium price of ceramic pottery mugs?

c Is the ceramic pottery mug industry in long-run equilibrium? Explain your answer.

7 A perfectly competitive industry has 100 identical firms in the short run, each of which has the short-run cost curves listed in Table 11.5.

TABLE **11.5**

Output (units)	Average Total Cost ($)	Average Variable Cost ($)	Marginal Cost ($)
11	20.5	13.1	
			12
12	19.8	13.0	
			14
13	19.3	13.1	
			16
14	19.1	13.3	
			18
15	19.0	13.6	
			20
16	19.1	14.0	
			22
17	19.2	14.5	
			24
18	19.5	15.0	
			26
19	19.8	15.6	
			28
20	20.3	16.2	
			30
21	20.7	16.9	

This short-run average total cost curve touches the long-run average cost curve at the minimum point on the long-run average cost curve as point *M* in Text Figure 11.9 on page 251. The industry demand schedule is the same in the long and the short run. Table 11.6 represents some points on the demand schedule.

TABLE **11.6**

Price ($)	Quantity Demanded
11	3,200
13	3,000
15	2,800
17	2,600
19	2,400
21	2,200
23	2,000
25	1,800
27	1,600
29	1,400
31	1,200

a What is the quantity of output corresponding to the firm's break-even point? the shutdown point? Explain your answers.

b What is the short-run equilibrium price in this market? Show how you found your answer.

c What amount of profit or loss is being made by each firm at the short-run equilibrium price? Is this industry in long-run equilibrium at its present size? Why or why not?

d Exactly how many firms will exist in this industry in the long run? Explain your answer. How much economic profit will each firm earn in the long run?

8 Suppose we observe a perfectly competitive industry in a long-run equilibrium when there is a permanent decrease in demand for the industry's product. There are no external economies or diseconomies. How does the industry adjust to a new long-run equilibrium? What happens to price, quantity, firm profits, and the number of firms during the adjustment process?

9 Consider a perfectly competitive industry in long-run equilibrium. All firms in the industry are identical.

a Draw a two-part graph illustrating the long-run equilibrium for the industry—part (a) on the left—and for the typical firm—part (b) on the right. The graph of the firm should include the *MC*, *ATC*, *MR*, and *LRAC* curves. Assume that the *LRAC* curve is U-shaped as it is in Text Figure 11.9 on page 251. Label the equilibrium price P_0, the equilibrium industry quantity Q_0, and the output of the firm q_0.

b Now, suppose there is a decline in industry demand. Using your graphs from part **a**, show what happens to market price, firm output, firm profits, and industry equilibrium quantity in the short run (assume that the shutdown point is not reached).

Then show what happens to market price, firm output, firm profits, and industry equilibrium quantity in the long run (assume that there are no external economies or diseconomies). What has happened to the number of firms?

10 In a perfectly competitive industry with no external benefits or costs, suppose output is restricted to a quantity less than the equilibrium quantity. Explain why this level of output is inefficient.

ANSWERS

True/False and Explain

1 T Each firm is price taker. (240)

2 F Individual firm demand curve horizontal. Industry demand curve downward-sloping. (240–241)

3 F Maximize economic profit. (240)

4 F Losses in short run but not long run. (245–246)

ⓒⓣ **5 F** True if $P <$ minimum *AVC*. False if $P >$ minimum *AVC* but $<$ minimum *ATC*. (245–246)

6 F As long as $P >$ minimum *AVC*. (246–247)

7 T Otherwise firm driven out of business by lower-cost firms. (250–251)

ⓒⓣ **8 T** *ATC* shifts upward with no ΔMC. Economic losses cause exit. (249–250)

9 F As new firms enter, supply shifts rightward, price falls and output each existing firms decreases. (248–249)

10 T Price rises above *ATC*, creating economic profit. (252–253)

11 F Short-run economic losses cause firms to exit, shifting supply leftward, raising price until economic losses eliminated. (252–253)

12 F Negatively sloped. (253–254)

13 F Efficient when $MB = MC$. (256–257)

14 F Efficient when sum of consumer surplus and producer surplus maximized. (256–257)

15 T $P = MB = MC$ and maximum sum of consumer and producer surpluses. (256–257)

Multiple-Choice

1 d Identical products. (240–241)

2 d So there is room for many (efficient) firms in the industry. (240)

3 **d** Firm can increase Q without ΔP, so MR from additional $Q = P$. (240–241)

ⓒⓣ 4 **c** Draw graph. Firm should choose lower Q where $P = MC$. If AVC at current Q = \$10, minimum AVC must be < \$10, so new Q at P > minimum AVC. (244–246)

5 **b** Since $MR = AR$, $AR > ATC$. Multiplying by Q yields $TR > TC$, so economic profit. (244–246)

6 **b** Firm stays shut down ($Q = 0$) until P reaches minimum AVC. (246)

ⓒⓣ 7 **a** **a** implies shutdown. Other answers possible with losses (**b**, **d**) or profits (**c**, **e**). (244–246)

8 **d** ($MC = P =$) $AR > ATC$. **a**, **b**, **c** not consistent with profit maximization. **e** implies losses. (244–246)

9 **e** If couldn't pay variable costs then below shutdown. If paying all variable and fixed costs then breaking even. (244–246)

10 **a** Definition. **c** is momentary supply curve. **d** is demand curve facing individual firm. (247)

11 **a** For one firm: $7 = 1 + 2Q_S$; $2Q_S = 6$; $Q_S = 3$. For 100 firms, $3 \times 100 = 300$. (247)

12 **c** Profit = TR (\$15 × 10) – TC (\$100 + \$50) = 0. (248–249)

ⓒⓣ 13 **d** TR (\$10 × 10) – TC (\$100 + \$50) = –\$50. Shutting down would bring bigger loss of \$100 (fixed costs). (248–249)

ⓒⓣ 14 **c** He is making long-run decision. **a**, **b** refer to short run. **d** false because *losses* are signal to move resources. (249–251)

15 **a** Definition long-run equilibrium includes zero economic profit. (249–251)

16 **b** Long-run equilibrium at intersection ATC, MC, and $LRAC$ curves. (250–251)

17 **e** Product produced in short and long run, revenues exactly cover all costs (including implicit costs). (249–251)

18 **b** As firms exit, supply shifts left, decreasing industry Q and raising P. In response to higher P, remaining firms increase Q. (252–253)

19 **c** Choose Q where $P = MC$. (252–253)

20 **d** Economic profit attracts new entry, causing falling P and increased output creates incentive to build larger, lower cost plant. (252–253)

21 **b** Long-run equilibrium at intersection $SRAC$, MC, and $LRAC$ curves. (252–253)

22 **d** Because decreasing costs as industry Q increases. (253–255)

23 **c** In long-run equilibrium, economic profit always zero. (252–255)

24 **d** **a**, **e** conditions perfect competition. **b**, **c** affect shape long-run supply curve but not efficiency. (256–257)

25 **e** When no external benefits or external costs, **a** and **b** are true; **c** is the equilibrium between demand and supply. (256–257)

Short Answer Problems

1 If a firm in a perfectly competitive industry charged a price even slightly higher than the market price, it would lose all of its sales. Thus it will not charge a price above the market price. Since it can sell all it wants at the market price, it would not be able to increase sales by lowering its price. Thus it would not charge a price below the market price since this would decrease total revenue and profits.

2 In a perfectly competitive industry, the existence of positive economic profit will attract the entry of new firms, shifting the industry supply curve rightward, causing the market price to fall and firm profits to decline. This tendency will exist as long as there is positive economic profit. Similarly, the existence of economic losses will cause firms to exit from the industry, shifting the industry supply curve leftward, causing the market price to rise and firm profits to rise (losses to decline). This tendency will exist as long as losses are being incurred. Thus, the only point of rest in the long run (the only equilibrium) occurs when economic profits are zero.

3 a Completed Table 11.1 is shown here as Table 11.1 Solution.

TABLE 11.1 SOLUTION

Quantity (units per day)	Total Cost ($)	Total Variable Cost ($)	Average Total Cost ($)	Average Variable Cost ($)	Marginal Cost ($)
0	12	0	—	—	
					12
1	24	12	24.00	12.00	
					8
2	32	20	16.00	10.00	
					10
3	42	30	14.00	10.00	
					12
4	54	42	13.50	10.50	
					14
5	68	56	13.60	11.20	
					16
6	84	72	14.00	12.00	

b Completed Table 11.2 is given here as Table 11.2 Solution. The values for profit are computed as total revenue minus total cost, where total revenue is price times quantity and total cost is given in Table 11.1.

TABLE 11.2 SOLUTION

Quantity (units per day)	Profit P = $9	Profit P = $11	Profit P = $15
0	**−12**	−12	−12
1	−15	−13	−9
2	−14	−10	−2
3	−15	**−9**	3
4	−18	−10	6
5	−23	−13	**7**
6	−30	−18	6

c If the price is $9, profit is maximized (actually loss is minimized) when the firm shuts down and produces zero units. If the firm chooses to produce, its loss will be at least $14, which is greater than the fixed cost loss of $12. If the price is $11, the firm is still unable to make a positive economic profit. The loss is minimized (at $9) if the firm produces 3 units. At this price, all of variable cost and part of fixed cost can be recovered. At a price of $15, the firm will maximize profit (at $7) at an output of 5 units per day.

4 The marginal analysis of profit maximization states that the firm should produce all units of output for which marginal revenue exceeds marginal cost. For a perfectly competitive firm, marginal revenue equals price, so (equivalently) the firm should produce every unit for which price exceeds marginal cost. If the price of output is $15, we can see from Table 11.2 Solution that the firm should produce 5 units. Since the marginal cost of moving from the 4th to the 5th unit ($14) is less than price ($15), the 5th unit should be produced. The marginal cost of moving to the 6th unit ($16), however, is greater than price. It should not be produced. The answer here is the same as the answer in **3c**.

5 a With only one variable input (labour), *AVC* (for any level of output) = (labour hours × wage rate). The requested table is Table 11.7.

TABLE 11.7

Output (per day)	*TVC* ($)	*TC* ($)	*AVC* ($)	*ATC* ($)	*MC* ($)
0	0	64	—	—	
					2.60
20	52	116	2.60	5.80	
					1.80
40	88	152	2.20	3.80	
					1.40
60	116	180	1.93	3.00	
					1.20
80	140	204	1.75	2.55	
					1.20
100	164	228	1.64	2.28	
					1.30
120	190	254	1.58	2.12	
					1.50
140	220	284	1.57	2.03	
					1.80
160	256	320	1.60	2.00	
					2.20
180	300	364	1.67	2.02	
					2.80
200	356	420	1.78	2.10	
					3.60
220	428	492	1.95	2.24	
					4.60
240	520	584	2.17	2.43	
					5.80
260	636	700	2.45	2.69	
					7.20
280	780	844	2.79	3.01	

b The graph appears in Figure 11.2. It also illustrates the answers to part **c**.

FIGURE **11.2**

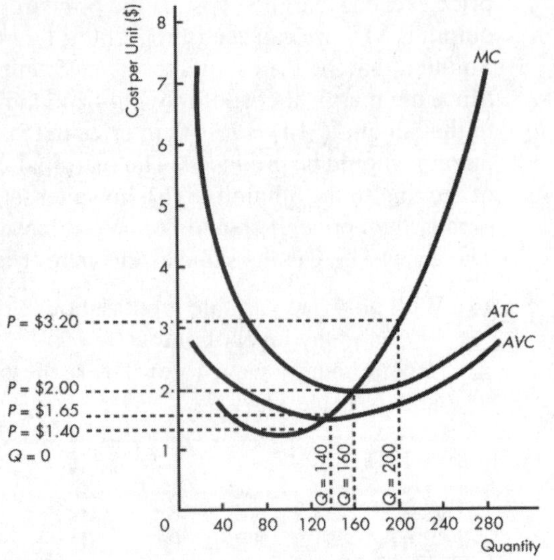

c In every case, at the profit-maximizing output, marginal revenue (which, for a price-taking firm in a perfectly competitive market, is the same as market price) is equal to marginal cost, provided that price is greater than average variable cost.

Profit "per unit of output" is the difference between average revenue (price) and average total cost at the level of output. Total profit is "per unit profit" × number of units of output. Economic profit might be zero or negative (a loss) and still be the best the firm can attain in the short run. The calculations of total profit at each price appear in Table 11.8.

TABLE **11.8**

Price ($)	Output Chosen	Per Unit Profit ($)	Total Profit ($)
3.20	200	1.10	220.00
2.00	160	0	0
1.65	140	–0.38	–53.20
1.40	0	0	–64.00

Note the following:

1. Marginal cost is $3.20 at approximately 200 units.
2. The per unit profit is *P* – *ATC*.
3. 160 units is the "break-even" level of output, where *MC* = minimum *ATC* and the firm is just covering all its opportunity costs.
4. At an output of 140 units, the firm continues to produce in the short run because it can more than cover its variable costs. If it produced zero units, its loss would be greater, $64, which is the amount of its fixed costs.
5. Any positive output increases losses when the price is below the shutdown price, which here is approximately $1.57. When price is less than minimum *AVC*, the firm would not only lose its fixed costs, it would also lose additional money on every unit it produced.

6 There are 60 identical price-taking firms. For every possible price (above minimum *AVC* of approximately $1.57), each firm will supply the quantity at which *P* = *MC*. We can derive (in Table 11.9) the industry supply schedule from the *MC* curve of an individual firm.

TABLE **11.9**

Price ($)	Quantity Supplied by 1 Firm	Quantity Supplied by 60 Firms
1.57	134	8,040
1.80	150	9,000
2.20	170	10,200
2.80	190	11,400
3.60	210	12,600
4.60	230	13,800
5.80	250	15,000
7.20	270	16,200

a The graph of the industry supply curve appears in Figure. 11.3, together with the industry demand curve.

FIGURE **11.3**

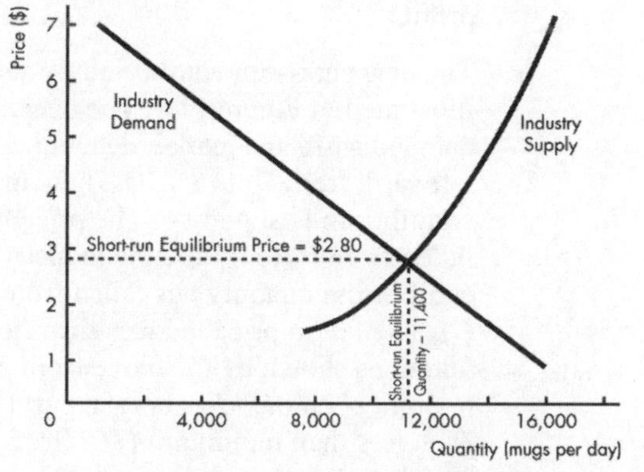

b The short-run equilibrium price is $2.80 (where a total of 11,400 mugs per day are supplied and sold; or 190 mugs per day supplied by each firm at *MC* of $2.80).

c At a price of $2.80 and output of 190, for each firm, $P > ATC$ where $ATC = \$2.06$. So all existing firms are making an economic profit after covering all opportunity costs including a normal profit. (See Helpful Hint 3.) The industry will attract new entrants because it offers more than normal profit. Even though the industry is in short-run equilibrium, it is *not* in long-run equilibrium because the number of firms has not "stabilized." New firms will enter the industry, the industry supply curve will shift rightward, and price will fall until no firm is making economic profit.

7 a The break-even point occurs at 15 units of output. At this level of output, *ATC* is at its minimum ($19) and is equal to *MC*. Since the *MC* of moving from the 14th to the 15th unit is $18, and the *MC* of moving from the 15th to the 16th unit is $20, we can interpolate the *MC* exactly at 15 units as midway between $18 and $20, or as $19. The shutdown point occurs at 12 units of output. At this level of output, *AVC* is at its minimum ($13) and is equal to *MC*. The interpolated value of *MC* at exactly 12 units of output is midway between $12 and $14, or is $13.

b The short-run equilibrium price is $25. This is the price at which industry quantity supplied equals quantity demanded as shown in Table 11.10.

TABLE **11.10**

P = MC ($)	Quantity Supplied by 1 Firm	Quantity Supplied by 100 Firms	Quantity Demanded
13	12	1,200	3,000
15	13	1,300	2,800
17	14	1,400	2,600
19	15	1,500	2,400
21	16	1,600	2,200
23	17	1,700	2,000
25	**18**	**1,800**	**1,800**
27	19	1,900	1,600
29	20	2,000	1,400

c At a price of $25, each firm produces 18 units of output. At 18 units, *ATC* is $19.50, so economic profit is being earned. The amount of profit is ($25 – $19.50 per unit =) $5.50 per unit. Total economic profit per firm is $5.50/unit × 18 units = $99. This means that new entrants will be attracted to the industry. We conclude that the industry is not in long-run equilibrium.

d Entry continues until economic profit is competed away, and all firms are operating at the minimum point of the *LRAC* curve (which, in this problem, is also the minimum point of the given short-run average total cost curve).

Minimum *ATC* for each firm occurs at 15 units of output, when $ATC = MC = \$19$, so price in the long run must be $19. At a price of $19, consumers demand 2,400 units (from Table 11.10). It follows that when the industry is in long-run equilibrium, there must be 2,400 units/15 units per firm = 160 firms in the industry, each producing 15 units of output, at zero economic profit.

8 The decrease in market demand causes the market price to fall. Since, in the initial long-run equilibrium, each firm was earning zero economic profit, the fall in price means that profits will fall and firms will now incur losses. Since the decrease in demand is permanent, these losses will induce some firms to leave the industry. This will shift the industry supply curve leftward, causing an increase in market price. The increasing price causes profits to increase for the remaining firms, so their losses will decline. The exit of firms continues until losses are eliminated. Costs have not been affected by the decrease in demand, so if there are no external economies or diseconomies, the price must continue rising until it reaches its original level in the new long-run equilibrium. The output of each firm will also equal its original level, but the equilibrium quantity at the industry level will be less because the number of firms has declined.

9 **a** A long-run equilibrium in a perfectly competitive industry is illustrated in Figure. 11.4.

Part (a) illustrates industry equilibrium at the intersection of industry demand (D_0) and industry supply (S_0): point *a*. The equilibrium industry quantity is labelled Q_0 and the equilibrium market price is labelled P_0.

Part (b) illustrates the situation for a single firm in long-run equilibrium. The firm is at point *a*', the minimum point of both the short-run average total cost curve (*ATC*) and the long-run average cost curve (*LRAC*). The firm is producing the output labelled q_0 and earning zero economic profit.

b The new short-run equilibrium is also illustrated in Figure 11.4. The decrease in demand shifts the market demand curve leftward, from D_0 to D_1. The new market equilibrium is at point *b*. The price has fallen from P_0 to P_1 and the industry equilibrium quantity has fallen from Q_0 to Q_1. The fall in price induces firms to reduce output as shown by the move from point *a*' to point *b*' on the *MC* curve in part (b). Since P_1 is less than minimum *ATC*, firms are incurring losses in the new short-run equilibrium.

The new long-run equilibrium is also illustrated in Figure 11.4. With short-run losses, firms will exit from the industry in the long run. This causes the industry supply curve to shift leftward, causing the price to rise and thus reducing losses. Firms continue to leave until the industry supply curve has shifted enough to eliminate losses, from S_0 to S_1. This gives a new long-run industry equilibrium at point *c* and the price has returned to its initial level, P_0, but industry quantity has fallen to Q_2.

FIGURE 11.4

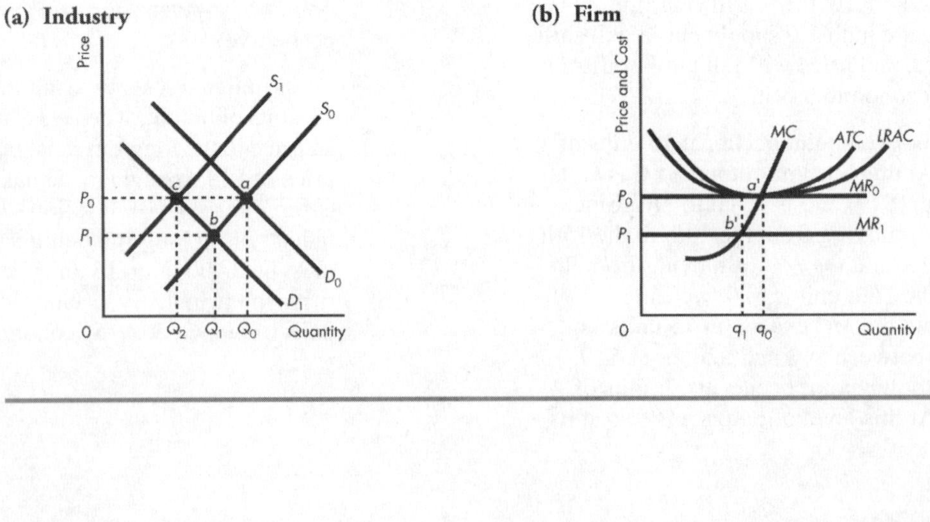

As firms exit and the market price rises, remaining firms will increase their output (moving up the *MC* curve from point *b'* to point *a'*) and their losses will be reduced. When sufficient firms have left the industry, the price will have risen (returned) to P_0 and firms will have returned to point *a'* in part (b). At this point, each firm is again earning zero economic profit and firm output has returned to q_0. But, since there are now fewer firms, industry equilibrium quantity is less.

10 Refer to Text Figure 11.12 on page 257. If output is restricted to a quantity less than Q^*, the value to consumers of an additional unit of the good is greater than P^* (from the lesser Q, go "up" to the *MSB* curve and "over" to the price axis to find the maximum price people are willing to pay). For that lesser Q, producers would be willing to supply additional goods for a price less than P^* (from the lesser Q, go "up" to the *MSC* curve and "over" to the price axis to find the minimum price producers are willing to accept). If more goods are produced and sold at any price in between those prices, consumers will be better off, because they value the goods more than the price paid, and producers will be better off because they receive a higher price than the minimum necessary to induce production. Consumers and producers could be made better off without making someone else worse off. Therefore at a quantity less than Q^*, there are unrealized gains from trade (more consumer and producer surplus is possible), and this level of output is allocatively inefficient.

Chapter 12 Monopoly

KEY CONCEPTS

Market Power

Monopoly is a model of market structure where the force of *competition* is absent and firms have extreme **market power**. Assumptions include industry with one supplier; no close substitutes; barriers to entry.

Monopoly can arise when

- no close substitutes for product.
- **barriers to entry**—constraints protecting firm from competition from potential new entrants.
  - Legal barriers to entry—for a **legal monopoly**, competition and entry restricted by *public franchise*, *government licence*, *patent*, or *copyright*.
  - Natural barriers to entry—a **natural monopoly** occurs when, due to economies of scale, one firm can supply the market at lower *ATC* than multiple firms can.

Price-setting strategies depend on type of monopoly:

- **Single-price monopoly**—must sell each unit of output at same price to all customers.
- **Price discrimination**—selling different units of output for different prices.

A Single-Price Monopoly's Output and Price Decision

Single-price monopoly charges same price for every unit output.

- Monopoly's demand curve is industry demand curve.
- Marginal revenue (*MR*) < price (*P*). To sell additional output, must lower *P* on *all* output.
- In moving down the monopoly's demand curve
  - when total revenue (*TR*) increasing, *MR* positive, $\eta > 1$.
  - when *TR* maximum, *MR* zero, $\eta = 1$.
  - when *TR* decreasing, *MR* negative, $\eta < 1$.
- Monopoly's technology and costs like firm in perfect competition.
- Profit-maximizing monopoly chooses output at which *MR* = *MC*, charges maximum price consumers willing to pay (on demand curve).
- Monopoly never operates in inelastic range of demand curve. Monopoly has no supply curve.
- Monopoly can make economic profit even in long run because barriers prevent entry of new firms.

Single-Price Monopoly and Competition Compared

Output and price:

- Single-price monopoly *Q* < competitive *Q*.
- Single-price monopoly *P* > competitive *P*.

Efficiency:

- Single-price monopoly inefficient compared to efficiency of perfect competition. Monopoly prevents gains from trade: restricts output, captures some consumer surplus, but creates *deadweight loss*—total loss of *consumer surplus* and *producer surplus* (revenue – opportunity cost production) below efficient levels.
- Social cost of monopoly greater than deadweight loss because of **rent seeking**—attempt to capture consumer surplus, producer surplus, or economic profit.

- If no barriers to rent seeking, cost of resources used rent seeking = value monopoly profit (with no rent seeking), so no economic profit.
- Social cost of monopoly = deadweight loss + resources used rent seeking

Price Discrimination

Price discrimination (selling different units of output for different prices) converts consumer surplus into economic profit for the monopoly. Examples include charging lower per-unit price on large order than small; discriminating among groups with different average willingness to pay.

Price discrimination requires:

- ♦ Product cannot be resold.
- ♦ Charge lower P to lower willingness-to-pay group. Charge higher P to higher willingness-to-pay group.

Perfect price discrimination—different price for each unit sold; obtains maximum price each consumer willing to pay; converts *all* consumer surplus into economic profit.

- ♦ *MR* curve same as demand curve.
- ♦ Same output and efficiency (zero deadweight loss) of perfectly competitive industry, but
  - all consumer surplus captured as economic profit.
  - rent seeking occurs that might eliminate economic profit.

Monopoly Policy Issues

Gains from monopoly:

- ♦ Increased innovation and technological change (in some cases)
- ♦ Economies of scale (decreased *LRAC* through increased *Q*)
- ♦ Economies of scope (decreased *ATC* through increased range of goods produced)

Natural monopolies may be regulated to achieve gains from monopoly but avoid worst inefficiencies. Possible rules:

- ♦ **Marginal cost pricing rule**—set price equal to marginal cost. Maximizes total surplus and is efficient, but not viable because firm incurs economic loss.
- ♦ **Average cost pricing rule**—set price equal to average total cost. Firm earns normal profit only. Inefficient, but better outcome than unregulated monopoly.

HELPFUL HINTS

1 The opposite extreme of perfect competition is monopoly. While in perfect competition there are many firms that can decide only on quantity produced but not on price, a monopoly is a single firm with the ability to set both quantity and price. These differences create differences in the revenue situation facing the monopoly. The cost curves for the two market structures are assumed to be the same.

Because there is only one firm, the industry demand curve is also the firm demand curve. Facing a negatively sloped demand curve, if a single-price monopoly wants to sell one more unit of output, it must lower its price. This has two effects on revenue. First, the sale of an additional unit will increase revenue by the amount of the price. However, since the firm must also *drop the price on previous units*, revenue on these will decrease. The net change in revenue, the marginal revenue, will be less than price and the marginal revenue curve will lie below the demand curve.

Combining this new revenue situation with our familiar cost curves from Chapter 10 yields the important Text Figure 12.4(b), which is reproduced below as Figure 12.1. Notice the following points about this graph.

FIGURE 12.1 MONOPOLY OUTPUT & PRICE

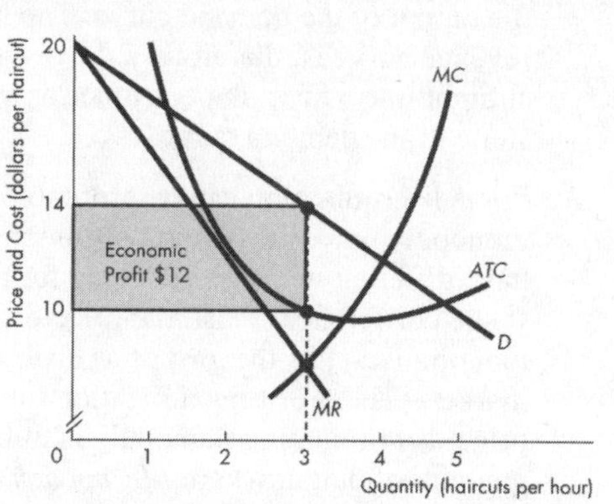

The profit maximization rule for a single-price monopoly is to find the quantity of output where $MR = MC$. This is the same rule that applies to a perfectly competitive firm.

For a perfectly competitive firm *MR* is also equal to price, so the intersection of *MR* and *MC* yields the profit-maximizing output and price. That is not true for the monopolist. *MR* is not equal to price, and once the profit-maximizing output is identified, the monopolist still has to set the price.

To find the profit-maximizing price, draw an imaginary vertical line up to the demand curve from the intersection of *MR* and *MC*. Then draw an imaginary horizontal line to the price axis to read the price.

Understanding what the vertical and horizontal distances of the economic profit area represent will make you less likely to make mistakes in drawing that area. The vertical distance is between the demand (or average revenue) curve and the average total cost curve. That distance measures average revenue minus average total cost, which equals average economic profit, or economic profit per unit. The horizontal distance is just the number of units produced. So the area of the rectangle (vertical distance × horizontal distance) = economic profit per unit × number of units = total economic profit. Do *not* make the mistake of drawing the vertical distance down to the intersection of *MC* and *MR*. That intersection has no economic meaning for the calculation of total economic profit.

2 There is an easy trick for drawing the marginal revenue curve corresponding to any linear demand curve. The price intercept (where $Q = 0$) is the same as for the demand curve, and the quantity intercept (where $P = 0$) is exactly *half* of the output of the demand curve. The marginal revenue curve is, therefore, a downward-sloping straight line whose slope is twice as steep as the slope of the demand curve.

3 Price discrimination can be profitable for a monopoly only if different consumer groups have different willingness to pay for the product. If such differences exist, the price-discriminating monopolist treats the groups as different markets. The profit maximization rule for a price-discriminating monopoly is to find the quantity of output where *MR in each market* = *MC*. Then, in each market, charge the maximum price the consumer group is willing to pay for that output (on demand curve). Different willingness to pay translates into different elasticities of demand between groups, yielding different prices in the two markets.

4 The absence of entry barriers into a perfectly competitive industry is the basis for the prediction that any short-run economic profit in perfect competition will be competed away in the long run. Conversely, the presence of entry barriers in monopoly is the basis for the prediction that monopoly profits can persist in the long run. However, when rent-seeking activity is taken into account, there may be no long-run economic profit, even in monopoly. Rent seeking is any activity aimed at obtaining existing monopoly rights or creating new monopoly rights. Competition among rent seekers bids up the cost of rent seeking until it just equals the value of the potential monopoly profits, leaving the rent-seeker-turned-monopolist with little or no economic profit.

SELF-TEST

True/False and Explain

Market Power

1 Monopoly can arise when there are close substitutes for a product.

2 If one firm can supply the market at a lower cost than multiple firms can, then there are natural barriers to entry.

3 Barriers to entry are essential to a monopoly.

A Single Price Monopoly's Output and Price Decision

4 Over the output range where total revenue is decreasing, marginal revenue is positive.

5 The supply curve of a monopoly firm is its marginal cost curve.

6 Once a single-price monopoly chooses its output, average revenue always equals price.

Single Price Monopoly and Competition Compared

7 A monopoly will always make economic profit.

8 In moving from perfect competition to single-price monopoly, part of the deadweight loss is due to a reduction in producer surplus.

9 Because of the existence of rent seeking, the social cost of monopoly is smaller than the deadweight loss.

10 When rent seeking is taken into account, economic profits from monopoly are guaranteed in the long run.

Price Discrimination

11 Price discrimination only works for goods that can be readily resold.

12 Price discrimination is an attempt by a monopolist to capture the producer surplus.

13 For a perfect price-discriminating monopolist, the demand curve is also the marginal revenue curve.

Monopoly Policy Issues

14 A monopoly industry with large economies of scale and scope may produce more output and charge a lower price than does a perfectly competitive industry.

15 If a regulator applies an average total cost pricing rule, a natural monopoly will earn normal profits only.

Multiple-Choice

Market Power

1 Which of the following is a *natural* barrier to the entry of new firms in an industry?
a licensing of professions
b economies of scale
c issuing a patent
d a public franchise
e all of the above

A Single-Price Monopoly's Output and Price Decision

2 In order to increase sales from 7 units to 8 units, a single-price monopolist must drop the price from $7 per unit to $6 per unit. What is marginal revenue in this range?
a $48
b $6
c $1
d –$1
e None of the above

3 If marginal revenue is negative at a particular output,
a price must be negative.
b the monopolist should increase output.
c the elasticity of demand is less than 1 at that output.
d demand must be elastic at that output.
e the monopolist should shut down.

4 Four monopolists were overheard talking at an expensive restaurant. Which of their statements below is a correct strategy for maximizing profits?
a "In my company, we don't increase output unless we know that the larger output will raise total revenue."
b "I think cost minimization is the key to maximizing profits."
c "We try to make the most of our equipment by producing at maximum capacity."
d "I don't really keep close tabs on total profits, but I don't approve any business deal unless it increases my revenue more than it increases my costs."
e None of the above.

5 A profit-maximizing monopoly will never produce at an output level
a where it would incur economic losses.
b where marginal revenue is less than price.
c where average cost is greater than marginal cost.
d in the inelastic range of its demand curve.
e in the inelastic range of its marginal revenue curve.

6 If a single-price monopoly has shut down, at the level of output where marginal cost and marginal revenue intersect, it *must be true* that
a marginal revenue is less than average variable cost.
b marginal cost is less than average variable cost.
c price is less than average variable cost.
d total revenue is less than total cost.
e all of the above are correct.

7 For the single-price monopoly shown in Figure 12.2, when profit is maximized, quantity is
a 3 and price is $3.
b 3 and price is $6.
c 4 and price is $4.
d 4 and price is $5.
e 5 and price is $4.

FIGURE **12.2**

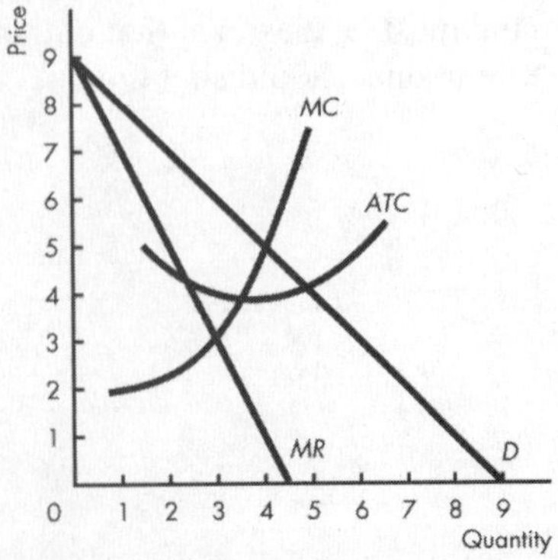

8 If the single-price monopoly shown in Figure 12.2 is maximizing profit, what is total economic profit?
a $3
b $4
c $6
d $9
e none of the above

9 A single-price monopolist will maximize profits if it produces the output where
a price equals marginal cost.
b price equals marginal revenue.
c marginal revenue equals marginal cost.
d average revenue equals marginal cost.
e average revenue equals marginal revenue.

10 If a profit-maximizing monopoly is producing an output at which marginal cost exceeds marginal revenue, it
a should raise price and lower output.
b should lower price and raise output.
c should lower price and lower output.
d is incurring losses.
e is maximizing profit.

11 A monopoly will go out of business in the short run if
a it is incurring an economic loss.
b *MR* is less than *AVC*.
c the price is less than *AVC*.
d the profit-maximizing level of output is in the elastic range of the demand curve.
e *MR* is less than *AR*.

Single-Price Monopoly and Competition Compared

12 Table 12.1 lists marginal costs for the XYZ firm. If XYZ sells 3 units at a price of $6 each, what is its producer surplus?
a $2
b $6
c $7
d $9
e $12

TABLE **12.1**

Quantity	Marginal Cost
1	2
2	3
3	4
4	5

13 Which of the following is true for a producing single-price monopolist but not for a producing perfect competitor?
- a The firm maximizes profit by setting marginal cost equal to marginal revenue.
- b The firm is a price taker.
- c The firm can sell any level of output at any price it sets.
- d The firm's marginal cost is less than average revenue.
- e None of the above.

14 Activity for the purpose of creating monopoly is
- a called rent seeking.
- b illegal in Canada.
- c called price discrimination.
- d called legal monopoly.
- e costless.

15 Taking rent-seeking activity into account, the social cost of monopoly is equal to the
- a deadweight loss from monopoly.
- b monopoly profit.
- c deadweight loss plus monopoly profit.
- d deadweight loss minus monopoly profit.
- e consumer surplus lost plus producer surplus lost.

16 Consider the industry demand curve in Figure 12.3. If the industry operates under perfect competition, which area in the diagram indicates consumer surplus?
- a *aek*
- b *dhk*
- c *dik*
- d *dih*
- e None of the above

FIGURE **12.3**

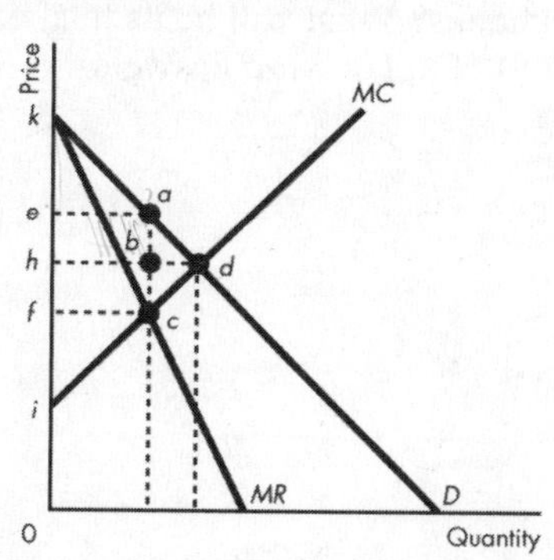

17 Consider the industry demand curve in Figure 12.3. If the industry operates under perfect competition, which area in the diagram indicates producer surplus?
- a *aek*
- b *dhk*
- c *dik*
- d *dih*
- e none of the above

18 Consider the industry demand curve in Figure 12.3. Which area in the diagram indicates the deadweight loss from a single-price monopoly?
- a *eacf*
- b *acd*
- c *abd*
- d *bcd*
- e none of the above

Price Discrimination

19 Which area in Figure 12.3 indicates the deadweight loss from a perfect price-discriminating monopoly?
- a *eacf*
- b *acd*
- c *abd*
- d *bcd*
- e none of the above

20 A perfect price-discriminating monopoly
- a has a demand curve which is also its average revenue curve.
- b will maximize revenue.
- c is assured of making a profit.
- d will produce the quantity at which the marginal cost curve intersects the demand curve.
- e will be allocatively inefficient.

21 When perfect price discrimination occurs, which of the following statements is *false*?
- a Buyers cannot resell the product.
- b The firm can distinguish between buyers.
- c The firm sets prices.
- d The firm captures consumer surplus.
- e Efficiency is worse than with single-price monopoly.

22 The output of a (not perfect) price-discriminating monopoly will be
- a less than a single-price monopoly.
- b more than a single-price monopoly, but less than a perfectly competitive industry.
- c the same amount as a perfectly competitive industry.
- d more than a perfectly competitive industry.
- e none of the above.

23 Many video stores charge a lower rental for Wednesday nights compared with weekends. This price discrimination is profitable only if the average willingness to pay for DVDs on Wednesdays is
- **a** greater than the average willingness to pay for DVDs on weekends.
- **b** less than the average willingness to pay for DVDs on weekends.
- **c** positive and the average willingness to pay for DVDs on weekends is negative.
- **d** negative and the average willingness to pay for DVDs on weekends is positive.
- **e** equal to one.

Monopoly Policy Issues

24 A monopoly has economies of scope if
- **a** average total cost declines as the firm's scale increases.
- **b** average total cost declines as output increases.
- **c** total profit declines as output increases.
- **d** average total cost declines as the number of different goods produced increases.
- **e** total profit declines as the number of different goods produced increases.

25 *Disadvantages* of monopoly include
- **a** economies of scope.
- **b** economies of scale.
- **c** diffusion of technological advances.
- **d** rent-seeking behaviour.
- **e** all of the above.

Short Answer Problems

1 Why is marginal revenue less than price for a single-price monopoly?

2 A single-price monopoly is the only seller of skyhooks in the Canadian market. The firm's total fixed cost is $112 per day. Its total variable costs and total costs (both in dollars per day) are shown in Table 12.2.

- **a** Complete the table by computing marginal cost, average variable cost, and average total cost. (*Remember:* Marginal cost should be entered *midway* between rows of output.)

TABLE **12.2**

Quantity	Total Variable Cost (*TVC*)	Total Cost (*TC*)	Marginal Cost (*MC*)	Average Variable Cost (*AVC*)	Average Total Cost (*ATC*)
9	135	247			
10	144	256			
11	155	267			
12	168	280			
13	183	295			
14	200	312			
15	219	331			
16	240	352			
17	263	375			
18	288	400			
19	315	427			
20	344	456			

- **b** Table 12.3 lists some points on the demand curve facing the firm, as well as the total cost information from part **a**. Complete the table by copying your values for marginal cost from Table 12.2 and by computing total revenue, marginal revenue, and economic profit. (*Remember:* Marginal revenue, like marginal cost, should be entered *midway* between rows of output.)

  What is the firm's profit-maximizing quantity of output? At what price will it sell skyhooks? What will be its total economic profit? Explain your answers.

TABLE 12.3

Price (P)	Quantity Demanded (Q_D)	Total Revenue (TR)	Marginal Revenue (MR)	Total Cost (TC)	Marginal Cost (MC)	Economic Profit (TR–TC)
57	9			247		
56	10			256		
55	11			267		
54	12			280		
53	13			295		
52	14			312		
51	15			331		
50	16			352		
49	17			375		
48	18			400		
47	19			427		
46	20			456		

c On the graph in Figure 12.4, plot the demand curve and the *MR*, *AVC*, *ATC*, and *MC* curves corresponding to the data in parts **a** and **b**. Show the equilibrium output and the area of economic profit on your diagram.

FIGURE 12.4

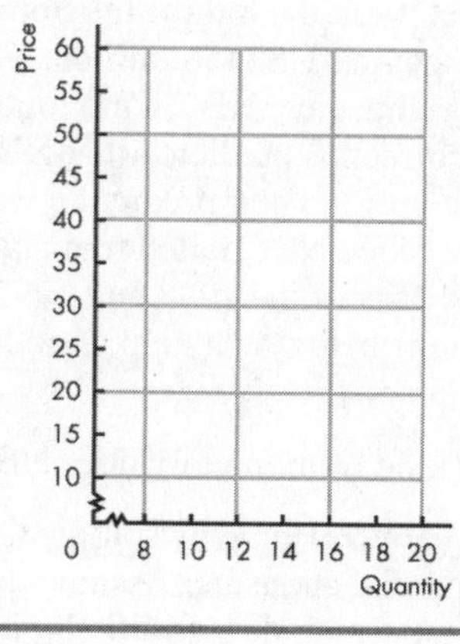

d The firm's cost curves are unchanged, but now consumer demand shifts. Table 12.4 lists some points on the new demand curve, as well as the total cost information from part **a**. Complete the table by copying your values for marginal cost from Table 12.2, and by computing the new values for total revenue, marginal revenue, and economic profit.

TABLE 12.4

Price (P)	Quantity Demanded (Q_D)	Total Revenue (TR)	Marginal Revenue (MR)	Total Cost (TC)	Marginal Cost (MC)	Economic Profit (TR–TC)
24.50	9			247		
24.00	10			256		
23.50	11			267		
23.00	12			280		
22.50	13			295		
22.00	14			312		
21.50	15			331		
21.00	16			352		
20.50	17			375		
20.00	18			400		
19.50	19			427		
19.00	20			456		
18.50	21			487		

What is the firm's new profit-maximizing quantity of output? At what price will it now sell skyhooks? What will be its total economic profit? Explain your answers.

e On the graph in Figure 12.5, plot the new demand curve and *MR* curve. Copy the *AVC*, *ATC*, and *MC* curves from Figure 12.4. Show the new equilibrium output and the area of economic profit on your diagram.

FIGURE **12.5**

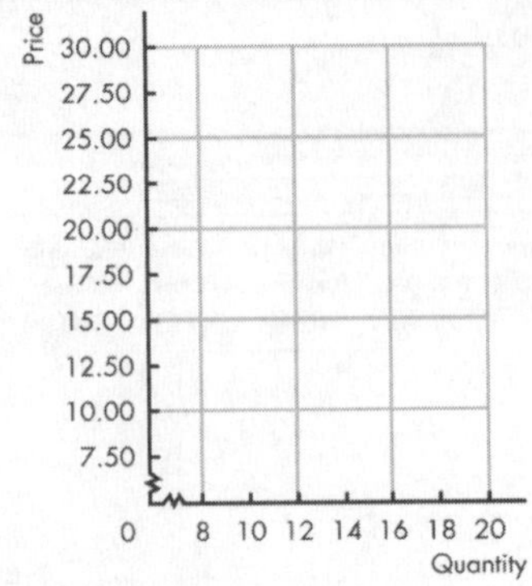

f Suppose demand falls even further so that the new demand curve equation is $P = 19 - 1/2Q_D$. On the graph in Figure 12.6, plot this demand curve and copy the *AVC* curve from Figure 12.4. Explain why the monopolist will shut down in the short

FIGURE **12.6**

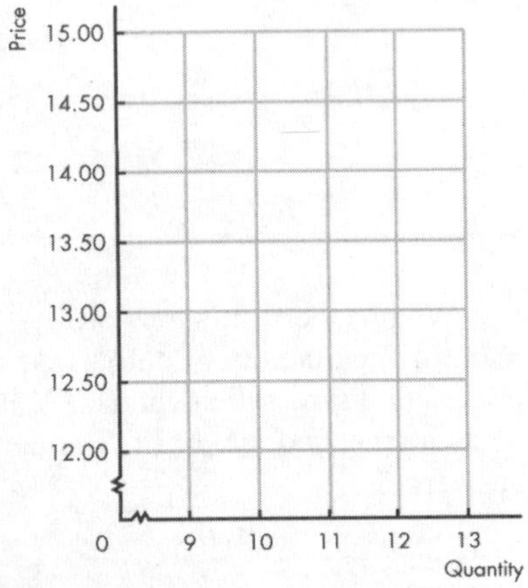

ⓒⓣ **3** You are given the following information about an industry consisting of 100 identical firms.

The demand curve facing the industry is

$$P = 36 - 0.01Q$$

The marginal revenue curve facing the industry is

$$MR = 36 - 0.02Q$$

The marginal cost curve of an individual firm is

$$MC = -12 + 2Q$$

The horizontal sum of the marginal cost curves of all of the firms in the industry is

$$MC = -12 + 0.02Q$$

Use this information to answer the following questions.

a Suppose all 100 firms are controlled by a single-price monopolist. Calculate the profit-maximizing quantity of output for the monopolist. Calculate the price per unit of output that the monopolist will charge.

b Suppose instead that the 100 firms operate independently as a perfectly competitive industry. Calculate the short-run equilibrium quantity of output for the industry as a whole. Calculate the short-run equilibrium price for the industry.

c *Without* using your answer about industry output to part **b**, calculate the short-run equilibrium output per firm.

d Compare the monopoly price and quantity outcomes with the perfect competition price and quantity outcomes.

4 Explain why the output of a competitive industry will always be greater than the output of the *same* industry under single-price monopoly.

ⓒⓣ **5** Before every Olympic Games, the International Olympic Committee (IOC) auctions off the rights to televise the Games to the highest bidder. NBC won the bid for the Summer 1996 Olympics, paying US$456 million. The television rights gave NBC a monopoly. Yet analysts (correctly) predicted that NBC would not make a profit. Their prediction was reasonable, since NBC failed to make a profit on similar telecasts of the 1988 and 1992 Olympics. The questions below will help to understand this apparent paradox.

a What kind of monopoly does NBC have?

b NBC earns revenue by selling airtime to commercial sponsors. Assume that NBC faces a normal, downward-sloping demand curve in selling 30-second commercial spots. Let's ignore for the moment the payment to the IOC and assume that marginal cost and average total cost of delivering the airtime are equal and constant. Draw a diagram representing NBC's profit-maximizing decision.

Although you do not have enough information to calculate precise numbers, indicate generally the quantity of commercial spots sold and the price per commercial spot.

c On your diagram, indicate the area representing economic profit. If the analysts' predictions were correct, what is the value of this area?

d Why did NBC fail to realize this economic profit?

6 Barney's Bistro has two kinds of customers for lunch: stockbrokers and retired senior citizens. The demand schedules for lunches for the two groups are given in Table 12.5.

Barney has decided to price discriminate between the two groups by treating each demand separately and charging the price that maximizes profit in each of the two submarkets. Marginal cost and average total cost are equal and constant at $2 per lunch.

a Complete Table 12.5 by computing the total and marginal revenue associated with stockbroker demand (TR_{SB} and MR_{SB}) as well as the total and marginal revenue associated with senior citizen demand (TR_{SC} and MR_{SC}). (*Remember:* Marginal revenue should be entered *midway* between rows.)

b What are the profit-maximizing output and price for stockbrokers?

c What are the profit-maximizing output and price for senior citizens?

d What is total economic profit?

e Show that the total economic profit in part **d** is the maximum by comparing it with total economic profit if instead Barney served: 1 additional lunch *each* to stockbrokers and senior citizens; 1 less lunch *each* to stockbrokers and senior citizens.

f What is the consumer surplus for stockbrokers? for senior citizens? for all customers?

ⓒⓣ **7** The stockbrokers complain bitterly about Barney's discriminatory pricing policy, and threaten to bring bag lunches unless Barney charges a uniform price to all customers. Barney buckles under to the pressure, and sits down with his calculator to figure out his profit-maximizing output and price as a single-price monopolist. Using the previous information in Short Answer Problem **6**, can you figure it out for him *without* looking at the hints below? If not, answer these questions.

TABLE **12.5**

	Stockbrokers			Senior Citizens		
Price (P)	Quantity Demanded (Q_D)	Total Revenue (TR_{SB})	Marginal Revenue (MR_{SB})	Quantity Demanded (Q_D)	Total Revenue (TR_{SC})	Marginal Revenue (MR_{SC})
8	0			0		
7	1			0		
6	2			0		
5	3			1		
4	4			2		
3	5			3		
2	6			4		
1	7			5		
0	8			6		

a Calculate Barney's demand schedule by adding up the quantity demanded by stockbrokers and senior citizens at each price. Construct a table similar to Table 12.5, with columns for price, quantity demanded, total revenue, and marginal revenue. (*Remember:* Marginal revenue should be entered *midway* between rows.)

b Marginal cost and average total cost remain unchanged at $2 per lunch. What are Barney's profit-maximizing output and price?

c What is Barney's total economic profit as a single-price monopolist? How does this compare with his total economic profit as a price-discriminating monopolist?

d What is the consumer surplus for all customers? How does this compare with the consumer surplus for all customers when Barney price discriminated?

ⓒⓣ 8 The price of the last unit sold and the quantity sold are exactly the same in an industry under perfect competition and under a perfect price-discriminating monopoly. Are consumers therefore indifferent between the two? Explain.

9 Figure 12.7 gives the demand, marginal revenue, and marginal cost curves for a certain industry. Your task is to illustrate how consumer and producer surplus are distributed under each of four ways of organizing the industry. In each case redraw any relevant part of Figure 12.7 and then (1) indicate the region of the graph corresponding to consumer surplus by drawing horizontal lines through it; (2) indicate the region corresponding to producer surplus by drawing vertical lines through it; and (3) indicate the region (if any) corresponding to deadweight loss by putting dots in the area.

a The industry consists of many perfectly competitive firms.

b The industry is a single-price monopoly.

c The industry is a price-discriminating monopoly charging two prices: P_1 and P_3.

d The industry is a perfect price-discriminating monopoly.

FIGURE 12.7

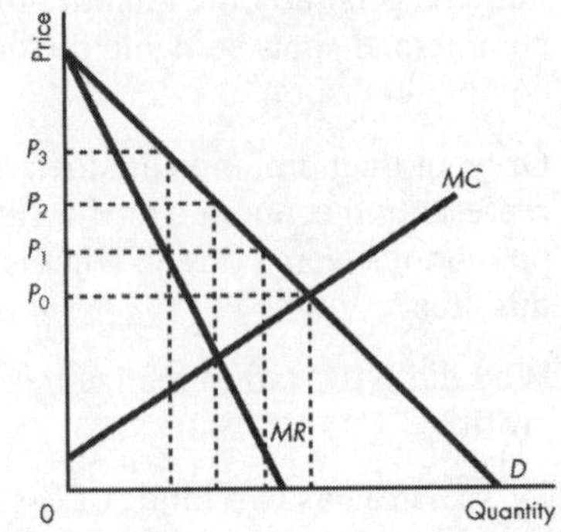

10 Under what circumstances would a monopoly be more efficient than a large number of competitive firms? Illustrate graphically such a situation where a monopoly produces more and charges a lower price than would be the case if the industry consisted of a large number of perfectly competitive firms.

ANSWERS

True/False and Explain

1 F When there are *no* close substitutes. (264)

2 T Definition of natural monopoly. (264–265)

3 T Without barriers to entry, other firms will enter industry, creating competition. (264–265)

4 F *MR* is negative. (266–267)

5 F Monopolist has no supply curve. (268–269)

ⓒⓣ 6 T Average of all (equal) prices of product = price. For any row in text Table 12.1, $AR = TR/Q = P$. (266–269)

ⓒⓣ 7 F Monopoly no guarantee economic profit if rent seeking is costly enough. (270–273)

8 T Area below competitive price and above *MC* for reduced output. (270–272)

ⓒⓣ 9 F Greater. Resources used in rent-seeking cost to society. (272–273)

10 F In equilibrium, economic profit may be totally eliminated by rent-seeking costs. (272–273)

11 F Can*not* be readily resold. (273–274)

12 F To capture consumer surplus and convert to economic profit. (273–274)

13 T Demand curve gives revenue for each successive unit sold (at different price). (275–276)

14 T Advantages of monopoly. (277–278)

15 T *P* = *AR* = *ATC*. Outcome inefficient because deadweight loss, but more efficient than unregulated monopoly. (278–279)

Multiple-Choice

1 b Others are legal barriers. (264–265)

2 d *TR* (*P* = \$7) = \$7 × 7 = \$49. *TR* (*P* = \$6) = \$6 × 8 = \$48. *MR* = Δ*TR* = \$48 – \$49. (266–268)

3 c Monopolist should decrease output. Shutdown decision premature since monopolist can change price. (268–269)

4 d *MR–MC* comparisons are key. Revenue **a** and cost **b** are important, but must be *compared* for profitability. (268–269)

5 d *TR* would be decreased needlessly. Monopolist could decrease *Q* and raise *P* to increase *TR*. (266–269)

6 c **a**, **b** irrelevant comparisons marginal and average quantities. **d** true if *TR* < *TVC*. (266–269)

7 b *Q* where *MR* = *MC*. Highest *P* consumers will pay for 3 units. (268–269)

ⓔ **8 c** (*AR* – *ATC*) × *Q* = (\$6 – \$4) × 3. (268–269)

9 c Rule for choosing output. (268–269)

10 a Draw graph. $Q_{current}$ > *Q* corresponding to *MR* = *MC*. (268–269)

11 c Shutdown rule same as perfect competition. (268–269)

ⓔ **12 d** Sum of (*P* – *MC*) for each unit output. (270–271)

ⓔ **13 d** **a** true for both. **b** true competitor only. **c** false for both. (270–271)

14 a Definition. Activity has costs. (272–273)

15 c Monopoly profit = resources used rent seeking. (272–273)

16 b Area above price but below demand (willingness to pay). (270–272)

17 d Area below price but above *MC*. (270–272)

18 b Sum of lost producer (*bcd*) and consumer (*abd*) surplus compared to competitive outcome. (270–272)

19 e Deadweight loss is zero. (275–276)

ⓔ **20 d** Same outcome as perfectly competitive industry, so **e** wrong. *D* = *MR* so **a** wrong. Profit maximizing so **b** wrong. (275–276)

21 e Efficiency same as perfect competition. (275–276)

22 b **c** true for perfect price discrimination. (273–275)

23 b Charge lower price with higher η and higher price with lower η. (273–275)

24 d Definition. (277–278)

25 d Others are advantages. Rent seeking diverts resources that could be used productively. (277–279)

Short Answer Problems

1 In order to sell an additional unit of output, a monopoly must drop the price. This has two effects on revenue: one positive and equal to price, and the other negative. Marginal revenue is the net effect, which must be less than price. First, the additional unit sold at the new lower price adds an amount to revenue equal to the price. But, a single-price monopoly must also lower the price to previous customers who would have paid more. The net effect on marginal revenue is equal to the price minus the loss of revenue from lowering the price to previous customers. This difference must necessarily be less than price.

2 **a** Completed Table 12.2 is given here as Table 12.2 Solution.

TABLE **12.2** SOLUTION

Quantity	Total Variable Cost (*TVC*)	Total Cost (*TC*)	Marginal Cost (*MC*)	Average Variable Cost (*AVC*)	Average Total Cost (*ATC*)
9	135	247		15.00	27.44
			... 9		
10	144	256		14.40	25.60
			... 11		
11	155	267		14.09	24.27
			... 13		
12	168	280		14.00	23.33
			... 15		
13	183	295		14.08	22.69
			... 17		
14	200	312		14.29	22.29
			... 19		
15	219	331		14.60	22.07
			... 21		
16	240	352		15.00	22.00
			... 23		
17	263	375		15.47	22.06
			... 25		
18	288	400		16.00	22.22
			... 27		
19	315	427		16.58	22.47
			... 29		
20	344	456		17.20	22.80

b Completed Table 12.3 is shown here as Table 12.3 Solution.

TABLE **12.3** SOLUTION

Price (*P*)	Quantity Demanded (Q_D)	Total Revenue (*TR*)	Marginal Revenue (*MR*)	Total Cost (*TC*)	Marginal Cost (*MC*)	Economic Profit (*TR–TC*)
57	9	513		247		266
			... 47		... 9	
56	10	560		256		304
			... 45		... 11	
55	11	605		267		338
			... 43		... 13	
54	12	648		280		368
			... 41		... 15	
53	13	689		295		394
			... 39		... 17	
52	14	728		312		416
			... 37		... 19	
51	15	765		331		434
			... 35		... 21	
50	16	800		352		448
			... 33		... 23	
49	17	833		375		458
			... 31		... 25	
48	18	864		400		464
			... 29		... 27	
47	19	893		427		466
			... 27		... 29	
46	20	920		456		464

Equilibrium output occurs where $MC = MR = 28$, $Q = 19$, $P = \$47$, economic profit = \$466 per day.

The profit-maximizing quantity of output occurs where marginal cost equals marginal revenue, at 19 units. The maximum price the firm can charge and still sell 19 units is \$47. This combination of quantity and price yields a total economic profit of \$466, which, as can be seen from the table, is the maximum possible profit.

c The requested diagram appears in Figure 12.4 Solution.

FIGURE **12.4** SOLUTION

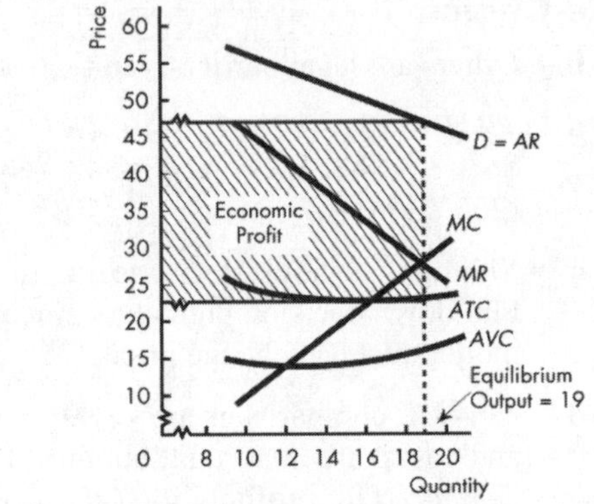

d Completed Table 12.4 is given here as Table 12.4 Solution.

TABLE **12.4** SOLUTION

Price (*P*)	Quantity Demanded (Q_D)	Total Revenue (*TR*)	Marginal Revenue (*MR*)	Total Cost (*TC*)	Marginal Cost (*MC*)	Economic Profit (*TR–TC*)
24.50	9	220.50		247		–26.50
			... 19.50		... 9	
24.00	10	240.00		256		–16.00
			... 18.50		... 11	
23.50	11	258.50		267		–8.50
			... 17.50		... 13	
23.00	12	276.00		280		–4.00
			... 16.50		... 15	
22.50	13	292.50		295		–2.50
			... 15.50		... 17	
22.00	14	308.00		312		–4.00
			... 14.50		... 19	
21.50	15	322.50		331		–8.50
			... 13.50		... 21	
21.00	16	336.00		352		–16.00
			... 12.50		... 23	
20.50	17	348.50		375		–26.50
			... 11.50		... 25	
20.00	18	360.00		400		–40.00
			... 10.50		... 27	
19.50	19	370.50		427		–56.50
			... 9.50		... 29	
19.00	20	380.00		456		–76.00

Equilibrium output occurs where $MC = MR = 16$, $Q = 13$, $P = \$22.50$, economic profit = –\$2.50.

The profit-maximizing quantity of output occurs where marginal cost equals marginal revenue, now at 13 units. The maximum price the firm can charge and still sell 13 units is \$22.50. This combination of quantity and price yields a total economic profit of –\$2.50 (an economic loss). As can be seen from the table, this is the minimum possible loss. The firm will continue to produce in the short run, because this loss is less than its shutdown loss, which would be \$112, the amount of its fixed cost.

e The requested diagram appears in Figure 12.5 Solution.

FIGURE **12.5** SOLUTION

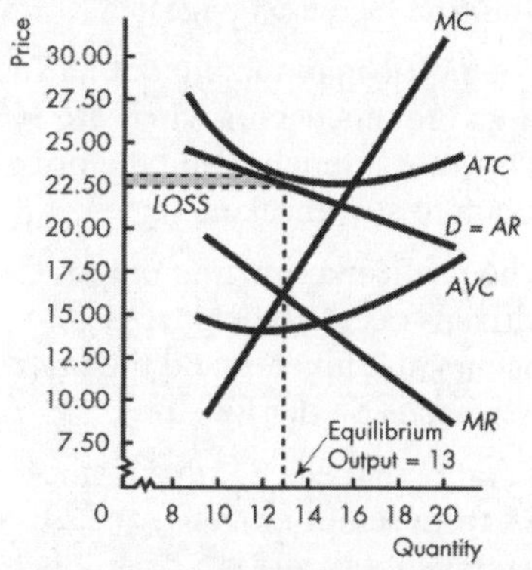

f The requested diagram appears in Figure 12.6 Solution. Since the demand curve is everywhere below the *AVC* curve, no matter what quantity of output the firm might produce, price will be less than *AVC*. This means that the firm will lose money on every unit produced in addition to losing its total fixed cost. The monopolist will minimize loss in this case by shutting down and losing just its fixed cost (\$112).

FIGURE **12.6** SOLUTION

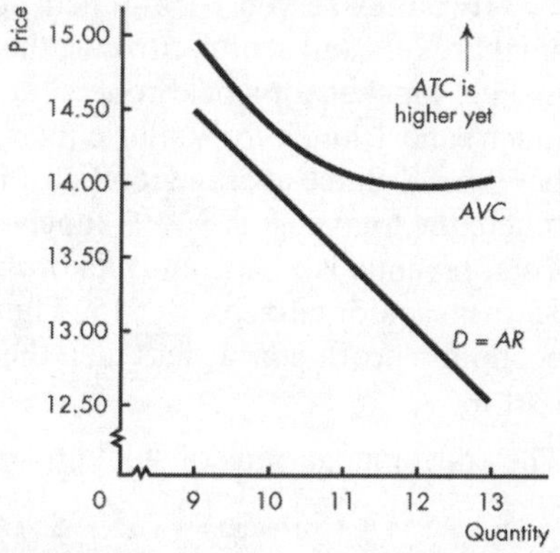

ⓒ **3 a** The monopolist will choose the quantity of output where marginal revenue equals marginal cost. To calculate this quantity, set the equation for marginal revenue equal to the equation for industry marginal cost (since the monopolist controls all of the firms).

$$36 - 0.02Q = -12 + 0.02Q$$
$$48 = 0.04Q$$
$$1{,}200 = Q$$

To calculate the price that the monopolist will charge, substitute the quantity 1,200 into the demand equation. This is the mathematical equivalent of graphically, after finding the quantity corresponding to the intersection of *MC* and *MR*, moving your eye up to the demand curve to read the price.

$$P = 36 - 0.01Q$$
$$P = 36 - 0.01(1{,}200)$$
$$P = 36 - 12$$
$$P = 24$$

b The perfectly competitive industry's short-run equilibrium quantity of output occurs where industry demand intersects industry supply. Set the industry demand equation equal to the industry supply equation, which is the horizontal sum of the marginal cost curves of all firms in the industry.

$$36 - 0.01Q = -12 + 0.02Q$$
$$48 = 0.03Q$$
$$1{,}600 = Q$$

To calculate the short-run equilibrium price for the industry, we can substitute the quantity 1,600 into either the industry demand equation or the industry supply equation. Using the industry demand equation yields

$$P = 36 - 0.01Q$$
$$P = 36 - 0.01(1{,}600)$$
$$P = 36 - 16$$
$$P = 20$$

Using the industry supply equation yields the same result:

$$P = -12 + 0.02Q$$
$$P = -12 + 0.02(1{,}600)$$
$$P = -12 + 32$$
$$P = 20$$

c If industry output is 1,600 units and there are 100 identical firms, then obviously the output per firm is 1,600 units/100 firms equals 16 units/firm. But the question specifically asks you *not* to use the information about industry output.

The other way to calculate the short-run equilibrium output per firm is to substitute the equilibrium price of 20 into the individual firm's marginal cost curve, which is also its short-run supply curve.

$$P = -12 + 2Q$$
$$20 = -12 + 2Q$$
$$32 = 2Q$$
$$16 = Q$$

d The monopoly price ($24) is higher than the perfect competition price ($20) and the monopoly quantity of output (1,200) is lower than the perfect competition quantity of output (1,600).

4 A competitive industry will produce the level of output at which the industry marginal cost curve intersects the demand curve facing the industry. A single-price monopoly will produce at the level of output at which the industry marginal cost curve intersects the monopoly marginal revenue curve. Since the marginal revenue curve lies below the demand curve, this implies a lower level of output in the monopoly industry.

ⓒⓣ **5 a** NBC had a legal monopoly, based on a public franchise—an exclusive right granted to a firm to supply a good or service.

b The requested diagram is shown in Figure 12.8. The quantity of commercial spots sold is Q_{CS} and the price is P_{CS}.

FIGURE **12.8**

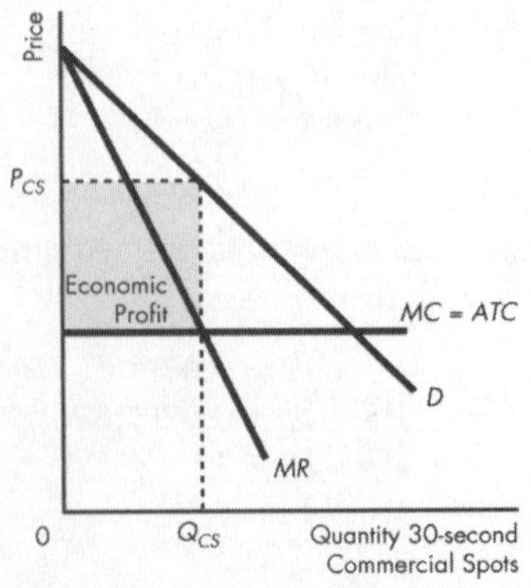

c The shaded rectangle above *ATC* and below P_{CS} in Figure 12.8 represents economic profit. That profit, which is based on costs that exclude the US$456 million payment to the IOC, will be US$456 million if the analysts are correct.

d NBC fails to make an economic profit because of the costs of rent seeking. NBC had to compete for the monopoly rights to televise the Olympics. It makes sense for bidders to continue to offer a higher price for those rights up to the point where the price of the rights equals the value of the economic profit to be earned from owning them.

6 a The completed table is given in Table 12.5 Solution (see next page).

b The profit-maximizing output for stockbrokers occurs when $MC = \$2 = MR_{SB}$. This is at 3 lunches and the price is $5 per lunch to stockbrokers.

c The profit-maximizing output for senior citizens occurs when $MC = \$2 = MR_{SC}$. This occurs at 2 lunches and the price to senior citizens is $4 per lunch.

d Total revenue is $15 from stockbrokers and $8 from senior citizens, or $23. Since average total cost is $2 per lunch, total cost is $2 × 5 lunches = $10. Thus total economic profit is $13.

e If Barney served 1 additional lunch each to stockbrokers and senior citizens, that would make 4 lunches for stockbrokers (at $4 per lunch) and 3 lunches for senior citizens (at $3 per lunch). Since average total cost is $2 per lunch, the total cost is $2 × 7 lunches = $14. Total revenue is $16 from stockbrokers and $9 from senior citizens, or $25. Thus total economic profit is $11, less than the $13 in part **d**.

If Barney served 1 less lunch each to stockbrokers and senior citizens, that would make 2 lunches for stockbrokers (at $6 per lunch) and 1 lunch for senior citizens (at $5 per lunch). Since average total cost is $2 per lunch, the total cost is $2 × 3 lunches = $6. Total revenue is $12 from stockbrokers and $5 from senior citizens, or $17. Thus total economic profit is $11, less than the $13 in part **d**.

f The consumer surplus of stockbrokers is

$$(\$7 - \$5) + (\$6 - \$5) + (\$5 - \$5) = \$3$$

TABLE 12.5 SOLUTION

	Stockbrokers			Senior Citizens		
Price (P)	Quantity Demanded (Q_D)	Total Revenue (TR_{SB})	Marginal Revenue (MR_{SB})	Quantity Demanded (Q_D)	Total Revenue (TR_{SC})	Marginal Revenue (MR_{SC})
8	0	0		0	0	
			7			0
7	1	7		0	0	
			5			0
6	2	12		0	0	
			3			5
5	**3**	**15**		1	5	
			1			3
4	4	16		**2**	**8**	
			–1			1
3	5	15		3	9	
			–3			–1
2	6	12		4	8	
			–5			–3
1	7	7		5	5	
			–7			–5
0	8	0		6	0	

The consumer surplus of senior citizens is

$$(\$5 - \$4) + (\$4 - \$4) = \$1$$

The consumer surplus of all customers is

$$\$3 + \$1 = \$4$$

7 a The requested table is given as Table 12.6 Solution.

TABLE 12.6 SOLUTION

Price (P)	Quantity Demanded (Q_D)	Total Revenue (TR)	Marginal Revenue (MR)
8	0	0	
			7
7	1	7	
			5
6	2	12	
			4
5	4	20	
			2
4	6	24	
			0
3	8	24	
			–2
2	10	20	
			–4
1	12	12	
			–6
0	14	0	

b The profit-maximizing output occurs when $MC = \$2 = MR$. This occurs halfway between a combination of 4 lunches at \$5 per lunch and 6 lunches at \$4 per lunch. Either combination yields the same economic profit. Let's look at the combination of 6 lunches at \$4 per lunch.

c Total revenue is \$4 per lunch × 6 lunches = \$24. Average total cost is \$2 per lunch. Total cost is \$2 × 6 lunches = \$12. Thus total economic profit is \$12. Barney's economic profit as a single-price monopolist (\$12) is less than his economic profit as a price-discriminating monopolist (\$13).

d From the demand curves we can tell that there is 1 customer (stockbroker) who values lunch at \$7, 1 customer (stockbroker) who values lunch at \$6, 2 customers (stockbroker and senior) who value lunch at \$5, and 2 customers (stockbroker and senior) who value lunch at \$4. The consumer surplus for all customers is

$$1(\$7 - \$4) + 1(\$6 - \$4) + 2(\$5 - \$4) + 2(\$4 - \$4) = \$7$$

This consumer surplus without price discrimination (\$7) is greater than consumer surplus with price discrimination (\$4).

ⓒ 8 While the quantity sold and the price charged to the last customer are the same for perfect competition and a perfect price discriminator, the distribution of consumer surplus is not the same. Since a perfect price discriminator charges each customer the most she is willing to pay, there is no consumer surplus. Any consumer surplus that would have occurred under perfect competition now accrues to the monopoly. Consumers would like to obtain more consumer surplus, and therefore pay less for the same amount. Consequently, consumers prefer perfect competition.

9 a Under perfect competition, price equals marginal cost. The amount of consumer surplus is given by the area under the demand curve but above the price (P_0) while the amount of producer surplus is given by the area above the *MC* curve but below the price; see Figure 12.7 Solution (a).

b If the industry is a single-price monopoly, price will be greater than *MC* and output will be less than under competition. Consumer surplus is still given by the area under the demand curve but above the price (P_2), while producer surplus is given by the area above the *MC* curve but below the price up to the monopoly level of output. The remaining part of the large triangle is a deadweight loss—the amount of surplus under competition that is lost under a single-price monopoly; see Figure 12.7 Solution (b).

c Similar reasoning allows us to establish regions in Figure 12.7 Solution (c) corresponding to consumer surplus, producer surplus, and deadweight loss.

d Under perfect price discrimination, all of the potential surplus is captured by the producer and there is no deadweight loss (or consumer surplus). See Figure 12.7 Solution (d).

FIGURE **12.7** SOLUTION

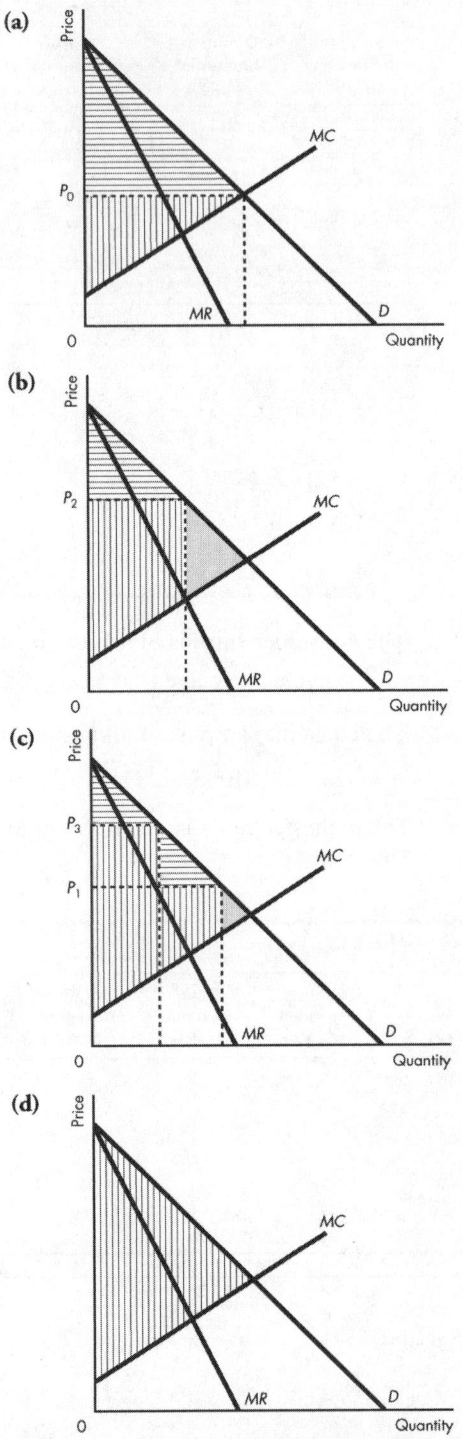

10 A monopoly would be more efficient than perfect competition if the monopoly has sufficient economies of scale and/or scope. Those economies must be large enough that the monopoly produces more than the competitive industry and sells it at a lower price. Figure 12.9 illustrates such a situation. The important feature is that the marginal cost curve for the monopoly must not only be lower than the supply curve of the competitive industry, but it must also be sufficiently lower so that it intersects the *MR* curve at an output greater than *C* (the competitive output). Such a situation could arise if there are extensive economies of scale and/or scope.

FIGURE 12.9

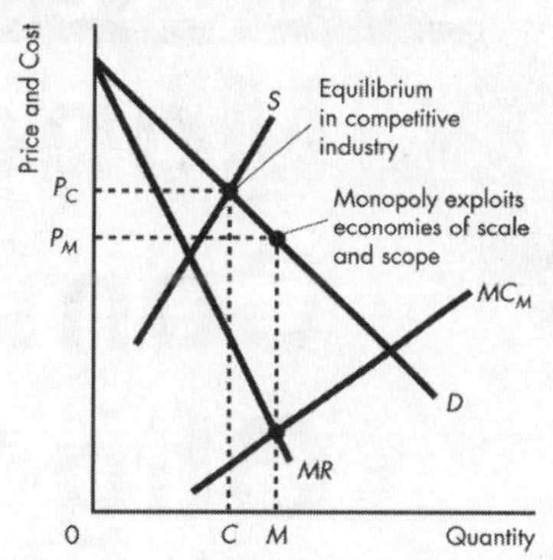

Chapter 13 Monopolistic Competition and Oligopoly

KEY CONCEPTS

Monopolistic Competition

- **Monopolistic competition** is a model of market structure in which many firms compete; there is **product differentiation** (firms make similar but slightly different products) giving firms some monopoly power; firms compete on product quality, price, and marketing; there is free entry and exit.
- Firm ignores other individual firms and collusion impossible because all have small market share.
- Firm faces downward-sloping demand curve.
- Marginal revenue curve $\neq$ demand curve.
- Firm can choose price and output.

Price and Output and in Monopolistic Competition

Outcomes:

- Profit maximization (or loss minimization): choose Q where $MC = MR$, charge highest possible price (on demand curve).
- Short-run economic profit possible, attracts entry, causing leftward shift demand (and MR) curves facing each firm.
- Short-run economic loss possible, some firms exit, causing rightward shift demand (and MR) curves facing each remaining firm.
- Long-run economic profit = 0, $P = ATC$. But
  - ATC not at minimum. Firm has *excess capacity*, producing *below* **capacity output** where ATC = minimum.
  - $P > MC$ by amount of markup.
- Inefficiency of monopolistic competition must be weighed against gain of greater product variety.

Product Development and Marketing

To restore economic profits, monopolistically competitive firms must continuously innovate and develop new products. New firms enter with similar products, compete away economic profits—the cycle continues.

Marketing expenditures on advertising and packaging (selling costs) are used to *create perception* of product differentiation even when actual product differences are small, and to **signal** quality.

- Selling costs are fixed costs that increase total costs, but average total cost might decrease if output increases enough.
- Selling costs might increase demand for firm's product, but might also decrease demand by increasing competition.

Inefficiencies of monopolistic competition (selling costs and excess capacity) must be weighed against gain of greater product variety.

What Is Oligopoly?

Oligopoly is model of market structure where few firms compete and *strategically interact*. Firm considers effects of its actions on behaviour of others and actions of others on its own profit.

- Natural or legal barriers prevent entry new firms.
- **Duopoly**—oligopoly market with two firms.
- **Cartel**—group of firms in collusive agreement.

Two Traditional Oligopoly Models

Kinked demand curve model assumes if firm raises price, no firms follow, and if firm cuts price, all firms follow.

- ♦ Result: each firm faces kinked demand curve, with kink at current *P*, *Q*.
- ♦ Prediction: sticky prices—kink causes break in *MR* curve so *MC* curve can vary within break without affecting price or quantity.

Dominant firm oligopoly model assumes one large firm with major cost advantage, many small firms.

- ♦ Predictions: large firm acts like monopoly, sets profit-maximizing price. Small firms take price, act like perfect competitors.

Oligopoly Games

Game theory analyzes strategic behaviour. Games have

- ♦ rules—specify permissible actions by players.
- ♦ **strategies**—actions such as raising or lowering price, output, advertising, or product quality.
- ♦ payoffs—profits and losses of players. **Payoff matrix** shows payoffs for every possible action by each player.
- ♦ outcome—determined by players' choices. In a **Nash equilibrium**, *A* takes best possible action given *B*'s action, and *B* takes best possible action given *A*'s action.

A "prisoners' dilemma" is a one-time, two-person game with a **dominant strategy equilibrium**. Each player has a dominant strategy (unique best strategy independent of other player's action) of cheating, that is, confessing.

- ♦ Prisoners' dilemma yields a Nash equilibrium outcome that is *not* in the best interests of the players.

In a duopoly game, each firm can *comply* with a **collusive agreement** to restrict output and raise price, or it can *cheat*.

- ♦ In one-time price-fixing game, prisoners' dilemma solution occurs—each firm has dominant strategy of cheating, even though both firms would be better off if they could trust each other and comply.
- ♦ Unlike prisoners' dilemma game, a game of chicken has a Nash equilibrium that is *not* a dominant strategy equilibrium.

Game theory can be used to analyze other choices for firms—how much to spend on research and development, on advertising, whether to enter or exit an industry.

Repeated Games and Sequential Games

In repeated game, other strategies can create **cooperative equilibrium** in which each firm complies with collusive agreement and makes monopoly profits. Requires firms to punish cheating in previous period.

- ♦ *Tit-for-tat strategy*—taking same action other player took last period. Lightest punishment.
- ♦ *Trigger strategy*—cooperating until other player cheats, then cheating forever. Most severe punishment.

Game tree—shows decisions made at first and second stages of sequential game—can be used to analyze sequential entry-deterrence game. In a **contestable market** there are few firms but free entry and exit so existing firms face competition from *potential* entrants. Existing firms may use strategies of

- ♦ set monopoly price, but risk entry of new firm.
- ♦ set competitive price and earn normal profit to keep out a potential competitor.
- ♦ **limit pricing**—set highest price that just inflicts loss on entrant. Compared to monopoly outcome, charge lower price and produce greater quantity in order to deter entry.

HELPFUL HINTS

1 Most industries are neither perfectly competitive nor pure monopolies; they lie somewhere between these two extremes. This does not mean that the last two chapters have been wasted. By examining firms under these extreme market structures, we now can discuss the wide range of industries between them in just one chapter.

The intermediate forms of market structure share many characteristics of perfect competition and/or monopoly. Consider the profit-maximizing rule of choosing the output where $MC = MR$. The rule applies not only in perfect competition and monopoly, but also in monopolistic competition, kinked demand curve, and dominant firm oligopoly models. Free entry leads to zero long-run economic profit in both perfect competition and monopolistic competition. The downward-sloping demand and marginal revenue curves of monopoly also apply to monopolistic competition, kinked demand curve, and dominant firm oligopoly models.

The extreme and unrealistic assumptions of models of perfect competition and monopoly allow us to isolate the impact of important forces like profit maximization and important constraints like competition and market demand. These forces and constraints also operate in more realistic market structures. But it was necessary to isolate these forces and constraints beforehand rather than attempt to immediately analyze "realistic" market structures like monopolistic competition and oligopoly, which would have been a confusing jumble of details and possible outcomes. It would have been like driving in a strange, large city without a road map.

2 In graphing a monopolistically competitive firm in long-run equilibrium, be sure that the *ATC* curve is tangent to the demand curve at the same level of output at which the *MC* and *MR* curves intersect. Also be sure that the *MC* curve intersects the *ATC* curve at the minimum point on the *ATC* curve.

3 This chapter uses elementary game theory to explain oligopoly. The prisoners' dilemma game illustrates the most important game theory concepts (rules, strategies, payoffs, outcome), which are then used in more complex game theory models like repeated and sequential games.

It is important to learn how to find the Nash equilibrium of a prisoners' dilemma–type game. Take the example of players *A* and *B*, where each player has to choose between two strategies—confess or deny. First set up the payoff matrix. Then look at the payoff matrix from *A*'s point of view. *A* does not know if *B* is going to confess or deny, so *A* asks two questions: (1) Assuming that *B* confesses, do I get a better payoff if I confess or deny? (2) Assuming that *B* denies, do I get a better payoff if I confess or deny?

If *A*'s best strategy is to confess, regardless of whether *B* confesses or denies, confessing is *A*'s dominant strategy. Next, look at the payoff matrix from *B*'s point of view. Let *B* ask the equivalent two questions, and find *B*'s dominant strategy. The combination of *A*'s dominant strategy and *B*'s dominant strategy comprises the Nash equilibrium outcome of the game.

4 The key insight of the prisoners' dilemma game is the *tension* between the Nash equilibrium outcome (where both players' best strategy is to confess because they can't trust each other) and the fact that both players could make themselves better off if only they would cooperate. All of the equilibrium situations we have examined up until now have been stable outcomes where all agents' self-interests (utility and profit) have been maximized. Remember, equilibrium is defined as a situation where there is no tendency to change. The Nash equilibrium of the prisoner's dilemma is different. Even though both players confess, their individual self-interests are not maximized. It is the additional possibility of strategic interaction (to trust or not to trust the other player) that creates the instability of outcomes.

The instability of outcomes in this simple game helps us to understand more complex market phenomena such as gasoline price wars. When gasoline station owners trust each other, prices remain relatively high and profits are maximized. But there is always an incentive to cheat on a collusive agreement. Once cheating begins, trust breaks down and owners are driven to the equilibrium outcome where all owners cheat, prices fall, and profits are reduced. Eventually, reduced profits lead owners to take a chance on trusting each other again, since they figure it couldn't be worse than existing low prices and profits. All stations raise their prices, and the cycle begins again. This instability of price and profit outcomes stems from the cycle of trust and non-trust. In other words, instability arises from strategic interaction between station owners.

SELF-TEST

True/False and Explain

What Is Monopolistic Competition?

1 Barriers to entry give monopolistically competitive firms some monopoly power.

2 Product differentiation gives monopolistically competitive firms some monopoly power.

Price and Output in Monopolistic Competition

3 In monopolistic competition, short-run profits attract new entry, shifting each individual firm's demand curve rightward.

4 Free entry is the key characteristic of monopolistic competition that produces excess capacity.

5 When a monopolistically competitive industry is in long-run equilibrium, economic profit is zero and price equals minimum average total cost.

Product Development and Marketing

6 Firms in monopolistic competition must innovate continuously to enjoy economic profits.

7 Selling costs always increase average total costs.

8 Advertising by monopolistic competitors is never allocatively inefficient.

What Is Oligopoly?

9 An oligopolist will consider the reaction of other firms before it decides to cut its price.

Two Traditional Oligopoly Models

10 The kinked demand curve model predicts that price and quantity will be sensitive to small cost changes.

Oligopoly Games

11 A Nash equilibrium occurs when *A* takes the best possible action given the action of *B*, and *B* takes the best possible action given the action of *A*.

12 If duopolists agree to collude, they can (jointly) make as much profit as a single monopoly.

13 For colluding duopolists in a nonrepeated game, the equilibrium is always for both firms to cheat.

Repeated Games and Sequential Games

14 For colluding duopolists in a repeated game, the equilibrium is always for both firms to cheat.

15 A limit pricing strategy sets the price that inflicts the highest loss on a new entrant.

Multiple-Choice

What Is Monopolistic Competition?

1 In monopolistic competition, firms
- **a** can collude.
- **b** strategically interact with other firms.
- **c** have an element of monopoly power.
- **d** face a kinked demand curve.
- **e** do all of the above.

Price and Output in Monopolistic Competition

2 For a monopolistically competitive firm in long-run equilibrium,
- **a** $P = MC$.
- **b** $MC = ATC$.
- **c** $AR = ATC$, but $P > MC$.
- **d** $MC = AR$, but $ATC > AR$.
- **e** none of the above is true.

3 Figure 13.1 represents a monopolistically competitive firm in short-run equilibrium. What is the firm's level of output?
- **a** Q_1
- **b** Q_2
- **c** Q_3
- **d** Q_4
- **e** zero

FIGURE **13.1**

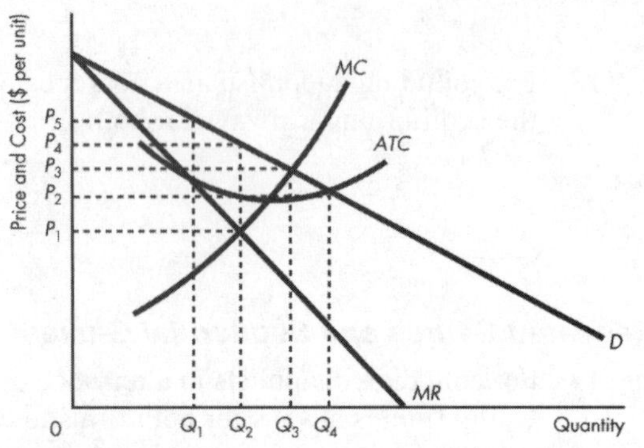

4 Figure 13.1 represents a monopolistically competitive firm in short-run equilibrium. What is the firm's economic profit *per unit*?
- **a** $P_4 - P_2$
- **b** $P_4 - P_1$
- **c** P_4
- **d** P_3
- **e** None of the above

5 Figure 13.1 represents a monopolistically competitive firm in short-run equilibrium. In the long run,
- **a** new firms will enter, and each existing firm's demand shifts leftward.
- **b** new firms will enter, and each existing firm's demand shifts rightward.
- **c** existing firms will leave, and each remaining firm's demand shifts leftward.
- **d** existing firms will leave, and each remaining firm's demand shifts rightward.
- **e** there will be no change from the short run.

6 Under monopolistic competition, long-run economic profit tends toward zero because of
- **a** product differentiation.
- **b** the lack of barriers to entry.
- **c** excess capacity.
- **d** inefficiency.
- **e** downward-sloping demand curves facing each firm.

7 In the long run, a monopolistically competitive firm will earn the same economic profit as
- **a** a monopolistically competitive firm in the short run.
- **b** a member of a cartel.
- **c** a pure price-discriminating monopolist.
- **d** a perfectly competitive firm.
- **e** none of the above.

8 Which of the following is true for perfect competition, monopolistic competition, and single-price monopoly?
- **a** homogeneous product
- **b** zero long-run economic profit
- **c** short-run profit-maximizing quantity where $MC = MR$
- **d** easy entry and exit
- **e** none of the above

9 In the long run, the firm in monopolistic competition will
- **a** face a perfectly elastic demand curve.
- **b** produce more than the quantity that minimizes *ATC*.
- **c** produce less than the quantity that minimizes *ATC*.
- **d** produce the quantity that minimizes *ATC*.
- **e** earn economic profit.

10 In the long run, a monopolistically competitive firm will produce the output at which price equals
- **a** marginal cost.
- **b** marginal revenue.
- **c** average variable cost.
- **d** average total cost.
- **e** **b** and **d**.

11 Which of the following characteristics is *not* shared by single-price monopoly and monopolistic competition?
- **a** firms face a downward-sloping demand curve
- **b** profit-maximizing quantity where $MC = MR$
- **c** equilibrium *ATC* above minimum *ATC*
- **d** positive long-run economic profit
- **e** positive long-run normal profit

Product Development and Marketing

12 Selling costs
- a are variable costs that increase total cost.
- b always increase demand for a firm's product.
- c always decrease demand by increasing competition.
- d always provide consumers with valuable services.
- e include marketing expenditures on advertising and packaging.

What Is Oligopoly?

13 Each of the following is a characteristic of monopolistic competition. Which is *not* a characteristic of oligopoly?
- a Each firm faces a downward-sloping demand curve.
- b Firms are profit-maximizers.
- c The sales of one firm will not have a significant effect on other firms.
- d There is more than one firm in the industry.
- e Firms set prices.

Two Traditional Oligopoly Models

14 Which of the following statements about the sections of kinked demand curve in Figure 13.2 is *correct*?
- a *AB* assumes new firms will enter the industry, while *BC* assumes no new firms will enter.
- b *AB* assumes no new firms will enter the industry, while *BC* assumes new firms will enter.
- c The kink between sections reflects market imperfections.
- d *AB* assumes other firms will match a price increase, while *BC* assumes other firms will not match a price decrease.
- e *AB* assumes other firms will not match a price increase, while *BC* assumes other firms will match a price decrease.

FIGURE **13.2**

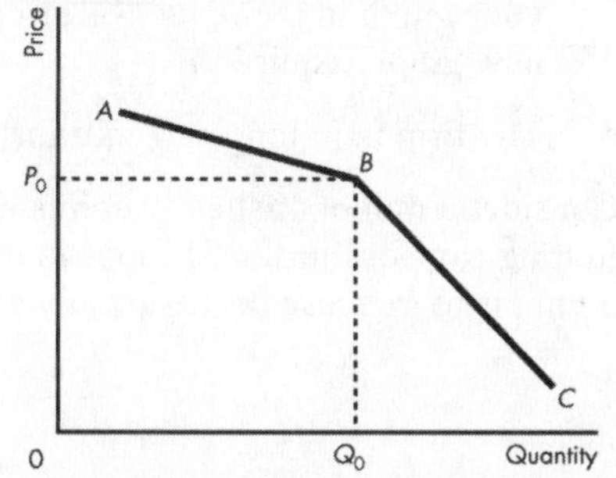

15 In the dominant firm model of oligopoly, the smaller firms act like
- a oligopolists.
- b monopolists.
- c monopolistic competitors.
- d perfect competitors.
- e a cartel.

Oligopoly Games

16 Which of the following is *not* common to all games?
- a rules
- b collusion
- c strategies
- d payoffs
- e the analysis of strategic interaction

17 In the prisoners' dilemma with players Art and Bob, each prisoner would be best off if
- a both prisoners confess.
- b both prisoners deny.
- c Art denies and Bob confesses.
- d Bob denies and Art confesses.
- e none of the above is done.

18 If a duopoly with collusion maximizes profit,
- a each firm must produce the same amount.
- b each firm must produce its maximum output possible.
- c industry marginal revenue must equal industry marginal cost at the level of total output.
- d industry demand must equal industry marginal cost at the level of total output.
- e total output will be greater than without collusion.

19 Table 13.1 gives the payoff matrix in terms of profit for firms *A* and *B*, when there are two strategies facing each firm: (1) charge a low price or (2) charge a high price. The equilibrium in this game (played once) is a Nash equilibrium, because
- a firm *B* will reduce profit by more than *A* if both charge a lower price.
- b firm *B* is the dominant firm.
- c the best strategy for each firm does not depend on the strategy chosen by the other.
- d there is no credible threat by either firm to punish the other if it breaks the agreement.
- e all of the above are true.

TABLE **13.1**

		Firm B: Low Price	Firm B: High Price
Firm A	Low Price	A: $2 B: $5	A: $20 B: –$15
Firm A	High Price	A: –$10 B: $25	A: $10 B: $20

20 Refer to the nonrepeated game in Table 13.1. In Nash equilibrium, what are firm *A*'s profits?
- **a** –$10
- **b** $2
- **c** $10
- **d** $20
- **e** indeterminate.

21 Refer to the nonrepeated game in Table 13.1. If both firms could agree to collude, what would firm *A*'s profits be?
- **a** –$10
- **b** $2
- **c** $10
- **d** $20
- **e** indeterminate.

22 The firms Trick and Gear form a cartel to collude to maximize profit. If this game is nonrepeated, the Nash equilibrium is
- **a** both firms cheat on the agreement.
- **b** both firms comply with the agreement.
- **c** Trick cheats, while Gear complies with the agreement.
- **d** Gear cheats, while Trick complies with the agreement.
- **e** indeterminate.

Repeated Games and Sequential Games

23 Consider the same cartel consisting of Trick and Gear. Now, however, the game is repeated indefinitely and each firm employs a tit-for-tat strategy. The equilibrium is
- **a** both firms cheat on the agreement.
- **b** both firms comply with the agreement.
- **c** Trick cheats, while Gear complies with the agreement.
- **d** Gear cheats, while Trick complies with the agreement.
- **e** indeterminate.

24 The equilibrium in Question **23** is called a
- **a** credible strategy equilibrium.
- **b** dominant player equilibrium.
- **c** duopoly equilibrium.
- **d** trigger strategy equilibrium.
- **e** cooperative equilibrium.

25 Limit pricing refers to
- **a** the highest price a monopolist can set.
- **b** the highest price that just inflicts a loss on a potential entrant.
- **c** a strategy used by entering firms in contestable markets.
- **d** the price determined in a kinked demand curve model.
- **e** none of the above.

Short Answer Problems

1 Consider a single firm in a monopolistically competitive industry in the short run. Using axes like those shown in Figure 13.3, draw a new graph for each of the following situations.

FIGURE **13.3**

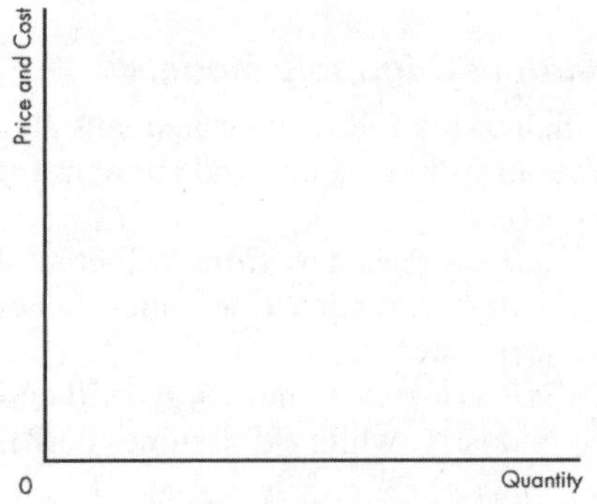

- **a** The firm is making an economic profit.
- **b** The firm is incurring a loss that will cause shutdown.
- **c** The firm is incurring a loss, but is still producing.
- **d** Starting from the situation in part **c**, explain what will happen in this industry and how your graph in part **c** will be affected. (No new graph required.)
- **e** The firm is in long-run equilibrium.

ⓒⓣ **2** Consider a monopolistically competitive industry in long-run equilibrium. Firm *A* in this industry attempts to increase profits by advertising.

a On the graph in Figure 13.4, show what will happen in the short run as a result of the decision to advertise. Briefly explain your graph.

FIGURE **13.4**

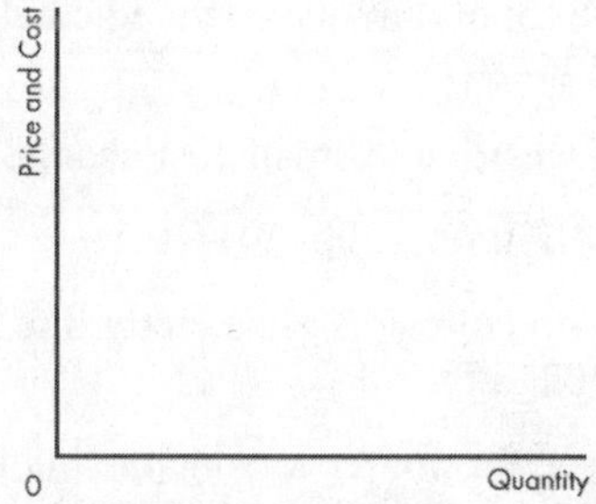

b If the firm is successful in raising profits in the short run, what will happen in the long run?

3 Compare the advantages and disadvantages of perfect competition and monopolistic competition in terms of efficiency.

4 In monopolistic competition, will a single product innovation guarantee long-run economic profits? Explain.

5 Consider the case of two colluding duopolists in a nonrepeated game. In Nash equilibrium, will the firms comply or cheat on the agreement? Explain why.

6 How can a price war that eliminates profits be explained using game theory?

7 A small prairie town has two bakeries—Always Fresh and Never Stale. Transportation costs are high relative to the price of bread, so the bakeries do not get any out-of-town competition; the local bread industry is a duopoly. Always Fresh and Never Stale have the same cost curves, and each currently makes an annual profit of $2,000.

Suppose that a new advertising service, Philomena's Flyers, starts up. If one bakery advertises in Philomena's Flyers, its annual profits will increase to $5,000, while the other bakery will lose $2,000. If both advertise, each will make a zero profit. If neither advertises, each bakery will continue to make an annual profit of $2,000.

a Represent this duopoly as a game by identifying the players, strategies, and possible outcomes.

b Construct the payoff matrix.

c What is the Nash equilibrium outcome? Explain.

8 Figure 13.5(a) gives the identical average total cost (*ATC*) curve for Always Fresh and Never Stale. Figure 13.5(b) gives the town's market demand curve for bread and the firms' joint marginal cost curve. Suppose that the two bakeries collude to maximize profit and agree to divide output equally for a single year.

FIGURE **13.5**

(a) *ATC* Curve for Each Bakery

(b) Market Demand for Bread and Firm's Joint *MC* Curve

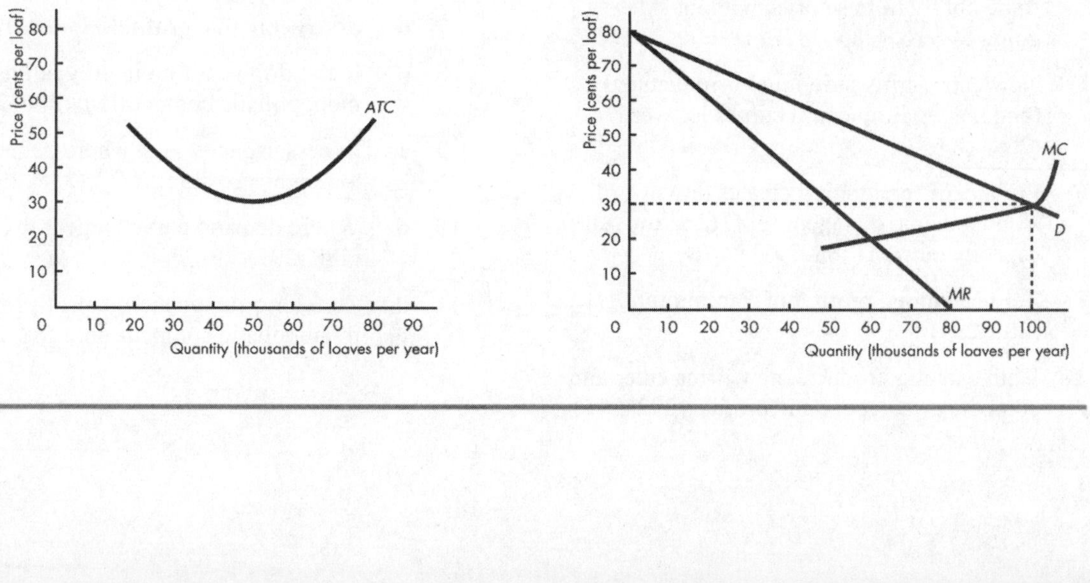

a How much will each bakery produce and what price per loaf will they charge?

b What is each bakery's average total cost and profit?

9 Now suppose that Never Stale convinces Always Fresh that demand has decreased and they must reduce their price by 10 cents per loaf in order to sell their agreed-upon quantity. Of course, demand has not decreased, but Always Fresh produces its agreed amount and charges 10 cents less per loaf. Never Stale, the cheater, also charges 10 cents less than before, but increases output sufficiently to satisfy the rest of demand at this price.

a How many loaves of bread does Never Stale produce?

b What is Always Fresh's average total cost and profit?

c What is Never Stale's average total cost and profit?

10 Return to the initial situation. The firms are preparing to enter into a *long-term* collusive agreement. Always Fresh credibly assures Never Stale that if Never Stale cheats in a repeated game, Always Fresh will undercut Never Stale's price as soon as the cheating is discovered. Would Never Stale want to cheat on the agreement now? Why or why not?

ANSWERS

True/False and Explain

1 F Free entry and exit in monopolistic competition. (286–287)

2 T Creates downward-sloping demand curve; some ability to raise price without sales going to zero. (286–287)

3 F New entry shifts individual firm demand (and marginal revenue) curves leftward. (288–289)

4 F Product differentiation creates downward-sloping demand tangent to *ATC* below full capacity output. (288–291)

5 F Zero economic profit, but *P* minimum *ATC*. (288–291)

6 T With existing products, new firms enter and compete away economic profits. (292–295)

7 F Selling costs are fixed costs that increase total costs, but if output increases enough, average total cost may decrease. (293–294)

8 F Depends on information versus persuasion content of advertising and gains from increased product variety. (292–295)

9 T Oligopoly involves strategic behaviour. (296–297)

10 F Insensitive to small cost changes. (298)

11 T Definition. (300–301)

12 T With collusion, act exactly like monopoly. (302–303)

13 T True for nonrepeated game but may be false for repeated game. (303–306)

14 F Tit-for-tat strategy yields cooperative equilibrium in repeated game. (309–311)

15 F Sets highest price that just inflicts (smallest) loss, since any loss deters entry. (310–311)

Multiple-Choice

1 c All other answers describe oligopoly. (286–287)

2 c Demand curve ($AR = P$) tangent to *ATC* and above *MC*. (288–289)

3 b Where $MC = MR$. (288–289)

4 a At Q_2, $AR - ATC$. (288–289)

5 a With new entrants due to economic profit, industry demand divided among more firms so each firm's demand curve shifts leftward. (288–289)

6 b **a** and **e** create possibility of economic profit, **c** and **d** are outcomes, not forces leading to zero economic profit. (288–291)

7 d Zero economic profit. (288–291)

8 c **b** and **d** false for monopoly. **a** false for monopolistic competition. (286–291)

9 c Excess capacity at *Q* where demand tangent to downward slope *ATC*. (288–291)

10 d Where demand curve tangent to *ATC*. (288–291)

11 d Zero long-run economic profit for monopolistic competition. (288–291)

12 e Selling costs are fixed costs that may increase or decrease demand, and may persuade consumers about exaggerated differences between products rather than provide valuable information. (294–295)

13 c Oligopoly involves interdependence between firms. (296–297)

14 e *AB* more elastic than *BC* because price changes unmatched. (298)

15 d Dominant firm sets price, smaller firms take that price as given. (298–299)

16 b No collusion in prisoners' dilemma. (300–308)

17 b Both denying would yield lesser jail terms, but doesn't happen because players cannot trust each other enough to collude. (300–301)

18 c See Text Figure 13.14(b). (303)

19 c Dominant strategy for each. (305–306)

20 b Both firms charge low price. (305–306)

21 c Both firms charge high price. (305–306)

22 a Similar to prisoners' dilemma outcome. (302–306)

23 b Cooperative equilibrium; each player responds rationally to credible threat of other. (309–311)

24 e Definition. (309–311)

25 b Definition. **c** would be true for existing firms. (310–311)

Short Answer Problems

1 a Figure 13.3 Solution (a) illustrates a monopolistically competitive firm making an economic profit in the short run. The important feature of the graph is that at the profit-maximizing output, price is greater than average total cost. Economic profit is the shaded area.

FIGURE **13.3** SOLUTION

(a)

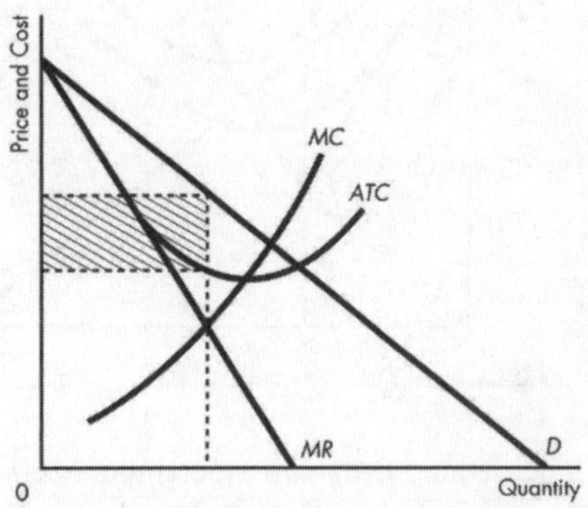

b Figure 13.3 Solution (b) illustrates a firm that will shut down in the short run since price is less than average variable cost at the profit-maximizing (loss-minimizing) level of output.

FIGURE **13.3** SOLUTION

(b)

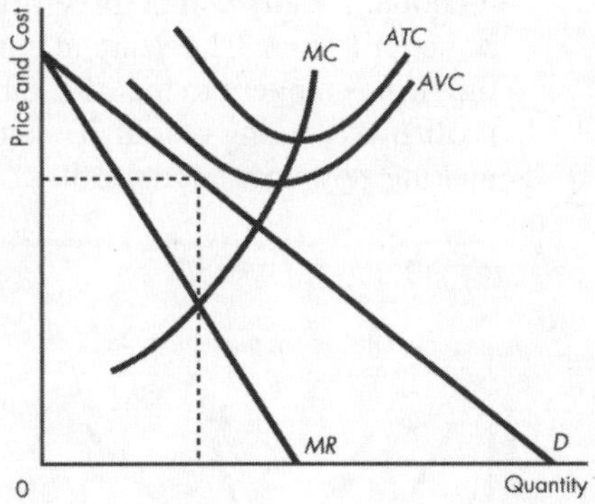

c Figure 13.3 Solution (c) illustrates a firm incurring a loss but continuing to produce. The loss is the shaded area. Note that, at the profit-maximizing output, price is less than *ATC* but greater than *AVC*.

FIGURE **13.3** SOLUTION

(c)

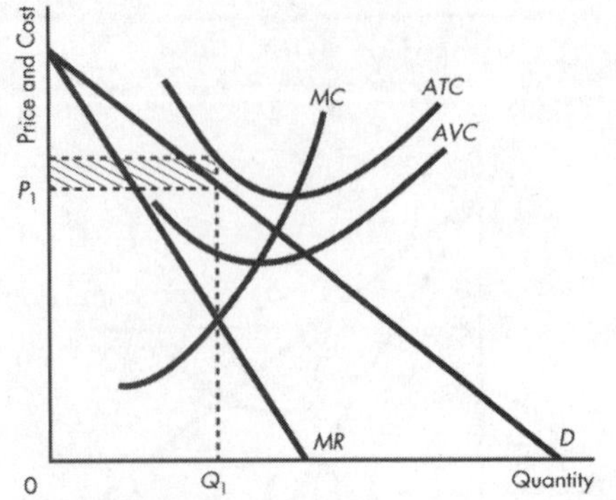

d Since firms are incurring a loss, firms will leave the industry. The demand curves facing each remaining firm will shift rightward as they each attract some customers of departing firms. As firms' demand curves shift rightward, losses are reduced. Firms continue to have an incentive to leave until losses are eliminated. Thus remaining firms' demand curves continue to shift until they are tangent to the *ATC* curve.

e Figure 13.3 Solution (d) illustrates a monopolistically competitive firm in long-run equilibrium. The demand curve facing the firm is tangent to the *ATC* curve at the profit-maximizing output. Thus the firm is making zero economic profit.

FIGURE **13.3** SOLUTION

(d)

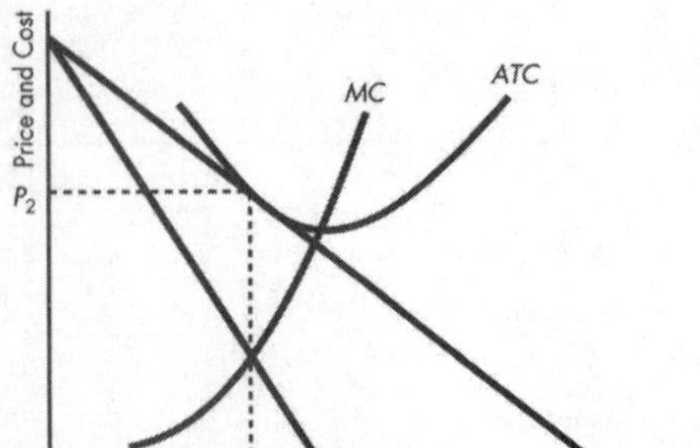

2 a Advertising will increase firm *A*'s cost, but also increase demand (it hopes). If the increase in demand (revenue) is greater than the increase in cost, firm *A* will increase its profit. Figure 13.4 Solution illustrates this situation. The initial curves are given by D_0, ATC_0, and MR_0.

Initially the firm is producing Q_0 and selling at price P_0 and making zero economic profit. Advertising, which is a fixed cost, raises the *ATC* curve to ATC_1 (*MC* does not shift), but also increases the demand and marginal revenue curves to D_1 and MR_1 respectively. The shift in the demand curve is sufficiently great that there is now positive economic profit at the new profit-maximizing level of output (Q_1). Economic profit is the shaded area.

FIGURE **13.4** SOLUTION

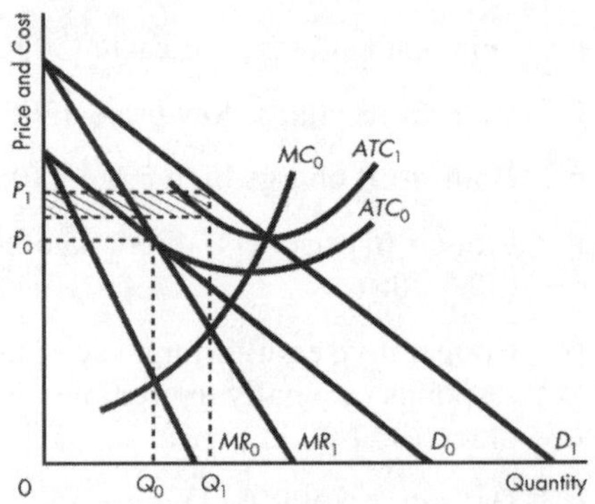

b Other firms will also begin to advertise to attempt to increase their profit (or recover lost profit). As all other firms advertise, the demand curve for our firm will shift back to the left as it loses some customers it gained. In the long run, once again, all firms will be making zero profit even after advertising.

3 The advantage of perfect competition is that it leads to production at minimum average total cost, while monopolistic competition leads to higher average total cost due to reduced output and high advertising expenditures.

The advantage of monopolistic competition is that it leads to greater product variety, which consumers value, while in a perfectly competitive industry there is a single, identical product produced by all firms. Monopolistic competition also leads to greater product innovation and, as a positive byproduct of greater advertising, valuable information to consumers. Thus the loss in allocative efficiency and greater advertising costs (higher *ATC*) in monopolistic competition have to be weighed against the gains of greater product variety, greater product innovation, and more valuable information provided to consumers.

4 No. In the short run, a firm in monopolistic competition will earn economic profit because its downward-sloping demand curve gives it some price power. But in the long run, economic profit attracts new firms that make close substitutes for the product. With free entry, new firms compete away the economic profit. To restore economic profit, monopolistically competitive firms must continuously innovate and develop new products.

5 Each firm's best strategy is to cheat regardless of the strategy of the other firm. Call the firms *A* and *B*. Firm *A* knows that if firm *B* follows the collusive agreement, *A* can increase its profit by cheating. If firm *B* cheats, then firm *A* knows that it must also cheat to minimize its loss of profit. Thus cheating is the dominant strategy for firm *A*. It is also the dominant strategy for firm *B*, so the Nash equilibrium is both firms cheat.

6 Game theory explains price wars as the consequence of firms in a colluding industry responding to the cheating of a firm. If one firm cheats by cutting its price, then all other firms will cut their prices, and a price war will ensue. Once price has fallen sufficiently (perhaps to the zero profit level), firms will again have a strong incentive to rebuild their collusion.

7 **a** The players are Always Fresh and Never Stale. Each firm has two strategies: to advertise or not to advertise. There are four possible outcomes: (1) both firms advertise, (2) Always Fresh advertises but Never Stale does not, (3) Never Stale advertises but Always Fresh does not, and (4) neither firm advertises.

b The payoff matrix is given in Table 13.2. The entries give the profit earned by Always Fresh (*AF*) and Never Stale (*NS*) under each of the four possible outcomes.

TABLE **13.2**

		Never Stale	
		Advertise	Not Advertise
Always Fresh	Advertise	*AF*: 0 *NS*: 0	*AF*: $5,000 *NS*: –$2,000
	Not Advertise	*AF*: –$2,000 *NS*: $5,000	*AF*: $2,000 *NS*: $2,000

c First, consider how Always Fresh decides which strategy to pursue. If Never Stale advertises, Always Fresh can advertise and make zero profit or not advertise and make a $2,000 loss. Thus Always Fresh will want to advertise if Never Stale does.

If Never Stale does not advertise, Always Fresh can advertise and make a $5,000 profit or not advertise and make a $2,000 profit. Therefore Always Fresh will want to advertise whether Never Stale advertises or not. Never Stale will come to the same conclusion. The Nash equilibrium is that both firms advertise.

8 **a** The firms will agree to produce 30,000 loaves each and sell at a price of 50 cents per loaf. We determine this by noticing (Figure 13.5b) that the profit-maximizing (monopoly) output is 60,000 loaves for the industry ($MR = MC$ at 60,000) and the industry price is 50 cents per loaf. Since the firms have agreed to divide output equally, each will produce 30,000 loaves.

b From Figure 13.5(a) we determine that, at 30,000 loaves, each firm's average total cost is 40 cents per loaf. Since price is 50 cents per loaf, profit will be $3,000 for each firm.

ⓒ 9 a At the new price of 40 cents per loaf, total quantity demanded is 80,000 loaves. Since Always Fresh continues to produce 30,000 loaves, this means that Never Stale will produce the remaining 50,000 loaves demanded.

b Since Always Fresh continues to produce 30,000 loaves, its average total cost continues to be 40 cents per loaf. With the new price also at 40 cents, Always Fresh will make a zero economic profit.

c Never Stale has increased output to 50,000 loaves, which implies average total cost of 30 cents per loaf. Thus, given a price of 40 cents, Never Stale's economic profit will be $5,000.

10 Given that the agreement is long-term, Never Stale would almost surely not cheat. The reason is that, while Never Stale could increase short-term profit by cheating, it would lose much more future profit if Always Fresh retaliates in a repeated game.

The key point is that Never Stale's behaviour changes, not because cost or demand have changed, but rather because Always Fresh's behaviour has changed in the repeated game. In duopoly and oligopoly, the best strategy for any firm depends on the behaviour of other firms.

CHAPTERS 9–13

Part 4 Wrap Up

Understanding Firms and Markets

PROBLEM

FIGURE **P4.1**

(a) Industry **(b) Firm**

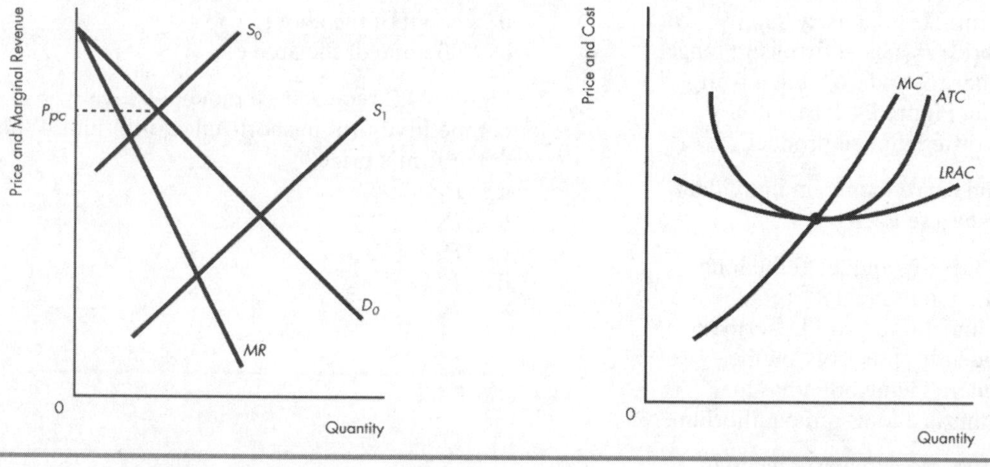

Despite significant differences between perfect competition, monopoly, and monopolistic competition, all of these market structures can be analyzed using the diagrams in Figure P4.1.

Figure P4.1(a) shows an industry in short-run equilibrium at the intersection of the demand (D_0) and supply (S_0) curves. Ignore for the moment the other supply curve (S_1) and the marginal revenue curve (MR). Long-run market demand is the same as short-run market demand. There are no external economies or diseconomies. Figure P4.1(b) shows the cost curves of one of many identical firms in the industry.

Let's first suppose this is a perfectly competitive (pc) industry.

a Describe the demand curve facing an individual firm; describe the marginal revenue curve.

b On Figure P4.1, identify and label the industry short-run equilibrium price (P_{pc}) (this is a giveaway!), output (Q_{pc}), and individual firm output (q_{pc}). Is each individual firm making a profit or loss? Explain.

c What happens in the long run? On Figure P4.1, identify and label the industry long-run equilibrium price ($P^{LR}{}_{pc}$), output ($Q^{LR}{}_{pc}$), and individual firm output ($q^{LR}{}_{pc}$).

Now suppose that the market in Figure P4.1(a) is supplied by a single-price monopolist (m) with a legal monopoly. S_1 is the monopolist's marginal cost curve. Ignore S_0 and part (b) of the figure.

d Describe the demand curve facing the monopolist; describe the supply curve of the monopolist.

e On Figure P4.1(a), identify and label the industry short-run equilibrium price (P_m) and output (Q_m).

f At Q_m, if the monopolist's average total cost is less than P_m, explain what happens in the long run. On Figure P4.1(a), identify and label the industry long-run equilibrium price ($P^{LR}{}_m$) and output ($Q^{LR}{}_m$).

g Compare the long-run allocative efficiency of this industry under monopoly versus under perfect competition. Identify any deadweight loss on the appropriate figure.

Finally, suppose that the industry in Figure P4.1(a) is supplied by many monopolistically competitive (mc) firms. The industry supply curve is S_0, and at price P_{pc}, each firm is in long-run equilibrium. Ignore S_1 and MR. Each firm has the cost curves in Figure P4.1(b), but produces a slightly differentiated product.

h Describe the demand curve facing an individual firm and draw it on Figure P4.1(b).

i On Figure P4.1(b), identify and label the long-run output (q_{mc}) for an individual monopolistically competitive firm. Describe one point that you can identify precisely on the marginal revenue curve facing an individual firm. Explain why this is a long-run equilibrium.

j Compare the long-run allocative efficiency of this industry under monopolistic competition versus under perfect competition. What consideration must be taken into account that is not taken into account for a monopoly?

MIDTERM EXAMINATION

You should allocate 48 minutes for this examination (24 questions, 2 minutes per question). For each question, choose the one *best* answer.

1 The supply curve for a single-price monopoly is
- **a** its marginal cost curve.
- **b** its marginal cost curve above minimum average variable cost.
- **c** its average variable cost curve.
- **d** its marginal revenue curve.
- **e** none of the above.

2 A successful price-discriminating firm must be able to
- **a** prevent consumer resale.
- **b** differentiate consumers with high price elasticity of demand and charge them low prices.
- **c** differentiate consumers with low price elasticity of demand and charge them high prices.
- **d** do all of the above.
- **e** do none of the above.

3 Figure P4.2 represents a monopolistically competitive firm in short-run equilibrium. What is the firm's price?
- **a** P_1
- **b** P_2
- **c** P_3
- **d** P_4
- **e** P_5

FIGURE **P4.2**

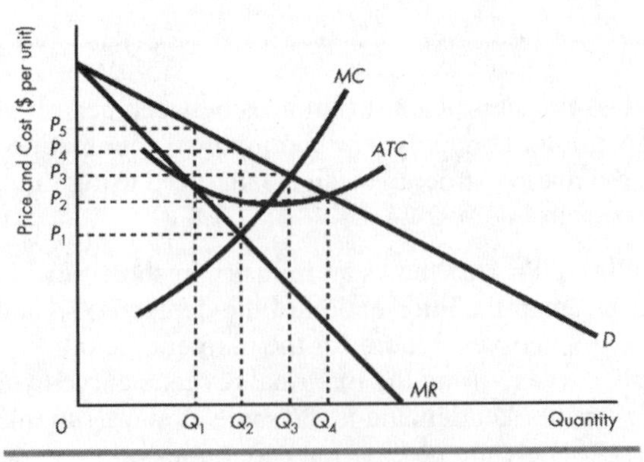

4 Figure P4.2 represents a monopolistically competitive firm in short-run equilibrium. In the long run, what is the firm's economic profit *per unit*?
- a $P_4 - P_2$
- b $P_4 - P_1$
- c P_3
- d P_2
- e none of the above

5 For a single-price monopolist, which of the following statements is *false*?
- a There is no unique one-to-one relationship between price and quantity supplied.
- b For any output greater than zero, $MR < AR$.
- c The industry demand curve is the monopolist's demand curve.
- d The intersection of *MR* and *MC* provides all information necessary for identifying the profit-maximizing quantity and price.
- e Total revenue is at a maximum where $MR = 0$.

6 A single-price monopoly never operates
- a on an elastic portion of the demand curve.
- b on a unit elastic portion of the demand curve.
- c on an inelastic portion of the demand curve.
- d at a quantity where marginal revenue is positive since total revenue is not at a maximum.
- e under any of the above conditions.

7 In a perfectly competitive industry of 100 firms, the demand curve facing the individual firm is
- a unit elastic.
- b identical to the industry demand curve.
- c 1/100 of the industry demand curve.
- d one where $AR = MR$.
- e none of the above.

8 If economic profits are being made by firms in a competitive industry, new firms will enter. This will shift
- a the industry demand curve leftward, causing market price to fall.
- b the industry demand curve rightward, causing market price to rise.
- c the industry supply curve leftward, causing market price to rise.
- d the industry supply curve rightward, causing market price to fall.
- e none of the above curves.

9 The kinked demand curve model
- a suggests that price will remain constant even with fluctuations in demand.
- b suggests how the current price is determined.
- c assumes that marginal revenue sometimes increases with output.
- d assumes that competitors will match price cuts and ignore price increases.
- e suggests none of the above.

10 In the prisoners' dilemma with players Art and Bob, the Nash equilibrium is
- a both prisoners confess.
- b both prisoners deny.
- c Art denies and Bob confesses.
- d Bob denies and Art confesses.
- e indeterminate.

11 In a perfectly competitive industry, the market price is \$5. An individual firm is producing the level of output at which marginal cost is \$5 and is increasing, and average total cost is \$25. What should the firm do to maximize its short-run profits?
- a shut down
- b expand output
- c contract output
- d leave output unchanged
- e insufficient information to answer

12 The long-run competitive industry supply curve will be positively sloped if there are
- a external economies.
- b external diseconomies.
- c no external economies or diseconomies.
- d external costs.
- e external benefits.

13 A perfectly competitive firm maximizes profit if
- a marginal cost equals price and price is above minimum average variable cost.
- b marginal cost equals price and price is above minimum average fixed cost.
- c total revenue is at a maximum.
- d average variable cost is at a minimum.
- e average total cost is at a minimum.

14 The more perfectly a monopoly can price discriminate, the
- a closer its output gets to the single-price monopoly output.
- b more efficient is the outcome.
- c more consumer surplus is converted to deadweight loss.
- d more producer surplus is converted to deadweight loss.
- e more producer surplus is captured as profit.

15 Selling costs in monopolistic competition
- **a** shift up the average total cost curve.
- **b** may be justified by the useful information provided to consumers.
- **c** may not provide benefits that justify the increased opportunity cost.
- **d** may attempt to increase product differentiation.
- **e** do all of the above.

16 The construction cost of a building is $100,000. The conventional depreciation allowance is 5 percent per year. At the end of the first year the market value of the building is $80,000. For the first year, the depreciation cost is
- **a** $20,000 to an accountant or an economist.
- **b** $5,000 to an accountant or an economist.
- **c** $5,000 to an accountant but $20,000 to an economist.
- **d** $20,000 to an accountant but $5,000 to an economist.
- **e** none of the above.

17 The marginal cost curve slopes upward because of
- **a** diminishing marginal utility.
- **b** diminishing marginal returns.
- **c** technological inefficiency.
- **d** economic inefficiency.
- **e** none of the above.

18 In economics, the long run is a time frame in which
- **a** one year or more elapses.
- **b** all resources are variable.
- **c** all resources are fixed.
- **d** there is at least one fixed resource and at least one variable resource.
- **e** all resources are variable but plant size is fixed.

19 A firm has $200 in explicit costs and sells the resulting output for $250. The normal rate of profit is 10 percent. Which of the following statements is *true*?
- **a** Implicit costs are $25.
- **b** Economic profits are $20.
- **c** Economic profits are $50.
- **d** Economic profits exceed accounting profits.
- **e** Explicit costs exceed implicit costs.

20 If *AFC* is falling *MC* must be
- **a** rising.
- **b** falling.
- **c** above *AFC*.
- **d** below *AFC*.
- **e** none of the above.

21 If all inputs are increased by 10 percent and output increases by more than 10 percent, it must be the case that
- **a** average total cost is decreasing.
- **b** average total cost is increasing.
- **c** the *LRAC* curve is positively sloped.
- **d** there are economies of scale.
- **e** there are diseconomies of scale.

22 In Table P4.1, which method(s) of making a medical hologram is/are technologically efficient?
- **a** 1 only
- **b** 2 only
- **c** 3 only
- **d** 1, 2, and 3
- **e** 1 and 3 only

TABLE **P4.1** THREE METHODS OF MAKING ONE MEDICAL HOLOGRAM

	Quantities of Inputs	
Method	**Labour**	**Capital**
1	5	10
2	10	15
3	15	5

23 Refer to Table P4.1. If the price of labour is $20 per unit and the price of capital is $10 per unit, which method(s) is/are economically efficient?
- **a** 1 only
- **b** 2 only
- **c** 3 only
- **d** 2 and 3 only
- **e** 1 and 3 only

24 In a contestable market, the
- **a** Herfindahl–Hirschman Index is always low.
- **b** Herfindahl–Hirschman Index is always high.
- **c** firm in the market earns large economic profits.
- **d** firm in the market might play an entry deterrence game.
- **e** firm in the market will not use a limit pricing strategy.

ANSWERS

Problem

a The individual firm's demand curve and marginal revenue curve is a horizontal line at P_{pc}.

b See Figure P4.1(b) Solution. Each firm is making economic profit because at output q_{pc}, price (P_{pc} = average revenue) is greater than average total cost.

c See Figure P4.1 Solution. In response to economic profit, new firms enter the industry, causing the industry supply curve to shift rightward until it reaches S_1. When price has fallen to $P^{LR}{}_{pc}$, economic profit has been eliminated and each firm is earning normal profit only.

d The monopolist's demand curve is the industry demand curve D_0. The monopolist does not have a supply curve since she can choose a combination of price and quantity.

e See Figure P4.1(a) Solution.

f Even though the monopolist is earning economic profit, nothing happens in the long run because legal barriers prevent new entry. Long-run equilibrium price and output are the same as short-run price (P_m) and output (Q_m).

g Monopoly is less efficient than perfect competition, by the shaded area of deadweight loss indicated on Figure P4.1(a) Solution.

h See Figure P4.1(b) Solution. Since the firm is in long-run equilibrium, the downward-sloping demand curve must be tangent to the *ATC* curve at the equilibrium price P_{pc}.

i See Figure P4.1 Solution. A profit-maximizing firm chooses the output (q_{mc}) where *MC* intersects *MR*. Hence the *MR* curve must intersect *MC* at q_{mc}. This is a long-run equilibrium because the firm is earning zero economic profit, so no incentive for entry or exit.

j Under monopolistic competition, *ATC* is higher (P_{pc}) than under perfect competition ($P^{LR}{}_{pc}$), implying less efficiency. However, the loss in allocative efficiency of monopolistic competition must be weighed against the gain in increased product variety.

Midterm Examination

1 e Monopoly has no supply curve. (266–269)

2 d See text discussion. (273–275)

3 d Highest possible price to sell Q_2. (288–290)

4 e Long-run economic profit per unit = zero. (288–290)

FIGURE **P4.1** SOLUTION

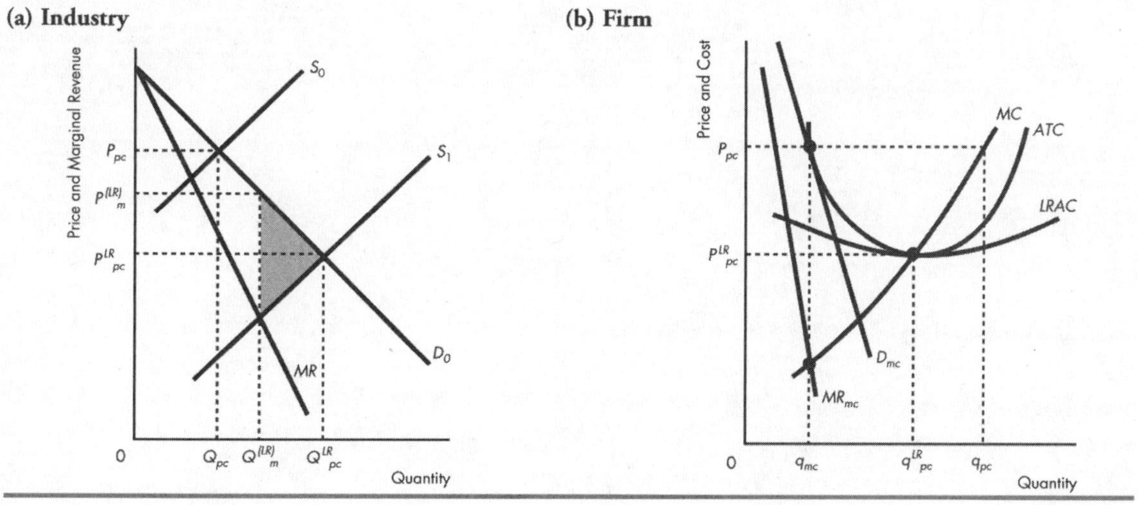

5 d Need demand curve to identify price. (266–269)

6 c If demand is inelastic then $MR < 0$. But MR must always be > 0 to intersect (positive) MC. (266–267)

7 d Horizontal at market price. Infinite elasticity. (240–241)

8 d Economic profit/loss signal for supply shifts. Profit attracts entry new firms. (248–251)

9 d **a** true if fluctuation in MC. MR always decreases with increasing Q so **c** false. (298)

10 a Outcome of game. (300–301)

11 e Firm at Q where $P = MC$, but losing \$ since $AR < ATC$. Need AVC information to determine if **a** or **d** correct. (244–247)

12 b Increasing costs as industry Q increases. (253–255)

13 a AFC irrelevant. Maximizing profit ≠ maximizing revenue. **d**, **e** might be true depending on P. (244–246)

14 b Perfect price discrimination has zero deadweight loss; all consumer surplus captured as profit. (275–276)

15 e Enhanced information and variety may or may not justify increased (opportunity) cost of selling costs. (292–295)

16 c Accountant's depreciation = (5%) × \$100,000. Economist's depreciation = Δ market value. (198–199)

17 b Diminishing marginal returns implies decreasing MP causing increasing MC. (226–228)

18 b Definition. All inputs and plant size variable. (220)

19 e Implicit costs = 0.10 (\$200) = \$20; economic profit = \$25; accounting profit = \$50. (198–199)

20 e AFC always falling; no necessary relation to MC. See Text Figure 10.5. (226–227)

21 d Definition downward-sloping $LRAC$. Since all inputs variable, **a** and **b** irrelevant. (232–233)

22 e 2 uses more labour and more capital than 1. (201–202)

23 a 1 costs \$200; 2 and 3 cost \$350. (201–202)

24 d HHI may be high or low since measures actual, not potential competition. Firm may use entry deterrence or limit pricing and will not earn large profits. (310–311)

Chapter 14 Competition Policy

KEY CONCEPTS

The Economic Theory of Government

Government economic activity attempts to correct **market failure**—failure of unregulated market to efficiently allocate resources. Five problems governments address:

- monopoly and oligopoly regulation—output restriction by monopolies and cartels preventing efficient allocation resources (Chapter 14).
- externalities—costs or benefits affecting others than the buyers and sellers of a good. Markets produce too many goods with negative externalities and too few goods with positive externalities (Chapter 15).
- *public goods*—can be consumed simultaneously by everyone; no one can be excluded. *Free-rider problem* causes markets to produce less than the efficient quantity of public goods.
- use of common resources—owned by no one and used by everyone; no one can be excluded. Markets fail to use common resources efficiently because no one has incentive to conserve what everyone else is free to use (Chapter 16).
- income redistribution—unregulated market economy produces an unequal distribution of income and wealth (Chapter 18).

Government failure can occur when government actions create inefficiency. *Public choice model* analyzes government as a political marketplace analogous to the economic marketplace. Actors are:

- voters—consumers of political marketplace. Express their preferences by voting, campaign contributions and lobbying.
- firms—also consumers of political marketplace. Express their preferences by campaign contributions and lobbying.
- politicians—entrepreneurs in political marketplace. Objective is to get and stay elected. Votes to politicians are like economic profits to firms.
- bureaucrats—producers in political marketplace. Officials in government, hired by politicians. Objective is maximize budget of their department.

Political equilibrium—choices of voters, firms, politicians, and bureaucrats are compatible, and no group can improve its position with a different choice.

Monopoly and Oligopoly Regulation

Forms of government intervention in monopolistic and oligopolistic markets:

- regulation—rules determining prices, product standards, and entry conditions.
- public ownership—publicly owned firms operated (in principle) in the social interest are **Crown corporations**.
- **anti-combine law**—makes some market behaviour (monopolistic practices) illegal.

Monopolistic practices create tension between consumer interests and producer interests. This tension is key to economic theory of regulation. Political marketplace in which monopoly and oligopoly are regulated has:

- demand for regulation—consumers demand regulation that increases consumer surplus, while firms demand regulation that increases producer surplus.
- supply of regulation—politicians supply regulations that increase their campaign funds and votes.

In political equilibrium, regulation might be in social interest or in self-interest of producers. There are two theories of political equilibrium:

- **social interest theory**—predicts regulations supplied to maximize total surplus and eliminate deadweight loss. Government acts in the social interest to eliminate waste and achieve efficient resource allocation.
- **capture theory**—predicts regulations supplied to maximize producer surplus and economic profit. Government "captured" by interests of producers, creating government failure and inefficient resource allocation.

Regulation and Deregulation

Government regulatory agencies set rules for prices, quantities, and market access.

Natural monopoly (because of economies of scale, one firm can supply the market at lower *ATC* than multiple firms can) can be regulated with the following rules.

- **Marginal cost pricing rule**—set price equal to marginal cost. Maximizes total surplus, but not viable because firm incurs economic loss.
- **Average cost pricing rule**—set price equal to average total cost. May be most efficient even though deadweight loss.
- **Rate of return regulation**—set price to achieve target rate of return on capital.
  - Ideally, yields normal profit only; same outcome as average cost pricing rule.
  - But there is a problem of incentives for firm to inflate cost (of capital) to yield economic profit.
- **Price cap regulation**—set price ceiling to achieve target rate of return on capital.
  - Gives firm incentive to keep costs under control. Replacing rate of return regulation.
  - Often combined with earnings sharing regulation that forces firms to share profits above target level with consumers.
- Evidence mixed, but regulated natural monopolies seem to earn profits equal to or greater than average, supporting more predictions of capture theory than public interest theory.

Cartel (collusive agreement among firms in an oligopoly to restrict output and raise price) can be regulated with the following rules.

- Set price and quantity at competitive levels (intersection of industry demand and *MC* curves). Social interest theory outcome.
- Set price and quantity to maximize profit (highest price associated with quantity at intersection of industry *MC* and *MR* curves). Capture theory outcome.
- Evidence mixed, but regulated cartels seem to earn profits equal to or greater than average, supporting more of predictions of capture theory than public interest theory.

Public Ownership

Publicly owned corporations can be operated with the following objectives.

- Efficiency—set price equal to marginal cost and subsidize the economic loss. Maximizes consumer surplus.
- Budget maximization with marginal cost pricing—set price equal to marginal cost but pad production costs to maximum. Allocatively efficient, but maximizes producer benefits.
- Budget maximization at zero price—increase output until price falls to zero. Inefficient (deadweight loss), results in overproduction and maximizes producer benefits.
- Evidence suggests publicly owned firms will overproduce and be less efficient than private firms. Recent tendency to privatize publicly owned firms.

Anti-Combine Law

Competition Act of 1986 distinguishes between

- criminal actions (conspiracy to fix prices, bid-rigging, false advertising), dealt with by courts.
- noncriminal actions (mergers, abuse of market position, exclusive dealing), dealt with by Competition Tribunal.

Evidence suggests anti-combine laws have served the social interest.

HELPFUL HINTS

1 Economists judge the success of the market (or any other institution) in terms of efficiency. Efficiency means that the economy is producing all goods and services up to the point where marginal cost equals marginal benefit. At an efficient outcome, no one can be

made better off without making someone else worse off.

When the market fails to achieve this "ideal" efficient outcome, we call it *market failure*. The market can fail by producing too little if the marginal benefit of the last unit exceeds the marginal cost. Or, the market can fail by producing too much if the marginal cost of the last unit exceeds the marginal benefit.

In this chapter (and in Chapters 15–16), we learn that governments can correct market failures, but can also create inefficiency. Since both markets and governments can fail, the relevant economic question in each case is: Which fails less?

2 Figure 14.1 depicts revenue and marginal cost curves for an industry. Use this figure to think of regulation as determining the division of the potential total surplus (the area of triangle *abc*) among consumer surplus, producer surplus, and deadweight loss.

FIGURE **14.1**

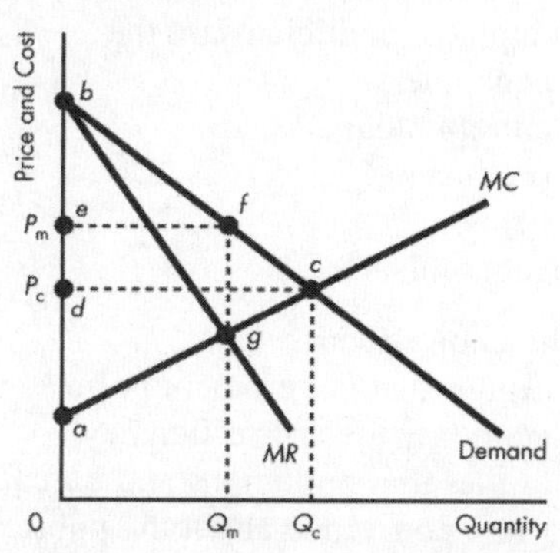

If the industry is perfectly competitive, then output will be Q_c and the market price will be P_c. Total surplus is maximized and is given by the area of triangle *abc*. Total surplus is equal to the sum of consumer surplus (triangle *dbc*) and producer surplus (triangle *adc*). There is no deadweight loss so efficiency is achieved.

If the industry is a profit-maximizing monopoly, output will be Q_m and the price will be P_m. In this case, total surplus is represented by the area of trapezoid *abfg*. Because of monopoly restriction of output, total surplus under monopoly is less than under competition. The difference is the deadweight loss from monopoly, the amount of total surplus that is lost when we go from competition to monopoly. The deadweight loss is given by the area of triangle *gfc*. Total surplus can be divided into consumer surplus (triangle *ebf*) and producer surplus (trapezoid *aefg*). Consumer surplus is quite small, but producer surplus is at a maximum.

Actual output is likely to be between these bounds. As output moves from Q_c to Q_m, consumer surplus decreases, while producer surplus and the deadweight loss both increase. If this industry is regulated, the social interest theory of intervention predicts output will be close to Q_c, while the capture theory of intervention predicts output closer to Q_m.

SELF-TEST

True/False and Explain

The Economic Theory of Government

1 Restriction of output by monopolies is an example of market failure.

2 The outcome resulting from the choices of voters, politicians, and bureaucrats is a political equilibrium.

3 In a political equilibrium, politician and lobbyists stop trying to change laws to their advantage.

Monopoly and Oligopoly Regulation

4 Government regulation will always move the economy closer to efficiency.

5 According to the capture theory, government regulatory agencies eventually capture the profits of the industries they regulate.

Regulation and Deregulation

6 For a natural monopoly, marginal cost is always less than average total cost.

7 The outcome of rate of return regulation is similar to marginal cost pricing.

8 Under rate of return regulation, firms can get closer to maximizing producer surplus if they inflate their costs.

9 Price cap regulation gives firms incentives to keep costs under control, and is replacing rate of return regulation.

10 Evidence of higher-than-normal rates of return for regulated natural monopolies matches the predictions of the capture theory.

11 Evidence that producers strongly support deregulation matches the predictions of the capture theory.

12 If industry prices and profits fall after deregulation, the regulation was likely serving the interest of consumers.

Public Ownership

13 An efficiently operated Crown corporation will maximize total surplus.

Anti-Combine Law

14 According to Canada's anti-combine laws, mergers and abuse of a dominant market position are criminal offences.

15 Anti-combine laws have helped achieve efficiency and serve the social interest.

Multiple-Choice

The Economic Theory of Government

1 Government economic activity can attempt to correct
- **a** free-rider problems.
- **b** monopoly.
- **c** externalities.
- **d** economic inequality.
- **e** all of the above.

2 In the public choice theory of the political marketplace, politicians are the
- **a** consumers.
- **b** entrepreneurs.
- **c** producers.
- **d** firms.
- **e** economists.

3 Public choice theory
- **a** argues that government policies move the economy towards efficiency.
- **b** argues that politicians and bureaucrats are more concerned about the public interest than individuals in the private sector.
- **c** argues that the public choices of government maximize net benefits.
- **d** applies tools of economic analysis to analysis of government behaviour.
- **e** applies tools of political analysis to analysis of economic markets.

4 Total surplus is maximized when
- **a** marginal cost equals marginal revenue.
- **b** marginal cost equals average total cost.
- **c** price equals marginal cost.
- **d** price equals average total cost.
- **e** price equals average variable cost.

5 For a monopoly, producer surplus is maximized when
- **a** marginal cost equals marginal revenue.
- **b** marginal cost equals average total cost.
- **c** price equals marginal cost.
- **d** price equals average total cost.
- **e** price equals average variable cost.

6 In a political equilibrium,
- **a** efficiency must be achieved.
- **b** no one wants to change their proposals.
- **c** firms will be making zero economic profit.
- **d** all parties agree that the appropriate level of regulation has been achieved.
- **e** all of the above are true.

Monopoly and Oligopoly Regulation

7 Regulation refers to
- **a** the discipline of the marketplace.
- **b** rules administered by a government agency.
- **c** selling a publicly owned corporation to private shareholders.
- **d** cartelization of a competitive industry.
- **e** the formation of monopolies.

8 The supply of economic regulation originates with
- **a** monopolists.
- **b** labour unions.
- **c** fair trade associations.
- **d** voters.
- **e** politicians and bureaucrats.

9 Which of the following is consistent with the social interest theory of regulation?
- **a** regulation of natural monopoly by setting price equal to marginal cost
- **b** regulation of competitive industry to increase output
- **c** regulation of airline industry by establishing minimum airfares
- **d** regulation of agriculture by establishing barriers to exit from the industry
- **e** none of the above

10 Which of the following is consistent with the capture theory of regulation?
- **a** regulation of natural monopoly by setting price equal to marginal cost
- **b** regulation of competitive industry to increase output
- **c** regulation of airline industry by establishing minimum airfares
- **d** regulation of agriculture by establishing barriers to exit from the industry
- **e** none of the above

11 The social interest theory of regulation predicts that government regulation will
- **a** maximize the interests of public officials.
- **b** maximize total surplus.
- **c** maximize producer surplus.
- **d** minimize producer surplus.
- **e** maximize consumer surplus.

Regulation and Deregulation

12 Which of the following is *not* a federal regulatory agency?
- **a** Atomic Energy Control Board
- **b** Canadian Radio-television and Telecommunications Commission
- **c** Petro-Canada
- **d** Canadian Transport Commission
- **e** National Farm Products

13 Which of the following is *least* likely to be a *natural monopoly*?
- **a** subway service
- **b** electric utilities
- **c** water and sewer service
- **d** taxicab service
- **e** cable TV service

14 A natural monopoly has
- **a** low fixed cost and low marginal cost.
- **b** low fixed cost and high marginal cost.
- **c** high fixed cost and low marginal cost.
- **d** high fixed cost and high marginal cost.
- **e** high fixed cost and increasing marginal cost.

15 Figure 14.2 gives revenue and cost curves for an industry. This industry is a natural monopoly because
- **a** one firm can supply the entire market at a lower price than can two or more firms.
- **b** there are decreasing returns to scale over the entire range of demand.
- **c** there are diseconomies of scale over the entire range of demand.
- **d** even a single firm will be unable to earn a positive profit in this industry.
- **e** all of the above are true.

FIGURE **14.2**

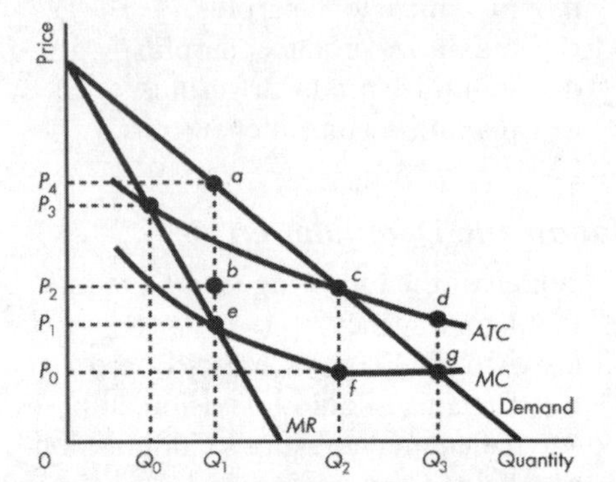

16 Consider the natural monopoly in Figure 14.2. If the firm is unregulated and operates as a private profit-maximizer, what output will it produce?
- **a** 0, because the firm incurs economic losses when $P = MC$
- **b** Q_0
- **c** Q_1
- **d** Q_2
- **e** Q_3

17 Consider the natural monopoly in Figure 14.2. If regulators set a price just sufficient for the firm to earn normal profits, what output will it produce?
- **a** 0, because the firm incurs economic losses when $P = MC$
- **b** Q_0
- **c** Q_1
- **d** Q_2
- **e** Q_3

18 Consider the natural monopoly in Figure 14.2. Total surplus is maximum when quantity is
- **a** Q_0 and price is P_3.
- **b** Q_1 and price is P_1.
- **c** Q_1 and price is P_4.
- **d** Q_2 and price is P_2.
- **e** Q_3 and price is P_0.

19 Consider the natural monopoly in Figure 14.2. If regulators use a marginal cost pricing rule, what line segment gives the amount of subsidy (per unit of output) required to keep the monopolist in business?
- **a** *ba*
- **b** *ea*
- **c** *fc*
- **d** *gd*
- **e** *eb*

20 Consider the natural monopoly in Figure 14.2. What region in the graph represents deadweight loss from an average cost pricing rule?
- **a** *abc*
- **b** *cdg*
- **c** *cfg*
- **d** *aeg*
- **e** none of the above

21 Consider the natural monopoly in Figure 14.2. Under price cap regulation, regulators will set the price at
- **a** P_0.
- **b** P_1.
- **c** P_2.
- **d** P_3.
- **e** P_4.

22 A monopolist under rate of return regulation has an incentive to
- **a** inflate costs.
- **b** produce more than the efficient quantity of output.
- **c** charge a price equal to marginal cost.
- **d** maximize consumer surplus.
- **e** maximize shareholder profits.

Public Ownership

23 A Crown corporation may be
- **a** operated to achieve economic efficiency.
- **b** operated to maximize its budget.
- **c** provincial.
- **d** federal.
- **e** all of the above.

24 A Crown corporation that maximizes its budget together with marginal cost pricing will
- a produce the efficient level of output.
- b produce more than the efficient level of output.
- c produce less than the efficient level of output.
- d maximize consumer surplus.
- e minimize production cost.

Anti-Combine Law

25 Anti-combine laws attempt to
- a support prices.
- b establish Crown corporations.
- c prevent monopoly practices.
- d establish fair trade laws.
- e regulate monopolies.

Short Answer Problems

1 Briefly compare an equilibrium in a political market with an equilibrium in a market for goods and services.

2 Regulation of monopoly is necessary because of the tension between the public interest and the producer's interest. Explain.

3 Suppose the government tried to eliminate monopoly profit by taxing each unit of monopoly output.

a What effect would this policy have on the quantity a monopolist produces and the price it charges?

b What is the effect on economic efficiency? Use a graph as part of your answer.

ⓔ ⓒⓣ 4 The demand for Aerodisks, a disk made from a unique material that flies a considerable distance when thrown, is given by the equation

$$P = 10 - 0.01Q_D$$

The corresponding marginal revenue (*MR*) equation is

$$MR = 10 - 0.02Q$$

The Aerodisk Company is a natural monopoly. The firm's total fixed cost is \$700 and the marginal cost is constant at \$2 per disk. (*Note:* This implies that average variable cost is also constant at \$2 per disk.) Suppose that the Aerodisk Company is *not* regulated.

a What will be the quantity sold and the price of an Aerodisk?

b How much is economic profit or loss?

c How much is producer surplus?

d How much is consumer surplus?

e How much is total surplus?

ⓔ ⓒⓣ 5 Now suppose that the Aerodisk Company becomes regulated and that the regulator uses a marginal cost pricing rule.

a What will be the quantity sold and the price of an Aerodisk?

b How much is economic profit or loss?

c How much is producer surplus?

d How much is consumer surplus?

e How much is total surplus?

6 Suppose that the regulator of the Aerodisk Company uses an average cost pricing rule.

a What will be the price of an Aerodisk and how many will be sold?

b How much is economic profit or loss?

c How much is producer surplus?

d How much is consumer surplus?

e How much is total surplus?

7 Since the Aerodisk Company will incur a loss under marginal cost pricing, the government must subsidize the production of Aerodisks for the firm to be willing to produce.

a What is the total subsidy necessary under a marginal cost pricing rule to leave the firm with zero economic profit?

b What is the amount of the deadweight loss associated with an average cost pricing rule?

ⓒⓣ c Which pricing rule is superior?

8 a Why is rate of return regulation equivalent to average cost pricing?

b Why is rate of return regulation being increasingly replaced by price cap regulation?

9 Figure 14.3 illustrates the industry demand, marginal revenue (*MR*) and marginal cost (*MC*) curves in an oligopoly. The industry is regulated.

a What price and quantity are predicted by the public interest theory of regulation? Why?

b What price and quantity are predicted by the capture theory of regulation? Why?

c Can you explain why the firms in this industry might demand regulation?

FIGURE **14.3**

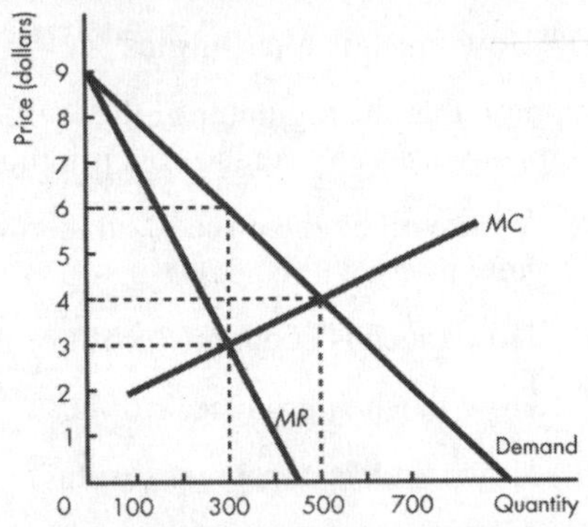

ⓔ **10** During its 1999 attempt to take over both Air Canada and Canadian Airlines, the Onyx Corporation tried to advance its cause by taking out expensive multi-page advertisements in both national newspapers arguing that its proposal was in the "best interests of Canadians." Which theory of economic regulation does Onyx's actions support?

ANSWERS

True/False and Explain

1 T Inefficient output. (324)

2 T Equilibrium outcome of political marketplace. (326)

3 F They continue to try and change laws, but do not find it worthwhile to *change the resources* devoted to these activities. (326)

4 F True according to social interest theory, false according to capture theory. (326–327)

5 F Industry captures more of total surplus. (326–327)

6 T That's why *ATC* is always downward-sloping. (328–329)

7 F More like average cost pricing. (330)

8 T Increased costs yield increased profits. (330–331)

9 T Specifies highest price firms allowed to charge; used in electricity and telecommunications industries. (330–331)

10 T Regulators act in interest of monopoly. (332)

11 F Matches public interest theory. (332–334)

12 F Serving producers. (333–334)

13 T Producing output where $P = MC$. (335–336)

14 F Noncriminal offences. Criminal offences include price-fixing, and false advertising. (338)

15 T See text discussion. (338–339)

Multiple-Choice

1 e **a–c** are market failures, **d** is perceived to be unfair and needing government action. (324–325)

2 b Voters are consumers, bureaucrats are producers/firms. (325–326)

3 d Views government as political marketplace with a (political) equilibrium outcome. (325–326)

4 c Pricing rule for efficiency; see Helpful Hint **2**. (324–326)

5 a Pricing rule for monopoly profit maximization; see Helpful Hint **2**. (324–326)

6 b See text discussion. (324–326)

7 b See text discussion. (326)

8 e Create legislation. (326–327)

9 a Only option that increases allocative efficiency. (326–327)

10 c Helps airline firms, not consumers. (326–327)

11 b Achieve allocative efficiency. (326–327)

12 c Previous Crown corporation, now privatized. (327–328)

13 d No major economies of scale. (328–330)

14 c Yielding always downward-sloping *ATC*. (328–329)

15 a Definition natural monopoly. (328–329)

16 c Where $MC = MR$. (328–332)

17 d Where $P = ATC$. (328–332)

18 e Where $P = MC$. (328–332)

19 d To cover loss per unit of output. (328–329)

20 c See Text Figure 14.3. (328–329)

21 c See Text Figure 14.5. (330–332)

22 a To increase profits; see Text Figure 14.4. (330–331)

23 e See text discussion. (335–337)

24 a See Text Figure 14.8. (335–337)

25 c See text discussion. (338–339)

Short Answer Problems

1 In both cases, equilibrium is a state of rest in the sense that no group has an incentive to change their choices. In equilibrium in an ordinary market for goods and services, neither demanders nor suppliers are able to make an exchange that will make them better off. Similarly, when a political market is in equilibrium, neither demanders (voters and firms as consumers) nor suppliers (politicians as entrepreneurs, bureaucrats as producers) are able to make an alternative choice that will make them better off.

2 It is in the public interest to achieve economic efficiency; to expand output to the level that maximizes total surplus. It is in the interest of the monopoly producer to restrict output in order to maximize producer surplus and thus monopoly profit.

Since these interests are not the same, monopoly must be regulated to achieve efficiency. The public interest theory of regulation suggests that this principle guides regulation of monopoly industries.

3 a Imposing a tax on each unit sold by a monopolist increases marginal cost. As a consequence the profit-maximizing monopolist will raise price and reduce the quantity produced.

b The tax will certainly reduce the profit of the monopolist and may even eliminate it, but it will make the inefficiency due to monopoly even worse. This is illustrated in Figure 14.4. The curve *MC* is the marginal cost curve before the tax. An unregulated monopolist will produce amount Q_2, while the economically efficient output is Q_3. The tax, however, causes the monopolist to reduce output from Q_2 to Q_1, which moves the market outcome farther away from efficiency.

FIGURE 14.4

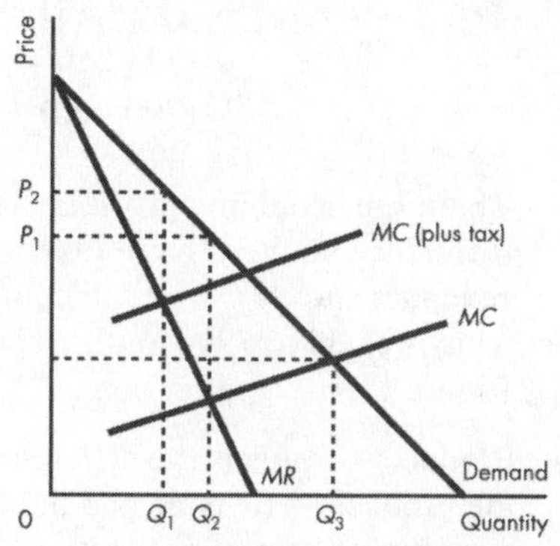

ⓔ ⓒⓣ 4 Figure 14.5 is helpful in answering questions about the Aerodisk market. It gives relevant revenue and cost curves for the Aerodisk Company.

FIGURE 14.5 AERODISK COMPANY

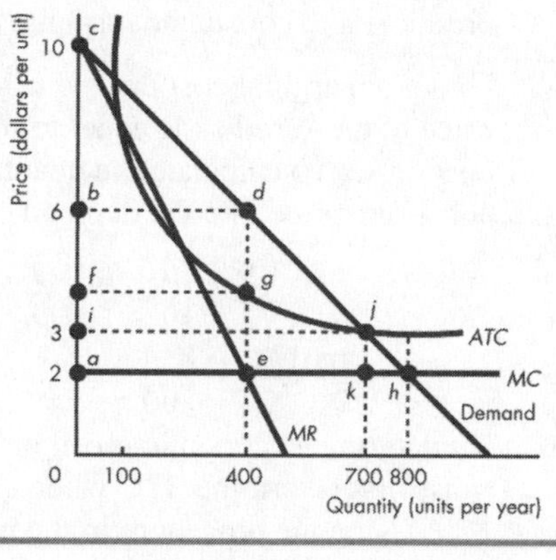

a In an unregulated market, the Aerodisk Company will choose output to maximize profit, where $MR = MC$. To calculate this output, set $MR = MC = 2$ and solve for Q:

$$10 - 0.02Q = 2$$
$$8 = 0.02Q$$
$$400 = Q$$

To calculate price, substitute $Q = 400$ into the demand equation:

$$P = 10 - 0.01Q_D$$
$$= 10 - 0.01\,(400)$$
$$= 10 - 4$$
$$= 6$$

400 Aerodisks will be produced and sold at a price of $6 each.

b To determine economic profit we first determine average total cost (*ATC*) when output (*Q*) is 400 units.

$$ATC = AFC + AVC$$
$$= (TFC/Q) + AVC$$
$$= (700/400) + 2$$
$$= 3.75$$

Therefore economic profit is the difference between price (average revenue) and *ATC* times the quantity sold. This is equal to $900 and is represented in Figure 14.5 by region *fbdg*.

c Producer surplus is the difference between the producer's revenue and the opportunity cost of production. Total revenue is $2,400 ($6 × 400 units) and total opportunity cost is $800 ($2 × 400 units). Thus producer surplus is $1,600. Graphically, producer surplus is the area of rectangle *abde* in Figure 14.5.

d Consumer surplus is the area in triangle *bcd* in Figure 14.5, $800.

e Total surplus is $2,400, the sum of producer and consumer surplus.

ⓔ ⓒⓣ **5** **a** Under a marginal cost pricing rule, the price of an Aerodisk is equal to marginal cost or $2. To calculate the quantity sold, substitute price into the demand equation:

$$P = 10 - 0.01Q_D$$
$$2 = 10 - 0.01Q_D$$
$$0.01Q_D = 8$$
$$Q_D = 800$$

b To determine economic profit or loss, we must first determine *ATC* when output is 800. Using the procedure in the previous problem we find at Q = 800, *ATC* is $2.875, which is greater than price by $0.875 (87.5 cents). Therefore the Aerodisk Company will incur a loss of $700 ($0.875 × 800). Alternatively, since *MC* is constant, if price is set equal to *MC* which is equal to *AVC*, the total loss will be just *TFC* or $700.

c Producer surplus is zero. Note that profits = producer surplus – total fixed costs.

d Consumer surplus is the area of triangle *ach* in Figure 14.5, $3,200.

e Total surplus is $3,200 (a maximum).

6 **a** Computation of *ATC* at various levels of output allows us to determine the *ATC* curve crosses the demand curve when $Q = 700$ and $ATC = \$3$. Thus under an average cost pricing rule, the price of an Aerodisk is $3 and 700 units will be sold.

b Since price equals average total cost, economic profit is zero.

c Producer surplus is $700, area *aijh* in Figure 14.5. Note that profits = producer surplus – total fixed costs.

d Consumer surplus is $2,450, the area of triangle *ijc* in Figure 14.5.

e Total surplus is $3,150.

7 **a** The total subsidy equals the loss under marginal cost pricing. In Short Answer Problem **5b** we computed this to be $700.

b The deadweight loss from the average cost pricing rule is the loss of total surplus relative to the marginal cost pricing rule. We have computed total surplus under marginal cost pricing ($3,200) in Short Answer Problem **5e** and total surplus under average cost pricing ($3,150) in Short Answer Problem **6e**. The deadweight loss is the difference: $50.

ⓒⓣ **c** It depends on the size of the deadweight loss associated with the taxes required to cover the subsidy under the marginal cost pricing rule. If the deadweight loss from these taxes exceeds $50, then the average cost pricing rule has a smaller deadweight loss and is superior. If the deadweight loss is less than $50, then the marginal cost pricing rule is superior.

8 a The key here is to recall that economic cost includes a normal rate of return. Because rate of return regulation sets a price that allows a normal rate of return, it is setting the price equal to average total cost.

b Under rate of return regulation, firms have an incentive to inflate their costs, since they are guaranteed a normal rate of return on all costs. A price ceiling in price cap regulation gives firms an incentive to operate efficiently and keep costs under control. Regulators try and set a price ceiling that yields the same output as (uninflated) average cost pricing. In case the price is set too high, price cap regulation is often combined with earnings sharing regulation, so profits above a target level must be shared with firms' customers.

9 a Social interest theory predicts that regulators set price and quantity to maximize total surplus. This means they choose quantity (and price) where *MC* is equal to demand. This corresponds to a quantity of 500 units and a price of $4 per unit.

b Capture theory predicts that regulators choose quantity and price to maximize the profit of the industry. This is the quantity a profit-maximizing monopolist would choose, 300 units, where *MC* = *MR*. The highest price that could be charged and still sell that quantity can be read from the demand curve: $6 per unit.

c Firms in the industry would demand regulation if the regulation increased profit to the industry. As we discovered in Chapter 13, cartels are unstable because there is always an incentive to cheat on output restriction agreements and it is difficult to enforce the agreements. If, however, firms in an industry can get the government, through regulation, to enforce a cartel agreement, they will want to do it.

Ⓒ **10** There is no single right answer to this question. Onyx's actions suggest that it was trying to influence the federal government to allow the takeover, by convincing Canadian citizens that a merged airline was in everyone's best interest. Obviously Onyx believed the takeover was in Onyx's interest, or it wouldn't have even tried. Since after the takeover there would have been only a single (monopoly) airline in Canada, the government would then have to provide some form of economic regulation. Because politicians respond to voters, if politicians believed that voters favoured the takeover, the politicians could support the takeover. Thus the advertisements, by swaying public opinion, were designed to ultimately influence the government/politicians. This line of reasoning is consistent with the capture theory.

On the other hand, the social interest theory suggests that any monopoly will be regulated in the society's best interest. For the airline monopoly to be approved in the first place (to take advantage of natural economies of scale), Onyx needed to convince the government (which would ultimately regulate its airline) that the takeover could work in the social interest.

Chapter 15 Externalities

KEY CONCEPTS

Externalities in Our Lives

Externality is cost or benefit from production activities or consumption activities that affects people who are not part of the original activity. Externalities may be negative or positive.

- **Negative externality**—imposes external cost.
  - negative production externality (pollution)
  - negative consumption externality (tobacco smoke)
- **Positive externality**—provides external benefit.
  - positive production externality (honeybees pollinating nearby fruit orchard)
  - positive consumption externality (flu vaccination)
- Externalities create market failure (*in*efficiency). Markets overproduce goods/services with negative externalities and underproduce goods/services with positive externalities.

Negative Externalities: Pollution

Many people assume all pollution must be stopped. Economic analysis of pollution, however, evaluates costs and benefits to identify efficient amounts of pollution.

- **Marginal private cost** *(MC)*—cost of producing additional unit of good/service paid by producer.
- **Marginal external cost**—cost of producing additional unit of good/service that falls on people other than the producer.
- **Marginal social cost** *(MSC)*—*MC* incurred by entire society; *MSC* = *MC* + Marginal external cost.

FIGURE **15.1** GOOD WITH AN EXTERNAL COST

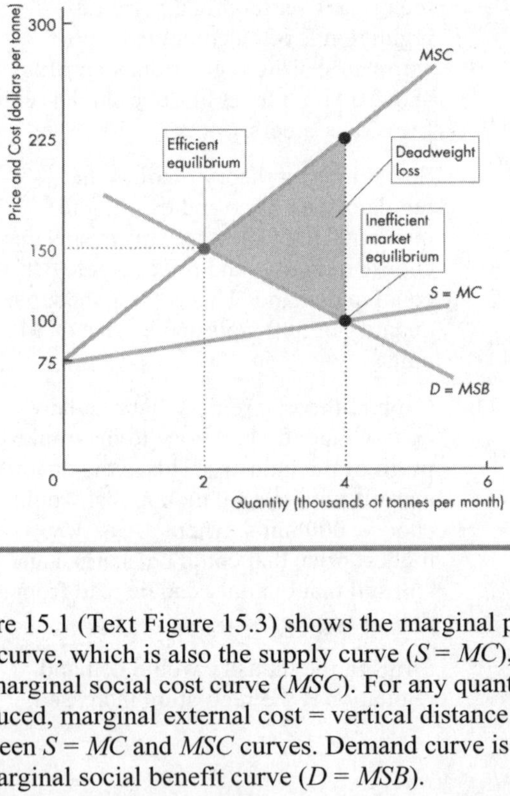

Figure 15.1 (Text Figure 15.3) shows the marginal private cost curve, which is also the supply curve (*S* = *MC*), and the marginal social cost curve (*MSC*). For any quantity produced, marginal external cost = vertical distance between *S* = *MC* and *MSC* curves. Demand curve is same as marginal social benefit curve (*D* = *MSB*).

- Efficient equilibrium (where *D* = *MSB* intersects *MSC*) takes into account all (private + external) costs.
- Private market equilibrium is inefficient (where *D* = *MSB* intersects *S* = *MC*) because does not take into account marginal external cost.
- Private market equilibrium produces too much of good with external cost and creates deadweight loss (from *MSC* > *MSB* for all units beyond efficient quantity).

Inefficiency from externalities can sometimes be reduced by establishing property rights.

- **Property rights** are a legally established title to ownership, use, and disposal of factors of production and goods and services.
- **Coase theorem**—If property rights exist and **transactions costs** (opportunity costs of conducting transactions) are low, there will be no externalities and private transactions are efficient. Who has property rights will *not* affect the efficiency of the outcome.

Where property rights cannot be established or transactions costs are high, other government actions can achieve efficiency even with negative externalities.

- Taxes—to create incentive for producers to cut back negative externalities, government can impose **Pigovian tax** equal to external marginal cost.
  - This makes *MSC* curve the relevant *MC* curve for polluting producer's decision, yielding output where *MSC* = *MSB*.
- Emission charges—set price per unit of pollution that polluter pays.
  - In practice, difficult to determine correct price.
- Marketable permits—each polluter given pollution limit (permit) that can be bought and sold.
  - Firms reducing pollution below their limit can sell "excess" reduction to other firms who then can pollute more. In competitive market for permits, price of permits = marginal external cost of pollution, yielding efficient outcome where *MSC* = *MSB*.

Positive Externalities: Knowledge

Knowledge from education and research creates private and social benefits.

- **Marginal private benefit** *(MB)*—benefit from additional unit of good/service received by consumer.
- **Marginal external benefit**—benefit from additional unit of good/service enjoyed by people other than the consumer.
- **Marginal social benefit** *(MSB)*—*MB* enjoyed by entire society; *MSB* = *MB* + Marginal external benefit.

FIGURE **15.2** GOOD WITH AN EXTERNAL BENEFIT

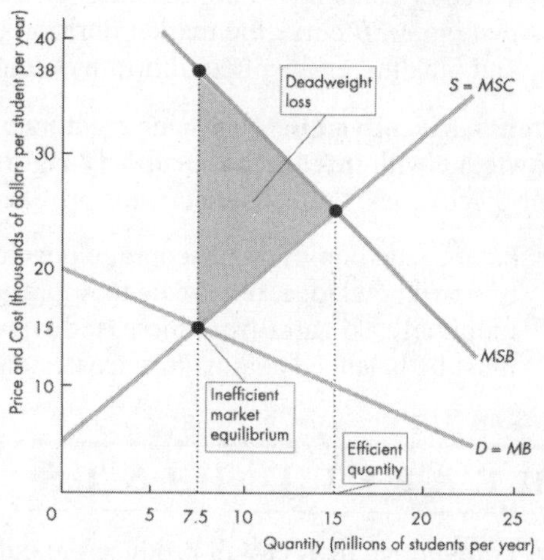

Figure 15.2 (Text Figure 15.7) shows the marginal private benefit curve, which is also the demand curve (*D* = *MB*), and the marginal social benefit curve (*MSB*). For any quantity consumed, marginal external benefit = vertical distance between *D* = *MB* and *MSB* curves. Supply curve is same as marginal social cost curve (*S* = *MSC*).

- Efficient equilibrium (where *MSB* intersects *S* = *MSC*) takes into account all (private + external) benefits.
- Private market equilibrium is inefficient (where *D* = *MB* intersects *S* = *MSC*) because does not take into account marginal external benefit.
- Private market equilibrium produces too little of good with external benefit and creates deadweight loss (from lost *MSB* > *MSC* for all units below efficient quantity).

Government actions can achieve efficiency even with positive externalities.

- **Public provision**—government provides the good/service (public education) and charges price below cost that equals marginal private benefit at the efficient quantity.
  - Additional cost paid by taxpayers, to yield total cost = *S* = *MSC*.
- **Subsidies**—payment by government to private producers of goods/services.
  - If subsidy equal to external marginal benefit, supply curve becomes *S* = *MSC* – subsidy, yielding efficient equilibrium quantity.

- **Vouchers**—government-provided tokens to households for buying specified goods/services.
  - Value of voucher = marginal external benefit, making *MSB* curve the market demand curve and yielding efficient equilibrium outcome.
- **Patents** and **copyrights**—provide creators of knowledge with **intellectual property rights** in their discoveries; help ensure creator profits.
  - Patents and copyrights encourage development of new knowledge, but create temporary monopoly, so gains from increased knowledge must be balanced against loss from monopoly.

HELPFUL HINTS

1 A competitive market will produce the quantity of output at which marginal private cost is equal to marginal private benefit. The allocatively efficient quantity is the quantity at which marginal social cost is equal to marginal social benefit.

The difference between *marginal social cost* and *marginal private cost* is marginal external cost, and the difference between *marginal social benefit* and *marginal private benefit* is marginal external benefit.

In most economic activities, people who are not part of the original activity are not affected, so there are no external costs or benefits. This means private and social costs and benefits coincide and competitive markets are efficient. However, when third parties are affected, there are external costs or benefits and competitive markets are *not* efficient. Markets overproduce goods/services with external costs (negative externalities) and underproduce goods/services with external benefits (positive externalities).

2 Competitive markets with externalities are not efficient because some of the costs or benefits are *external*. If those costs or benefits could be *internalized* somehow, then the market would be efficient. There are two main approaches to internalizing externalities discussed in this chapter.

The first is to establish and strictly enforce property rights. Then costs imposed on people who are not part of the original activity can be recovered through the legal process and will be paid by those involved in the activity: the costs become internal (private).

The second approach to internalizing externalities is to tax activities that generate external costs and subsidize activities that generate external benefits. By charging a tax equal to the external costs, the entire cost becomes internal. Similarly, by paying a subsidy equal to the external benefits, the entire benefit becomes internal.

3 Figure 15.1 in Key Concepts shows the production of a good with a negative externality (pollution). Note that *the efficient level of pollution is not zero*—efficient Q is *not* $Q = 0$. Generally, costs saved by reducing pollution to zero are less than the benefits lost (benefits from consuming goods whose production created pollution as a byproduct).

SELF-TEST

True/False and Explain

Externalities in Our Lives

1 Externalities arise only from production.

2 Flu vaccination is an example of a positive production externality.

3 A negative production externality imposes an external cost.

Negative Externalities: Pollution

4 If the production of a good involves no external cost, then marginal social cost is equal to marginal private cost.

5 If negative externalities exist, marginal social cost and marginal external cost are equivalent.

6 Externalities often arise from the absence of private property rights.

7 Assigning property rights always solves the problem of a negative externality.

8 Pigovian taxes creates incentives for producers to cut back negative externalities.

9 Firms with a low marginal cost of reducing pollution will buy marketable pollution permits.

10 When external costs are present, the private market produces more than the efficient level of output.

11 The efficient quantity of pollution is zero.

Positive Externalities: Knowledge

12 The existence of external benefits means that marginal social cost is greater than marginal private cost.

13 The private market equilibrium for goods with external benefits has deadweight loss, but the private market outcome with external costs has no deadweight loss because too many goods are produced.

14 Patents encourage invention and innovation.

15 Copyrights contribute to the development of knowledge so they have no economic cost.

Multiple-Choice

Externalities in Our Lives

1 An externality is a cost or benefit arising from an economic activity that falls on
- **a** consumers but not producers.
- **b** producers but not consumers.
- **c** free riders.
- **d** rivals.
- **e** none of the above.

2 The production of too few goods with positive externalities is an example of
- **a** market failure.
- **b** government failure.
- **c** producer sovereignty.
- **d** consumer sovereignty.
- **e** external costs.

3 Which of the following illustrates the concept of external cost?
- **a** Bad weather reduces the size of the wheat crop.
- **b** A reduction in the size of the wheat crop causes income of wheat farmers to fall.
- **c** Smoking harms the health of the smoker.
- **d** Smoking harms the health of nearby nonsmokers.
- **e** Public health services reduce the transmission of disease.

Negative Externalities: Pollution

4 The income elasticity of demand for a better environment is
- **a** negative.
- **b** zero.
- **c** positive.
- **d** trendy.
- **e** impossible to know without additional information.

5 Levels of acid rain caused by air pollution are
a less than efficient levels due to external costs.
b less than efficient levels due to external benefits.
c more than efficient levels due to external costs.
d more than efficient levels due to external benefits.
e decreasing the earth's average temperature.

6 Figure 15.3 shows demand for good *A* as well as the marginal private cost (*MC*) and marginal social cost (*MSC*) associated with production of good *A*. Production of the sixth unit of output generates an *external*
a cost of $1.50.
b cost of $3.00.
c cost of $6.00.
d benefit of $3.00.
e benefit of $6.00.

FIGURE **15.3**

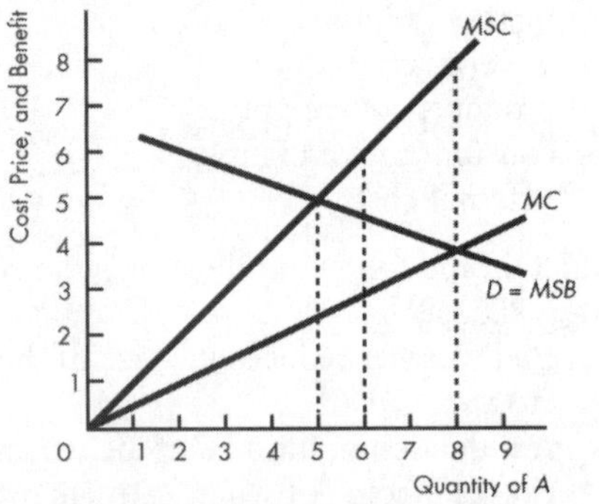

7 In Figure 15.3, how many units of good *A* will be produced in an unregulated market?
a 0 units
b 5 units
c 6 units
d 8 units
e impossible to calculate without additional information

8 In Figure 15.3, what is the efficient quantity of good *A*?
a 0 units
b 5 units
c 6 units
d 8 units
e impossible to calculate without additional information

9 At the current level of production of buckyballs, marginal social benefit is less than marginal social cost. To achieve allocative efficiency,
a buckyballs should be taxed.
b buckyballs should not be produced.
c output of buckyballs should increase.
d output of buckyballs should decrease.
e property rights in buckyballs should be established.

10 The production of too many goods with negative externalities is an example of
a redistribution.
b consumer sovereignty.
c producer sovereignty.
d public failure.
e market failure.

11 An externality is
a the amount by which price exceeds marginal private cost.
b the amount by which price exceeds marginal social cost.
c the effect of government regulation on market price and output.
d someone who consumes a good without paying for it.
e a cost or benefit that arises from an activity but affects people not part of the original activity.

12 The marginal private cost curve (*MC*) is a positively sloped straight line starting at the origin. If marginal external costs per unit of output are constant, the marginal social cost curve is a positively sloped straight line
a parallel to and above *MC*.
b parallel to and below *MC*.
c starting at the origin and above *MC*.
d starting at the origin and below *MC*.
e identical to *MC*.

13 A market economy tends to __________ goods with negative externalities and __________ goods with positive externalities.
a overproduce; overproduce
b overproduce; underproduce
c underproduce; overproduce
d underproduce; underproduce
e produce; consume

14 Policies for correcting problems of negative externalities include all of the following *except*
a emission charges.
b patents.
c quantitative limits.
d Pigovian taxes.
e marketable permits.

15 A battery acid producer pollutes the water upstream from nude swimmers belonging to the Polar Bear Club. If transactions costs are low, the quantity of pollution will be efficient

- **a** only if Ronald Coase is a member of the Polar Bear Club.
- **b** only if Ronald Coase is not a member of the Polar Bear Club.
- **c** only if water property rights are assigned to the producer.
- **d** only if water property rights are assigned to the Polar Bear Club.
- **e** if water property rights are assigned either to the producer or the Polar Bear Club.

16 Refer to Table 15.1. If the fertilizer market is perfectly competitive and unregulated, output (in tonnes) is

- **a** 1.
- **b** 2.
- **c** 3.
- **d** 4.
- **e** 5.

TABLE **15.1** CHEMICAL FERTILIZER MARKET

Output (tonnes)	Marginal Private Benefit ($)	Marginal Social Benefit ($)	Marginal Private Cost ($)	Marginal Social Cost ($)
1	140	140	50	80
2	120	120	60	90
3	100	100	70	100
4	80	80	80	110
5	60	60	90	120

17 Refer to Table 15.1. Fertilizer has a per-unit marginal external

- **a** cost of $100.
- **b** benefit of $100.
- **c** cost of $30.
- **d** benefit of $30.
- **e** cost of $0.

18 Refer to Table 15.1. The efficient output of fertilizer (in tonnes) is

- **a** 1.
- **b** 2.
- **c** 3.
- **d** 4.
- **e** 5.

Positive Externalities: Knowledge

19 The marginal private benefit curve (*MB*) is a negatively sloped straight line. If marginal external benefits per unit of output are positive and decreasing with additional output, the marginal social benefit curve is a negatively sloped straight line

- **a** parallel to and above *MB*.
- **b** parallel to and below *MB*.
- **c** above and steeper than *MB*.
- **d** above and flatter than *MB*.
- **e** below and flatter than *MB*.

20 Figure 15.4 shows the demand curve for good *B*, the marginal social benefit (*MSB*) curve, and marginal private and social cost (*MC* = *MSC*) curve. How many units of good *B* will be produced and consumed in an unregulated market?

- **a** 0
- **b** 3
- **c** 5
- **d** 6
- **e** 9

FIGURE **15.4**

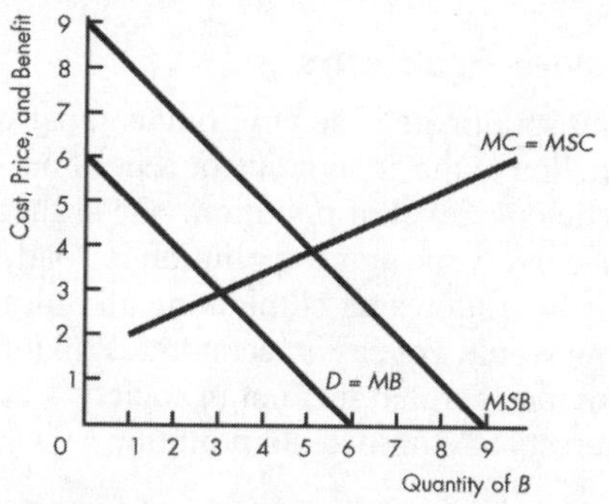

21 In Figure 15.4, what is the efficient quantity (in units) of good *B*?

- **a** 0
- **b** 3
- **c** 5
- **d** 6
- **e** 9

22 In Figure 15.4, which of the following government policies would induce the market to achieve allocative efficiency?

- **a** Tax the production of *B* at $3 per unit.
- **b** Tax the production of *B* at $4 per unit.
- **c** Provide vouchers for consumption of *B* at $1 per unit.
- **d** Provide vouchers for consumption of *B* at $3 per unit.
- **e** Provide vouchers for consumption of *B* at $4 per unit.

23 Policies to achieve allocative efficiency when there are external benefits include
- a intellectual property rights.
- b subsidies.
- c public provision.
- d all of the above.
- e none of the above.

24 Knowledge, as a factor of production,
- a displays diminishing marginal productivity.
- b creates external costs.
- c has costs totalling those paid to the patent holder.
- d is encouraged by intellectual property rights.
- e is all of the above.

25 When market failure occurs, government will act to reduce inefficiency. This is a prediction of a
- a fair results theory of government behaviour.
- b fair rules theory of government behaviour.
- c social interest theory of government behaviour.
- d public choice theory of government behaviour.
- e rent-seeking theory of government behaviour.

Short Answer Problems

ⓒⓣ 1 Your roommate is an environmentalist who is appalled at the economic concept of an "efficient" level of pollution. She argues that since everyone agrees pollution is "bad," society must work towards eliminating all pollution. How would you, as an economics major, convince her that it is not in society's best interests to eliminate all pollution?

2 The production of steel also produces pollution and generates external costs. Suppose government attempts to solve the problem by imposing a tax on steel producers. At the after-tax level of output, we observe the original marginal social cost curve is below the demand curve. Is the after-tax level of output efficient? If not, should steel production, and therefore pollution production, be increased or decreased?

3 Explain how a tax can be used to achieve efficiency in the face of external costs.

4 Two prairie pioneers, Jethro and Hortense, have adjacent fields. Because they get along so well and always work out any problems that arise, they have not bothered to put up a fence. Then one day Jethro buys a new pig, Babe. Babe sometimes wanders into Hortense's field and eats her corn. If Babe would only stay on Jethro's farm, he would eat valueless garbage. Suppose that Babe eats $500 worth of Hortense's corn per year (a negative externality imposed on Hortense) and that to build a fence between the farms costs $300. No property rights to keep animals off the fields have been established yet.

- a If the property right is given to Jethro so Babe can continue to wander, will Hortense build a fence? Explain.
- b If, instead, the property right is given to Hortense, so that she can charge Jethro for the corn Babe eats, will Jethro build a fence? Explain.
- c Explain how this example illustrates the Coase theorem.

ⓔ ⓒⓣ 5 Lever Sisters Company produces Flatulost, a popular room deodorizer. Unfortunately, the production process releases sulfur dioxide into the atmosphere. The marginal private cost (*MC*) to Lever Sisters of producing Flatulost is

$$MC = 1Q_S$$

The marginal social cost (*MSC*) is

$$MSC = 3/2Q_S$$

The demand curve for Flatulost (there are no external benefits) is

$$P = 12 - 1/2Q_D$$

Q_S is the quantity of Flatulost supplied, P is the price of Flatulost in dollars, and Q_D is the quantity demanded.

- a In an unregulated market, what is the equilibrium quantity of Flatulost? the equilibrium price?
- b To achieve allocative efficiency, what should be the equilibrium quantity of Flatulost? the equilibrium price?
- c Compare the unregulated market quantity and price with the allocatively efficient quantity and price.
- d The government wants to impose a tax on Flatulost to achieve the allocatively efficient quantity of output. What should the tax be?

6 Governments publicly provide education for free, or at least at a price (tuition) much less than cost. What is the economic argument that supports this policy?

7 The first two columns of Table 15.2 give the demand schedule for education in Hicksville, while the third column gives the marginal social cost. Since education generates external benefits, marginal social benefit given in the last column is greater than marginal private benefit.

TABLE **15.2** EDUCATION IN HICKSVILLE

Quantity (number of students)	Marginal Private Benefit ($)	Marginal Social Cost ($)	Marginal Social Benefit ($)
100	500	200	800
200	400	250	700
300	300	300	600
400	200	350	500
500	100	400	400
600	0	450	300

a Represent the data in Table 15.2 graphically.

b What equilibrium price and quantity would result if the market for education is unregulated?

c What is the allocatively efficient quantity of students in Hicksville?

8 In an attempt to address the inefficient level of education in Hicksville, the town council decides to publicly support schooling. The council offers a $200 voucher to each student who buys a year of education.

a Draw the new marginal private benefit curve, which includes the voucher, on your graph and label it MB_1.

b What are the approximate new equilibrium price and quantity?

9 The Hicksville town council increases the voucher to $400.

a Draw another marginal private benefit curve, which includes the voucher, on your graph and label it MPB_2.

b What are the approximate corresponding equilibrium price and quantity?

c What level of voucher will achieve the efficient quantity of education?

10 What are the benefits and costs of creating intellectual property rights for the creation of new knowledge?

ANSWERS

True/False and Explain

1 **F** Externalities can arise from production or consumption and be negative or positive. (346)

2 **F** Positive consumption externality. (346)

3 **T** Positive production or consumption externality provides external benefit. (346)

4 **T** *MSC* = *MC* + marginal external cost. (349)

5 **F** *MSC* = *MC* + marginal external cost. (349)

6 **T** Property rights allow recovery of (external) costs. (350–351)

7 **F** True if transactions costs low; false otherwise. (350–351)

8 **T** See text discussion. (352–353)

9 **F** Firms with low marginal cost of reducing pollution sell permits; firms with high marginal cost of reducing pollution buy. (352–353)

10 **T** Where *MC* (instead of *MSC*) intersects demand. (349–350)

11 **F** Efficient quantity where *D* = *MSB* intersects *MSC* production (including pollution). (349–350)

ⓔ 12 **F** External benefits affect *MSB*, not *MSC*; *MSB* = *MB* + marginal external benefit. (353–355)

ⓔ 13 **F** Both have deadweight loss; with external costs, deadweight loss is excess *MSC* over *MSB* for units produced beyond efficient quantity. (349–350, 353–355)

14 **T** Intellectual property rights overcome positive externality problem of knowledge. (357)

15 **F** Copyrights are monopolies with associated inefficiencies; but benefits new knowledge presumed to outweigh costs of monopoly. (357)

Multiple-Choice

1 **e** Falls on people who are not part of original activity. (346)

2 **a** Markets fail to produce efficient quantity of goods with positive externalities. (345–346)

3 d Cost falls on people not part of original activity. (346)

4 c Better environment is normal good so $\eta_y > 0$. (347)

5 c Market overproduction of good with negative externalities (external costs). (347–350)

6 b Vertical distance between *MSC* and *MC* at $Q = 6$. (349–351)

7 d Where *MC* intersects demand. (349–350)

8 b Where *MSC* intersects demand. (349–350)

9 d Draw graph. Don't know if positive, negative, or any externality. (349–353)

10 e Failure to achieve allocative efficiency because external costs not taken into account in private, market decisions. (349–351)

11 e Definition. (346–352)

12 a *MC* shifts leftward by vertical distance equal to marginal external cost per unit. (349)

13 b Outcomes of market failure. (350, 354–355)

14 b Patents correct problems of positive externalities. (352–353)

15 e This is the Coase theorem. (350–351)

16 d Where $MB = MC = 80$. (349–351)

17 c $MSC - MC$ is constant in this example. (349–351)

18 c Where $MSB = MSC$. (349–351)

19 c Similar to text Figure 15.6. (353–354)

20 b Where *MC* intersects demand. (353–355)

21 c Where *MC* intersects *MSB*. (353–355)

22 d Shift *MC* rightward by vertical distance between *MSB* and demand. (355–357)

23 d All move output to where $MSB = MSC$. (355–357)

24 d No diminishing marginal productivity; creates external benefits; patent monopoly creates loss from restricted use. (357)

25 c Public interest to achieve efficiency. (381, 355–357)

Short Answer Problems

1 We all want to eliminate pollution, *ceteris paribus*, but every action, including reducing pollution, has a cost. Once again, the key concept underlying the economic argument is opportunity cost. What is the opportunity cost of reducing pollution, or, what does society have to give up to achieve a pollution-free environment?

Small reductions in pollution are relatively inexpensive—eliminating lead from gasoline and paint, conserving energy to reduce output from coal-fired electrical plants, etc. But to eliminate all pollution would mean eliminating all cars and airplanes, outlawing all power except solar and hydroelectric power, shutting down most factories, etc. The cost of eliminating *all* pollution is enormous, and that additional cost is far greater than the additional benefits from further reductions in pollution. Therefore some level of pollution is efficient. Pollution is part of the opportunity cost of the benefits we receive from driving or flying instead of walking, from enjoying the comfort of air conditioning in hot weather, and from enjoying goods produced in factories. The efficient level of pollution balances the marginal social cost of the pollution against the marginal social benefit of the production and consumption associated with that level of pollution.

2 Since the marginal social cost curve is below the demand curve at the after-tax output, marginal social cost is less than marginal benefit. This means that the tax has been set too high; it has been set at a level in excess of the external cost. As a result, the after-tax level of steel production will be less than the efficient level. The level of steel production and pollution production should be increased by decreasing the amount of the tax.

3 The existence of external costs means that producers do not take into account all costs when deciding how much to produce. If a tax is levied that is exactly the amount of the external cost, the cost will no longer be external. As a result, the producer will take it into account and be induced to produce the efficient quantity.

4 a Hortense will build a fence. Although the fence costs \$300 per year, it saves her the \$500 in lost corn that Babe would otherwise eat.

b Jethro will build a fence. The $300 per year is less than the $500 per year he would now have to pay Hortense for Babe's wanderings.

c The Coase theorem states that if transactions costs are low and property rights are established, there are no externalities and an efficient outcome occurs regardless of who is assigned the property right. Because Jethro and Hortense can work out their problems amicably, transactions costs are low. The outcome of building a fence eliminates the negative externality of the wandering pig and occurs regardless of which pioneer is assigned the property right. The outcome is efficient because, for this one decision, the $300 cost to society of the fence is less than the $500 cost of consumed corn.

5 a In an unregulated market, the equilibrium quantity would be determined by the intersection of the supply (*MC*) and demand curves. In equilibrium, $Q_S = Q_D = Q^*$. Setting the *MC* equation equal to the demand equation yields

$$1Q^* = 12 - 1/2Q^*$$
$$3/2Q^* = 12$$
$$Q^* = 8$$

To solve for the equilibrium price (P^*), substitute Q^* into the demand (or into the *MC*) equation.

$$P^* = 12 - 1/2Q^*$$
$$P^* = 12 - 1/2\ (8)$$
$$P^* = 8$$

b In order to achieve efficiency, *MSC* must equal marginal social benefit (*MSB*). Since there are no external benefits, the demand curve is also the *MSB* curve. In equilibrium, $Q_S = Q_D = Q^*$. To find the equilibrium quantity, set the *MSC* equation equal to the demand equation.

$$3/2Q^* = 12 - 1/2Q^*$$
$$2Q^* = 12$$
$$Q^* = 6$$

To solve for the equilibrium price (P^*), substitute Q^* into the demand (or into the *MSC*) equation.

$$P^* = 12 - 1/2Q^*$$
$$P^* = 12 - 1/2\ (6)$$
$$P^* = 9$$

c Compared with the efficient outcomes, the unregulated market produces too much Flatulost (8 units versus 6) and the product sells at too low a price ($8 versus $9).

d The tax should be equal to the cost differential (*MSC* – *MC*) at the optimum output of 6 units. Since the *MSC* curve = 1.5 × *MC* curve, the tax should be 50 percent.

6 Government subsidizes education heavily. The economic argument is that education generates external benefits. When individuals are educated, society at large receives benefits beyond the private benefits that accrue to those choosing how much education to obtain.

7 a Figure 15.5 is a graphical representation of the data in Table 15.2. The demand for education is given by the marginal private benefit curve (labelled *MB*), the marginal social cost curve is labelled *MSC* and the marginal social benefit curve is labelled *MSB*. Ignore the other curves for now.

FIGURE **15.5**

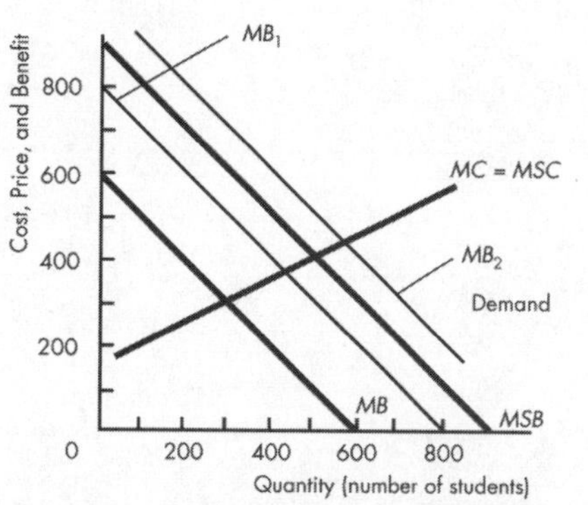

b In an unregulated market, equilibrium price and quantity are determined by the intersection of the *MB* and *MC* curves. The equilibrium price is $300 and the equilibrium quantity is 300 students.

c Since there are no external costs, the efficient quantity is determined by the intersection of the *MSC* and *MSB* curves. Efficiency is attained at a quantity of 500 students.

8 a The voucher increases the marginal private benefit to each student by the amount of the voucher, $200. The new *MB* curve, labelled MB_1, is included in Figure 15.5.

b The new equilibrium after the $200 voucher is at the intersection of the *MSC* and MB_1 curves. The price of a unit of education is approximately $370 and there are approximately 430 students.

9 a With a voucher of $400 per student, the *MB* curve shifts to MB_2 in Figure 15.5.

b With this voucher the equilibrium is at the intersection of the *MSC* and MB_2 curves. The corresponding price of a unit of education is approximately $430 and the number of students is approximately 570.

c In order to achieve an efficient outcome, the voucher must make the *MB* curve coincide with the *MSB* curve. This requires a voucher of $300 per student.

10 Intellectual property rights create incentives for individuals to create new knowledge by granting the inventor a limited monopoly to benefit from the application of her idea. Without the property right, anyone could freely use the idea and there would be little profit to the inventor. The limited monopoly, although necessary as an incentive to produce knowledge, has a social cost—the restriction of knowledge-based output below the efficient, competitive quantity.

Chapter 16 Public Goods and Common Resources

KEY CONCEPTS

Classifying Goods and Resources

A good/service/resource is either

- ♦ **Excludable**—can prevent others from consuming it, or
- ♦ **Nonexcludable**—can*not* prevent others from consuming it

and is either

- ♦ **Rival**—one person's consumption decreases amount available for others, or
- ♦ **Nonrival**—one person's consumption does *not* decreases amount available for others

These characteristics are used to classify all goods/services/resources into four types:

- ♦ **Private good**—rival and excludable. Example: a hot dog.
- ♦ **Public good**—nonrival and nonexcludable; can be consumed simultaneously by everyone; no one can be excluded. Example: national defence.
- ♦ **Common resource**—rival and nonexcludable; a unit can be used only once, but no one can be excluded from using other available units. Example: ocean fish.
- ♦ Natural monopolies—nonrival and excludable; with economies of scale and low marginal cost, increased consumption reduces cost, but buyers can be excluded. Example: cable television.

Public goods create **free-rider** (someone who consumes without paying) **problem**—no one has an incentive to pay for a public good.

Common resources create **tragedy of the commons**—overuse and depletion of a resource because no one has an incentive to conserve its use.

Public Goods and the Free-Rider Problem

Efficient quantity of public good occurs where net benefit is maximized or where marginal benefit equals marginal cost of public good.

- ♦ *Total benefit* is total $ value placed on public good.
- ♦ *Net benefit* is total benefit – total cost.
- ♦ *Marginal benefit* is increased total benefit from a unit increase in public good.
- ♦ The economy's marginal benefit curve of a public good is the *vertical* sum of individual marginal benefit curves.

Provision of public goods:

- ♦ Private provision of a public good creates a free-rider problem and provides less than the efficient quantity of the good.
- ♦ Government provision can provide an efficient quantity of a public good, where politicians compete for votes of well-informed voters.

The quantity of government provision of a public good generally depends on political marketplace and actions of voters, politicians, and bureaucrats.

- ♦ Politicians follow **principle of minimum differentiation**—tendency for competitors to make themselves identical to appeal to maximum number voters/clients.
- ♦ Voters may be **rationally ignorant**—deciding *not* to acquire information because cost of acquisition > expected benefit. Then politicians, influenced by bureaucrats and special-interest lobbyists, may allow inefficient overprovision of a public good.

Types of political equilibrium:

- ♦ Social interest theory—predicts governments achieve efficiency because voters are fully informed.
- ♦ Public choice theory—predicts governments create inefficiency because voters are rationally ignorant.

Common Resources

The tragedy of the commons—overuse and depletion of a resource—occurs because when no one owns a resource, no one has an incentive to conserve its use. The overfishing of Atlantic cod fish is an example.

- ♦ Sustainable production is rate of production that can be maintained indefinitely. For cod, maximum sustainable catch occurs where marginal catch (per boat) is zero.
- ♦ Overfishing occurs where maximum sustainable catch starts decreasing and marginal catch is negative. Text Figure 16.5 shows the maximum sustainable catch at 5,000 boats.

FIGURE 16.1
Efficient Use of a Common Resource

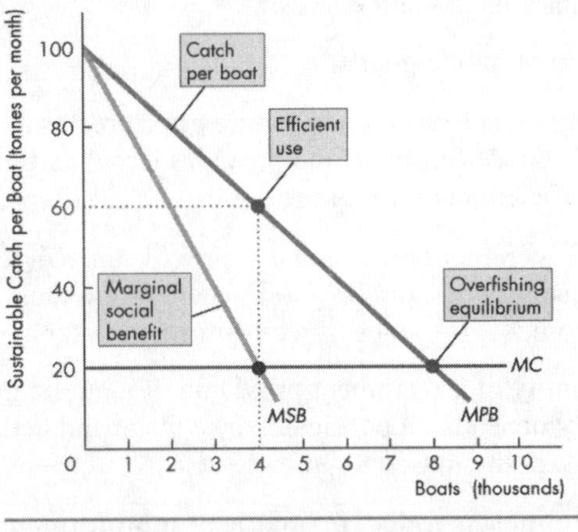

Figure 16.1 (text Figure 16.7) shows the tragedy of the commons outcome (overfishing equilibrium) and the efficient use outcome. The marginal cost curve (*MC*) shows the monthly opportunity cost of operating a boat (including normal profit) measured in tonnes of fish. The marginal private benefit (*MPB*) curve shows the average monthly catch per boat. The marginal social benefit (*MSB*) curve shows the change in total catch when one more boat goes fishing.

- ♦ Marginal catch (*MSB*) is less than average catch (*MPB*) because each additional boat decreases the catches of boats already fishing. Those decreases must be subtracted from the catch of the additional boat to calculate the marginal social benefit of the last boat.
- ♦ Overfishing equilibrium—the unregulated equilibrium use of a common resource, is the quantity where $MC = MPB$. Overfishing occurs because the equilibrium of 8,000 boats is greater than the maximum sustainable production of 5,000 boats.
- ♦ Efficient use—the efficient use of a common resource is the quantity where $MC = MSB$, or 4,000 boats.

Efficient use of a common resources requires incentives that confront users with the marginal social consequences of their actions. Three main incentive methods:

- ♦ Property rights—assigning private property rights to a resource makes the *MSB* curve the same as the owner's *MPB* curve, so owner will use resource efficiently. But difficult to assign enforceable property rights to the ocean or atmosphere.
- ♦ Quota—government sets quota at efficient quantity. Problems include incentives to cheat by increasing output, and differing marginal costs among producers, so efficient producers might not get proper share of quotas.
- ♦ **Individual transferable quota (ITQ)**—production limit assigned to an individual, who can sell quota to someone else. Market price of ITQ will equal marginal private benefit minus marginal cost at the efficient quantity, so producers with higher marginal costs will not produce.

HELPFUL HINTS

1. All goods provided by the government are not necessarily public goods. A public good is defined by being *nonrival* and *nonexcludable*, not by whether or not it is publicly provided. For example, many communities provide swimming pools and residential garbage pickup. Neither of these is a pure public good despite the fact that each may be provided by the government. In other communities, the same services are provided by the private market.

2. The nonrival and nonexcludable properties of pure public goods imply that we obtain the marginal benefit curve for the economy as a whole differently than for private goods.

For a private good, to obtain the demand curve for the whole economy, we sum the individual marginal benefit (demand) curves *horizontally*. For example, at a price of $7, suppose Max demands 5 units of a private good, Lisa demands 5 units, and total demand is 10 units. Because the private goods are rival and excludable, the units Max consumes must be different from the units Lisa consumes, and therefore must be added together to get total market demand.

But for a public good, to obtain the economy's marginal benefit curve we sum the individual marginal benefit curves *vertically*. For example, for the fifth unit of a public good, suppose Max is willing to pay $7 and Lisa is willing to pay $7. Because public goods are nonrival and nonexcludable, both Max and Lisa can consume the fifth unit simultaneously. The total benefit from consuming the fifth unit is $7 + $7 = $14.

3 The key to the graph explaining the tragedy of the commons—overuse and depletion of a resource—is understanding why the marginal social benefit (*MSB*) curve lies below the marginal private benefit (*MPB*) curve. The *MPB* curve shows the *average* monthly catch per boat. The *MSB* curve shows the *change* in total catch when one more boat goes fishing.

The relationship between *MSB* and *MPB* for a common resource is similar to the relationship in Chapter 12 between marginal revenue and average revenue for a single-price monopoly. The downward-sloping demand curve facing a single-price monopoly is also its *average* revenue curve. To sell one more unit of output, the firm must lower its price. But this has two effects. First, the sale of an additional unit will increase revenue by the amount of the price. However, since the firm must also *drop the price on previous units*, revenue on these will decrease. The net change in revenue, the marginal revenue, is less than the price and the marginal revenue curve will lie below the demand (average revenue) curve.

When a new boat goes out to catch fish, this has two effects. First, the quantity of fish will increase by the amount of the new boat's catch. However, each additional boat on the water *decreases the catches of previous boats fishing*, and those decreases must be subtracted from the catch of the new boat to calculate its marginal social benefit. The net change in the catch, the marginal catch (*MSB*), is less than the average catch (*MPB*) and the *MSB* curve will lie below the *MPB* curve.

SELF-TEST

True/False and Explain

Classifying Goods and Resources

1 Cable television service is nonrival and excludable.

2 A movie you watch in a mostly empty theatre is both nonrival and nonexcludable.

3 Public goods create the tragedy of the commons.

Public Goods and the Free-Rider Problem

4 Goods supplied by government are defined as public goods.

5 The excludability feature of goods leads to the free-rider problem.

6 The existence of public goods gives rise to the free-rider problem.

7 The economy's marginal benefit curve for a public good is obtained by adding the marginal benefits of each individual at each quantity of provision.

8 The private market will produce much less than the efficient quantity of pure public goods.

9 According to public choice theory, not only is there possibility of market failure, there is also the possibility of "government failure."

10 Political parties tend to propose fundamentally different policies to give voters a clearer choice.

Common Resources

11 When the sustainable catch of fish is at a maximum, the marginal catch is zero.

12 The marginal private benefit (*MPB*) curve shows the change in total catch when one more boat goes fishing.

13 For a common resource, marginal private benefit is greater than marginal social benefit.

14 The efficient use of a common resource is the quantity where $MC = MSB$.

15 Individual differences in marginal cost prevent an ITQ system from delivering an efficient outcome.

Multiple-Choice

Classifying Goods and Resources

1 When a city street is not congested, it is like a(n)
a external good.
b internal good.
c rival good.
d private good.
e public good.

2 A private good is
1 rival.
2 nonrival.
3 excludable.
4 nonexcludable.
a 1 and 3
b 1 and 4
c 2 and 3
d 2 and 4
e 1 only

3 A common resource is
1 rival.
2 nonrival.
3 excludable.
4 nonexcludable.
a 1 and 3
b 1 and 4
c 2 and 3
d 2 and 4
e 2 only

4 A public good is
1 rival.
2 nonrival.
3 excludable.
4 nonexcludable.
a 1 and 3
b 1 and 4
c 2 and 3
d 2 and 4
e 4 only

5 Which of the following goods is nonexcludable?
a city bus
b toll bridge
c lighthouse
d art museum
e all of the above

Public Goods and the Free-Rider Problem

6 Governments provide pure public goods like national defence because
- **a** governments are more efficient than private firms at producing such goods.
- **b** of free-rider problems that result in underproduction by private markets.
- **c** people do not value national defence very highly.
- **d** of the potential that private firms will make excess profits.
- **e** of external costs.

7 The quantity of public goods produced by an unregulated market tends to be
- **a** less than the efficient quantity.
- **b** equal to the efficient quantity.
- **c** greater than the efficient quantity.
- **d** that which maximizes total public benefit.
- **e** that which maximizes net public benefit.

8 The market demand curve for a *private* good is obtained by summing the individual marginal
- **a** cost curves horizontally.
- **b** cost curves vertically.
- **c** benefit curves horizontally.
- **d** benefit curves vertically.
- **e** benefit curves diagonally.

9 The economy's total demand curve for a *public* good is obtained by summing the individual marginal
- **a** cost curves horizontally.
- **b** cost curves vertically.
- **c** benefit curves horizontally.
- **d** benefit curves vertically.
- **e** benefit curves diagonally.

10 The efficient scale of provision of a public good occurs where
- **a** total benefit is at a maximum.
- **b** total benefit is at a minimum.
- **c** marginal benefit is at a maximum.
- **d** marginal benefit minus marginal cost equals zero.
- **e** marginal cost is at a minimum.

11 Refer to Figure 16.2 which shows the total cost and total benefit of proposals for building four different-sized high schools. The proposal with the largest net benefit is
- **a** *A*.
- **b** *B*.
- **c** *C*.
- **d** *D*.
- **e** impossible to identify without additional information.

FIGURE **16.2**

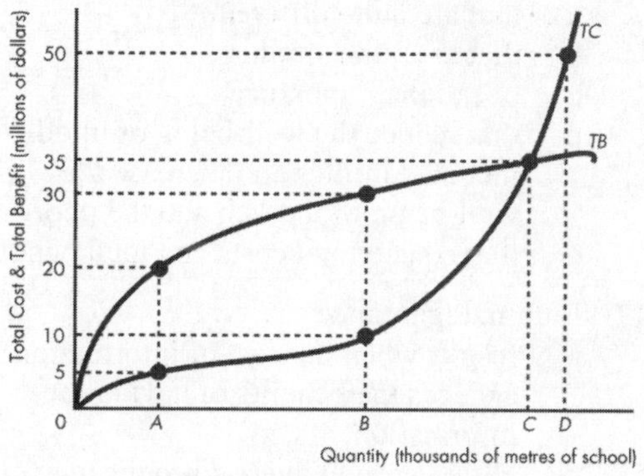

12 Refer to Figure 16.2 which shows the total cost and total benefit of proposals for building four different-sized high schools. The proposal most likely to appeal to voters in an election is
- **a** *A*.
- **b** *B*.
- **c** *C*.
- **d** *D*.
- **e** impossible to identify without additional information.

13 Refer to Figure 16.2 which shows the total cost and total benefit of proposals for building four different-sized high schools. The proposal that best meets the goals of the school district's bureaucrats is
- **a** *A*.
- **b** *B*.
- **c** *C*.
- **d** *D*.
- **e** impossible to identify without additional information.

14 According to public choice theory, a voter will favour a candidate whose political program is
- **a** perceived to offer the greatest personal benefit to the voter.
- **b** best for the majority of the people.
- **c** closest to the efficient use of resources.
- **d** favoured by the median voter.
- **e** all of the above.

15 Competitors who make themselves identical to appeal to the maximum number of voters illustrate the principle of
- **a** maximum differentiation.
- **b** minimum differentiation.
- **c** rational ignorance.
- **d** nonrivalry.
- **e** excludability.

16 Competition between two political parties will cause those parties to propose policies
- **a** that are quite different.
- **b** that are quite similar.
- **c** of rational ignorance.
- **d** that reduce the well-being of middle-income families and increase the well-being of the rich and the poor.
- **e** that equate total costs and total benefits.

17 Rational ignorance
- **a** results when the cost of information exceeds the benefits of having the information.
- **b** allows special interest groups to exert political influence.
- **c** combined with special-interest groups can yield inefficient provision of public goods.
- **d** results in all of the above.
- **e** results in none of the above.

18 If voters have similar views and are well informed, the quantity of national defence provided by the government will tend to be
- **a** greater than the efficient quantity.
- **b** less than the efficient quantity.
- **c** the least costly quantity.
- **d** the quantity that maximizes net benefit.
- **e** the quantity that maximizes the Ministry of Defence budget.

19 On any given spending issue subject to a vote, the median voter is the one who favours
- **a** the least spending.
- **b** the most spending.
- **c** the efficient level of spending.
- **d** the average level of spending.
- **e** spending more than the level favoured by half the voters and less than the level favoured by half the voters.

Common Resources

20 The tragedy of the commons is the absence of incentives to
- **a** reduce marginal cost of common resources.
- **b** prevent under use of common resources.
- **c** prevent over use of common resources.
- **d** discover new common resources.
- **e** export wool in sixteenth-century England.

21 For a common resource like fish, marginal private benefit of an additional boat is the __________ and the marginal social benefit is the __________.
- **a** catch per boat; total fish caught
- **b** total fish caught; change in total catch from an additional boat
- **c** change in total catch from an additional boat; catch per boat
- **d** catch per boat; change in total catch from an additional boat
- **e** change in total catch from an additional boat; total fish caught

22 In the equilibrium for a common resource with no government regulation,
- **a** marginal social benefit is greater than marginal private benefit.
- **b** marginal social benefit equals marginal private benefit.
- **c** marginal social benefit equals marginal cost.
- **d** marginal social benefit is greater than marginal cost.
- **e** marginal private benefit equals marginal cost.

23 When the sustainable catch of fish is at a maximum, the marginal catch is
- **a** rising.
- **b** falling.
- **c** zero.
- **d** positive.
- **e** negative.

24 For a common resource like fish, marginal cost includes
- **a** the opportunity cost of maintaining a boat.
- **b** the opportunity cost of operating a boat.
- **c** normal profit.
- **d** all of the above.
- **e** none of the above.

25 Which of the following methods is *not* used to achieve the efficient use of a common resource?
- **a** assigning property rights
- **b** quotas
- **c** subsidies
- **d** individual transferable quotas
- **e** all of the above are used to achieve the efficient use of a common resource

Short Answer Problems

1 Explain the four types of goods that result from the distinctions between excludable and nonexcludable and between rival and nonrival.

2 Explain the *nonrival* and *nonexcludable* features of a pure public good.

3 What is the free-rider problem?

4 Heritage Apartments has 100 residents who are concerned about security. Table 16.1 gives the total cost of hiring a 24-hour security guard service as well as the marginal benefit to each of the residents.

TABLE **16.1**

Number of Guards	Total Cost per Day ($)	Marginal Benefit per Resident ($)	Marginal Benefit to All Residents ($)
1	300	10	
2	600	4	
3	900	2	
4	1,200	1	

a Why is a security guard a public good for the residents of Heritage Apartments?

b Why will zero guards be hired if each of the residents must act individually?

c Complete the last column of Table 16.1 by computing the marginal benefit of security guards to all of the residents together.

ⓒ 5 Now suppose that the residents form an Apartment Council that acts as a governing body to address the security issue.

a What is the optimal (allocatively efficient) number of guards? What is the net benefit at the optimal number of guards?

b Show that net benefit is less for either one less guard or for one more guard than for the optimal number of guards.

c How might the Apartment Council pay for the guards?

6 Two candidates are competing in an election for president of the Economics Club. The only issue dividing them is how much will be spent on the annual Economics Club party. It is well known that the seven voting members of the club (*A* through *G*) have the preferences in Table 16.2. These are strongly held preferences about exactly how much should be spent on the party.

TABLE **16.2** ECONOMICS CLUB PREFERENCES

Voting Member	Proposed Amount ($)
A	10
B	20
C	30
D	40
E	50
F	60
G	70

a How much will each candidate propose to spend?

b To demonstrate that your answer to part **a** is correct, consider the outcome of the following two contests.

i Candidate 1 proposes the amount you gave in part **a** and candidate 2 proposes $1 less. Which candidate will win? Why?

ii Candidate 1 proposes the amount you gave in part **a** and candidate 2 proposes $1 more. Which candidate will win? Why?

c Suppose the Sociology Club is also electing a president and the same single issue prevails. It is well known that the seven voting members of the Sociology Club have the following strongly held peferences regarding exactly how much should be spent on their party (see Table 16.3).

TABLE **16.3** SOCIOLOGY CLUB PREFERENCES

Voting Member	Proposed Amount ($)
T	0
U	0
V	0
W	40
X	41
Y	42
Z	43

How much will each of the two candidates propose in this case?

7 Explain why it may be rational for voters to be ignorant.

8 Table 16.4 gives three alternative income distributions for five individuals, *A* through *E*. Currently income is distributed according to distribution 1 (the first column of the table). Consider alternative proposed distributions 2 and 3, one at a time.

TABLE **16.4**

Individual	Distribution 1 ($)	Distribution 2 ($)	Distribution 3 ($)
A	0	200	150
B	200	300	250
C	400	350	450
D	700	600	600
E	1,000	850	850

a If distribution 2 is proposed as an alternative to distribution 1, will it have majority support? Why or why not?

b If distribution 3 is proposed as an alternative to distribution 1, will it have majority support? Why or why not?

9 What is the tragedy of the commons problem, and why does it occur? Use the example of ocean fisheries to illustrate your explanation.

10 Figure 16.3 shows the marginal cost, marginal private benefit and marginal social benefit curves for Atlantic Halibut fish, a common resource.

FIGURE **16.3**

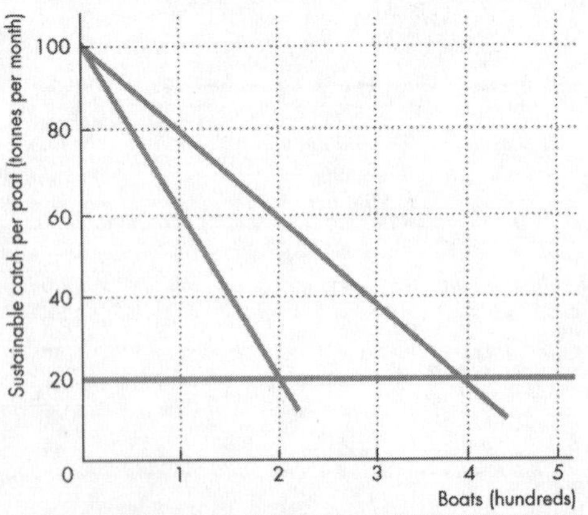

a Label each curve.

b What is the private equilibrium number of boats and the sustainable catch per boat?

What is the efficient number of boats and the efficient sustainable catch per boat?

c If the government were to act, what quota achieves the efficient outcome?

d If the government issues individual transferable quotas (ITQ), what is the market price of an ITQ?

ANSWERS

True/False and Explain

1 T Your use of cable does not affect me, but buyers can be excluded from service. (364)

2 F Nonrival because your attendance does not affect others' access to tickets, but those not paying can be excluded. (364)

3 F Public goods create free-rider problems; common resources create tragedy of the commons. (375)

4 F By definition, public goods are *nonrival* and *nonexcludable*. But governments also supply swimming pools, which are rival and excludable goods (see Helpful Hint 1). (369)

5 F Nonexcludability creates free-rider problem. (365–366)

6 T Nonexcludability means no incentive for anyone to pay. (365–366)

7 T See Helpful Hint 2. (365–366)

8 T Because no accounting for external benefits. (366–367)

9 T Believe government agents act in own interest, not necessarily public interest. (369)

10 F Propose similar policies as vote-maximizing strategy appealing to median voter. (367–368)

11 T See Text Table 16.1, point *F*. (370–371)

12 F Definition of marginal social benefit (*MSB*) curve. (370–372)

13 T Marginal social benefit is less than marginal private benefit because each additional user of a resource decreases quantity caught by all previous users. (372–373)

14 T Efficient use of common resource does not overuse the resource. (372–373)

15 F Low cost producers are willing and able to pay more for quotas, so producers with higher marginal costs will not produce. (374–375)

Multiple-Choice

1 e Nonrival and nonexcludable. Congestion creates rivalry. (364)

2 a See Text Figure 16.1. (364)

3 b A unit of a common resource can be used only once, but no one can be excluded from using other available units. (364)

4 d Can be consumed simultaneously by everyone; no one can be excluded. (364)

5 c Can't prevent ships from seeing the light. (364)

6 b Would not be profitable for private firms. (365–366)

7 a Private production unprofitable because of free-rider problem. (365–366)

8 c Because private goods rival and excludable, quantities consumed by each individual at each price are different and must be added to get total market demand. (365–367)

9 d Because public goods nonrival, can sum marginal benefit to each individual. See Text Figure 16.3. (365–367)

10 d Equivalent to maximum net benefit. (365–367)

11 b Largest *TB* – *TC*. (365–367)

12 b Maximizes net benefit. (365–369)

13 d Public choice theory assumes bureaucrats maximize budget (*TC*). (365–368)

14 a Voter, like consumer, assumed concerned only with own self-interest. (369)

15 b Definition of principle. (367)

16 b Vote maximizing by using principle of minimum differentiation. (367–369)

17 d **a** definition, **b**, **c** outcomes of rational ignorance. (368)

18 d Government will respond to demands of voters. (367–369)

19 e Median = exactly halfway between. (365–369)

20 c Prevent over use and depletion because common resources rival and nonexcludable. (370–372)

21 d See definitions. (370–373)

22 e See Text Figure 16.6; *MSB* is not considered in private decisions. (370–372)

23 c See Text Table 16.1; like other mathematical functions, maximum total value occurs when marginal value equals zero. (370–371)

24 d Definition. (371)

25 c Common resources overused because too inexpensive, so subsidies would make overuse worse. (373–375)

Short Answer Problems

1 (1) *Private good*—rival and excludable. Example: a hot dog. (2) *Public good*—nonrival and nonexcludable; can be consumed simultaneously by everyone; no one can be excluded. Example: national defence. (3) *Common resource*—rival and nonexcludable; a unit can be used only once, but no one can be excluded from using other available units. Example: ocean fish. (4) *Natural monopolies*—nonrival and excludable; with economies of scale and low marginal cost, increased consumption reduces cost, but buyers can be excluded. Example: cable television.

2 A good is nonrival if its consumption by one person does not reduce the amount available for others. Nonexcludable means that if the good is produced and consumed by one person, others cannot be excluded from consuming it as well.

3 The free-rider problem is the problem of unregulated markets producing too little of a pure public good because there is little incentive for individuals to pay for the good. There is nothing to prevent the person from being excluded from consuming the good, or from getting a free ride.

4 a A security guard is a public good because, in this case, it is nonrival and nonexcludable. It is nonrival because one resident's *consumption* of the security provided by a guard does not reduce the security of anyone else. It is nonexcludable because once a security guard is in place, all residents enjoy the increased security; none can be excluded.

b If each resident must act individually in hiring a security guard none will be hired because each resident receives only $10 in benefit from the first guard, which costs $300 per day.

c The entries in the last column of Table 16.1 Solution are obtained by multiplying the marginal benefit per resident by the number of residents, 100. This multiplication is the numerical equivalent of summing the individual marginal benefit curves vertically for each quantity of guards.

TABLE **16.1** SOLUTION

Number of Guards	Total Cost per Day ($)	Marginal Benefit per Resident ($)	Marginal Benefit to All Residents ($)
1	300	10	1,000
2	600	4	400
3	900	2	200
4	1,200	1	100

ⓔ 5 a If the Apartment Council hires each guard for whom the marginal benefit exceeds the marginal cost, they will hire the optimal number of guards. The marginal cost of each additional guard is $300. The marginal benefit of the first guard is $1,000, so he will be hired. Similarly, the marginal benefit of the second guard is $400, and she will be hired.

The marginal benefit of the third guard, however, is only $200, which is less than marginal cost. Therefore the efficient (optimal) number of guards is two. For two guards, the net benefit is $800: total benefit ($1,400) minus total cost ($600).

b For one guard, net benefit is $700: total benefit ($1,000) minus total cost ($300). For three guards, net benefit is also $700: total benefit ($1,600) minus total cost ($900). Thus the net benefit of $800 is greatest for two guards.

c The Apartment Council might pay for the guards by collecting a security fee of $6 per day from each of the 100 residents in order to hire two security guards.

6 a Each candidate will propose spending $40 since that is the preference of the median voter (voter *D*).

b i Candidate 1 will win because *D*, *E*, *F*, and *G* will vote for that candidate because $40 comes closer to matching their preferences than the $39 proposed by candidate 2. Only *A*, *B*, and *C* will vote for candidate 2.

ii Candidate 1 will win because *A*, *B*, *C*, and *D* will vote for that candidate while only *E*, *F*, and *G* will vote for candidate 2.

c Once again, the candidates will both propose spending $40 on the party since that is the preference of the median voter. Note that in this case, the median voter's view is not "average."

7 Most issues have only a small and indirect effect on most voters. In such cases it is irrational for a voter to spend much time and effort to become well informed because the additional cost would quickly exceed any additional benefit. Only if the voter is significantly and directly affected by an issue will it pay to become well informed. As a result, most voters will be rationally ignorant on any given issue.

8 a Only *A* and *B* are better off under distribution 2. Distribution 2 will receive the support of only *A* and *B* with *C*, *D*, and *E* opposed. Note that the median voter (*C*) is worse off under distribution 2.

b Distribution 3 will receive majority support since it makes the median voter better off. It will be supported by *A*, *B*, and *C* and opposed by *D* and *E*.

9 The tragedy of the commons—the overuse and depletion of a common resource—occurs because when no one owns a resource, no one has an incentive to conserve its use. For example, as more boats fish, the average quantity of fish that one boat catches (marginal private benefit) decreases. But no individual takes account of the decrease in the average catch because each is concerned only with his own catch. As a result of ignoring the social consequences of any decision to fish, additional boats go out fishing until their

marginal private benefit (average catch per boat) equals the marginal cost of fishing. When that many boats fish, marginal cost is greater than marginal social benefit, overfishing occurs, and the common fish resource is depleted.

10 a See Figure 16.3 Solution. It shows the marginal cost, marginal private benefit and marginal social benefit curves for Atlantic Halibut fish, a common resource.

FIGURE 16.3 SOLUTION

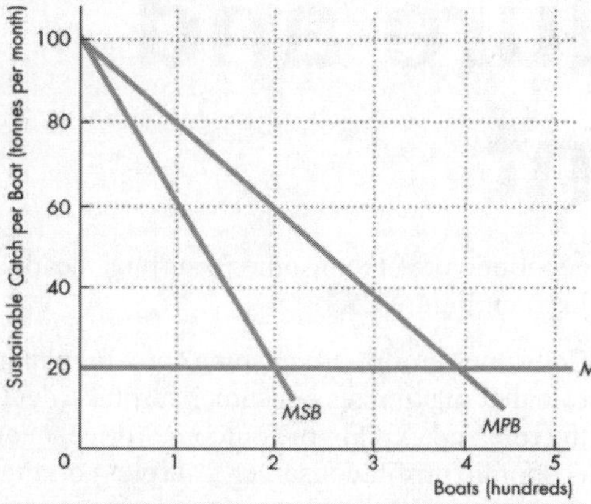

b The private equilibrium number of boats (400) is determined by the intersection of the *MC* and *MPB* curves. The sustainable catch is 20 tonnes per boat. The efficient number of boats (200) is determined by the intersection of the *MC* and *MSB* curves. The efficient sustainable catch (60 tonnes per boat) is determined reading "up" from 200 boats and "over" to the *MSB* curve.

c The quota that achieves the efficient outcome is set for the quantity at which *MC* equals *MSB*—200 boats each catching 60 tonnes of halibut.

d The market price of an individual transferable quota (ITQ) equals the *MPB* – *MC*, at the quota level of fish. The government issues ITQs to 200 boats, so the ITQ market price = 60 tonnes – 20 tonnes = 40 tonnes of halibut.

CHAPTERS 14–16

Part 5 Wrap Up

Understanding Market Failure and Government

PROBLEM

The Canadian Radio-television and Telecommunications Commission (CRTC) is holding public hearings on renewing the licence of Cretin's Choice Cable TV Company. You have been hired to help the CRTC evaluate the contradictory claims made by different interest groups in testimony to the commission. Figure P5.1 shows the best available information about costs and revenues for Cretin's Choice.

FIGURE **P5.1** CRETIN'S CHOICE

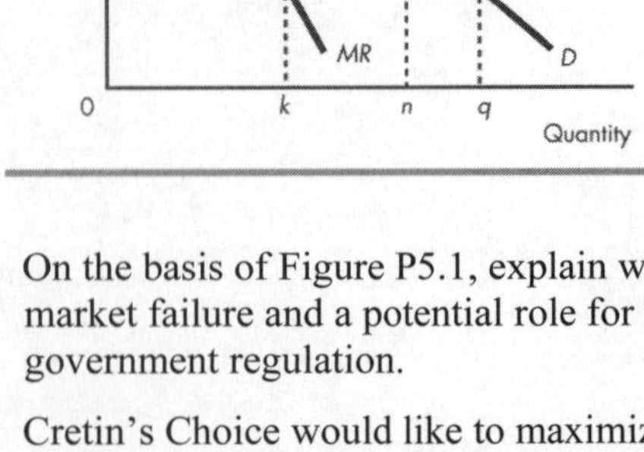

a On the basis of Figure P5.1, explain why there is market failure and a potential role for government regulation.

b Cretin's Choice would like to maximize its profits. Identify the firm's profit-maximizing rule and explain the outcome (price, quantity, economic profit, consumer's surplus, deadweight loss) on Figure P5.1.

c Consumer groups are pushing for a regulatory rule that maximizes consumer surplus. Identify the rule and explain the outcome (price, quantity, economic profit, consumer's surplus) on Figure P5.1. If the CRTC adopts the rule, what options might you suggest that would keep the cable company in business?

d Any CRTC regulation rule has to appear to meet the social interest goal of efficient use of resources. Identify the rule (other than marginal cost pricing) that comes closest to achieving this goal and explain the outcome (price, quantity, economic profit, consumer's surplus, deadweight loss) on Figure P5.1.

e While Cretin's Choice wants maximum profits, it recognizes the CRTC's need to *appear* to use the regulatory rule in part **d**. What argument can you expect to hear from Cretin's Choice? Use Figure P5.1 to explain.

f If, despite your advice to the contrary, the CRTC accepts the industry argument in part **e**, what theory of regulation is supported?

g After years of the type of regulation in part **f**, the CRTC deregulates Cretin's Choice's market. If rates of return increase, what theory of regulation is supported?

MIDTERM EXAMINATION

You should allocate 32 minutes for this examination (16 questions, 2 minutes per question). For each question, choose the one *best* answer.

1 The free rider problem for a public goods means that
- **a** the good is rival.
- **b** the good is excludable.
- **c** an unregulated market produces the efficient quantity.
- **d** an unregulated market produces less than the efficient quantity.
- **e** an unregulated market produces more than the efficient quantity.

2 A noisy party that irritates the neighbors is an example of a
- **a** negative production externality.
- **b** positive production externality.
- **c** negative consumption externality.
- **d** negative production externality.
- **e** mistake to not invite the neighbors.

3 Total surplus is the sum of
- **a** the gain from trade accruing to consumers and the gain from trade accruing to producers.
- **b** the gain from regulation and the gain from anti-combine laws.
- **c** revenues received by firms and government subsidies.
- **d** consumer payments and producer profit.
- **e** none of the above.

4 Consider the natural monopoly in Figure P5.2. Producer surplus is a maximum when quantity is
- **a** Q_0 and price is P_3.
- **b** Q_1 and price is P_1.
- **c** Q_1 and price is P_4.
- **d** Q_2 and price is P_2.
- **e** Q_3 and price is P_0.

FIGURE **P5.2**

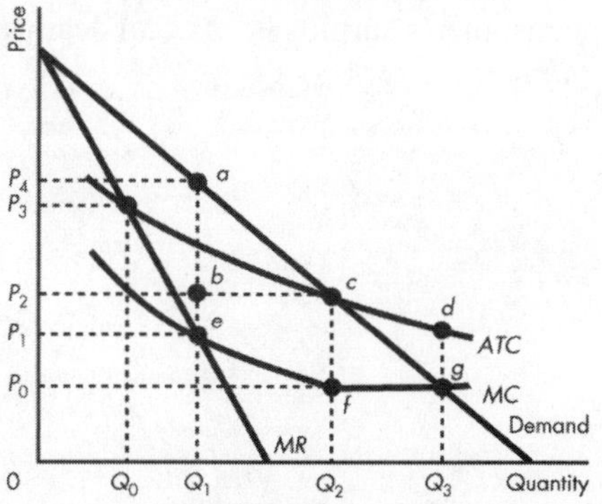

5 According to the economic theory of bureaucracy, bureaucrats
- **a** aim to maximize the budget of their bureau.
- **b** aim to maximize total surplus.
- **c** aim to privatize Crown corporations.
- **d** will operate Crown corporations to underproduce compared to private firms.
- **e** will be rationally ignorant.

6 In the efficient use of a common resource,
- **a** marginal social benefit is greater than marginal private benefit.
- **b** marginal social benefit equals marginal private benefit.
- **c** marginal social benefit equals marginal cost.
- **d** marginal social benefit is greater than marginal cost.
- **e** marginal private benefit equals marginal cost.

7 Refer to Figure P5.3. The unregulated outcome in the paper market is
- **a** quantity = 40, price = 11.
- **b** quantity = 40, price = 13.
- **c** quantity = 50, price = 12.
- **d** quantity = 50, price = 14.
- **e** quantity = 60, price = 13.

FIGURE **P5.3** PAPER MARKET

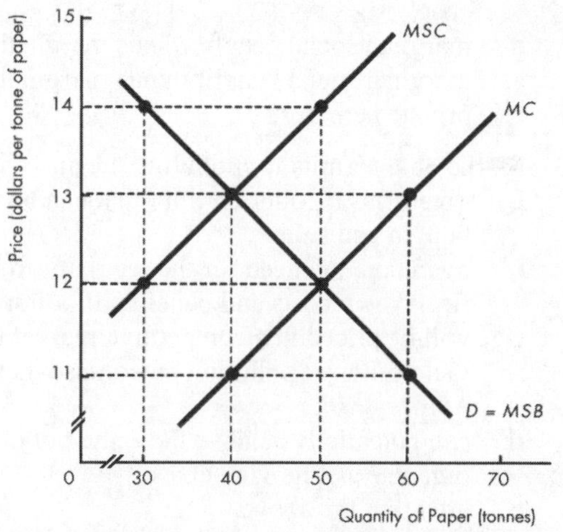

8 Refer to Figure P5.3. A tax of __________ per tonne is necessary to achieve the efficient output of __________ tonnes of paper.
- **a** \$14; 50
- **b** \$14; 30
- **c** \$13; 40
- **d** \$2; 50
- **e** \$2; 40

9 Social interest theory predicts the political process minimizes
- a producer surplus.
- b consumer surplus.
- c total surplus.
- d deadweight loss.
- e efficient use of resources.

10 The factor of production least likely to display diminishing marginal productivity is
- a land.
- b labour.
- c capital.
- d entrepreneurship.
- e knowledge.

11 According to the Coase theorem, if transactions costs are low and property rights exist,
- a negative externalities cause deadweight losses.
- b positive externalities cause deadweight losses.
- c private transactions are efficient.
- d public transactions are efficient.
- e the efficient level of pollution will be zero.

12 The market price at the quota quantity of an individual transferable quota (ITQ) equals the
- a marginal private benefit.
- b marginal social benefit.
- c marginal private benefit minus marginal cost.
- d marginal social benefit minus marginal cost.
- e marginal social benefit minus marginal private benefit.

13 Marketable permits for polluting the air
- a give firms a pollution limit that can be bought and sold.
- b overcome the need for the regulator to know firms' own costs and benefits of pollution.
- c will be priced in a competitive market to yield efficient pollution outcomes where $MSC = MSB$.
- d can potentially achieve the same pollution outcome as Pigovian taxes.
- e are all of the above.

14 The *total benefit* of a given level of provision of a public good can be obtained by
- a adding the marginal benefit of each level of provision up to the given level.
- b adding the marginal benefit of each level of provision and then subtracting the marginal cost of each level of provision.
- c adding the net benefit of each level of provision up to the given level.
- d multiplying net benefit by the quantity of the public good provided.
- e none of the above methods.

15 Voters are asked to vote for either proposition *A* or proposition *B*. Proposition *A* will win if it
- a is closer the efficient use of resources.
- b is supported by bureaucrats.
- c is preferred by the median voter.
- d generates greater social benefits than social costs.
- e generates the fewest negative externalities.

16 Policies for correcting problems of positive externalities include
- a emission charges.
- b vouchers.
- c marketable permits.
- d Pigovian taxes.
- e all of the above

ANSWERS

Problem

a Market failure is the inability of an unregulated market to efficiently allocate resources. Cretin's Choice is a natural monopoly with economies of scale. While only a monopoly can achieve the economies of scale, in the absence of regulation, it will restrict output, increase price, and create a deadweight efficiency loss.

b The profit-maximizing rule is to choose the quantity of output where $MC = MR$ and charge the highest possible price. On Figure P5.1, price is *b*, quantity is *k*, economic profit is *bcgf*, consumer's surplus is *abf*, and deadweight loss is *fhp*.

c The marginal cost pricing rule (set price equal to *MC*) maximizes consumer surplus. On Figure P5.1, price is *e*, quantity is *q*, loss per unit is *op*, and consumer's surplus is *aep*. The firm is making a loss and will not voluntarily stay in business. You could suggest that the company be allowed to price discriminate or that it receive a government subsidy (financed by taxes that would create a deadweight loss elsewhere).

d An average cost pricing rule sets price equal to *ATC*. On Figure P5.1, price is *d*, quantity is *n*, economic profit is zero, consumer's surplus is *adl*, and deadweight loss is *lmp*. If this deadweight loss is less than the deadweight loss associated with subsidizing the marginal cost pricing rule in part **c**, then the average cost price rule comes closest to achieving efficient use of resources.

There are two main forms of average cost pricing rules. One is rate of return regulation, which allows a normal rate of return on the cost of capital. The other is price cap regulation, which sets a price ceiling (where *ATC* intersects the demand curve) to achieve target rate of return on capital.

e Cretin's Choice will argue that their costs are much higher than those reflected in the *ATC* curve of Figure P5.1. The company will inflate its costs and argue that its real *ATC* curve is higher and just tangent to the demand curve at point *f*. If the CRTC accepts this argument and applies the average cost pricing rule, the regulated price and outcome will be the same as the monopolist's own profit-maximizing rule in part **b**.

The advantage of price cap regulation is that by setting a price ceiling, the firm has an incentive to operate efficiently and keep costs under control. The difficulty with price cap regulation is in setting the price just right—too low results in reduced output and inefficiency, while too high results in economic profits. For this reason, price cap regulation is often combined with earnings sharing regulation that forces firms to share profits above the target level with consumers. That gives some flexibility to setting the price slightly high while still yielding an outcome in the social interest.

f If the CRTC accepts the industry argument in part **e**, the capture theory of regulation is supported.

g If, after deregulation, rates of return increase, the social interest theory of regulation is supported.

Midterm Examination

1 d Public goods are nonrival and nonexcludable. No incentive for people to pay, so no profitable private production. (364–366)

2 c Imposed by consumers of "party services." (346)

3 a Consumer surplus plus producer surplus; see Chapter 14, Helpful Hint **2**. (326–327)

4 c Private monopoly outcome. (328–329)

5 a See text discussion. (335–337)

6 c See Text Figure 16.7. (372–373)

7 c Where $D = MSB$ intersects MC. (349–350)

8 e $2 per tonne tax (vertical distance between *MC* and *MSC*) makes firm's *MC* equal to *MSC*. Output where $D = MSB$ intersects *MSC*. (350–352)

9 d Or maximize total surplus (efficient use of resources). (369)

10 e Because of external benefits. (357)

11 c There are no externalities. Level of pollution where $MB = MSC$. (350–351)

12 c This makes the user pay the full opportunity cost of using the common resource. (374–375)

13 e See text discussion. (352–353)

14 a **b**–**d** involve irrelevant costs. (365–366)

15 c 50 percent of votes plus 1. (365–368)

16 b Others for negative externality problems. (355–357)

Chapter 17 Demand and Supply in Factor Markets

KEY CONCEPTS

Factor Prices and Incomes

Factors of production, or resources (labour, capital, land, entrepreneurship) are hired by firms to produce output.

Demand and supply in competitive factor markets for labour, capital, and land determine those factor prices (*PF*) (wages, interest, rent) and quantities (*QF*).

- ♦ Factor income = (*PF* × *QF*).
- ♦ Factor price for entrepreneurship is normal profit. Economic profit/loss is residual income going to firm's owners.

Changes in demand and supply:

- ♦ Increased demand for factor increases *PF*, increases *QF*, and increases income.
- ♦ Decreased demand for factor decreases *PF*, decreases *QF*, and decreases income.
- ♦ Increased supply of factor decreases *PF*, increases *QF*, and increases income if $\eta_D > 1$; decreases income if $\eta_D < 1$.
- ♦ Decreased supply of factor increases *PF*, decreases *QF*, and decreases income if $\eta_D > 1$; increases income if $\eta_D < 1$.

Labour Markets

Demand for factors is a **derived demand**, stemming from demand for goods and services produced by a factor and driven by firms' profit-maximizing objective.

- ♦ **Marginal revenue product** (*MRP*) is extra revenue from employing one more unit of labour.
  - $MRP = MP \times MR$
  - For a perfectly competitive firm, $MR = P_{output}$. So $MRP = MP$ (additional output produced by employing additional unit of labour) $\times P_{output}$.

Equivalent conditions for profit maximizing:

- ♦ Firm hires additional units of labour up to quantity of
  - factor where *MRP* = wage rate (*W*)
  - output where *MR* = *MC*
- ♦ Firm's demand curve for labour is identical to downward-sloping marginal revenue product curve of labour.
- ♦ Firm's long run demand for labour curve (MRP_L curve) shifts rightward if
  - increased P_{output}.
  - technological change increases *MP* labour.
  - increased price of substitute factor of production.
  - decreased price of complement factor of production.

Market demand curve for labour is horizontal sum of quantities of labour demanded by all firms at each wage rate.

$$\text{Elasticity of demand for labour} = \left| \frac{\%\ \Delta \text{ quantity labour demanded}}{\%\ \Delta \text{ wage rate}} \right|$$

Demand for labour will be more elastic

- ♦ when production is more labour-intensive (wages a greater percentage of total cost).
- ♦ the greater the elasticity of demand for the final product.
- ♦ the greater the substitutability of capital for labour in the long run.

Supply of labour determined by households' decisions allocating time between labour supply (work) and leisure.

- ♦ Wage rate is *opportunity cost of leisure*.
- ♦ At wage rates above household's *reservation wage*, household supplies labour.

- *Substitution effect* from higher wage induces increased quantity labour supplied.
- *Income effect* from higher wage induces decreased quantity labour supplied.
- When wage rises, quantity labour supplied increases when substitution effect > income effect.
- Individual household labour supply curve is *backward-bending* when income effect > substitution effect.

Market supply of labour curve is horizontal sum of all household supply curves. Upward-sloping over normal range of wage rates.

- Supply of labour curve shift rightward if
  - increased adult population.
  - technological change or increased capital in home production.

Capital Markets

Capital markets coordinate household's saving decisions (supply of financial capital) and firm's investment decisions (demand for financial capital to buy physical capital equipment).

"Price of capital" determined by equilibrium of supply and demand in capital markets = real interest rate.

Demand for capital depends on future marginal revenue products of physical capital. Firms compare future marginal revenue products with present cost of capital.

- **Discounting** is conversion of future amount of money to its present value.
- **Present value** of future amount of money is amount that, if invested today, will grow as large as future amount, taking account of earned interest.

$$\text{Present value} = \frac{\text{Amount money available } n \text{ years}}{(1 + r)^n}$$

Firms decide whether to buy physical capital by evaluating net present value.

- **Net present value** (*NPV*) = future flow of marginal revenue product – purchase price.
- If net present value positive, firm buys capital good and increases profit.
- Higher interest rate lowers *NPV* and decreases quantity of capital firms demand (movement up along capital demand curve).

Market demand curve for capital shows relationship between quantity of capital demanded and the interest rate, *ceteris paribus*.

Supply of capital determined by households' saving decisions. Households supply financial capital that firms use to buy physical capital equipment.

- Quantity of financial capital supplied determined by
  - income—higher income yields higher saving.
  - expected future income—when current income > expected future income, saving is higher.
  - interest rate—higher interest rates yield higher saving.

Market supply of capital curve shows relationship between quantity of capital supplied and interest rate, *ceteris paribus*. Supply of capital shifts rightward due to

- increases in income or population.
- increases in middle-aged proportion of population.

Natural Resource Markets

Economists call all natural resources *land.*

- **Renewable natural resource** can be used repeatedly and not be depleted.
- **Nonrenewable natural resource** can only be used once and cannot be replaced.

Supply of renewable resources fixed and perfectly inelastic, so price determined by demand. But to individual competitive firm, supply of land perfectly elastic at market price.

Supply of nonrenewable natural resources depends on stock and flow supply.

- *Stock*—known quantity that exists at a given time. Perfectly inelastic.
- *Flow* supply—rate of use. Perfectly elastic at price equal to present value of expected price next period.

Because flow supply perfectly elastic, current period's price = present value next period's price.

- *Hotelling Principle*—price of natural resource expected to rise at rate = interest rate. But actual price may fluctuate from expected price because of unexpected technological change.

Income, Economic Rent, and Opportunity Cost

Economic rent is income received by factor owner above amount required to induce supply. Income required to induce supply is opportunity cost of factor of production.

- Total income = opportunity cost (area under supply curve) + economic rent (area above supply curve but below factor price).
- The more inelastic the supply of factor of production, the greater portion of its income is economic rent.
- Rent (price paid for services of land or a building) is distinct from economic rent (component of income of any factor of production).

HELPFUL HINTS

1 Be careful to distinguish between the marginal revenue product of a factor of production and the marginal revenue of a unit of output. The marginal revenue product of a factor of production is calculated by multiplying marginal revenue and marginal product ($MRP = MR \times MP$). The intuition is this: marginal product tells us how much more output we receive from using more of a factor, and marginal revenue tells us how much more revenue we receive from selling each unit of that additional output. Therefore *MP* times *MR* tells us how much more revenue we receive (the *MRP*) from using more of the factor of production.

2 This chapter gives a broad overview of characteristics common to competitive markets for the factors of production labour, capital, and land. Profit-maximizing firms will hire labour up to the point where marginal revenue product (*MRP*) is equal to the marginal cost (*MC*) of labour. Since marginal cost is the wage rate of labour (*W*), $MRP = W$ in a competitive labour market.

3 The most important graph in this chapter appears in Text Figure 17.3, reproduced here as Figure 17.1. Using the example of Max's Wash 'n' Wax, the figure demonstrates that a firm's demand for labour curve is the same as its marginal revenue product curve of labour.

FIGURE 17.1

(a)

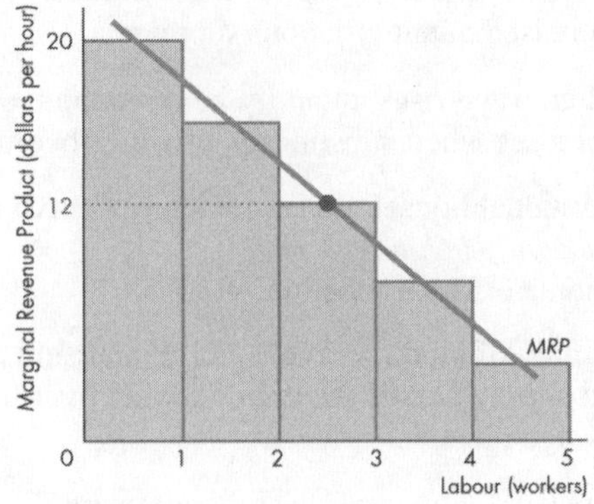

(a) Marginal revenue product

(b)

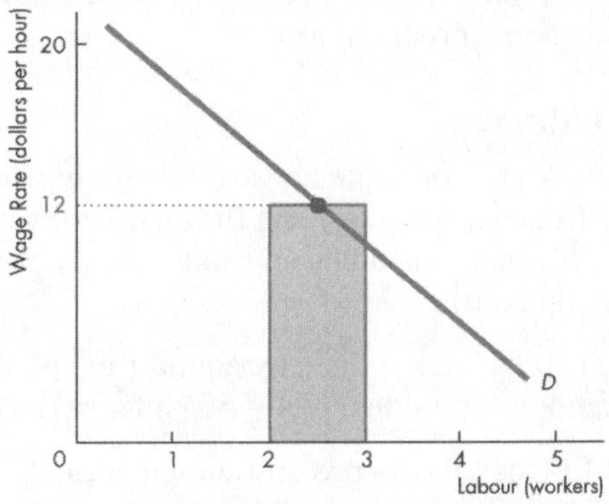

(b) Demand for labour

Part (a) shows the marginal revenue product curve (*MRP*) based on the numbers in Text Table 17.1 on page 390. Notice that the values for *MRP* are plotted midway between the labour inputs used in their calculation. For example, the *MRP* of moving from 0 to 1 labourer is 20, so the value of 20 on the *MRP* curve is plotted midway between 0 and 1 labourers.

Part (b) constructs Max's demand for labour by asking how much labour Max will hire at alternative wage rates. Since Max is a profit maximizer, he will hire labour up to the point where the marginal revenue product of labour is equal to the wage rate. For example, if the wage rate is $10 per hour, Max will hire 3 workers since marginal revenue product is $10 when 3 workers are hired. Other points on the labour demand curve can be obtained in similar fashion. The result is that the labour demand curve is the same as the *MRP* curve.

4 The concept of present value is essential in thinking about the value today of an investment or of future amounts of money. It gives us a method of comparing investments that have payments at different points in time. The intuition behind present value is a dollar today is worth more than a dollar in the future because today's dollar can be invested to earn interest. To calculate the value today of an amount of money that will be paid in the future, we must discount that future amount to compensate for the forgone interest. The present value of a future amount of money is the amount that, if invested today, will grow as large as the future amount, taking into account the interest that it will earn.

5 The profit-maximizing condition of hiring a factor of production until $MRP = MC$ must be adapted when a firm buys capital equipment. The reason is capital usually operates over more than one period and generates marginal revenue products distributed over time. The purchase price, however, must be paid now. In order to compare the purchase price (MC) with the stream of marginal revenue products, we must compute the present value of that stream.

In the case of capital equipment used over more than one period, the profit-maximizing condition becomes: buy an additional unit of capital as long as the present value of the stream of marginal revenue products is greater than the purchase price of the unit of capital. Since the net present value (NPV) of an investment is defined as the present value of the stream of marginal revenue products minus the purchase price of capital, an equivalent condition is: *Buy capital equipment as long as its net present value is positive.*

SELF-TEST

True/False and Explain

Factor Prices and Incomes

1 Economic profit is the factor price of entrepreneurship.

2 An increase in the supply of labour always increases labour income.

Labour Markets

3 A firm's average revenue product curve is also its demand for labour curve.

4 Demand for labour is more elastic when demand for the final product is more inelastic.

5 A household supplies no labour at wage rates below its reservation wage.

6 A backward-bending supply of labour curve occurs when the income effect dominates the substitution effect.

Capital Markets

7 If the price of a unit of capital exceeds the present value of its marginal revenue product, a profit-maximizing firm should buy it.

8 If a household's current income is low compared with its expected future income, it will save very little.

9 The supply curve of capital shows the relationship between the quantity of physical capital supplied and the interest rate, other things remaining the same.

Natural Resource Markets

10 Natural resources can only be used once and cannot be replaced.

11 The market supply of a particular piece of land is perfectly elastic.

12 The Hotelling Principle states that the price of hotel stocks is expected to rise at a rate equal to the interest rate.

Income, Economic Rent, and Opportunity Cost

13 Economic rent is not the same thing as the rent you pay for an apartment.

14 If the supply of a factor of production is perfectly inelastic, its entire income is opportunity cost.

15 If Lloyd Robertson would be willing to read the news for \$100,000 per year, and he is paid \$2,100,000 per year to do so, he is earning economic rent of \$2,000,000.

Multiple-Choice

Factor Prices and Incomes

1 Factor prices are wages for labour, rent for land,
- **a** normal profit for capital, and interest for money.
- **b** dividends for capital, and interest for money.
- **c** interest for capital, and normal profit for entrepreneurship.
- **d** interest for capital, and economic profit for entrepreneurship.
- **e** economic profit for capital, and normal profit for entrepreneurship.

2 The supply of a factor of production is very elastic. An increase in demand for that factor results in a
- **a** large increase in quantity supplied and small increase in price.
- **b** small increase in quantity supplied and large increase in price.
- **c** large increase in supply and small increase in price.
- **d** small increase in supply and large increase in price.
- **e** small increase in supply and small increase in price.

Labour Markets

3 An example of derived demand is the demand for
- **a** sweaters derived by an economics student.
- **b** sweaters produced by labour and capital.
- **c** labour used in the production of sweaters.
- **d** sweater brushes.
- **e** none of the above.

4 A profit-maximizing firm will continue to hire units of a factor of production until the
- **a** marginal cost of the factor equals its marginal product.
- **b** marginal cost of the factor equals its average revenue product.
- **c** average cost of the factor equals its marginal revenue product.
- **d** marginal cost of the factor equals its marginal revenue product.
- **e** factor's marginal revenue product equals zero.

5 A firm's marginal revenue product of labour curve is also its
- **a** marginal cost curve for labour.
- **b** labour demand curve.
- **c** labour supply curve.
- **d** output supply curve.
- **e** average revenue curve.

6 If the price of its output falls, a perfectly competitive firm will employ
- **a** less labour, causing the wage to fall.
- **b** less labour, causing the marginal product of labour to rise.
- **c** less labour, causing the marginal product of labour to fall.
- **d** more labour, causing the marginal product of labour to rise.
- **e** more labour, causing the marginal product of labour to fall.

7 A technological change that increases the marginal product of labour will shift the labour
a demand curve leftward.
b demand curve rightward.
c supply curve leftward.
d supply curve rightward.
e supply and demand curves rightward.

8 The larger the proportion of total cost coming from labour, *ceteris paribus*, the
a more elastic the demand for labour.
b less elastic the demand for labour.
c more elastic the supply of labour.
d less elastic the supply of labour.
e lower the demand for labour.

9 If the wage rate increases, the *substitution* effect will give a household an incentive to
a raise its reservation wage.
b increase leisure and decrease work.
c increase work and decrease leisure.
d increase both work and leisure.
e decrease both work and leisure.

10 If the wage rate increases, the *income* effect will give a household an incentive to
a raise its reservation wage.
b increase leisure and decrease work.
c increase work and decrease leisure.
d increase both work and leisure.
e decrease both work and leisure.

11 As the wage rate rises, a household will have a backward-bending labour supply curve if
a the income effect reinforces the substitution effect.
b the wage rate rises above the reservation wage.
c the substitution effect dominates the income effect.
d the income effect dominates the substitution effect.
e leisure is an inferior good.

12 The labour supply curve facing the individual firm in a perfectly competitive labour market is
a upward-sloping.
b backward-bending.
c first upward-sloping and then backward-bending as the wage increases.
d vertical.
e horizontal.

13 If the desire for leisure increased, the wage rate would
a rise and employment would fall.
b rise and employment would rise.
c fall and employment would fall.
d fall and employment would rise.
e fall and employment may rise or fall.

Capital Markets

14 If the annual rate of interest is 10 percent, what is the present value of $100 received one year from now?
a $90
b $90.91
c $95.45
d $100
e $110

15 If the present value of $500 received one year from now is $463, what is the annual interest rate?
a 5 percent
b 8 percent
c 10 percent
d 20.8 percent
e 37 percent

16 The higher the rate of interest, the
a higher the net present value of an investment.
b lower the present value of the flow of marginal revenue products of an investment.
c greater the quantity of capital demanded.
d greater the marginal revenue product of capital.
e lower the marginal revenue product of capital.

17 Firms will invest as long as net present value
a exceeds the rate of interest.
b equals the rate of interest.
c is less than the rate of interest.
d is positive.
e is zero.

18 The supply curve of capital is
a upward-sloping.
b downward-sloping.
c perfectly elastic.
d perfectly inelastic.
e backward-bending.

19 Technological advances increase both the demand for capital and the supply of capital by the same amount. As a result, the interest rate __________ and the quantity of capital __________.

a rises; increases
b remains constant; increases
c increases; remains constant
d falls; increases
e remains constant; decreases

Natural Resource Markets

20 Which of the following is a nonrenewable natural resource?

a coal
b land
c water
d trees
e none of the above

21 If the market for a nonrenewable natural resource is currently in equilibrium, the price of the resource

a is equal to the marginal revenue product of the resource.
b is expected to rise at a rate equal to the interest rate.
c is expected to fall at a rate equal to the interest rate.
d will actually rise at a rate equal to the interest rate.
e will actually fall at a rate equal to the interest rate.

Income, Economic Rent, and Opportunity Cost

22 Economic rent is the

a price paid for the use of a hectare of land.
b price paid for the use of a unit of capital.
c income required to induce a given quantity of a factor of production to be supplied.
d income received above the amount required to induce a given quantity of a factor of production to be supplied.
e opportunity cost of a factor of production.

23 Consider the supply schedule of a factor of production given in Table 17.1. If 4 units are supplied at a price of $8 per unit, what is the opportunity cost of the factor of production?

a $8
b $12
c $20
d $32
e none of the above

TABLE **17.1**

Price of Factor ($)	Quantity of Factor Supplied
2	1
4	2
6	3
8	4
10	5

24 Consider the supply schedule of a factor of production given in Table 17.1. If 4 units of the factor are supplied at a price of $8 per unit, what is the economic rent?

a $8
b $12
c $20
d $32
e none of the above

25 The income of a factor of production in relatively inelastic supply will consist of

a opportunity cost only.
b economic rent only.
c more opportunity cost than economic rent.
d more economic rent than opportunity cost.
e equal amounts of opportunity cost and economic rent.

Short Answer Problems

1 Table 17.2 gives the total and marginal product schedules for a firm that sells its output and buys labour in competitive markets. Initially the price at which the firm can sell any level of output is $5 per unit and the wage rate at which it can purchase any quantity of labour is $15 per unit.

TABLE **17.2**

			P = $5		P = $3	
Quantity Labour (L)	Output (Q)	Marginal Product (MP_L)	Total Revenue (TR)	Marginal Revenue Product (MRP_L)	Total Revenue (TR)	Marginal Revenue Product (MRP_L)
0	0					
		12				
1	12					
		10				
2	22					
		8				
3	30					
		6				
4	36					
		4				
5	40					
		2				
6	42					

a Complete the first two blank columns in Table 17.2 by computing the TR and MRP_L corresponding to a price of output = \$5.

b The marginal revenue product of labour (MRP_L) can be computed by either of the following formulas:

$$MRP_L = \Delta TR/\Delta L$$

$$MRP_L = MR \times MP_L$$

where ΔTR = the change in total revenue, ΔL = the change in labour, MR = marginal revenue, and MP_L = marginal product of labour. Show that these two formulas are equivalent for the case when the quantity of labour changes from 1 to 2 units.

c If the firm maximizes profit, what quantity of labour will it employ? How much output will it produce?

d If total fixed cost is \$125, what is the amount of profit?

e What is its profit if the firm hires one more unit of labour than the profit-maximizing quantity? one less unit of labour than the profit-maximizing quantity?

f Draw a graph of the firm's demand for labour and the supply of labour to the firm and illustrate the profit-maximizing labour decision.

2 Now, suppose that the market demand for the output of the firm in Short Answer Problem **1** decreases, causing the price of output to decrease to \$3 per unit. The total and marginal product schedules remain unchanged.

a Complete the last two blank columns in Table 14.2 by computing the TR and MRP_L corresponding to price of output = \$3.

b If the wage remains at \$15 per unit of labour, what is the profit-maximizing quantity of labour that the firm will hire? How much output will it produce?

c Total fixed cost continues to be \$125. What is the amount of profit?

d Will the firm shut down in the short run? Explain.

e Draw a new graph of the firm's demand for labour and supply of labour and illustrate the new profit-maximizing labour decision.

3 The price of output for the firm in Short Answer Problem **2** remains at \$3, but the wage now rises to \$21 per unit of labour. The total and marginal product schedules remain unchanged.

a What happens to the demand curve for labour (the MRP of labour curve)?

b Under these circumstances, what is the profit-maximizing quantity of labour that the firm will employ? How much output will it produce?

c Total fixed cost continues to be \$125. What is the amount of profit?

d Draw a graph of the firm's demand for labour and supply of labour and illustrate the new profit-maximizing labour decision.

ⓔ ⓒⓣ **4** A perfectly competitive firm in long-run equilibrium produces flubits using only two factors of production—labour and capital. Each factor is sold in a perfectly competitive factor market. Labour costs \$30 per unit and capital costs \$50 per unit.

a Assuming the firm has hired the profit-maximizing quantity of capital in part **b** of this question, the marginal revenue product of labour curve is

$$MRP_L = 110 - 8/5Q_L$$

where MRP_L is the marginal revenue product of labour and Q_L is the quantity (in units) of labour employed. How many units of labour does the firm employ?

b Assuming the firm has hired the profit-maximizing quantity of labour in part **a** of this question, the marginal revenue product of capital curve is

$$MRP_K = 125 - 75/40Q_K$$

where MRP_K is the marginal revenue product of capital and Q_K is the quantity (in units) of capital employed. How many units of capital does the firm employ?

c The price of a flubit is \$10.

i How many flubits is the firm producing? (*Hint:* Remember that the firm is in long-run equilibrium.)

ii What is the marginal (physical) product of the 25th unit of labour hired?

ⓒⓣ **5** Using substitution and income effects, can you predict the effect on a household's quantity of labour supplied if the wage rate *decreases*? Explain.

ⓒⓣ **6** Why isn't the factor price for capital the price of the specific pieces of capital equipment that the firm buys?

ⓒⓣ **7** Larry's Lawn Care is considering the purchase of additional lawn mowers. These lawn mowers have a life of two years and cost $120 each. Marginal revenue products for each year are given in Table 17.3.

TABLE **17.3**

Number of Lawn Mowers	*MRP* in First Year	*MRP* in Second Year	*NPV* (r = 0.05)	*NPV* (r = 0.10)	*NPV* (r = 0.15)
1st	100	80			
2nd	80	64			
3rd	72	62			

a Complete Table 17.3 by computing net present values (*NPV*) if the interest rate is 5 percent (r = 0.05), 10 percent (r = 0.10), or 15 percent (r = 0.15).

b How many lawn mowers will Larry's Lawn Care purchase if the interest rate is 15 percent? 10 percent? 5 percent?

c Construct an approximate lawn mower demand curve for Larry's Lawn Care by graphically representing the three points identified in part **b** and drawing a curve through them.

8 Why does the quantity of capital demanded increase when the interest rate falls?

ⓒⓣ **9** *The Globe and Mail* reported that prices for hockey tickets for the Toronto Maple Leafs were the highest in the NHL. Are the prices of Toronto Maple Leafs tickets high because player salaries are high, or are player's salaries high because ticket prices are high? Explain.

10 Table 17.4 gives the market labour demand and supply schedules.

TABLE **17.4**

Wage Rate (dollars per hour)	Quantity of Labour Supplied (hours)	Quantity of Labour Demanded (hours)
0	0	240
1	20	200
2	40	160
3	60	120
4	80	80
5	100	40
6	120	0

a What is the equilibrium wage rate and the quantity of labour employed?

b What is the total amount of income received by labour in this market?

c Represent the market graphically. Identify the equilibrium wage and quantity of labour.

d Based on your graph from part **c**, how much of labour income is opportunity cost? How much is economic rent?

e Now suppose that the demand for labour increases by 60 hours at each wage rate.

i What are the new equilibrium wage rate and quantity of labour?

ii What is the new total amount of labour income?

iii How much of this income is opportunity cost? How much is economic rent?

ANSWERS

True/False and Explain

1 F Normal profit. Economic profit is residual income to firm's owners, who may include the entrepreneur. (388)

2 F True if $\eta_D > 1$, false if $\eta_D < 1$. (388)

3 F Marginal revenue product curve is demand for labour curve. (391)

4 F Labour demand more elastic when product demand more elastic also. (394)

5 T Reservation wage minimum needed for labour supply. (394–395)

6 T Upward-sloping when substitution effect > income effect. (394–395)

7 F Reverse is true. (398–400)

8 T Saving for greater future consumption not sensible if expect to be better off in future anyway. (402–403)

9 F Between quantity of financial capital and the interest rate. (402)

10 F False for renewable natural resources (true for nonrenewable). (403)

11 F Perfectly inelastic. (403–404)

12 F Definition applies to price of natural resources. (404–405)

13 T Economic rent is income received by any factor owner above amount required to induce supply. (406)

14 F Entire income is economic rent. (406–407)

15 T Excess of income over opportunity cost necessary to induce supply. (406–407)

Multiple-Choice

1 c Definition. (388)

2 a Movement up along flat supply curve. (388)

3 c Factor used as input to production. (388–389)

4 d Where supply curve of factor to firm (*MC*) intersects demand curve for factor (*MRP*). (380–392)

5 b Shows quantity labour demanded at each wage rate. (390–391)

ⓒⓣ **6 b** Labour demand curve shifts leftward. Labour supply curve horizontal to individual firm. Because of diminishing *MP*, *decreased* quantity *L* causes *rise* in *MP*. (392–393)

7 b At a given wage, firm will demand increased quantity of labour because *MRP* now higher (since *MP* has increased). (392–393)

8 a Higher wage causes greater increase in both total costs and product *P*, leading to greater decrease in both sales and labour hired. (394)

9 c Substitute work for leisure because opportunity cost leisure increases. (394–396)

10 b Consume more normal goods, including leisure, so working less. (394–396)

11 d Income and substitution effects work in opposite directions, so tendency to increase leisure and decrease work dominates. (394–396)

12 e Because firm small part of labour market, can buy as much labour as desired at market wage. (394–396)

13 a Labour supply would shift leftward. (394–396)

14 b $PV = \$100/(1 + 0.1)$. (398–399)

15 b $\$463 = \$500/(1 + r)$. Solve for *r*. (398–399)

16 b Reverse **a**, **c** true. *r* does not directly affect *MRP* capital, only its present value. (398–400)

17 d Present value exceeds purchase price of capital. **a**, **b**, and **c** are nonsense comparisons. (400)

18 a See Text Figure 17.7. (402)

19 b Equal rightward shifts of both demand and supply curves. (403)

20 a Others are renewable natural resources. (403)

21 b This is Hotelling Principle. For current equilibrium, *actual* future prices may or may not follow *expected* prices.(404–405)

22 d Definition. Price paid for land use is rent. (406–407)

23 c $2 + $4 + $6 + $8. (406–407)

ⓒⓣ **24 b** Total income ($32 = 4 × $8) minus opportunity cost ($20). (406–407)

25 d Draw graph with steep supply and compare areas above and below supply curve at equilibrium *PF* and *QF*. (406–407)

Short Answer Problems

1 **a** The completed columns for *TR* and MRP_L corresponding to a price of output = $5 are shown in Table 17.2 Solution. The values for *TR* come from multiplying the quantity of output by the price of output ($5). The values for MRP_L between any two quantities of labour come from dividing the change in *TR* by the change in quantity of labour, or by multiplying *MR* ($5) by MP_L.

TABLE **17.2** SOLUTION

			P = $5		P = $3	
Quantity Labour (L)	Output (Q)	Marginal Product (MP_L)	Total Revenue (TR)	Marginal Revenue Product (MRP_L)	Total Revenue (TR)	Marginal Revenue Product (MRP_L)
0	0		0		0	
		... 12		... 60		... 36
1	12		60		36	
		... 10		... 50		... 30
2	22		110		66	
		... 8		... 40		... 24
3	30		150		90	
		... 6		... 30		... 18
4	36		180		108	
		... 4		... 20		... 12
5	40		200		120	
		... 2		... 10		... 6
6	42		210		126	

b From part **a**, the formula $MRP_L = \Delta TR/\Delta L$ yields a marginal revenue product of labour of 50 when the quantity of labour changes from 1 to 2 units. To confirm that the second formula ($MRP_L = MR \times MP_L$) gives the same answer when the quantity of labour changes from 1 to 2 units, substitute in the values for *MR* ($5, the price of an additional unit of output) and MP_L (10 units of output). This yields the same marginal revenue product of labour as above; $5 × 10 units = $50.

c The firm maximizes profit by employing labour up to the point where the *MRP* of labour is equal to the marginal cost of labour (the wage rate). That point occurs at 5 units of labour. The *MRP* of moving from 4 to 5 units of labour is 20, and the *MRP* of moving from 5 to 6 units of labour is 10. In moving from 4 to 5 units, $MRP > MC$ so the firm should hire the 5th unit. But in moving from 5 to 6 units, $MRP < MC$, so the firm should not hire the 6th unit. Thus by interpolation, the *MRP* at exactly 5 units of labour is 15 (midway between 20 and 10). So when 5 units of labour are employed, the *MRP* of labour is equal to the wage rate ($15). Given that 5 units of labour are employed, the profit-maximizing output will be 40 units (from Table 17.2 Solution).

d To calculate profit, first calculate total revenue and then subtract total cost. Total revenue is $200 (40 units of output × $5 per unit) and total cost is also $200—sum of total variable (labour) cost of $75 (5 units of labour × $15 per unit) and total fixed cost of $125. Thus profit is zero.

e If the firm employs one more unit of labour (6 units), total revenue will be $210 (42 units of output × the $5 price). Total cost will be the $125 fixed cost plus $90 in total variable cost (6 units of labour × $15 wage rate) or $215. Thus profit will be negative $5 ($5 loss).

If the firm employs one less unit of labour (4 units), total revenue will be $180 (36 units of output × the $5 price). Total cost will be the $125 fixed cost plus $60 in total variable cost (4 units of labour × $15 wage rate) or $185. Thus profit will be negative $5 ($5 loss).

f The graph of the firm's labour employment decision appears in Figure 17.2. The demand for labour is the firm's MRP_L curve which is labelled D_0 (D_1 will be discussed in Short Answer Problem **2**).

Notice that the values for *MRP* are plotted midway between the corresponding quantities of labour. For example, *MRP* of 60 is plotted midway between 0 and 1 units of labour.

Since the firm purchases labour in a perfectly competitive labour market, the supply of labour to the firm is perfectly elastic at the market wage rate. The labour supply curve is labelled $W = \$15$. The profit-maximizing decision is at the intersection of these curves, and corresponds to a wage rate of $15 and a quantity of labour employed of 5 units.

FIGURE **17.2**

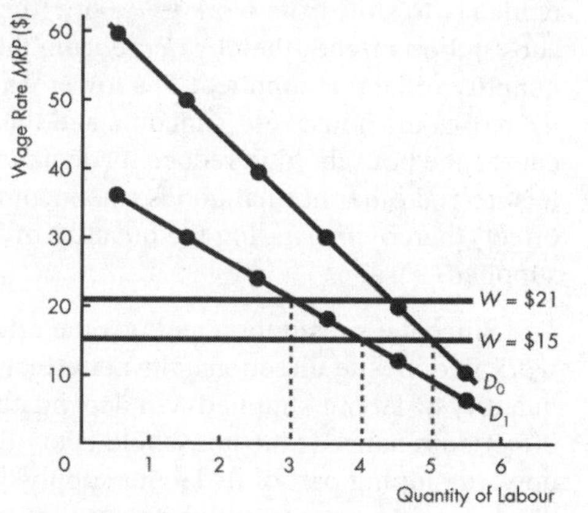

2 a The completed columns for *TR* and MRP_L corresponding to price of output = $3 are shown in Table 17.2 Solution. The values for *TR* come from multiplying the quantity of output by the price of output ($3). The values for MRP_L between any two quantities of labour come from dividing the change in *TR* by the change in quantity of labour, or by multiplying *MR* ($3) by MP_L.

b If the wage rate remains at $15, the profit-maximizing quantity of labour will fall to 4 units since MRP_L equals the wage rate at 4 units of labour. The *MRP* of moving from 3 to 4 units of labour is 18, and the *MRP* of moving from 4 to 5 units of labour is 12. Thus, by interpolation, the *MRP* at exactly 4 units of labour is 15 (midway between 18 and 12). Given that 4 units of labour are employed, the profit-maximizing output will be 36 units (from Table 17.2 Solution).

c Profit equals total revenue minus total cost. Total revenue is $108 (36 units of output × $3 per unit) and total cost is $185—sum of total variable (labour) cost of $60 (4 units of labour × $15 per unit) and total fixed cost of $125. Thus profit is –$77, or a loss of $77.

d The firm will not shut down since total revenue ($108) is enough to cover total variable cost ($60) and part of fixed cost. If the firm shut down, it would lose $125 of fixed cost rather than just $77.

e The graph of the firm's labour employment decision appears in Figure 17.2. The new demand for labour is given by the firm's new MRP_L curve, labelled D_1. The supply of labour has not changed; it continues to be horizontal at $15, the competitive market wage. The new profit-maximizing decision is at the intersection of these curves and corresponds to a wage rate of $15 and quantity of labour employed of 4 units.

3 a Since marginal revenue and the marginal product of labour are unaffected by a change in the wage rate, the demand curve for labour (the *MRP* of labour) will remain at D_1.

b If the wage rate rises to $21, the profit-maximizing quantity of labour will fall to 3 units since MRP_L equals the wage rate at 3 units of labour. Given that 3 units of labour are employed, the profit-maximizing output will be 30 units (from Table 17.2 Solution).

c Profit equals total revenue minus total cost. Total revenue is $90 (30 units of output × $3 per unit) and total cost is $188—sum of total variable (labour) cost of $63 (3 units of labour × $21 per unit) and total fixed cost of $125. Thus profit is –$98, or a loss of $98.

d See Figure 17.2. The relevant labour demand curve continues to be D_1, but the labour supply curve reflects the rise in the competitive wage rate; it is now horizontal at a wage rate of $21 (labelled $W = \$21$). The new profit-maximizing decision is at the intersection of these curves and corresponds to a wage rate of $21 and a quantity of labour employed of 3 units.

ⓔⓒⓣ 4 a By assuming that the firm has already hired its capital, we know (in principle) fixed costs and can calculate the profit-maximizing quantity of the variable factor of production (labour) by setting the MRP_L equal to the wage rate ($30).

$$30 = 110 - 8/5Q_L$$
$$8/5Q_L = 80$$
$$Q_L = 50$$

b By assuming that the firm has already hired its labour, we can treat labour as the fixed cost and treat capital as the variable factor of production. Calculate the profit-maximizing quantity of the capital by setting the MRP_K equal to the cost of a unit of capital ($50).

$$50 = 125 - 75/40Q_K$$
$$75/40Q_K = 75$$
$$Q_K = 40$$

c i The fact that the firm is in long-run equilibrium provides the key to calculating the quantity of flubits produced. In long-run equilibrium, the firm earns zero economic profit, so total revenue is exactly equal to total cost.

We can calculate total cost by adding the costs of the (only) two factors of production. Labour cost is 50 units of labour × $30 per unit or $1,500. Capital cost is 40 units of capital × $50 per unit or $2,000. Total cost is therefore $3,500.

Total revenue must also be equal to $3,500. Since total revenue (*TR*) is just the price of output (*P*) times quantity sold (*Q*), we can calculate *Q* by substituting in the values we have for *TR* ($3,500) and *P* ($10).

$$TR = P \times Q$$
$$\$3{,}500 = \$10 \times Q$$
$$Q = 350$$

ii To calculate the marginal product of the 25th unit of labour, we begin by calculating the marginal *revenue* product of the 25th unit of labour. Substituting $Q_L = 25$ into the equation for MRP_L yields

$$MRP_L = 110 - 8/5(25)$$
$$= 110 - 40$$
$$= 70$$

One definition of the marginal revenue product of labour is the marginal product of labour (MP_L) times marginal revenue (*MR*) or $MRP_L = MP_L \times MR$. Rearranging to solve for MP_L yields

$$MP_L = MRP_L/MR$$

Substituting in the values for the marginal revenue product of the 25th unit of labour (70) and for *MR* (the price of output $10) yields

$$MP_L = 70/10$$
$$MP_L = 7$$

ⓒⓣ 5 No, we can't predict the effect on the household's quantity of labour supplied. If the wage rate decreases, the opportunity cost of leisure decreases and households will have a tendency to shift from work to leisure (the substitution effect), thereby *decreasing* the quantity of labour supplied. The lower wage also decreases the household's income and thus causes the household to reduce its demand for leisure and other normal goods (the income effect) thereby *increasing* the quantity of labour supplied.

Since the substitution and income effects work in opposite directions, the net effect on the quantity of labour supplied will depend on which effect dominates. If the household is on the upward-sloping part of its labour supply curve, the decrease in wages will decrease the quantity of labour supplied. But if the household is on the backward-bending part of its labour supply curve, the decrease in wages will increase the quantity of labour supplied.

ⓒⓣ 6 In general, factor prices represent the opportunity cost to the firm of *using* that factor. Wages are the cost of using labour and rent is the cost of using land. The cost of using a piece of capital equipment bought by the firm is the interest that must be paid (explicitly or implicitly) on the funds tied up in the purchase of the equipment. Capital equipment lasts for a long period of time. The cost of capital during any one period is not the purchase price of the equipment; it is the cost of the funds tied up in the equipment over the period.

ⓒ **7 a** Completed Table 17.3 appears here as Table 17.3 Solution. *NPV* is calculated as the present value of the stream of marginal revenue products resulting from an investment, minus the cost of the investment. For lawn mowers with a two-year life, the *NPV* is calculated using the following equation:

$$NPV = \frac{MRP_1}{1 + r} + \frac{MRP_2}{(1 + r)^2} - P_L$$

In this equation, MRP_1 and MRP_2 are the marginal revenue products in the first and second years respectively, and P_L is the price of a lawn mower. The values of MRP_1 and MRP_2 are given in Table 17.3 for the first, second, and third lawn mowers and P_L is given as $120. The values for *NPV* given in Table 17.3 Solution are obtained by substituting these values into the above equation and evaluating the expression for alternative values of *r*, the interest rate.

TABLE **17.3** SOLUTION

Number of Lawn Mowers	MRP in First Year	MRP in Second Year	NPV (r = 0.05)	NPV (r = 0.10)	NPV (r = 0.15)
1st	100	80	47.80	37.02	27.45
2nd	80	64	14.24	5.62	–2.04
3rd	72	62	4.81	–3.31	–10.51

b If the interest rate is 15 percent, only one additional lawn mower will be purchased since the second lawn mower has negative net present value. If the interest rate is 10 percent, two lawn mowers will be purchased, and if the interest rate is 5 percent, three lawn mowers will be purchased.

c The approximate lawn mower demand curve is illustrated in Figure 17.3. The curve indicates that, at an interest rate of 15 percent, one lawn mower will be demanded. At an interest rate of 10 percent, two lawn mowers will be demanded and, at an interest rate of 5 percent, three lawn mowers will be demanded.

FIGURE **17.3**

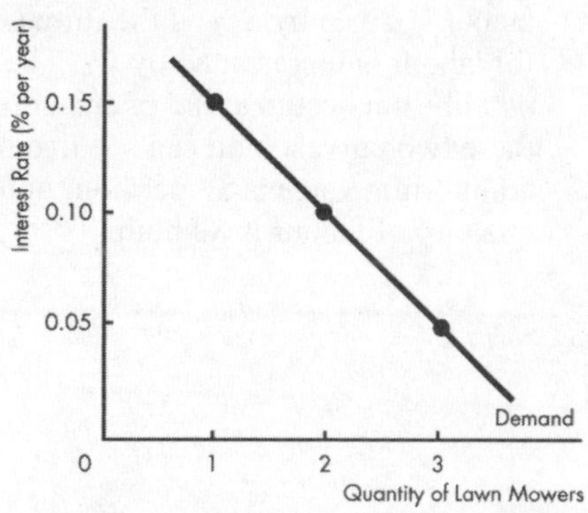

8 Profit-maximizing firms will demand capital as long as the present value of the stream of future marginal revenue product from the new capital exceeds the purchase price of the new capital; in other words, as long as its net present value is positive. Since a lower interest rate implies that the present value of any given future stream of marginal revenue product will be larger, the net present value will be positive for a *larger* number of additional capital goods and thus more capital will be purchased. Therefore the quantity of capital demanded increases as the interest rate falls.

ⓒ **9** Player salaries are high because ticket prices are high. The full explanation combines demand and supply. The demand for NHL-calibre players is high, because team owners know that fans will pay high prices to see those players. The supply of talented NHL-calibre players is relatively inelastic, so, combined with the high demand, much of the income earned by NHL players is economic rent rather than payment for opportunity cost.

It is only because owners (who care about profits) know that they can charge high ticket prices (and television fees), that they compete against each other in bidding up the salaries of relatively scarce star players. That bidding for resources in relatively inelastic supply produces economic rents for the players.

10 a The equilibrium wage rate is $4 per hour and the quantity of labour employed is 80 hours.

b Total income is $320 ($4 per hour × 80 hours).

c The supply and demand curves for labour are given in Figure 17.4. The supply of labour is given by S_0 and the initial demand for labour is represented by D_0. The equilibrium occurs at the intersection of these two curves. You can see that the equilibrium wage is \$4 per hour and the quantity of labour is 80 hours.

FIGURE **17.4**

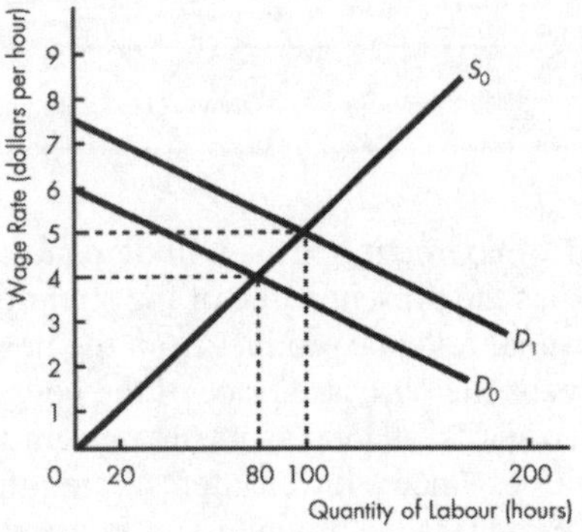

d Given that the labour supply curve is a 45° line starting at the origin, half of income is opportunity cost (the area below the supply curve) and the other half is economic rent (the area above the supply curve). Since income is \$320, each of these is \$160.

e **i** Each entry in the last column of Table 17.4 will increase by 60 units. The new equilibrium wage rate is \$5 per hour and the new equilibrium quantity of labour is 100 hours. The new labour demand curve appears in Figure 17.4 as D_1.

ii Total income is now \$500 (\$5 per hour × 100 hours).

iii Once again the slope of the labour supply curve (which has not changed) implies that income is split evenly between opportunity cost and economic rent. Each will be equal to \$250.

Chapter 17 Appendix: Labour Unions

KEY CONCEPTS

Market Power in the Labour Market

Labour unions are organized groups of workers.

- *Closed shop*—firms can hire only union members.
- *Union shop*—firm can hire non-union members, but they must eventually join the union.
- *Open shop*—employees not required to join union or pay union dues.
- **Rand Formula** requires all workers in a closed shop to pay union dues whether or not they join the union.
- *Collective bargaining*—process of negotiation between unions and employers.

Labour unions' objectives are increasing compensation, improving working conditions, and expanding job opportunities. Methods of achieving objectives include

- restricting supply of labour.
- increasing demand for union labour or making demand more inelastic by
  - encouraging import restrictions.
  - supporting minimum wage laws and immigration restrictions.
  - increasing product demand.
  - increasing marginal product of union members.

Monopsony—market structure in which there is a single buyer. Firm that is only employer in town is monopsonist in the labour market.

- To hire more labour, monopsonist must pay a higher wage. Marginal cost of labour curve (*MCL*) for monopsonist is upward-sloping and above and steeper than the market supply curve of labour.
- Profit-maximizing rule for monopsonist is to hire quantity of labour where *MCL* curve intersects *MRP* curve, then offer lowest wage for which labour will work (on supply curve).
- For monopsonist, employment and wage are lower than for competitive labour market. More elastic supply of labour means less *opportunity* for monopsony to cut wages, to reduce employment, or to increase economic profit.

Adding union to a monopsony labour market can create **bilateral monopoly**, in which wage determined by relative bargaining strength firm and union.

- Highest possible wage where *MCL* intersects *MRP*. Lowest possible wage is pure monopsony wage.
- Adding a minimum wage law to a monopsony labour market can actually increase wages and increase employment.

HELPFUL HINTS

1 This appendix introduces the concept of a monopsonist, a firm that is the only buyer in a market, such as labour. The monopsonist faces an upward-sloping supply curve of labour. As a result, its marginal cost of labour curve (*MCL*) is different from the labour supply curve.

There is a close parallel between (a) the relationship between the labour supply curve and the *MCL* curve for the monopsonist and (b) the already familiar relationship (Chapter 12) between the demand curve and the marginal revenue curve (*MR*) for the monopolist. Both sets of relationships stem from the assumption of a single price for labour or output in the relevant market.

The monopolist, as the only seller in an output market, faces a downward-sloping demand curve. The marginal revenue from the sale of an additional unit of output is *less* than the selling price because the monopolist must *lower* the price on all previous units as well. Thus the *MR* curve lies *below* the demand curve for the single-price monopolist.

For the monopsonist in a labour market, the marginal cost of hiring an additional unit of labour is *higher* than the wage because the monopsonist must *raise* the wage on all previous units of labour as well. Thus the *MCL* curve lies *above* the supply of labour curve for the monopsonist.

Another way to think about this parallel is that the supply/*MCL* relationship (and the resulting wage versus *MRP* relationship) is just the demand/*MR* relationship (and the resulting price versus *MC* relationship) flipped upside-down.

SELF-TEST

True/False and Explain

Market Power in the Labour Market

1 A closed shop refers to a firm that is not operating because its workers are on strike.

2 Unions support minimum wage laws in part because they increase the cost of low-skill labour, a substitute for skilled union labour.

3 Most union workers earn about 40 percent more than nonunion workers in comparable jobs.

Monopsony

4 For a firm that is a monopsonist in the labour market, the supply curve of labour is the marginal cost of labour curve.

5 The more elastic labour supply is, the less opportunity a monopsonist has to make an economic profit.

6 In a monopsonistic labour market, the introduction of a minimum wage that is above the current wage will raise the wage but reduce employment.

7 In the case of bilateral monopoly in a labour market, the wage depends on the bargaining strength of the two traders.

Multiple-Choice

Market Power in the Labour Market

1 The Rand formula made
- **a** collective bargaining compulsory.
- **b** it compulsory for all workers in a partially unionized plant to pay union dues.
- **c** binding arbitration legal.
- **d** strikes and lockouts illegal under some circumstances.
- **e** none of the above.

2 A working arrangement in which all workers must be members of the union before they can be hired by the firm is called a(n)
- **a** open shop.
- **b** closed shop.
- **c** union shop.
- **d** craft shop.
- **e** professional association.

3 Which of the following would unions be *least* likely to support?
- **a** increasing the legal minimum wage
- **b** restricting immigration
- **c** encouraging imports
- **d** increasing demand for the goods their workers produce
- **e** increasing the marginal product of union labour

4 A union is formed to restrict labour supply in a previously perfectly competitive labour market. If the union succeeds in raising the wage,
- **a** employment will fall.
- **b** employment will rise.
- **c** employment will not change.
- **d** the total wage bill will rise.
- **e** the total wage bill will fall.

Monopsony

5 Figure A17.1 illustrates a monopsonist in the labour market (*MCL* = marginal cost of labour). The profit-maximizing wage rate and quantity of labour hired will be
- **a** $4 per hour and 800 hours of labour.
- **b** $4 per hour and 400 hours of labour.
- **c** $7 per hour and 600 hours of labour.
- **d** $9 per hour and 400 hours of labour.
- **e** none of the above.

FIGURE **A17.1**

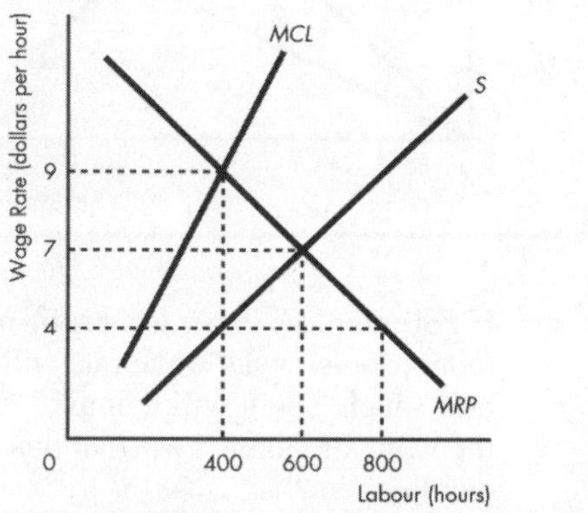

6 If the labour market illustrated in Figure A17.1 became competitive, the equilibrium wage rate and quantity of labour hired would be
- **a** $4 per hour and 800 hours of labour.
- **b** $4 per hour and 400 hours of labour.
- **c** $7 per hour and 600 hours of labour.
- **d** $9 per hour and 400 hours of labour.
- **e** none of the above.

7 If a union forms to face the monopsonist in Figure A17.1, the situation is one of
- **a** binding arbitration.
- **b** derived demand.
- **c** duopoly.
- **d** collusive oligopoly.
- **e** bilateral monopoly.

8 If a union and the monopsonist in Figure A17.1 agree to collective bargaining, the outcome will be an hourly wage
- **a** of $7.
- **b** between $4 and $7.
- **c** between $4 and $9.
- **d** between $7 and $9.
- **e** of $9.

9 When compared with a competitive labour market with the same marginal revenue product and labour supply curves, a monopsonist labour market has a(n)
- **a** lower wage and lower employment.
- **b** lower wage and higher employment.
- **c** higher wage and lower employment.
- **d** higher wage and higher employment.
- **e** indeterminate outcome.

10 If a strike or lockout occurs in a bilateral monopoly situation, it is usually because the
- **a** demand for labour is relatively inelastic.
- **b** demand for labour is relatively elastic.
- **c** supply of labour is relatively inelastic.
- **d** supply of labour is relatively elastic.
- **e** union or firm has misjudged the bargaining situation.

11 For the monopsonist employer illustrated in Figure A17.2, the profit-maximizing wage rate and quantity of labour hired will be
- **a** $9 per hour and 300 hours of labour.
- **b** $8 per hour and 350 hours of labour.
- **c** $8 per hour and 500 hours of labour.
- **d** $7 per hour and 400 hours of labour.
- **e** $6 per hour and 300 hours of labour.

FIGURE **A17.2**

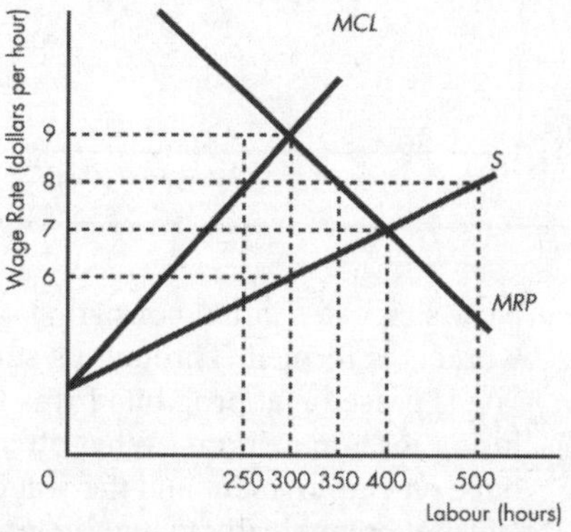

12 Suppose the government passes a minimum wage law that prohibits anyone from hiring labour at less than $8 per hour. In Figure A17.2, the marginal cost of labour (*MCL*) for the monopsonist
- **a** is not affected.
- **b** equals $8 only from 0 to 250 hours of labour.
- **c** equals $8 only from 0 to 350 hours of labour.
- **d** equals $8 only from 0 to 500 hours of labour.
- **e** shifts up by a vertical distance of $8.

Short Answer Problems

1 Members of labour unions earn wages well above the minimum wage. Even so, why is it in the interest of a union to support increases in the legal minimum wage?

2 Initially we observe an industry facing a competitive labour market in which the supply of labour comes from two sources: domestic workers and foreign workers. All workers have similar skills. Also assume that the output of the industry competes with imported goods.

a In Figure A17.3, graphically represent the initial competitive labour market. Draw the labour demand and supply curves and identify the equilibrium wage rate and level of employment.

FIGURE **A17.3**

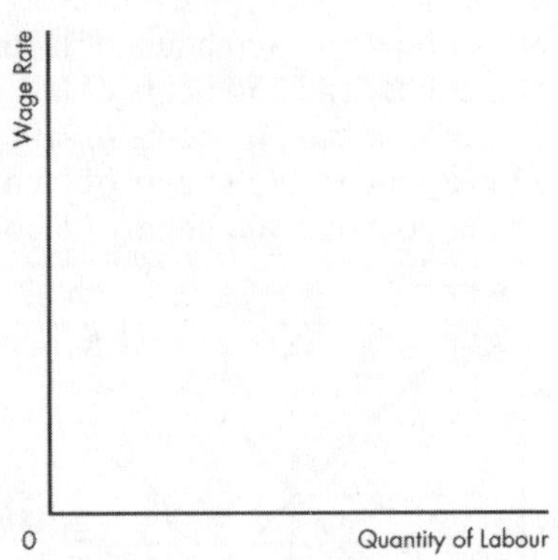

b Now suppose a union consisting of domestic workers is formed. Through its support a law is passed that prohibits firms from hiring foreign workers. What effect will this have on employment and the wage rate? Illustrate graphically using the graph in part **a**.

c Finally, the industry and union support the passage of a law that legally restricts imports that compete with industry output. Using the same graph, show the consequences for the wage rate and employment.

3 Pollutionless Paper is a pulp and paper mill that employs almost all of the labour in a small town in New Brunswick. The town's labour market, which approximates a monopsony, is illustrated in Figure A17.4, where *S* is the supply curve of labour, and *MRP* and *MCL* are Pollutionless Paper's marginal revenue product of labour and marginal cost of labour curves, respectively.

FIGURE **A17.4**

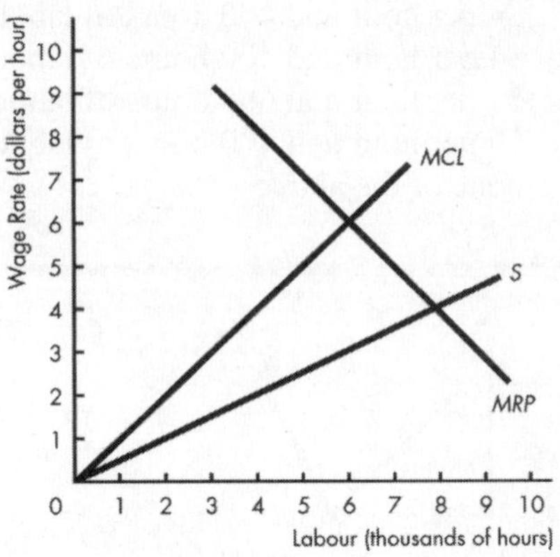

a If Pollutionless Paper is a profit-maximizing monopsonist, what wage rate will it pay and how much labour will it employ? What is the value of labour's *MRP* at this level of employment?

b If the town had a competitive labour market with the same *MRP* curve, what would the equilibrium wage rate and the level of employment be? Compare these outcomes with the monopsony outcomes in part **a**.

4 Consider the following alternatives for the labour market in Figure A17.4.

a Suppose the government imposes a minimum wage of $4 per hour. What wage rate will Pollutionless Paper pay and how much labour will it employ? Compare these outcomes with the monopsony outcomes in Short Answer Problem **3a**.

b Suppose there is no legal minimum wage, but the workers form a union. If the union tries to negotiate a higher wage rate while maintaining employment at the monopsony level, what is the maximum wage rate that Pollutionless Paper will be willing to pay? What is the minimum wage rate that the union will accept?

5 Consider the negotiations between Pollutionless Paper and the union in Short Answer Problem **4b**.

a What determines the wage rate that will actually be paid?

b If Pollutionless Paper and the union are equally strong and realize it, what will the wage rate likely be?

c If Pollutionless Paper and the union are equally strong, but the union mistakenly believes it is stronger, what is the likely outcome of negotiations?

d If Pollutionless Paper and the union are equally strong, but Pollutionless Paper mistakenly believes it is stronger, what is the likely outcome of negotiations?

ANSWERS

True/False and Explain

1 F Firm that can hire only union workers. (413)

2 T Increased price of substitute creates increased demand for union labour. (413–415)

3 F Union–nonunion wage differential in comparable jobs is 10 to 25 percent. (415–416)

4 F *MCL* curve is above supply curve of labour. (416–417)

ⓒⓣ **5 T** Greater η labour supply means smaller differences between *MCL* and wage. (416–417)

ⓒⓣ **6 F** Wages and employment both increase; true for competitive labour market. (416–418)

7 T See text discussion. (417–418)

Multiple-Choice

1 b See text discussion. (413)

2 b Definition. (413)

3 c Increasing imports substitutes for domestically produced goods, decreasing demand for domestic, union labour. (414–415)

4 a Leftward shift supply decreases employment. Impact on wage bill depends on elasticity of demand for labour. (414–415)

5 b *QL* where *MCL* intersects *MRP*. Firm pays lowest wage required for labour to supply that *QL* (on supply curve). (416–417)

6 c Where *S* intersects *MRP*. (416–417)

7 e Firm is only buyer of labour, union is only seller of labour. (417–418)

8 c Between minimum firm can achieve ($4) and maximum union can achieve ($9). (417–418)

9 a See Text Figure A17.3. (417–418)

10 e **a–d** may affect relative bargaining strength but do not cause strikes or lockouts. (417–418)

11 e *QL* where *MCL* intersects *MRP*. Firm pays lowest wage required for labour to supply that *QL* (on supply curve). (416–417)

ⓒⓣ **12 d** *MCL* horizontal at minimum wage until intersects *S*. Firm must then raise wage to get increased quantity supplied labour. (417–418)

Short Answer Problems

1 An increase in the minimum wage will increase the cost of hiring low-skill labour, which will tend to increase demand for high-skill labour which is a substitute.

2 a The initial competitive demand for labour and supply of labour curves are D_C and S_C respectively, in Figure A17.3 Solution (ignore the other curves for now). The equilibrium wage rate is W_C and the competitive equilibrium level of employment is QL_C.

FIGURE **A17.3** SOLUTION

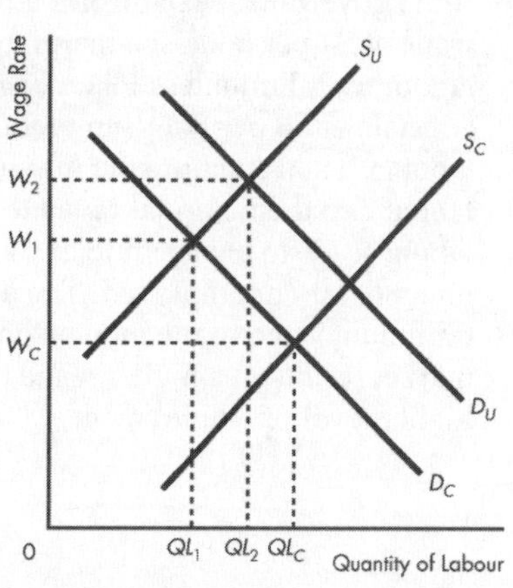

b If a law is passed prohibiting firms from hiring foreign workers, the labour supply curve (now under a union) will shift leftward (to S_U in Figure A17.3 Solution). This will raise the wage rate to W_1 and decrease the quantity of labour employed to QL_1.

c Restrictions on imports will increase demand for the product produced in the industry and thus increase the derived demand (*MRP*) of labour in the industry. In Figure A17.3 Solution this is a shift from D_C to D_U. The result is a further increase in the wage rate to W_2 and increase in employment to QL_2. Whether the quantity of labour hired now exceeds the initial competitive quantity depends on the magnitude of the shift in the labour demand curve.

3 a A profit-maximizing monopsonist will hire additional labour up to the point where *MCL* equals *MRP*. Referring to Figure A17.4, this means that Pollutionless Paper will hire 6,000 hours of labour. To hire that quantity of labour, the labour supply curve *S* tells us that the wage rate must be $3 per hour. This is less than the $6 per hour marginal revenue product of labour.

b In a competitive labour market, the wage rate would be $4 per hour and 8,000 hours of labour would be employed. The competitive labour market results in a higher wage rate and a higher level of employment than the monopsony outcomes.

4 a If the government establishes a minimum wage at $4 per hour, the marginal cost of labour to Pollutionless Paper becomes constant at $4 per hour (up to 8,000 hours of labour). Thus equating the marginal cost of labour and the marginal revenue product of labour leads to a wage rate of $4 and 8,000 hours of labour employed. The addition of a minimum wage to the monopsony labour market results in a higher wage rate and a higher level of employment.

b The maximum wage rate Pollutionless Paper is willing to pay for 6,000 hours of labour is $6 per hour (the *MRP* of that amount of labour). The minimum wage rate that the union will accept for 6,000 hours of labour is $3 per hour (the supply price of that amount of labour).

5 a The wage rate that will actually be paid as the outcome of bargaining depends on the relative bargaining strengths of the firm and union. Bargaining strength depends on costs (from lockouts and strikes) that each side can inflict on the other if there is a failure to agree.

b Pollutionless Paper and the union will split the difference between $6 and $3 and agree on a wage rate of $4.50.

c If the union holds out for more than a $4.50 wage rate, Pollutionless Paper will likely lock out the workers.

d If Pollutionless Paper holds out for less than a $4.50 wage rate, the union will likely strike. When lockouts or strikes occur, it is usually because one side has misjudged the situation.

Chapter 18 Economic Inequality

KEY CONCEPTS

Measuring Economic Inequality

Measures of economic inequality look at

- **market income**—wages, interest, rent and profit before paying income taxes.
- **total income**—market income + cash payments to households by governments.
- **after-tax income**—total income – tax payments by households to governments.

Distribution of after-tax household income in Canada in 2003 was positively skewed.

- *Mode* (most common) income was $15,000–$19,999.
- *Median* income was $39,700.
- *Mean* income was $48,400.

There is a great deal of inequality of income and wealth. The degree of inequality is measured by the Lorenz curve.

- The **Lorenz curve** for income (wealth) graphs the cumulative percentage of income (wealth) against the cumulative percentage of households.
- The 45° "line of equality" represents a hypothetically equal distribution of income (wealth).
- The farther the Lorenz curve from the line of equality, the more unequal the distribution.
- The distribution of wealth in Canada is even more unequal than the distribution of income.

Wealth is the *stock* of assets owned by an individual. Wealth includes *human capital* as well as financial assets. *Income* is the *flow* of earning received by an individual from his or her stock of wealth.

- Data used to construct wealth distributions do not include human capital and therefore overstate wealth inequalities.
- Distributions of annual income and wealth are more unequal than distributions of lifetime income and wealth.
- Even correcting for these factors, there are significant inequalities in distributions of income and wealth in Canada, with the income shares of the richest 20 percent of households rising since 1980.

Poverty exists when families cannot buy adequate food, shelter, and clothing.

- Poverty is a relative concept and is measured by the **low-income cutoff** (families spending 55 percent or more of their income on food, shelter, and clothing). On average in Canada since 1980, 17 percent of families have incomes below the low-income cutoff.
- Most important factors influencing poverty are source of income, household type, and sex and age of household head.

The Sources of Economic Inequality

Income inequality arises from differences in human capital, or skill differentials in labour markets.

- Demand—high-skilled labour has higher marginal revenue product (*MRP*) and demand curve than low-skilled labour. Vertical distance between demand curves = *MRP* of skill.
- Supply—high-skilled labour has more *human capital*, which is costly to acquire. Supply curve high-skilled labour is above supply curve low-skilled labour by vertical distance = compensation for cost of acquiring skill.
- Wages (equilibrium of demand and supply) higher for high-skilled labour.

Wage differentials between men and women can be partly explained by

- ♦ human capital differences—differences in schooling (mostly eliminated), work experience, and job interruptions (lessened recently).
- ♦ discrimination—results in lower wages and employment for those discriminated against.
- ♦ differences in degree of specialization—because of social conventions men have specialized in earning income, while women have divided their time between earning income and household activities (bearing and raising children and household chores).

Wealth inequality increases between generations because

- ♦ assets can be inherited but debt cannot.
- ♦ of *assortative mating* (marrying within one's own socioeconomic class).

Income Redistribution

Income is redistributed by governments through income taxes, income maintenance programs, and subsidized services.

- ♦ Income taxes can be
  - **progressive**—marginal tax rate increases with higher-level income.
  - **regressive**—marginal tax rate decreases with higher-level income.
  - **proportional** (*flat-rate tax*)—marginal tax rate constant at all levels income.
- ♦ Income maintenance programs include social security, employment insurance, and welfare.
- ♦ Subsidized services (provision of goods and services below cost) such as education and health care services reduce inequality.

Income distribution *after taxes and benefits* redistributes income to the very poor considerably, reducing the inequality of the *market income* distribution.

Income redistribution creates a **big tradeoff** between equity and efficiency. Redistribution uses scarce resources and weakens incentives, so a more equally shared pie results in a smaller pie.

HELPFUL HINTS

1 Statistics used to construct Lorenz curves do not always give an accurate picture of inequality. You should understand why a distribution of wealth that excludes the value of human capital gives a distorted picture relative to the distribution of income. You should also understand why the distribution of annual (static) income gives a distorted picture relative to the distribution of lifetime (dynamic) income. Finally, you should understand why the distribution of before-tax, before-benefits income gives a distorted picture relative to the distribution of after-tax, after-benefits income.

SELF-TEST

True/False and Explain

Measuring Economic Inequality

1 The farther the Lorenz curve from the 45° line, the more equal the distribution of income.

2 In Canada, measured income is more equally distributed than measured wealth.

3 Wealth distribution data exclude human capital and thus *overstate* inequality.

4 Income is a stock of earnings.

5 The lifetime distribution of income is more equal than the annual distribution of income.

The Sources of Economic Inequality

6 Human capital is capital equipment constructed by human workers.

7 The demand for low-skilled workers is to the left of the demand for high-skilled workers.

8 The vertical distance between the labour supply curves for high-skilled and low-skilled workers is the marginal revenue product of the skill.

9 The larger the marginal revenue product of skill and the more costly it is to acquire, the smaller the wage differential between high-skilled and low-skilled workers.

10 Assortative mating makes the distribution of wealth more unequal over time.

Income Redistribution

11 Under a proportional income tax, total taxes rise as income rises.

12 Under a progressive income tax, the marginal tax rate does not change as income rises.

13 A regressive income tax redistributes income from the rich to the poor.

14 Compared with the market distribution of income, government taxes and benefits reduce the inequality of income distribution.

15 In general, reducing income inequality by redistributing income from the rich to the poor will lead to greater production of goods and services.

Multiple-Choice

Measuring Economic Inequality

1 Which diagram is used by economists to illustrate the distribution of income or wealth?
- **a** Lorenz curve
- **b** normal bell-shaped distribution
- **c** Sophia Loren curve
- **d** low-income cutoff curve
- **e** none of the above

2 In Figure 18.1, the richest 20 percent of all households receive what share of all income?
- **a** 10 percent
- **b** 20 percent
- **c** 30 percent
- **d** 40 percent
- **e** none of the above

FIGURE **18.1**

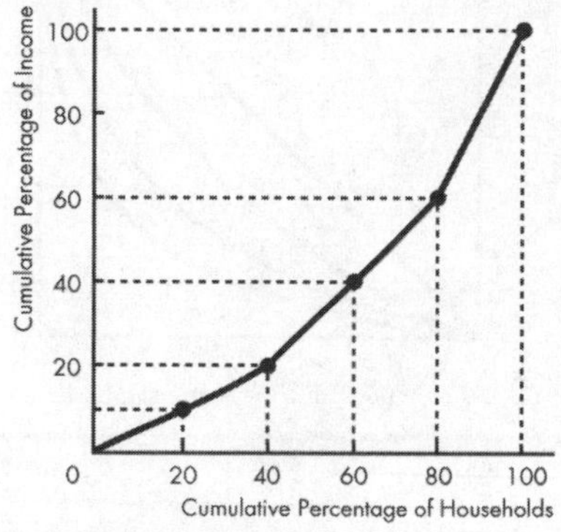

3 In Figure 18.1, the poorest 20 percent of all households receive what share of income?
a 10 percent
b 20 percent
c 30 percent
d 40 percent
e none of the above

4 In Figure 18.1, the middle 20 percent of all households receive what share of income?
a 10 percent
b 20 percent
c 30 percent
d 40 percent
e none of the above

5 The curve in Figure 18.1 represents the
a line of fairness.
b line of equality.
c learning curve.
d wage differential curve.
e Lorenz curve.

6 Consider the Lorenz curves in Figure 18.2. Which Lorenz curve corresponds to the greatest income *inequality*?
a *A*
b *B*
c *C*
d *D*
e impossible to tell without additional information

FIGURE **18.2**

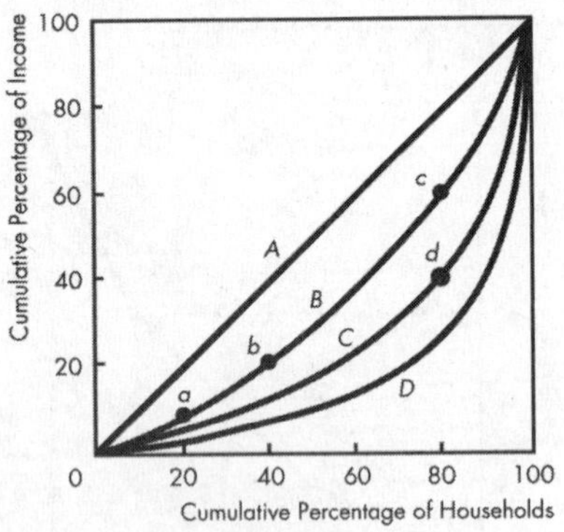

7 In Figure 18.2, what is curve *A* (a straight line) called?
a market distribution line
b line of equality
c fairness line
d low-income cutoff line
e none of the above

8 Which point in Figure 18.2 indicates that the richest 20 percent of households earn 40 percent of the income?
a *a*
b *b*
c *c*
d *d*
e none of the above

9 The distribution of *annual income*
a understates inequality because it does not take into account the household's stage in its life cycle.
b understates inequality because it does not take into account the distribution of human capital.
c overstates inequality because it does not take into account the household's stage in its life cycle.
d overstates inequality because it does not take into account the distribution of human capital.
e is an accurate measure of inequality.

10 The distribution of *wealth*
a understates inequality because it does not take into account the household's stage in its life cycle.
b understates inequality because it does not take into account the distribution of human capital.
c overstates inequality because it does not take into account the household's stage in its life cycle.
d overstates inequality because it does not take into account the distribution of human capital.
e is an accurate measure of inequality.

11 Which distribution would show the most *equality*?
a stock of financial wealth
b stock of human capital
c annual income
d lifetime income
e all show same degree of equality

12 Wealth differs from income in that
a income is a stock, wealth is a flow.
b wealth is derived from income.
c income is what you earn, wealth is what you own.
d income is what you own, wealth is what you earn.
e wealth is preferable to income.

13 The most important factor influencing the duration of poverty is
- **a** source of income.
- **b** householder type
- **c** age of householder.
- **d** education of householder.
- **e** labour force status.

The Sources of Economic Inequality

14 Refer to Figure 18.3. For any given quantity of labour employed,
- **a** the elasticity of demand is lower for high-skilled workers than for low-skilled workers.
- **b** wages will be lower for high-skilled workers than low-skilled workers.
- **c** wages will be higher for high-skilled workers than low-skilled workers.
- **d** the vertical distance between the curves is the compensation for the cost of acquiring skill.
- **e** the vertical distance between the curves is the present value of human capital.

FIGURE **18.3**

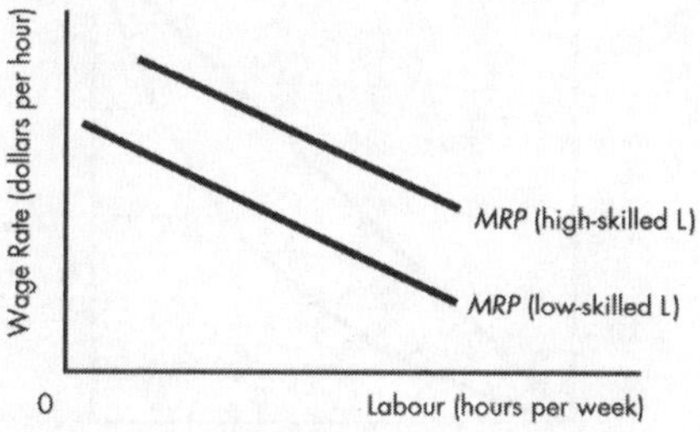

15 The vertical distance between the two supply curves in Figure 18.4
- **a** is the compensation for the cost of acquiring skill.
- **b** is the *MRP* of skill.
- **c** is the result of discrimination against low-skilled workers.
- **d** is the result of subsidies for high-skilled workers.
- **e** will disappear if there is free entry in the high-skilled market.

FIGURE **18.4**

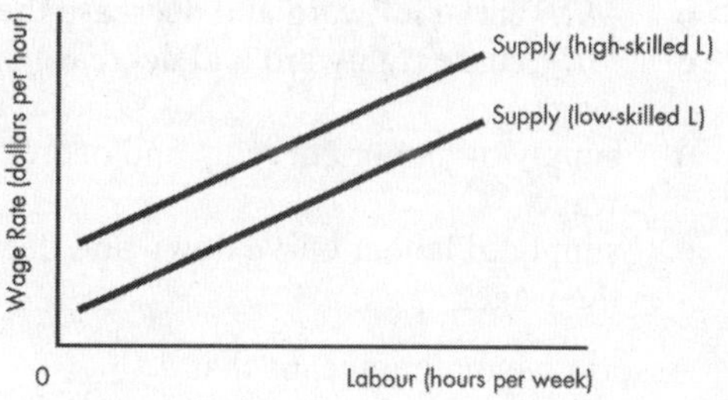

16 Refer only to the information in Figure 18.4. For any given wage rate, more hours of
- **a** low-skilled labour will be demanded than high-skilled labour.
- **b** high-skilled labour will be demanded than low-skilled labour.
- **c** low-skilled labour will be supplied than high-skilled labour.
- **d** high-skilled labour will be supplied than low-skilled labour.
- **e** low-skilled labour will be supplied if the *MRP* of skill increases.

17 Which of the following is *not* a reason why the wage of high-skilled workers exceeds the wage of low-skilled workers?
- **a** The market for high-skilled workers is more competitive than the market for low-skilled workers.
- **b** The marginal revenue product of high-skilled workers is greater than that of low-skilled workers.
- **c** The cost of training high-skilled workers is greater than the cost of training low-skilled workers.
- **d** High-skilled workers have acquired more human capital than low-skilled workers.
- **e** The demand curve for high-skilled workers lies to the right of the demand curve for low-skilled workers.

18 Wage differentials between males and females can be explained by
- **a** educational differences.
- **b** human capital differences.
- **c** degree of specialization differences.
- **d** discrimination.
- **e** all of the above.

19 If discrimination takes the form of restricting a group's access to education and training, the effect on this group of workers will be to shift their
 a *MRP* curve rightward and increase the wage.
 b *MRP* curve leftward and decrease the wage.
 c *MRP* curve rightward and decrease the wage.
 d supply of labour curve up and decrease the wage.
 e supply of labour curve down and decrease the wage.

20 Assortative mating means that
 a poor men tend to marry rich women.
 b rich men tend to marry rich women.
 c rich men tend to marry poor women.
 d same-sex marriages occur because "like attracts like."
 e same-sex marriages are prohibited.

Income Redistribution

21 If the marginal tax rate increases as income increases, the income tax is defined as
 a progressive.
 b proportional.
 c negative.
 d regressive.
 e excessive.

22 In Table 18.1, which tax plan is proportional?
 a Plan *A*
 b Plan *B*
 c Plan *C*
 d Plan *D*
 e impossible to calculate without additional information

TABLE **18.1**

Current Market Income	Tax Payment Plan A	Tax Payment Plan B	Tax Payment Plan C	Tax Payment Plan D
0	0	0	0	200
1,000	100	100	200	200
2,000	200	400	200	200
4,000	400	1,600	200	200

23 In Table 18.1, which tax plan is progressive?
 a Plan *A*
 b Plan *B*
 c Plan *C*
 d Plan *D*
 e impossible to calculate without additional information

24 Which of the following *reduces* the inequality of income or wealth relative to the market distribution?
 a government payments to the poor
 b a regressive income tax
 c large inheritances
 d assortative mating
 e all of the above

25 Redistribution of income from the rich to the poor will lead to a reduction in total output. This is known as the
 a market distribution.
 b Robin Hood principle.
 c inheritance principle.
 d big tradeoff.
 e capitalist dilemma.

Short Answer Problems

1 Consider the worlds of Vulcan and Klingon. The Vulcan Lorenz curve is given in Figure 18.5, and the Klingon income distribution data are given in Table 18.2.

FIGURE **18.5**

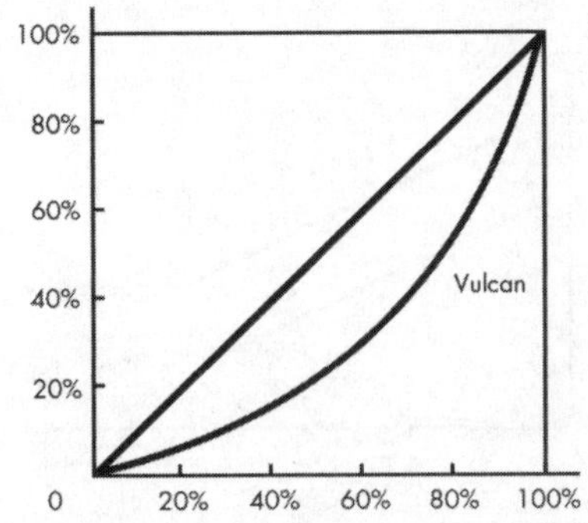

TABLE **18.2** KLINGON INCOME DISTRIBUTION

Household Income Rank	Percentage Share Total Income
Lowest 20%	10%
Second 20%	10%
Middle 20%	20%
Fourth 20%	30%
Highest 20%	30%

 a Label the axes of Figure 18.5 and explain what the diagonal line represents.

 b Using the data from Table 18.2, draw the Klingon Lorenz curve on Figure 18.5.

2 Chapter 5 describes two approaches to ideas about fairness—fair results and fair rules.

a Describe briefly each idea about fairness.

b Using only the information in Short Answer Problem **1**, which idea(s) about fairness can be used to judge Vulcan and Klingon? Which world is more fair according to the idea(s)?

3 Explain the differences and connections between the concepts of wealth and income.

4 Table 18.3 gives information regarding the distribution of income in an economy which generates $100 billion in total annual income.

TABLE **18.3** TOTAL HOUSEHOLD INCOME

Percentage of Households	Total Income (billions of $)	Income Share (%)	Cumulative Percentage of Households	Cumulative Percentage of Income
Poorest 20%	5			
Second 20%	10			
Third 20%	15			
Fourth 20%	20			
Richest 20%	50			

a Complete the last three columns in Table 18.3.

b Draw the Lorenz curve for income in this economy and label it *A*.

5 Now suppose a progressive income tax is levied on the economy. The distribution of after-tax income is given in Table 18.4. We assume none of the revenue is redistributed to families in the economy. Note that total after-tax income is $71 billion.

TABLE **18.4** AFTER-TAX HOUSEHOLD INCOME

Percentage of Households	After-Tax Income (billions of $)	After-Tax Income Share (%)	Cumulative Percentage of Households	Cumulative Percentage of After-Tax Income
Poorest 20%	5			
Second 20%	9			
Third 20%	12			
Fourth 20%	15			
Richest 20%	30			

a Complete Table 18.4.

b Draw the Lorenz curve for after-tax income on the same graph you used for Short Answer Problem **4b** and label it *B*.

c What effect has the progressive income tax had on inequality?

d What is the size of the "big tradeoff" in this case?

6 Finally, suppose that, in addition, the government redistributes all revenue so that the after-benefits (after-tax) income distribution is given in Table 18.5. For example, those in the poorest group receive benefits income of $10 billion so their after-benefits income becomes $15 billion.

TABLE **18.5** AFTER-BENEFITS HOUSEHOLD INCOME

Percentage of Households	After-Benefits Income Share (billions of $)	After-Benefits Income Share (%)	Cumulative Percentage of Households	Cumulative Percentage of After-Benefits Income
Poorest 20%	15			
Second 20%	16			
Third 20%	18			
Fourth 20%	20			
Richest 20%	31			

a Complete Table 18.5.

b Draw the Lorenz curve for after-benefits income on the same graph you used for Short Answer Problems **4b** and **5b** and label it *C*.

c What effect has income redistribution through benefits payments had on inequality?

7 Consider an economy consisting of 100 individuals who are identical in every way. Each lives to be 80 years of age and no older. Between birth and the age of 20 years they earn zero income; between the ages of 21 and 35 each earns an annual income of $30,000; between the ages of 36 and 50 each earns an annual income of $40,000; between the ages of 51 and 65 each receives an annual income of $60,000; and between the ages of 66 and 80 each receives an

annual income of $20,000. At any given time there are 20 individuals in each of the five age groups. For simplicity, assume there are no bequests. This information is summarized in Table 18.6.

TABLE **18.6** LIFETIME INCOME PATTERNS

Age Group (years)	Number in Age Group	Individual Annual Income ($)
0–20	20	0
21–35	20	30,000
36–50	20	40,000
51–65	20	60,000
66–80	20	20,000

a Draw the Lorenz curve for lifetime income in this economy and label it *A*.

b Draw the Lorenz curve for annual income in this economy and label it *B*.

c Which of these is a better measure of the inequality among individuals in this economy? Why?

8 Figure 18.6 shows the demand and supply of low-skilled and high-skilled labour. D_L and D_H are the demand curves for low-skilled and high-skilled workers respectively, and S_L and S_H are the supply curves for low-skilled and high-skilled workers respectively.

FIGURE **18.6**

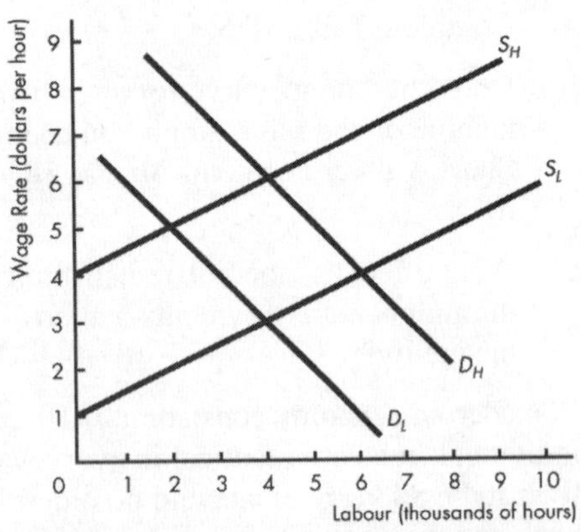

a What is the *MRP* of skill if 5,000 hours of each kind of labour are hired?

b What amount of extra compensation per hour is required to induce the acquisition of skill at the same level of hiring?

c What are the equilibrium wage and quantity of labour in the market for high-skilled labour?

d What are the equilibrium wage and quantity of labour in the market for low-skilled labour?

9 Suppose you are working for the Minister of Post-Secondary Education. She is constantly told by student groups that because university and college students have some of the lowest incomes in society, the government should make additional large income transfers to students. The Minister, who knows her economics, asks you to write up the economic arguments *against* the student groups' position. What are they? Can you think of any economic arguments in favour of society supporting larger transfers to students?

10 Why is there a "big tradeoff" between equity and efficiency?

ANSWERS

True/False and Explain

1 F More unequal. (421–423)

2 T See text discussion. (420–422)

3 T Human capital wealth is more equally distributed than financial wealth. (420–421)

4 F Income is a flow of earning from a stock of wealth. (422)

5 T Differences in life cycle stages make annual income more unequal. (423)

6 F Human capital is people's accumulated skills and knowledge. (426–428)

7 T Because the marginal revenue product of low-skilled workers is lower than that of high-skilled workers. (426–427)

8 F Vertical distance = compensation for cost of acquiring skill. (426–427)

9 F The larger the wage differential. (426–428)

10 T Wealthy people seek wealthy partners, increasing concentration of wealth. (430)

11 T Marginal tax rate constant, but total taxes increase. (431)

12 F Marginal tax rate rises with higher incomes. (431)

13 F From poor to rich. (431)

14 T See Text Figure 18.10. (432)

15 F Lower production due to the big tradeoff. (433)

Multiple-Choice

1 a Definition. (421–423)

2 d 100 percent – 60 percent of cumulative income. (420–423)

3 a 10 percent – 0 percent of cumulative income. (420–423)

4 b 40 percent – 20 percent of cumulative income. (420–423)

5 e Definition. (420–423)

6 d Curve farthest from 45° line. (420–423)

7 b Definition. (421–422)

8 c Moving from 80 percent to 100 percent of households (richest 20 percent) moves income from 60 percent to 100 percent of total (40 percent). (420–423)

9 c Human capital affects distribution of wealth, not income. (422–423)

10 d Life cycle biases distribution income, not wealth. (422–423)

11 d Lifetime income more equally distributed than annual income or than any wealth distribution in a given year. (422–423)

12 c Wealth is a stock, income a flow derived from wealth. (422)

13 d High school completion is key. (425)

14 c Reverse **a** true. **d** applies to supply. **e** nonsense. (426–428)

15 a See Text Figure 18.8(b). (426–427)

16 c No demand curves on figure. Increased *MRP* skill shifts demand, not supply. (426–428)

17 a Wage differences not due to competitive differences. In any case, greater competitiveness would cause fall in high-skilled wages. (426–428)

18 e All can contribute to differentials. (427–430)

19 e Education and training would increase human capital and shift supply curve labour up. (427–430)

20 b Marriage within a socioeconomic class. (430)

21 a Definition. (431)

22 a Taxes are always 10 percent of income. (431)

23 b With higher income, tax rate increases from 0 percent, to 10 percent, to 20 percent, to 40 percent. (431)

24 a Others increase inequality. (431–433)

25 d See text discussion. (433)

Short Answer Problems

1 a See Figure 18.5 Solution. The diagonal line represents hypothetical income equality.

b See Figure 18.5 Solution.

FIGURE **18.5** SOLUTION

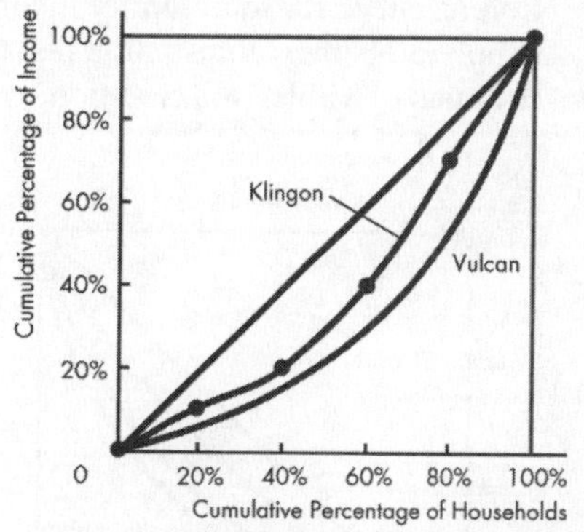

2 a According to the fair-results idea, there should be equality of incomes. According to the fair-rules idea, there should be equality of opportunity.

b Since we have information only on income outcomes and not on the processes or opportunities leading to those incomes, only the fair-results idea can be used to judge Vulcan and Klingon. Since the Klingon Lorenz curve is closer to the line of equality, the Klingon world is more fair according to the fair-results idea.

3 Wealth is the *stock* of assets owned by an individual, while income is connected in that an individual's income is the earnings that flow from her stock of wealth.

4 a Table 18.3 is completed as Table 18.3 Solution. The income share for each group of families is the total income of that group as a percentage of total income in the economy ($100 billion). The cumulative percentage of income (last column) is obtained by adding the percentage income share of the group (from the third column) to the total percentage income share of all poorer groups of families.

TABLE **18.3** SOLUTION
TOTAL HOUSEHOLD INCOME

Percentage of Households	Total Income (billions of $)	Income Share (%)	Cumulative Percentage of Households	Cumulative Percentage of Income
Poorest 20%	5	5	20	5
Second 20%	10	10	40	15
Third 20%	15	15	60	30
Fourth 20%	20	20	80	50
Richest 20%	50	50	100	100

b The curve labelled *A* in Figure 18.7 is the Lorenz curve for total family income. This simply plots the values in the last two columns of Table 18.3 Solution.

FIGURE **18.7**

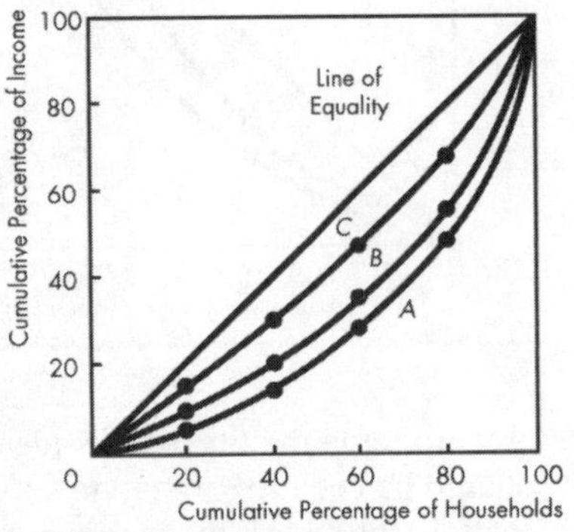

5 a Table 18.4 is completed as Table 18.4 Solution.

TABLE **18.4** SOLUTION
AFTER-TAX HOUSEHOLD INCOME

Percentage of Households	After-Tax Income (billions of $)	After-Tax Income Share (%)	Cumulative Percentage of Households	Cumulative Percentage of After-Tax Income
Poorest 20%	5	7	20	7
Second 20%	9	13	40	20
Third 20%	12	17	60	37
Fourth 20%	15	21	80	58
Richest 20%	30	42	100	100

b The curve labelled *B* in Figure 18.7 is the Lorenz curve for after-tax household income.

c The progressive income tax has reduced inequality by taking a larger percentage of income from higher income groups.

d The "big tradeoff" is the fact that a more equally shared pie results in a smaller pie. While the after-tax distribution is now more equal, total income has been reduced from $100 billion to $71 billion. The $29 billion loss is the cost of the big tradeoff, due to the costs of administering the redistribution program and the deadweight loss from weakened work incentives.

6 a Table 18.5 is completed as Table 18.5 Solution.

TABLE **18.5** SOLUTION
AFTER-BENEFITS HOUSEHOLD INCOME

Percentage of Households	After-Benefits Income Share (billions of $)	After-Benefits Income Share (%)	Cumulative Percentage of Households	Cumulative Percentage of After-Benefits Income
Poorest 20%	15	15	20	15
Second 20%	16	16	40	31
Third 20%	18	18	60	49
Fourth 20%	20	20	80	69
Richest 20%	31	31	100	100

b The curve labelled *C* in Figure 18.7 is the Lorenz curve for after-tax, after-benefits household income.

c Income redistribution through benefits payments has reduced inequality.

7 a Since each individual in the economy earns exactly the same lifetime income, the Lorenz curve for lifetime income coincides with the line of equality and is labelled *A* in Figure 18.8.

FIGURE **18.8**

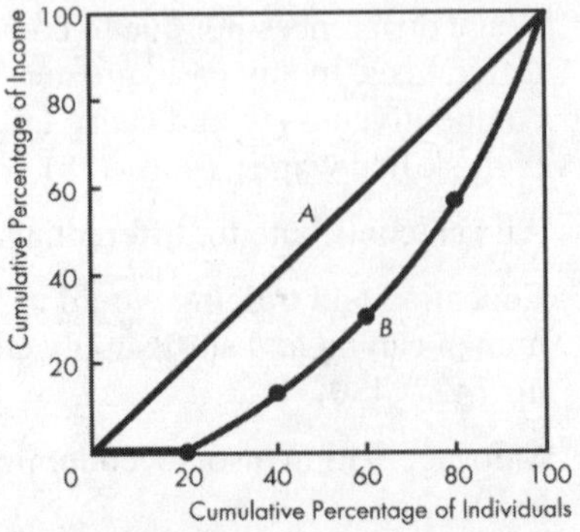

b The Lorenz curve for annual income is labelled *B* in Figure 18.8. It reflects that the poorest 20 percent of individuals, those aged 0–20 years, receive 0 percent of the annual income; the second-poorest 20 percent, 60–80 years, 13 percent; the third-poorest 20 percent, 21–35 years, 20 percent; the fourth-poorest 20 percent, 36–50 years, 27 percent; and the richest 20 percent, 51–65 years, 40 percent.

c The distribution of lifetime income is a better measure of the degree of inequality. In this imaginary economy all individuals are identical (equal), a fact reflected in equal lifetime incomes. The only reason annual income distribution in this economy is not equal is because individuals are at different stages of identical life cycles.

8 a The *MRP* of skill is the difference between the *MRP* of high-skilled versus low-skilled labour; the vertical distance between the demand curves for high-skilled and low-skilled labour. In Figure 18.6, the *MRP* of skill is $3 per hour when 5,000 hours of each kind of labour are employed.

b Since labour supply curves give the minimum compensation workers are willing to accept in return for supplying a given quantity of labour, the extra compensation for skill is the vertical distance between the supply curves of high-skilled and low-skilled labour. At 5,000 hours of employment for both kinds of labour, this is $3 per hour.

c In equilibrium in the market for high-skilled labour, the wage rate will be $6 per hour and employment will be 4,000 hours of labour. This occurs at the intersection of the D_H and S_H curves.

d In equilibrium in the market for low-skilled labour, the wage rate will be $3 per hour and employment will be 4,000 hours of labour. This occurs at the intersection of the D_L and S_L curves.

9 The request by students for more income transfers is related to many of the issues in this chapter. The first issue is the distribution of annual income versus lifetime income. Post-secondary students are relatively poor at this stage of their career, but can expect to earn far-above-average incomes for the rest of their lives. So on the basis of lifetime income (which is a more comprehensive measure than annual income), there is no good argument for transfers.

The reason behind these higher lifetime incomes is that post-secondary education is an investment in human capital for the individual paying the tuition. As an investment, the payoff comes later in life in the form of higher average incomes. Statistics show that the annual real rates of return (after allowing for inflation) for an investment in post-secondary education are 5 to 10 percent, a better return than almost any other investment you are likely to make (See text page 427).

Post-secondary students who will receive these high rates of return already receive transfers from government in the form of subsidized education. While tuition fees have been rising sharply over the past decade, the annual undergraduate university tuition in Ontario of around $5,000 covered only a small fraction of the more than $20,000 it cost the government to supply that education.

Thus, from the material in this chapter there are many arguments *against* further income transfers to post-secondary students.

The most important argument in favour of further government support (subsidizes and transfers) for post-secondary education is that there are benefits to society as a whole from having a well-educated workforce and citizenry that are greater than the benefits to the individual receiving the education. This argument was developed in Chapters 15 and 16 in the discussion of public goods and positive externalities.

10 If greater equity means increasing the equality of income, it can only be achieved by income redistribution; the income of some must be taxed in order to make transfer payments to others. However, there are incentive effects that reduce the total amount of income available to be distributed.

If productive activities such as work are taxed, there will be a tendency to reduce time spent in those activities. Furthermore, any redistribution program would require resources to administer it and thus leave fewer resources for other productive activities. Thus we arrive at the insight that a more equally shared pie results in a smaller pie.

CHAPTERS 17–18

Part 6 Wrap Up

Understanding Factor Markets

PROBLEM

FIGURE **P6.1** LABOUR MARKETS FOR PROGRAMMERS

(a) Left-Handed **(b) Right-Handed**

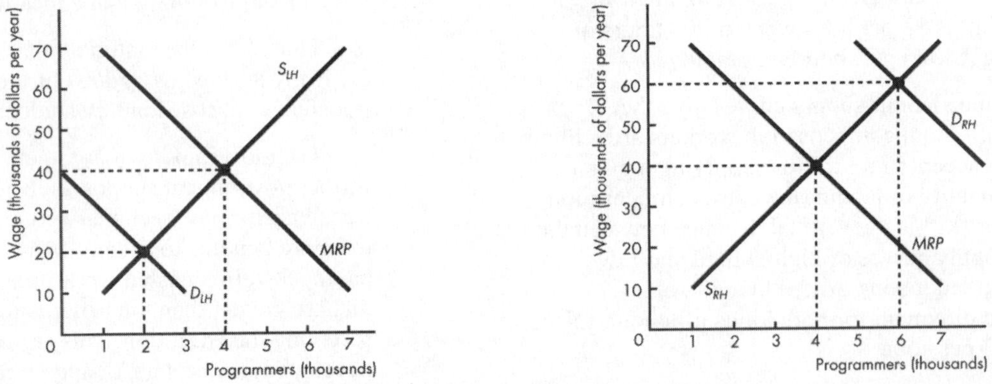

Suppose the computer software industry uses only two inputs—programmers (labour) and computers (capital). All programmers, whether left-handed or right-handed, have computer science degrees, are equally skilled and productive, and have the marginal revenue product (*MRP*) curve in Figure P6.1(a) and (b).

Software firms (run mostly by right-handers) discriminate against left-handed programmers, believing (wrongly) that left-handers are less productive than right-handers. Figure P6.1(a) shows the supply curve of left-handed programmers and firms' demand curve for left-handed programmers.

Software firms also discriminate in favour of right-handed programmers, believing (wrongly) that right-handers are more productive than left-handers. Figure P6.1(b) shows the supply curve of right-handed programmers and firms' demand curve for right-handed programmers.

a What is the relationship between the wage and the marginal revenue product for left-handed programmers? for right-handed programmers?

b Explain the competitive forces that would tend to eliminate this form of discrimination, even without government legislation.

c If owners of firms are so strongly prejudiced against left-handers that they are willing to accept lower profits rather than employ left-handers, will competitive forces eliminate this discrimination?

d The government introduces pay equity legislation, designed to equalize wages between left-handers and right-handers. The legislation includes an educational program to inform firms of the true and equal productivity of all programmers, regardless of their "handedness." If the program is successful, what will be the wage of programmers? the employment of left-handed programmers? the employment of right-handed programmers?

e With equalized programmer wages, what is now the relationship between the wage and the marginal revenue product for left-handed programmers? for right-handed programmers? What other meaning does *pay equity* have besides paying different groups equal wages?

f As a result of the pay equity legislation, what has happened to the *average* wage of programmers?

g As a result of the pay equity legislation, what has happened to the average wage of *left-handed* programmers? Explain the impact on the decisions of left-handers to invest in human capital.

MIDTERM EXAMINATION

You should allocate 26 minutes for this examination (13 questions, 2 minutes per question). For each question, choose the one *best* answer.

1 Refer to Figure P6.2. If demand for a factor of production increases from D_0 to D_1, the *change* in the opportunity cost of using the resource is
- **a** area *ihfc*.
- **b** area *jcfk*.
- **c** area 0*fk*.
- **d** area 0*fh*.
- **e** none of the above.

FIGURE **P6.2**

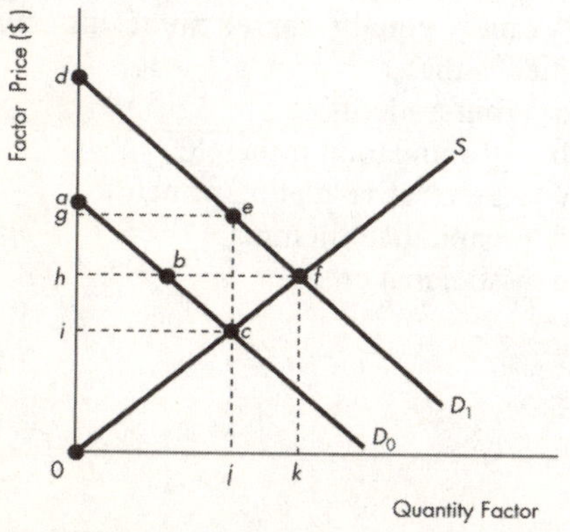

2 Household savings are larger when either current income is
- **a** low compared with expected future income or interest rates are high.
- **b** low compared with expected future income or interest rates are low.
- **c** high compared with expected future income or interest rates are high.
- **d** high compared with expected future income or interest rates are low.
- **e** above or below the reservation wage.

3 Wealth is the
- **a** large flow of income earned by the rich.
- **b** large stock of income available to the rich.
- **c** stock of assets owned by an individual.
- **d** flow of assets to an individual from labour.
- **e** flow of assets to an individual from capital.

4 Refer to Figure P6.3. For any given wage,
- **a** the elasticity of demand for high-skilled workers is greater than the elasticity of demand for low-skilled workers.
- **b** more high-skilled workers will be hired than low-skilled workers.
- **c** more low-skilled workers will be hired than high-skilled workers.
- **d** the horizontal distance between the curves is the compensation for the cost of acquiring skill.
- **e** the horizontal distance between the curves is the *MRP* of skill.

FIGURE **P6.3**

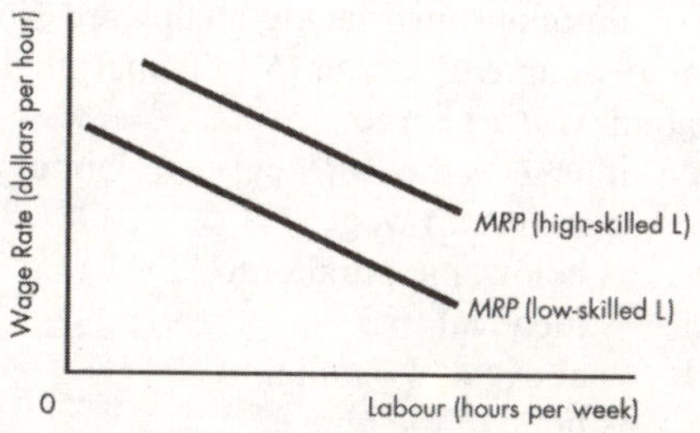

5 Consider the Lorenz curves in Figure P6.4. Which point indicates that the richest 20 percent of families earn 60 percent of the income?
- **a** *a*
- **b** *b*
- **c** *c*
- **d** *d*
- **e** none of the above

FIGURE **P6.4**

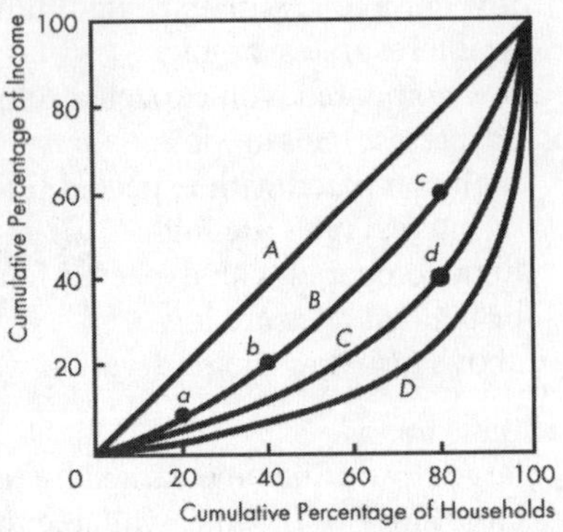

FIGURE **P6.5**

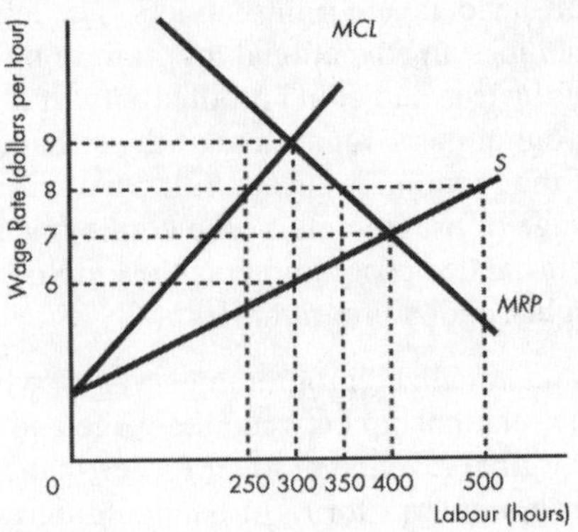

6 The demand curve for a factor of production will shift leftward as a result of a(n)
- **a** decrease in the price of the factor.
- **b** increase in the price of the factor.
- **c** increase in technology.
- **d** increase in the price of output.
- **e** decrease in the price of output.

7 A profit-maximizing firm hires labour in a competitive labour market. If the marginal revenue product of labour is greater than the wage, the firm should
- **a** increase the wage rate.
- **b** decrease the wage rate.
- **c** increase the quantity of labour it hires.
- **d** decrease the quantity of labour it hires.
- **e** diminish the marginal revenue product of labour.

8 For a monopsonist facing an upward-sloping supply curve of labour (*S*), the marginal cost of labour (*MCL*) curve
- **a** intersects the *MRP* curve of labour at the equilibrium wage.
- **b** is below and parallel to *S*.
- **c** is identical to *S*.
- **d** is above and parallel to *S*.
- **e** is none of the above.

9 Suppose the government passes a minimum wage law that prohibits anyone from hiring labour at less than $8 per hour. In Figure P6.5, the monopsonist will hire
- **a** 250 hours of labour.
- **b** 300 hours of labour.
- **c** 350 hours of labour.
- **d** 400 hours of labour.
- **e** 500 hours of labour.

10 If the marginal tax rate decreases as income increases, the income tax is defined as
- **a** progressive.
- **b** proportional.
- **c** negative.
- **d** regressive.
- **e** redistributive.

11 Which of the following is *not* part of an individual's stock of wealth?
- **a** stock of assets
- **b** flow of earnings
- **c** human capital
- **d** physical assets
- **e** financial assets

12 If the net present value of a new machine is positive,
- **a** the firm should not buy the machine.
- **b** the present value of the machine's stream of marginal revenue products is greater than the purchase price.
- **c** the present value of the machine's stream of marginal revenue products is less than the purchase price.
- **d** a and **b**.
- **e** a and **c**.

13 "A more equally shared pie results in a smaller pie" is the
- **a** big tradeoff.
- **b** Robin Hood principle.
- **c** assortative mating principle.
- **d** capitalist dilemma.
- **e** socialist creed.

ANSWERS

Problem

a For the 2,000 left-handed programmers employed, the wage ($20,000 per year) is much less than the marginal revenue product of $60,000 per year. For the 6,000 right-handed programmers employed, the wage ($60,000 per year) is much more than the marginal revenue product of $20,000 per year.

b A nondiscriminating firm could earn higher profits by employing more left-handed programmers as long as their marginal revenue product exceeds the wage. Similarly, profits will increase by employing fewer right-handed programmers as long as their wage exceeds their marginal revenue product. The competitive outcome would be a wage of $40,000 per year for every programmer, and employment of 4,000 left-handed and 4,000 right-handed programmers.

c No. Firms can continue to discriminate if they "pay" for the discrimination in the form of lower profits.

d A successful education program alters firms' beliefs about left-handed and right-handed programmers and moves the demand curves to the true *MRP* curves. The outcome will be the same as the competitive outcome—a wage of $40,000 per year for every programmer, and employment of 4,000 left-handed and 4,000 right-handed programmers.

e The wage is equal to the marginal revenue product for every programmer. Pay equity also means each labourer being paid an amount *equal* to the value of his or her marginal revenue product.

f Before legislation, the average yearly wage of programmers was a weighted (by employment) average of the wages of left-handers and right-handers.

$$\frac{(\$20{,}000 \times 2{,}000) + (\$60{,}000 \times 6{,}000)}{8{,}000} = \$50{,}000$$

After legislation, the average yearly wage has fallen to $40,000.

g The average yearly wage of left-handed programmers has increased from $20,000 to $40,000. This creates an incentive for more left-handers to invest in the necessary human capital (computer science degrees) to become programmers, increasing the quantity supplied of left-handed programmers.

Midterm Examination

1 b Increase in area under supply curve. (406–407)

2 c See text discussion. (402)

3 c Wealth is a stock of assets. Assets are stocks, not flows (**d**, **e**); income is a flow, not stock (**b**). (422–423)

4 b Reverse **a** true. **d** true for vertical distance between supply curves. **e** true for vertical distance between demand curves. (426–428)

5 d Moving from 80 percent to 100 percent of families (richest 20 percent) moves income from 40 percent to 100 percent of total (60 percent). (421–423)

6 e Lower price of output lowers *MR* which in turn lowers *MRP*. **a** and **b** move along curve, **c** and **d** shift curve rightward. (393)

7 c Hiring more labour increases profit since *MRP* > *MC*. **a** and **b** wrong because competitive firm can't change wage; **e** nonsense. (391–392)

8 e *MCL* is above, but not parallel to *S*. *MCL* intersects *S* at equilibrium *QL*, not wage. (416–418)

9 c New *MCL* flat at $8 until it hits *S* curve yielding *QL* where new *MCL* intersects *MRP*. (416–418)

10 d Definition. (431)

11 b Flow of earnings is *income* from individual's stock of wealth. (422–423)

12 b Definition. Firm should buy machine. (399–401)

13 a Tradeoff between equity and efficiency arises because redistribution uses scarce resources and weakens incentives. (433)

Chapter 32 Trading with the World

KEY CONCEPTS

Patterns and Trends in International Trade

Imports are goods and services we buy from other countries, **exports** are what we sell to other countries.

- Canada's major exports and imports are motor vehicles and capital goods, our major trading partner is the United States.
- Trade includes trade in services, such as tourism.
- **Net exports** = value of exports – value of imports.

The Gains from International Trade

Countries can produce anywhere on or inside production possibilities frontier (*PPF*).

- Slope of *PPF* = Δ *y*-axis variable/Δ *x*-axis variable = opportunity cost of one more *x*-axis variable.
- A country has comparative advantage in production of good for which it has lowest opportunity cost.

A country gains from trading by buying goods from countries with lower opportunity costs and selling the goods for which it has lower opportunity cost.

- **Terms of trade** = quantity needed to export to buy 1 unit of imports.
- Countries pay for their imports with their exports—value of exports = value of imports.
- Countries react to new terms of trade by producing more exported good and less imported good.
- *Both* countries gain by specializing—both can therefore *consume outside* their *PPF*.
- Most trade can be explained by comparative advantage, but much trade is trade in similar goods, due to diversified tastes and economies of scale.

International Trade Restrictions

Governments protect domestic industries by restricting trade with tariffs and nontariff barriers.

- Tariffs have been decreasing due to **General Agreement on Tariffs and Trade** (international treaty to limit trade restriction), its successor the **World Trade Organization**, and the **North American Free Trade Agreement**.

Tariffs are taxes on imported goods.

- Tariffs increase import price, decreasing imports, increasing domestic production.
- Net losses to importing country because new price > original import price.
- Tariffs lower imports in home country and exports to foreign country.

Nontariff barriers restrict supply of imports, which increases domestic price and domestic production.

- **Quotas** set import quantity restriction, with quota licences distributed by home country.
- **Voluntary export restraints** (VERs) set export quantity restrictions, with foreign distributors having export licences.

The Case Against Protection

Trade restrictions are used despite losses of gains from trade for three somewhat credible reasons—to protect **infant industries**, prevent foreign companies from **dumping** their products on world markets at prices less than cost, and to save jobs in import-competing industries.

A country may restrict trade for the following less credible reasons:

- ♦ To protect strategic industries for national security.
- ♦ To compete with cheap foreign labour.
- ♦ To bring diversity and stability.
- ♦ To penalize lax environmental standards.
- ♦ To protect a national culture.
- ♦ To prevent rich countries from exploiting developing countries.

The biggest problem with protection is that it invites retaliation from other countries.

- ♦ There are two reasons for trade restrictions:
  - Tariff revenue is an attractive tax base for governments in developing countries.
  - To protect groups/industries that suffer disproportionately under freer trade.
- ♦ In Canada, employment insurance and interprovincial transfers provide some compensation for losses due to free trade.

The Balance of International Payments

The balance of payments accounts measure Canada's international transactions.

- ♦ Current account—net exports + net interest payments + net transfers.
- ♦ Capital account—foreign investment in Canada – Canadian investment abroad.
- ♦ Official settlements account—net changes in Canada's official international reserves (government's holdings of foreign currency). If official reserves increase, official settlement balance is negative.
- ♦ Current account balance + capital account balance + official settlements balance = 0.
- ♦ To pay a current account deficit we must borrow from abroad or decrease official reserves.

International finance categories of countries:

- ♦ Flow categories:
  - Net borrower—borrowing more from rest of world than lending in current year (capital account surplus).
  - Net lender—lending more to rest of world than borrowing in current year (capital account deficit).
  - Being a net borrower not a problem if it is to finance investment that generates higher income to pay debts, as has been recent case in Canada.
- ♦ Stock categories:
  - Debtor nation—has borrowed more than lent to rest of world over its history.
  - Creditor nation—has lent more than borrowed to rest of world over its history.

Current account balance is primarily determined by net exports ($NX = X - M$).

- ♦ Via circular flow, net exports ($X - M$) = private sector balance ($S - I$) + government sector balance ($NT - G$).
- ♦ Government budget deficit and current account deficit move together (twin deficits).

The North American Free Trade Agreement

Despite protectionism pressures, Canada has a free trade agreement with the United States and Mexico.

- ♦ This agreement involves
  - Reducing common tariffs to zero in phases.
  - Reducing nontariff barriers.
  - Freer trade in energy and services.
  - Future negotiations on subsidies.
  - A dispute-settling mechanism.
- ♦ Total effects of the agreement are unknown at the moment, but they do include large increases in the total volume of trade, with significant changes in some sectors.

HELPFUL HINTS

1 This chapter applies the fundamental concepts of opportunity cost and comparative advantage from Chapter 2 to the problem of trade between nations. The basic principles are the same for trade between individuals in the same country and between individuals in different countries.

Many people involved in debates about trade seem confused by the concept of comparative advantage, partially because they implicitly consider *absolute advantage* as the sole reason for trade. A country has an absolute advantage if it can produce all goods using less inputs than another country. However, such a country can still gain from trade. Consider California and Saskatchewan. California has a better climate and, with widespread irrigation, has an absolute advantage in the production of all agricultural products. Indeed, California frequently has more than one harvest a year! This absolute advantage would seem to imply that California has no need to trade with Saskatchewan. Saskatchewan, however, has a *comparative advantage* in the production of wheat. Therefore California will specialize in fruits and trade them for wheat. California could easily grow its own wheat, but the opportunity cost would be too high—the lost fruit crops. By specializing and trading, both California and Saskatchewan can gain.

2 One of the crucial results of this chapter is that both countries can gain from trade. This gain occurs because the post-trade price is between the two countries' pre-trade opportunity costs. We can see this gain illustrated in Text Figure 32.3, in which the equilibrium price of a car is 3 tonnes of grain, between the pre-trade opportunity costs of 1 tonne and 9 tonnes.

Students are often puzzled by where to put the price when working through these types of examples. How did the authors come up with the value of 3? In a sense, it is an arbitrary value, one they just plucked out of a hat. Given the logic of voluntary trade, it must be between the two pre-trade values of 1 and 9. However, by redrawing the export supply and the import demand curves with different slopes, the authors might have arrived at a value of 6 tonnes. This result would have been equally logical, and equally valid.

In the real world, the strength of the demand for specific products by the consumers of each country will determine the slopes of the export supply and import demand curves, and determine just where the equilibrium price is set. In your examples, either you will be able to pick where you want the price to be (given that it must be between the two pre-trade opportunity costs) or you will be given some specific information telling you where the price is.

3 An important economic effect of trade restrictions is that a tariff and a quota have the same effects. A voluntary export restraint (VER) is also a quota, but it is one imposed by the exporting country rather than by the importing country.

All trade restrictions raise the domestic price of the imported goods and reduce the volume and value of imports. They also reduce the value of exports by the same amount as the reduction in the value of imports. The increase in price that results from each trade restriction produces a gap between the domestic price of the imported good and the foreign supply price of the good.

The difference between the alternative trade restrictions lies in which party captures this excess. In the case of a tariff, the government receives the tariff revenue. In the case of a quota imposed by the importing country, domestic importers who have been awarded a licence to import capture this excess through increased profit. When a VER is imposed, the excess is captured by foreign exporters who have been awarded licences to export by their government.

4 The major point of this chapter is that there are considerable gains from free trade. Why then do countries have such a strong tendency to impose trade restrictions? The key is that while free trade creates overall benefits to the economy as a whole, there are both winners and losers. The winners gain more in total than the losers lose, but the losers tend to be concentrated in a few industries.

Given this concentration, free trade will be resisted by some acting on the basis of rational self-interest. Even though only a small minority benefit while the overwhelming majority will be hurt, it is not surprising to see trade restrictions implemented. The cost of a given trade restriction to *each* of the majority will be individually quite small, while the benefit to *each* of the few will be individually large. Thus the minority will have a significant incentive to see that restriction takes place, while the majority will have little incentive to expend time and energy in resisting trade restriction.

5 To understand the source of pressures for trade restrictions, let us summarize those who win and lose from trade restrictions.

Under the three forms of restrictions (tariffs, quotas, and VERs) *consumers* lose, because the price of the imported good increases. *Domestic producers* of the imported good and their factors of production gain from all three, because the price of the imported good increases. *Foreign producers* and their factors of production lose under all three schemes, because their export sales decrease. Under quotas and VERs, the *holders of import licences* gain from buying low and selling high (they may be foreign or domestic). *Government* gains tariff revenue under tariffs and, potentially, votes under other schemes.

Given this list, it is hardly surprising that the main supporters of trade restrictions are domestic producers and their factors of production.

SELF-TEST

True/False and Explain

Patterns and Trends in International Trade

1 When a Canadian citizen stays in a hotel in France, Canada is exporting a service.

The Gains from International Trade

2 If a country can produce all goods cheaper than other countries, it will not benefit from trade.

3 Trading according to comparative advantage allows all trading countries to consume outside their *PPF*.

4 If Atlantis must give up 3 widgets to produce 1 watch and Beltran must give up 4 widgets to produce 1 watch, Atlantis has a comparative advantage in the production of watches.

International Trade Restrictions

5 When governments impose tariffs, they are increasing their country's gain from trade.

6 A tariff on a good will raise its price and reduce the quantity traded.

7 A quota will cause the price of the imported good to decrease.

The Case Against Protection

8 Japan is dumping steel if it sells steel in Japan at a lower price than it sells it in Canada.

9 Since Mexican labour is paid so much less than Canadian labour, entering into a free trade agreement with Mexico guarantees Canada will lose jobs to Mexico.

10 Elected governments are slow to reduce trade restrictions because there would be more losers than gainers.

The Balance of International Payments

11 There can be no such thing as a balance of payments surplus/deficit, because by definition a *balance* of payments must always *balance*.

12 A larger government sector deficit always leads to a higher current account deficit.

13 If a nation is a net borrower from the rest of the world, it must be a debtor nation.

14 If Canada borrows more from the rest of the world than it lends to the rest of the world, Canada has a capital account surplus.

The North American Free Trade Agreement

15 The impact of the North American Free Trade Agreement has been significant changes in some sectors, but no overall change in the total volume of trade.

Multiple-Choice

Patterns and Trends in International Trade

1 Which of the following is a Canadian service export?
- a A Canadian buys dinner while travelling in Switzerland.
- b A Swiss buys dinner while travelling in Canada.
- c A Canadian buys a clock made in Switzerland.
- d A Swiss buys a computer made in Canada.
- e A Canadian buys a Canadian computer in Switzerland.

The Gains from International Trade

2 In Atlantis, 1 unit of capital and 1 unit of labour are required to produce 1 watch, and 2 units of capital and 2 units of labour are required to produce 1 widget. What is the opportunity cost of producing one watch?
- a the price of 1 unit of capital plus the price of 1 unit of labour
- b 1 unit of capital and 1 unit of labour
- c 2 units of capital and 2 units of labour
- d 1/2 widget
- e 2 widgets

3 Refer to Figure 32.1. The opportunity cost of 1 beer in Partyland is __________, and the opportunity cost of 1 beer in Cowabunga is __________.
- a dependent on where on the *PPF* we measure it; dependent on where on the *PPF* we measure it
- b 100 pizzas; 25 pizzas
- c 3 pizzas; 1 pizza
- d 1 pizza; 1 pizza
- e 1 pizza; 1/3 pizza

FIGURE **32.1** PARTYLAND AND COWABUNGA—*PPF* FOR BEER AND PIZZA

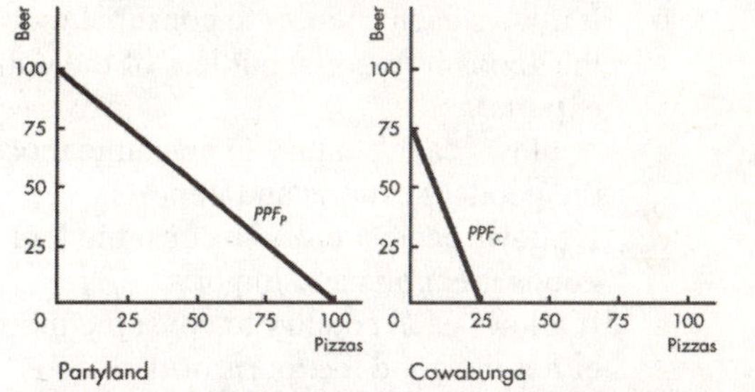

4 Refer to Figure 32.1. The opportunity cost of 1 pizza in Partyland is __________, and the opportunity cost of 1 pizza in Cowabunga is __________.
- a dependent on where on the *PPF* we measure it; dependent on where on the *PPF* we measure it
- b 100 beers; 25 beers
- c 3 beers; 1 beer
- d 1 beer; 1 beer
- e 1 beer; 3 beers

5 Refer to Figure 32.1. If trade occurs between Partyland and Cowabunga,
- a there will be a lot of drunk turtles.
- b Partyland will supply both pizza and beer, because it has a comparative advantage in both.
- c Cowabunga will supply both pizza and beer, because it has a comparative advantage in both.
- d Partyland will supply pizza, and Cowabunga will supply beer.
- e Partyland will supply beer, and Cowabunga will supply pizza.

6 Refer to Figure 32.1. If trade occurs between Partyland and Cowabunga, the terms of trade will be
- a 1 beer for 1 pizza.
- b 1 beer for 1/3 pizza.
- c 1 beer for 3 pizzas.
- d somewhere between 1 beer for 1 pizza and 1 beer for 3 pizzas.
- e somewhere between 1 beer for 1 pizza and 1 beer for 1/3 pizza.

7 Compared to no trade, how does international trade change the consumption possibilities of each country?
- a It allows each country to consume more of the goods it exports, but less of the goods it imports.
- b It allows each country to consume more of the goods it imports, but less of the goods it exports.
- c It allows each country to consume more of the goods it exports and imports.
- d It allows each country to consume less of the goods it exports and imports.
- e It allows each country to consume more of either the good it exports or the good it imports, but not both.

International Trade Restrictions

8 Consider Table 32.1. Under free trade, the international price of donut holes would be $_________ per hundred donut holes, and _________ million holes would be exchanged.
- a 0.75; 6
- b 1.00; 3
- c 1.25; 4
- d 1.25; 5
- e 1.50; 4

TABLE **32.1** INTERNATIONAL TRADE IN DONUT HOLES

International Price (dollars per 100 holes)	Glazeland's Export Supply of Holes (millions)	Snorfleland's Import Demand for Holes (millions)
0.50	1	10
0.75	2	8
1.00	3	6
1.25	4	4
1.50	5	2
1.75	6	0

9 Consider Table 32.1. Snorfleland's donut hole producers convince their government that there is a need to protect the domestic industry from Glazeland's cheap imports. (They argue that holes are a crucial food group.) In response, Snorfleland's government sets an import quota of 3 million donut holes. The resulting price of a donut hole in Snorfleland will be $_________ per hundred holes, and domestic production of donut holes will _________.
- a 0.75; decrease
- b 0.75; increase
- c 1.25; remain unchanged
- d 1.38; increase
- e 1.38; remain unchanged

10 A tariff on watches which are imported by Atlantis will cause the
- a demand curve for watches in Atlantis to shift leftward.
- b demand curve for watches in Atlantis to shift rightward.
- c supply curve of watches in Atlantis to shift leftward.
- d supply curve of watches in Atlantis to shift rightward.
- e demand and the supply curve of watches in Atlantis to shift leftward.

11 When a *quota* is imposed, the gap between the domestic price and the export price is captured by
- a consumers in the importing country.
- b the domestic producers of the good.
- c the government of the importing country.
- d foreign exporters.
- e the domestic importers of the good.

12 When a *voluntary export restraint* agreement is reached, the gap between the domestic import price and the export price is captured by
- a consumers in the importing country.
- b the domestic producers of the good.
- c the government of the importing country.
- d foreign exporters.
- e the domestic importers of the good.

13 When a *tariff* is imposed, the gap between the domestic price and the export price is captured by
- a consumers in the importing country.
- b the domestic producers of the good.
- c the government of the importing country.
- d foreign exporters.
- e the domestic importers of the good.

The Case Against Protection

14 Which of the following is *not* an argument for protectionism?

a to protect strategic industries
b to save jobs in import-competing industries
c to gain a comparative advantage
d to allow infant industries to grow
e to prevent rich nations from exploiting poor nations

15 The biggest problem with protection is that

a it invites retaliation from trading partners.
b losers are not compensated.
c it worsens environmental standards.
d it can worsen national security.
e it lowers wages.

16 Why is international trade restricted?

a because government revenue is costly to collect via tariffs
b in order to get higher consumption possibilities
c to realize the gains from trade
d due to rent-seeking
e because free trade creates economic losses on average

The Balance of International Payments

17 $NX =$

a $C + I + G$
b $(S + I) - (NT + G)$
c $(G - NT) + (I - S)$
d $(S - I) + (G - NT)$
e none of the above

18 Suppose Canada initially has all balance of payments accounts in balance (no surplus or deficit). Then Canadian firms increase their imports from Japan, financing that increase by borrowing from Japan. There will now be a current account

a surplus and a capital account surplus.
b surplus and a capital account deficit.
c deficit and a capital account surplus.
d deficit and a capital account deficit.
e deficit and a capital account balance.

19 The country of Mengia came into existence at the beginning of year 1. Given the information in Table 32.2, in year 4 Mengia is a

a net lender and a creditor nation.
b net lender and a debtor nation.
c net borrower and a creditor nation.
d net borrower and a debtor nation.
e net lender and neither a creditor nor a debtor nation.

TABLE **32.2**

Year	**Borrowed from Rest of World (billions of dollars)**	**Lent to Rest of World (billions of dollars)**
1	60	20
2	60	40
3	60	60
4	60	80

20 Assuming that Mengia's official settlement account is always in balance, in which year or years in Table 32.2 did Mengia have a current account surplus?

a year 1
b year 2
c years 1, 2, and 3
d years 1 and 2
e year 4 only

21 If Mengia's official settlement balance was in deficit every year, for which year or years in Table 32.2 can you say for sure there was a current account surplus?

a year 1
b year 2
c years 2 and 3
d years 1 and 2
e years 3 and 4

22 Suppose that a country's government expenditures are $400 billion, net taxes are $300 billion, saving is $300 billion, and investment is $250 billion. This country has a government budget

a surplus and a private sector surplus.
b surplus and a private sector deficit.
c deficit and a private sector surplus.
d deficit and a private sector deficit.
e surplus and a private sector balance.

23 The distinction between a debtor or creditor nation and a net borrower or net lender nation depends on

a the distinction between the level of saving in the economy and the saving rate.
b the distinction between the level of saving in the economy and the rate of borrowing.
c the distinction between the stock of net borrowing and the flow of net borrowing.
d the distinction between exports and imports.
e nothing really; they are the same.

24 If the current account is in deficit, and the capital account is also in deficit, the change in official reserves is
- **a** negative.
- **b** positive.
- **c** probably close to zero, but might be either negative or positive.
- **d** zero.
- **e** not affected.

The North American Free Trade Agreement

25 Examining the implementation of the North American Free Trade Agreement has revealed
- **a** Canada has been severely damaged by the agreement.
- **b** Canada has been helped enormously by the agreement.
- **c** free trade does not work.
- **d** all losers from free trade will be compensated.
- **e** large increases in trade, benefiting consumers, but costing some jobs.

Short Answer Problems

1 Why can *both* parties involved in trade gain?

2 Suppose Atlantis imposes a tariff on its imports of watches from Beltran. How does the tariff affect the domestic price of watches, the export price, the quantity imported, the quantity of watches produced domestically, and Atlantis's exports to Beltran?

3 It is often argued by union leaders that tariffs are needed to protect domestic jobs. In light of your answers to Short Answer Problem **2**, evaluate this argument.

4 The international transactions of a country for a given year are reported in Table 32.3.

TABLE **32.3**

Transaction	Amount (billions of dollars)
Exports of goods and services	100
Imports of goods and services	130
Transfers to the rest of the world	20
Loans to the rest of the world	60
Loans from the rest of the world	?
Increases in official reserves	10
Net interest payments	0

- **a** What is the amount of loans from the rest of the world?
- **b** What is the current account balance?
- **c** What is the capital account balance?
- **d** What is the official settlements balance?

5 Consider a simple world in which there are two countries, Atlantis and Beltran, each producing food and cloth. The *PPF* for each country is given in Table 32.4.
- **a** Assuming a constant opportunity cost in each country, complete the table.
- **b** What is the opportunity cost of food in Atlantis? of cloth?
- **c** What is the opportunity cost of food in Beltran? of cloth?
- **d** Draw the *PPF*s on separate graphs.

TABLE **32.4** ATLANTIS AND BELTRAN—*PPF* FOR FOOD AND CLOTH

Atlantis		Beltran	
Food (units)	Cloth (units)	Food (units)	Cloth (units)
0	500	0	800
200	400	100	600
400		200	
600		300	
800		400	
1,000		—	—

6 Suppose that Atlantis and Beltran engage in trade.
- **a** In which good will each country specialize?
- **b** If 1 unit of food trades for 1 unit of cloth, what will happen to the production of each good in each country?
- **c** If 1 unit of food trades for 1 unit of cloth, draw the consumption possibilities frontiers for each country on the corresponding graph from Short Answer Problem **5**.
- **d** Before trade, if Atlantis consumed 600 units of food, the most cloth it could consume was 200 units. After trade, how many units of cloth can be consumed if 600 units of food are consumed?

7 Continue the analysis of Atlantis and Beltran trading at the rate of 1 unit of food for 1 unit of cloth.

a If Atlantis consumes 600 units of food and 400 units of cloth, how much food and cloth will be consumed by Beltran?

b Given the consumption quantities and the production quantities from Short Answer Problem **6b**, how much food and cloth will Atlantis and Beltran import and export?

8 Figure 32.2 gives the import demand curve for shirts for Atlantis, labelled *D*, and the export supply curve of shirts for Beltran, labelled *S*.

a What is the price of a shirt under free trade?

b How many shirts will be imported by Atlantis?

FIGURE **32.2**

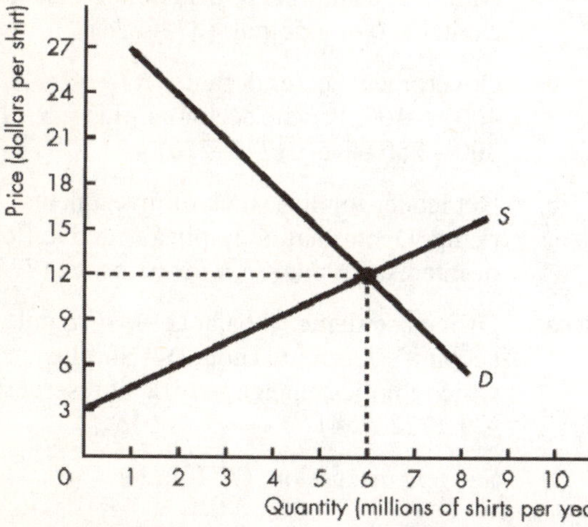

9 Suppose the shirt makers in Atlantis of Short Answer Problem **8** are concerned about foreign competition and, as a result, the government of Atlantis imposes a tariff of $9 per shirt.

a Using Figure 32.2, show what will happen to the price of a shirt in Atlantis.

b What is the price the exporter will actually receive?

c How many shirts will be imported by Atlantis?

d What is the revenue from the tariff? Who captures it?

10 Suppose that instead of a tariff, Atlantis imposes a quota of 4 million shirts per year.

a With the aid of a new graph, show what will be the new price of a shirt in Atlantis.

b What price will the exporter actually receive?

c How many shirts will be imported by Atlantis?

d What is the difference between the total amount paid by consumers and the total amount received by exporters—the "excess profit"? Who captures it?

ANSWERS

True/False and Explain

1 F Canada is importing (using) a service. (756)

2 F If comparative advantage exists, gains from trade exist. (757–762)

3 T Countries will specialize and trade to consume outside *PPF*. (757–761)

4 T Atlantis has a lower opportunity cost (3 widgets < 4 widgets) = lost widgets per unit of gained watches. (758–759)

5 F Trade restrictions reduce gains from trade. (764–766)

6 T Tariff shifts export supply curve leftward, which increases price and decreases quantity traded. (763–766)

7 F Quota decreases supply, which increases price. (766)

8 F Dumping would be selling in Canada at lower price than in Japan. (768)

9 F We must also examine the productivity of workers in each country, and Canadian workers are more productive. (768)

10 F They will be slow because losers' losses are individually much greater than winners' gains. (770–771)

ⓔ **11 F** Overall flow of money in/out of country = sum of the three balances of payment must balance. Individual balances may be in deficit/surplus/balance. (772–774)

ⓒⓣ **12 F** Twin deficits tend to move together, but depends on reaction of private sector surplus/deficit. (775–776)

13 F May or may not be true. Net borrower implies *current* net borrowing > 0. Debtor nation implies sum of *all* net borrowing > 0. (774)

14 T Definition—note which way the money is flowing. (772–774)

15 F There has been a large increase in the total volume of trade. (776–777)

Multiple-Choice

1 b **a** and **c** are imports, **d** and **e** are exports of a *good.* (756)

2 d Opportunity cost measures in foregone goods, not inputs. (757–758)

3 e Opportunity cost of 1 more beer = lost pizza. For Partyland, going from 0 beer to 25 beers costs 25 pizzas (one for one). Do same calculation for Cowabunga. (757–758)

4 e Same type of calculation as in **3**. (757–758)

5 d Each specializes where they have comparative advantage (lowest opportunity cost). (757–759)

ⓒⓣ **6 e** Terms of trade between the opportunity costs in each country at the pre-trade equilibrium. (757–759)

7 c Consumption possibilities frontier is outside *PPF*. (759–761)

8 c Equilibrium is where export supply = import demand. (764–766)

9 d Equilibrium is where quota = import demand increases price. Higher domestic price increases domestic production. (766)

10 c Tariff increases domestic price = export price + tariff, or a shift leftward in supply curve. (764–765)

11 e Under quota, domestic government allocates the licence to import. (766)

12 d Because they have right to export. (766)

13 c They collect tariff revenue = import price – export price. (764–765)

14 c See text discussion. (767–770)

15 a See text discussion. (767–770)

16 d See text discussion. (770–771)

17 e $(S—I) + (NT - G)$ from equality of injections and leakages in circular flow. (775–776)

ⓒⓣ **18 c** Imports > exports implies current account deficit. Borrowing > lending implies capital account surplus. (Think about which direction money is flowing.) (772–774)

19 b Current lending > borrowing implies net lender. Sum of past borrowing > sum of lending implies debtor nation. (772–774)

20 e Official settlements balance = 0 implies current account surplus = capital account deficit, which occurs only when lending > borrowing. (772–774)

ⓒⓣ **21 e** Since current account + capital account + official settlements account = 0, when official settlements is a deficit, to be sure current is a surplus, it must be the case that capital is 0 or a deficit. (772–774)

22 c Government sector deficit = $NT - G = 300 - 400 = -100$. Private sector surplus = $S - I = 300 - 250 = +50$. (775–776)

23 c Net lender implies stock of investments rising. Debtor nation implies negative flow of interest payments on investments. (774)

24 a Official settlements balance = –(Capital account + Current account) = Surplus, which implies change in official reserves < 0. (772–774)

25 e See text discussion. (772–773)

Short Answer Problems

1 For two potential trading partners to be willing to trade, they must have different comparative advantages; that is, different opportunity costs. Then they will trade and both parties will gain. If the parties do not trade, each will face its own opportunity costs. A price at which trade takes place must be somewhere between the opportunity costs of the two traders. This result means that the party with the lower opportunity cost of the good in question will gain because it will sell at a price above its opportunity cost. Similarly, the party with the higher opportunity cost will gain because it will buy at a price below its opportunity cost.

2 A tariff on an imported good will *raise its price to domestic consumers* as the export supply curve shifts leftward. The export price is determined by the original export supply curve. As the domestic price of the good increases, the quantity of the good demanded decreases, and thus the relevant point on the original export supply curve is at a lower quantity and a *lower export price*. This lower quantity means that the quantity imported decreases. The increase in the domestic price will also lead to an *increase in the quantity of the good supplied domestically*.

When Atlantis imposes a tariff on its imports of watches, not only does the volume of imports shrink, but also the volume of exports of widgets to Beltran will shrink by the same amount. Thus a balance of trade is maintained. The export price of watches received by Beltran and the quantity exported decreases when a tariff is imposed. This decrease in the price and the quantity exported means that the income of Beltran has decreased. This result implies that the quantity of widgets (Atlantis' export) demanded by Beltran will decrease and thus Atlantis' exports decline.

3 This argument has some truth to it. As Short Answer Problem **2** shows, the tariff will lead an increase in domestic production of the protected good, which will lead to an increase in jobs in that industry. However, as Short Answer Problem **2** also shows, the same tariff will reduce foreign income, and reduce foreign purchases of our goods, reducing our exports and our export production, reducing jobs in the export industry. The net effect on jobs is unclear, but it is definitely not large.

4 **a** Current account balance + Capital account balance + Official settlements balance = 0, or (100 – 130 – 20) + (Loans from rest of world – 60) + (–10) = 0, so Loans from rest of world = 120.

b The current account balance is a $50 billion deficit: exports minus imports minus transfers to the rest of the world plus net interest payments to the rest of the world.

c The capital account balance is a surplus of $60 billion: loans from the rest of the world minus loans to the rest of the world.

d Because official reserves increased, the official settlements balance is –10.

5 **a** Completed Table 32.4 is shown here as Table 32.4 Solution. The values in the table are calculated using the opportunity cost of each good in each country. See **b** and **c** below.

TABLE **32.4** SOLUTION

Atlantis		Beltran	
Food (units)	**Cloth (units)**	**Food (units)**	**Cloth (units)**
0	500	0	800
200	400	100	600
400	300	200	400
600	200	300	200
800	100	400	0
1,000	0	—	—

b To increase the output (consumption) of food by 200 units, cloth production (consumption) decreases by 100 units in Atlantis. Thus the opportunity cost of a unit of food is 1/2 unit of cloth. This opportunity cost is constant as are all others in this problem, for simplicity. Similarly, the opportunity cost of cloth in Atlantis is 2 units of food.

c In Beltran a 100-unit increase in the production (consumption) of food requires a reduction in the output (consumption) of cloth of 200 units. Thus the opportunity cost of food is 2 units of cloth. Similarly the opportunity cost of cloth in Beltran is 1/2 units of food.

d Figure 32.3, parts (a) and (b) illustrate the production possibilities frontiers for Atlantis and Beltran, respectively labelled PPF_A and PPF_B. The rest of the diagram is discussed in the solutions to Short Answer Problems **6** and **7**.

FIGURE **32.3**

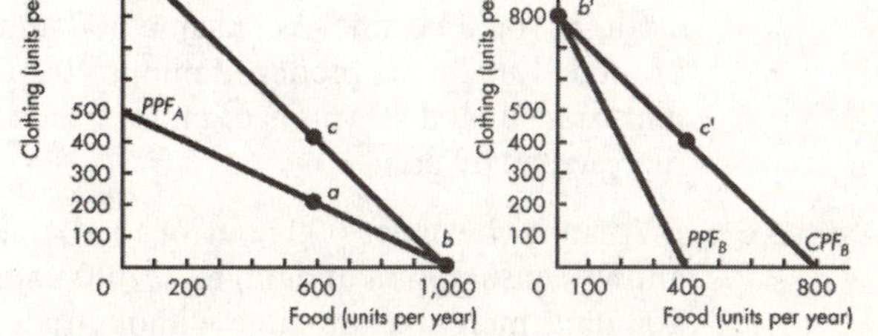

6 a We see from the solution to Short Answer Problems **5b** and **c** that Atlantis has a lower opportunity cost (1/2 unit of cloth) in the production of food. Therefore Atlantis will specialize in the production of food. Beltran, with the lower opportunity cost for cloth (1/2 unit of food), will specialize in cloth.

b Each country will want to produce every unit of the good in which they specialize as long as the amount they receive in trade exceeds their opportunity cost. For Atlantis, the opportunity cost of a unit of food is 1/2 unit of cloth, but it can obtain 1 unit of cloth in trade. Because the opportunity cost is constant, Atlantis will totally specialize by producing all of the food it can: 1,000 units per year, point *b* in Figure 32.3(a). Similarly, in Beltran, the opportunity cost of a unit of cloth is 1/2 unit of food but a unit of cloth will trade for 1 unit of food. Since the opportunity cost is constant, Beltran will totally specialize in the production of cloth and will produce 800 units per year, point *b*' in Figure 32.3(b).

c The consumption possibilities frontiers for Atlantis and Beltran, labelled CPF_A and CPF_B, are illustrated in Figure 32.3, parts (a) and (b) respectively. These frontiers are straight lines that indicate all the combinations of food and cloth that can be consumed with trade. The position and slope of the consumption possibilities frontier for an economy depend on the terms of trade between the goods (one for one in this example) and the production point of the economy.

The consumption possibilities frontier for Atlantis (CPF_A), for example, is obtained by starting at point *b* on PPF_A, the production point, and examining possible trades. For example, if Atlantis traded 400 units of the food it produces for 400 units of cloth, it would be able to consume 600 units of food (1,000 units produced minus 400 units traded) and 400 units of cloth, which is represented by point *c*.

d If Atlantis consumes 600 units of food, trade allows consumption of cloth to be 400 units, 200 units more than possible without trade. The maximum amount of cloth that can be consumed without trade is given by the production possibilities frontier. If food consumption is 600 units, this outcome is indicated by point *a* on PPF_A. The maximum amount of cloth consumption for any level of food consumption with trade is given by the consumption possibilities frontier. If food consumption is 600 units, this outcome is indicated by point *c* on CPF_A.

7 a Since Atlantis produces 1,000 units of food per year (point *b* on PPFA), to consume 600 units of food and 400 units of cloth (point *c* on CPFA) it must trade 400 units of food for 400 units of cloth. This outcome means that Beltran has traded 400 units of cloth for 400 units of food. Since Beltran produces 800 units of cloth, this result suggests that Beltran must consume 400 units of food and 400 units of cloth (point *c*' on CPF_B).

b Atlantis exports 400 units of food per year and imports 400 units of cloth. Beltran exports 400 units of cloth per year and imports 400 units of food.

8 a The price of a shirt under free trade will occur at the intersection of Atlantis' import demand curve for shirts and Beltran's export supply curve for shirts. This result occurs at a price of $12 per shirt.

b Atlantis will import 6 million shirts per year.

9 a The effect of the $9 per shirt tariff is to shift the export supply curve (*S*) leftward. This outcome is shown as a shift from *S* to *S*' in Figure 32.2 Solution. The price is now determined by the intersection of the *D* curve, which is unaffected by the tariff, and the *S*' curve. The new price of a shirt is $18.

FIGURE **32.2** SOLUTION

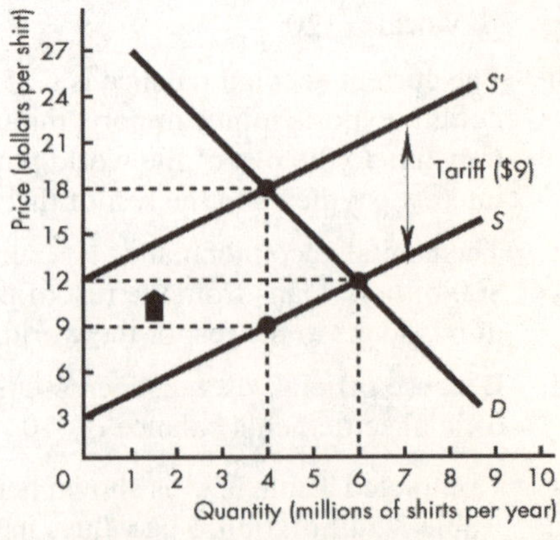

b Of this $18, $9 is the tariff, so the exporter only receives the remaining $9.

c Atlantis will now import only 4 million shirts per year.

d The tariff revenue is $9 (the tariff per shirt) × 4 million (the number of shirts imported), which is $36 million. This money is received by the government of Atlantis.

10 a The quota restricts the quantity that can be imported to 4 million shirts per year regardless of the price; it is represented by a vertical line in Figure 32.4 (which corresponds to Figure 32.2). The market for shirts will thus clear at a price of $18 per shirt.

FIGURE **32.4**

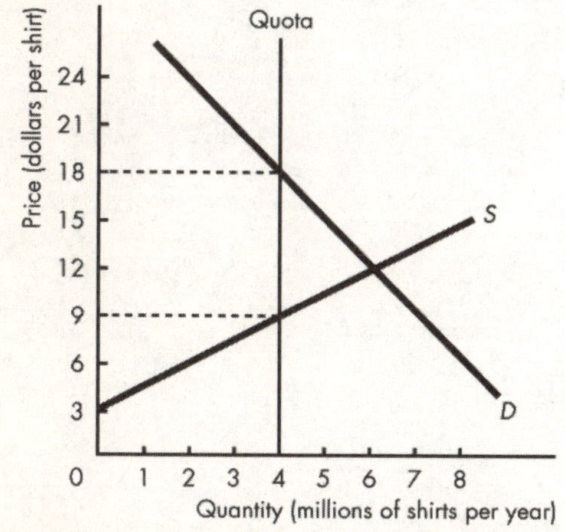

b This $18 price is received by the people who are given the right to import shirts under the quota. The amount received by the exporter is $9, given by the height of the *S* curve at a quantity of 4 million shirts per year.

c Atlantis will import 4 million shirts per year, the quota limit.

d The "excess profit" is $9 per shirt (the $18 received by the importer minus the $9 received by the exporter) × 4 million shirts, which is $36 million. This profit is captured by the importers who have been rewarded by the government of Atlantis because they have been given the right to import under the quota. This licence is essentially a right to make an "excess profit."